Outlaw Territories

Outlaw Territories

Environments of Insecurity/
Architectures of Counterinsurgency

Felicity D. Scott

ZONE BOOKS · NEW YORK

2016

ZONE BOOKS
633 Vanderbilt Street
Brooklyn, NY 11218

Printed in the United States of America.

Distributed by The MIT Press,
Cambridge, Massachusetts, and London, England.

Library of Congress Cataloging-in-Publication Data

Scott, Felicity Dale, 1965–
Outlaw territories : environments of insecurity/ architectures of counterinsurgency / Felicity D. Scott.
pages cm
Includes bibliographical references and index.
1. Architecture and society—History—20th century.
2. Architecture and globalization—History—20th century.
3. Architecture—Human factors—History—20th century.
4. Space (Architecture)—Social aspects—History—20th century. I. Title.
NA2543.S6S385 2016
720.1'.03—dc23

2015028486

To Marcus P. E. Scott (1964–2014)

Contents

INTRODUCTION
"Apocalypse Juggernaut, Hello" 9

I *Instruments of Environmental Control* 35

II *Code Wars* 73

III *Woodstockholm* 115

IV *Battle for the Earth* 167

V *Third World Game* 225

VI *"Cruel Habitats"* 283

VII *DISCOURSE, SEEK, INTERACT* 339

VIII *Dataland (and Its Ghosts)* 383

CONCLUSION
Passages and Passengers 431

Acknowledgments 443

Notes 447

Index 537

INTRODUCTION

"Apocalypse Juggernaut, Hello"

> We are told that the environment has the incomparable merit of being the first truly *global problem* presented to humanity. A *global problem*, which is to say a problem that only those who are organized on a global level will be able to solve. And we know who they are. These are the very same groups that for close to a century have been the vanguard of disaster.
>
> —The Invisible Committee, *The Coming Insurrection* (2009)

In January 1970, American entrepreneur Stewart Brand published a "supplement" to the *Whole Earth Catalog* entitled "The Outlaw Area."[1] Launched in 1968, Brand's catalog quickly became a catalytic piece of media infrastructure for sponsoring alternative lifestyles and the back-to-the-land commune movement. Fueled by the period's rhetoric of crisis and survival, it also amplified and fed that rhetoric back to a large audience. "The Outlaw Area" included the catalog's usual array of "tools" to empower the individual to "conduct his own education, find his own inspiration, shape his own environment, and share his adventure with whoever is interested"—hence fashioning lines of flight, or so it was widely assumed, from the power of "government, big business, formal education [and] church." Additionally, the edition included Brand's reflections on the notion of outlaw areas, "Apocalypse Juggernaut, Hello," wherein he identified a central nexus of ecological catastrophe and population explosion. "As if the spirits of our ancestors weren't trouble enough," he posited of rising anxiety about the future, "now we're haunted by the ghosts of our descendants." His solution to scripting a better future: "try stuff," even "try everything." "One thing we need is better outlaws."[2]

Figure 0.1 *Whole Earth Catalog* production studio, Menlo Park, CA. Taken on May 28, 1971 as they worked on the *Last Whole Earth Catalog* (AP Photo / Richard Drew).

Figure 0.2 Interior of shelter at Wheeler Ranch commune, with Charlotte and Bryce, c. 1969. From *Open Land: A Manifesto* (Wheeler Ranch Defense Fund, c. 1969) (Sylvia Clarke Hamilton).

According to Brand, complications with this plan arose from constraints imposed by law or, more specifically, by laws that did not account for a historical emergency in which, many prophesied, Earth and humanity faced certain destruction within the next thirty years. "Reasonable laws made by reasonable men in reasonable times proscribe trying everything," he suggested, adding, "For a good reason: people get hurt trying stuff. If you're bound to try stuff anyway, then either you're working directly for City Hall or you're an outlaw, or both."

Brand's ambivalent association of government and outlaws as agents fostering invention—one blurring the boundary between legality and illegality—might seem a peculiar place to begin a book interrogating architecture's inscription within an emergent apparatus of global environmental governance and the management of (unsettled) populations. But even in his brief reflections on outlaw areas and the ambiguous subjectivities occupying them, we can identify symptomatic evidence of this matrix that bears on the story that follows. A media-savvy figure who surfaces repeatedly in this book, Brand sought a strategic role within this apparatus (the *Whole Earth Catalog* being only the first of many initiatives), and in so doing offered telling clues to its operations. His acknowledgment of the potential indistinction between City Hall and outlaws alluded to the complex relationship between the actions of government and the police, on the one hand, and the actions of people (not always citizens) operating or positioned outside the law, on the other. It also pointed to the ambivalence at work in his entrepreneurial activities, which spanned from the catalog to recent ventures such as the Global Business Network. Did these two factions unwittingly form a knowing, if perverse mirror image of each other? Did one side learn from the strategies of the other? Positioned within a common zone of indeterminacy, as he saw it, they were less opposed than mutually intertwined.

Like the *Whole Earth Catalog*, Brand's speculations on the concept of an outlaw area were avowedly indebted to American inventor and futurologist R. Buckminster Fuller, whose experimental work and enigmatic persona switched back and forth between government and countercultural arenas at the time. In 1966, as cited by Brand in "The Outlaw Area," Fuller explained to *New Yorker* critic Calvin Tomkins that social and technological development—such as that spurred when a "minority" of humanity first "went to sea"—takes place beyond national borders, in domains beyond the reach of the law. The joint expansion of maritime power and European colonialism—an example that Fuller celebrated repeatedly—is testimony to his insight. "All improvement has to be made in the outlaw area," Fuller insisted of the need for venturing into extraterritorial zones, blithely overlooking the concomitant political resonances and legacy of violence. "You can't reform man, and you can't improve his situation where he is. But when you've made things so good out there in the outlaw area that they can't help being recognized, then gradually they get assimilated."[3] Fuller was speaking primarily of advances born of military technologies—transportation, communications, shelter—and of their assimilation into contemporary forms of life, what he famously read as "weaponry arts" becoming "livingry arts." It was a process that, as we will see, repeatedly underlay the normalization or generalization of states of exception and with it the ongoing militarization of the everyday milieu under the rubric of security.[4]

Brand identified as "present outlaw areas" marginal geographical locations—outer space, oceans, deserts, jungles, and so on—as well as scientific knowledge, the mind, and "other state-of-the-art frontiers whose languages are still foreign to lawmakers." Raising the specter of imminent catastrophe and violence, he concluded, citing a common futurological fantasy and a Cold War isolationist defense strategy (one revived post 9/11), "If the famines do indeed start coming down in the mid-70's, things are going to be too tense (fortress America) to try stuff in a friendly way any more. We'll need to have operationally developed a spectrum of open strategies before then." Although outer space increasingly caught Brand's imagination, as evident in his anthology *Space Colonies* of 1977,[5] here he set out three other examples of open strategies: a "Dope Academy" to test frontiers for the mind and two territorial fantasy games, each advancing neosovereign spaces in which the usual rule of law was suspended—the Outlaw Area and Place.

Brand described the Outlaw Area as "a geographical place where anything goes. Let's say it's an island." He identified two constituencies for this setting with "minimal prior form": criminals and hippies. "For society it functions as a human dumping station. When a guy gets a jail sentence he has the choice of serving the sentence or being deported to the Island.... Yessir, put all the bad apples in one bad apple barrel. For the individual it serves as an always possible alternative to the situation he's in. He can simply split for the Island and take his chances there."[6]

Trying to imagine what sort of environment the Outlaw Area might be, he invoked "the history of Australia, once a penal colony," and the contemporary underworld, suggesting it might take the form of "either a dictatorship or warfare of rival gangs" or that "the Island might become an Aquarian haven for the most useful pioneers...bending reality off into unimaginable directions with no restrictions save the harsh ones of nature. Could become our best school." Illustrating the latter outcome was a photograph of a naked pregnant woman and a shirtless, longhaired man, residing with a couple of chickens in a low-tech, dirt-floored shelter at Wheeler Ranch commune in Northern California. It was taken from *Open Land: A Manifesto*, to which we will return in Chapter 2. Implied was that prisons, colonies, ganglands, and communes shared a condition of illegality and, insofar as inhabitants could be deported, they shared a condition of foreignness or even statelessness. Moreover, violence might erupt at any moment.

His second example, Place, by contrast, would be owned and managed by the Place Company—a private governing body that regulated occupants' activities and wellbeing and to whom they paid rent. Brand conceived of Place as an experiment in microcosm with new economic and political paradigms: operating cybernetically, it presented a "system that generates systems," an environment in which strategies and tactics would emerge spontaneously through interaction, requiring no moment of political decision or political construction. Located in a remote mountain valley without automobile access, but "intimately linked to [the world] by communication," this multiplayer, evolutionary logistical game was divided between East Place and West Place (presumably a reference to Cold War divides). As Brand explained, "The first action at Place is to build a big fence, not around it, but down the middle of it. The fence (unlike Berlin's) has numerous open gates, holes, tunnels, arches—a very permeable wall." Place Company, he added, "bears the same relation as referees to a football game. Their function is to keep the game fair, determine the minimum rules and enforce them minimally, and bear no alliance to either side but to the life of the

Figure 0.3 Whole Earth Jamboree with Earth Ball, 1978 (© Roger Ressmeyer/CORBIS).

game." Like football, moreover, Place had an audience and media presence to help fund the enterprise. The company could also evict players. Derived from an event called "World War IV"—an agitprop game in which two teams pushed around a six-foot ball painted as Earth—Place sought to demonstrate a "fluid adversary model" of social and political life in which players participated in a competitive battle but, the other side willing, could switch to the opposite team. Enmity was always provisional. "The content of the game of Place," he concluded, referring to his claim for outlaw areas, "is trying stuff." Stressing the interdependence at play here, he added, "Whatever one side tries, occurs in close view of the other, who may incorporate it or try something opposite or grandly ignore it or defect and join it."[7]

Brand did not speculate on what potential defectors were to do when they were not accepted by the other team, when they were perceived as threats—as strangers, foreigners, criminals, invaders, enemies, or even terrorists—and when the wall became less permeable, serving instead as a form of defense, discrimination, or even repression.[8] What happened when rules were not respected, when they were asymmetrical, or when violence erupted in such a space, desublimating the lack of distinction between the fictional regulations and lawlessness, marking the undecidability of rule and exception? Assuming the political neutrality of Place's management system (itself a political fiction) and of systems that generated systems, he didn't ask what happened when checkpoints served particular ends, controlling and regulating movements, creating what Etienne Balibar characterizes with respect to our contemporary world order as "differentiated restrictions" to mobility according to "the utility and the reliability of the groups and individuals concerned from the point of view of hegemonic structures."[9] Nor did Brand question the regulatory role of media, something he understood very well.

At once an allegory of Cold War battles, of Earth's finitude and interdependence, of the capacity of media to sponsor a postnational space, and of the United Nations as a platform upon which contemporary territorial battles were played out, Brand's Place was also, I want to argue, haunted by geopolitical transformations for which environmental catastrophes and population explosions served as a code, triggering anxiety for many in the West at that moment. This was further evident in the two initiatives that followed "Apocalypse Juggernaut, Hello": Liferaft Earth, a weeklong "hunger game" staged in California the previous year, and Earth People's Park, a project to "free some land, and not just a little," named after Berkeley's People's Park "saga," but with a global ambition. We will return to both in Chapter 3 when looking at Brand's attempts to intervene in environmental debates at the 1972 United Nations Conference on the Human Environment in Stockholm.

While for Brand such islands and mountain valleys formed urgent and still semi-utopian "open ends" for social experimentation, less-utopian versions of outlaw areas, simulated places, and zones of indistinction were proliferating elsewhere: "human dumping grounds," battlefields and their electronic counterparts, environmental wastelands, and apartheid urbanisms.[10] These are what I call "outlaw territories," using the term to mark the linking of politics, populations, and environments within them. Sites of precarity, these included refugee, detention, and resettlement camps, arenas of civil war and guerilla insurgencies, occupied territories, areas under martial law, so-called urban "ghettos," squatter settlements, and other residues of structural inequity and environmental injustice, including company headquarters and social-scientific laboratories. Most (but not all) were born not of Cold War divides as such, but rather of the more complex or ambivalent topologies emerging between the First and Third Worlds or between the Global North and the Global South. Moreover, even after Brand's example of repressive structural divides—the Berlin Wall—was so spectacularly destroyed in 1989, and with it, supposedly, Cold War antagonisms, walls and other forms of discrimination continued to proliferate in what Wendy Brown has theorized as complex markers of a waning of sovereignty.[11] (One is also reminded of Walter Benjamin's "dialogue" with Carl Schmitt, particularly Benjamin's frequently cited remark, "The tradition of the oppressed teaches us that the 'state of emergency' in which we live is not the exception but the rule.")[12]

At the time of Brand's reflections, Western critics recognized the paranoid sense of "threat" elicited by encounters with the Third World. In Hans Magnus Enzensberger's words:

> The imperialist nations see the time coming when they will be only a small minority when compared to the rest of the world and their governments fear that population pressures will become a source of political and, in the last analysis, military power.... The "politics" of population have never been free of irrational and racist traits; they always contain demagogic elements and are always prone to arouse atavistic feelings.[13]

As many new countries joined the UN during the 1960s, having gained independence from colonial rule, while other populations continued their struggles for liberation, and with rising calls for socioeconomic and political justice in the developing world (for whose citizens these atavistic feelings had long been evident), calls for security and counterinsurgency measures proliferated within the West, permeating not only the popular imagination, but also, as we will see, architectural discourses and practices.

Environmentality Games

Outlaw Territories: Environments of Insecurity / Architectures of Counterinsurgency is stationed at this admittedly peculiar nexus where North American environmental, socioeconomic, and political ideals, along with scientific research, technological experimentation, and management and communication strategies that seek to operate at a global scale come together with dissident voices seeking to readjust or intervene in this playing field. At once heterogeneous and interconnected, all parties responded, implicitly or explicitly, to broader geopolitical transformations brought about by the deterritorializing forces of postindustrial technologies and neoliberal capitalism after World War II, and it is this connection as it relates to architecture that I want to unpack. Investigating institutional, academic, professional, and countercultural responses to the period's rising urban unrest in both the First and the Third Worlds, *Outlaw Territories* excavates specific moments in what is undoubtedly a much larger story of the roles played by architects and the built environment in the emergence of a multifaceted, dispersed, global governing apparatus. Each chapter seeks to identify practices, events, or technologies related to the emergence of techniques and policies for monitoring and managing environments and populations, thus speaking to what Michel Foucault identified in his contemporaneous work on biopolitics and governmentality (more on which below) as a fully fledged "environmentality."[14]

The staging of the content to follow often retains a North American point of departure. It does so not to shore up the centrality of the United States to all such discourses, but to recognize and contribute to interrogating the role it plays as a global superpower in forging hierarchies and dominating economic and political battlefields, effectively acting as the referees of Brand's Place Company, but hardly the keeping the game "fair."[15] Yet if the United States serves as a starting point, it will be through encounters with the developing world (both direct and indirect) that we trace shifts in both political and architectural or urban discourses seeking to maintain dominance and to quell dissent, both within the United States and beyond its borders. In the wake and midst of numerous decolonization struggles and guerilla insurgencies and at the height of the US-led war in Vietnam and Cambodia and the associated protests, architecture occasionally emerged as a target of countercultural refusal on account of its inherent normativity. It also became heavily imbricated with military, legal, and other institutional apparatuses, as well as with scientific and technological research dedicated to questions of international management and security. To this end, and in dialogue with precedents in the field, the book recasts the role of architecture from that of simply or unwittingly designing elegant or functional forms or engaging innovative and effective organizations and technologies in troubled contexts to one of providing strategic expertise.[16] We will thus follow a set of institutions, events, conflicts, technologies, policies, and media strategies as they surfaced within and had impacts upon cultural, semantic, material, and subjective domains. Through these coordinates, we will seek to understand how architecture (in the broad sense of the term) interfaced with or contributed to this apparatus and how it became a symptom of it.

Architecture

Architecture has long served both as a means of protection or defense against the environment (both "natural" and man-made) and simultaneously as a discipline whose concern was the materialization, organization, and representation of the life taking place within that milieu, whether at the scale of furniture, houses, apartment buildings, institutional headquarters, cities, or, occasionally, nations. Architecture is a political technology, one that remains endowed, quite literally, with the task of regulating the health, socialization, and productivity of a country's citizens. This is not a new story. Modern architecture earlier sought an expanded role in government, as evident with the establishment in 1928 of the Congrès International d'Architecture Moderne (CIAM). Founded, or so the story goes, following what Le Corbusier called the "Palais des Nations 'affair'"—the scandalous appointment of *other* architects to design a new headquarters for the League of Nations in Geneva the previous year—CIAM articulated a new, international "battlefront," in effect a world parliament of modern architects seeking to ensure architecture a better foothold in governmental and intergovernmental organizations.[17]

In the wake of World War II, CIAM did not gain consultation status with the newly founded UN, which was awarded instead to a rival organization, the Union Internationale des Architectes (UIA), still the primary nongovernmental liaison for the profession.[18] As Ijlal Muzaffar has detailed, the UIA "later provided many returning colonial planners as experts for UN missions."[19] By the early 1950s, we find CIAM turning to the rhetoric of "habitat"; its ninth congress convened in 1953 as La Chartre de l'Habitat, attempting to update its functionally oriented La Charte d'Athènes. In this context, the Groupe d'Architectes Modernes Marocains (GAMMA) presented Habitat du plus grand nombre, a project addressed to uprooted rural populations then living in *bidonvilles* on the outskirts of Moroccan cities. Vladmir Bodiansky, a GAMMA member soon to align with Team 10, a group of architects who confronted CIAM's bureaucratic approach to urbanism with new paradigms indebted to social sciences, reported to the UN soon after on the subject of how architecture might be reconceived in less abstract, more regional terms under this rubric.[20] At this point, however, architecture's role remained largely circumscribed by familiar professional practice, even if often tending toward planning.

In the case of the late 1960s and 1970s, we are faced with a situation in which the scale of environmental concern expanded exponentially, as registered in tropes such as the "whole Earth" and the pervasive rhetoric of Spaceship Earth or in the equally postsovereign territory forged by global capitalism and institutions like the Ford Foundation and the UN. Although Fuller, for example, had long prided himself on thinking not only in international, but in "world-around" terms, this global imaginary now became far more common, architecture's client becoming "humanity" as such. It is thus not incidental to this story that the UN became increasingly concerned not only with questions of international security and war, but also, as evident in the series of "world conferences" convened during the 1970s, with the management of environments, populations, food, women, the sea, and, in turn, human habitats.[21] Following the reconstruction of war-torn Europe and in response to calls for economic parity and justice, the UN—and with it the United States and its economic allies—worked to install solutions to environmental and urban problems in the developing world firmly within global economic and political apparatuses they could steer. While Le Corbusier sold his "radiant city" vision to industrialists, bankers, and governments as a counterrevolutionary strategy—"Architecture or Revolution. Revolution can be avoided"—something similar can be found in the evolving discourses of "human settlement" and "habitat" addressed to humanity at large.[22] Armed with scientific and technical data and engaging new, flexible technological paradigms and techniques of management, architecture sought a vocation for its artifacts and expertise within this context. Intimately connected with the exercise of political power within shifting geopolitical frameworks, it came to serve a multinational clientele in its globalizing mandate.

The transformation of geographical scale and increased attention to humanity and "life itself" did not leave the conception of an architectural object or practice unchanged, and it is this transformation and its capacity to speak more broadly about historical forces that I want to explicate. While many architectural coordinates will remain familiar, we will frequently venture far beyond the conventional institutions and discourses of architectural history to identify and analyze power relations at stake and the ways in which they become inscribed within architecture and territories and upon bodies and populations. Although a destabilizing gesture for some, the goal of such disciplinary decentering is to gain further visibility of the complex web of economic and political strategies informing architecture at that moment and within which it operated. Reflecting on Foucault's reading of social apparatuses as at once shifting and variable lines of force and of subjectification, Gilles Deleuze potently reminds us in "What Is a Dispositif?": "We belong to these apparatuses and act in them."[23] With architecture now understood within a global matrix of forces (environment, development, migration, war, poverty, communications technology, computerization), the pressures exerted upon domiciles and habitats, and hence the historical conditions manifest in houses and cities, sometimes rendered the appearance of the resultant "architecture" even more contested and strange. Unlike their utopian modernist forerunners in functional planning and hygienic housing estates, these artifacts soon became almost unspeakable as a concern for the discipline proper, which retreated into the historical and semantic experiments of postmodernism, a call to order that itself forms an equally symptomatic, if more legible architectural response to those very same globalizing forces.[24]

World Architecture

To tell this story, we begin with recognizably *architectural* examples of the profession working in the service of global management: Kevin Roche's designs for the Ford Foundation Headquarters and One United Nations Plaza in New York. Channeling environmental, political, and geopolitical conditions that these institutions sought to control, including urban instabilities and social radicalism, the buildings speak to the relationship of US philanthropic organizations and international governing institutions to the expansion of neoliberal capitalism in the 1960s and 1970s. Chapter 2 turns to the other side of this equation, looking at Open Land communes, which in their attempted exodus from such urban instability and the governing apparatuses seeking to control it recognized and, with some precision, fought against the manner in which techniques of power operate on the body and psyche of the subject in their most intimate domains. Theatrically performing what Foucault was to call "counterconducts" and adopting strategies of "voluntary primitivism"—as evident in the photograph illustrating "The Outlaw Area"—these communards experimented with alternative shelter technologies and explicitly nonnormative forms of life. In dialogue with what they termed "cybernation," they presciently spoke to the biopolitical contours of the increasingly administered environment in the United States, their struggles eliciting a violent response from the state. The next two chapters turn to the 1972 Stockholm conference, followed by two chapters on Habitat: The United Nations Conference on Human Settlements (Habitat) of 1976, and then two final chapters address architectural and urban research at the Massachusetts Institute of Technology (MIT). I want to outline the importance of these UN conferences and MIT in slightly more detail before underscoring what was at stake for architecture.

A landmark event in the history of environmental politics, the Stockholm conference marked at once the moment of an increased role for nongovernmental organizations (NGOs) within the UN, the integration of (and polemical interruptions staged by) voices from the Third World in environmental and population debates, and the political mobilization of the figure of Earth as an ecological system. That mobilization sought not only to foster environmental awareness, but to launch neoliberal challenges to extant regimes of national sovereignty upon which the UN was founded. The rising sense of vulnerability of humanity's global habitat provided the occasion for the UN to step in and help governments develop the political and economic infrastructure through which to manage the "whole Earth" on its behalf, with systems-based paradigms of ecology, electronic monitoring networks, and scientific management serving as tools with which to do so. In addition to introducing the UN conference, which took place under the motto "Only One Earth," Chapter 3 details Brand's transposition of Earth People's Park and other trappings of the American counterculture into this media-saturated international forum. Tracing the complex topology between official and unofficial or "counter" conferences, I detail the traction attained by Brand's "environment yes, politics no" platform within the UN conference, particularly among the US delegation, as well as the complex semantic and problematic political logics at work in the Tent City settlement that he set up on the outskirts of Stockholm to manage itinerant populations.

Chapter 4 traces a series of struggles between conflicting nongovernmental agents at the conference, including protests against the "ecocide" then being systematically wrought in Vietnam by US military forces, groups promoting neo-Malthusian "limits to growth" arguments and computer-driven management tools developed at MIT, interventions by Third World scientists against Euro-American population discourses, and an exhibition demonstrating more overtly political forms of alternative technologies and shelter. Issues of pollution and population control and the protection of the natural environment that dominated Western environmental discourses encountered distributive-justice claims from developing nations and radical activists, including an unanticipated resistance to environmental standards as a pretext for discriminatory trade policies or as potentially sponsoring "pollution havens" in developing countries; multiple calls for technology transfer, as well as for reparations arising from earlier exploitation of resources and environmental damage, whether by colonial occupiers or multinational corporations; and battles over the inclusion of considerations not only of ecocide, but also of apartheid, colonial and neocolonial aggression (or expansion), racism, warfare, and genocide. All, various parties insisted, were forces affecting the environment and hence properly environmental concerns. Erupting into visibility, these debates were quickly countered by the United States in defense of the UN's

Development Decade initiative, an initiative spurred in 1961 by President John F. Kennedy as a strategy to enfranchise poor countries on the capitalist side of the Cold War divide, which was then entering its second decade. Hence, we find figures such as Robert S. McNamara—the US secretary of defense during the escalation of the Vietnam War and then president of World Bank—stressing the imperative of growth and development aid to quell such political challenges.

The rhetoric of planetary togetherness—shared by the counterculture and those seeking dominant positions of global governance—was again very much on view at Habitat, wittingly or unwittingly mirroring the interests of US-led global capitalism, the violent contours of which remain hauntingly familiar in the present. "One of the most hopeful developments of the Seventies," British economist Barbara Ward emoted at Habitat, "is the degree to which world society has begun to examine, seriously and together, what one might call the basic facts of 'planetary housekeeping.'"[25] As Chapters 5 and 6 demonstrate, by 1976, when faced with growing evidence of economic and environmental damage born of foreign aid and development programs, it became clear to many that Earth's self-appointed caretakers had other goals in mind.[26] Chapter 5 focuses on Ward and Fuller, each promoting paradigms of global interdependency; the instrumentalization of alternative and countercultural practices at Habitat Forum (the NGO arena) to support the UN's development narratives; and counterclaims staged by the Group of 77 and the Palestine Liberation Organization, an organization representing the period's quintessential figures of "unsettlement." Desublimating in different ways the biopolitical governing apparatus sought by the UN in the domain of shelter, each forged positions in what I cast as a "Third World Game." Again the United States sought to close down political openings, insisting that settlements were merely technical matters. Chapter 6 looks at a competition and exhibition of architects' designs for self-help housing strategies in the Philippines. With architects cast as experts on human unsettlement, it shows that even experimental trajectories were brought into alignment with the development apparatus promoted by the UN and the World Bank.

The final two chapters address another nexus of architectural expertise, insecurity, environmental control, technology, social-scientific research, and geopolitics, focusing on the Architecture Machine Group (ArcMac) at MIT and its research funded by the US government and military agencies. Chapter 7 investigates ArcMac's relation to the Urban Systems Lab and integration into Big Science initiatives at the institute. Looking beyond the ostensible neutrality of systems-based analysis and quantitative methodologies—methodologies replete with the rhetoric of objective evaluation and rationalized design responses, with a seamless ability to modulate across fields ranging from art installations and pollution barometers to data on race and poverty, and with claims to institute new prospects for "choice" and "participation"—the chapter traces a symptomatic acknowledgment and simultaneous bracketing of contemporary injustices and instabilities, both in the United States and globally. Emerging during a period threatened by urban insurrection at home and abroad in which military technologies and government funding were increasingly geared to countering urban insecurity, it asks: For whom were such cybernetic and systems-based environments being invented?

Chapter 8 turns to the Aspen Movie Map, explicating the relation of this groundbreaking interactive environment to the Entebbe hijacking episode in 1976 and Israel's calls, in response, for a War on Terror. While ArcMac's work was typically cast in the language of disinterested monitoring and rationalized design responses, the Movie Map is further evidence that the technologies and methods deployed arose from an economic and political matrix that was far from neutral. A vanguard not only in the experimental use of computers in architecture, ArcMac research operated at the cutting edge of instrumenting technologies of data collection, spatial data management, and input and output, as well as perceptual and cognitive psychology. "Technology moves faster than laws," Brand noted triumphantly of this research a few years later, "All new technologies are outlaw areas. All new communications technologies are political dynamite."[27]

My ambition in bringing these stories together is not to demonstrate unequivocally how architecture came to serve as a tool for neoliberal capitalism, but to ask how discourses and techniques at work within different streams of environmental and architectural research and "human settlement" activism functioned (knowingly or otherwise, and often ambivalently) within the logics of globalization. In this sense, the stories offer cautionary tales. They are told in large part at the micro level as each chapter seeks to identify and understand power relations and historical forces at play in a specific context. The research is in this sense situated in its historical moment, with newspaper accounts, critical reviews, reports, institutional and personal archives, period interviews, photographs, films, and other contemporary documentation serving as primary source material. However, the research also aims to have a contemporary bearing, because the stories intersect in complicated ways with current critical and political concerns. Indeed, one ambition of *Outlaw Territories* is to understand how certain discourses, practices, technologies, conflicts, and dynamics became institutionalized to the point of remaining entirely familiar within contemporary capitalism. Yet while we can identify familiar concerns and constellations amid the messy historical contingencies in which they are grounded, the terms rarely align neatly, giving rise to instructive ambiguities.

The tragic litany of concerns arising decades earlier that continue to haunt the present are well known: the mobilization of security threats (real or imagined) in order to declare states of emergency, institute new policies and laws, or breach sovereignty, as evident in the wake of the attacks on September 11, 2001; the capillary expansion and illegal deployment of surveillance technologies and practices, as demonstrated in part by leaked documents from Prism, the US National Security Agency program of digital surveillance and data collection; the growing indistinction between military and police strategies and technologies, with the resultant militarization of urban environments (including the suspension of laws to which police are normally bound) and its uneven impact upon the civil rights of minority populations; the launch and devolution of US-led and distinctly asymmetrical wars in Iraq and Afghanistan under the rubric of the War on Terror; ongoing struggles against Israel's illegal occupation of Palestinian territory and the ongoing support by the United States for state violence mocking international law; the neocolonial perpetuation of structural underdevelopment under the rubric of economic Realpolitik, security, and development policy; the renewed embrace of environmental discourses and their asymmetrical instrumentation in biopolitical techniques of governance; the uprooting of populations and their forced migrations due to warfare and political conflict, environmental crises, and economic inequities, along with the spaces of exception to which they give rise—camps, tent cities, squatter settlements, quarantine areas, and more; the proliferation of walls, including those around Gaza and within the Occupied Territories in Palestine, between the United States and Mexico, and so on; and the production of new subjectivities both in line with and against this apparatus of control. All find precedents within but are necessarily slightly out of sync with the material to follow.

Territorial Insecurity

Paul Virilio identified techniques of power at play and at stake within this emergent global *dispositif* decades ago, and I want to recall a few salient points from his writing, marking a precedent within architectural discourse engaged with the work of Foucault. In "The Overexposed City" (1984), a text alluding to ArcMac research, Virilio cautioned, "It is too easily forgotten that more than being an ensemble of techniques designed to shelter us from inclemency, architecture is an instrument of measure, a sum of knowledge capable of organizing society's space and time by pitting us against the natural environment," a material dimension then, as he put it, "enter[ing] into open conflict with the structural capacities of mass communication."[28] The previous decade, in *L'insécurité du territoire* (1976), Virilio mentioned the Stockholm conference when explicating mechanisms deployed in the wake of World War II to facilitate the global expansion of a US-led Western economic system, first to Europe—in managing postwar reconstruction under programs such as the Marshall Plan—then to the developing world in the form of aid. Working to institute structural underdevelopment elsewhere, this process entailed a collapse of the distinction between wartime and peacetime economies in which he identified the replacement of the overt violence of "total war" with the structural violence of "total peace," a twentieth-century version of the eighteenth-century phenomenon of "perpetual peace" that Foucault identified, following Kant, in his study of liberalism.[29]

"As early as the first months of 1947," Virilio argued, "Senator Pepper (Democrat, Florida) defined plans for aid: they formed part of a non-declared state of war. Henry Wallace presented them as 'answering more to the needs of the American Navy for petroleum than to the nutritional needs of Greek or Turkish children.'"[30]

Affording veto powers and a police function to the permanent members of the UN Security Council, strategic economic and military advantages were built into the new institution of global governance. (We are reminded of the limits of Brand's "fluid adversary model" as it attempted to translate World War IV into a game of inventing rules for life.) "As with total war," Virilio argued, "it will be possible to wage total peace from above and afar. Decolonization, promoted in the name of 'the right of nations to self-determination' . . . will only in reality be the *end of a cohabitation.* A new segregation . . . which permits the extension of the status of ghetto to entire continents."[31] As with a declared end to total war, "successful decolonization" did not return living conditions to a prior state. Rather, "after destruction and ruin of the habitat, [one] finds the obligatory insertion of subjects into the new milieu forced upon them. This is the profound sense that must be associated with Nixon's words, 'We are not imperialists, we only want to offer a way of life.'"[32] Moreover, unlike traditional warfare, at stake in "total peace" was not a struggle to defend or annex territory, but to manage life itself within that new milieu: "the war of milieu is succeeded by war waged on the milieu—nature, society."[33] Virilio suggested in the course of his argument that the deterritorializing logic characteristic of naval warfare expanded onto land with aerial attacks, citing an arc from mustard gas used by European powers in the earlier twentieth century to defoliating agents recently deployed by US forces in Vietnam.

When Virilio turned to the Stockholm conference, it was not with reference to ecocide (hotly debated at the conference), but to "the administration of fear" and with it the attempted evacuation of the precondition of politics. For the "directors of the suicidal state," he posited, the "coming together of the international experts, as in Stockholm, has, perforce, no meaning. . . . The statistical curves can soar vertiginously toward the end of the planet, and after? Thought is dried up."[34] His reference was presumably to the alarming graphs of exponential growth and collapse in environmental systems that were produced by Jay Forrester and his Systems Dynamics team at MIT for the Club of Rome's *Limits to Growth*, to which we return in Chapter 4.[35] At stake in mobilizing fear was not returning to better or healthier forms of life or saving the natural environment, but deploying a "constant ascent of statistics toward planetary death" in the interests of the state.[36] (Hence his footnote citing McNamara as exemplary.)[37] Underscoring the undecidability of the civil and the military, Virilio explained: "The exploitation of the malaise of man *vis-à-vis* his environment (maladjustment, new urban situation, pollution, insecurity, desocialization, overpopulation, etc.), malaise more and more widespread, a repulsive force more and more powerful and expressive which tends to replace the contempt for the milieu by the fear of it, comes . . . to superimpose itself exactly on the new military schema."[38]

It was in his remarks on humanitarian aid in *L'insécurité du territoire*, however, that Virilio's dialogue with Foucault becomes most apparent. Offering only provisions "indispensible for life," Virilio argued, humanitarian aid positioned populations not as citizens or subjects of law, but rather as units of biological survival: "for the man thus exposed, assistance has become survival, non-assistance a condemnation to death."[39] In the "new milieu forced upon them," aid became a means for integrating bodies into the apparatus of capital as new labor pools.[40] Control over the subject's habitat, as with the regulation of his movement in this "instrumental structure," became the means to sustain life, to exploit it, or to strike a man dead: "water, air, the movement or stopping of the body becoming the right of life or condemnation to death."[41] A nice summation of World Bank policy at this moment.

Spatial and urban tropes pervaded Foucault's historical and philosophical writings, as is often noted, including his work from the late 1970s on biopolitics, biopower, and governmentality (his reading of how techniques of power and of government are exercised within territories and over populations and ultimately bodies). Concepts such as environment and habitat haunt this work, as well, and I want to outline a few key instances, since they return, less overtly, throughout this book.[42] In his 1975–76 lectures at the Collège de France, *Society Must Be Defended*, Foucault spoke directly to environment and habitat in a manner that might help us understand why they emerged in the 1970s as central to institutions of global governance, as evident in the UN conferences and the expertise therein sought. "Biopolitics' last domain," Foucault proposed, is "control over relations between the human race, or human beings insofar as they are a species, insofar as they are living beings, and their environment, the milieu in which they live." After identifying "geographical, climatic, or hydrographic" factors as relevant, he stressed that at stake was "the problem of the environment to the extent that it is not a natural environment, that it has been created by the population and therefore has effects on that population. This is, essentially, the urban problem."[43]

Speaking to the figure of "man" suspended at once within a biological environment and "human historicity," Foucault also addressed this nexus of life and environmental control in *The History of Sexuality*. "There is no need either to lay further stress on the proliferation of political technologies that ensued," he explained of the micropolitical logics at work, "investing the body, health, modes of subsistence and habitation, living conditions, the whole space of existence."[44] It was, he noted, "as managers of life and survival, of bodies and the race, that so many regimes have been able to wage so many wars, causing so many men to be killed."[45] As we know, Foucault continued to develop readings of spatial organization as strategies of management throughout the late 1970s: his lectures from 1977 and 1978, published as *Security, Territory, Population*, detailed connections between town planning, scarcity, security, circulation, and the rise of the modern conception of population; those from the following year, published as *The Birth of Biopolitics*, extended his articulation of population, police, and liberal forms of governance. Also at this time he directed an edited volume, *Politiques de l'habitat (1800–1850)*, derived from collaborative research.[46] All remain decisively marked by the period's evident nexus of neoliberalism, globalization, and militarism. In addition to tracing centuries-long transformations in the arts of government, Foucault implicitly spoke to recent events: he recognized in struggles for liberation from colonial rule and against neocolonial incursions such as those playing out in Latin America, Africa, and Indochina an asymmetrical, but creative battle against dominant relations of power.

When asked by Paul Rabinow the following decade to clarify what he meant by suggesting that architecture became political in the late eighteenth century, Foucault acknowledged that architecture had been political before, but at this moment, one could recognize "the development of reflection upon architecture as a function of the aims and techniques of the government of societies."[47] From the eighteenth century on, he argued, questions of urbanism, collective facilities, hygiene, and domestic architecture became proper to political discussions on the art of government, "the model of the city" itself becoming "the matrix for the regulations that apply to a whole state."[48] But this model reached limits as a paradigm of management. With the emergence of liberalism and new notions of "society," and in turn with the introduction of the railway, communication, and electrical networks, he argued, "the links between the exercise of political power and the space of a territory, or the space of cities," shifted to the point where architects were no longer, as he put it, "the technicians or engineers of the three great variables—territory, communication, and speed. These escape the domain of architects."[49] Foucault did not mean that architecture now operated beyond such vectors. Indeed, as he noted, although architects were no longer in control of these historical forces and the *dispositif* of power to which they gave rise, such "techniques of power" remained "invested in architecture."[50]

Even if Foucault was correct that certain forces had escaped the domain of architecture, this condition of being superseded by other environmental factors—communication and transportation technologies, economic paradigms, expanded geopolitical organizations, even climate—in terms of its relevance to the art of governing does not render architectural objects less able to speak to questions of politics and techniques of power. Rather, they now speak differently about them. Architecture—as a discipline, a practice, and a discourse—remains porous to historical transformation, and it is partially on account of such "investment" that as a site of historical research, architectural and urban formations, as well as technologies of shelter or dwelling, provide cogent vehicles for tracing emergent techniques of power. Moreover, in the late 1960s and 1970s, architects sought to return control over such forces to their domain. We can thus interrogate architectural artifacts and discourses, as well as their circulation in media, for ways in which they interface with historical forces not as dominant tools of governance, but as secondary ones operating within the same apparatus. To do so does not reduce the need to ask what role aesthetic and formal dimensions play within architecture, but it entails the productive burden of attending to an expanded matrix of discourses and forces affecting the discipline.

Equally importantly, it is on account of being so thoroughly invested with and implicated in contemporary forces that architecture can also work at times to cut across such vectors, to interrupt or politically rearticulate dominant techniques of power from within or from without, albeit if only momentarily. My ambition in what follows is not just to elucidate a picture of ever-tightening environmental control and of passive victims of state (or nonstate) power, but also to trace the emergence, tactically or otherwise, of interstices, counterconducts, counterdiscourses, and other forms of creative resistance in order to speak to the production of alternatives, or what Deleuze and Félix Guattari—who avowedly derived their theorization of deterritorialization and reterritorialization from *L'insécurité du territoire*—called lines of escape or flight.[51] This is not done in order to situate such acts and discourses merely as updated versions of heroic narratives of modern architecture serving as a force of progressive change or even as necessarily triumphant, let alone to affirm hippie fantasies of liberation. All have served at times to bracket more nuanced readings of the politics at play. Rather, while in the first instance my ambition is to identify points at which the discipline fell knowingly or unwittingly into a cynical apparatus or *dispositif* of power (thereby offering a map, so to speak, of the minefield), in the second instance, it is to suggest that architecture can relate otherwise to this very same apparatus, that it can serve to redirect it or make it function for other ends.[52]

At stake in Foucault's reading of power relations as fluid and strategic games, rather than power as the property of individuals or inherent to institutional frameworks, as Maurizio Lazzarato elucidates, was insisting that ethical and political agency could emerge from the instabilities and mobilities of positions in a field of players. Foucault's conception of power, that is, entailed the imminent possibility of a strategic reversibility of power and with it a potential undermining of the status quo. Hence the importance of his tripartite distinction between modalities of power—"states of domination" (the focus of conventional notions of how power operates), strategic relations of power, and techniques of government that in some sense mediate between the other two. Concomitant with this conception of power as unstable and as effectively reversible was recognition of the productive or creative function of resistance, something to which I will return throughout the book. No longer "conceptualized only in terms of negation," as Foucault put it, resistance can be reconceived as an active form of participation catalyzing processes of transformation: moreover, if not necessarily giving rise to states of liberation as such, creative acts can open onto new forms of life.[53]

Architecture has once again taken up the interrelated mantles of environmentalism and humanitarianism, even seeking lessons and prospects in ideologies of sustainability, informal settlements, emergency situations, and other threats of insecurity. Questions of Big Data, data management, and computerization remain dominant concerns; its protagonists operate in a global domain. The question at stake in *Outlaw Territories* is thus not (or not always) whether architects should simply withdraw from or refuse biopolitical techniques of power, but rather how they might more effectively and more critically operate within such apparatuses. It asks what else architecture might bring to the table, what other tactics remain open to it. These questions surface in various ways and in the context of specific actions and events, insisting that architecture need not necessarily function in alignment with a normative apparatus, that it can at times be deposed from such a role. Moreover, as a historian, it is my hope that in excavating a set of technologies, discourses, events, and practices from the 1960s and 1970s—which, however conceptually resonant, necessarily remain detached from the urgencies of the present—one can open space for a mode of reflection that offers insight into and that retains traction on the contemporary. To acknowledge a debt to Balibar, the hope is that within such a discursive space, one can forge theoretical tools, even conceptual weapons, by which to enter the space of this contemporary battlefield both within and beyond architecture, thereby questioning and even unsettling dominant narratives and rhetorical valences.

A related ambition is to render more legible the complex interplay and occasional affinities between theory and philosophy, on the one hand, and life, history, and experience, on the other, as they pertain to architecture. Such affinities emerge in *Outlaw Territories* as historical symptoms or clues that point to critical stakes; they serve as moments of intelligibility, crystallizations of historical and political forces at work that, to reiterate, remain all too familiar today and, whether we like it or not, form the context within which architecture is produced and the context necessary to understand its machinations.

Finally, I want to distinguish such interventions from Brand's calls for "better outlaws." For him, agents seeking alternative mechanisms—whether working at City Hall or living in "outlaw areas" such as Earth People's Park—ultimately served the evolution of a dominant apparatus, as is evident in his later celebration of ArcMac under the rubric of the outlaw. The "outlaw territories" in the stories that follow are found, in Brand's sense, both in domains regulated by government—whether City Hall, the state, or intergovernmental institutions—and those "colonized" by hippies and the counterculture who imagined they somehow escaped normative codes. A range of sites and institutions served as testing grounds for experimenting with practices seeking to explode conventional modes of life or otherwise to harness a condition of exceptionality, including places where what Brand allegorized as City Hall turned to military means.[54]

Central to my approach, then, is identifying the manner in which, buoyed by a growing sense of environmental or territorial insecurity, mechanisms are invented or put in place—whether in the form of institutions, policies, technologies, forms of organization, aesthetics, even paradigms of "settlement"—that have aimed to quell much-feared insurgencies under the rubric of maintaining "peace." Even when departing from conventional forms of governance or administration (as in City Hall), we find that outlaw areas remained equally, if differently marked by relations of power, and it is these that rarely have received enough attention. Territory, as Foucault suggested, "is no doubt a geographical notion, but it's first of all a juridico-political one: the area controlled by a certain kind of power."[55] Resistance, in turn, has to be political, constructed and negotiated. It does not simply *evolve* in outlaw areas, or even in outlaw territories.

So we begin with the analysis of two buildings—the Ford Foundation Headquarters and UN Plaza—that from the outside look rather innocuous, but if we listen to contemporary accounts, manifest particular disquiet, forming another chapter in the story of modern architecture's response to a geopolitical order radically transformed in the aftermath of World War II. We find architecture not only operating in the service of clientele with a global reach (although that is not incidental), but also, in effect, as a tool within an emergent apparatus of territorial management and security.

CHAPTER ONE

Instruments of Environmental Control

Jolted by images of protesters clashing with heavily armed police officers in [Ferguson] Missouri, President Obama has ordered a comprehensive review of the government's decade-old strategy of outfitting local police departments with military-grade body armor, mine-resistant trucks, silencers and automatic rifles.... Following the attacks of September 11, 2001, the government regarded the police as the frontline forces in a new war.

—Matt Apuzzo and Michael S. Schmidt, *New York Times*, August 24, 2014

Preparing an exhibition at New York's Museum of Modern Art, *Work in Progress: Philip Johnson, Kevin Roche, Paul Rudolph*, Arthur Drexler, director of the Department of Architecture and Design, interviewed the Irish-born and commercially successful American architect Kevin Roche. The exhibition, which opened in October 1970, included the Kevin Roche–John Dinkeloo and Associates' United Nations Center (UN Center) in New York, a project commissioned by the recently formed United Nations Development Corporation (UNDC) for a site directly across First Avenue from the United Nations Headquarters. Before turning to the UN Center and to Roche's related design for the Ford Foundation Headquarters, completed a few years earlier and located only a few blocks away, Drexler initiated the conversation in a seemingly oblique way. Assuring Roche that he was more interested in discussing "attitudes about the art of architecture" than "the problems of the world," Drexler asked how he would "now go about teaching architecture in view of the general upheaval and commotion" brought about by student radicalism and protest movements.[1] The period's widespread unrest and dissent was on the minds of many in the American establishment, whose access to resources and power was a target of contemporary struggles. Channeling the growing sense of insecurity within the profession and the society it served, Drexler's question elicited a telling response. In sometimes subtle, sometimes astonishingly frank terms, Roche spoke to architecture's function within a contemporary matrix of power.

The two institutions around which their conversation revolved—the Ford Foundation and the UN—were major players in the reshuffling of economic and geopolitical power after World War II. Roche's other clients, including the US Air Force, the Federal Reserve Bank, and many formidable US and multinational corporations—IBM, Bell Labs, Union Carbide, Exxon Chemical, General Foods Corporation, John Deere Financial Services, Conoco Inc. Petroleum, J.P. Morgan, Bank of America, and more—were also key to the expansion of US interests to a global arena.[2] All operated within an expansive territory in which American corporate architecture (born in the wake of high modernism, a point to which I will return) was very much at home and which it helped to construct. In what follows, after identifying some key points from the MoMA interview, I want to outline the manners in which Roche's work for the Ford Foundation and the UN quite literally embodied and sought to contribute to neoliberal processes of globalization. "I think that you would first of all have to determine," Roche responded to Drexler, "what role architecture is supposed to be playing." The discipline's interests, and hence its pedagogy, he stressed, were no longer confined to "image requirements," engineering solutions, and environmental control, let alone to "simply providing shelter" (as he egregiously positioned the role of "indigenous architecture"). Rather, as he put it, stressing the perils of population growth, architecture should "participate in the solution of major social problems."[3] It had to begin with politics and the political process.

Politics, Roche clarified, "establishes the basic intention of what our society is going to do and what its objectives are," intentions embodied in institutions of government. The architect's role, he believed, should be to help steer those goals, to assist the "pilot" in establishing the proper direction for governance while also helping to "modify" or "re-direct the system."[4] Roche's concepts of politics and of redirecting the system, of course, were not aligned with the "radical students": quite the opposite. To explain further the architect's role, he invoked the slightly deceptive figure of a pyramid: at the top was "expertise in the organization of the forces of the country so that those forces can be applied," beneath which, in order, were "technicians who can be assembled and organized to put their management capability into the whole thing," followed by "design technicians," then "workers" putting designs into effect, and finally the occupants, those to be governed.[5] Architecture, that is, was seen as a mediating device between governors and the governed, a technology to incorporate occupants into systems of organization and management designed by the few as they sought to institute techniques of power.

Drexler and Roche's conversation turned to the finitude of natural resources—Drexler invoking the prescience of R. Buckminster Fuller and the need for resource management—and to Roche's anxiety about an imminent Orwellian scenario, a *1984*-like "super bureaucracy . . . almost automatically lessening individual freedom," and his thoughts on limits to social justice.[6] Although Roche's stated ideal was "the society which respects the brotherhood of man," in which "nobody starves to death," this did not mean "making everybody totally equal." While equality "in terms of rights or in terms of law" was to be respected, to him, it did not translate well into economic and technical domains. In the Ford Foundation and UN of the period he found perfect allies. "It is nice to have this kind of discussion," Roche told Drexler, confident of his worldly approach, "because it puts architecture and it puts our environment and it puts our lives . . . in a little bit better perspective." Architecture, the environment, and life all indeed appear in heightened perspective once inscribed within such a *dispositif* wherein aesthetic questions appeared to wane. "How much difference does it really make whether a building is beautiful?" Roche posited rhetorically of such a supplementary virtue, adding "does it really make a difference if we have what we call good architecture?"[7]

Drexler believed that it did make a difference, but in defending the "art" of architecture, he recodified aesthetic functions; citing a landmark of modernist aesthetics, he posited that Ludwig Mies van der Rohe's Barcelona Pavilion refuted conventional function by offering itself as the medium of display. Roche remained unconvinced, stating that he "would not get involved in building a monument, whether it is to six million Jews or whether it is to John F. Kennedy," because building monuments remains a "marginal" activity.[8] Recognizing that such media were only one facet of a larger apparatus, Roche had his eye on a more powerful role in modifying or redirecting the system.

Both men agreed that in contrast to the radical students' idealism, and in spite of claims made on its behalf, contemporary architecture (at least within their orbit) was not revolutionary, but rather served "present society." Whether looking at the work of Philip Johnson, Paul Rudolph, Robert Venturi, or Paolo Soleri, they conceded, when faced with the job of making buildings, architects tended to operate within the system, resorting to formal or sculptural models in so doing. If, Roche proposed, Soleri "invents the life to occupy the sculpture," Johnson "accepts what the life will give him and makes his sculpture for it."[9] Roche's work departed from both. Invoking the Ford Foundation Headquarters, he indicated that his design manifests the "ruthless logic" of highway construction, evident in its scale and calculated approach to technology, materials, and economics. However, it was not the size or construction technique that marked the building's affiliation with a broader apparatus: at twelve stories, significantly lower than zoning laws allowed, it was rather modest. More important was its unprecedented organizational strategy of wrapping the program around an enclosed, glazed atrium, a gesture repeated for the UN Center complex. Referring to Fuller domes as precedents, Roche reminded Drexler that city-scale enclosures, such as that Fuller envisaged for Manhattan, were not yet affordable, and he explained of the UN Center, "we are just doing a little skin around our little piece of the world.... So that as well as having garden space, like Ford, which is in a conditioned environment, we have the shopping space and the theater entrances and just building space... all in the same conditioned environment."[10]

At first glance, these conditioned environments seem relatively innocuous, and in some respects, they were. But as with the ruthless logic of highway construction, demarcating their "little piece of the world" was a calculated and symptomatic response to the social, urban, environmental, and territorial instabilities they sought to manage. Haunting their glazed walls and conditioned environments were anxieties about sustaining hierarchies of power and, we might add, about architecture's capacity to serve as an "instrument"—the term comes from Roche—to perpetuate that stratification while helping to modify and redirect the system to particular ends. The

Figure 1.1 Kevin Roche–John Dinkeloo and Associates (KRJDA), Ford Foundation Headquarters, New York, 1963–68 (Ezra Stoller / Esto).

City of New York, Roche noted, responded positively to his enclosures, strategizing to institute zoning legislation to encourage such "super arcades" in place of zoning that encouraged plazas. The paradigm of a publically accessible, although privately owned, outdoor space (derived the previous decade from Mies's Seagram Building) no longer seemed adequate to environmental or security concerns.[11]

Reviewing *Work in Progress: Philip Johnson, Kevin Roche, Paul Rudolph*, Ada-Louise Huxtable noted, "It is an Establishment show in every sense of the word: sponsor, architects and clients." At stake, she indicated, was not the architects' competence or talent, which was evident. "What is seriously questioned," she wrote, "is

Figure 1.2 Installation view of the exhibition *Works in Progress: Architecture by Philip Johnson, Kevin Roche, Paul Rudolph.* October 2, 1970–January 3, 1971. The Museum of Modern Art, New York. Photographic Archives (Alexandre Georges. Digital image © The Museum of Modern Art/licensed by SCALA/Art Resource, NY).

their goals."[12] Noting the "considerable impassioned rock-throwing at the reputations" of Roche and his cohort and the recent arson of Rudolph's Art and Architecture Building at Yale,[13] she wrote, "The approved goals of the present generation are social and environmental reform through architectural practice." Drexler's show, in its focus on the art of architecture, remained "on the side of the monument."[14] "There will be many who will dismiss much of this work as irrelevant to a society in crisis," Huxtable concluded, "Picket lines have been formed for less." Although out of sync with the approved goals of a younger generation and less dramatic than burning Rudolph's Yale building, the architecture on display was marked in other ways by what Wolf von Eckardt referred to in his review as "all that young and black anger." To him, the "impact" of dissent could be seen not in "some arty new style," but in the buildings' "structural clarity and simplicity" in the implied call to order.[15]

As is evident in the Ford Foundation Headquarters and UN Center, we should take Roche literally when he insisted that any aesthetic or formal dimensions of his designs were subservient to the task of capturing and controlling contemporary forces—economic, social, political, territorial—and that the client was the key source of that power.[16] He believed that architects had to recognize those forces and the *dispositif* to which they gave rise and had to design instruments or mediating devices to marshal them in order to integrate people within environments in such a manner as to further a client's ambition.

I want to turn now to the Ford Foundation to unpack this a little further. With a mandate of sponsoring the worldwide "spread" of democracy and with it American economic growth, the Ford Foundation's focus shifted during the 1950s from the reconstruction of Europe under the US-led Marshall Plan to become involved with development aid for the Global South, operating as the long arm of the Truman Doctrine by "injecting money quietly into the operating arms of other non-profit institutions."[17] As Ford Foundation president McGeorge Bundy put it in 1968, "We believe in foreign aid on every ground—of humanity, of peace, and of our own American interest."[18] Recognizing the centrality of the UN to this mission, the foundation injected enormous funding into UN programs, including its UN Center expansion designed by Roche in the late 1960s and 1970s.

The Military-Industrial-Philanthropic Complex

Anticipating a huge injection of funds following the death of Henry Ford (1863–1947), in 1948, the Ford Foundation's board of trustees hired Rowan Gaither to study how it could best define its policies and programs and use its resources in the service of advancing its charter: "human welfare."[19] Once characterized as "a man with a mind like an I.B.M. machine," Gaither functioned at the heart of the military-industrial-academic complex: he was an attorney who served as assistant director of the Massachusetts Institute of Technology's Radiation Laboratory during World War II and, after the war, coordinated the conversion of the Air Force's Research and Development arm into the RAND Corporation, where he went on to be chairman.[20] Like the foundation's board and executive officers, the committee members that Gaither assembled were powerful businessmen and academics, often closely related to or themselves former members of government or military bodies involved with foreign policy and national security decisions.[21] Direct beneficiaries of the national mobilization of industry and technoscientific research following US entry into World War II, they, too, derived from an interconnected elite who continued to manage the country's war machine as it expanded during the 1950s and 1960s in the service of maintaining national security and American technological and economic supremacy, or so-called "Total Peace."[22] The famous "Gaither Report" appeared in 1949: equating the advancement of human welfare with the spread of liberal democratic principles, it declared nothing less than "world peace" to be the foundation's objective.[23] Fueled by the period's Cold War tensions, the foundation pursued the spread of US-led democracy and free-market capitalism by establishing institutional mandates and economic structures throughout the world, hoping thereby to counter the reach of Communist counterparts in the Soviet Union and China.[24]

The world was entering a period of permanent war, war operating in domains other than the strictly military (such as the environment) and coming to structure legal codes and institutional norms. Here, we might say, was a succinct demonstration of Michel Foucault's inversion of Clausewitz: while Clausewitz declared that warfare is the continuation of politics or policy by other means, Foucault recognized the reverse. Policy or politics is a continuation of warfare by other means. In this case, structural underdevelopment and economic colonialism would replace conventional occupation to ensure the status quo.[25] Warfare, as Antonio Negri noted of a generalized condition, "is the crisis that becomes the *dispositif* of capitalist order."[26]

The Gaither Report explained that in pursuing the foundation's goals, "many traditional concepts, such as that of sovereignty, will be subject to scrutiny and redefinition," and it identified as key areas of support in this regard: "education and training of persons for high level policy making in international affairs, plans for aid to underdeveloped areas of the world, and measures to increase international understanding and open the channels of world communication."[27] The foundation's first president, Paul G. Hoffman, formerly President Truman's appointee as administrator of the Marshall Plan, even spoke of "waging peace on the information front."[28] Under this auspice they funded publications, exhibitions, and the education of technocratic elites throughout the world and hence, by extension, the spread of ideologies and institutional frameworks favorable to capitalism. They also funded research and teaching of foreign "languages, literatures, arts, music and philosophies" in the United States. "Our hopes for peace," the foundation argued, marking a strategic shift from ill-fated notions of fortification to cultural infiltration, "rest upon the deep understanding which will come from such knowledge, and not in the erection of Maginot lines, however formidable."[29]

Increasingly central to Ford's "soft" agenda was support for "non-Western studies," particularly social-science research, or what they called "the scientific study of man."[30] This research informed US counterinsurgency strategy and the destabilizing of hostile governments. "Greater knowledge of human behavior, and techniques for acquiring and utilizing such knowledge," the Gaither Report explained of this expanded arsenal, "would be exceedingly useful in the fields of government, business, and community affairs."[31] "Life itself," it added, would "provide the laboratory for basic research."[32] Foundation-sponsored research in the social sciences, from questions of "minority tensions and race relations" to those addressed to health, housing, and education, thus fed US national security strategy as it shifted its focus toward social engineering on the civilian front, both domestically and internationally, situating us within the realm of what Foucault theorized as biopolitical regulation.[33] The

Gaither Report highlighted support for the newly founded United Nations as the key instrument of security: "the maintenance of peace depends in large part upon the willingness and ability of nations to improve and strengthen the United Nations to the point where that organization becomes, in fact, the structure of a world order of law and justice."[34]

Although during the early 1950s, the Communist threat was thought primarily to come from Eastern Bloc countries and from the Marxist ideology spreading in South Asia, particularly in India, recently liberated from British colonial rule,[35] by the end of the decade, as noted above, the foundation turned to focus on the threat of Communism taking hold throughout the Third World, including developing nations in Africa, the Middle East, Asia, and Latin America. In addition to programs in Europe and India, it initiated activities in Africa in 1958, following Ghana's independence from the British Empire, and in turn, the next year, in Latin America, following Fidel Castro's victory in Cuba.[36] A 1961 follow-up study, *The Ford Foundation in the 1960s*, concluded that on account of the "acceleration of science, technology, and weapons development, and the emergence of explosive political, social, and economic forces throughout the world" the foundation had to enlarge its territorial scope: "in an era when both problems and solutions disdain national boundaries, it must be prepared to act globally."[37] It also sponsored so-called "population studies" or "population control," around which the anxieties of the Western World crystallized during the late 1960s.[38] With enormous income generated from Ford Motor Company stocks during the 1950s and 1960s and suspended between government and business, the foundation was in an extremely powerful position of influence, with grants (or their withholding) becoming key instruments to direct (or redirect) national and foreign policy.[39]

By 1967, the year the new Ford Foundation Headquarters in New York opened, the neoliberal ideology of development driving Ford-sponsored aid programs was already controversial, especially as exploitation affiliated with rapid modernization and what one foundation advisor referred to as "a world order congenial to American ideals, interests, and security" became apparent.[40] Take, for instance, the "Green Revolution" funded by the Ford and Rockefeller Foundations as well as by the United States Agency for International Development (USAID). The Green Revolution introduced technologies and management practices from industrialized agriculture—chemical fertilizers and pesticides, irrigation, as well as "high-yield" grain varieties—into developing countries, making huge profits for multinational corporations and increasing rural-urban migration, often to disastrous effect. Using selectively bred crops that were dependent on chemicals and not sensitive to regional light conditions—and hence could be successfully planted in many parts of the globe—this program established a highly toxic method of increasing crop yield that not only led to immense profits for chemical corporations such as Standard Oil (which put together agricultural packages as part of this program), but explicitly aimed to thwart agrarian reform initiatives tied to socialist politics. Although the yields at times helped alleviate famine, they had devastating effects on the bodies of those handling the chemicals (cancer was rife), as well as on small-scale and traditional agricultural methods, traditional diets and ways of life, and biodiversity. Moreover, the foundation's cultural programs, such as the Congress for Cultural Freedom, were now known to be covert operations of the CIA.[41] With growing social unrest in the United States, and as the US-backed Vietnam War escalated, the new world order of "permanent peace" sought by Ford no longer appeared simply to operate in the service of the lofty goal of "human welfare," a point uniformly passed over at the time by the architectural establishment.[42]

Toward a New Architecture

Having sought advice from Pietro Belluschi, dean of the School of Architecture and Planning at MIT (a connection mediated by Julius A. Stratton, the institute's president), in July 1963, the Ford Foundation commissioned Kevin Roche to design their headquarters on a parcel of land on East Forty-Second Street between First and Second Avenues.[43] At the time, Henry Heald was the foundation's president, with John J. McCloy acting as chairman of the board. Both had previously worked with modern architects. As president of the Armor Institute in Chicago, Heald had commissioned Mies to design a new campus during its transformation into the Illinois Institute of Technology; as US high commissioner for Germany from 1949 to 1952, during which he oversaw the creation of the

Federal Republic of Germany, McCloy sponsored the founding of the Hochschule für Gestaltung in Ulm. (A US assistant secretary of war from 1941 to 1945 and president of the World Bank from 1947 to 1949, McCloy was better known for his wholesale pardoning of Nazi criminals, especially powerful industrialists.) After meeting with Heald, McCloy, and other executive officers in August 1963, Roche wrote asking if in the interest of better understanding the foundation's ambitions, the executives could answer the question: "What five things do you consider most important about the Foundation, particularly with reference to the spirit of the Foundation as it will be reflected in this building?" The question was not addressed to "building methods," Roche clarified. His concern, rather, was to understand the institution's goals in "the broadest possible philosophical terms," since the building would "inevitably become the symbol of the organization."[44] The executives' responses revolved around tropes and clichés such as progress, efficiency, originality, courage, integrity, freedom of inquiry, education, world scope, and human betterment.[45]

Of the responses circulated anonymously to Roche, one stood out—most likely McCloy's. Although organized under similar categories—human welfare, social action, education, the arts, and invention—each "attribute" was put forward as a challenge to the architect. First, the respondent explained, given the "world-wide" and "far flung" nature of the foundation's concerns, "no mean parochial building" could speak to human welfare. The building had to emanate its ambitions on a global scale. Second, he noted that unlike governments, which "must await the slow ground swell of public opinion and then deal with the crisis," the foundation could operate at the "leading edge" of "Social Action"; it could enter "the arena while the issue is still unsettled," preempting and steering still-fluid social concerns, and as such, "a monument is premature." Third, he recommended that since "no word more than *Teaching* describes the foundation's spirit and modus operandi," "the building itself should teach." Fourth, he explained, "In the international confrontation of science-based cultures," the foundation "had thrust upon it—the role of keeper of the culture until the wars are ended," and hence the building "must nourish the eye." Finally, on the question of invention, he positioned the foundation as "the largest pool of risk capital in the world." Equipped with funds to test ideas that were "still below the surface of public knowledge and expose them to the test of public reaction," it could even "speed" change, serving as "a wholesaler in the market of ideas." Offering the architect extraordinary license, he set out a culminating challenge: "If we're talking about risk capital, the building itself should be another venture of the Foundation in risk"; it should anticipate "whatever will emerge to save our urban centers, to make them humane and habitable."

The recommendation concluded by underscoring the building's role in responding to the impending urban crisis, reiterating the challenge to demonstrate nothing less than "the next step in the volution [sic] of urban shelter," to produce "a prototype of the shape of things to come in urban architecture." Following recent Civil Rights struggles and in the midst of a massive demographic shift born of the Second Great Migration of African Americans to urban areas and of so-called "white flight" from them, the 1960s was the moment of widespread anxiety regarding the future and security of American cities. In 1962, the foundation added "Problems of Urban Growth" to its sponsorship areas, and in 1967, the year the new headquarters opened, it responded to the "social ferment in the nation's cities" by setting up a program in "University Urban Studies." During its first year, it gave away $13.5 million to four universities, including funds to establish the Urban Systems Lab at MIT and through it to sponsor counterinsurgency projects addressed to the national context, as well as to Latin America and Southeast Asia.[46]

By 1967, McGeorge Bundy had succeeded Heald as president, and Stratton had replaced McCloy as chairman of the board.[47] From 1961 to 1966, before taking up the position at the foundation, Bundy had served as national security advisor for the Kennedy and Johnson administrations, in which capacity he notoriously had encouraged the escalation of US involvement in Vietnam. While Bundy's contribution to the 1967 *Annual Report* concluded by celebrating their new building, he began with what he considered the nation's primary social problems: racial equity and "black nationalism." Referring to the "terrible riots of 1967," he noted, "the subject is still under review, as I write, by a distinguished commission, and we have been proud to help in some of the supporting research it wanted."[48] When reviewing the new building, *Washington Post* reporter Nicholas von Hoffman situated Bundy's philanthropic agenda at this nexus of race and the security complex.

Figure 1.3 Police in riot gear patrol Plymouth Avenue during race riots in North Minneapolis, Minnesota, July 21, 1967 (© Minnesota Historical Society/CORBIS).

Figure 1.4 Armored personnel carrier patrolling downtown Plainfield, New Jersey, July 17, 1967 (AP Photo/John Duricka).

> It's he who led the Foundation into attempting to do some useful things in the area of race relations. In so doing he was implementing the desires of that portion of the American ruling class that is usually called the Eastern Establishment. These are the couth, polished fellows who believe in fair play and enough social change to prevent the mobs on the streets from stealing their money. (The Foundation's all-white board is composed of people like Robert McNamara, Roy E. Larsen, Chairman of Time, plus the heads of a number of other big, profitable organizations). They're ... the best kind of leaders corporate liberalism has been able to produce.[49]

Roche's building sought to provide an antidote or secure environment in the face of this unrest. Moreover, its garden soon came to be read in terms of environmental discourses rising in prominence following the 1962 publication of Rachel Carson's *Silent Spring*. Resonating between allusions to such threats and their solution, the building spoke to the growing need for the instruments of global governance that the foundation staff was simultaneously working to institute.

Crystal Palaces

Responding to the Ford Foundation's program, ethos, and site, Roche distributed the offices in a ten-story, L-shaped configuration along the west and north sides of the midblock plot. The eleventh floor, which ringed the building, was dedicated to higher-level executive offices, including the president's office, with the top floor housing the chairman of the board, as well as meeting and dining areas. These spaces faced onto a spectacular and at the time unprecedented indoor garden, the other two sides of which were composed of sheer glass walls hung from above to enclose a 160-foot-high volume topped by a skylight and encompassing six million cubic feet.[50] Covering a full third of an acre, the greenhouselike environment was designed by landscape architect Dan Kiley, designer of the courtroom for the Nuremberg Trials.[51] It was planted with temperate species, including a giant magnolia tree and a stand of eucalyptus trees, as well as rhododendrons, ferns, and other species "chosen to convey a familiar, rather than an exotic feeling."[52] In "The Outside-In Building," Joan Lee Faust cited Kiley's remark that the landscaping "express[ed] a natural, but controlled atmosphere."[53] In "... Where You Go Inside to Get Outdoors," Sara Davidson speculated that in the garden, it was "perpetually Spring."[54] Housing 37 trees, 999 shrubs, 148 vines, 21,954 groundcover plants and 18 aquatic plants for the pool, the garden was organized in eleven distinct zones, the health of each regulated by artificial-fertilizer injectors and an irrigation system "automatically controlled by timers."[55] Replete with an elaborate air-conditioning system, the environment was kept at a comfortable temperature for the human occupants (between fifty-five and ninety degrees), many of whose office windows opened directly onto the space.

This setup produced symptomatic divides within the critical establishment. The provision and management of the garden was typically received as a benevolent contribution to the public good, praised as an expression of civic idealism, or seen as a polemical departure from the plaza model inaugurated by Mies's Seagram Building the previous decade. But the intensively controlled environment provoked other reactions. Von Hoffman explained, for instance, that "the only air-conditioned forest in this city or maybe in the world flourishes lush in seasonless tranquility inside the Ford Foundation building." The effect of this "glass-enclosed, man-mastered environment," he continued, was like "Shangri-la; a place where the corrosive action of nature, where the unfairness of life, where the motion of time with its cycles of death and regeneration are stayed, if not completely abrogated. It is here in quiet glass chambers that the Ford Foundation's 400-plus employees do their serene work of charity, glancing down at the perpetually green forest where it never rains."[56]

For other critics, this retreat from the urban environment raised the specter of environmental catastrophe. As William Zinsser wrote in "A Grant to Beauty,"

> Inevitably, the garden seems not quite real, shielded behind a veil of glass from the birds and the noises beyond. But perhaps it is a herald of what our future cities will be like, for our present cities are beginning to choke on their own air, a mixture of fumes and soot that few plants will tolerate and man doesn't like much better. So it may be that our salvation lies in the experiment that has just begun on East 42nd Street. Entire blocks will be glassed over, planted with greenery and controlled by thermostat—and there, in the still and filtered atmosphere, we will breathe easily once again and reclaim our old belief that urban life is livable.[57]

Figure 1.5 Plants arriving at Ford Foundation Headquarters, New York, 1966 (© Bruce Davidson / Magnum Photos).

Figure 1.6 Garden in the Ford Foundation Headquarters, designed by Dan Kiley, 1964–68. Photo January 15, 1968 (John Duprey / NY Daily News via Getty Images).

That the Ford Foundation Headquarters continued to resonate in such terms was apparent in "The Cleanest Air in Town . . . and It's Polluted" of 1970. Ed Wallace reported that although hippies were still attracted to the space, where they prayed to the flowers, signs of pollution had emerged, as manifest in the leaves of the camellia plants, among others. He also recounted an attempted addition of bird life by one elderly lady, who released parakeets into the garden. Within a couple of days, he noted, the chirping stopped.[58] The perpetual spring remained a silent one.

For Roche, the configuration served both to provide a garden as an amenity for foundation staff and to structure sightlines within the organization and hence an in-looking sense of community. Von Eckardt described Roche's ambition as providing "tangible contact with nature and a sense of belonging and participation in the place and organization where they work."[59] The goal, as Roche put it, was to articulate "a sense of the individual identifying with the aims and intentions of the group"[60]—identifying, that is, not with those to whom they ministered aid, but with the foundation itself and its global ambitions. When plans were first unveiled, Huxtable reported: "'It will be possible, in this building,' says Kevin Roche . . . 'to look across the court and see your fellow man or sit on a bench in the garden and discuss the problems of Southeast Asia. There will be an awareness of the whole scope of the foundation's activities.'"[61] Others, too, noted that this suspension—of the city, of the seasons, of office workers—within a controlled, internalized environment translated into a sense of control at the global scale. As Joan Silver reported for the *Village Voice*,

> Fred E. Crossland, Program Officer for Special Projects in Education, has an office which does face the court. He likes it. "You are able to see urban and rural settings and two different seasons of the year at the same time. With the kind of work we're involved in, this gives me a broader outlook on life. It makes me recognize that the world and the problems we're grappling with here are not limited to time, season, or place. It helps me keep thinking in global terms.[62]

Just as the environmental control mechanisms produced at once a sense of security—that Ford was taking care of its occupants amid hostile conditions, that one's urban habitat was safe—and

Figure 1.7 KRJDA, Ford Foundation Headquarters, New York, 1963–68. View from executive floors (courtesy of KRJDA).

simultaneously a certain unease, the building's spatial topology, switching back and forth between continuity and disjunction, here and there, resonated uncannily with the foundation's postwar mandate of expanding US interests within a global arena.

In "Charity Begins at Home," *Progressive Architecture* critics Jim Burns and C. Ray Smith spoke to the "huge scale" evoked by the building, noting that the ambiguity between the inside and outside gave the feeling of being suspended "like a fly in amber" between the court, with its "glistening hive of offices rising around one," and the United Nations beyond. "Am I to experience *all* this at once?" they queried in a psychedelic tone, noting a sense of "continual involvement" and "all-in-oneness" that extended as far as "the entire world of Foundation causes." "It is exciting, and perhaps can be a little unsettling to some," they concluded of a waning sense of the individual that resulted.[63] Far from intending to produce an experience of limitless scale, Roche, to reiterate, sought a sense of belonging to a hermetic community, like a family. "After all," he stated to Zinsser, stressing a connection to the workers' productivity, "they spend much of their life there. It's their other family. Everybody wants to belong and to contribute. That's when they're happiest and do their best work."[64] Repeatedly likening his building to a big house for the office family, Roche explained, "we ended up with a solution which creates its own environment."[65] Alfred (Fred) Friendly—the Ford Foundation's television advisor and founding head of the Marshall Plan's Information Program, offered another metaphor of isolation. Coming to work, he explained, was "like being on an ocean liner. It's like walking around with a martini in your hand."[66]

The building's resulting panoptic quality was alluded to by many critics and also caused a sense of unease. If, as Zinsser suggested, referring to Bundy's office, there might be "some pleasure in keeping tabs on the boss, it is a transaction that works both ways: the boss is not only seen, but all-seeing."[67] Davidson turned to this loss of privacy, reporting, "'At first I thought I'd feel self-conscious—like being in a fishbowl,' a receptionist on the eighth floor said, 'but it hasn't worked out that way. Everybody goes about his work, and you get an overall feeling of closeness." "A young man," she recounted of the multidirectional lines of sight, "leans over the balcony and gestures to a lower floor. 'I can see what my secretary is doing,' he said. 'So

Figure 1.8 KRJDA, Ford Foundation Headquarters, New York, 1963–68. Interior wall of atrium, January 10, 1968 (Ben Heller © Bettman/CORBIS).

can I,' a friend answers, 'she's looking back at you.'"[68] Defending his project, Roche explained to Heinrich Klotz and John Cook that for the foundation's "common aim to be reinforced" in a world transformed by television, it was important for "each to be aware of the other."[69] Klotz responded, invoking "Big Brother": "it might work adversely in that they not only communicate, but also control each other, even spy on each other."[70] Roche insisted that people soon acclimatized. Shifting the conversation away from the Orwellian scenario, he stated: "That really doesn't happen. Its rather like being in your bathing trunks that first day of summer when you're not in such great shape; but the larger the crowd is, the less nervous you are about it, especially if everybody else is in the same situation. You don't feel quite so exposed."[71] Klotz remained unsatisfied by this acculturation argument, adding, "Couldn't such a situation create the pressure to conform? The one who pulls the blinds is considered a separatist?"[72] Many reviews began with stories of secretaries anxious about taking too long at lunch or of executives not being able to have their secretaries say they were out, but all noted that there was little evidence of occupants pulling their blinds.[73]

What Silver called the "atmosphere of total visibility" elicited other behaviors, keying into contemporary forms of desire. As she speculated with evident irony in "A Crystal Palace for Visible Man," the building was "perhaps the ultimate expression of a contemporary phenomenon, the Visible Man," a subject for whom "privacy is less important than being noticed. He enjoys attention more than seclusion. Anonymity is disaster. He likes being interviewed, polled, watched, photographed, and listened to." Who, she queried rhetorically of this figure at home in a spectacular media environment, "would have figured on the Ford Foundation building him a definitive preserve?" It was no longer that "the rich and powerful lived in splendid isolation," she explained, since the Visible Man "works in plain view." Wryly playing on this ambivalent, if not simply cynical condition, she wrote, "Life in a goldfish bowl? Lack of privacy? Enforced togetherness? The Foundation employees prefer to speak of 'a sense of community' and an awareness of the organization as a cooperative enterprise."[74] If Ford Foundation employees gained a sense of community by looking at others who, like themselves, were contributing to their common cause, the work undertaken by those looking and performing in this spectacular Crystal Palace, unlike the walls, was far from transparent. It is hard to resist recalling Manfredo Tafuri here, who, following Walter Benjamin, declared with confidence that the great exhibitions, arcades, and department stores of the nineteenth century, "were certainly the places in which the crowd, itself become a spectacle, found the spatial and visual means for a self-education from the point of view of capital."[75] Here, too, we might say, capitalism was at once capturing, mobilizing, and in some instances launching strategic models of subjectivity.[76]

Although invoking Sir Joseph Paxton's Crystal Palace of 1851 in her title, Silver made only passing mention of it as a nickname for the headquarters. Huxtable earlier invoked the referent when announcing with celebration that the foundation "has built itself a splendid, shimmering Crystal Palace." Applauding the "large American foundation, with royal resources," as "a kind of corporate Medici" for late twentieth-century culture, she believed that Ford's patronage gave rise to "a humanistic, rather than an economic environment," a claim that is difficult to sustain.[77] While the Ford Foundation, like other segments of corporate America, enjoyed the scale and influence of royal resources at this moment, the Italian Renaissance is a less apt precedent for its patronage than the imperial ambitions of Victorian England for which the Crystal Palace was conceived.

Derived from Paxton's greenhouse designs, notably those creating artificial climates at Chatsworth for tropical plants (botanical bounties of the British Empire), the Crystal Palace is a landmark within early twentieth-century narratives of architectural modernism emerging from the glass-and iron industrial structures of the nineteenth century. (Roche channeled this ethos in his reference to the scale and rigor of highway structures such as bridges). Among the most influential narratives was that of Sigfried Giedion, who in *Space, Time and Architecture* declared as fully justified Lothar Buchar's 1851 prediction that "the Crystal Palace is a revolution in architecture from which a new style will date."[78] Underscoring the importance of new aesthetic responses that it elicited, Giedion cited Buchar as prescient again in respect to modern architecture: "We see a delicate network of lines without any clue by means of which we might judge their distance from the eye or the real size."[79] In addition to undermining the capacity to perceive "actual size or distance," the organization and light blue coloring of its structural members gave rise to another dazzling effect: "all materiality is blended into the atmosphere."[80] Giedion recognized a similar dematerialization of the landscape and its dissolution into infinity in the work of J. M. W. Turner, noting that while Turner's paintings were less abstract, "an equivalent insubstantial and hovering effect is produced."[81]

Giedion celebrated the Crystal Palace as introducing a sense of "grandeur" and "gentleness" to the industrial milieu, effectively masking or sanitizing its social, subjective, and environmental effects. This first international exhibition, officially called the Great Exhibition of the Works of Industry of All Nations, reflected for him "the courage and enterprise of the early Victorian period," its prefabricated systems

Figure 1.9 The Great Nave of the Crystal Palace, London, 1851. Photographed during move to Sydenham, 1854 (Philip Delamotte © Victoria and Albert Museum, London).

of elements demonstrating the efficient and rational logic of a highly developed industrial nation. Yet Giedion's remarks extended beyond ideological, aesthetic, and technological observations. He rightfully noted that the Crystal Palace's international character was born of "the principle of free trade" and predicated upon the emergence of a global marketplace. It was a "product of the liberal conception of the economy: free trade, free communication, and improvement in production and performance through free competition."[82] Although he recognized as overly confident the expectation that the exhibition might (through encouraging such "freedom") "solve all the problems of the world," Giedion did not speak to contradictions at play between what he cast as the "urge to master the earth's resources and draw out all its wealth" and Prince Consort Albert's more idealistic hope that it might "unite the human race."[83]

The Crystal Palace *was* instrumental in forging a certain union or interconnectedness, a point not lost on Karl Marx, for whom the exhibition was exemplary of the imperialist tendencies of industrial capitalism. (Decades after Giedion, Giorgio Agamben read "the 'bluish halo' that envelops the Crystal Palace" as "but a visualization of the aura that bathes the commodity fetish," speculating additionally that Marx's theorization of the commodity fetish's phantasmagorical character derived from his encounter with the 1851 exhibition.)[84] Stressing the British context, Paul Young explains: "the Crystal Palace was seen as a cartographic validation of free trade's new world order, setting out an Anglocentric industrial and cultural mission at the same time as it further opened the world to British hegemonic ambition."[85] Associated with the rhetoric of a "glorious humanity" and with claims to a peaceful and progressive new world order through industrial enterprise, the Crystal Palace, with its grand scale and enchanting environment, was a mediatic vehicle for establishing an interdependent, but distinctly hierarchical global capitalist system. "For [Immanuel] Wallerstein, as for Marx," Young recalls, "capitalism's capacity to forge connections on the global stage resulted in a world system characterized by territorialized exploitation and uneven development."[86] While sponsoring new forms of interstate negotiation and exchange, and while far from a unified manifestation of different cultures, the Crystal Palace's imperial vision of industrialization and modernization was far from peaceful or equitable: sponsoring dependency and uneven economic and technological development, it was exploitative, violent, and coercive.

As the British Empire collapsed following World War II and as the industrial world encountered the rise of multinational corporations and the information revolution, the Ford Foundation stepped in to build new crystal palaces, those no longer displaying industrial goods, but revealing new operatives in an emergent neoimperial enterprise as it expanded under the opportunistic rubric of development aid, resource management, and security.[87] Mobilizing the rhetoric of peace, progress, and human betterment on a global scale, what went on in the foundation's atmosphere of total visibility involved a carefully calculated deterritorialization and reterritorialization, one not unrelated to Roche's suggestion that while he believed in the "brotherhood of man," it did not mean "making everybody totally equal." The work undertaken in these beautiful glazed offices and perhaps even discussed in its garden had profound ramifications elsewhere, particularly in decolonized territories whose resources and labor pools were becoming increasingly valuable to the West.

In 1968, Kenneth Frampton pointed to the ambivalent relation of the Ford Foundation Headquarters to the constituencies it served, recognizing its "pervasive sense of confidence" as paradoxical evidence of "its underlying sense of *insecurity*." "The *Third World* would have no place here," he reckoned of its "exclusive and hermetic" character. "One cannot but conclude that consciously or unconsciously, the Ford Foundation and its architects knew what they were doing," he deduced of its relation to the public and to the "ordinary objects of our industrial civilization." Himself torn between the evident formal mastery of the architecture and the elitism that it harbored, Frampton concluded that it was a "house of Ivy League values and good intentions, dedicated to the dispensation of private profit for the public good, hermetically sealed in an unreal world, which is not only open to unfortunate external misinterpretations, but which may well also distort, through its all pervasive yet delusive sense of security, its own internal perception of the reality in which it must operate."[88] However, we might read this semantic ambivalence and even the distorted perception of reality (its bracketing) not as a contradiction per se, but rather as central to the building's function, for in its simultaneous presentation of mastery and vulnerability, openness and closure, presence and distance, the building found its cynical vocation, one mirroring its underlying intentions in appealing to the public good. Despite the many readings focused on the building's hierarchical form and classical geometry as a visible expression or symbolism of the foundation's princely power[89] or even those celebrating its innovative use of Cor-ten steel, such characteristics were secondary to its capacity to capture and control contemporary forces and subjects within them, to act, as Roche himself put it, as an instrument for the "organization of forces, political, economic, and technical forces."[90] "Nineteenth-century ambiguity," Tafuri reminds us, "consists wholly in the unrestrained exhibition of a false conscience."[91]

United Nations

The proximity of the Ford Foundation Headquarters to the UN Headquarters, the latter designed in the late 1940s by Wallace K. Harrison in association with an international board of consultants and completed in 1952, was self-conscious and strategic.[92] Not only was the UN important to the foundation's goals, the foundation hoped to align the global missions of the two organizations in the public's mind, thereby deriving an air of legitimacy. Roche's design for the Ford Foundation departed from the UN's modernist paradigm, yet he paid careful attention to the complex when planning the approach to his building, from the upper levels of which were panoramic views of the UN Secretariat.[93] Moreover, even before its headquarters was complete, the Ford Foundation started purchasing parcels of land between Forty-Third and Forty-Fifth Streets in anticipation of the UN expansion. Pursuing this initiative in association with the Rockefeller Brothers Fund, the Carnegie Corporation, and the US mission to the UN under the umbrella of the East River–Turtle Bay Fund, Inc., they commissioned Roche to undertake studies of the area's development potential.[94] At the request of Governor Rockefeller and Mayor John Lindsay, Roche's initial planning studies fed into the creation of the UNDC by the New York state legislature. With McCloy as chairman of its board of directors, the UNDC was a public-private partnership with the ability to use eminent domain and issue tax-free bonds to fund the development. To many, this arrangement led simply to a "land grab" driven by commercial real estate interests.[95] After delays resulting from the

Figure 1.10 KRJDA, UN Center, New York, 1969. Rendering with Ford Foundation Headquarters in lower left (courtesy of KRJDA).

Figure 1.11 View across East River to United Nations Headquarters, 1947–53, and One United Nations Plaza, New York, 1969–75 (Ronald Livieri).

1967 Arab-Israeli War, in 1968, Roche was formally commissioned by the UNDC to design the expansion, his two commissions thus being closely related to each other in far more ways than the provision of an atrium or greenhouse.[96] Both served the interests of a matrix of powerful players seeking to script the emergence of a new world order.

A 1969 brochure for the UN development announced: "For nearly a quarter century New York City has been the center of decisions affecting the lives and welfare of people of all nations. Since 1946, when the United Nations decided to make its headquarters here, the tragedies and the hopes of mankind have been mirrored in the handsome headquarters buildings along the East River." One outcome of those tragedies and hopes was the doubling of UN member nations, primarily through the addition of new nation-states born of liberation struggles, leading to a huge upsurge of delegates and visitors and hence, the brochure posited, to "severe overcrowding."[97] Under the title "A Crystal Palace for the UN," *Progressive Architecture* reported in 1970, "Like the countries it serves, the United Nations has undergone a population explosion," a symptomatic allusion not only to expanded member nations, but to the anxiety regarding population growth, particularly in developing nations.[98] Responding to this growth, the program included offices and hotels to serve the building's primary constituencies—expanded UN missions, dignitaries, and nongovernmental organizations (NGOs)—along with a range of facilities including a visitors center, theaters, restaurants, sports facilities (even a rooftop swimming pool) and shops. Harking back to the Crystal Palace, the brochure announced: "International stores will display and sell crafts and other merchandise from all over the world. Nations, too, will have an opportunity to display products and tell the story of their challenges and achievements. The entire area will become a permanent world's fair in miniature."[99]

Although often likened to the Ford Foundation Headquarters in its pervasive use of glass and provision of an atrium, the UN Center was not designed as a preserve for Visible Man, at least not in the material sense. Early accounts stressed the need for added security for diplomats and heads of state, whose "limos zip into a special enclosed drive-in area, its heavy doors slam shut, and, without seeing so much as a soul, they can rush into a reserved elevator."[100] In April

1968, Kathleen Teltsch reported that Roche's designs aimed "to help fulfill the United Nation's desire for improved security arrangements," noting that "it will be possible for a visiting diplomat to be accommodated at the hotel and reach the United Nations directly through an underground passageway."[101] Four years later, in "New Building for U.N. Aims at Security Fears," she reported: "A skyscraper to be constructed overlooking the United Nations will allow tenants to work, confer, live, eat, shop and swim without stepping outside the premises."[102] Soviet and Arab delegations, among others, she noted, had been subject to "attacks and harassment," hence the need for a conditioned environment appropriate to the new world order. Underscoring its hermetic nature, Roche noted: "The idea is to supply all the facilities and services needed to sustain life so the diplomats can get along comfortably for a week, or as long as they choose, without having to venture outside."[103] Early plans called for an enclosed bridge spanning First Avenue to connect directly with the UN as a security measure. Protection of visiting foreign dignitaries, Teltsch wrote, was "a growing concern in recent years, to the point where the enclosed crosswalk is expected to be made of bulletproof glass."[104]

Moreover, the UN Center was no longer, strictly speaking, transparent, even if its glazed walls produced aesthetic effects resonant with those Giedion celebrated in the Crystal Palace. Unlike Paxton's nineteenth-century structure and the Ford Foundation Headquarters, the towers were designed to be clad in reflective glass that, the brochure anticipated, would help the "new construction blend into its environment." "The immense, faceted forms of its three joined office towers and connecting hotel wing," Huxtable explained of an early scheme for the "superbuilding," "would be covered with a sleek skin of reflecting glass panels, giving the city back to itself in a kind of monumental architectural dissolve. The building is a superb tour de force, a giant trick with mirrors."[105] Diana Agrest later read mirror-glass buildings as producing a "false contextualization": the image they reflect was to her a "message without a code, a continuous endless message."[106] However, that message operated at a metalevel, speaking to the architecture of global capital. (Roche had initially hoped to use red and blue glass—the most common color of flags, he claimed—but later settled for green in deference to the Secretariat building across the street).

Huxtable expanded upon her reading of the UN Center in "Sugar Coating a Bitter Pill." Evidently increasingly conflicted over the merits of the work, she began: "I suppose only a super-scrooge could take exception to the superproject that the [UNDC] has come up with to solve the UN's space and security problems in New York. You would have to be against the pursuit of peace, the brotherhood of nations and man, and the importance of the UN internationally and to New York—6,000 income-producing visitors a day and $6-million in increased taxes to the city."[107]

Questioning why over half the square footage was devoted to commercial office space in order to subsidize the "gargantuan" development, she scoffed at Roche's "beautiful monster, created by monstrous economics." In addition to being "inimical to the city's best environmental interests," the architect had given "glittering architectural form" to such economic reasoning. Here, as she put it, was a "commercial mold" opportunistically "turned into a monument by the architect."[108] But while the tower gave form to monstrous economics, its aesthetic logic retained fluidity, as earlier called for at the Ford Foundation.

Even before the first phase of the UN Center was complete, Vincent Scully questioned the strange inaccessibility or distancing at play in Roche's work, pointing to its "scalelessness... absolute abstraction, disquieting remoteness."[109] In "Thruway and Crystal Palace" of 1974, he critiqued the technocratic bent in the architect's "highway-inspired buildings" such as the Ford Foundation. While seeming to admire its "truly Babylonian courtyard," he read Roche's buildings as "*schema*, idealized abstractions applied to their particular functions," which "derive from Kevin Roche's experience of America."[110] That is, these superscaled projects and "greenhouse city spaces" manifest something about postwar America—what Scully referred to as "the truly inhuman scale of modern corporate society as it actually is."[111] Rendering visible or even desublimating something about that corporate society, Roche's work "created arresting images of it which reveal more about it to us than we knew before." Among those revelations was the increasingly disembodied locus and logic of power. Power, Scully remarked, referring to Greek sculptures of young male nudes and their military counterpart, "does not reside in the *kouros* or even in the soldier any longer." Roche's designs, he proposed,

> instinctively embody something which has no body at all, but in which the real operating force of modern society lies: its massive depersonalized groupings, its vast computerized abstractions, and the essential emptiness of its presidential chair. It is the special power of Roche-Dinkeloo's buildings not simply to reflect such realities, as for example the average building of today may be said to do, but to comment on them through a curiously implacable set of expressive forms, to find visual symbols for them, and to make them emotionally unforgettable through that intensification of reality which is art. One would not want those buildings to lose such qualities, disquieting though what they have to say may sometimes be.

Roche and Dinkeloo, Scully concluded of the work's aesthetic qualities, "make the kind of art that money likes."[112]

The first phase, One United Nations Plaza, was completed in 1976. Describing the building, Paul Goldberger returned to qualities that Giedion celebrated in the Crystal Palace, but added a haunting valence. The tower was clad in "a skin of bluish-green reflective glass arranged in a gridiron pattern of panes so as to obscure any sense of floor divisions, or even any sense of scale at all, from the outside. The glass covers everything like a great shining blanket, and its pattern offers no hint as to the goings-on inside" rendering the building "almost weightless."[113] The following decade, Francesco Dal Co turned to the building's phantasmagoric and spectral qualities, calling it "an estranged figure, destined to appear in the New York skyline as a phantom." "The apparition constructed by Roche," he posited of its disquieting nature, "resembles an enormous block of shaped ice hovering among the clouds, a foggy condensation of the smog of the city."[114] Recognizing something similar, William Marlin added a positive inflection to the gossamerlike qualities of the reflective glass skin as it reflected capitalism. Acknowledging that the building undermined modernist axioms, such as expressing functional distinctions or delineating floors, to him, this "friendly neighborhood skyscraper" (presumably alluding to Spider-Man's ambiguous character) refused the idea "that a building, like the news report, should 'tell it like it is.'"[115] Why should a building tell the truth? he implicitly asked. The "quizzical quality" of the surface served, instead, to deflect attention to the earlier UN buildings and stealthily mirror forces at work in its New York surroundings.

As Roche avowed to Drexler, he saw architecture's role as that of serving clients and hence, in his case, quite literally as instrumentalizing the power of American institutions and corporations. He was even more explicit about this closeness to capitalism when talking with Klotz and Cook. As "a social tool," he stated, architecture is "very much a part, even an appendage, of the general movement of society." Casting the discipline as an "instrument" intimately tied to "governing organizations," he believed its role should be that of "*harness*[*ing*] the forces of society to build portions of the city. . . . It's really a matter of *organizing*."[116] "That sounds like an Establishment answer," Cook responded, for it implied that "an architect must then get into that stratum of society which runs it." Roche's clients were, as noted, representative of such a governing stratum. Having worked with and for them, moreover, he understood, consciously or unconsciously, that power no longer operated exclusively from the top down or always in a strictly legible or semantic register, but strategically and horizontally—one didn't "tell it like it is." "When you say something is Establishment," Roche replied, "I don't know what that really means," suggesting rather that the "instrument" of which he spoke was "an organization of forces, political, economic, and technical forces." There was, of course, still a sector of American society that one could call the establishment in the early 1970s, and we have seen an interrelated and revolving cast of such characters shifting between the Ford Foundation, the United Nations, US government agencies and military posts, multinational corporations, and MIT. All were involved with the organization of forces that Roche deemed relevant to the discipline. What he comprehended, to reiterate, was that given this *dispositif*, the architect must learn to recognize those forces, to understand how such instruments are structured, how their objectives are established, who participates in the apparatus of power, and how.

Although architects, too, thus had to operate tactically within a shifting battlefield, to Roche, the discipline retained a stabilizing role: "In a society which also has an inheritance of violence, and destruction, and fracture of moral standards," he stated, "architecture must help stabilize." When Klotz queried, "Does that imply that an architect cannot be revolutionary? Must he accept and affirm the society in which he finds himself?" Roche skirted the question, explaining that new buildings are expensive and involve a lot of people, and "in order to accomplish that, an architect has to harness all available energies."[117] We might read the stabilization of which Roche spoke not simply as a form of material fixing in place, such as architecture might conventionally have produced in bricks and mortar or through a monument, but as part of a strategy for maintaining hierarchies of power in a radically unstable and ambivalent economic and political environment. His work for the Ford Foundation and UN helped stabilize techniques of power then fueling American economic expansion under the rubric of security, an expansion cynically sponsored in the name of democracy and humanity.

Architecture or Revolution?

Introducing a 1975 monograph on Kevin Roche–John Dinkeloo and Associates, Henry-Russell Hitchcock attempted to position the office's practice with respect to its modernist forebears, finding it necessary to distinguish the work from the "heroic" period of modernism in early twentieth-century Europe. "Unlike that of the advanced architects of the 1920s," Hitchcock proposed, lamenting that progressive concepts had come to an end, the work was "not future-slanted; they have been and still are building for the here and now."[118] If, as he put it, alluding to Le Corbusier's *Vers une architecture*, European modernists had been striving "Toward a New Architecture," Roche and Dinkeloo's architecture "represents essentially the future of their elders become our present."[119] To underscore the distinction, Hitchcock imagined what that heroic generation might think when encountering the work. They

> would have been amazed at the backers that this later architecture was finding, annoyed and doubtless shocked that an architecture they had associated with a socially reformed world should be receiving the support of such clients as the Federal Reserve Bank and the Ford Foundation. . . . These would have been rather naïve, extra-architectural responses, and negative rather than positive, resulting on the one hand from envy and, on the other, from the feeling that there must have been some sort of "sell-out" for an architecture descended from theirs to receive such support.[120]

Hitchcock himself played a key role in rendering modernism palatable to American corporate clients through his 1932 MoMA exhibition, cocurated with Philip Johnson, *Modern Architecture:*

International Exhibition. Indeed, his codification of an "international style" notoriously contributed a fatal blow to progressive notions of modern architecture, replacing ideals of social transformation with a rational aesthetic suitable for the corporate world.[121] But this was not the end of the story. What his commentary on Roche elucidated, like Drexler's question to the architect five years earlier, was the degree to which those "extra-architectural" dimensions had returned to the fore. Architectural criticism, let alone history, could no longer confine its readings to heroic narratives and the men and buildings that populated them. Understanding architecture, as Roche knew, meant tracing out a different map and a broader matrix of forces.

Roche's Ford Foundation Headquarters and UN Center situate us, historically speaking, at (or right after) this turning point of American late modernism—the moment when, as Hitchcock conceded, one could no longer assume an allegiance, even cynically, between modernist aesthetics and progressive social ideals. Both buildings were constructed during a period of social and political turmoil and even insurrection in the United States. The civil rights struggles, antiwar dissidence, and environmental activism that surfaced in reviews and interviews were born of a growing discontent with socioeconomic injustices and environmental destruction fueled in large part by the neoimperial economic agendas of US foreign policy and powerful corporations such as the ones for whom Roche worked. There was also a growing recognition among powerful economic and political actors that calls for justice and self-determination from the developing world posed a rising threat. To the establishment, both domestic and foreign dissent potentially posed an economic and hence a security threat, a threat that, in different ways, the Ford Foundation (as a philanthropic organization) and the UN (as an interstate institution dedicated to maintaining peace and fostering human rights, development, and humanitarian aid) sought to quell. Harnessing anxieties regarding urban unrest and environmental control, Roche's architecture stepped in to this arena to provide a reassuring image of peace and stability, assuring anxious citizens and policy makers in the United States that world order could be maintained. My point is not that architecture cannot operate to progressive ends, but that it tended to do so only in certain hands and for certain clients. The problem arises when architects assume the mantle of outdated heroic narratives, erecting glazed facades and white houses that, wittingly or unwittingly, and fueled by critics, contribute to this cynicism.

In many respects, Roche offered an updated answer to Le Corbusier's famous question in *Vers une architecture*: architecture, or revolution? He, too, believed that "revolution could be avoided." But he understood that "extra-architectural" forces had changed since the time of high modernism. Le Corbusier's idea that affordable housing provided by a rationalized industrial modernism might save bankers from the discontent of the working classes no longer had traction. While seeking pacification, Roche's architecture aimed to serve his clients otherwise. That Roche sought to advance their agenda was evident in his comments in an interview in *Office Age*. "Workers, first of all, can become more productive. A corporation's employees are its greatest creative resource. This fact should be used, and must be used, in order for a corporation to exploit its potential." Hence, in architecture, "anything done has to be justified in terms of improved productivity."[122] The architect's role thus was to serve his clients and the systems within which they operated, to (as he put it) "harness" contemporary forces and keep workers productive in those "all-executive" environments, replete with pleasant gardens and lunchrooms, as they extended their reach worldwide.

The Ford Foundation and the UN were not simply wealthy clients, but instruments of economic liberalism and powerful players in a new world order and its postsovereign and biopolitical governing logics, and Roche's architecture served forces of capitalist expansion, actualizing the desires of what Tafuri and Dal Co termed "the new American clientage," something perhaps better characterized not as a "system of big corporations," but as a military-industrial-academic-philanthropic complex. "The artificial 'nature' inserted into the heart of Manhattan is no less false," they scoffed, "than the pretenses to community welfare that the architects resort to as justification."[123] Following the postwar reconstruction of Europe, as noted earlier, the UN, like the Ford Foundation, turned increasingly to the problem of "development" or modernization in Third World countries. Both institutions played key roles in structuring the economic and technical character of that development and ensuring the dominance of American economic and political interests in a globalizing world. Hence Bundy's remark: "We believe in foreign aid on every ground—of humanity, of peace, and of our own American interest."[124]

It was not, however, only late-Marxist architecture critics such as Tafuri and Dal Co who recognized foul play within the period's architecture and the system it served. The next chapter turns to countercultural practices affiliated with the Open Land movement in Northern California that tell a different, but not unconnected story. Although it seems an unlikely connection, we will find that while establishment institutions and architects remained haunted in some senses by radicalism, the opposite was also true. These communards recognized with some precision and sought, in effect, to invert the techniques of power and neoliberal economic apparatus at work within that system. They recognized, implicitly or explicitly, that harbored in the strategic openness and ambivalence of the emergent biopolitical apparatus was the potential for critical forms of harnessing or redirection, even quite literally the potential for reversals of power. Architects such as Roche did not have a monopoly over environmental tactics on this battlefield, and it remains important to trace moments when architecture and the built environment were put to other ends. For even if the Open Land communards were far less powerful and less resilient than Roche and his clients, their story reminds us that ethical and political choices are at work in how people position themselves within such an apparatus. The questions we need to ask—old questions, but still good ones—are for whom did they work, and to what ends?

CHAPTER TWO

Code Wars

In June 1970, Sara Davidson published the story of her encounter with the Open Land movement in *Harper's Magazine*. Entitled "Open Land: Getting Back to the Communal Garden," the article recounted the journalist's recent visits to Wheeler Ranch in Northern California and Freedom Farm in Washington State, along with a brief conversation in Menlo Park with Stewart Brand, editor of the *Whole Earth Catalog*. It concluded with a short note on the movement to establish Earth People's Park, spearheaded by the Hog Farm commune's Hugh Romney (aka Wavy Gravy). Pursuing an ideal of "no authorities and no rules," Earth People's Park, as Davidson explained, hoped to open large tracts of communal land and hence to offer "a way out of the disaster of the cities, a viable alternative."[1] *Harper's* was not the first mainstream press coverage of the ideals and struggles of contemporary agrarian communards. Indeed, like their urban counterparts in Berkeley, San Francisco's Haight-Ashbury, and New York's East Village, this aspect of hippie culture proved attractive to media, soon spreading from alternative press such as *The Modern Utopian*, *The Green Revolution*, and *Mother Earth News* to *Life*, *Time*, the *San Francisco Chronicle*, the *New York Times*, and beyond.[2] Davidson's article is of interest here for its focus on the battles of the Open Land movement—on attempts to cede private property rights to a largely undefined domain of communal stewardship and to make land available rent free for anyone to use, not just in California and the Pacific Northwest, but eventually nationally and even globally. Such attempts met a rapid and increasingly violent response by the state.

Offering her impressions of Wheeler Ranch, Davidson recalled a sign near the community garden reading "Permit not required to settle here."[3] Many had taken up the call to occupy land free of charge, building makeshift structures or setting up temporary dwellings from tents and teepees to customized school buses and vans in this ambiguous territorial zone. The dwellings, Davidson wrote of the scene she encountered, "are straight out of Dogpatch—old boards nailed unevenly together, odd pieces of plastic strung across poles to make wobbly igloos, with round stovepipes poking out the side. Most have dirt floors, though the better ones have wood." The occupants themselves had a similarly poverty-ridden, even preindustrial, if slightly theatrical (or fictional) appearance, wearing, as she put, "hillbilly clothes, with funny hats and sashes," outfits also described as "pioneer clothes."[4] The scene in the patchworklike garden, she went on to suggest, "presents the image of a nineteenth century tableau: women in long skirts and shawls, men in lace-up boots, coveralls, and patched jeans tied with pieces of rope, sitting on the grass playing banjos, guitars, lyres, wood flutes, dulcimers, and an accordion. In a field to the right are the community animals—chickens, cows, goats, donkeys, and horses."[5] Emerging from a society that long placed a premium on social and technological modernity—whether in agricultural and land-management practices, housing techniques, clothing habits, consumption and entertainment, or standards of hygiene—how are we to understand this peculiar and willing "regression," this identification that ran so clearly against the grain of ideals of progress?

Wheeler Ranch was not alone in adopting such anachronistic and seemingly vernacular customs and aesthetic trappings or in adopting an ethos of communal property and the minimal exploitation of resources. Indeed, these practices were characteristic of many back-to-the-land "pioneers" and have typically been read as manifestations of an escapist desire to return to simpler modes of existence in response to increasingly hostile urban environments or as simply Romantic searches for a life more meaningful than the spiritual void characteristic of their parents' generation. While these widespread sentiments were important motivating factors in returning to the land, I want to suggest that one might revisit the critical and political valence of their nonnormative lifestyles. We might read the Open Land movement as a symptomatic and tactical response to historical forces, as demonstrating a form of counterconduct that (wittingly or unwittingly), in its attempts to loosen the grip of the state's

Figure 2.1 Low-tech shelters at Wheeler Ranch commune, c. 1969. From *Open Land: A Manifesto* (Wheeler Ranch Defense Fund, c. 1969) (Sylvia Clarke Hamilton).

Figure 2.2 Bill and Gay Wheeler, Wheeler Ranch commune, c. 1970 (Bob Fitch Photographic Archive, © Stanford University Libraries).

regulatory apparatus, articulated a precise form of knowledge about contemporaneous biopolitical techniques of power and governance.

At a moment once again marked by the legacy of US-led neo-imperial warfare on foreign territory, a seemingly ever-increasing range (and reach) of social and political regulation under the auspice of security (both of territories and of populations), widespread concerns over the environment and the exploitation of natural resources, and struggles against the imminent foreclosure of any remaining global commons or public domain—from land, air, and sea to the digital realm—these historical paradigms of counterconduct and the response of the state seem to warrant revisiting. Not in the sense of providing models of refusal or dissidence (for conditions have fundamentally changed), but as sites at which to investigate emergent techniques of power. Although only a small sector of the back-to-the-land movement, Open Land offers a provocative way to investigate practices that emerged in response to an increasingly administered environment, hence outlining stakes raised by the nation's "internal exodus" of the late 1960s.[6] What sorts of ethics, I think we need to ask, were at work in the Open Land movement and why did such attempts to "open" or "free" the land elicit such rapid and often violent responses from the state?

Exodus from official systems of managing land and the built environment—from property rights and trespass laws to building codes and health and safety regulations—was not as easy as declaring "Permit not required to settle here," as soon demonstrated at Wheeler's. Indeed, the sign served less as a performative or speech act in the sense theorized by J. L. Austin (actually declaring the land to be free of the need for permits) than it did as a polemical and political gesture.[7] It was at once a manifesto for freeing the land or ceding it (back) to the commons and an invitation to participate in testing the limits of the tolerance of the police and the legal system (let alone of the neighbors) for the commune's battle against the private ownership of land and for their unconventional behavior. And the local authorities (like the neighbors) fought back, giving rise to what came to be known as "code wars" and with them an escalating set of tactical and countertactical maneuvers between the commune and local and state governing institutions. During this battle, the ad hoc shelters and other nonnormative structures (we cannot quite call this architecture) emerged as strategic components of

Figure 2.3 Sonoma County officials arriving at Wheeler Ranch, 1969 (Bob Fitch Photographic Archive, © Stanford University Libraries).

countercultural refusal and of the local government's defense against it. While these low-tech shelters proved to be powerful matériel on the part of the communards—easy to produce, affordable, and garnering both anxiety and publicity—they proved ultimately insufficient against the laws regulating human habitation, which quickly came to replace the charge of harboring dangerous persons as the police and the legal system's most effective weapon.

Davidson ended her account of Wheeler Ranch by recounting that she had accompanied commune members to a court appearance for "charges of assaulting a policeman when a squad came to the ranch looking for juvenile runaways and Army deserters." Although the judge had declared a mistrial in this instance, she noted that "the county fathers are not finished, though. They are still attempting to close the access road to Wheeler's and to get an injunction to raze all buildings on the ranch as health hazards."[8] County officials would eventually triumph on both fronts; with the exception of Bill Wheeler's studio (protected as the legal owner's private residence), all buildings were later demolished, and the access road was closed to all but Wheeler and a few select guests. Normalcy of occupation was enforced.

Happiness People

Wheeler Ranch was not the first property in Sonoma County to have "opened" its land to those wishing to depart from urban life and join an alternative rural community.[9] Nor was it the first to have elicited a crushing response from law enforcement and the judiciary system. When Bill Wheeler opened his 320-acre property in the winter of 1967 to whomever wished to settle there, he did so partially in response to the rapid foreclosure of Morning Star Ranch, an earlier attempt to forge a "liberated" territory within the United States. In the spring of 1966, Lou Gottlieb and Ramon Sender declared Gottlieb's ranch to be Open Land, a place without rules, regulations, or organization. In a sympathetic article on Morning Star and its "happiness people" published by the local *Press Democrat* newspaper, Gottlieb was described as "a patriarch who doesn't govern, a landlord who doesn't charge."[10] Morning Star was to be a utopia of the nongoverned, a nonhierarchical community, a place existing far beyond the domain of patriarchs and landlords, as well as of extant social and material norms. Gottlieb, a former singer with the Limeliters, and Sender, an important protagonist in the early development of electronic music and synthesizers at the San Francisco Tape Music Center, met at the legendary Trips Festival at San Francisco's Longshoremen's Hall in January 1966. Sender was a principal organizer (along with Stewart Brand) of this three-day, acid-fueled experiment with overcoming the ego through alternative consciousnesses and electronic environments. The lineup included Brand's *America Needs Indians*, the Merry Pranksters and their psychedelic symphony, Open Theater, the "God Box," Ann Halprin, Gordon Asby, The Stroboscopic Trampoline, the Grateful Dead, and more.[11]

In retrospect, this point of departure seems far from incidental: many within the counterculture attested that LSD played a significant role in sponsoring their rejection of mainstream values in favor of a sense of oneness with the Earth and its peoples.[12] Moreover, Morning Star remained haunted by the sense that electronic technologies and computerization heralded a future of pure automation, a future in which human labor would be replaced by machines. "The people here," Gottlieb remarked to a journalist while touring the commune's "primitive houses," "are the first wave of an ocean of technologically unemployables. The cybernation is in its early snowball stages."[13] That human labor would become outmoded on account of "cybernation" harbored, on the one hand, a utopian promise: freedom from work and from scarcity. And in retrospect, the embrace of manual labor—building houses, farming the land, doing it yourself—reads as a compensatory shift away from that very "cybernation," a largely unself-conscious, if for many therapeutic attempt to deal with the prospect of a withdrawal of material activities by the first generation for whom this shift toward the vicissitudes of immaterial labor was not only imminent, but palpable.[14]

On the other hand, there was the recognition of a dystopian underside heralded by advanced technologies—the eradication of opportunities for work and the loss of the dignity of labor, and beyond this, the specter of atomic and nuclear warfare. This sense of a looming threat of being forced into a condition of basic survival gives a very different valence to the embrace of archaisms and the identification with less privileged persons that was characteristic of what they termed "voluntary primitivism." The two sides of this equation were not necessarily opposed. Sender noted that

Figure 2.4 Ramon Sender playing the Buchla Box at the Trips Festival, San Francisco, January 1966 (Susan Elting Hillyard).

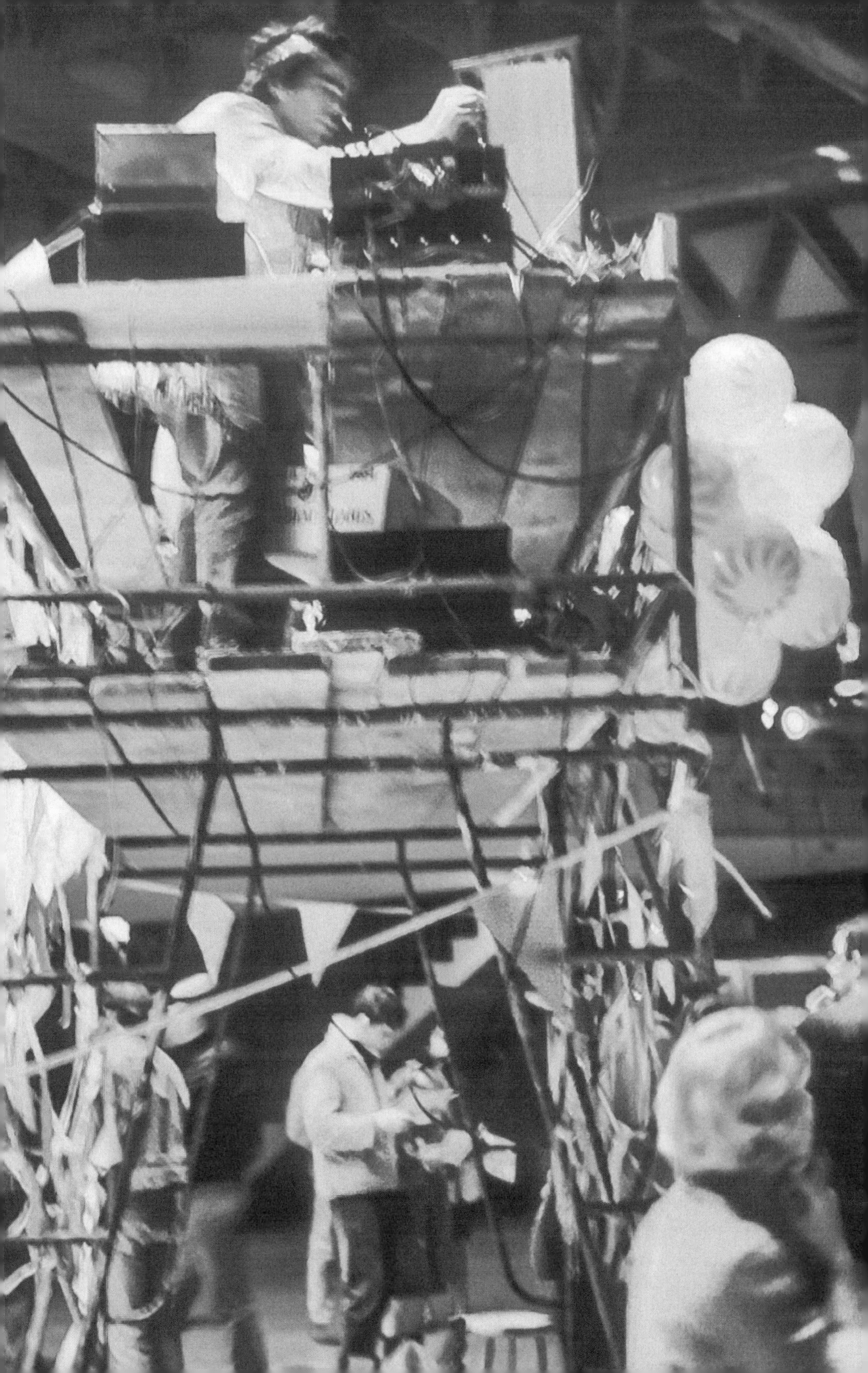

"voluntary primitivism" "could only evolve within an economy of abundance, such as the United States today. It proposes a synthesis of the technologically sophisticated life style with a voluntary return to the ancient, tested ways."[15] Here, in a microcosm, was a strange, distorted reiteration of the radical ruptures and unjust adjacencies emerging in global access to technology and the shifting topology of relations between industrial and postindustrial modes of production. Although voluntary for those living within an economy of abundance, for many others—whether the poorer sector of the American populace or the rapidly industrializing areas of the Third World, including countries recently gaining independence from colonial rule and increasingly becoming industrial labor pools—such "primitivism" was hardly voluntary, raising the question of how to read the identification with social injustice or the identification "down," whether with poor farmers, with itinerant populations, with Native Americans, with the nineteenth century, or with survivors of a nuclear apocalypse.

LATWIDN

The history of Morning Star and Wheeler Ranch has been recounted in detail elsewhere.[16] Here, I want to recall a few prescient details in trying to address what might have been at stake in the particular conjunction of an attempted opening or freeing of the land, an underdeveloped form of shelter, rejection of many aspects of modernity, and the ethics of "care"—at once of the land, of the planet, of other persons, and of the self. Morning Star's ethos of openness was presented as the principle of LATWIDN—"land access to which is denied no one." As claimed in *Open Land: A Manifesto*, "We found out that, if you told no one to leave, the land (the *vibes*) selected the people who lived on it. We also found out that in this supportive, *no rules* environment, hostilities could find little breeding ground."[17] Private ownership of property and exploitation of the land for profit came to be thought of not just as the unjust appropriation of the commons, but as the cause of a loss of innocence, or, in Gottlieb's words, as an "original sin." The "landlord role," he posited, "may be the core of the wrong relationship to the earth's surface.... We are talking about the *fons et origo* of an ecological mistake that could render the planet uninhabitable by homo sapiens—in legal terms, 'fee simple' which conveys to the title holder 'absolute dominion over the land.'"[18]

Figure 2.5 Family of the Mystic Arts commune members, 1969 (John Olson/The LIFE Picture Collection/Getty Images).

LATWIDN derived in part from the Diggers' Free City, and Morning Star attracted a number of Diggers who grew fresh vegetables both for bartering with neighbors and for their urban food giveaways in San Francisco. Gottlieb also acknowledged historical predecessors, situating Morning Star as "continuing the tradition of the intentional community—Brook Farm, Oneida, New Harmony."[19] Yet he stressed that Morning Star marked a distinct form of departure. "If the people are assembled on the basis of any kind of trip, it's old hat. It immediately becomes a sort of 19th century closed community, closed intentional community, and that trip's been done."[20] To Davidson he insisted that in prioritizing free rent, "Open land has no historical precedent. When you give free land, not free food or money, you pull the carpet out from under the capitalist system." Invoking the anxiety this produced, Gottlieb continued: "Once a piece of land is freed, 'no trespassing' signs pop up all along the adjoining roads."[21] "No Trespassing" signs, he declared, "are the cause of war, racial strife and marital unhappiness."[22] To Richard Fairfield, editor of *The Modern Utopian*, Gottlieb reiterated that free rent "is the most potent lever for the transformation of our society."[23]

Following a mention of the "Morning Star colonists" in *Time*'s famous July 7, 1967, cover story on hippies, the thirty-two-acre property quickly attracted large numbers of residents and visitors and with them the attention (and wrath) of Sonoma County officials. In late June 1967, Gottlieb had been charged with operating an organized camp in violation of state public health regulations. Upon being arrested, he wryly announced: "If they find any evidence of organization here, I wish they would show it to me."[24] Having constructed a bathroom and fixed up the kitchen facilities in an attempt to be in accordance with the law, Gottlieb pleaded no contest to the initial charges on September 12. But within hours of the plea, the "hippie colony" was raided by what one paper called "a small army of county officials," including Sheriff John Ellis, sheriff's deputies, probation officers, FBI officers, the director of environmental health, building inspectors, a Sonoma County supervisor, Municipal County Judge James E. Jones, and others.[25] Signs were posted condemning the structures, and residents were given twenty-four hours to evacuate. It was following this raid that many of Morning Star's early settlers moved to Wheeler Ranch, others moving to New

Figure 2.6 Morning Star Ranch commune members, 1967. From *Open Land: A Manifesto* (Wheeler Ranch Defense Fund, c. 1969) (Sylvia Clarke Hamilton).

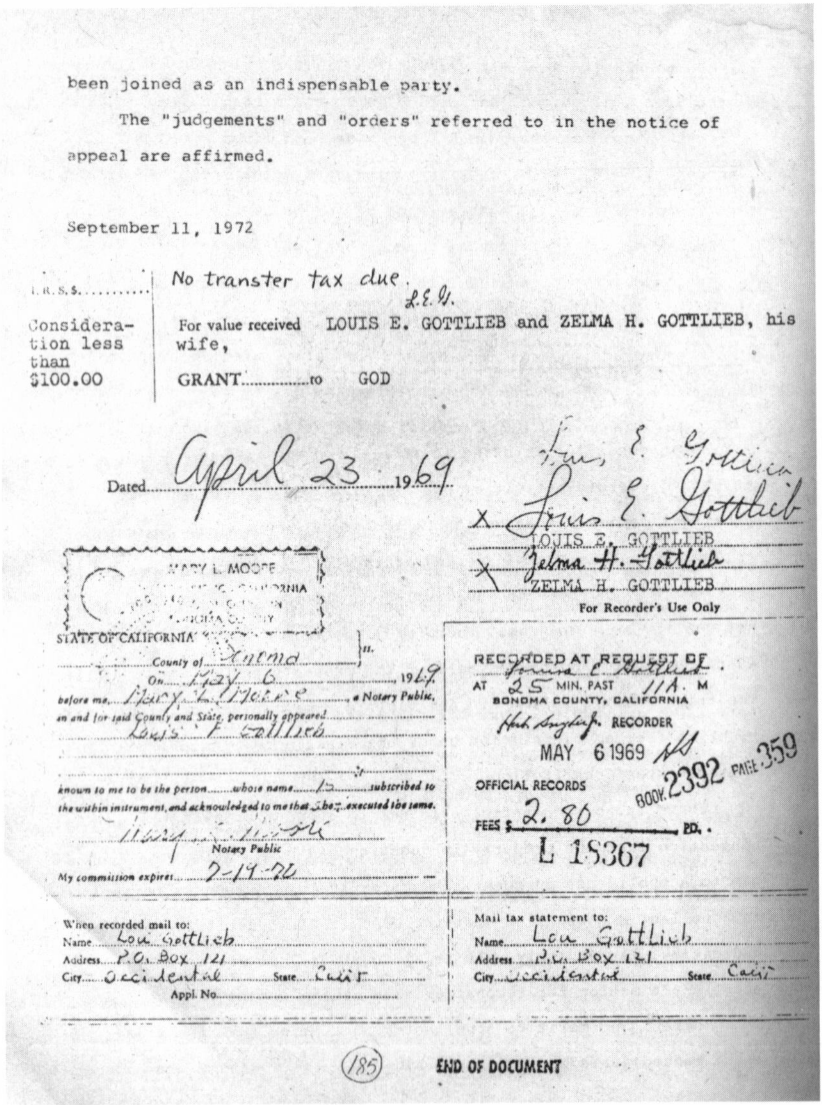

been joined as an indispensable party.

The "judgements" and "orders" referred to in the notice of appeal are affirmed.

September 11, 1972

I.R.S.$..........

Considera-tion less than $100.00

No transfer tax due.

L.E.G.

For value received LOUIS E. GOTTLIEB and ZELMA H. GOTTLIEB, his wife,

GRANT............to GOD

Dated April 23 1969

Louis E. Gottlieb

x Louis E. Gottlieb

LOUIS E. GOTTLIEB

x Zelma H. Gottlieb

ZELMA H. GOTTLIEB

MARY L. MOORE

STATE OF CALIFORNIA

County of Sonoma } ss.

On May 6 1969

before me, Mary L. Moore, a Notary Public, in and for said County and State, personally appeared Louis E. Gottlieb

known to me to be the person whose name is subscribed to the within instrument, and acknowledged to me that he executed the same.

Mary L. Moore

Notary Public

My commission expires 7-19-72

For Recorder's Use Only

RECORDED AT REQUEST OF Louis E. Gottlieb

AT 25 MIN. PAST 11 A. M

SONOMA COUNTY, CALIFORNIA

Herb Snyder Jr. RECORDER

MAY 6 1969

OFFICIAL RECORDS

BOOK 2392 PAGE 359

FEES $ 2.80 PD.

L 18367

When recorded mail to:

Name Lou Gottlieb

Address P.O. Box 121

City Occidental State Calif

Appl. No.

Mail tax statement to:

Name Lou Gottlieb

Address P.O. Box 121

City Occidental State Calif

(185) END OF DOCUMENT

Figure 2.7 Signature page of deed granting Morning Star Ranch to God, 1969. From Unohoo, Coyote and the Mighty Avengers, *Morning Star Scrapbook* (Occidental, CA: Friends of Morning Star, c. 1973) (courtesy Ramon Sender).

Mexico and founding Morning Star East amid a growing field of Southwestern communes.[26] Those remaining or subsequently arriving were repeatedly raided and rounded up, and the property was repeatedly condemned. The organized camp charge was eventually dropped, but further charges followed—from contempt of court and trespass to fire and safety code violations; anything to discourage this nuisance.

In January 1969, with Gottlieb still refusing to remove people forcibly from the land on the grounds that it went against his religious beliefs, twenty-one people were arrested on charges of violating a Superior Court order to vacate. Faced with ever-mounting violations and fines, in May, Gottlieb (whose name translates as "God loves") went to the county courthouse and deeded the land to God in a notorious attempt to render the property public domain, to return it to the commons. This savvy legal maneuver served to stay the injunctions for a period, with judges unwilling to declare that God doesn't exist. But in July 1970, Sonoma County Superior Court Judge Kenneth Eymann ruled that "whatever be the nature of the Deity, God is neither a natural nor an artificial person capable of taking title (of Morningstar Ranch) under existing California law"[27] and instructed local authorities to carry out the writ against the property and demolish all inhabited structures with the exception of Gottlieb's studio, understood as his private residence. Gottlieb denounced the ruling as "idolatry," "blasphemous," and "sacrilegious," but appeals to the freedom of religion also proved useless.[28] As the communards observed, Sonoma County had "started a broad-based policy of repression, including a punitive and discriminatory enforcement of the health and building codes.... It became a political issue for Sonoma County's officials to rid themselves of their *undesirable* neighbors."[29]

Bulldozing the unskilled, ad hoc settlements at Morning Star and Wheeler's can be read, on a first-order level, as simply a way to remove structures considered to be threats to human health and safety and unfit for human habitation, as an instance of the state acting on behalf of the welfare of its citizens, as a simple act of enforcing the law when faced with buildings not up to code. (Such regulatory codes do, of course, play an important role in keeping people safe and slumlords in check.) Yet if we are to judge by the vehemence of the county's response, the stakes were higher than the health and safety of those choosing to live in such conditions. For the communards, these structures were a principal means for articulating prospects for and disseminating images of alternative modes of life. They were strategic and mediatic vehicles in their attempts to withdraw from the state's regulation of the environment, tactical weapons in the battle over opening land. Building codes and bulldozers, in turn, became strategic weapons in the state's defense against these "attacks" on mainstream American values.

But this raises the question of whether what we are seeing is something like the intentional destruction of a built environment as a means of destroying a corresponding culture, something like an act of war that, were it a war between states, would be prohibited by the Geneva Convention. Before deeding the land to God, Gottlieb in fact proposed deeding Morning Star to the county as a museum of folk architecture, a gesture seeking to preserve these eccentric structures as a form of testimony, to protect its "cultural heritage" from the code wars. And we might note that whether we recall the destruction of low-income inner-city neighborhoods as crime-filled "ghettoes" under the rubric of urban renewal or (in a distinct register) the destruction of Palestinian refugee camps on the basis of their harboring terrorists or of Vietnamese villages as giving cover to Communist insurgents, the bulldozer was a key twentieth-century technology for the intentional destruction of ways of life deemed crucibles of insecurity, a key technology of urbicide.[30] To try to unpack the issues raised here, I want to return and take a closer look at what informed these highly idiosyncratic built assemblies and how they might have posed a challenge to security—of land prices, of the health of the population, of moral and social values, of the productivity and hence profitability of the workforce.

A Philosophy of Architecture

A section of *Open Land: A Manifesto* entitled "Our Beleaguered Homes" outlined the ethos of self-build, no-code homes. "How about building yourself a house? No, no, you don't need money, architect, plans, permits. Why not use what's there?" Suggesting that in the mild climate of Northern California one could simply join the blue jays and squirrels in the branches of trees or dig a hole hidden from the cops, the text asserted that "man has a nest-building instinct just like the other animals, and it is totally frustrated by our lock-step

Figure 2.8 Bulldozing of shelters at Morning Star Ranch. From Unohoo, Coyote and the Mighty Avengers, *Morning Star Scrapbook* (Occidental, CA: Friends of Morning Star, c. 1973) (Sylvia Clarke Hamilton; courtesy Ramon Sender).

County photos of 'illegal' structures

Figure 2.9 Sonoma County photos of 'illegal' structures at Morning Star Ranch. From Unohoo, Coyote and the Mighty Avengers, *Morning Star Scrapbook* (Occidental, CA: Friends of Morning Star, c. 1973) (courtesy Ramon Sender).

society whose restrictive codes on home-building make it just about impossible to build a *code* home that doesn't sterilize, insulate, and rigidify the inhabitants.... So it falls down in the first wind storm. The second one won't. Dirt floors are easy to keep clean. Domes are full of light and air."[31] While the cost of materials and a do-it-yourself ethos certainly informed the nonnormative character of the ad hoc constructions springing up at Morning Star, Wheeler's, and beyond, as this manifesto suggests, their forms cannot be explained simply as the product of a lack of building expertise, although this did of course often factor in. The teepees, lean-tos, tents, open-sided A-frames, simple tarpaulins, tree houses, geodesic structures, vans, school buses, brushwood hogans, and "other miscellaneous shelters, including a Cadillac hearse, being used as homes"[32] were, to reiterate, not simply expediencies, but a form of protest, one that took the form of demonstrating alternative modes of life.

In a short article in *Communitarian*, Bill Wheeler noted of the commune's rejection of conventional building practices, "Two-by-fours sixteen inches on center just does not make any sense to us." And he went on to suggest that they had been actively seeking, testing, and theorizing an alternative. "As California and the whole country is progressively filling up with plastic architecture, impersonal and cold plus prohibitively expensive, we feel we must present a viable alternative of free and happy homes that everyone joins in and builds. One of the most significant aspects of Wheeler Ranch," he continued, "has been this evolution and practice of this philosophy of architecture."[33] To Gottlieb, too, as told to Dick Torkelson, "The 16-inch stud makes life duller than it has to be." While discussing the folk-art merits of structures built on tree stumps or covered with plastic, they came across a house with a "stop work" notice tacked to its front, prompting Gottlieb to lament, "Building codes and conformance laws are troublesome." Troping upon the ideals of architectural modernism, Gottlieb suggested with humor, "This is an experiment in lowest cost housing."[34]

The "philosophy of architecture" developed at (and largely shared by) Wheeler's and Morning Star in fact worked against many central tenets of architectural modernity: functional distribution of programmatic elements (bathrooms, kitchens, bedrooms, dining room, and so on); use of modern technologies and materials; standardization, rationalization, and mass production; structural stability;

Figure 2.10 Hippies at Wheeler Ranch commune, c. 1970. This image was appropriated in a famous Superstudio collage for *Fundamental Acts: Life, Supersurface* of 1972. (Bob Fitch Photographic Archive, © Stanford University Libraries).

and even standards of plumbing, lighting, and hygiene. Or where they were adopted—in the use of new materials such as plastic, the demarcation of a "functional" nook for meditation, or in the literal dissolution of interior and exterior spaces in open walls—they could be read only as unwittingly parodic. Most had no kitchens or sanitary facilities, and their materials and forms were intentionally "funky." Following the failure of the dream of a codified, regulated, technologically advanced and universal modernism to achieve the goal of housing for all, its unregulated hippie other was stepping up to fill the gap left by both the state and capitalism.

Modernist environmental ideals of access to light and air were key terms with which institutions such as the Congrès International d'Architecture Moderne (CIAM) lobbied both the profession and governments, justifying the discipline's role in social, hygienic, and economic terms. And these ideals persisted. However, the statistically driven logics of building rationalization and regulation (those operating, or so it was thought, below the radar of aesthetic codes) were increasingly coupled during the late 1950s and 1960s with the discipline's embrace of the human and social sciences and facilitated by the data-processing capacities of the modern computer. Spreading from Western Europe and North America to less industrialized countries, this globalizing logic infiltrated architectural pedagogy and thinking through programs such as the Architectural Association's Department of Tropical Architecture, as well as through publications and "think tanks" such as Constantin Doxiadis's Ekistics project, and, in turn, global development agencies such as those affiliated with the UN.[35] We will return to this nexus in later chapters. I mention it here for two reasons: in the first instance, these forms of rationalization marked exactly the points at which architecture was deployed within a logic of governmentality, giving it a role in what Foucault theorized as the biopolitical regulation of the population. In the second instance, it brings us back to the identification "down," in this case, with the pressures on developing countries.

In a remarkable text on the alternative architecture of the communes, William Chaitkin invoked a connection to (or projection onto) architecture's shifting roles with respect to "development." He noted that "what was expected was found: vernacular revival, simplified self-build, and low-gain energy systems—all on the de-industrialized model of an 'underdeveloped country' of communes." To him, the buildings on hippie communes represented a form of "vernacular nostalgia" (one shared at that moment by many architects), implicitly recognizing that with modern housing, "demonstrable connections between natural environment, human habitat, and human culture had been lost."[36] Although, as noted above by Wheeler, climate informed these structures, they often used local materials, and they emerged from within a self-identified cultural group (a group identifying, like many within the counterculture, with a new "tribalism"), these forms of habitation were not vernacular or regional in the strict sense of the terms, but they certainly seemed nostalgic.[37] (They were too idiosyncratic to be vernacular, and they adopted forms such as teepees largely for semantic associations.)[38] Climate was not invoked to inform adaptation of structures to a region or under the auspice of a technoscientific rationality, in which calibrations of heat, humidity, wind, rainfall, and so on would serve to functionalize techniques of control over the environment, as in studies associated with tropical architecture. The mild climate of Northern California had simply alleviated the burden of expertise, or so it was assumed, facilitating departure from the trappings of modern society and encouraging closeness to the earth.

From the perspective of architectural history, this dislocation produces an interesting anomaly: these shelters were not, to reiterate, vernaculars, for they neither evolved over time from encountering cultural and climatic forces nor were they handed down over generations. They were also, of course, far from high architecture in the institutionalized sense of the discipline and its role in Western culture. We could simply call them pseudovernacular, but there seems to be an opportunity here to resituate them conceptually away from tropes of cultural authenticity, regional specificity, and naturalization (humans returning to some instinctual relation to nature) that tend to characterize many vernacular discourses and the communards' own claims, and instead to interrogate their modes of identification and appropriation, refusal, and mediation. We can see seem them as responding, albeit in a very different way, to a historical condition in which, as architects including Robert Venturi, John K. Rauch, Denise Scott-Brown, and Charles Moore argued around the same time, relevant tropes would not be climate and region, but forces such as communication technologies and capitalism.[39] Like those early harbingers of architectural postmodernism, the communards understood their individualized shelters to harbor "meaning."[40] Moreover, like early postmodern engagements with information technology, Open Landers sought architecture appropriate to a way of life that was flexible and open to adaptation to the environment and to new circumstances, hence, the aesthetic archaisms at work were also always and already coupled with postindustrial paradigms, or what the communards called "cybernation."[41] To be clear: I don't want to suggest that these low-tech, idiosyncratic, and often quite bizarre structures were not the product of historical forces at work. Indeed, I think they were precisely that, but to understand them, we need to push their conceptualization in a different direction.

The tendency toward openness, informality, and flexibility was less a means of decoupling bodies from traditional sites of industrial labor (indeed, their activities remained distinctly manual) than a training ground for that "cybernation," giving rise to a paradoxical coupling of archaisms and post-Fordist dynamics. By the end of the 1960s, moreover, this nexus was firmly instituted in the *Whole Earth Catalog*, and the heterogeneous and seemingly individualistic character of the communards' ad hoc structures could no longer be read as simply chaotic. Beyond their open organization, consistencies included: the adoption of self-build approaches, use of recycled or found materials, ad hoc assembly, the appropriation of vernacular forms, knowledge of alternative technologies, and, often, mobility. The fascination with teepees, yurts, log cabins, geodesic domes, tensile structures, barrios, early American tools, and systems-based notions of the environment existed before the *Whole Earth Catalog*, but it quickly became an important mediator and magnifier—not least the section on shelter and land use, edited by Lloyd Kahn, who went on to publish *Domebooks* and the magazine *Shelter*. Studies on vernacular architecture, notably, Bernard Rudofsky's *Architecture without Architects* of 1964 and Paul Oliver's *Shelter and Society* of 1969, along with publications presented as valuable for starting communes, such as Ian McHarg's *Design with Nature* of 1969, the broadsheet *The Green Revolution* (billed as "A world-wide effort for decentralization and rural revival"), and treatises on how to weave, make pottery, grow organic food, deliver babies, and more, together offered an integrated field of knowledge. In the context of the rural

Figure 2.11 *Morning Star Scrapbook*, c. 1973. Health inspectors and A-frame shelter at Morning Star Ranch. From Unohoo, Coyote and the Mighty Avengers, *Morning Star Scrapbook* (Occidental, CA: Friends of Morning Star, c. 1973) (Sylvia Clarke Hamilton; courtesy Ramon Sender).

communards' often limited access to, if not rejection of, mainstream channels of media—television, magazines, newspapers—the *Whole Earth Catalog* took on a heightened function in producing a mediated, though dispersed community.

Voluntary Primitivism

I want to come back here to "voluntary primitivism," a term coined by Sender and central to the Open Land communes' conceptualization of ideal relations between humans and their environments. As Fairfield explained, at Morning Star and Wheeler's, voluntary primitivism meant

> living in harmony with the four elements—earth, air, fire and water . . . building your own biodegradable home out of mud and twigs and dead branches and old lumber. This means giving up electricity, gas, running water and the telephone as well as other modern conveniences. Living on the land also means conditioning your body to withstand cold and damp weather, carrying your own water for drinking and your own wood for cooking. It means planting and harvesting your crops with muscle and not machinery.[42]

Sara Davidson also included "rolling loose tobacco into cigarettes, grinding their own wheat, baking bread, canning vegetables, delivering their own babies, and educating their own children," as well as giving up rock music. "No one brushes his teeth more than once a week," she noticed at Wheeler's, "and then they often use 'organic toothpaste,' made from eggplant cooked in tinfoil."[43] Life was an endless cycle of manual labor.

In addition to developing highly ritualized child-birthing practices, the communards attempted to abandon other aspects of modern medicine. Refusing what Foucault theorized as the increasing "medicalization" of the body,[44] they were, for instance, "experimenting with herbs and Indian healing remedies to become free of manufactured medicinal drugs."[45] Going back to the land meant, in addition, a level of intimacy with the elements, even at the cost of discomforts that architecture would traditionally defend the subject against: "Houses shouldn't be designed to keep out the weather," Davidson recalled Wheeler saying. "We want to get in touch with it."[46] That conditioning one's body to the land, often literally to the earth or ground, meant a level not only of physical uneasiness, but also of exposure to disease was evident to Davidson, who, in recounting the problems arising at Wheeler's, symptomatically alluded to the less developed neighbor of the United States: "Because of the haphazard sanitation system, the water at Wheeler's is contaminated, and until people adjust to it, they suffer dysentery, just as tourists do who drink the water in Mexico. There are periodic waves of hepatitis, clap, crabs, scabies, and streptococcic throat infections."[47] Wheeler, however, remained adamant about maintaining a relation to the earth unmediated by modern sanitary technology. Even after toilets were installed to satisfy legal requirements, he scoffed: "I wouldn't go in one of those toilets if you paid me. It's very important for us to be able to use the ground, because we are completing a cycle, returning to Mother Earth what she's given us."[48] Limits were soon reached, such as when Sender's young child developed pneumonia from their habit of sleeping on the ground. And at one point, a potentially fatal infectious intestinal disease was found at Morning Star, at which point, four occupants reported to the local community hospital.[49]

We might ask, then, what sort of ethics of care of the self and of the land was at work here. How are we to understand this type of risk? One partial answer to this question involves the widespread and often phantasmatic attribution of healing powers to the land, the idea that the land would heal both itself and the humans who lived in close association to it. Beyond the problematic mysticism, such an ideology quickly translates into ceding responsibility to "nature." A less problematic counterpart to this was the argument that modern society has caused its own types of illness—physical, social, and psychological. Refusing concerns over sanitary regulations as ideological, Gottlieb remarked, "they speak of health.... But they know they are not the curers of disease—they are the producers of it."[50] *Open Land: A Manifesto* was even more explicit, suggesting these practices offered a line of flight from or therapeutic alternative to the normative disciplinary institutions of contemporary society:

> The more complex a society becomes the more important it becomes to allow folks to return to ancestral ways whenever the stresses and strains of modern living begin to drive them sick or crazy. In the enlightened world of the 1970's, as leisure becomes compulsory, the voluntary return to the soil will replace the ghetto-jail-nuthouse syndrome. Conditioned by their fast, competitive culture to unnatural living rhythms,

Americans find themselves falling sick and dying prematurely in a *diseased* society.[51]

Faced with the commune's foreclosure, Gottlieb appealed to the courts to accept their strange ways by arguing that the Open Land movement could save the state money, replacing the need for jails and other institutions proliferating to deal with these forms of contemporary "dis-ease." Reiterating the imminent obsolescence of the country's youth, he prophesied that it might serve as a means to stem violence. "The day may arrive," he explained, "when transferring ownership of small remote portions of Public Land to God will provide appropriate tribal sanctuary for some of the desperate, technologically unemployable, inner city inhabitants—a constructive alternative to incendiary rioting."[52]

As mentioned above, one central premise of Morning Star was that the land would select its inhabitants and teach them how to become its stewards. Noting that its proper legal form was "waqf—Arabic for divine ownership of immovable property," Open Land, Gottlieb explained, "was an attempt to solve the principle problem of communal organization, namely, who stays and who's gotta go, by letting the land choose its inhabitants thereby forming a tribe."[53] Population would thus effectively be self-organizing, or so it was assumed, albeit mediated through the land; people would leave when conditions deteriorated enough, and those remaining would learn to live with each other. Shared ancestry, customs, and care of the land, such as that characteristic of the Native American tribes with whom hippies often identified, were to be replaced by the spontaneous emergence of shared ideals. In the meantime, under the pressure of a massive influx of people and with it the accumulation of waste by less conscientious residents and visitors, as well as the destruction of trees, the leveling of ground for campsites, and problems of multiple campfires in a fire-prone region, the land and its inhabitants experienced a significant level of environmental distress. As architect and cofounder of Ecology Action, Chuck Herrick recounted: "with the great number of people on the land, the two inadequate toilets [at Morning Star] were literally inundated by a river of shit," with unburied fecal matter accumulating on the property contributing to serious health hazards.[54]

At one point, Herrick ran ecology courses for the commune. In line with the period's systems-based ecology, he argued for an ecological understanding of nature that took into account the dynamics of multiple interrelated systems. His courses were "discontinued because the pressure of existing problems was so acute that they had to be dealt with through action rather than talk."[55] Herrick's views on the need for population planning and ecological management conflicted with those of Gottlieb and Sender, who believed that "control and regulation of the land and people are undesirable and unnecessary."[56] In one aspect, Gottlieb and Sender's prophecy proved correct. Herrick observed that the social stress and threat of disease caused by the overcrowding of the original structures spawned the rapid construction of other shelters. Yet in the meantime, Morning Star had become a microcosm of accelerated environmental crisis, not only a testing ground for creating new selves, but fuel for the period's widespread fear that the Earth was facing the threat of a global population explosion that might prove fatal to the environment. The subject, to which we will return in later chapters, was popularized by Paul Ehrlich's best-selling *The Population Bomb* of 1968, which, promoted by the *Whole Earth Catalog*, fostered anxiety regarding growth in developing countries.

Futures Past

As mentioned above, Native Americans played a large role in the hippie imaginary: on the one hand, they represented alternative social relations (tribalism), closeness to nature, and a nonproprietary relation to the land. "It's like the Indians—land held in trust for all to enjoy," Gottlieb explained.[57] When, in September 1971, Gottlieb prepared a legal brief about deeding Morning Star to God, he noted that such an act "recreates in the consciousness of white people the attitude toward nature of the indigenous people of this hemisphere."[58] And the teepee, to reiterate, (also a prominent *Whole Earth Catalog* item) served as a privileged icon for alternative modes of life. "The tipi in fact became the standard tent of the counterculture, accommodating the new nomadism," Chaitkin pointed out, wryly adding, "although the twenty-foot-long poles of the Plains Indians' buffalo-hide tipis were dragged behind their ponies, not loaded into psychedelic vans."[59] On the other hand, beyond these forms of mimicry, Native Americans were occasionally invoked as a fellow underclass in American society with whom they claimed affinity as victims: "Morning Star took on more and more the aspect of a besieged native village," they reported after inspectors had come to close the place down.[60] There is little doubt that this identification with Native Americans was intended to be a sympathetic one. But these identifications, which often involved a problematic naturalization, if not simply mythical projections, did not typically open a space of political encounter. Contemporary social justice issues and rights struggles—concerning, for instance, land, environmental damage, financial and technological resources, medical care, or housing—received only limited visibility. Furthermore, it was not only Native Americans with whom these communards identified or from whom they borrowed shelter forms or other cultural trappings. As we have seen, one also repeatedly finds enlisted (often interchangeably and often contradictorily) tropes pertaining to developing countries, barrios, shantytowns, America in the nineteenth century, or America following a nuclear apocalypse or ecological catastrophe.

What Davidson called a "sense of imminent doomsday" was widespread among the counterculture, its prevalence evident in *Whole Earth Catalog* sales.[61] "I can report that sales on *The Survival Book* are booming," Brand announced to her, "it's one of our fastest moving items."[62] Open Land communards repeatedly underscored that they adopted "primitive" habits as part of a game plan of training for survival, developing knowledge appropriate for life after the end of modern technology, or so it was assumed. "We are running a pilot study in survival," Gottlieb remarked to one journalist, reiterating that "the hippies are the first wave of the technological unemployed."[63] Morning Star's experimental structures, he insisted, were "not [those of] ghetto dwellers.... These people are developing a life-style that will save you some day."[64]

But these identifications with Native Americans and anxiety over technology don't account for the uncanny return of cultural trappings (from clothing to tools to log cabins) from nineteenth-century American pioneers. That hippie "tribalism" often appeared in conjunction with a frontier mentality reminds us that nostalgia can be highly problematic, in this case, hauntingly recalling the nineteenth-century migration west and the violent struggles with aboriginal peoples over access to and privatization of the land under the rubric of Manifest Destiny. The hippies, William Hedgepeth ominously

Figure 2.12 Lorien commune members, 1969 (© Dennis Stock / Magnum Photos).

remarked, had "begun the new colonization of the continent,"[65] one ambiguously identifying at once with the colonized and the colonizers. Moreover, when, in their search for cheap land, the commune movement expanded throughout the Southwest, the threat of this second wave of "settlement" was not lost on the native population or earlier Spanish-speaking settlers, whose unromantic contemporary living conditions and political and economic status were unlikely to benefit.

Karl Marx might serve to remind us here that this was not the first time such a symptomatic revival occurred in the course of revolutionary social projects. As noted in *The Eighteenth Brumaire of Louis Bonaparte*,

> Tradition from all the dead generations weighs like a nightmare on the brain of the living. And just when they appear to be revolutionizing themselves and their circumstances, in creating something unprecedented, in just such epochs of revolutionary crisis, that is when they nervously summon up the spirits of the past, borrowing from them their names, marching orders, uniforms, in order to enact new scenes in world history, but in this time-honored guise and with this borrowed language.[66]

What, then, was it about the nineteenth century that captured the imagination of hippies, even if subconsciously weighing it down like a lingering nightmare? Was it a compensatory guilt regarding treatment of the native people; a mythical model of a simpler, rural life and existence less burdened by transformation in the technological milieu; an identification with political and economic struggles fostered by the evident inequity born of the rapid expansion of industrial capitalism; the emergence of so many alternative and intentional communities, including many that left cities to return to the land; the identification with a period of availability of free land, of a frontier for pioneers to settle and farm; or perhaps the romance of the outlaw and the possibility of a life somehow beyond the long arm of the law and of the increasingly capillary reach of governmental regulation, whether related to hygienic standards, the regulation of births, educational norms, or the development of codes for the organization of towns and construction of dwellings?

All perhaps played a part, and what they seem to share is a symptomatic and often contradictory relation to American history, or at least to the mythology of the founding of the nation. As Walt Odets explained in his foreword to "Utopia, U.S.A," this was a distinctly American story. "Their pioneering spirit has long been fundamental to America and they are moved, in part, by the same American spark which fires the foolish men at NASA. America began as a commune, and communal experiment here is nothing really new." But if America began as a commune, and if exhibited here was the same expansionist spirit driving the search for new territory from the eighteenth century to NASA's exploration of outer space, why were hippies so disturbing? Why, as Odets posited, could communes and their largely middle-class American occupants be read as "a *threat* to America"? Why could hippies "terrorize" us? As he queried rhetorically, "Who are these freaks who insult our best American Hopes with their self-ordained poverty?"[67]

Exit or Voice

"Dropping out" was widely read as a form of laziness born of affluence, a simple refusal of productivity in favor of idleness. And in many cases, it might well have been. But if such practices harbored a form of apathy or *ennui*, to recall Marx's son-in-law Paul Lafargue's nineteenth-century critique of the "consequences of over-production"—against which he proclaimed the "right to be lazy"—they might also be understood at times as moments of radical disobedience or engaged withdrawals from extant work ethics, normative lifestyles, and their functioning within capitalist modes of productivity.[68] I am thinking here of the argument made by Paolo Virno, who has posited that such lines of flight could take on a political cast when acts of withdrawal, subtraction, or defection became coupled with the founding of new social and political "republics," new collectivities, even new publics outside the regulation of state control. Exodus, he argues, does not involve opposing or protesting the government in order to overthrow it and take its place. (It is not dialectical in this manner.) Rather, it institutes a *positive* form of production, the production of a "non-State Republic."[69] Virno's examples are the mass defection from the factory and move back to the land in North America in the middle of the nineteenth century—an "exit" that to Marx had posed a paradoxical aberration with respect to capitalist social relations, confounding capitalists' ability to establish a viable labor pool[70]—along with the refusal of work by Italian youth in the 1970s. In both cases, he remarks, "preestablished roles were deserted and a 'territory' unknown to the official maps was colonized."[71] While not wanting to gloss over the problematic nature of the communards' identifications with alterity or their lack of understanding of environmental issues discussed above, I want to try to unpack this form of exodus further.

Virno's thesis drew not only on Marx, but also on Albert O. Hirschman's reading of two dominant responses to dissatisfaction with a product or service within competitive economic systems: voice (protesting management, direct confrontation) and exit (going elsewhere, withdrawal). Like Marx, he read the "exit option" as a distinctly American phenomenon. The United States, he explained, "owes its very existence and growth to millions of decisions favoring exit over voice."[72] "In a real sense," Louis Hartz posited (as cited by Hirschman), "physical flight is the American substitute for the European experience of social revolution."[73] And like Marx again, Hirschman believed this drive was fueled by the promise of access to land free for settling. "The exit from Europe," he explained, "could be re-enacted within the United States by the progressive settlement of the frontier, which Frederick Jackson Turner characterized as the 'gate of escape from the bondage of the past.'"[74] This ideology had persisted: "Even after the closing of the frontier, the very vastness of the country combined with easy transportation make it far more possible for Americans than for most other people to think about solving their problems through 'physical flight' than either through resignation or through ameliorating and fighting *in situ* the particular conditions into which one has been 'thrown.'"[75]

According to Hirschman's thesis, recent "voice" movements such as "black power" were thus a radical novelty in America, especially insofar as they sought a "collective stimulation" and hence the social advancement of a particular minority group, as opposed to individual socioeconomic advancement through departure from urban ghettoes. When Hirschman turned to address briefly the phenomenon of hippie culture, he recognized another shift, one producing a convolution in the distinctly "American" character of exit.

> In this perspective, the present day "cop-out" movement of groups like the hippies is very much in the American tradition; once again dissatisfaction with the surrounding social order leads to flight rather than fight, to withdrawal of the dissatisfied group and to its setting up a separate "scene." Perhaps, the reason for which these groups are felt to be "un-American" is not their act of withdrawal, but, on the contrary, their *demonstrative* "otherness" which is sensed as an attempt to influence the square society they are rejecting. By making their exit so

> spectacular, by oddly combining *deviance* with *defiance*, they are actually closer to voice than was the case for their pilgrim, immigrant, and pioneer forebears.[76]

That is, according to Hirschman, hippies worked toward activating exit through protest or voice, a voice in the sense of a spectacular or theatrical image of their deviance or otherness. Under the appearance of withdrawal, they had in fact been sending messages that spoke the language of a perhaps more dangerous political confrontation.

To many hippies, recent protest movements had proven largely ineffective in transforming modes of governance, and they frequently distinguished their own form of withdrawal from earlier struggles on the Left. As Davidson recounted: "Lou Gottlieb, who was once a Communist party member, says, 'The entire Left is a dead end.' The hippie alternative is to turn inward and reach backward for roots, simplicity, and the tribal experience."[77] Hedgepeth, too, read this as a paradigm shift:

> their rebellion is of a new and general pattern as different from older social revolutions as guerilla warfare is from conventional combat. The older type—which can be considered "vertical insurgency"—takes place when the low-ranking discontents in society set out to secure for themselves the benefits or whatever privileges they desire that are enjoyed only by those in higher positions of established authority. The present pattern of rebellion—or "lateral insurgency"—takes place when the discontents simply go off in another direction and develop their own values and counter-institutions in absolute disregard for the established system. The establishment, therefore, is left without the ability to control the rebels by offering or withholding social privileges.[78]

The hippie's weapon, he suggested, was "indifference" to the values and rewards of mainstream society. But just as despair at the failure to achieve radical social transformation through civil disobedience and the democratic political process led to the radicalization of the protest movement—with the emergence of militant and nationalist groups such as the Black Panthers, the Symbionese Liberation Front, the Weather Underground, and more, and the shift from protest marches to guns and bombs—with the Open Land communards, we find them questioning whether they, too, would be forced to turn to other strategies in the face of a crushing response by the state.

Territory

"Is our message" to our children, Sender reflected when faced with eviction from Wheeler Ranch, "to be that there is no escape from the rules and regulations of a rigid and authoritarian future?" One alternative conceived by the communards, understood as a peaceful endgame to Open Land struggles, was to forge exit strategies or open new frontiers not within the United States, but beyond its national borders. "We all belong to the same planet," Sender posited, "and its name is The Open Earth."[79] Following her visits to Open Land communes, Davidson reported that their ambition was not only to open land in California, New Mexico, Oregon, and Washington: "Gottlieb plans to buy land and deed it to God in Holland, Sweden, Mexico and Spain." "We're fighting against the territorial imperative," Gottlieb asserted to Davidson, referring to evolutionary biologist Robert Ardrey's 1966 book, *The Territorial Imperative: A Personal Inquiry into the Animal Origins of Property and Nations.*[80] "If we defend the title to our land or the sovereignty of our country," Ardrey spuriously claimed of mankind's instinct for survival and his genetic disposition to defend territory, "we do it for reasons no different, no less innate, no less ineradicable, than do lower animals."[81] Ardrey's thinly veiled diatribe against Communism and his pernicious deployment of animal biology to justify militarism and capitalist expansion was a good target for Gottlieb to fight against. *The Territorial Imperative* even included a championing of the Vietnam War, apologias for European colonialism, and support for South Africa's apartheid government. "The hippies should get the Nobel Prize for creating this simple idea," Gottlieb stressed of their counterethos.[82] (In the 1980s, Ardrey's thinking was adopted by white supremacist group Northwest Territorial Imperative, which sought to make the American Northwest an exclusively "Aryan" terrain.)

In 1971, Gottlieb went so far as to tie Open Land's expansionist goal to challenging sovereign borders, insisting that their practices could force the territorial imperative to "transfer into its opposite."

> Now the only thing wrong with open land, as far as I can see so far, is there's not enough of it. I have a kind of mystical conviction that there is a proper set of coordinates on the earth's surface for every

> consciousness. You know, the right place for you to be.... Just because we're born in Bengal, doesn't mean that's where we're supposed to be. I feel that doing away with no trespassing signs is a step in the right direction. After that comes state and national boundaries. I really feel they are tremendously artificial and they are lethal in our time, because they perpetuate this horrible old obsolete territorial imperative that's just turned murderous on us now.[83]

Although cast as a refusal of the murderous war in Indochina, in this expansionist logic, we begin to find an uncanny reiteration of (or perhaps counterimage to) the forces of globalization, raising the question of how such tactical interventions could retain their critical valence when recast as a strategy of global colonization.

War

Open Land was initially conceived as a utopian experiment. Yet it quickly came to operate as a battlefield, a site of mêlée with county authorities. When, in May 1971, the county razed structures at Morning Star, Gottlieb again "struck an ominous chord" as one journalist noted. "'This was peaceful. But think how easy [sic] it could have changed. One insane act—and...' he swept an outstretched arm toward the cluster of officials standing some 50 yards away. 'Sooner or later, it will no longer be a peaceful confrontation. Someday... It will be bestial—worse than the Civil War.'"[84] Gottlieb indicated that opening land was always and already conceived as a nonviolent form of militancy: "Morning Star is a training replacement center, or rest and recuperation area, for the army of occupation in the war against the exclusive ownership of land."[85] Wheeler reiterated and extended this theme, suggesting that the struggle with Sonoma County over the communal use of land was already akin to a state of civil or guerilla warfare, the clash of two ideologies with radically unequal military strength. Boldly likening the commune to the Viet Cong, he declared: "We're an underground movement. We're going to take some very hard blows for sure. It's not inconceivable that the County will succeed in tearing down all the buildings on the Ranch.... But we are a form of guerilla warfare and we're going to take our losses."[86]

In this context, Wheeler recalled a meeting with a Sonoma County supervisor at the tax window who associated Open Land tactics with revolutionary battles: "You know, we've *got* to fight against you," the supervisor said. "Every revolution that's ever happened has had resistance against it, and if you think this one's going to be any different you're crazy." "I thought about it," Wheeler added, "And he's right—we need it. It's gotta happen that way. For us to come together we've got to fight for what we believe in, in the same way the Israelis fought for what they believed in."[87] Although the comparison with Israel was symptomatic of a widespread fascination among hippies with kibbutzim as a paradigm of communalism and with the founding of a new country, it also reminds us of the important and complicated set of issues regarding the relation of the utopian imaginaries of these "pioneers" and settlers to native populations.

Morning Star and Wheeler Ranch had become not simply an "outlaw area" in Brand's terminology, but was deemed "Outlaw Territory" by the state.[88] Indeed, beyond accusations of providing shelter to those sought by the law—for which it was repeatedly raided without search warrants, prompting Wheeler to accuse the county of civil rights abuses—Open Land was quite literally conceived as such a place.[89] It was an attempt to open territory beyond the reach (and protection) of legal codes, an attempt to demarcate and declare an extraterritorial enclave in which the usual rule of law and the functioning of the state legislature could somehow be suspended. As Gottlieb proposed during an interview: "What we need in this country are statute free sanctuaries, because many people who fall ill in this country fall ill from an allergy to statutes; there has never been a society that has been as burdened by statutes."[90] While they sought escape from the impact of regulatory codes, refusing to abide by statutes deemed oppressive, if not harmful to one's person, these formulations raise the question of what sort of legal protection and citizenship rights were assumed to remain. Are we faced here with something like a perverse mirror image of declaring martial law, or of the state's ability to suspend the usual functioning of the law through declaring a "state of emergency"? Can we read these hippie colonies, that is, to have formulated a camp in the expanded sense theorized by Giorgio Agamben, wherein "the functional nexus" between territory, the state, and citizenship (nation) becomes unsecured? Certainly, the communards hoped to complicate a simple topology of citizen and foreigner, or inside versus outside America, to produce a new spatial arrangement that "remains constantly outside the normal state of law."[91] While the communards' frequent claims to being refugees or immigrants on their own soil were largely rhetorical, when compounded with attempts under the rubric of voluntary primitivism willingly to forego what were, in principle, rights guaranteed by international law—the right to adequate housing, health care, and more—we might begin to ask whether a segment of the population is unwittingly appealing here to a right *not* to have rights, not to be subject to or subject of the law, to be (to invoke Hannah Arendt) "the scum of the earth."[92]

Morning Star and Wheeler's were treading a fine line between civil disobedience and a total disregard for the institutions of the law and its enforcement, the institutions through which civility is maintained and citizens are protected and represented, but also, as they acknowledged, through which dominant techniques of power and the normalizing function of the state operate to particular (and, to the communards' minds, oppressive) ends. Motivating these actions, as we have seen, was the belief that a propertyless relation to land would lead to a distinct form of social organization (tribalism) and new geopolitical relations (Open Earth). But we need to ask, of course, how such a self-organizing system could ensure that what would come to replace that governmental rationality and its attendant institutions would be equitable, nonhierarchical, or even nonviolent relations and systems of organization. What sort of political space, I think we need to ask, were Open Land communes actually imagining? What sort of prospects for political participation remained? How could these new communities possibly escape a situation in which other structures of power rushed in to refill that power vacuum? Such a dynamic was all too familiar from the many charismatic figures within the counterculture who emerged to fill the void left by the eradication of normative social and political structures or from the often remarked persistence of entirely hierarchical, stereotyped gender relations, to which were frequently attributed natural differences between the sexes.

Philosophy of Architecture: How Communes Fail

I want to come back in concluding to underscore what might be at stake in these struggles over Open Land for architecture. I have attempted to trace the manner in which the forms of life and counterconducts practiced by Open Landers worked with some precision upon key components of what Foucault theorized as the biopolitical regulation of the population. Rejecting normative and scientifically justified approaches to health, hygiene, education, sanitation, birthrates, labor, housing, natural resources, agriculture, and the organization of the environment, Open Land communards were *not*, I want to stress, fighting for access to or equitable inclusion within the system. Rather, they were actively withdrawing from the institutions, practices, and sites through which micropolitical techniques of power had developed under a modern form of governmental rationality. They were withdrawing from the points at which these techniques systematically met the body and psyche of contemporary subjects in their everyday lives. Open Land thus also implicitly questioned the relation between the state's more benevolent role in ensuring the health and welfare of its citizens and the forms of control it exerted over them in the name of maintaining productivity, or more precisely, maintaining profitability for the capitalist machinery.

Although invoking Foucault's analysis of biopolitics, I am not trying to suggest that Open Land communards were somehow Foucauldian. They did write manifestoes to rationalize their practice, demonstrated most evidently in the claim to a "philosophy of architecture" or in Gottlieb's seven-page legal brief detailing his arguments for deeding Morning Star to God. Their arguments appealed not to historical or theoretical concepts, but to insights emerging from what Gottlieb referred to as "ongoing encounters" within their lived practice or lived experience, or at least the prospect of developing experimental testing grounds in order to live as such. Deeding land to God, he explained, pointing again to the transforming sociotechnological milieu, "establishes laboratories for the definition, defense and demonstration of an alternative life-style consonant with human dignity for the time in the not-too-distant future when leisure will be completely compulsory due to the inevitable take-over of repetitive labor by our 'happy-slave'-cybernated industry."[93] We know that Foucault was familiar with alternative and communal lifestyles emerging in Northern California, visiting at least one commune while teaching at Berkeley in the 1970s. His research, by contrast, was characterized by a close-grained historical tracing and analysis of emergent forms of power and a theorization of what was at stake in their transformations—from a sovereign to a disciplinary and in turn to a biopolitical regime, or more properly, to a condition in which these had become complexly layered within modern forms of governmentality. Despite significant differences in conceptual tools, motivation, and modes of practice, the historical coincidence of the communards' struggles and Foucault's theorization was perhaps not incidental; both recognized the contemporary functioning of a biopolitical form of management and regulation. Foucault had traced its genealogy; Open Land had sought to interrupt its contemporary functioning.

Many of these communards believed that in working against the grain of the normative logics inscribed within conventional architectural and urban forms and instituted through planning and building codes, alternative structures in themselves facilitated a mode of liberation from forces that "sterilize, insulate, and rigidify the inhabitants." There are many reasons to be suspicious of such functionalist claims—claims that the forms themselves were liberating. We need think only of the degree to which structures such as geodesic domes and the wood-butcher aesthetic became rather mainstream in Northern California by the 1970s, assimilated without significantly altering modes of life. Yet it does seem that at the moment of their emergence, these practices identified points within the architectural process in which contemporary forms of governmentality impinged most directly upon the subject, where techniques of power were most evident within the organization and regulation of the built environment. And it is perhaps in this register (rather than, say, their aesthetic value or simplistic ideas of their liberatory function) that such alternative built environments offer lessons for thinking about architecture and the built environment, lessons regarding how buildings might not simply serve to give a spatial form to dominant institutions and techniques of power, but how they might also operate as tactical maneuvers within or sites of refusal of official forms of social and ideological regulation. Could architecture, that is, articulate something like a *counterdispositif*? Or does such a strategic reversal of power remain the domain of counterconducts, rather than built forms and their organization?

Whether successful or not, in contravening normative modes of organizing the built environment, these peculiar hippie dwellings revealed domestic habitation to be a potential point of insecurity in the biopolitical apparatus. (Who would have thought that people would choose to cede private property to the commons and to embrace a lifestyle and an architecture of "primitivism" in America?) As evident to Sonoma County officials, these shelters spoke to the fact that the "system" was under attack, hence provoking court injunctions, fines, and extensive legal deliberations regarding the hippies' occupation of the land and, in turn, producing legislation to govern forcibly their standards of living (while leaving others in squalor elsewhere). Far from facilitating a "statute free sanctuary," Open Land communes prompted local and state governing bodies to fight to preserve their integrity or even to strengthen and expand legal statutes, even rendering Morning Star "Outlaw Territory, so defined by Sonoma County itself."[94] While the environmental aspects of the struggles over Open Land remain unrecoverable as viable practices (and my purpose here is not programmatic in this sense), and while hippies' claims often remained shrouded in a problematic mysticism and appeal to nature, for a historian, these lived practices nevertheless retain a remarkable value, helping trace a type of historical experience (and a mode of refusal) of the functioning of regulatory and normative mechanisms of the state as they meet the built environment. That is, these encounters help render visible operations of political power and control while simultaneously revealing the complexities and limitations of attempting simply to withdraw from or overcome them. As the communards recognized, the county's response was motivated not by ensuring care of the land, its inhabitants, and the environment as such, but was inseparable from the maintenance or even expansion of political power, power that, Foucault recognized, remains invested in architecture.

Despite the successful crushing of Morning Star and Wheeler's, we might still ask whether the "code wars" were in fact won by the state. The widespread fascination with living on communes and returning to the land soon subsided. However, as Steve Durkee suggested of the Lama commune, these experimental communities left behind "accurate maps of the territory."[95] Some of these maps are being recovered by a new generation seeking to leave the city and found ecovillages, to fight the closing of the commons, to renew the Open Land movement, or to extend related ambitions to questions of intellectual property in the Information Age.[96] These maps, as we have seen, harbor many flaws and disturbing points of blindness, and certainly they need to be redrawn, their user's guides updated. The state is of course familiar with them, too. But they also harbor lessons regarding the need to recognize critically and with great specificity the complex matrix of forces at work in a particular historical and geopolitical condition, and it is in this sense that I have recovered them here. That such recoveries come heavily mediated through archival traces and that they appear as fragments is exemplified in other, parallel, nonmimetic revisitings and retrievals, such as the work of artist Martin Beck.[97] In interrogating what he calls "utopian socialities," Beck reminds us simultaneously of their distance from us—these are not specters to be reanimated in any simple sense—and of the degree to which they have instituted certain imaginaries regarding forms of social organization that continue to haunt us.[98] Although the matrix of forces within which Open Land communes operated and in relation to which they struggled has in turn been transformed since the early 1970s, such updated vectors are, strictly speaking, organizing the milieu in which we live, and hence, they remain the battleground in which architecture, too, operates.

CHAPTER THREE

Woodstockholm

> In less than a month, more than 100,000 peopled moved into a tent city by the airport in Bangui, Central African Republic, because of the threat of violence.
>
> —Adam Nossiter, *New York Times*, January 14, 2014

In "Getting Back to Earth," an article published in the *Washington Post and Times Herald*, journalist Daniel Zwerdling reflected enthusiastically upon one of the so-called alternative conferences or counterconferences that had run concurrently with the United Nations Conference on the Human Environment held in Stockholm from June 5 to June 16, 1972. "If living at peace with the environment begins at home," he remarked, invoking a popular ethic of personal responsibility,

> then the most encouraging progress in Stockholm wasn't made in the gilded parliamentary halls of the United Nations Conference but on a muddy old airport field called Skarpnack. Here the Hog Farm, a commune which travels about America in battered old school buses, erected their Tent City–Sweden, home for the ecofreaks who flocked to Stockholm as unofficial and uninvited guests of the environmental conference.
>
> It was a model in clean environmental living: great canvas tents and an Indian tepee, a geodesic dome fashioned from wood strips and beer cans, giant bins of throwaway bottles for landfill and mounds of human excrement and garbage which would return to the earth as compost. Hog Farmers made and mended their own clothes (natural fibers, of course), repaired their own buses (25 years old, at least) and cooked with wood fuels.[1]

Figure 3.1 Hog Farm Tent City encampment at Skarpnäck, Sweden, June 1972 (Tommy Broeng).

While we might question whether traveling the country in battered old school buses was environmentally sound, let alone transporting them along with fifty commune members to Stockholm, it is not surprising that the highly theatrical and media-savvy "lifestyle" demonstrations of the Hog Farmers at Skarpnäck might have appealed to the American journalist. Such ecotactics and counterconducts had by this time enjoyed a half-decade or more of mainstream press coverage, and Zwerdling's account in many ways fell back on well-worn mass-media portrayals of American hippie culture and the back-to-the-land environmental activism of the late 1960s. These familiar tropes were in fact precisely what the Hog Farm had been brought there to convey, invited to Stockholm under the auspices of Stewart Brand's initiative the Life Forum to, as Barry Weisberg scoffed, "create a better show."[2]

The Life Forum would be only one of many alternative platforms hoping to supplement and to trouble the circumscribed range of environmental issues that had been identified, synthesized, and proposed for discussion at the UN conference. Motivating the creation of the Miljöforum (Environment Forum) and the Folkets Forum (People's Forum), as well as the activities of groups such as Pow-Wow, Dai Dong, the Oi Committee, and others, was the recognition that missing from the UN agenda were adequate considerations of the economic and political roots of environmental distress, including the impact of defense spending, warfare, and social and distributive injustices. Numerous contemporary accounts puzzled over the status and expanded range of political actors at play, trying to understand just how the claims made at the counterconferences would interface with or affect official UN proceedings. Indeed, the prospect of an encounter between governmental delegates, scientific experts, and countercultural and radical voices marked the political imaginary of this event even before it began. In a *Village Voice* article, symptomatically titled "Woodstockholm '72: The Subject Is Survival," Ross Gelbspan and David Gurin speculated in the month leading up to the conference that anywhere "from 5000 to 150,000 people—high-level government leaders, earth-concerned scientists from around the world, journalists (about three to every UN delegate), non-official environmentalists, and intellectual leaders, freaks, poets, holy men, conservationists, and revolutionaries—will converge to talk about ways to heal the planet and avert devastation for the next population-doubling generation of potentially starving and unhoused people."[3]

Newsweek's special feature, "The Big Cleanup: The Environmental Crisis '72," perpetuated this characterization of a potentially unruly, if transient mass gathering at the event itself, positing a strange hybrid outgrowth of the famous Woodstock music festival as it encountered the scientific, political, and media establishment: "At the railroad and airline terminals last week, motley groups of hippies, radicals and ecofreaks were mingling with scientists, diplomats, politicians and newsmen from 109 [sic] nations.... The whole scene suggested a complex cross between a scientific convention, a summit conference and rock festival."[4] "Wags," the article reiterated, "are calling the gathering 'Woodstockholm.'" *Time* magazine would also invoke the neologism, connecting it to the Hog Farm's Tent City and activities at Skarpnäck.[5]

The reference to Woodstock was not incidental: as Brand's press release covering the commune's participation in the Life Forum announced, the Hog Farm enjoyed a certain fame from having fed, organized, and controlled the crowds of youth that descended on upstate New York in August of 1969. Brand loudly prophesied, in turn, a similar mass migration to Stockholm, estimating the arrival of "100,000 to 400,000 youth" and campaigning the Swedish authorities to allow the Hog Farm to take charge.[6] By this time a countercultural celebrity, Brand was in fact a driving force behind this much-anticipated population swell. As reported in the *Voice*, "the Life Forum leaders are calling for a mass migration to Sweden 'to provide a living reality-model of people taking care of each other.'"[7] The Hog Farm's role at the UN conference, Brand proposed, "is to help wherever it is needed: with field kitchens in the parks, with liaison between the municipality and street populations, with free stage organization and activities, with medical and drug First Aid, with on-going recycling[,] clean-up and other ecological projects, with information dispersal, with anything that leads to people feeling good and helping each other."[8] From their adoption of alternative cooking and shelter technologies—the latter including stylized teepees, geodesic domes, and customized buses and tents—and distinctly nonnormative appearance, to their Digger-inspired free-food giveaways, free-stage theatrical demonstrations, and nomadic and/or communal modes of living, the Hog Farm was, indeed, retracing

Figure 3.2 Stewart Brand during Life Forum event at United Nations Conference on the Human Environment, Stockholm, June 1972 (Bjorn Gustafsson).

familiar countercultural ground, this time performing "care" and "love" before a global audience in order to help them "feel good" while considering the state and fate of the environment.

According to *Newsweek*, which stressed the importance of the environmental movement "mov[ing] off the streets and into the legislatures, the courts and the corporate boardrooms," the spectacularized nature of this countercultural element came with a certain risk: "if the circus elements of Woodstockholm managed to overshadow the substance of the conference," the editors warned, "the loss would be immense."[9] The countercultural element would not, as it turned out, entirely overshadow the UN conference proper, but it would at times redirect attention.[10] In the first instance, as I want to demonstrate in what follows, under Brand's careful management, new alliances were forged between the UN, the US delegation, and the Life Forum, coming together around a "politics no, environment yes" approach that sought to keep that attention on resource management and away from topics deemed political or divisive by the US delegation. In the second instance, those "circus" elements encountered hostile reactions from other environmental activists and nongovernmental actors in Stockholm, reactions revealing not only political differences, but also strategic positions in an emergent battlefield of environmental politics. Whether understood as potentially distracting "sideshows" to the main UN events, as principled and even ethical alternatives (as with Zwerdling's account of the Hog Farm), or as verification of the environmental movement's status as a powerful political constituency and hence as evidence of the growing impact of nongovernmental voices upon the UN, the multiple, conflicting, and occasionally competing outer conferences were hardly incidental to the UN's shepherding of interstate deliberations. "History may not find it clear," Frances Gendlin noted in *Science and Public Affairs: Bulletin of the Atomic Scientists*, "which was the main event and which the sideshow."[11] As suggested by the rhetoric of circuses, sideshows, and voices, the modes of communication were not unimportant—theatrical performances, demonstrations, costumes, teach-ins, exhibitions, films, publications, press releases, alternative declarations, and even built environments each operated as strategic components within this apparatus.

In addition to the Hog Farm, the Life Forum sponsored a number of other programs, including the publication of Mary Jean

Haley's *Open Options: A Guide to Stockholm's Alternative Environmental Conferences*,[12] a "salon" that was run by celebrity birth-control and overpopulation activist Stephanie Mills and that included Beat poets Gary Snyder and Michael McClure, events by the Black Mesa Defense Committee addressing environmental pressures on indigenous Americans, and antiwhaling activities organized by Project Jonah. My aim in recovering this material is not to privilege the distinctly American genealogy of theatrical ecotactics within which Life Forum activities are readily legible and whose legacy surfaces at times in environmental activism today. Calling into question Zwerdling's celebratory account of Brand's mobilization of the American counterculture in Stockholm, the ambition is to ask how such tactics might be troubled by other (equally, if differently symptomatic) paradigms of nongovernmental politics and environmental activism that were "driven by a shared determination not to be governed *thusly*."[13]

To do so, I want to resituate Hog Farm's Tent City as well as the Life Forum–sponsored antiwhaling demonstrations back into the expanded set of environmental debates that marked the institutional, visual, and discursive matrix of the UN conference and both its semiofficial and unaccredited "sideshows," a matrix in which Brand's strategies become increasingly comprehensible. While what follows rarely speaks to architecture directly, the hope is to identify emerging connections between environmental and architectural paradigms as mediated through the UN in response to geopolitical transformations. These would become more evident (although more complicated) four years later with Habitat: The United Nations Conference on Human Settlements. Human settlements were initially part of the Stockholm conference agenda and appeared in key documents, but during the course of events, the topic was deferred. Traces remain in the interstices, leaving clues regarding architecture's role, knowing and otherwise, in this story of global environmental management.

Only One Earth

The Stockholm conference took place under the motto "Only One Earth."[14] Motivated by the growing recognition in the late 1960s (primarily among industrialized nations) of an impending and potentially global "ecological crisis," the conference was initiated in 1968 by the Swedish delegation to a summer session of the United Nations Economic and Social Council (ECOSOC) and ratified by the UN General Assembly on December 3, 1968.[15] Thus, although Weisberg could wryly note that "it was almost as if the carefully controlled but colorful Earth Days in the U.S. over the last two years had been dress rehearsals for what went on in Stockholm," the initial proposal preceded this widespread popularization of environmental issues. Harnessing that popular support to other ends, the UN used the occasion of a growing fear of environmental emergency to institute mechanisms of resource management and a paradigm of developmentalism at the level of ratified international policies. In December 1970, Maurice Strong, a wealthy Canadian industrialist and former oilman then overseeing Canada's external aid program to developing countries, was appointed secretary general of the conference.[16] With the ambition of forging a worldwide consensus, Strong, according to many accounts, played an active diplomatic role, exerting a forceful hand in an effort to overcome growing divides—not only along the familiar East-West axis characteristic of Cold War battles, but across the (to many) less expected, but increasingly evident and convoluted North-South distinction between industrialized countries and their less developed counterparts.[17]

The UN's Preparatory Committee met four times to set the official agenda, synthesizing literally hundreds of thousands of pages of national reports into a streamlined set of largely scientific and technical (and hence supposedly neutral) concerns regarding the state of the global environment and recommendations for new legal and institutional frameworks to manage its future. This included the establishment of Earthwatch, a global monitoring system to collect and manage data on contaminants, climate change, animal and plant life, resources, and the decline of genetic diversity. The two main conference documents were an "Action Plan" for environmental controls and agreements and a draft Declaration on the Human Environment. The latter, which Strong described as a "carefully constructed consensus,"[18] was a not legally binding document that, he hoped, might achieve the same sort of ethical mandate for environmental issues that the UN's 1948 Declaration on Human Rights had achieved for the notion of universal rights. These highly edited and, in one reviewer's words, "prefabricated"[19] documents served as the basis for deliberations among the 113 nations that arrived in

Stockholm. As one author explained, tying this to 1960s ideologies, they amounted to "a mandate to the United Nations to save 'Spaceship Earth.'"[20]

For the United States and other industrialized countries that held sway at the UN, at stake was establishing paradigms of environmental discourse and mechanisms of governance that would defray rising political challenges and dissipate claims to distributive justice, in effect quelling dissent and allowing them to maintain access to crucial natural resources in the developing world, such as oil. In addition to Strong's skillful efforts in consensus politics, claims to the universal nature of environmental concerns served as cause to exclude questions considered political or divisive that might derail the process, confining agendas to the realms of science, technology, management, development processes, and institutional frameworks. Expertise in all was dominated by Northern countries. Before returning to Brand and the Hog Farm, I want to outline Strong's strategy, for it is against this backdrop that we can best read the integration of Brand's Life Forum agenda and, in turn, the cracks that began to emerge in this picture of consensus.

New World Order

"Marshall McLuhan is famous for the observation that 'the medium is the message,'" explained legal scholar and UN advisor Richard Gardner at a May 1972 hearing on the UN conference before the US Senate Committee on Foreign Relations. "Strong is the originator of another phrase," he continued, "'the process is the policy.' Its relevance to the UN is evident. While public attention focused on the Stockholm conference, the process of getting to Stockholm may have even greater long-term significance than the conference itself."[21] Policies and the process of instituting them were central to Strong's scripting of moves on this battlefield. If new policies were not put in place, he warned, conflict and war would ensue. Under Strong's guidance, academic expertise, media strategies, technological developments, legal and economic protocols, data collection and analysis, and nongovernmental organizations all fed the institutional machinery of the UN to promote a certain vision of environmental problems.

In *Did We Save the Earth at Stockholm?* Peter Stone, Strong's senior information advisor for the conference, recalled that the UN

Preparatory Committee remained cautious regarding the "political consequences" of "uncontrolled participation" by nongovernmental organizations (NGOs), other experts, and concerned citizens in Stockholm. Environmental groups, Strong and Stone acknowledged, had been instrumental in raising awareness of environmental issues to the point where such an intergovernmental discussion could happen at all, and both understood NGOs to be a potential means of making the conference "more newsworthy and exciting."[22] In fact, Stone explained, "I rather felt that unless there were an off-stage chorus of environmentalists the Press and television men might not come at all."[23] Stone's initial plans for augmenting public interest included a McLuhan-inspired "'global village' meeting by television," a Will Burtin–designed information facility replete with "audio-visual model of the complex interlocking cycles of the planetary environment," and a closed-circuit television station—"Environment '72"—to render the conference a "big environmental teach in."[24] Although Stone's audiovisual programming was rejected, Strong's process of forging a media-NGO complex to mobilize public opinion was enormously successful: press coverage was extensive, in the buildup to the conference, during the event, and in its aftermath.

Beyond attracting media, Strong told the Friends of the Earth, NGOs "stimulated a two-way exchange of ideas and information." "We must leave here," he continued, "with an awakened sense of this new dynamic breaching the barriers between those who make the official decisions and those who are affected by such decisions. If we do that, it may well have a more far-reaching impact on the affairs of Planet Earth than any of the more technical decisions we have reached."[25] If barriers between governments and the governed were breached in Stockholm, this two-way exchange was not a free or open-ended dialogue, nor was it intended to be. Strong established the Environment Forum, a semiofficial conference for NGOs to which we return in Chapter 4, to regulate such breaching and to monitor and contain the mounting threat of countervoices. He also commissioned *Only One Earth: The Care and Maintenance of a Small Planet* in May 1971 to set the conceptual narrative for conference participants, NGOs, media, and the general public.[26] Written by British economist Barbara Ward and French-born, US-based biologist René Dubos, the best-selling book was sponsored by the

Ford Foundation and the International Bank for Reconstruction and Development, aka the World Bank.

Armed with Western notions of progress and "the weight of scientific proof," *Only One Earth* set out a picture of planetary interconnectedness and imminent catastrophe.[27] Its grand narrative of a unified, interdependent planetary system spanned from prehistoric plasma forming into the planet and the first rain falling on Earth to the rise of worldwide economic and communication systems and nuclear weapons. Now threatening the fragile balance of Earth's ecology, the book posited, was pollution born of industry, population growth, rapid urbanization, and the density of cities, as well as patterns of human migration. Among the dominant threats, in the authors' estimation, was the possibility that the two-thirds of people who lived in developing countries—whose consumption they likened to "Neolithic man"—might start to demand even half the resources consumed per capita in the developed nations of the world. "Suppose seven billion try to live like Europeans or Japanese? Suppose they seek American standards of automobile use"? they warned with unchecked hubris of the threat from "the modernizing 'South' of our planet," stressing that it would "alter dangerously and perhaps irreversibly, the natural systems of his [technological man's] planet upon which his biological survival depends."[28]

The book's production was coordinated by Strong and the International Institute for Environmental Affairs (IIEA), an organization founded under the sponsorship of Robert O. Anderson, chairman of Atlantic Richfield, and renamed the International Institute for Environment and Development (IIED) under Ward's subsequent directorship. The IIEA was a think tank born of the Aspen Institute for Humanistic Studies, and like its point of origin, it was dedicated to maintaining the world-leadership status of business elites by providing them access to a wider field of knowledge.[29] The IIEA left a strong imprint on *Only One Earth* and on the conference.[30] It put together a committee of 152 "scientific and intellectual leaders" from fifty-eight countries to offer input into the manuscript. Among them were Aurelio Peccei, an Italian industrial manager and economist affiliated with Olivetti and Fiat and president of the Club of Rome; presidents of oil companies, such as Imperial Oil Ltd. of Toronto; chairmen of international chambers of commerce; social scientists such as Daniel Bell and Margaret Mead; and engineers, physical scientists, educators, management specialists, economists, and lawyers. There were also five experts on "human settlements": Constantin Doxiadis, Martin Meyerson, Lewis Mumford, Jorge Hardoy, and Kenzo Tange.

Spaceship Earth

Tasking the UN conference with "formulat[ing] the problems inherent in the limitations of the spaceship earth," *Only One Earth* invoked Adlai Stevenson's famous July 1965 speech to ECOSOC in Geneva, delivered while he served as US ambassador to the UN and five days before his death.[31] (A longtime friend and advisor of Stevenson, Ward has been credited as its ghostwriter, and she counted among her advisees Robert McNamara and multiple US presidents.)[32] "We travel together, passengers on a little spaceship," Stevenson remarked of Earth, "dependent upon its vulnerable reserves of air and soil; all committed for our safety to its security and peace; preserved from annihilation only by the care, the work, and I will say, the love we give our fragile craft."[33] Offering an eloquent figure of the vulnerability of humanity's interconnected habitat, the figure of Spaceship Earth served in the interim as the title to Ward's 1966 book, *Spaceship Earth*, and to R. Buckminster Fuller's *Operating Manual for Spaceship Earth* of 1969.[34]

Turning to the role of worldwide media in fomenting discontent among the poor, Ward and Dubos also silently cited less familiar clauses from Stevenson's speech. As he ominously suggested of the "vast contradictions" of rich and poor: "On their resolution depends the survival of us all."[35] In Ward and Dubos' assessment,

> If developing peoples were as ignorant as Pharaoh's slaves of how "the other half" lives, they might toil on without protest. But the transistor and the satellites and world-wide TV have put an end to that kind of ignorance. Can we rationally suppose that they will accept a world "half slave, half free," half plunged in consumptive pleasures, half deprived of the bare decencies of life? Can we hope that the protest of the dispossessed will not erupt into local conflict and widening unrest?[36]

Ward and Dubos were less interested in overcoming these contradictions than they were in managing their impact. The only positive note or "breakthrough" in their account was the Green Revolution of chemically assisted, genetically engineered crops. Backed by the Ford Foundation and the World Bank, the Green Revolution had by this time come under significant attack as wreaking social, economic, and environmental havoc in developing countries, primarily benefitting multinational corporations and sponsoring dependency. Although they acknowledged problems, to Ward and Dubos, it was to be encouraged as ultimately leading to successful development and hence quelling potential unrest.

Strong stressed that *Only One Earth* was not an official document, but "the work of individuals, serving in their personal capacities without restraints imposed upon officials of governments and international agencies."[37] As Stone noted glibly with respect to the long arm of the IIEA, *Only One Earth* was "very professional. It led one to understand and sympathize with the captains of industry and their economic rationalizers who have got us into our present pickle."[38] Alluding to solutions, Strong opened the Stockholm conference by announcing the need for "new concepts of sovereignty" that took into account the Earth's physical interdependency, along with "new international means for better management of the world's common property resources."[39] Although saving Earth was in everyone's interest, to Strong, such interdependency was not a reason to establish an even playing field, but to institute a well-regulated one, rendering the ramifications of such postsovereign paradigms of management distinctly asymmetrical.

The IIEA, which represented those captains of industry and economic rationalizers, sponsored the Distinguished Lecture Series at the UN conference, featuring Ward and Dubos, along with Peccei, the British scientist and policy advisor Lord Zuckerman, and other "citizens of the world." The seven talks appeared as a volume edited by Strong, *Who Speaks for Earth?*[40] Answering the question of who might speak, he invited Ward and Dubos to make a presentation at the UN conference, the only "citizens" to do so. Ward's assistant, David Satterthwaite, recalled with pride that although UN rules prohibited her from speaking at the plenary session, "the organizers ingeniously suspended the official proceedings so she could speak," a point confirmed by Strong.[41] Along with Margaret Mead, Ward led a collective of NGOs that issued an alternative declaration calling for a more permanent role for NGOs, including probusiness think tanks like the Aspen Institute and reformist scientists, engineers, and management experts with whom Strong remained affiliated.[42]

Prefacing the US State Department's report for the UN conference, *Safeguarding Our World Environment*, President Richard Nixon celebrated another contribution to fostering "world environmental consciousness," declaring: "We are now growing accustomed to the view of our planet as seen from space—a blue and brown disk shrouded in white patches of clouds. But we do not ponder often enough the striking lesson it teaches about the global reach of environmental imperatives. No matter what else divides men and nations, this perspective should unite them."[43] The planetary insecurity conveyed by Stevenson was indeed further catalyzed in 1968 by NASA's release of photographs of Earth taken from Apollo spacecraft by American astronauts, their release often credited to Brand's 1966 campaign of buttons reading "Why haven't we seen a photograph of the whole Earth yet?"[44] To many, these photographs rendered comprehensible for the first time the scientific claim that the planet functions as a closed ecological system. These images all too seamlessly lent themselves both to a countercultural environmental consciousness—exemplified in their appearance on the cover of Brand's *Whole Earth Catalog*—and to advancing mechanisms of global governance then being sought by both the United States and the United Nations. Nixon used them to promote the World Environment Fund to "stimulate international cooperation," committing $100 million toward a "centralized coordination point" for UN environment activities, including the anticipated new administrative body (the United Nations Environment Program [UNEP]) and Earthwatch. With the United States in the lead of remote sensing systems and data management, Earthwatch sat comfortably with US foreign policy.

Along with Strong's strategies to forge consensus and the seductive figures of a unified planet, the UN's demarcation of conference debates to focus on technical concerns served forcefully not only to suppress conflict, but to bracket historical relations and mask structural inequalities in the service of maintaining a vast imbalance of power. Yet the violent contradictions of rich and poor, exacerbated under a globalizing capitalism, erupted into debates in Stockholm, opening Strong's carefully constructed platform, at least momentarily, to critical challenges. As Barry Commoner rightly predicted, "ecological crusaders are about to clash with seekers of social justice." Delegates and "the world," he speculated, "are certain to be

Figure 3.3 View of Earth taken by an astronaut on the Apollo 8 mission, December 22, 1968 (NASA).

Figure 3.4 Stewart Brand selling "Why Haven't We Seen a Photograph of the Whole Earth Yet?" buttons, San Francisco, April 1966 (© Bill Young/San Francisco Chronicle/Corbis).

reminded that there is much more to the environmental crisis than the monitoring of pollutants, control of effluents, or tax incentives," because environmental questions have an "uncanny way in which, if pressed to their source they bring sharply into focus the long-standing, unresolved conflicts that trouble the world," a world "still, tragically dominated by poverty, racial conflict, and war."[45] We will come back to these interruptions in the narrative in Chapter 4.

Strong's extensive work mobilizing consensual political support for the conference and its aims from Third World delegations and his framing of environmental discourses and demands were largely successful, and the declaration and action plan were approved with minor modifications. Under his leadership, the UN validated paradigms of global environmental governance seeking to manage threats to economic growth in (or the political power of) dominant Western nations as posed either by ecological crusaders or those seeking social justice. "Despite ideological, political, economic or religious differences," *Science and Public Affairs* reported, "the delegates of 114 [sic] nations at the Conference were able to agree on an Action Plan and a Declaration of Principles based on the common realization that the Earth is a closed, ecological system and man continues to modify it only at his peril."[46] However, it was in the context of challenges posed by the developing world and by other political activists working against injustice that Strong learned from Brand, whose palliative and media-savvy tactics proved closely in alignment with mainstream US goals.

Mass Migration

To come back, then, to the Hog Farm and the Life Forum and how they played into this cynical scenario: Brand's ambition for the Stockholm conference was to transplant to European soil and to a global arena replete with expanded media presence the ethos of mass transience and alternative modes of life foregrounded in his *Whole Earth Catalog*, as well as festivities characteristic of the so-called "Woodstock Nation," replete with rock bands, street-theater companies, and countercultural celebrities. His strategy did not seek a contestatory political platform, but rather a corrective to radical political activities. It was to demonstrate a lifestyle aiming, in the words of his ally Allen Ginsberg, at a "transformation of world consciousness," rather than at "political action."[47] Brand has been celebrated for launching alternative print publications that in modeling "ecological" systems of information and exchange heralded the digital communities of the Internet.[48] Operating as a feedback mechanism for publicizing services, technologies, and knowledge, the *Whole Earth Catalog* was an effective mechanism of control, governing not only access to resources for "survival," but conceptual terms through which they sponsored alternative modes of life. Ever the entrepreneur, Brand considered the Stockholm conference to be "an unusual opportunity" for gaining "world wide visibility" for the catalog's "whole earth" ideology, a giant networking event for "unprecedented exchange of environmental information."[49] Stockholm would convene a global marketplace for the whole-Earth faith. Yet his underlying motivation remained murky, even confusing.

Brand's initial preparatory work in fact led to bitter confrontations with Swedish groups with whom he sought alliances. In May 1972, the *Village Voice* reported:

> a loose collection of happenings called "Household Earth" or "Life Forum" is being put together for Stockholm. Originally it was to be a part of the People's Forum planned by a coalition of Swedish leftists groups. But that alliance disintegrated when the American counter-culture contingent of Stewart Brand (compiler of the Whole Earth Catalog), David Padwa (a counter-culture lawyer working with the Black Mesa Defense Fund), and Melissa Savage went to Stockholm to meet with organizers from Sweden's new left. Apparently Brand passed out copies of the [*Whole Earth*] Catalog at a meeting and someone opened the book to a page advertising books on grass-growing. The ideologues freaked and accused Household Earth people of being CIA plants, intending to spread drugs around Stockholm.[50]

As evident from a People's Forum session entitled "The Destructive Role of Hog Farm," Swedish radical groups believed that "the US government was using drugs to dim the political consciousness."[51] Weisberg recounts that Brand, Padwa, and Savage (Life Forum coordinator and associate at the *Whole Earth Catalog*) approached the People's Forum in March "with an offer of $40,000 if they could share the building in which Folkets Forum was to be conducted, receive endorsement from Folkets Forum, arrange tent facilities in the parks for the alleged '100,000 to 400,00[0] youth' Brand

Figure 3.5 Stewart Brand on screen in media center during the United Nations Conference on the Human Environment, Stockholm, 1972. From *Clear Creek*, October 1972 (Ann Dowie).

[anticipated] would descend on Stockholm, and establish a name register for all activists entering Stockholm."[52]

Haley, who previously worked at *Clear Creek* magazine, recalls that Padwa's suggestion "that Life Forum offer information clearinghouse services during the conferences where the NGO and counter conference groups from all over the world could register, share contact information, meet each other and leave messages... did not say useful networking to the Swedes. It absolutely screamed CIA," as did the money they could access. The announcement that "they were bringing 50 Hog Farmers in to handle crowd control, drug freakouts and drug analysis" had a similar effect. "Swedish activists and political youth felt strongly that drugs were a CIA plot to turn people into idle do nothings who would be too stoned to throw off the yoke of the oppressor capitalists.... They were not flower children," Haley explains.[53] In addition to working with Black Mesa, Padwa was a representative of the Kaplan Fund, which in the mid-1960s was accused of being a conduit for the CIA.[54] With Life Forum funding coming both from Brand's Point Foundation, a channel for profit from the *Whole Earth Catalog*, and the Kaplan Foundation, the scene was set for a disastrous encounter with members of the Scandinavian Left.[55]

Moreover, the mass migration to Woodstockholm paradoxically, or perhaps simply cynically, posed the threat that Stockholm would become a model in miniature of the global ecological crisis. As Brand suggested, "Stockholm can build, or destroy, a faith."[56] Management was the key, and it was here that the Hog Farm was to play a role in providing that "living reality-model of people taking care of each other." The *Voice* reported that the Life Forum aimed to "charter two planes—one from California and one from the East Coast—to fly Americans to Stockholm."[57] The prospect of planeloads of Americans—commune members, rock bands, street-theater companies, environmental activists, hippies, and so on—let alone tens of thousands of other youths arriving for the UN event, was initially alarming not only to city authorities, but to the UN and to the US delegation, the latter expressing concern that on account of this mass migration the conference "does not become a highly charged political atmosphere of a divisive kind."[58] Beyond the specter of an environmental catastrophe like that at Woodstock (which was left strewn with garbage), Brand's alarmist claims that tens of thousands

Figure 3.6 & 3.7 Army tents with Hog Farm bus and teepees at Tent City; Hog Farm buses and Free Stage at Tent City, Skarpnäck, June 1972 (Anders Willgård).

Figure 3.8 Police presence during United Nations Conference on the Human Environment, Stockholm, June 1972 (Bjorn Gustafsson).

of youths were expected to show up convinced the police of an imminent security threat, to which they responded with excessive police presence.[59] In John Lewallen's words, "The city was crawling with platoons of cops, with the Swedish National Guard on stand-by alert."[60] The "mass international invasion of hippies," as he characterized the problem, never took place, but in the meantime, Brand successfully cast the Hog Farm's intervention in terms of "crowd control" and hence as in alignment with the security concerns of local police and other authorities, who by many accounts maintained "friendly relations" with the commune, even when faced with accusations of their promoting drug use.[61] Calling attention to the rhetoric of pacification, Weisberg noted, "In the words of the Chief of Police of Operations: 'They are nice people, they wish to cooperate. They don't intend to cause any disturbances. Instead, as far as the Hog Farm is concerned, they wish to quiet other people.'"[62] Like the police, but sporting an antiestablishment appearance, the Hog Farm was there to keep order.

Long a disciple of R. Buckminster Fuller and his entrepreneurial vision, Brand was unapologetic about his rejection of politics. He made his position clear as early as a 1969 conversation published in *Rolling Stone* and took care to reiterate his "non-political" position while in Stockholm.[63] In "A Visit to the Life Forum HQ," Alfred Heller recounted a conversation with Brand at the Life Forum's downtown venue. Heller had asked Hog Farm member Calico how she felt about the UN conference, receiving the answer that she "doesn't believe in government." Savage tried to clarify that "the politics of the Hog Farm itself are complicated." At which point Brand interjected: "I don't agree with that.... The Hog Farm is non-political. Everything we do is non-political. The 'Whole Earth Catalog' was non-political although everybody kept trying to tell me it was a political document."[64] Weisberg, too, albeit for different reasons, stressed the Life Forum's apolitical stance: "the greatest contrast to the Folkets Forum was not the United Nations—where political issues were at least acknowledged," he wrote, "but a collection of Americans brought to Stockholm under the auspices of Life Forum."[65] Although, as he indicated, the People's Forum and PowWow regarded the UN conference as "an opportunity to educate people to the connection between politics and ecology... this was not the Hog Farm's intention": "As one Hog Farmer explained condescendingly, 'Political action is representative, Hog Farm action is direct, one to one.'"[66] As many commentators noted, this was not simply a tactic of "direct action," but a "politics no, environment yes" ideology, one seeking individual planetary "consciousness" and an unmediated feeling of care for Spaceship Earth.

For Weisberg, such a position had a predilection not only to usurp more familiar leftist political discourses, but also to remain blind to (or unwilling to address) questions of social and distributive justice. "Hog Farm's message, that we must return to an idyllic, less industrial way of life," he proposed, "was lost on delegates from countries struggling for simple survival."[67] The Hog Farm's "identification down," their adoption of tents, teepees, and obsolescent forms of cooking, dressing, and transportation as a form of care of the self and of the land, was in many regards in line with the "voluntary primitivism" operating in Open Land communes and back-to-the-land activism of the mid to late 1960s. As detailed in Chapter 2, such practices served not to demonstrate rights claims for access to or inclusion within a dominant system, but rather as attempts to withdraw from the institutions and lifestyles through which micropolitical techniques of power interfaced with their bodies and psyches. Those alternative modes of life and their architectural manifestations remained problematic in many regards, but we can read them not only as symptomatic, if dissident, responses to a biopolitical regime, but also as tactical vehicles for the production and dissemination of images of something like a *counterdispositif*. My aim here is to ask what happens when such tactics are detached from the sociopolitical and technological milieu of the United States (from which they derived their specificity and political traction) and repositioned in an international arena where they encounter other voices, other concerns, and other tactics. Their aesthetic was not lost on those struggling for survival, and I think we need to pay attention to their semantic resonances and their strategic deployment by Brand. Having served as a Pentagon photojournalist following his military service, Brand understood mass media and put it to work on this battlefield.

Encampments

Convinced by Brand's arguments, the City of Stockholm provided the Hog Farm with a site at the abandoned airfield in Skarpnäck, on the outskirts of the city, a safe one-hour subway ride away from the main UN conference venues, along with approximately a hundred and seventy-five army tents to house the transient population. As *San Francisco Chronicle* writer Harold Gilliam recounted in "Eco-Trips at Hog Farm," after reaching the end of the subway system and being guided through "a maze of housing compounds and wood lots" by bemused local residents, he "found an encampment of army tents set up by Stockholm officials, a scattering of brightly colored mountain tents, a large tie-dyed teepee and some psychedelic-painted buses. The Hog Farm," he continued, "is a commune of about 50 long-haired young people and several over-30s" who specialize as "trouble-shooters and crowd-coolers."[68] There he met Wavy Gravy, described by Brand as the commune's "wise fool," then busy dressing up one of the Day-Glo painted buses as a giant whale for a demonstration the following day, along with Lou Todd, the Hog Farm's so-called "straw boss."[69] "We've set up a life-support system," Todd explained to the reporter of their method of defusing threats, "we feed everybody free, we have a free stage.... This is our way to take the heat off and keep violence out of the streets." The commune's function, he explained, confirming its palliative and consensual agenda, "is to effect consciousness-change among large numbers of people, to give people a living experience of a cooperative group-energy project, to show them how good that feels, to show them that sharing and cooperating is a much better approach to getting things done than competing with each other."[70] Describing the scene as "a colorful collection of Woodstock graduates, former Merry Pranksters and other assorted acid-heads, eco-freaks, save-the-whalers, doomsday mystics, poets and hangers-on," Rowland, too, commented on the idealistic mystical or New Age ethos that pervaded the group, which, he noted, "had come to Stockholm—mostly from the U.S.—to help the conference 'get it on,' to try to imbue the historic debates with the spirit of transcendentalism and humility before nature that the American counter-culture had lately been espousing."[71]

The Hog Farm proved an ideal vehicle for Brand. The commune was founded around 1966 when Wavy Gravy (then Hugh Romney) and three other "dropouts" made a deal to tend a pig farm in the foothills of the San Gabriel Mountains in Southern California in exchange for free rent. According to the magazine *Avant-Garde*, it quickly became the "grooviest hippie commune in America." Composed, as *Avant-Garde* put it, of a "motley cantonment of geodesic domes, tents, trailers, huts, and a cinderblock farmhouse," it had "assumed the proportions of a post-escape base camp. Drifters, refugees from less fortunate communes, friends, and strangers seeking a crash moved in."[72] Romney, a veteran street-theater performer, played "Commissioner of Talk" for this "experiment in utopian living." They also experimented with an ad hoc appropriation of Eastern religions, which, as *Avant-Garde* suggested, "seems to work for them. They seek to live in accord with the *Tao*, egoless identification with a World Consciousness to which reality is continuous change," with all decisions being made "with the help of the *I Ching*."[73] Seeking to undermine hierarchical leadership structures (though not traditional gender divisions), Hog Farm members instituted a rotating system of daily "dance masters," who ran the farm, and "dance mistresses," who ran the kitchen, both chosen by spinning a wheel and together in charge of running the camp. Out of this emerged the practice of a rotating "power day," playing out fantasies of being "god for 24 hours."[74]

The commune soon acquired a bus and hit the road to put on theatrical "freak-shows" and, in turn, elaborate psychedelic light shows—later called "life shows"—for a wider audience. Harnessing their Merry Prankster legacy, the self-proclaimed "citizens of Earth" eventually left the farm (and their increasingly hostile neighbors) behind entirely to become a nomadic show replete with domes, teepees, tents, an inflatable house, costumes, props, generators, lights, and the cameras, projectors, microphones, loudspeakers, and other electronic equipment necessary for such theatrical generation of "whole" or "cosmic consciousness." They even took a pig, Pigasus, along as a mascot, soon to serve as the Yippees' nominee at the 1968 Democratic Convention in Chicago.[75] The ideals of global unity or consensus and the replacement of political conflict by "cooperative group energy" pursued by the Hog Farm and the environmental and media techniques they employed to pursue them were intended as progressive, but are, in retrospect, far from unproblematic, even if less so than Brand's cynical redeployment of them in Stockholm.

In detailing the Hog Farm's "skill in serving large crowds of transients," Brand listed in addition to Woodstock a series of other "accomplishments": "their money-raising and faith-raising efforts for

Figure 3.9 Wavy Gravy and other Hog Farmers in Stockholm, June 1972 (Bjorn Gustafsson).

Earth Peoples Parks, their week of crowded starvation for the Hunger Show (Liferaft Earth), their peace-keeping activities on numerous battlefields such as Newark, Chicago, and Washington DC, their innumerable shows and presentations in America and Europe, and their helping journey to the heart of need in East Pakistan and Nepal last year,"[76] precedents I want briefly to recall.

Earth People's Park sought to expand upon the Open Land movement ideals of LATWIDN ("land, access to which is denied no one"). As recalled in the "The Outlaw Area" issue of the *Whole Earth Catalog*, the "Earth Peoples Park idea originated largely at the Sympowowsium," organized by Hog Farmer Tom Law, which in November 1969 "brought together organizers and promoters of festival events" such as Woodstock.[77] Based on the "idea of using the fantastic power and profits of rock music to free a piece of the planet," with the Ford Foundation identified as another possible source of funds, Earth People's Park entailed "the idea of acquiring and returning one small segment of Mother Earth back to herself." Moreover, it was to be a "nationLESS piece of Earth in a sectioned-off world," its inhabitants likewise identified with a new global tribe, rather than as citizens of a nation.[78] The antigovernance ambition at Earth People's Park was described as "a sort of basic anarchism: a sociological experiment in whether a group of strangers can live under the most primitive conditions without rules or government to guide them, for there is no boss or manager here, nor any governing body."[79]

While conceived as a means of liberating land from capitalist rule, the idealistic project of "freeing a piece of Mother Earth" quickly encountered other voices that complicate this picture. "One black guy" in the preparatory group, the *Whole Earth Catalog* recounted, eliding his name, "thought that the Earth Park idea was *nice*, but it was running away from the real problems of hunger and oppression."[80] In March 1970, the *Los Angeles Free Press* announced that the original idea for creating an Earth People's Park on a large tract of land in New Mexico had been abandoned. "Recent meetings in San Francisco with New Mexican Chicanos and Indians have convinced EPP organizers that an influx of white settlers would be regarded as another land rip-off." "Most of the locals," the article added of attempts to reverse this colonization, "sympathize with or support Reles Tijerina and La Alianza in their right to regain the land stolen from them by U.S. invaders."[81] The connection to the Hog Farm's activities in Skarpnäck was direct: they went to Stockholm to raise money and support for the Earth People's Park. The Tent City was, quite literally, to be a testing ground for the so-called Woodstock Nation's expansion beyond the United States, part of an ambition to achieve a permanent, global, post-territorial network of free spaces on Earth. "The Hog Farm may be found," Brand had indicated, at "Rainbow Junction, Earth Peoples Park (temporary), Stockholm."[82]

Are You Ready to Die?

In addition to the Hog Farm's promotion of a vision of global, post-territorial unity that, unfortunately, resonated with (without effectively interrupting) neoliberal ideals, Brand promoted a neo-Malthusian rhetoric of population control. The next precedent he cited as evidence of the Hog Farm's skills, Liferaft Earth, took place in October 1969 and took the form of a weeklong voluntary communal fasting game to simulate famine, with a departure from the group cast as a death. "Its intent," Brand recalled in "The Outlaw Area," "was to make very personal the matter of population control," but to project that personal act into the public sphere by harnessing media attention. "The stadium," he acknowledged, "was the news media, so a certain amount of theater (i.e. plot) was designed in." In addition to Wavy Gravy and other Hog Farmers, support came from Stephanie Mills (famous for announcing at her commencement speech at Mills College in 1969, after reading Paul Ehrlich's *The Population Bomb*, that her contribution to the planet would be to bear no children), from other individuals dedicated to population control, and from establishment environmental groups such as the Friends of the Earth and the Sierra Club. Beyond celebrity support, "Further visual interest—useful for TV and wirephotos," Brand noted, "was provided by Earth posters, the door for the event with its sign 'Are You Ready to Die,' and a splendid model of the inflated 10,000 sq. ft. polyethylene pillow that we planned to hold the event in."[83]

Filmed by Robert Frank, the Hunger Show eventually landed in the parking lot of a poverty-program office in Hayward, California. Local fire marshals rejected as a fire hazard the large inflatable pillow initially proposed to house the event, so the Southcoast Pneumads (soon to join the Ant Farm architectural collective) produced a "stage" ringed by a four-foot-high inflatable wall, a camp to contain

Figure 3.10 Liferaft Earth set up in Hayward, California, 1969. From *Berkeley Tribe*, October 17–23, 1969 (Peggy Miller).

the starving hordes. The scene was also replete with Earth flags and a giant inflatable globe. Bearing one of NASA's Apollo images, the Earth flag had just been added to the sales list of the Whole Earth Truck Store and was cast as a flag that, unlike those of nations, states, and the UN, represented "just people." A visitor stated, "I don't know if I'd die for it, but it's the first flag I've seen that I don't feel it somehow excludes me."[84] In addition to mediation, yoga, and participating in the Hog Farm's communal "gong-bong" breathing exercise, in which people would hold hands in a circle and breathe rapidly to effect a collective dizziness, entertainment included "a UN starvation movie on a sheet hung from the poverty center balcony," a recording of Franz Kafka's "Hunger Artist," and reading *The Population Bomb*, a prominent sales item in the catalog.[85] Brand's account of the event was illustrated with an Oxfam photograph of an emaciated child, captioned "In case there's some question what Liferaft Earth was about, it was about this" and accompanied by notes on a population bibliography and entries for publications on abortion and voluntary sterilization.

It was not surprising that Ehrlich was a key reference here. Brand studied with the biology professor while a student at Stanford in the late 1950s, at which point Ehrlich was still, as Fred Turner notes, "concentrating on the fundamentals of butterfly ecology and systems-oriented approaches to evolutionary biology."[86] Ehrlich attributed the shift in his concerns from insect populations to human overpopulation to an epiphany while traveling in Delhi, during which the intense activities of urban life in India "gave the scene a hellish aspect." With a cadence speaking of near panic, he recalled: "The streets were alive with people. People eating, people washing, people sleeping. People visiting, arguing and screaming. People thrusting their hands through the taxi window, begging. People defecating and urinating. People clinging to buses. People herding animals. People, people, people, people."[87] Deploying alarmist rhetoric, *The Population Bomb* called for compulsory methods of birth control, should voluntary ones fail to stem what he called the "cancer of population growth."[88] Through Ehrlich, Brand was introduced to the systems and cybernetic-based approaches to ecology that came to characterize not only his environmental thinking, but also the networking culture of the *Whole Earth Catalog*. Liferaft Earth suggests that systems thinking was not the only legacy of

Ehrlich at work—that the neo-Malthusian population bomb thesis also haunted his approach to environmental questions, or at least his alarmist presentation of them.

Mobilizing Shame

The third example raised by Brand as evidence of the Hog Farm's expertise and their relevance to his Life Forum initiative is equally, if differently, problematic. The Hog Farm's use of what might be called "parodic humanitarianism" in its journey to the "heart of need" in the East reveals uneasy slippages between the group's ideals and the visual language that they employed to promote them. Wavy Gravy offered a brief description of the trip in his 1974 book *The Hog Farm and Friends*, explaining that "the plan was to move food and doctors to East Pakistan, where the flood had just receded, killing a million and leaving the rest homeless and hungry." Their (mock) humanitarian mission was supposed both to resemble, but constitutively depart from those of groups such as the Red Cross: "Our best show has always been dinner, and doctors were needed," Wavy Gravy recalled, "but first on the menu, and that [sic] we could leave, was our love. We never believed that we could feed millions, but merely our presence and the sense of the press could embarrass great countries to take care of business."[89] The Hog Farm, it seems, planned to deploy a key tactic of human rights activism—mobilizing shame—in which visibility afforded by exposure through mass media was intended to rally public opinion regarding the violation of rights or mass human suffering and in turn to bring pressure to act on governments or intergovernmental institutions.[90] However, the Hog Farm's would-be humanitarian actions (if we can call love that) were interrupted before they could begin: "a war beat us to it and borders were closed," Wavy Gravy explained. The group continued on instead ("next slide please," as he put it) to Nepal, Wavy Gravy telling the story of their turn to hiking, of blowing bubbles for children, and of creating an Earth People's Playground.[91]

As with Liferaft Earth and even Earth People's Park, with the Hog Farm's mission to mobilize shame by traveling to East Pakistan (now Bangladesh), we find ourselves in a quandary regarding how to understand the relation between the idealism informing their project—bringing attention to hunger and suffering, attempting to provide land rent free—and the ambiguous nature of the mass-media tactics employed to do so. "So what difference does it make, for those of us who have to respond," Thomas Keenan asks of distinct instances of recent media overexposure and a loss of distance during humanitarian actions, "when the technologies of exposure become opportunities for performance, exhibition, self-exposure? What becomes of shame?" Keenan posits that despite risking ethical uncertainties, "aesthetic categories are relevant here. The aesthetic finds itself in extreme proximity to the ethico-political now; that proximity is perhaps discomforting to some, but it is also the condition of any serious intervention."[92] The Hog Farm's parodic performance of humanitarian aid and its redeployment of the visual language of dissent reminds us that even if aesthetic meaning remains unstable, and even if reception cannot be, strictly speaking, controlled, this does not exempt us from seeking to articulate the conditions of a "serious intervention." This is not to oppose a serious intervention to one taking the form of parody or irony; quite the opposite. It is to suggest (as Keenan does elsewhere[93]) the need to take irony seriously, in this case, the need to distinguish between interventions that, while harboring this risk, are articulated with a knowing precision regarding context and interventions that are not.

Wavy Gravy's account is illustrated with photographs of the Hog Farm's bus in Nepal, by a tie-dyed teepee installed in Turkey, replete with an Earth flag, and so on, images speaking of the multiple (and culturally insensitive) displacement of these artifacts into foreign contexts. They were attempts to spread the word about a new global consciousness and its idealistic ethos of peace and love, an unbounded, egoless love derived by the Hog Farm (and others) from idiosyncratic readings of Eastern religions. In May 1968, the *East Village Other* published a declaration exemplifying this ethos, inviting its readers to sign a "Constitution, for the Spaceship Earth." Indebted to Fuller, it concluded: "we have full power to make love rather than war, recall all the resources which have been installed in military complexes, cooperate with one another, generate operators' [sic] manuals for the spaceship Earth and guides to the Universe."[94] But achieving such idealistic ends is perhaps not as simple as replacing war with love, or even politics (or policy) with love.

Love is not self-evidently a political category, and the ends to which it is put remain as unstable as aesthetic practices. Although, to invoke Freud, we can read this love of humanity as symptomatic of a discontent with contemporary civilization, its efficacy as a humanitarian force (or as a political, let alone democratic platform) remains obscure. "The 'oneness with the universe'" that, as Freud argued, constitutes the "ideational content" of such an "oceanic feeling" as that of a love for all humanity "sounds like a first attempt at a religious consolation, as though it were another way of disclaiming the danger which the ego recognizes as threatening it from the external world."[95] Friend and enemy distinctions dissolve, conflict is eliminated, peace is automatic. Here, too, however, we might interrogate the nature of that perceived threat and insist on taking responsibility for one's representation of it—not to close down the potential for disagreement, but to render visible its contours, for this notion of humanity (and of a world without conflict) is perhaps less efficacious as a tool in the service of peace and justice than it is an image of forced consensus, of a state free from any moment of dissensus, a system without the means for its citizens to question forces underpinning it.[96] Humanity, Carl Schmitt argued decades earlier, is not "a political concept, and no political entity or society and no status corresponds to it."[97] If on the one hand this refusal of politics might seem to imply the elimination of war (in the argument that "humanity as such cannot wage war because it has no enemy, at least not on this planet"), on the other hand, as Schmitt expounded, "the concept of humanity is an especially useful ideological instrument of imperialist expansion, and in its ethical-humanitarian form it is a specific vehicle of economic imperialism."[98]

Life Forum's demonstrations in Stockholm appealed to humanity as such and to the ethos of making "love not war." However, although a *Time* reporter could stress the absurdity of any thought that the "youthful environmentalists at the abandoned airport" were dangerous, their presence raised anxiety. "The violent demonstrations the police feared never came," he reported. "Instead, the students put on gentle 'eco-skits' to dramatize 'eco-catastrophes.' In one, for example, a girl painted as a skeleton and accompanied by drums and cymbals danced a warning about the radioactive fallout from French nuclear-bomb tests in the Pacific."[99] As Stone recalled, the sense of threat nevertheless led Swedish authorities to react, "and one day . . . outside the New Parliament Building a busload of police arrived to break up a group of hippie musicians who were playing nothing more revolutionary than a selection from *Hair*."

"Security men," he added, "opened mail first and you could never get anywhere without passes." Although at the time this appeared absurd or irritating, that soon changed. In Stone's words: "the more recent memory of the Olympic Games and postal bombs has made one much more appreciative in retrospect."[100] The connection might give us pause; as we know from the violent responses to antiglobalization activists, in their attempts to interject other perspectives into the reception of institutions such as the World Bank, the International Monetary Fund, or the World Trade Organization, it is not only violent terrorist acts that elicit such anxieties: civil disobedience and rights struggles have also come to be treated as terrorist or security threats.

Tent City

In "A Crying Need for Quiet Conferences," Ehrlich reflected upon "the pleasantly relaxed atmosphere of the Tent City organized for nonofficial 'delegates' by the Hog Farm commune" in Stockholm, reiterating that all was "peaceful."[101] The psychedelic teepees, customized buses, and geodesic domes were all familiar icons of countercultural modes of life, particularly in Northern California, where Ehrlich taught. While the Hog Farm's environment proved unthreatening to him, unlike the chaotic scene in Delhi that motivated his neo-Malthusian crusade, the impression might not have struck other viewers as simply a peaceful atmosphere. Tents and geodesic domes were key technologies for rapid deployment during both military actions and humanitarian crises; to some, they were hauntingly familiar not from hippie communes and Woodstock-like gatherings, but from other encampments.

Photographs of the Hog Farm's encampment depict a field of tents behind cyclone fencing, as well as geodesic domes, old buses, and people cooking with low-tech devices for hungry masses lining up to eat. Here, indeed, were images depicting those "potentially starving and unhoused people" whom Gelbspan and Gurin identified as informing emerging environmental concerns. They further desublimate the Tent City's resonance with emergency shelters and temporary sites for disaster relief and the management of refugees or housing of soldiers. And they resonate with images of tent cities circulating decades later, such as Camp Bucca, America's largest detention facility during the Iraq War, which housed five thousand prisoners of the "War on Terror" in that nation's southern desert. Along with Camp Cropper, sited on the military base attached to the Baghdad International Airport, the camp was for "security detention," for "holding without charge people believed to pose a potential risk to security," a category recognized neither by Iraqi or American law.[102] To this we might add the refugee camps housing millions fleeing violence in Syria, Central and Eastern Africa, Afghanistan, Ukraine, and beyond. That is, the images spoke (and speak) at once to humanitarian crises and warfare, not only in Indochina (very much on the mind of activists in Stockholm), but also in other sites or camps emerging during states of emergency.

Brand understood the semantic ambiguity that the Hog Farm's camp might produce, acknowledging a potential slippage, but believing it to have been solved. To Brand, "Sweden is not a convincing model of environmental management. 'Sweden gives me the creeps,' he said. 'The way people think here does not coincide with natural processes. Stockholm wanted to put the tents out at Skarpnack in rows like a concentration camp. We stopped that. The Hog Farm stopped that. Now they're in a circle.'"[103] The Hog Farm had long used circular configurations to generate "whole consciousness." Domes provided the infrastructure for this function (or fiction). As Romney recalled, "We built a big dome (a domelette next to what we're into *now*) out of rubber hose, wooden dowels, and this enormous yellow parachute under which we would gather in circles and search for our center."[104] But Brand's connection of circular (or partially circular) organizations to "natural processes"—rather than, say, mystical, constructed, or cultural ones—remains tenuous.

Ian Hogan, an architect promoting alternative technologies with PowWow, picked up on the semantic ambiguity of Life Forum's camp. "I was simply astounded," he stated, to "see a teepee made of machine-made cloth and tie-dyed fashionable hippie colors, with fresh logs which had been stripped out of the Swedish forest by a bunch of American freaks." Hogan saw a subliminal reference to Native Americans: "The Hog Farm has been reacting to American authoritarianism for so long that they no longer see what they are doing...they parked their buses in a horseshoe, like covered wagons preparing for attack by Indians. The open end of the horseshoe is the high stage where the band plays. All of this is of course symbolic."[105] The ambivalent association between the Hog Farm's

Figure 3.11 Hog Farm's Tent City, Skarpnäck, 1972 (Henrik Henrikson).

Figure 3.12 Hog Farm buses at Tent City, Skarpnäck, June 1972 (Henrik Henrikson).

stylized appropriation of indigenous artifacts and the violent history of settlement or colonization in America underscores the complicated and far from utopian picture of nomadic ways of life at play here. As noted in the previous chapter, this ideological identification with Native Americans pervaded the counterculture, fostering a litany of crude projections. The very figure of a Woodstock Nation alluded to claims of Native American sovereignty derived from civil rights struggles and black nationalism, movements adopting strategies of symbolic action for asserting self-determination in the face of imposed forms of governance.[106]

The Native Americans that Brand brought to Stockholm hoped to publicize the environmental damage wrought by industrialization, as well as its impact on their culture. The delegation included Hopi and Navajo activists then (and still) fighting strip mining of the Black Mesa mountain by Peabody Coal, as well as Pit River Indians struggling with Pacific Gas and Electric over seven planned coal-burning power plants. Intended to service Las Vegas and Los Angeles, the bright lights of which loomed large in the architectural imaginary, the industrial plants threatened to pollute the environment and devastate water supplies in the fragile desert ecosystem.[107] The Hopi and Navaho, Haley wrote in *Open Options*, "are a small, underdeveloped sub-country, contained within one of the world's great powers." After noting that they aimed to speak to the plight of other North American indigenous populations and Chicano culture in the American Southwest, along with the "genocide being practiced on Brazilian Indians," she suggested that while "typical of the fate of American Indians throughout the history of the United States," their story "is equally illustrative of the fate of Third World people everywhere."[108]

However, Black Mesa's activities did not forge an easy alliance with "Third World people everywhere," especially when integrated into the Life Forum matrix. As noted in *Clear Creek*, they "came to sharp differences at the Third World (Oi Committee) session of the Alternative Conference" and "withdrew 'because the Committee was...so attuned to science and technology that they would not listen to the spiritualism we were trying to project.'"[109] Once integrated into the "life show," or appearing in Hog Farm's "American Indian Night," however, Native American spiritualism and Native Americans' struggles against injustice were reduced to a spectacle of alterity affiliated with the search for New Age consciousness. This was not new: we have seen it in the reduction of teepees to sales items in the *Whole Earth Catalog*, and the arrogation featured as well in Brand's *America Needs Indians*—a multimedia show to simulate "cosmic consciousness" performed at the 1966 Trips Festival in which he mobilized an imagined affinity between Native American culture and the electronically mediated "tribalism" espoused by Fuller and McLuhan.[110] *Time*'s article "Woodstockholm" pointed to this valence within their theatrical (if heartfelt) appropriation: "Chief Rolling Thunder, an honorary Shoshoni medicine man, chanted invocations while 50 members of the Hog Farm, a peregrinating U.S. commune, threw tobacco into a camp fire, a ritual that is supposed to ward off violence."[111]

"Comin' Together" with Whales

On June 7, Joan McIntyre's antiwhaling initiative Project Jonah staged Whale Night, a "whale show" on the Hog Farm's brightly lit, roughly hewn "free stage" in Skarpnäck. From the sound system she broadcast audiotape recordings of the haunting sounds of humpback whales, the creaks, moans, and groans of their plaintive songs intended to mobilize a mediated empathy for these endangered creatures. Based in Northern California, Project Jonah was funded by Brand's Point Foundation. McIntyre introduced two guests: first was San Francisco beat poet Michael McClure, a guest of the Life Forum; second was President Nixon's former secretary of the interior, Walter Hickel, a prominent member of the US delegation to the official UN conference. The audience at the Hog Farm's Tent City was notably expanded that night: in addition to colorfully dressed hippies and the marginal characters that the city relocated to the encampment for the duration of the conference were numerous members of the press, distinguished scientists such as Dubos, leaders of establishment conservation groups such as Peter Scott of the World Wildlife Fund (WWF), as well as UN and government delegates who directed their limousines to depart from official downtown venues and head to Skarpnäck. "It was the smart place to be that night," Stone noted.[112]

McClure, in his own words, "read some grahhhhr poetry and two whale poems," the latter including "prolonged moans and groans."[113] As recounted by Stone, McClure's poems "ended with the word

Figure 3.13 Maurice Strong at Life Forum's "Whale Night," Hog Farm Tent City's Free Stage, Skarpnäck, June 5, 1972 (UN Photo by Yutaka Nagata).

'gyre' which we understood was what whales say to each other. He repeated the word 'gyre' into the microphone something over thirty times, very slowly and very clearly. It was eerie to say the least, especially as the audience sitting on the damp grass listened intently."[114] Hickel shifted the tone somewhat, recounting his success in halting whale killing by Americans and announcing that it would be "a crime beyond belief if in the same decade that man walked on the moon he also destroyed the largest creature on earth."[115] Hickel was referring to his last act as secretary of the interior: In November 1970, having been forced to step down from Nixon's cabinet (reputedly after criticizing the president's handling of antiwar protestors and the Kent State massacre), he signed a bill adding eight giant whale species to the Endangered Species List, thus preventing the importation of products derived from them.[116]

The mood was thus set for the evening's main event. As Gilliam reported, Brand, "clad in long-fringed Buckskin and Emperor Norton hat" stepped up to the mike to introduce the "surprise guest"—none other than the secretary general of the UN conference, Maurice Strong. Having mounted the platform to appear between Brand and the Hog Farm's Wavy Gravy "in his cap and bells," the "short, dapper Canadian, a wealthy businessman in his business suit, might have felt uncomfortable," Gilliam noted, but "he rose to the occasion magnificently."[117] Far from questioning the appropriateness or efficacy of this so-called "freak show" as a form of citizen activism, Strong celebrated it as a paradigm of nongovernmental participation in UN debates. As recounted by Gilliam,

> "I must say I feel more at home here tonight," he beamed, "than I have since I arrived in Stockholm." Loud cheers. "What you're doing out here is very very important to us. This conference is a conference of governments, and governments are moved to do what people force them to do. They will do as much about these problems as they feel people like you are going to require them to do."
>
> "What you're doing here goes far beyond the plight of the whale himself, because the whale faces today the plight that mankind may well be facing in this generation."
>
> More yells from the crowd, which by now numbered perhaps 1000. Strong complimented Brand's *Whole Earth Catalog*, "which I've admired for a long time. My kids read this stuff: they never bother reading mine." Wavy Gravy pounded his "scepter" on the stage in approval.[118]

Expressing envy of the freedom enjoyed by young people and the "wish [that] I could spend the rest of my stay out here," Strong then departed to prolonged cheering. Stone noted that the "applause overloaded the microphone on my tape recorder and came out as a crackling rippling noise."[119] Everyone was happy, consensus achieved. Strong flanked by Brand and Wavy Gravy was good press, perpetuating his image of a pluralist and the claim to a consensual incorporation of other voices. Saving whales is of course to be applauded. My point is not to critique such goals or even the media tactics used to reach them, but to understand the ends toward which those tactics were deployed in Stockholm.

According to *New York Times* reporter Walter Sullivan, Strong's commentary "reached across the generation gap and his audience, rich in beards, long hair and blue jeans."[120] Stressing the strange encounter between a "former petroleum magnate" and a display of alternative shelter technology, Zwerdling alluded to the heterogeneous mix: "Strong bubbled, as he looked out over the tents and the tepee."[121] However, Strong might have been less comfortable visiting the exhibition on alternative technology (AT) staged at the Moderna Museet Filialen by PowWow, addressed in the next chapter. "At Skarpnak on that warm June night," Gilliam concluded, "the whales had brought the Establishment face-to-face with the Counterculture, Bay Area style, and the vibrations were good."[122] Notably absent from this celebrated event at what *Time* dubbed a "whole earth conference" were not only radical voices from Europe and the United States, but government delegates, NGOs, or other citizenry from the Global South.[123] Indeed, in retrospect, it was a rather homogenous mix of characters for a "world conference," composed of those assuming the right to set the conference agenda and to speak on behalf of the Earth.

Project Jonah's Whale Night was timed to rally support for an upcoming vote at the UN conference to recommend a ten-year moratorium on commercial whaling, an agenda considered by many in the North to be among the most important mandates at the conference, one that might influence an International Whaling Commission meeting later in June.[124] The morning after Whale Night, Project Jonah staged Whale Walk, an antiwhaling march launched from Skeppsholmen Island and traveling past the Riksdagshuset (the Old Parliament building, the main UN conference venue) and through the city. Pointing to its slightly outmoded character, McClure likened the rally to "a 1965 be-in," and in part, it looked quite like one, yet as with Whale Night, some protagonists were unlike be-in fellow travelers of the previous decade, their presence symptomatic of the alliance with the Life Forum and of a shift in environmental politics. Strong and Hickel led the Whale Walk alongside Russell Train, Nixon's primary representative at the UN conference. Then chairman of the newly founded Council on Environmental Quality, Train was a key player in environmental conservation in the US political establishment.[125] The theatrical antiwhaling demonstration featured a Hog Farm commune bus dressed up in black plastic and sporting a large tail to resemble a whale's, along with "youths carrying flowers and either making whale noises or crying 'Val! Val!' the Swedish word for whale and the ancient cry of Norwegian whalers."[126]

The UN resolution for a moratorium on whaling passed fifty-three to zero, with three abstentions (Japan, South Africa, and Portugal—the first a major whaling country, the latter two disenfranchised on account of hostility toward apartheid and colonialism in Africa). The Soviet Union, the other major whaling nation, boycotted the conference following the exclusion of East Germany. "The U.S. delegation saw the question of the whales as a perfect opportunity to become ecology activists," Weisberg wrote. "The U.S. had a moratorium on whale hunting; it was an issue that allowed Train to maintain his conviction that 'I am personally an environmentalist, not a politician.'"[127] The United States had no national stake in whaling, and Project Jonah "was the kind of success the U.S. delegation hoped the U.N. conference would be. Ecological problems were to be considered apart from their economic and political roots."[128] Rowland reiterated Weisberg's reading of the alliance: "It was interesting, if discouraging," he remarked, "to observe how the official American delegation to the U.N. conference adopted this 'politics no, environment yes' attitude represented by Brand and his followers, as a means of avoiding or obscuring potentially embarrassing political issues which, for a major imperialist nation like the United States, were legion."[129]

Ehrlich credited the antiwhaling march as the nongovernmental action having "the greatest impact on official proceedings" in Stockholm.[130] Given his relation to Brand, Ehrlich's advocacy is not surprising, and the Whale Walk was a significant media event, one that pressured governments to align with the US-led antiwhaling initiative and provided an image of US-led consensus. Channeling a flower-power cliché, another archaism from 1960s activism, Ehrlich wrote that with the Whale Walk, the unofficial contingent at the environment conference overcame official barriers, managing to pass "through police cordons by presenting the bemused cops with bouquets of flowers."[131] The topology at play in Stockholm, however, was far more complicated than any simple line dividing UN officials and government delegates from nongovernmental and countercultural voices. Indeed, if one were to offer a metaphor, it would not take the form of a division or opposition and its breaching (as Strong, too, suggested), but of a shifting configuration of players seeking to gain a position of advantage within an emerging apparatus of global environmental governance.

I am not suggesting that battle lines were not drawn in Stockholm. Indeed, they were. But they took the character of shifting and tactical alliances. The perceived threats to environmental control and the strategies sought by dominant players to manage them were not akin to those pertaining to traditional security measures, historical modes of warfare, or even simply interstate diplomacy, upon which the UN had been founded. Rather, in a geopolitical landscape that had radically changed following World War II and with a conception of Earth informed by NASA photographs, systems-based and cybernetic-based paradigms of ecology, among other factors, political battles (like military ones) had taken a different form. Writing for *Rolling Stone*, McClure offered a compelling characterization of this topology in Stockholm.

> The [Stockholm Conference] and the milieu surrounding it is like a super-complex double moebius strip crumpled up into a tight wad. (Or like an octopus turned inside out). One gets on one of the surfaces and starts moving. All of the surfaces are one surface and you keep crawling, tracking, and gliding over the byzantine labyrinth. You can move from meeting Secretary General Maurice Strong in a painted bus at the Hog Farm to an intellectual discussion of Alaskan cultural imperialism with a native whale hunter in the lobby of the shabby but cerebrally hot Hotel Regent.[132]

Singing "gyre," whales, it seems, exhibited an ironic sense of humor, speaking allegorically to the ever-shifting spiral turn or vortex of environmental concerns in which their fate was caught up. In "Stockholm Revealed," Lewallen offered a different, if not unrelated figure of interconnectedness, writing of "a Kafkaesque drama of shifting identities and obscure motives, a cross-cultural struggle for power, prestige, and attention, acted out by the leaders of the environmental movement in the Western world."[133]

Buoyed by the success of the antiwhaling resolution, the Hog Farm proposed "Resolution Number 86-A: A Ten-Year Moratorium on the Killing of Human Beings."[134] Mimicking the language of UN resolutions, their "Declaration of Life" began, "We, the people of the world who recognize no national or international boundaries, borders, access restrictions, or ownership of our Mother, the Earth."[135] It was reproduced in *Forum*, surrounded by images of demonstrators in face paint and costumes, others nude, dancing with drums and banjos, along with Wavy Gravy in his signature "jester's cap and patch-work romper suit."[136] It was presented with great theatrics to Strong, their new ally. A smiling, business-suited Strong shook his fist, surrounded by youths and accompanied by Brand in floral shirt and feathered top hat. *Forum* recorded Strong's performance: "'I hope this message will get through to the whole world' said . . . Strong to the thousands gathered at Sergels torg. . . . Clearly very moved, Strong went on: 'I love your message. I feel the sense of love in the message.'"[137] Following the presentation, the Holy Modal Rounders, a folk-psychedelic duo brought by the Life Forum, played to a joyous crowd.[138]

In "Getting Back to Earth," the article with which we began, Zwerdling celebrated the Hog Farm's agitprop theatrical performances and lifestyle demonstrations as paradigms of personal responsibility. "'I guess you could say we're a sort of show,' says Lou Todd, a member of the family. 'Only with no distinction between life and the show.'" Todd repeated the trope to *Forum*, speaking of "a show with no distinction between life and the show."[139] This "life show" demonstrated the joy born of an "environment yes, politics no" ideology; while pointing to the question at the heart of the UN conference—how to regulate "life itself"—it shifted the discourse away from interrogating institutions seeking to govern environments and populations and toward the domain of entertainment. As in Liferaft Earth, their bodies, along with the Day-Glo buses, tents, teepees, free stage and other equipment, were less tools to escape or

Figure 3.14 Maurice Strong, Stewart Brand, and Hog Farm members at "Life Fest," Stockholm, June 1972 (Bjorn Gustafsson).

cut across the vectors of emerging biopolitical techniques of power than props in this mediatic enterprise.[140] Could we say that Brand and the Life Forum occupied the mass media differently, otherwise? Perhaps: the real question is, to what ends?

Territorial Insecurity

I want to come back, in concluding, to Brand's invocation of Life-raft Earth and Earth People's Park as precedents for the Hog Farm's capacity to manage the makeshift environment and its itinerant population in Stockholm, both of which he profiled in "The Outlaw Area" issue of the *Whole Earth Catalog*. Whether taking the form of a mock-humanitarian crisis zone (Liferaft Earth and its Hunger Show) or a space to be liberated from state rule and returned to an emergent tribal "humanity" (Earth People's Park), both were conceived as forms of outlaw territory, literally as spaces transformed during a state of emergency or staged beyond the reach of the law. Beyond its resonance with the mythology and libertarian ethos of the American frontier, the term "outlaw area," as we have seen, entered the *Whole Earth* lexicon via Fuller. In Fuller's conception of Spaceship Earth, environments such as the ocean and in turn outer space would exist, at least initially, "outside the law," with military battles over the occupation or control of such territories being the source of or occasion for technological advancement. It was these "weaponry arts" that, he repeatedly declared, gave rise to the "livingry arts" that form industrial humanity's very milieu.[141] Whether derived from technologies of colonial (and neocolonial) expansion or motivated by contemporary Cold War defenses, the result was the same: a thoroughgoing incorporation of military technology into the matrix of contemporary forms of life.

Fuller was not wrong in believing that such technological advancements—including those derived from cybernetics and computerization—would come to form the organizational matrix of an increasingly dispersed global *dispositif* of power then driving the post-Fordist economy. To his way of thinking, this was to be celebrated without question as part of a long march of technological progress toward universal human emancipation, including the overcoming of geographical distance and of cultural distinctions. Beyond his blindness to the politics of alterity, Fuller failed to recognize the inertia inhering in hierarchies of power. Technological change would not lead to the smooth universal space of which Fuller dreamed but to new forms of administration. Such an idealization of a territory beyond the reach of law and the normalizing forces of government thus returns us to the question of what sort of political space was at work in Skarpnäck, what sort of rights the Hog Farm (and Brand) imagined this "outlaw" population might retain in their "living reality model" of caring for the environment. I have pointed a number of times to the widespread ethic of taking personal responsibility adopted by the counterculture, and I think we need to ask how the particularity and personal nature of such an ethos might (or might not) have a bearing on nongovernmental politics in this context. (Recall that we are not here in the domain of the feminist challenge, "The personal is political," which would explicitly make an articulation with rights issues and the public realm.)

In a widely cited text "Why Tribe?" Life Forum participant Gary Snyder connected this trope of personal responsibility to an emergent tribalism. "The tribe," he wrote, "proposes personal responsibilities rather than abstract central government, taxes and advertising-agency-plus-Mafia type international brainwashing corporations."[142] He dated the emergence of this phenomenon to "the increasing insanity of the modern nations" after World War I and articulated its adherents' modes of disidentification with the state within a genealogy of critiques of Western industrial civilization that began with interwar Marxism, passing through a fascination with Buddhism and Hinduism to end with the embrace of heretical Gnostic and esoteric movements. Together, these constituted a "Great Underground" whose spirit could be recognized in hippies populating Golden Gate Park. "In America of course," "Why Tribe?" begins, "the word has associations with the American Indians, which we like. This new subculture," he goes on to clarify, "is in fact more similar to that ancient and successful tribe, the European Gypsies—a group without nation or territory which maintains its own values, its language and religion, no matter what country it may be in."[143] Snyder did not suggest how such tribalism might interface with or otherwise produce an encounter with "abstract central governments" or with international legal codes overseeing the actions of those "international brainwashing corporations." Indeed, there is a good chance that he had little interest in so doing. His precedents for this new tribalism—Native Americans and the European

Roma—however, might offer lessons in how taking responsibility for one's actions can relate to frameworks for political participation and/or the public sphere, even if not in simple terms. The rights claims put forward under the rubric of Indian nationalism and Romani demands to be recognized by the UN as a nation without a state both explicitly involved a "detourning" of traditional modes of governance, effectively, a reversal of techniques of power.[144]

Snyder's examples might also be productively troubled by the history of violence against these and other ethnic and cultural groups, populations for whom the decoupling of territorial organizations from the nation-state, as sought by Earth People's Park, had been not voluntary, but forced. Like Native Americans, Roma have suffered centuries of discrimination. Despite their arrival in Europe during the fifteenth century, as Sean Nazerali reminds us, they are "still regarded by many as foreigners and strangers," as outcasts, and "the darkest period of Romani history was World War II," when, along with Jews, they were transported to concentration camps.[145] To understand what is at stake here, I want to turn briefly to Hannah Arendt's seminal text "The Decline of the Nation-State and the End of the Rights of Man," which addressed the plight of people forcibly "ejected from the old trinity of state-people-territory that," as she noted, "still formed the basis of European organization and political civilization."[146] It is a philosophical text that identifies the importance of the period following World War I to this disruption in relations between nations, citizens, and territory, albeit in very different terms from Snyder's.

Arendt traced the plights of minority groups, stateless persons, and refugees in Europe, those who were not easily assimilated during the construction of a unified political body or who, under fascism, were forcibly denationalized. Without the right of asylum, some had become, in her words, outlaws "by definition." There are many things one could unpack from this text with regard to what Arendt identified as a "new global political situation," but here I want to turn to her recognition of the emergence of a disturbing topology for which the text is widely cited. Deprived of the trappings of civilization, "rightless people" were "thrown back into a peculiar state of nature." Without access to a political community, they had become, in her words, "nothing but human," at once a "human being in general... *and* different in general, representing nothing but his own absolutely unique individuality." This condition of being rightless had a disturbing spatial correlate: as she explained, "the internment camp—prior to the second World War the exception rather than the rule for the stateless—has become the routine solution for the problem of domicile of the 'displaced persons.'" Given their status as "outlaw by definition," Arendt posited, "the only practical substitute for a nonexistent homeland was an internment camp. Indeed, as early as the thirties this was the only 'country' the world had to offer the stateless."[147] Ad hoc shelters such as tents, cantonments, and, in turn, their translation into permanent, if far from homely structures, we might add, became the recognizable architectural infrastructure of those "countries," homes for those without citizenship.

The Hog Farm's Tent City and the Earth People's Park of which it formed a component were conceived during a different historical moment from those camps discussed by Arendt. The "unsettlement" they registered and the transient constituency for which they offered a domicile on so-called "House Hold Earth" was not, of course, that of the forcibly displaced, but typically a group of white, educated, disenchanted people who were voluntarily seeking to withdraw from normative and environmentally damaging lifestyles and from extant economic and geopolitical organizations. They identified as citizens of a Woodstock Nation or simply of Earth, as outside of a political polity or democratic process. While the Hog Farm's outlaw area forms an almost diametrically opposed condition to the violent exclusions of which Arendt wrote, the Tent City emerged as a strange sort of semantic, spatial, even architectural residue of the territorial insecurity inscribed within the "new global political situation" of which she spoke, the contours and strange topologies of which remain, as Giorgio Agamben reminds us, in a more extended form today, whether in the reuse of public spaces for detention or in gated communities. "This principle," he proposed, "is now adrift: it has entered a process of dislocation" or of a dislocating localization of spaces of exception in which, as he put it, "we can expect not only new camps but also always new and more delirious normative definitions of the inscription of life in the city."[148] As a historical artifact, the Hog Farm's Tent City was not just a lifestyle demonstration or "show," but both a symptom of such territorial insecurity and an apparatus for controlling it.

Despite their radical appearance to some at Stockholm, the Hog Farm was *not*, to invoke Foucault's argument in "Confronting Governments: Human Rights," bringing "the testimony of people's suffering to the eyes and ears of governments"—suffering that, as Foucault announced, "grounds an absolute right to stand up and speak to those who hold power." And indeed, this was not necessarily their aim in Stockholm. Yet the images they produced of nonnormative modes of life resonated ambiguously with such suffering and with the insecurity for which it was a harbinger. They did not do so either with adequate irony or in a manner that would confront governments. "It's true that good governments appreciate the holy indignation of the governed, provided it remain lyrical," Foucault explained. "Experience shows," he continued, "that one can and must refuse the theatrical role of pure and simple indignation that is proposed to us."[149] Under Brand, the Hog Farm's depoliticized performance of countercultural protest served as a red herring, reminding us of the need to pay attention not only to the captivating images of theatrical counterconducts and counterenvironments that have long operated as efficient vehicles for garnering attention, but also to the ambiguous political ends to which they are or might be deployed.

What the Life Forum initiative rendered visible in Stockholm, whether self-consciously or not and whether cynically or simply unwittingly, was that it was indeed "life" itself that was at stake in the biopolitical paradigm of management sought by the UN. The "human" in the term "human environment," they made evident, is not *necessarily* a political subject who would question the laws or protest the actions of particular governments, but something closer to the "population" that Foucault recognized during the 1970s as long the subject of techniques of governmentality. Trained in the life sciences, Brand might have understood that "life" had become the subject of explicit calculation under a biopolitical regime, in this case, directed toward management of the environment, built or otherwise, and the populations within it. Collected in the *Whole Earth Catalog* was information for managing health, education, food, and shelter, offered not in opposition to this dominant logic, but (to reiterate) as something like its uncanny mirror image. In the context of the Stockholm conference, wherein, as we will see in the next chapter, environmental issues had taken on multiple and conflicting political casts, the portrayal of "survival" in the Hog Farm's Tent City resonated all too strongly with and hence potentially fueled prevalent neo-Malthusian anxieties of population explosion and limited resources, anxieties often directed at countries recently liberated from or still struggling to gain independence from colonial rule. That is to say, the lifestyle images presented by these self-styled "refugees" from the American way of life can be read not only as attempts to withdraw from biopolitical regulation into an outlaw area, but also as vehicles, witting or unwitting, for the desublimation of the very environmental violence that characterized the global impact and neoimperial imperative of that same logic: poverty, environmental catastrophe, displacement, genocide, and warfare. It was these forces that many of the other alternative voices in Stockholm worked actively and structurally to interrupt.

CHAPTER FOUR

Battle for the Earth

> Remember the population explosion? . . . Well, concerns about population seem to be creeping back. As the threat of climate change has evolved from a fuzzy faraway concept to one of the central existential threats to humanity, scholars like Professor [Joel E.] Cohen have noted that reducing the burning of fossil fuels might be easier if there were fewer of us consuming them.
>
> —Eduardo Porter, *New York Times*, August 6, 2014

In "The Browning of Stockholm: America Takes Its Ecology Show Abroad," Barry Weisberg turned to the overwhelming presence of Americans at the United Nations Conference on the Human Environment, something commented upon in many accounts. "There were more Californians alone at the conference than participants from all of Africa; more journalists from the U.S. than from all the underdeveloped countries combined," he remarked, adding that Americans dominated the drafting of official documents, "monopolized microphone time at the plenary sessions," and co-opted media attention.[1] With Americans occupying the best hotels, Stockholm, he lamented, seemed almost like a US colony. Through both the Environment Forum set up by the UN as a semiofficial platform to enfranchise nongovernmental voices and the alternative conferences, Americans transplanted not only wildlife conservation efforts, back-to-the-land ideologies, and freak shows but also, with equally unparalleled arrogance, the neo-Malthusian population debates (what Weisberg called "the endless ego combat between Barry Commoner and Paul Ehrlich") and resource-depletion concerns characteristic of different factions of the US "ecology crusade." Together, as he put it, this "not only created a cornucopia of

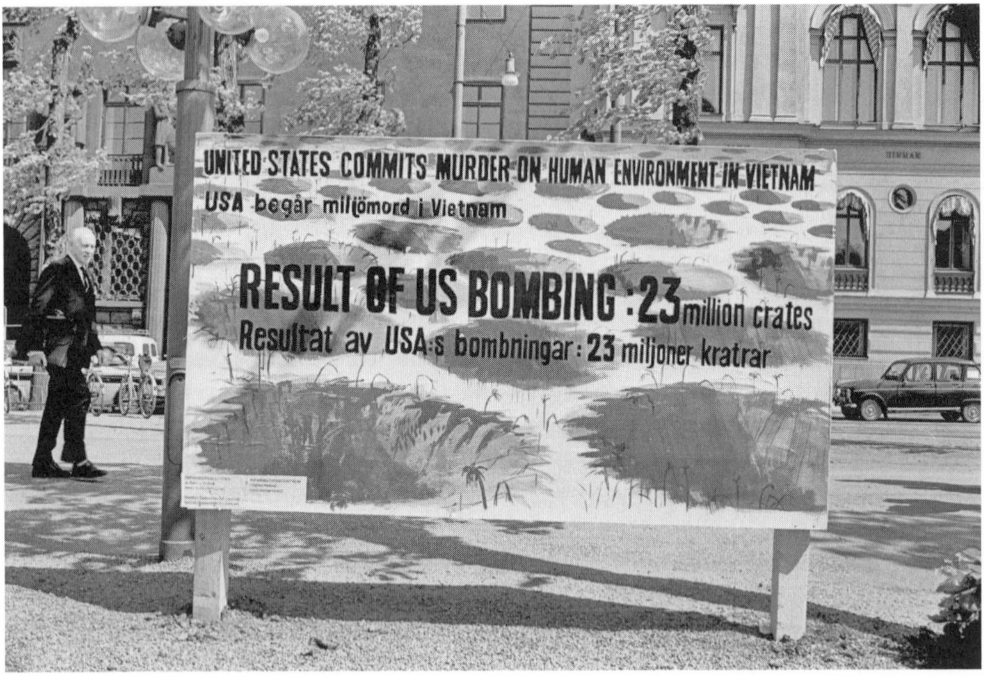

Figure 4.1 Anti-war billboard in Stockholm, June 1972 (Bjorn Gustafsson).

confusion that revealed the inadequacy of [the American] notion of an ecology crusade, but also diverted attention from what people from the rest of the world had come to discuss—the political and economic roots of the environmental disorder spreading like a plague through their countries."[2]

The Environment Forum was composed of lectures, panel debates, film programs, exhibitions, workshops, and "public hearings," and it published a daily newsletter, *Forum: Environment Is Politics*. Offering a space for questions deemed too politically sensitive to be addressed by national delegates, it was "a platform for an open and unconstrained discussion about contemporary environmental problems," according to executive secretary Elisabeth Wettergren, and was intended to "serve as a complement to the UN conference."[3] It offered NGOs the opportunity to present views to government delegates (should they choose to attend) and simultaneously to world media through the vast press gathered for the UN event.[4] Having invited submissions from NGOs, Wettergren received an enormous number of proposals on divisive issues related to "chemical and biological warfare, urbanization, population, etc."[5] Reputedly following a staff "mutiny" over the ensuing chaos, Commoner's organization, the Scientists' Institute for Public Information (SIPI)—a group committed to sponsoring public debates regarding scientific responsibility and postwar scientists' often uncritical participation in the military-industrial complex—were given a prominent role in organizing the forum.[6] In turn, Commoner invited the Oi Committee International, a group of young, predominantly Third World scientists committed to expanding the discourse on development and environment from technological approaches and "traditional concerns with the physical and natural environment" to include "socio-economic, political and cultural causes" of environmental damage and questions of Third World self-determination.[7] Reorganized thematically, the final program included events related to ecocide; limits to growth; population control; indigenous rights; anti-apartheid and national liberation struggles; industrial workplace issues; toxic metals; a replay of Whale Night; alternative technologies; and, on the final day, architect Paolo Soleri speaking on "alternative futures."

"The UN took the initiative to arrange their own *alternative* alternative shortly after they heard about our plans," Stockholm-based collaborative PowWow argued, referring to their role in establishing the People's Forum to inject radical debates into the conference. Although applauding the prospect of a diversity of viewpoints in the Environment Forum, the group read its establishment as a compensatory or palliative gesture and expressed concern that it "may confuse things and blur the distinction between the UN Conference (which includes as a side show the Environment Forum) and the criticism of it."[8] By June, the three camps that PowWow identified—the UN conference for governments, the Environment Forum for NGOs, and the People's Forum for "people"—had been joined by Stewart Brand's Life Forum, Dai Dong, and John Lewallen's Convention on Ecocidal War, further blurring those distinctions and creating complicated alliances, the contours of which I want to trace in order to render more legible the positions at play.

Weisberg was largely correct that the Stockholm conference remained dominated by Americans. Yet the picture was more complicated than a simple transference of a US-led ecology crusade, as others recognized. "The environmental crisis is a signal that we have run out of ecological credit, that it is time to pay the debt to nature or go into bankruptcy. This much is now well known," Commoner posited in *Harper's Magazine*. Shifting such pecuniary metaphors toward alternatives to the consensual politics and narratives of planetary togetherness promoted by the UN, Commoner continued,

> What is just beginning to become apparent is that the debt cannot be paid in recycled beer cans or in the penance of walking to work; it will need to be paid in the ancient coins of social justice—within nations and among them. In this sense, the environmental crisis has become the world's most dangerous political issue, as it wrenches back into open view the brutality of racial competition for survival, the incompatibility between the economic goals of entrepreneur and worker, the tragic absurdity of war.... If nations must, on ecological grounds, become more dependent on each other's indigenous goods, how can we avoid the ancient evils of international exploitation? As these issues are brought into the view of the world at Stockholm, new steps can be taken toward making the peace among men that must precede a peace with nature.[9]

Commoner was reiterating a controversial argument made during his 1970 Earth Day speech at Brown University and published in *The Closing Circle.*[10] As reported in *Time*, in Stockholm, too, he "urged a near Utopia. 'To solve the environmental crisis,' he said, 'we must solve the problems of poverty, racial injustice and war.'"[11] Commoner's reconciliation of environmental care and social justice did not come to pass: the response to "the world's most dangerous political issue" would not take the form of instituting peace as such, either among men or with nature, or of alleviating injustice, but of new forms of control ("perpetual peace") over global flows of resources now cast as an issue of national and international security. But during the course of the conference, as I want to trace in this chapter, other discourses and technologies entered that battlefield—some progressive, some not—to expand the terrain of environmental concerns beyond those of the US ecology crusade and to disrupt the narrative set out in Barbara Ward and Rene Dubos's *Only One Earth* and embodied in Secretary General Maurice Strong's desired policies, as detailed in the previous chapter. As I hope to set out here, in what is necessarily a complicated story, positions within this battlefield were at once separate and interconnected, and from them, Strong would draw lessons for a new paradigm of global management.

Ecocide

In his critique of the saturation of the United Nations Conference on the Human Environment by Americans, Weisberg quoted British architect Ian Hogan, then working with PowWow: "At every level of the Conference the American presence is felt, either overtly or covertly, and that presence is felt in every conversation." Hogan's point was not that the conference had adopted an American stand, but that facilitated by Swedish Prime Minister Olaf Palme's speech to the plenary session on opening day, a prevalent anti-Americanism dominated and steered conversations both at the Environment Forum and at the official UN conference. In Hogan's words: "Everyone here openly detests the Americans and so you get away from environmental considerations and spend your time on anti-Americanism."[12]

Directly countering Strong's attempts to replace points of conflict with an ideology of planetary togetherness, Palme turned to the question of war, treading on territory that to some was a breach of diplomacy. "It is terrifying that, to quote the draft declaration," he told assembled delegates and press, "'immense resources continue to be consumed in armaments and armed conflict, wasting and threatening still further the human environment.'" After noting recent disarmament debates in Geneva, he stated: "The immense destruction brought about by indiscriminate bombing, by large scale use of bulldozers and herbicides is an outrage sometimes described as ecocide, which requires urgent international attention. It is shocking that only preliminary discussions of this matter have been possible so far in the United Nations.... We fear that the active use of these methods is coupled by a passive resistance to discuss them."[13]

Ecological warfare, Palme insisted of the systematic effort by the United States to destroy the Vietnamese environment, must "cease immediately." Noting that "the charges of ecological warfare levied by the Prime Minister are plainly directed at the United States," the chairman of the US delegation, Russell Train, offered a quick rebuke to Palme's "gratuitous politicizing of our environmental discussions," remarks he claimed were out of place and inappropriate for a host government. Attempting to shift the focus back to a supposedly neutral domain, after protesting that "I am personally an environmentalist, not a politician," he declared: "I wish to see us work together in a spirit of positive cooperation for development and for global environmental protection. The injection of a highly charged issue by the Prime Minister can only do a disservice to this objective."[14] Yet it was clear to many that environmental issues were intimately tied to war and national security, whether in the mobilization of the threat posed by the scarcity (real or imagined) of natural resources such as oil and food that was then informing national security policy or in the US war machine's brutal strategy of environmental destruction.

It was not the first time that the Swedish Prime Minister had spoken out against US strategy in Vietnam, nor would it be the last.[15] In this instance, Palme was purportedly inspired to do so after meeting American scientists Egbert W. Pfeiffer and Arthur H. Westing, who arrived in Stockholm immediately before the UN conference to attend the International Commission of Enquiry into US Crimes in Indochina.[16] The meeting was timed to raise the visibility of the environmental dimensions of the Vietnam War at the UN conference, questions suppressed by the United States, over which the UN had little power.[17] "Indochina is today a testing ground for all the

Figure 4.2 Air Force jet spraying Agent Orange near Saigon, now Ho Chi Minh City, Vietnam, October 14, 1968 (© Bettmann/CORBIS).

Figure 4.3 Vietnamese village bursting into flame under spread of phosphorous explosives dropped during American air strike, January 1, 1966 (Larry Burrows/The LIFE Picture Collection/Getty Images).

Figure 4.4 Secretary of Defense Robert McNamara pointing to map of Vietnam at a press conference, April 26, 1965 (Marion S. Trikosko/Library of Congress Prints and Photographs Division).

terrible means of destruction at disposal by the U.S. government," Gunnar Myrdal explained as chairman of the commission. "When we protest against the destruction and the crimes, we do it for the peoples of Indochina who are the victims. But we also protest for the sake of ourselves, of our children and of future generations."[18] Myrdal was alluding to a key trope in debates on ecocide, a term launched by American botanist Arthur Galston in 1970 to connect the intentional destruction of the environment (as the milieu of life) to crimes against humanity. It was not only Vietnam that was threatened by the expanding US military-industrial arsenal against popular struggles in the Third World, they argued, hoping to garner wide support, but humanity and its earthly milieu: ecocide was at once a global environmental and a global security threat.[19] Papers by Pfeiffer and Westing, along with political scientist John H. E. Fried, biochemist J. B. Neilands, antiwar activist Fred Branfman, and the head of International Voluntary Services in Vietnam, Don Luce, further outlined the history, nature, intensity, and immense scope of the US military's multifaceted "pacification" strategy as it systematically and intentionally, if often indiscriminately, wreaked havoc on Indochinese environments and populations.

Key components of US counterinsurgency strategy detailed by the commission were the use of herbicides and defoliants to destroy plant life under the code name Operation Ranch Hand—including plants giving cover or sanctuary to insurgents, food crops, and resources such as mangroves and nipa palms used for housing;[20] the "Rome Plow" program of massed bulldozers that flattened villages, farms, and trees, including hardwood forests and rubber plants;[21] carpet bombings by B-52 bombers and F-4 Phantom jets, supported by a stratified array of specialized aircraft, deployed for antipersonnel missions and to execute widespread craterization that rendered land useless for agriculture;[22] the intentional "generation of refugees" with no option but to move to camps and urban concentrations under US control; and the automation of detection and response systems exemplified in General William Westmoreland's "electronic battlefield." Together, the strategies and technologies of this war machine—directed, at least initially, toward guerilla operations and wars of national liberation, but targeting civilian peasant populations and often undertaken in association with weak, corrupt, and dependent client regimes—effected an unprecedented modification of the environment. Human environments and urbanization emerged as systematic sites and weapons of war; distinctions between military and civilian realms dissolved.[23]

In addition to explicating US military strategy and documenting atrocities, the commission aimed to establish a UN convention banning ecocide as a war crime, a proposal first advanced in February 1970 by Galston at the Conference on War and National Responsibility in Washington, DC.[24] Precedents included the 1907 Hague Convention; the 1925 Geneva Protocol for the Prohibition of the Use in War of Asphyxiating, Poisonous or other Gases, and of Bacteriological Methods of Warfare; the UN's Nuremberg Principles, detailing war crimes and crimes against humanity as punishable under international law; the 1948 UN Convention on the Prevention and Punishment of the Crime of Genocide, defining genocide with respect to intent; and the 1949 Geneva Convention updating definitions of humanitarian protections of civilians in war zones.[25] As Fried, formerly special legal consultant at the US War Crimes Tribunals in Nuremberg, explained of the Genocide Convention, although most of the acts proscribed were already forbidden by existing international law, the creation of a specific term marked "genocide" as especially condemned by the world community, hence serving as a "weapon, an instrument of ultimate indignation" to mobilize public opinion, and ultimately, it was hoped, formally outlawing it would act as a deterrent in the future. Defining ecocide, the commission hoped, might have a similar effect.

Although the United States successfully excluded ecocide and the war in Indochina from the UN conference agenda, these issues, Weisberg reported, "without question dominated the thoughts of almost everyone attending."[26] Weisberg had recently edited *Ecocide in Indochina: The Ecology of War*, a 1970 anthology detailing how older counterinsurgency strategies gave way to techniques bent on destroying the enemy's culture, food crops, settlements, and territory. Such warfare, he noted, "knows no simple boundaries," recognizes no clear battle lines, whether those between military and civilian, friend and enemy, war and peace, or nation and beyond; hence, "national confrontations become global survival issues."[27] Without the ability to distinguish military targets from civilian ones, such deterritorialized war was waged on the entire society and the milieu sustaining human life. A product of what Westmoreland termed "military-industrial-academic-scientific cooperation," these experimental strategies, Weisberg explained, pointing to a growing paranoia driving a shift in US strategy from retaliation and deterrence to counterinsurgency, aimed to "enable America to fight 'brushfire' guerilla warfare around the globe."[28] While less visually dramatic than atomic war, and, he believed, paralleling the more widespread destruction of the Earth by the American chemical industry, such techniques were evidence of the extreme violence inherent to the rule of political management.[29] Ecocide, Weisberg confirmed, is "the very negation of life itself."[30] Indeed, the term "ecocide" rendered all too literal the ambivalence at the heart of scientific and technical knowledge, its capacity to switch between care for humans and their environments and their destruction.

Sweden was a hotbed of opposition to the US-led war in Vietnam, and during the UN conference, many alternative venues hosted ecocide-related events, creating convoluted associations rivaled only by the antiwhaling movement. United Swedish National Liberation Front groups invited Pfeiffer and Westing to present at the People's Forum on June 7, along with Stockholm-based lawyer and secretary general of the commission Hans-Göran Franck and anti-ecocide activist and author of *Ecology of Devastation: Indochina* (1971) John Lewallen.[31] On June 12, the Environment Forum hosted a panel with Pfeiffer, Westing, Lewallen, and international law professor Richard A. Falk, bringing the topic into a semiofficial domain.[32] Lewallen, formerly a refugee-relief volunteer in South Vietnam, organized the two-day Convention on Ecocidal Warfare, which took place on June 13 and 14. Pfeiffer and Westing featured prominently again, along with Luce, Branfman, and Falk. Held under the auspice of Dai Dong (a group moving fluidly between the People's Forum, the Environment Forum, and the Life Forum), the convention was funded by Stewart Brand, rendering it another player in the Kafkaesque drama surrounding the conference.[33]

If, as Lewallen noted of Brand's Life Forum, he initially "suspected . . . a sinuous plot, led by personages funded in part by what seemed to be a CIA money channel, to distort and discredit our presentation of the stark reality of the devastation of the human environment of Indochina," the situation became even more severely disorienting as the organizers themselves were accused by Swedish radicals of CIA affiliation on account of their connection to

Brand.[34] As Rowland recounted, "*Folkets Forum* organizers presented evidence which they said showed that not only Life Forum, but also S.I.P.I. (Commoner's group) had received funding from the notorious Kaplan Foundation. The organizers concluded from this that the C.I.A. had tried to manipulate the course of events at Stockholm by taking the spotlight away from those (like themselves) who had been arguing that an improved human environment demanded an end to capitalism."[35] "I think it is very possible the CIA *was* in among us," Lewallen concluded, "but it would be nearly impossible, and probably a waste of time, to sort truth from fantasy now."[36] With Brand refusing to protest US bombing of Vietnam, the picture remained murky.[37]

Urbanization

The Friends of the Earth noted that participants in Lewallen's convention "had some question about the origin of the new war machine, some believing that the US military simply backed into it and others tracing it to an early Rand Corporation study on counter-insurgency methods."[38] The idea that the United States "simply backed into it" was tied to conservative political scientist Samuel P. Huntington. Lewallen cited his comments in the journal of US international relations and foreign policy, *Foreign Affairs*, at the People's Forum. As Huntington explained:

> In an absent-minded way the United States in Viet Nam may well have stumbled upon the answer to "wars of national liberation." The effective response lies neither in the quest for conventional military victory nor in the esoteric doctrines and gimmicks of counter-insurgency warfare. It is instead forced-draft urbanization and modernization which rapidly brings the country in question out of the phase in which a rural revolutionary movement can hope to generate sufficient strength to come to power. Time in South Vietnam is increasingly on the side of the Government. But in the short run, with half of the population still in the countryside, the Viet Cong will remain a powerful force which cannot be dislodged from its constituency so long as the constituency continues to exist.[39]

Huntington's prediction of the imminent success of this US client state was misguided, but his reading of US strategy exhibited insight.

Figure 4.5 Water-filled bomb craters from B-52 strikes in rice paddies and orchards west of Saigon, now Ho Chi Minh City, Vietnam, January 1, 1966 (AP Photo/Henri Huet).

As Noam Chomsky characterized that strategy, "to crush the people's war, we must eliminate the people."[40] Alluding to the oft-cited aphorism of counterinsurgency attributed to Mao Tse-tung—"a guerilla swims among the people as a fish swims in water"—Falk returned the environment to this equation: "not only must the sea be drained to imperil the fish, but its life-supporting ecology must be destroyed as well." "Environmental devastation," Falk concluded, "is a virtually inevitable byproduct of a sustained campaign of counterinsurgency."[41] The psychophysical correlation of humans and their environment, he added, connected genocide and ecocide in US strategy.

It is not difficult to understand why the United States and the United Nations would be so invested in bracketing out references to the Vietnam War, especially given the central role of Robert S. McNamara, former US secretary of defense and then head of World Bank. McNamara's name even graced an electronic environmental barrier in Vietnam between north and south, the "McNamara Line." At a moment of rising environmental consciousness and a systems-based understanding of ecological interconnections, the fact that environmental systems and with them "human settlements" were simultaneously being targeted as sites of war was simply too cynical, rendering environmental research open to suspicion of militarism.[42] Following public outcry over the use of chemical agents in the war—2,4-D, 2,4,5-T, cacodylic acid, picloram, and mixtures such as Agent Orange, Agent Blue, and Agent White—Operation Ranch Hand, with its programs to deny both cover and food to the Viet Cong, largely came to an end by the summer of 1971. Yet the intentional destruction of the environment continued under the expanded Rome Plow program, its name derived from the manufacturer of the "Rome plow" in Rome, Georgia: "The basic tool of the landclearing [sic] operations in Vietnam," Westing explained, "is the 20-ton D-7E Caterpillar tractor fitted with a massive 11-foot wide, 2.5-ton 'Rome plow' blade equipped with a special 3-foot splitting lance or 'stinger,' and with 14 tons of added armor."[43] Other models were double this weight and size. Able to cut through forests and towns, the equipment moved in formation through the landscape to ensure even destruction, transgressing Hague regulations that explicitly forbid indiscriminate devastation in both occupied territories and nonoccupied enemy terrain. As reported in the *New*

York Times, the result of army units such as the Jungle Eaters was "to leave the soil bare, gray and lifeless."[44] Bombing continued, as well, with statistics that belie any claims of a just war: in addition to civilian lives lost, Westing estimated munitions expenditures between 1965 and 1971 to involve the explosion of 26 billion pounds, or 584 pounds of munitions per person in Indochina. The more than 23 million craters produced covered an area of 423,000 acres.[45]

Together, the chemical burning, bulldozer scarring, bombing, and craterization rendered the earth scorched, uninhabitable, and almost moonlike. Add to this the terror induced by designating "free-fire zones" subject to indiscriminate bombing or land mines,[46] and we see the contours of the US strategy recognized by Huntington, bent on destroying the very milieu of Vietnamese physical and social life and hence forcing rural-to-urban migration and "modernization."[47] While many rural peasants were forced to flee under such conditions, others were rounded up en masse by military troops and transported to refugee camps or to so-called "strategic hamlets," later termed "new life hamlets," before their houses and farms were destroyed to discourage return. To Jean-Paul Sartre, these were simply "two names for the same concentration camps."[48] In addition to those displaced into refugee camps and other US-planned settlements built in close proximity to US troops to secure a labor force, many South Vietnamese fled the violence of the countryside to the now superdense city of Saigon, rendering statistics of those forcibly displaced largely unknowable. It was, as Lewallen suggested, "war-bred urbanization."[49] "As one who witnessed the Tet-Offensive of 1968," he speculated at the Environment Forum, "I believe the main cause of this tremendous refugee movement is the certainty in people's minds that all villages, towns and cities taken by the liberation army will be destroyed by U.S. bombers."[50] Only US-controlled territory was marginally safe. Luce estimated that up to a third of the population was affected by programs designed to create refugees and force urbanization, human unsettlement thus joining environmental destruction as a systematic weapon of war.

One of the few detailed accounts of this violent process of uprooting and urbanization was that of Jonathan Mirsky in *The Nation*. Of the January 1967 destruction of the village of Ben Suc and the displacement of its residents, he reported: "Great brown bulldozer swirls replace the village."[51] Mirsky described the stark contrast between the "lunatic wasteland" of destruction wrought by the war and the human environment's prior condition, which he described as "neatly articulated rice paddies, canals, the normal colors of nature," including trees and people amid picturesquely sited "hamlets and villages, densely strung together." An equally harsh contrast was created by the resettlement camp Lai Chu, which was "supposed to be a model, a 'showcase.'" "The gridlike pattern of Lai Chu in its grassless, treeless, waterless, red-brown setting deceives the airborne observer into thinking he is looking down onto an army camp. Five hundred and eighteen families live here in cement-block, aluminum roofed, one-room 'dwellings.'"[52] The houses, Mirsky noted, were built by the refugees themselves with American-supplied materials, each family offered a plot of land by the government to encourage this self-help enterprise and expected to grow peanuts and sweet potatoes, neither part of their diet. "To the surprise of the Americans," he recounted, "only 100 of the 518 families have claimed their deeds. 'They don't seem enthusiastic about farming,'" desiring rather to return to their destroyed village and farm rice.[53] As Chomsky ironically quipped of the situation: "We, in our magnanimity, are using our modernizing instruments, bombs and artillery, to lead the suffering peasants to the promised land of resettlement and refugee areas, while the ferocious Viet Cong—mere 'village thugs,' as the MIT political scientist, Ithiel [de Sola] Pool, explains...—cruelly drive them back to their homes."[54] Resisting such alienating conditions, many refugees returned to destroyed areas, their lives rendered increasingly precarious amid treacherous free-fire zones. Other critics recognized lingering traces of the ideology of Manifest Destiny, replaying violence once directed against Native Americans on US soil: As foreign editor Robert Moskin noted in *Look*, reporting on a visit to another refugee camp in Vietnam, here, "America's historic westward-driving wave has crested."[55]

Systems Environments

At the Convention on Ecocidal War, Lewallen offered his reading of what might have allowed the US military to back into the "Devastation Model of Counterinsurgency," "depriv[ing] the 'insurgent' of the elements... which support his life." It was, as he put it, a "practical application of systems theory," adding, "the most significant

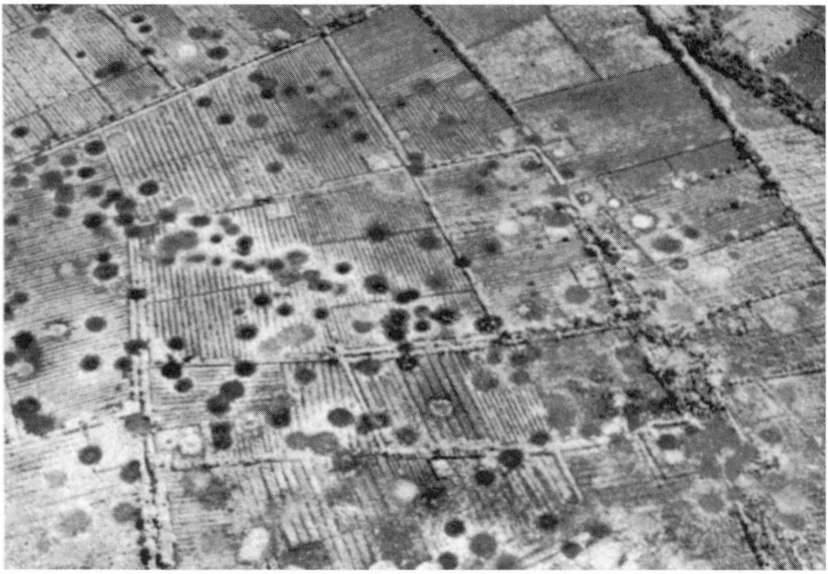

Figure 4.6 Bomb craters in Vietnamese landscape, c. 1970. From Barry Weisberg, *Ecocide in Indochina*, 1970 (Gordon Orians).

Figure 4.7 United States Army plows clearing field northwest of Cu Chi, Vietnam, May 10, 1971 (AP Photo).

application of American systems theory is the U.S. Defense Department's Indochina War program."[56] Distancing *his* conception of the network of forces at play in ecological webs and human environments from a systems-theory understanding of interdependence, he recalled that the latter "can view our planet, in the words of Jay W. Forrester, author of *World Dynamics* and leading systems-theorist, as a 'multiple-loop feedback system,' but as yet it cannot view our world as a whole." Systems theory, he posited, "has become a means of shutting our minds from reality, the more dangerous because it seems all-inclusive."[57] Lewallen spoke from experience, having worked in a think tank in Washington, DC., one of many during the 1960s deploying systems theory and social scientific knowledge in the service of a "pseudoscience of 'counterinsurgency.'"[58]

Lewallen concluded about the contemporary apotheosis of this paradigm: "The ultimate development of practical systems theory in Indochina is what General William Westmoreland has called the 'automated battlefield'—the sensors, computers, drones, laser-guided bombs, and other technological war systems which are presently operative."[59] This fluid and dispersed apparatus of sensors, armaments, and servomechanisms required new techniques of management, another area of Forrester's expertise, as we will see. Hence, Westmoreland established the position of systems manager to coordinate the army's activities in the field of developing an integrated, automatic battlefield system.[60] Justified in part by mounting domestic opposition to the war due to American casualties, the electronic battlefield offered a "substitution of American technology for American manpower."[61] This tactical shift from soldiers' bodies to electronic systems and prosthetics allowed the United States to pursue its military goals of pacification, giving rise to a further depersonalization of warfare. Target selection was now the domain of electronic and mechanical devices—acoustic and seismic sensors, starlight scopes for night vision, and urine sniffers reacting to ammonia, sensors that transmitted signals to "the electronic aircraft which relay them to computer technicians either on the ground or in the electronic ships themselves."[62] Weapons delivery systems were also increasingly automated or operated remotely, the air force then beginning to experiment with "remotely piloted vehicles," unmanned aircraft that are the precursors to today's drones.[63] As Lewallen lamented, positioning these technologies within the landscape, here was "a

Figure 4.8 Resettlement camp, Vietnam, c. 1970. From Barry Weisberg, *Ecocide in Indochina*, 1970 (Orville Schell).

countryside seeded with sensors and bomblets, swept with radar and infrared spotlights and laser beams; artillery rounds, air strikes, and naval fire crashing down on blips and rustles monitored by electronic surveillance; and field troops pushing buttons and pulling switches as they fulfill their specialized roles as automatic data processors and information storers and retrievers. The killers are physically and emotionally separated from the killed."[64]

Westmoreland had set out his vision for the electronic battlefield during an October 1969 speech in Washington, DC. Stressing its surveillance capacities and temporal modalities, he explained:

> On the battlefield of the future, enemy forces will be located, tracked, and targeted almost instantaneously through the use of data links, computer assisted intelligence evaluation, and automated fire control. With first round kill probabilities approaching certainty, and with surveillance devices that can continually track the enemy, the need for large forces to fix the opposition physically will be less important.... I see battlefields or combat areas that are under 24 hour real or near real time surveillance of all types. I see battlefields on which we can destroy anything we locate through instant communications and the almost instantaneous application of highly lethal firepower.[65]

A few months earlier, Leonard Sullivan, deputy director of research and development for South East Asian Matters, reported to Congress on this environmental research.

> These developments open up some very exciting horizons as to what we can do five or ten years from now: When one realizes that we can detect anything that perspires, moves, carries metal, makes a noise, or is hotter or colder than its surroundings, one begins to see the potential.... You begin to get a "Year 2000" vision of an electronic map with little lights that flash for different kinds of activity. This is what we require for this "porous" war, where the friendly and the enemy are all mixed together.[66]

Resonating with Buckminster Fuller's futuristic vision for the World Game (to which we turn in Chapter 5), this "electronic map with little lights that flash for different kinds of activity" was not intended to produce an equitable distribution of resources. This totally monitored environment was the endpoint of a new landscape of postindustrial technology and management systems, able to detect and monitor humans and their activities, but not to distinguish friend from enemy in its collection of data. The environment itself was again conceived as an instrument of war.

Speaking to the asymmetry inherent to such a "porous" war, Chomsky stressed the neocolonial logic of US military strategy as it served the country's economic expansion: "The techniques of which Westmoreland, Sullivan and [Douglas] Pike are so proud of are, of course, designed for use against a special kind of enemy: one who is too weak to retaliate, whose land can be occupied. These 'Year 2000' devices, which Westmoreland describes as a quantum jump in warfare, are fit only for colonial wars."[67] As Chomsky knew, US counterinsurgency doctrine derived from colonial wars in Algeria and beyond, wars won by insurgents despite their asymmetrical access to matériel. Supported by the Advanced Research Projects Agency, in 1963, the RAND Corporation published David Galula's *Pacification in Algeria, 1956–1958*, a personal account of the military and psychological components of his counterinsurgency and pacification strategy, believing it relevant to insurgencies then faced by the United States in Southeast Asia and Latin America. (They reissued the document in 2006 on the occasion of the US-led War in Iraq.)[68] Galula gained experience in counterinsurgency warfare in a number of arenas before being sent to North Africa: during China's people's revolution led by Mao Tse-tung, in French Indochina, in the Malay Peninsula (then under British possession), during the civil war in Greece, and even during the Huk Rebellion in the Philippines. In addition to being a consultant to RAND's Social Science Department, in 1962, he was appointed a research associate at Harvard University's Center for International Affairs, for which he wrote another key document informing US strategy: *Counter-Insurgency Warfare: Theory and Practice*, in 1964.[69] (Architectural research at MIT followed a similar trajectory, as detailed in Chapters 7 and 8: adopting interdisciplinary think-tank models, data collection, and servomechanisms, architects dreamed of developing electronic environmental systems able to detect the presence, movement, and identity of occupants and to deploy computers, servomechanisms, and management strategies in response—not, we can presume, in the interest of creating "automatic murder machines," but informed by MIT faculty such as Forrester and Pool and aligned with apparatuses of control and pacification.)

"Malthus in — Malthus out"

Only One Earth was not the only publication rushing to influence environmental discourse in advance of the conference. In addition, there was Forrester's *World Dynamics*, mentioned by Lewallen, and (related to it) the notorious, but popular "doomsday report," *The Limits to Growth: A Report for the Club of Rome's Project on the Predicament of Mankind*, prepared by MIT scientists for Aurelio Peccei and the Club of Rome.[70] As with *Only One Earth* and Paul Ehrlich's *The Population Bomb*, both carried neo-Malthusian messages of alarm regarding limits to resources and hence to industrial development, messages intended to rally Western audiences under the rubric of scarcity and imminent environmental catastrophe and hence the threat of global insecurity and war. "Although environmentalists from industrialized nations applauded" such doomsday reports, Norman Faramelli recalled, they "were poorly received by the Third World representatives and many leftists from industrialized nations" who recognized not only a blindness to social justice, but the goals implicit in such reports.[71] The former camp repeatedly dismissed the latter as paranoid conspiracy theorists, naïve, or irresponsible, unwilling to make sacrifices necessary to avoid disaster.

Many popular attempts to mobilize fear of an ecological emergency born of industrial waste and the so-called population explosion drew upon interdisciplinary expertise, including systems-based models of ecology and UN statistics to encourage politically unpalatable policies. *The Limits to Growth* and *World Dynamics*, however, prominently introduced computer simulation using feedback-based "world models" to produce terrifying graphs of the imminent catastrophe inherent in exponential growth. Heralded from MIT, an institution at the forefront of computing and hence of the military-industrial-academic complex, both enjoyed the authority of Big Science.[72] When diagramed in terms of exponential growth, natural resources such as oil reserves and minerals necessary to the economic growth of industrial nations suddenly looked limited or threatened, with concomitant dependency on foreign resources raising the specter of risks to state security.[73] Computer modelers and systems analysts emerged as indispensable technocrats on whom to call for strategic policy ideas and steady-state solutions, both considered necessary to avoid catastrophe or war.

In June 1970, Forrester presented his Systems Dynamics paradigm at a Bern meeting of the Club of Rome, believing it offered relevant techniques to model what the club conceived as "the predicament of mankind."[74] Founded in 1968, the Club of Rome described itself as "an informal, multinational, non-political group of scientists, economists, planners, educators and business leaders," its vocation as "the good of mankind . . . in a world which is rapidly emerging as a whole, integrated system."[75] Peccei stressed the value of systems concepts for alleviating the crisis born of new technologies and the planetary reach of their effects: humanity was courting disaster, he proposed, unless it understood the "dynamic interdependencies" of Earth's overlapping systems and brought that knowledge to the attention of the "main decision centers of the world."[76] The club's statutes underscored that decision centers were their primary audience, aiming to "influence as much as possible the conduct of world affairs in a more rational and humane direction."[77] When Peccei invited Forrester to join the club in March 1970, he detailed its symptomatic constellation of concerns: security and military build-up; atmospheric pollution; increasing cultural, economic, and technological gaps; "the frightening increase of population over a finite planet"; and, referring to protest movements, "the younger generations' widespread rebellion against the way human affairs are presently conducted."[78] Forrester responded enthusiastically, noting affinities with his recent study of cities, *Urban Dynamics* of 1969, the findings of which prompted the invitation.[79]

Forrester was a pioneering computer engineer who reputedly created the first computer graphic animation. In the late 1940s, he directed Project Whirlwind in MIT's Servomechanisms Laboratory—the first digital computer able to display text and images in real time on a video monitor. He went on to direct its successor, MIT's Digital Computer Laboratory, and for classified research, Division 6 (Digital Computer Division) of the Lincoln Laboratory in the 1950s. In 1956, he moved to MIT's Alfred P. Sloan School of Management, where, in the context of research on industry and urbanism, he synthesized recent developments at the nexus of engineering and social science—theories of information feedback and self-regulating control systems, knowledge of human decision-making processes and their relation to information in a subject's environment, experimental mathematical modeling and simulation of complex systems, and electronic digital computing—to found the cybernetic management paradigm called Systems Dynamics. With Ford Foundation support, he developed methods of corporate policy design based in feedback-loop structures, published as *Industrial Dynamics* in 1961.

After meeting former Boston mayor John F. Collins, a visiting scholar at MIT, Forrester extended this research to urban areas, using as parameters industry, housing, and people (including subsets of managerial-professional, labor, and underemployed). When these parameters were fed into his simulation of the city, its behavior yielded the following "discoveries": slum housing should be demolished to discourage the influx of the underemployed and to make way for industry, and low-cost housing programs should likewise be avoided in order to "limit the inward population flow."[80] "Very often one finds that the policies that have been adopted for correcting a difficulty are actually intensifying it rather than producing a solution," Forrester concluded in *Urban Dynamics*, insisting that the behavior of complex systems is often counter to ethical norms and social-justice concerns, but should nevertheless inform policy.[81] What he dismissed as "humanitarian impulses coupled with short-term political pressures," such as provision of job training, low-cost housing, and financial aid, simply exacerbated urban problems, he claimed. Dismissing urban studies and with it history and politics as external to the choice of parameters and systems operation, Forrester believed the computer offered more rational, less biased solutions.[82] That is, problems should be solved in the domain of management; politics was obsolete. Nowhere was the Second Great Migration—the period's enormous rural-to-urban migration of African Americans—mentioned, nor did civil rights struggles and other significant historical movements appear, yet these were implied targets of Forrester's project and motivation for its funding. Rehearsing his vision in Bern, again cast as a paragon of political and academic neutrality, Forrester used the example of Pruitt-Igoe, a massive urban housing project in St. Louis, Missouri, designed by Minoru Yamasaki and completed in 1956, to explain that according to his model, its construction exacerbated urban problems by attracting low-income people to the area.[83] Shortly after, in December 1971, its demolition—a landmark in narratives of the end of modern architecture—was agreed upon by government bodies and was put into effect immediately before the Stockholm conference.[84]

Figure 4.9 Demolition of Pruitt-Igoe public housing complex by dynamite, April 21, 1972 (© Bettman/CORBIS).

Spurred by the Club of Rome to expand his model from the urban to the global scale, Forrester reputedly sketched his World1 model on the back of an envelope during his flight back from Switzerland, much as an architect might do.[85] World1 simulated at world scale interrelationships between population, pollution, food, capital investment (industrialization), and natural resources. Soon after, Forrester hosted seminars and workshops at MIT on Systems Dynamics and computer modeling for a Club of Rome delegation. Data and data banks, he speculated while preparing, do not give rise to theories. Strategies for social design should come from management systems.[86] Activist interventions, he noted, recalling capitalism's ability to contain and learn from dissent, would remain ineffective, for complex systems are able to react, "distort," and adjust their parameters in order to defeat contestation. During the July workshop, Forrester and his former student Dennis Meadows presented key concepts—systems, models, information, data, positive and negative feedback loops, growth, equilibrium, decay, and complex social systems—with other sessions demonstrating how they played out in *Urban Dynamics* and Forrester's updated model, World2. Their colleague Gerald Barney ran specialized presentations and workshops on the "Malthus model," reminding us of the explicit connection to population control.

In expanding his methodology from corporate policy and urban systems to World2's planetary scale, Forrester quite literally scaled up and adjusted his conception of management to offer computer-based techniques for governing Earth. His thesis was rushed to publication under the title *World Dynamics* in 1971, hence preempting *The Limits to Growth*, but not enjoying its widespread popular audience or publicity campaign. The simple graph on its cover made his point clear: increase in population corresponded to decreased quality of life for current residents. Claiming commonality among the behavior of feedback-based systems ecologies on many scales, Forrester offered a template of "world behavior" that positioned social and political dimensions as points of interference, in the face of which the system merely had to adjust or compensate in order to return to equilibrium, effectively neutralizing dissent. As one contemporary critic noted, "Forrester's impatience with democracy is frequently apparent."[87] Forrester insisted, moreover, that as with precedents in "mental models," his World Models,

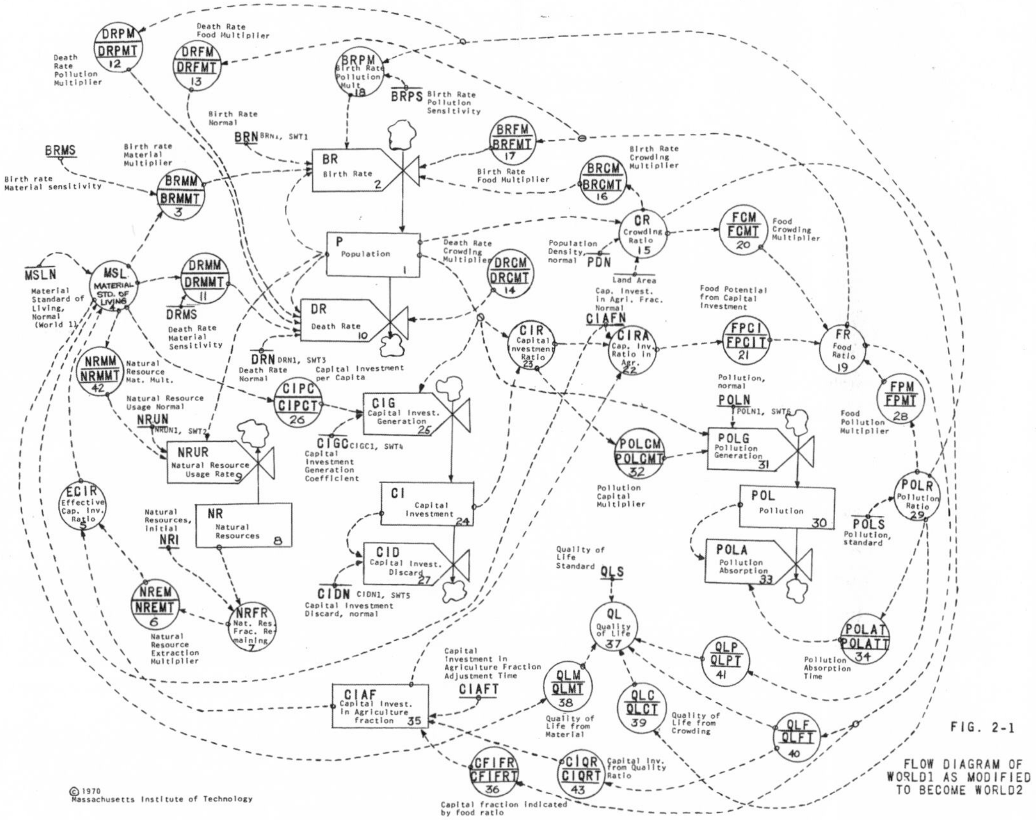

Figure 4.10 Flow diagram of World1 as modified to become World2, 1971 (courtesy of MIT Libraries, Institute Archives and Special Collections, Cambridge, Massachusetts, Jay Wright Forrester Papers; all rights reserved).

though incomplete, offered the best available platforms for directing government policy.[88]

Forrester's concluding simulations demonstrated once again the need to be "cautious about rushing into programs on the basis of short-term humanitarian impulses. The eventual result can be anti-humanitarian."[89] While the "humanitarian paradox" in which aid unintentionally prolongs suffering or exacerbates a process such as ethnocide remains an important specter haunting contemporary humanitarian interventions, here we are faced with an argument based in self-protection.[90] Choosing between "present residents and potential in-migrants," he reiterated in 1973, was essential to solving urban problems, whether nationally or globally; "the interurban control of population movement is the internal counterpart of international control of population movement."[91] Although, as he conceded, this might seem undemocratic, immoral, discriminatory, or selfish, Forrester saw no other solution, asking, "But what are the alternatives?"[92]

Convinced by Systems Dynamics and its ability to influence policy and armed with a $250,000 grant from Volkswagen, the Club of Rome commissioned a team of MIT scientists headed by Meadows to undertake a one-year research project in advance of the Stockholm conference and develop an interactive model of the world's environmental predicament.[93] Meadows, along with his wife and member of the team, Donella Meadows, were active members of Zero Population Growth (ZPG), an organization cofounded in 1968 by Ehrlich. After detailing positive and negative feedback loops within and among systems deemed relevant—population, pollution, land, and industrial, service, and agricultural capital—Meadows and the team synthesized them into an aggregate diagram of global interdependency called World3, or the World Model, a centerpiece of *The Limits to Growth*. The World Model used Forrester's notations and, although acknowledging gaps in the system, likewise deemed other forces irrelevant to the computer's calculations. The pervasive "clouds" or puffs of smoke in the model represented, as they put it, "sources or sinks that are not important to the model behavior."[94] Those clouds or sinks, I want to posit, marked social, cultural, and political forces to which the model remained blind, their evacuation from the diagram informing a particular conception of world order and the management policies that Systems Dynamics sought to institute within it.

Forrester and his Systems Dynamic group were confident of the accuracy, objectivity, and political neutrality of their data input and programming. It was not they, but the unbiased computer that forecast catastrophic breakdowns of Earth's life-support systems if current rates of population growth, resource consumption, and environmental pollution were not curtailed. The computer models convinced many. In his recollection of the Stockholm conference, *The Plot to Save the World*, Wade Rowland found Systems Dynamics to reveal logics of "such universal application to man's policies for managing his environment that it might almost be termed a law of nature."[95] However, other critics in Stockholm recognized that the simulations of exponential growth, albeit couched as possible futures, not necessary ones, were neither natural nor neutral, their underlying ambition was not only to protect planet Earth. In either case, their point was clear: to maintain quality of life in the West, drastic if unpopular measures were necessary elsewhere.

As reported in *Forum* under the title "Garbage In, Garbage Out," "The M.I.T. report ... was viciously attacked" during an Environment Forum panel, John Lambert calling it a "computer mystification," not "an objective basis for policy making." Only physical, quantifiable elements, the commentary noted, were fed in. What came out of the computer thus mirrored pernicious assumptions and instructions fed in. As another critic put it: "Malthus in—Malthus out."[96] While *Forum* reported that American economist Herman Daly called for "depletion quotas," there was no trace of what Landing Savane of Senegal, Jose de Castro of Brazil, or other Third World voices contributed to the discussion. The *Stockholm Conference Eco* offered some clues, reporting "swingeing and bitter criticism particularly from speakers from the nonindustrialized countries" regarding lack of Third World participation in decision making, noting their critiques of industrialization, colonial exploitation, the parasitism of foreign aid, and the fact that "the multinational corporation in the third world is the main enemy."[97]

In a UN plenary session the next day, Robert McNamara offered a different critique of *Limits to Growth*. Given his experience at the World Bank and the Department of Defense, McNamara recognized that the United States stood to profit from expanding its industrial paradigms. There was no evidence, he insisted, dismissing the "alarmists" and their MIT computer models, that economic growth in developing countries "will necessarily involve an unacceptable burden either on their own or anybody else's environment."[98] As reported in *Eco*, McNamara dismissed the "main prop" of conservation arguments. "'Mathematical modeling is useful. But it is only as useful as the validity of its assumptions and the comprehensiveness of its inputs.' Apparently," the *Eco* scoffed in response, adopting Forrester's terminology, "he bases his own decisions on a mental model more valid and comprehensive than the elaborate systems-dynamics model that he seems not to have studied."[99]

McNamara's point was not that social justice should inform those assumptions, although he cleverly mobilized this rhetoric. "Hundreds of millions of individual human lives—with all their inherent potential—are being threatened, narrowed, eroded, shortened and finally terminated by a pervasive poverty," he explained with typical eloquence.[100] To him, those human lives were critical calculations in the development apparatus, potential low-cost labor pools necessary for industrial expansion. Channeling the populist metaphors and doomsday alarmism of *Only One Earth*, McNamara announced, "We have come to see our planet as 'spaceship earth.' But what we must not forget is that one-quarter of the passengers on that ship have luxurious first-class accommodations and the remaining three-quarters are traveling in steerage. That does not make for a happy ship." The "penalties of prolonged injustice," he warned, were inevitable: "Restlessness will edge toward rebellion, and reason will give way to violence," proving "catastrophically costly to rich and poor alike." The poor had to be integrated into the system. To ward off allegations of inattentiveness to environmental pressures, McNamara established the Environmental Office and the post of environmental advisor at the World Bank, asserting that no conflict existed between environmental and development aims.[101] Given the bank's disastrous record of environmental management in the following decades, these moves appear either as short-term palliatives or as cynical. Well versed in the role of development aid in the expansion of multinational corporations and the vast profits they stood to gain through access to resources (including labor) and dependency, it remained in the interest of McNamara and the bank's largest shareholder, the United States, to undermine calls for limits.

Monster Cities

On June 13, Aurelio Peccei delivered the final lecture in the Distinguished Lecture Series sponsored by the International Institute for Environmental Affairs on the theme of "human settlements." Not only was his talk one of the few semiofficial appearances of the topic; it rendered explicit his neo-Malthusian agenda.[102] Troping on Systems Dynamics notions of exponential growth, Peccei opened with a nightmarish fiction: with barely disguised anti-immigration sentiment and xenophobia, he told a story of planet Earth being invaded by "cunning and adaptive" creatures that imitated the "original world inhabitants." Realizing their usefulness, Earthlings stopped fighting them and integrated them instead into the workforce. But quickly, their numbers expanded, effectively doubling Earth's population, producing "Apocalypse on a massive scale—famine, pestilence, war and death."[103] The story, he proposed, bore "a striking resemblance to the situation building up in the real world," wherein the Earth's population was expected to double within four decades. Hence, Peccei continued, he was "haunted by the vision of 6 or 7 billion people crowding our globe by the year 2000... and the very human problem of settling them... in this terrestrial abode."[104]

Like Forrester, Peccei refracted his narrative back and forth between world and urban scales. He prophesied the "formation of unprecedented, fantastic, immense conurbations," "colossal megalopolises" and "monster cities" born of "rampant" population growth and urbanization. Most problematic to him was that these future cities "would be a hundredfold more complex and impervious to management than our present-day cities, which already baffle us."[105] What was necessary to manage this complexity and its "life-and-death challenges to our future," he proposed, was a new, global optic, one that would facilitate greater insight into "Man-Society-Nature-Technology integrated systems."[106] Turning, like McNamara, to the metaphor of Spaceship Earth, with its "first-, second-, and other-class passengers," Peccei tried to shift the discourse again, playing out the "growth-and-collapse" behavior modeled by Forrester and the MIT study.[107] After paying lip service to questions of justice, he underscored the need for a powerful response given the threat of insecurity posed by the ship's deteriorating environment and increasing omens of "revolutionary reshufflings" among "rebellion-prone multitudes," as with earlier disruptions of society's vertical structuring. "The mood and mentality on Spaceship Earth may one day change," he proposed of the need for counterinsurgency strategies, "from that of [an ocean] liner to that of a *lifeboat*."[108] "A lifeboat can hold only so many people," Garret Hardin (another neo-Malthusian population alarmist) argued a few years later, deploying this pernicious metaphor to claim that America (itself born of revolutionary reshufflings) might sink should aid to the poor deplete its resources or should migration from poor countries continue.[109]

"War and civil strife" were inevitable, Peccei speculated, if "the second wave of human population which will invade the planet in the next three or four decades does not find a place to settle."[110] But finding a place in which to settle was not so easy, and he identified as enormous "the job of building the houses, schools, hospitals, churches, and churchyards, and the roads, ports, bridges and transport systems, and of erecting the factories and reclaiming the lands required by this population doubling." Architects, planners, and engineers in the audience might have had their interest piqued at this point. But Peccei was not calling for more architecture and infrastructure: such construction was presented as an improbable task, requiring a level of construction matching two "billenia" within three decades; population control, he insisted, would be more feasible and more effective.[111] Peccei concluded with a Hollywood vision: if limits were not respected, as proven by the MIT computer simulations, "I am afraid that humankind will face the danger of a Darwinian 'Battle for the Earth,' a scramble among people and nations to secure space, resources, life chances."[112] It was a sentiment echoed by the Euro-American establishment, and it was precisely what came to the fore during the eruption of the Commoner-Ehrlich debate at the Environment Forum.

Disagreements

The Commoner-Ehrlich debate revolved around the relative impact of the socially irresponsible use of polluting technologies versus overpopulation as the root cause of environmental crisis. It exploded a few months earlier in a highly public manner. Ehrlich coauthored a critique of Commoner's *The Closing Circle* for publication in *Science and Public Affairs: Bulletin of the Atomic Scientists*, which Commoner preemptively printed along with a scathing response in his own journal, *Environment*.[113] Commoner alluded to this in *Harper's* when mentioning the "white man's hangup" about being "crowded out of his secure and comfortable niche in the world."[114] In that context, he invoked not Ehrlich, but Hardin, famous for his antiwelfare diatribe of 1968, "The Tragedy of the Commons," a text often celebrated naively in sustainability debates.[115] After quoting Hardin's call for implementing "breeding control" in the interests of saving American civilization, Commoner cited another inflammatory passage: "How can we help a foreign country to escape overpopulation?" Hardin queried, mirroring Forrester's position on humanitarian aid. "Clearly, the worst thing we can do is send food. The child who is saved today becomes a breeder tomorrow. We send food out of compassion; but if we desired to increase the misery of an overpopulated nation, could we find a more effective way for doing so? Atomic bombs," he insidiously concluded, "would be kinder. For a few moments the misery would be acute, but it would come to an end for most of the people, leaving a very few survivors to suffer thereafter."[116]

Anxieties regarding population growth, as noted earlier, had been fueled by Ehrlich's *The Population Bomb*,[117] which translated in many people's minds and language into demands for population control in Third World countries. Hence the Organization for African Unity's allusion to attempts to halt "the advance of the 'colored peril.'"[118] For Commoner and the Oi Committee, such calls for coercive birth-control methods were not only misguided and morally unsupportable, but failed to recognize the origins of the population explosion in the exploitative nexus of industrialization and colonialism, or what Commoner referred to as "demographic parasitism."[119] Hence, the Oi Committee queried rhetorically, referring to the second-class status of industrializing and newly liberated countries in UN deliberations, whether the underlying ideology was simply "primogeniture in the family of man."[120]

The Oi Committee recognized that despite inclusion of Third World delegates, the conference was likely to remain dominated by Western interests, other priorities remaining either all but structurally excluded from the agenda or fundamentally framed within traditional Euro-American discourses so as to pose no challenge.[121] In response, they issued a counterdeclaration, arguing that the UN remained under the control of "expansionist industrial and military states which oppress the peoples of the exploited world." Referring to *The Limits to Growth*, they, too, refused "models of stagnation proposed by certain alarmist Western ecologists, economists, industrialists and computer fans," underscoring that the Green Revolution sponsored by the World Bank and the Ford Foundation simply served industrial powers.[122]

On June 14, the *Eco* launched an attack on "the rule of the Forum by pseudo-leftist elitists who claim to speak for the Third World," asking, "How did Barry and his band of lesser commoners come to take over the Environment Forum and turn a potential meeting place for many views into a semi-Marxist monologue?"[123] While illicit or too radical to some, the actions of Commoner and the Oi Committee gave rise to important moments of disagreement and dissensus. On June 9, Ehrlich was scheduled for a press conference and lecture at the Environment Forum under the title "Population: The Skeleton in Stockholm's Closet," to be followed by a panel discussion with Erland Hofsten of Sweden and Savane of Senegal. Sponsored by establishment NGOs—the World Wildlife Fund (WWF), the International Union for the Conservation of Nature and Natural Resources, and International Planned Parenthood Federation—it was to be chaired by Englishman Peter Scott of the WWF.[124] By the time Ehrlich arrived—reputedly dragged from the Grand Hotel by Wettergren—"a Third World revolution had just taken place."[125] Accounts of what happened differ. In the *Eco*'s account, "right in the midst of a press conference, the Oi boys (and girls) moved in a posse on to the platform and took over the meeting, adding four of their number to the three panelists who already were 2–1 against the view that population and environment should be related."[126] *Forum* noted that Dora Obi Chizea, then president of the African Environmental Association and a medical student at Temple University, Philadelphia, "physically took the chair, next to Peter Scott," while Taghi Farvar, an Iranian ecologist and student in Commoner's Center for the Biology of Natural Systems in Washington University, St. Louis, "seized the mike to announce that the panel had been changed to include more third world people."[127] According to *Time*, "A woman biologist from Nigeria, aided by four burly colleagues, startled the audience by seizing Ehrlich's microphone and declaring that birth control was merely a way for the industrial powers to remain rich by preserving the status quo. Peace was restored after Ehrlich conceded that the U.S. should curb its own consumption of natural resources before urging population controls on developing countries."[128]

Consistent across accounts of the event is that a member of the group seized the microphone and claimed a right on behalf of Third World people to challenge Ehrlich's discourse and his right to speak on their behalf. Attributing agency elsewhere, the *Eco* called it a "debunking" masterminded by Commoner, characterized as lurking in the background and "ventriloquising to his puppet army by means of scribbled instructions."[129] Francis Gendlin reiterated *Eco*'s account, referring to Commoner as "masterminding the Third World uprising against Ehrlich."[130] Launching accusations of neglecting free speech, Stone wrote, "Ehrlich was howled off the platform," and Scott "had physically to resist any attempt to depose him in favor of someone from the floor."[131] The language of takeover, uprising, deposing, and seizing control resonates with more than just acts of bullying: desublimating Western anxieties regarding liberation struggles and the threats they posed to extant hierarchies, all are associated with revolutionary struggles. No accounts recognized a legitimate claim to participate in framing the debate.

Celebrating Ehrlich's role in "awaken[ing] the world to the threat of the population bomb," the founding director of Friends of the Earth, David Brower, recalled that Ehrlich "considered his day in Stockholm the bleakest in his career."[132] Ehrlich himself expressed surprise at the "almost hysterical resistance" of less developed countries to limits-to-growth arguments.[133] The Environment Forum's potential for rational discussion among NGOs about "the fundamental problems besetting Spaceship Earth," he argued, was thwarted when his panel "was forcibly taken over by members of the 'pseudo-leftist' group," the following session also ending up "controlled by the 'Third World group.'" In addition to Farvar, Chizea, Hoften, and Savane, Ehrlich listed among the final panelists Yusaf ah Eraj (Kenya), Fred T. Sai (Ghana), and Caspar Brook, director of the British Family Planning Association who, while calling for control elsewhere "assure[d] the audience that Englishmen would not consider the population problem in making their family-size decisions."[134]

Ehrlich rightly criticized Brook for his lack of responsible leadership. Brook's position, however, manifests more than just an incident of poor judgment. Reminding us of the persistence of colonial mindsets, it spoke precisely to the need for political struggles, even platforms for what Farvar called "reeducation."[135] The *Eco* further exemplified ways in which Western claims to rationality or common sense shored up structures of privilege, scoffing that environmentalism was regarded by nonindustrialized countries as a "plot by the rich to hang on to wealth won by despoiling the environment, while depriving the poor of the fruits of development, in the name of ecological purity."[136] Such a "plot" was dismissed as an irrational or paranoid phantasm: it is unlikely that conspiratorial schemes could be simply overheard, their perpetrators identified, their plans properly exposed in any evidentiary sense. Yet we can recognize strategic moves by dominant players—subtly steering discourses, harnessing media, and instituting new paradigms of governance and policies to support them. We might simply call such moves "universalism," another front of Western imperialism advancing under the language of humanitarian good.[137] By the early 1970s, we can also identify in these strategies the forces of globalization, neocolonialism, neoliberalism, or even "Empire" and recognize, if not the authors of a plot or design as such, those who stand to profit and those who suffer their effects.[138]

Recalling the Commoner-Ehrlich debates in Stockholm, Michael Egan stresses Commoner's commitment to "public discourse and the value of disagreement." Although questioning the scientist's handling of the situation, Egan recognized that the stakes were high. Commoner, he argues, "was concerned that substantial attention to population questions would divert attention from what he considered to be the more pressing environmental issues: polluting technology and a capitalist means of production that endorsed growing world poverty and a concentration of wealth."[139] Whether orchestrated by Commoner or initiated by Chizea, Farvar, and others, what took place in the Environment Forum was not simply a silencing of Ehrlich or the foreclosure of his right to free speech. Nor can we can support a reading of such dissent as an illegitimate takeover by paranoid "Third Worlders" oblivious to population pressures. Rather, the act of intercepting the microphone, reworking the panel's constituency, and redirecting discussions regarding population control from the supposedly neutral realm of scientific facts and statistics claimed by Americans and Englishmen to the arena of socioeconomic and political factors, including race, created an interruption or opening within the Environment Forum and, we might say, fostered the emergence of a new kind of political space.

I am thinking here of Thomas Keenan's reading of how "the uninvited come to take a rightful place in politics" in "Drift: Politics and the Simulation of Real Life."[140] I don't want to collapse these examples—Keenan is writing about a remarkable speech act at the Fifth International Conference on AIDS in Montreal (1989), in which persons with AIDS, excluded from the proceedings, took the stage and successfully declared the conference open by mimicking the performative language of such declarations. Rather, I want to ask to what degree the performative utterance of declaring a right to inclusion and successfully taking control over the content of a discussion on population also forcefully altered the very context or demarcation of the political space represented by the Environment Forum. To what degree also had the Oi Committee harnessed to productive ends the ambiguities or structural paradox of rights claims—the question of who has the right to make a declaration or rights claim, to speak on behalf of others. For here, too, a group whose concerns were bracketed or were edited and contained "claimed, and enacted, the right to claim rights, the right to politics."[141] "The active end of exclusion," Keenan writes, "meant that a new public sphere opened up, accomplished a mutation in the conditions in which AIDS discourse (including science) was spoken and received."[142] And, as with the Montreal example, what happened in Stockholm was not simply a matter of "the triumph of 'free speech,' of liberal-democratic institutions, of individuals finally being able to speak in their true voices and make their own claims, an assertive subjectivity that refuses exclusion or censorship and cannot, ultimately, be contained or repressed."[143] These events suggest more than a simple form of inclusion or visibility within the mainstream, for that was achieved by Strong's insistence on a consensual Third World participation: they marked the emergence of a form of activism that disrupted the conventional mapping of a scientific and political terrain, even rewrote the terms of relations between dominant discourses and their minor (in this case Third World) counterparts. They opened a distinct space for politics. As Keenan argues, "the struggle over the limits of this space, over access to the stage of politics, is in fact the political struggle."[144]

Earthwatch

After the Stockholm conference, Senators Claiborne Pell and Clifford Case, both members of the US delegation, delivered their report to the Committee on Foreign Relations. They noted with regard to the approval of Earthwatch, a major initiative for knowledge exchange, that many developing countries expressed concern that monitoring stations would violate their territorial sovereignty and "might be utilized for subversive purposes."[145] Earthwatch was presented as a distributed system designed to detect, collect, analyze, and disseminate environmental data necessary for global management strategies. Monitoring pollutants and resources in the atmosphere, soil, and water, it was to be composed of dispersed base stations coordinated with data from ships, high-flying aircraft, and Earth-oriented satellites. The US Department of State report described the initiative as follows:

> Air and water sampling stations, vital statistics, studies of animal population and movement—all this will call for international networks, carefully coordinated to standardize data and to concentrate the search on information that is really needed. The most advanced monitoring technology will be required, including the use of earth satellites. The result, over a period of years, will be a steadily unfolding picture of our earthly environment and man's effect on it—a picture that governments can rely on as a guide to cooperative action against the ecological dangers which threaten them all.[146]

Again reminiscent of the World Game, that unfolding picture was a strategic resource. In Rowland's words, "Earthwatch would collect data on a global basis and feed it to a central location (the U.N.'s computer complex in Geneva) where it could be interpreted objectively to provide the international community with information necessary for rational policy-making."[147]

Earthwatch's surveillance capacities relied upon and reflected the advancement and expansion of communication and remote-sensing technologies driven by the US military-industrial complex and its space program, raising the question of who would be in control of data collected at those base stations and for what purpose it would be deployed, and thus the specter of possible military applications. That countries within the developing world expressed concern is not surprising, especially given that as Pell and Clifford noted, a US amendment to the action plan implied the use of environmental technologies as weapons of war: "The U.S. amendment appears to provide a loophole whereby any country could conduct covert military weather modification operations without any form of international control or responsibility."[148] The question to be asked is whose interest these technomanagerial systems served. It is not that data collection is necessarily pernicious, but we should pay attention to techniques of power at play within the apparatus in which technologies operate. Swedish ecologist Bengt Lundholm suggested as much a few months after the Stockholm conference. In an otherwise optimistic keynote address detailing the value of remote-sensing technologies to international environmental affairs, he concluded, "Unfortunately, we are in relation to remote sensing once more in a situation where the technical development is much more advanced than the political tools with which to handle this development.... If politics doesn't catch up with technology, remote sensing might be used in a way that would pose additional threats to the global environment."[149] Lundholm's point has relevance beyond remote sensing: at stake was not how to suppress or refuse technological developments or even environmental paradigms, but how to identify and put pressure on dominant techniques of power and on the economic and political ends to which they were put.

Alternative Architecture

That environmental technologies derived from and retained military or colonial applications, hence feeding development paradigms driven by corporations bent on exploitation, is not, of course, a new story. Nor is the cynical mobilization of security and emergency conditions to breach sovereignty, collapse distinctions between civilian and military, and institute alternative forms of governance—in effect, to create outlaw territories—unique to this picture. War, capitalism, imperialism, and disaster have been long affiliated; their technologies, conceptual tools, and management strategies interrelated. Less often commented upon is the relation of architecture and so-called human settlements to this emergent apparatus of global environmental management. We have seen how the built environment emerged within the interstices of debates on ecocide and limits to growth. I want to turn now to the presence of architects in the more conventional sense at the Stockholm conference, beginning with Paolo Soleri, then turning to architects affiliated with Pow-Wow, the latter demonstrating that environmental care, resource management, and even questions of social justice could take on more politically progressive valences.

The Environment Forum presented Soleri during the closing days of the conference, promoting his utopian concept of arcology, or ecological architecture. Soleri recently had enjoyed widespread public attention in the United States following the 1969 publication of his gigantic-format book, *Arcology: The City in the Image of Man*, and the 1970 Corcoran Gallery exhibition, *The Architectural Vision of Paolo Soleri*, replete with drawings up to 160 feet long. Known for his mystical, metaphysical, and abstruse thinking, the Italian-born, US-based experimental architect presented a slide show and lecture in Stockholm under the title "Alternative Futures," followed by a workshop on his gigantic visionary cities.[150] He called for complex, hyperdense, self-contained, and cybernetically managed urban agglomerations, megastructures leaving vast areas of pristine open space between them, a model that Galula might have approved as ideal for counterinsurgency needs.[151]

In 1972, Soleri had just begun construction of a prototype arcology called Arcosanti in the Arizona desert, a model utopian city built manually and, reputedly, largely by using unpaid student labor. Reviewing Soleri's book and exhibition, urban historian Dana White offered a summary, stripped of what he rightfully called Soleri's "extravagant vocabulary": "The expansion of a totally industrialized urban order across the earth's surface has reached a critical point; in its wasteful advance, it has polluted the environment and corrupted society itself; therefore, mankind must not only halt this suicidal warfare against its planet, but it must also pull back to create a new order of human living, one based upon the principles of ecology and architecture—that is, arcology."[152]

For White, arcology resonated at once with vernacular architecture depicted in Bernard Rudofsky's 1964 exhibition *Architecture without Architects* and with the *Whole Earth Catalog*, which featured both Rudofsky's and Soleri's catalogs as items for sale. Soleri's visionary cities occupied an ambivalent terrain between preindustrial and postindustrial landscapes, sponsoring both the trappings of alternative lifestyles and the technologies of environmental control. From Arcosanti I, a seven-acre megastructure housing 1500 people, to Babelnoah, an 18,000-acre megastructure comprising a metropolis for 6 million people and rising up to 400 stories high, Soleri's cities, while having a slightly archaic quality, were envisaged as futuristic high-tech creatures, giant cybernetic organisms run by automated systems and avowedly premised on the increasing miniaturization of technical systems. In this regard, they implied coordination of data and management. The architect's utopian ambition, White stressed of its largely formal conception, was not immediately concerned with "altered social organizations and institutions," but with "altered artifacts and the organization of space."[153]

In *Megastructure: Urban Futures of the Recent Past*, British critic Reyner Banham took Soleri's arcology to task on this point. Despite their alternative aesthetic packaging—a vocabulary seductive to back-to-the-land and antiurban sentiments—Banham insisted that Soleri's cities were far from alternative in conception. Indeed, they bore the hallmarks of technocracy. In its programmatic abstraction and rigidity, arcology remained to Banham a modernist archaism, reducing its occupants to statistics much as Pruitt-Igoe did and to which he likened it. Noting Soleri's support from the "academic/capitalist Establishment of professional futurologists," Banham went as far as identifying the operative abstraction of arcology with what allowed Herman Kahn to make "thermonuclear war 'thinkable.'"[154]

Soleri was an unusual architectural protagonist to promote at the first "world conference" on the human environment. Given both the appeal of arcology's aesthetics of alterity—a depoliticization functioning much like Life Forum's spectacular primitivism—and the unlikely possibility that its urban paradigms would replace extant norms in the West, we can see why it might have been palatable to the Environment Forum. Moreover, Soleri vocally mobilized the figure of a global emergency requiring dramatic response: problems related to natural resources, land conservation, commuting distance, pollution, climate control, waste, cost, obsolescence, the technical advancement of underdeveloped countries, leisure, racial and class segregation, medical care, aggression, even survival itself, he insisted, all were solved under the continuous roofs of arcologies.[155] Furthermore, Soleri, implicitly refusing the need for political interventions, speculated that the cybernetic age would allow developing countries simply to skip over the industrial era into a new age of leisure. Writing for *Harper's*, William Irwin Thompson (who later invited Soleri and Strong to his compound, Lindisfarne, in Colorado) celebrated Soleri's creative approach to capitalism, dismissing hippie communes as merely extensions of suburbia for acidheads and leftist radicals as unable to forge effective new visions. To Thompson,

Soleri's program for a new urbanism, which he believed to be rooted in ancient civilization, even provided an answer to Peccei's limits to growth.[156] Populations could both grow and be contained, pacified.

Alternative Technology

Although PowWow played a central role in founding the People's Forum, conflicts among its members left them marginalized by the time of the UN conference.[157] With the exception of event listings in *Forum*, there was little coverage of their efforts and little trace in the subsequent historical record.[158] Yet PowWow activities stand, in retrospect, not only as a rare instance of an architectural contribution in Stockholm, but as among the most precise critiques of the apparatus sought by Strong and his allies. PowWow staged three interventions: a counterinformation press center in Skeppsholmen—distributing leaflets headed "Don't Trust the UN Conference";[159] June 4 solidarity actions in Copenhagen, Sydney, London, New York, San Francisco, Tokyo, and Stockholm, which articulated a very different figure of a global, if decentralized activist network; and, what I want to focus on here, an exhibition on *mjukteknologi* (soft, or alternative technology) entitled *För en Teknik i Folkets Tjänst!*—Toward a People's Technology.

A groundbreaking exhibition on alternative technology (AT), *För en Teknik i Folkets Tjänst!* was organized by PowWow members led by Björn Eriksson in association with British specialists led by architect Peter Harper. Other participants included Varis Bokalders, Godfrey Boyle, Michael Crisp, Barbara Hammond, Ian Hogan, Per Janse, and Chris Ryan.[160] On June 12, in association with the exhibition and following a panel on nuclear energy, oil trade, and world politics entitled "Energy and Environment," the People's Forum hosted two PowWow sessions. The first critiqued the contemporary capitalist apparatus within which technology was developed and operated, offering prospects for alternative political structures. The second featured decentralized production in contemporary China and the technologies and political autonomy associated with it. Finally, PowWow ran seminars on the use of wind power and alternative modes of transportation during the final days of the UN conference. Together, these activities forged a knowing (if preliminary) dialogue with the matrix of technology, management, and policies at work in the UN conference.

Figure 4.11 Paolo Soleri, Xehaedron Housing City model, c. 1969 (Bob Peterson/ The LIFE Images Collection/Getty Images).

För en Teknik i Folkets Tjänst! was located in the Moderna Museet Filialen, a short-lived experimental annex of Moderna Museet situated in a barracks building on Skeppsholmen and curated by Pär Stolpe, himself a driving force behind the AT show. Stolpe was hired by Pontus Hultén to run the Filialen and through this alternative venue to introduce into the museum more radical social and political concerns, including protest actions, countercultural activities, free speech, and Third World movements. Among the shows he hosted, marking its leftist and anticolonial agenda, was *Mitt hem är Palestina* (My home is Palestine).[161] As Stolpe detailed in a report on the Filialen's forced closing, *För en Teknik i Folkets Tjänst!* included a range of AT displays in many formats: text and image panels, collaged murals, models, posters, installations, maps, slides, pamphlets, and books.

Entering the show, visitors were presented with an introductory text outlining the ambitions of the exhibition as it sought to transform simultaneously both the means and the relations of production, to promote technological change in alliance with creating "a social and political system that serves the people's real needs." As Pow-Wow explained, "We are interested in technological changes that could promote the following goals: workers' control, fulfillment through creative work; community cooperation; independent economic development; low specialization; low energy use; local self-sufficiency; resource conservation; environmental quality; recovery from industrial collapse; low risk of major technological disasters; activities subversive to the capitalist system."[162]

Following a wall-sized collage depicting urban alienation, visitors were presented with exhibits dedicated to the Multrum System of converting feces and kitchen waste into compost; hydroponics and low-impact food sources; hand looms and natural fibers for clothing; alternative energy (solar, tidal, methane, and wind); housing, with an emphasis on energy efficiency, traditional building materials, and materials derived from industrial waste, as well as biotechnic housing estates; and an AT research community in Wales formalized the next year as the Center for Alternative Technology. Further sections depicted a village in Skansen (Stockholm's outdoor exhibit of vernacular architecture), a model of a village in Sweden's Dalarna region demonstrating the application of technologies on display, and a large screened area presenting Chinese village technologies as an exemplary coordination of alternative technologies and societies.[163] Finally, a section was given over to a workshop, with tools and provisions and a table inviting ideas and contributions from visitors. In line with the period's participatory ethos, the show was designed for it to grow and transform in collaboration with the audience.

In addition to practical demonstrations, PowWow's ambition was to initiate a theoretical framework for the incipient field of alternative technology.[164] On June 13, *Forum* ran "Alternative Technologies," wherein Harper outlined the project of redefining the role of technology in relation to contemporary techniques of power: at stake was not simply the invention of technologies, but instituting a technological paradigm that operated outside the existing "profit system" and its forms of exploitation—of labor, of resources, of the social good.[165] Exponents of AT were not, he underscored, against technological efficiency or advancement: while some of their experiments currently looked "archaic, primitive or just laughable," the idea was "not to 'go back,'" but, he insisted, to develop technologies in the context of progressive social change, rather than in the service of capitalist exploitation. Central to this transformation, AT activists believed, were strategies of decentralization—putting technologies into the hands of the users to promote political autonomy. In a preparatory document, Eriksson and Harper listed as key the relation of AT to "workers' self management," "revolutionary practice," "Third World conditions," and overcoming "commercial resistance to alternative technologies."[166]

Turning to the state of AT research in industrial countries, Harper identified strategies within the exhibition that, while rather innocuous and naive in appearance, strategically pointed to techniques for withdrawing from the biopolitical apparatus:

> Re-design of houses using "free" local materials...; use of methane gas from human and animal wastes; use of trees to generate energy from the wind; production of high-quality food with no chemicals or machines on very little land and an aquaculture-horticulture rotation; use of soybeans and other legumes to enrich soil nitrogen and provide high-quality protein; replacement of pesticides by inter-cropping; re-opening of canals for transport; house designs for communal organization to reduce needs for energy and materials; mixed living house and green house; use of natural fibers in place of synthetic ones; ecological rather than engineering approach to medicine.

MILJÖFÖRSTÖRING

Reversing trajectories along which multinational corporations sought to organize the postwar milieu, the list can be read as a form of critique, rather than simply as a practical program. Each practice targeted powerful industrial players: construction firms, gas and private utility companies, agribusiness, the petroleum industry, automobile and transport companies, pharmaceutical corporations, and more, all of which retained vested interests in continuing and expanding current directions of modernization. (The promotion of ecological medicine, for instance, hoped to undermine the role of "synthetic chemical insecticides such as DDT," then part of the US machinery driving ecocide.)[167] At a moment when technology transfer to the Third World was promoted by the UN's Development Decade, multinational corporations, and NGOs under the rubric of "appropriate technology," PowWow's position implicitly questioned the profit-driven expansion of industries dependent upon technology transfer.[168] Just as the Marshall Plan helped to integrate Europe into a US-led economic system, the transfer of science, technology, and managerial paradigms to developing countries was a centerpiece of Ford Foundation–sponsored Cold War era US foreign policy hoping to reconstruct the Global South in alignment with American capitalism and to produce dependency. "It remains an open question," Harper thus concluded, marking PowWow's political agenda, "whether we should start work on the technical side before or after the revolution."

Reporting on the Stockholm conference, *The Christian Science Monitor* condescendingly referred to PowWow's "pictorial exhibit" in an article on the need for a "global viewpoint." Pointing to a central paradox, the article noted,

> Here are picturesque concepts for a return to a kind of non-polluting, do-it-yourself, homespun life style. To representatives of developing countries, this looks very much like the "anti-people" technology of underdevelopment they are anxious to outgrow. Ask PowWow members about this, and you get embarrassed vagueness in reply. None of them wants to suggest that developing countries remain poor. Beyond rather unspecific suggestions for a change in total, world, life-styles, they have no handy solution to this dilemma.[169]

It is not surprising that PowWow and the British AT figures did not have handy solutions to such enormous issues, and indeed, they

Figure 4.12 Miljöförstöring (Environmental Pollution) exhibit in *För en Teknik i Folkets Tjänst!*, Moderna Museet Filialen, Stockholm, June 1972 (Bjorn Gustafsson).

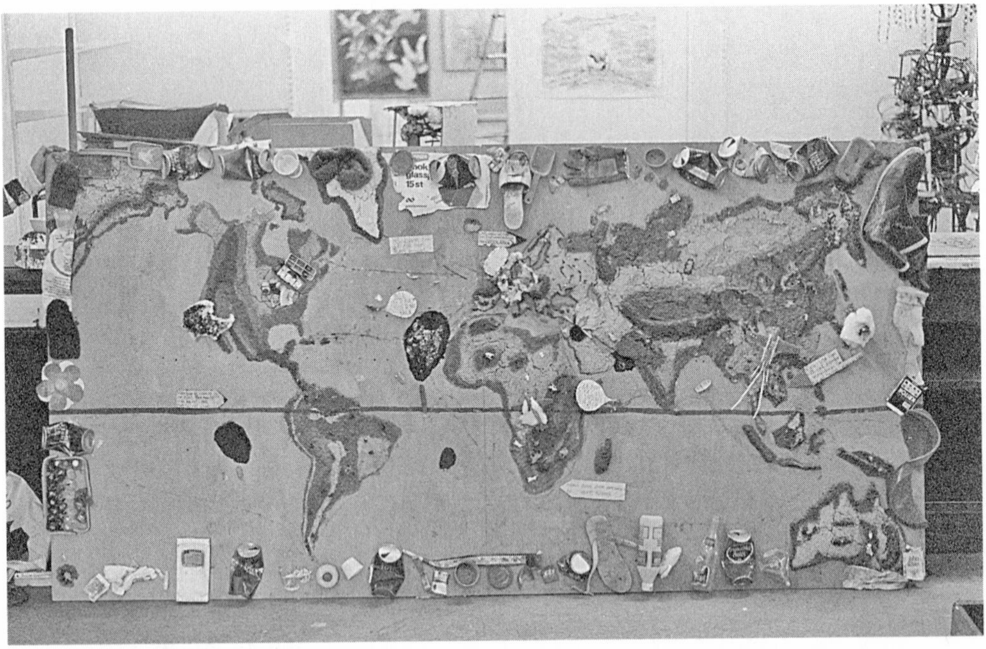

Figure 4.13 Mural in *För en Teknik i Folkets Tjänst!*, Moderna Museet Filialen, Stockholm, June 1972 (Bjorn Gustafsson).

cast *För en Teknik i Folkets Tjänst!* as a platform for provoking relevant discussion and research. Erikkson and Harper admitted that the heterogeneous and at times contradictory tendencies brought together under the rubric "alternative technologies" did not "add up to a coherent philosophy, but never mind. The intent of the exhibition is exploratory."[170]

What Harper identified as the archaic or "primitive" appearance of the provisional technologies on exhibit in the Filialen should not be conflated with the mediatic and theatrical qualities of the "primitive" lifestyle displays in the Hog Farm's Tent City in Skarpnäck. While the alternative equipment used in both resonated with underdevelopment or poverty, PowWow hoped to sponsor a trajectory of technological development that did not turn to New Age ideals of oneness or celebrate the aesthetics of alterity, but rather, to reiterate, promoted a different socioeconomic and political matrix. Staged as a series of anticapitalist interventions they did not seek alternatives to political action, but alternative tools for it. In other words, the exhibition sought a political valence that was largely eradicated in the Life Forum through Brand's spectacular, but palliative deployment of countercultural aesthetics and tactics. *För en Teknik i Folkets Tjänst!* offered an "environment yes, politics yes," message. Yet failing to harness the media, increasingly instrumental to the UN's apparatus, that message gained little immediate traction. PowWow's technologies and methods were also not seeking the "voluntary primitivism" of Open Land communes, even if their appearance seemed similar. Like Open Land communes, PowWow's ambition *was* to withdraw from the extant apparatus of capitalist development. But rather than identifying down, their "alternative" practices sought to put political pressure on those pushing exploitative technologies, including technologies targeted for developmental programs. While presented in the format of an exhibition, always and already a media format, both PowWow's content and its display harbored little of the media savvy not only of Open Land communards, but of Brand's Life Forum activities and the Hog Farm's "life show."

"Perhaps 'alternative' is not a very good generic name to use," PowWow mused in the context of the Filialen exhibition, "but it is the only one vague enough to cover the wild zoo of gadgets, materials, processes, skills, principles and philosophies that we feel to be groping in roughly the right direction."[171] AT, as the remarks implied, was not new. In 1972, however, it was largely a fringe activity, operating on the margins of the environmental movement, architecture, and engineering, and hence at home in the Filialen. They identified a diverse range of nascent "gropings": new alchemy, soft technology, countertechnology, people's technology, ecologically based technology, biotechnics, natural technology, utopian technology, independent technology, self-help technology, radical hardware, appropriate technology, intermediate technology, living technology, and community technology. Harper reiterated this diversity in *Forum*, paying attention to the political dimension and distinction of each of their claims. He also alerted the reader to their potentially ambivalent deployment, noting "such ideas can be misused."[172] Easily stripped of dimensions such as political autonomy and self-determination, AT and the striated socioeconomic structure that such low-tech images suggested proved profoundly ambiguous.

Harper and Boyle (an editor of *Undercurrents*) soon adopted the term "Radical Technology" as a substitute for AT in attempting to mark its move away from "pure gadgetry" and inscribe technological innovations within "a total movement towards a new form of society."[173] Environmental historian Francis Sandbach read this adoption as reflecting AT's antiestablishment intent, noting that its timing coincided with a moment "when the 'technological fix' aspects of the 'ecology/scientistic' approach (solar power, wind power, alternative housing, and so on) started to become part of establishment policy."[174] Although corporate interests would soon win the struggle against the rise of less profitable alternatives, especially by influencing energy policy, the popularity of E. F. Schumacher's *Small is Beautiful: Economics as if People Mattered* of 1973 and the panic set off by the OPEC oil crisis that year meant there was a brief moment in the 1970s when AT entered the mainstream. Hence the 1974 appointment of Sim Van der Ryn, president of the Farrallons Institute in Northern California, as state architect of California and Governor Jerry Brown's establishment of a short-lived Office of Appropriate Technology in 1976.[175] As an index of AT's rise, we can also cite the 1976 exhibition at Moderna Museet, *ARARAT: Alternative Research in Architecture Resources, Art and Technology*, restaged later that year as the Scandinavian contribution to the Venice Biennale. A major exhibition of AT was also developed for Habitat Forum, the venue for NGO participation at the 1976 United Nations Conference on Human Settlements.

Casting their contribution to the Stockholm conference as a "revolutionary struggle," PowWow sought a broad-based cultural revolution from below, a grassroots struggle to facilitate the decentralization of power by involving "the broad masses of the people in creating a new way of life."[176] In Stockholm, critics regarded the explicitly anticapitalist positions of both PowWow and the People's Forum as too far to the political left to have traction on governments or simply dismissed them as naïve. Referring to PowWow as "an entertaining body formed in Stockholm a year before" and as "keen on windmills," Stone recalled, "They wanted to change consumption patterns, production methods and create new ways of life. They blazed with earnestness and sincerity and made one wish that the world really were so simple."[177] The world, of course, was not so simple. But neither was PowWow so naïve about the political maneuvering and technocratic bias in Stockholm, even if their media strategy showed little such savvy. Anticipating "the tyranny of the dominant culture," their *Newsletter* read conference preparations as "a masterpiece of political opportunism" to structure debates among government delegations and ensure the "postponement of politically sensitive issues."[178] The ratification of an action plan and the establishment of Earthwatch, they speculated, "are likely to be little more than endless compromise and marketing of political and economic interests within the power structures. And it will all go on behind a veil of quasi-discussion on the environmental issues."[179] In this, they were largely accurate.

Human Settlements

Ward and Dubos dedicated a chapter of *Only One Earth* to human settlements, anticipating that the topic would remain on the conference agenda. The term derived from Constantin Doxiadis, whose paradigm of Ekistics, or the science of human settlements, was not only a central reference for them, but also an important precursor for Strong's conception of global environmental management.[180] Doxiadis hovered in the background, serving not only as an expert consultant for *Only One Earth*, but as a member of the Club of Rome. He also sponsored connections between many figures at play: in addition to Ward, Dubos, and Mead, Doxiadis counted among guests at his famous interdisciplinary powerhouse "symposions," as they cruised through the Aegean, McNamara, Fuller, Pell, Marshall McLuhan, and others.[181] Fellow Club of Rome member Senator Pell stressed the importance of foregrounding Ekistics in Stockholm during a meeting of the US Senate Committee on Foreign Relations, although this did not take place.[182] Indeed, the subject, and with it architects, took a back-row seat, ultimately relegated to another conference.

In their chapter entitled "Problems of Human Settlements," Ward and Dubos spoke to the rise of squatter settlements, situating the phenomenon within contradictions between the sovereignty desired by Third World countries and planetary "interdependence." But the symbolism of nationhood was not enough, they argued of a poor nation's ability to ensure prosperity and sovereignty within the "planetary system," for unlike already developed countries, they would never enjoy "free bonuses of land and minerals" or "the forceful growth of trade in markets kept open by colonial links and protection which first gave the present developed states their overwhelming predominance in economics and politics."[183] Rather than challenging injustices born of what they rightfully identified as an "inherited postcolonial order," Ward and Dubos proposed, instead, that developing countries operate *within* this global economic system, in effect remaining dependent upon it. Naturalizing hierarchies resulting from "physical interdependences," they argued that "this techno-economic environment is as much a fact about planetary society as the air over nations or the seas that wash their shores."[184] Squatter settlements were and remain an outgrowth of global economic interdependence, yet there is nothing natural about these violent residues of the uneven process of globalization.

In her plenary address as chairperson of the Philippine delegation, "Only One Earth: For Whom?" Senator Helena Z. Benitez reminded the UN that representatives of developing countries had "come to Stockholm in a hopeful and cooperative spirit, having been assured that there is no conflict between the needs of sound development and of good environment." The UN's stated commitment to economic development helped counter Third World countries' anxieties while reminding them of the economic benefits derived from alignments with the West. Benitez chaired the Stockholm conference's first committee, tasked with agendas related to planning and the management of human settlements for environmental quality, which received little priority.[185] In the course of her plenary speech, she, too, turned to the violent underside of development paradigms, pushing for the UN to pay more attention to the matter: "Uncontrolled population exodus from rural to urban areas, not to mention increase of population per se," she explained, "has spawned slums, squatter settlements and shanty towns in already congested cities, aggravating environmental deterioration and what has been aptly described as 'the pollution of poverty.'"[186] While this specter was largely kept in check in Stockholm, it would forcefully return four years later in Vancouver.

World Priorities, or Learning from Dissent

Capitalizing on political lessons derived from the conference, Strong published "One Year After Stockholm: An Ecological Approach to Management" in *Foreign Affairs*. After citing the rousing language of rights and responsibilities in the Declaration on the Human Environment, he turned to the power of NASA's Apollo images. It was only in 1969, he recalled, that

> the consciousness of millions around the world was heightened dramatically by the view of Planet Earth as seen from outer space—that exhilarating yet sobering sight of a small, finite Spaceship Earth with its living cargo sustained by a unitary, limited and vulnerable life-support system. For the first time we began to see that all mankind literally is in the same boat—that the world community is faced with its first truly global problem. It was the truth that ecologists and poets before them had been trying to tell us: in nature everything is tied together.[187]

Strong acknowledged that questions of pollution, wildlife, and population growth had been complicated by the poverty and underdevelopment manifest in housing, health care, food, education, and employment in developing countries. "We have the representatives of the poor of the world to thank, then," he posited, "for expanding both Stockholm's and the world's environmental awareness."[188] However, this new realization of how "everything is tied together" did not translate into environmental justice or benevolent governance. Quite the reverse.

Despite sharp political divides over the ideological underpinnings of Western calls for population control, Strong identified as the "foremost example" of "positive action" the "spreading effort to control population growth." "The continuation of [population] growth in many parts of the world at a time when the borders of virtually all nations are being closed to large-scale immigration," he suggested of its potential for conflict, is an issue that "will generate mounting pressures on international life."[189] He identified another implied threat to US power that might mobilize *Foreign Affairs* readers: uneven distribution of natural resources, including petroleum and pollution-free areas. (In a world of environmental limits, pollution-free zones in less developed countries were an economic resource, for they were attractive sites for industrial development.) The environmental issue, Strong warned, thus "points up some potentially large-scale shifts in comparative advantage which could give the developing countries significant new leverage in negotiating better arrangements with the rich countries."[190]

Strong's proposal in the wake of Stockholm was *ecological* management, a term still resonating with the common good. Ecological paradigms, he insisted, were appropriate to the "transnational" character of environmental threats and "the complexity inherent in a high-technology society."[191]

> New patterns of organization in an era of societal management must be based on a multitude of centers of information and of energy and power, linked together within a system in which they can interact with each other. Whether it be called a "systems concept" or an "ecological concept," this idea of management is not simply a new gimmick, but a necessary accommodation of our traditional linear concepts of management.[192]

Moving from feedback-based institutional networks to post-Fordist tropes, he concluded, "The outcome must lead not to bigger and bigger bureaucracies, or greater centralization, but toward broader participation in managing complexity—not to more and more rigid hierarchies but toward flexible arrangements for pursuing the cooperative way of life."[193] Central to his argument was fostering a shift from top-down, hierarchical, centralized, or bounded structures of power—whether governmental or intergovernmental agencies, academic disciplines, or other institutions—to fluid, variegated, distributed, but integrated forms of organization—not, as PowWow wished, in the interest of political autonomy, but to expand the reach of his desired management apparatus. Likening this network and its "horizontal" and "trans-sectoral" lines of communication to the environment itself in an attempt to naturalize its valence, he reiterated, "What is required now is the addition of the ecological dimension to the management of man's activities."[194]

Strong was still calling for new paradigms of sovereignty. But in addition to deriving lessons from dissenting parties, his consensus strategy now coupled concepts of the Earth's physical interdependence (and hence vulnerability) with new weapons: cybernetic and systems-theory–based management paradigms such as Systems Dynamics. Systems thinking not only came with the authority of science, its supposedly comprehensive model of interaction offered effective means of naturalizing interrelations. Questions of history, politics, and injustice could be acknowledged while remaining bracketed away from the decision-making process as not relevant to the system's operation. Prefacing *The Plot to Save the World*, Strong distanced his ideal from a conventional world government: "We are not moving towards an ephemeral supra-nationalism, but towards a wider, deeper, and more realistic conception of the responsibilities of individual nation-states towards their neighbors, and towards the preservation and enhancement of life on this planet."[195] Avoiding environmental catastrophe and calling upon nation-states to take responsibility for their actions are both important and noble goals. If, as Strong suggested, Spaceship Earth should not be forced to have a single captain—a world president to steer humanity—the mechanisms of governance he sought nevertheless would serve as dispersed forms of control in the hands of dominant players, those seeing enemies and insurgencies everywhere and with them ongoing territorial insecurity. While the Life Forum sought the eradication of sovereign boundaries under the rubric of environmental care and New Age humanitarian aid, with "good vibes" among tribes replacing legal codes and governmental politics, Strong's allies in the business and scientific world—voicing concern about insecurity born of resource scarcity, postwar geopolitical shifts, and population growth—sought a future for Western notions of progress and multinational corporations in a global, systems-based, managerial form of governance and a marketplace no longer constrained by the nation-state.

The postsovereign paradigm sought by Strong and his allies sought to expand the capillary reach of US-led capitalism, its dominant institutions now armed with data banks, scientific knowledge, UN sanctions, and a more nuanced understanding of the political risks and opportunities inhering in environmental concerns. These institutions functioned, to reiterate one last time, not in the interests of ensuring distributive justice, alleviating environmental degradation, or regulating forces affecting what we now call climate change, but to ensure major players' continuing access to resources. In the wake of independence struggles, control over resources for economic growth supplanted the colonial appropriation and governing of territory and (potentially) overt or interstate warfare as an insidious mechanism of maintaining global power. Such access was not simply a question of management, to underscore the point again, but came under the opportunistic rubric of security, hence its relevance to *Foreign Affairs*.[196] The post-9/11 US-led war in Iraq is perhaps the most palpable example of actions in the name of the environmental roots of security and hence of the potential violence inhering in an unchecked discourse of resource management.

With Strong intimately tied to the oil industry and at a moment when George H. W. Bush was head of the US Mission to the UN, PowWow's questioning of dominant energy sources and the military-industrial apparatus they served pointed to the heart of geopolitical struggles. By contrast, the Life Forum–sponsored antiwhaling initiative, to recall another node in this matrix, posed no threat to the US economy. Where the Life Forum, the Club of Rome, and even Soleri retained the upper hand over PowWow was in understanding media strategy to be a necessary part of any arsenal. Media were not only communication tools, but weapons, technologies to be tactically adapted within both mainstream and alternative networks, even employed to create networks, as Brand's *Whole Earth Catalog* demonstrated. It was a media war as much as a technological one: to succeed on this battleground, one needed to engage that register, too.

In Barry Weisberg's opinion, Third World representatives successfully demonstrated in Stockholm that the adverse ecological consequences of aid programs were "not a case of careless technology, but a technology conceived and implemented to perpetuate [economic and political] imbalance," and he celebrated their sophisticated "view of the super-powers who have always shaped their destiny." While to his mind "nobody was listening," those superpowers do seem to have been paying attention, as evident in the conference's long-range outcome.[197] Strong was appointed executive director of the newly founded United Nations Environment Programme the following year, stepping down in 1975 to head Petro-Canada; he was also a member of the Brundtland Commission and involved in its 1987 report, *Our Common Future*.[198] In turn, he served as secretary general of the UN Conference on Environment and Development, aka the Earth Summit, in Rio de Janeiro, Brazil, in 1992. If we add to this his background in the oil industry, we find a trajectory that helps us understand how failures to address environmental issues and their relation to development within the UN remained so hauntingly similar across two, even four or more decades.

The Stockholm conference established a paradigm of global, if distinctly asymmetrical environmental politics that remains, largely speaking, with us today, a biopolitical paradigm that extended certain states' interests in regulating the health and productivity of populations and in managing their natural resources and milieu into an expanded, worldwide domain. With the moral authority of ensuring the care of the planet and its biosphere—a cause one could (and should in principle) rally behind—it was not only international institutional frameworks, monitoring systems, and legal mandates for governing the environment that were established. We can also identify a logic of "environmentality" wherein environmental concerns and scientific expertise played into the service of a global form of governance—of populations, of resources, of nature, of human settlements—maintaining structural underdevelopment in the name of economic and territorial security. We can also identify a growing recognition among already powerful economic and political actors that with the rise in power of the nonaligned movement calls for justice and self-determination from the Global South posed a type of imminent threat. It was this threat that reached a critical point at the Habitat conference four years later.

Figure 5.1 View of Habitat Forum, Jericho Beach, Vancouver, June 1976 (Stephen Shames/Polaris).

CHAPTER FIVE

Third World Game

> We came here for a serious purpose related to human settlements. We do not feel it would be appropriate for this conference to be addressing a political problem.
> —Stanley Schiff, "Palestine Issue Erupts Again," 1976

> In advanced capitalist and Third World countries alike, intermediate technology and self-help philosophies are . . . put forward as a solution: build your own house, grow your own food, bicycle to work, become an artisan, and so on. To those in the Third World who have done all these things and who are still rarely far from starvation, such appeals to be more self-reliant must seem a rather curious form of radicalism!
> —Rod Burgess, 1978

British architect Ian Hogan traveled to Vancouver on the occasion of Habitat: The United Nations Conference on Human Settlements, which opened on May 31 and ran until June 11, 1976. Referring to Habitat as "the left-over tail-end of the agenda" of the UN's environmental conference in Stockholm four years earlier, he expected to find a continuation of the dialogue between the official UN event and its now customary "side-show" or "fringe event," in this case, Habitat Forum, a parallel or "autonomous" conference for NGOs and the public.[1] The fringe that brought environmental concerns to world attention in Stockholm, Hogan stated in *Architectural Design*, included People's Forum, the alternative technology exhibition at the Moderna Museet, and "three bus loads of US West Coast Clowns, Wavy Gravy and assorted refugees from the Kool Aid Acid Test."[2] Yet the environmental movement "born," or so he believed, of First World activism in Stockholm, and the ability for that fringe to address the "core," had not survived the transition to Habitat. Habitat Forum *appeared* distinctly alternative; it was housed five miles away from official downtown venues at Jericho Beach in abandoned Canadian Air Force seaplane hangars colorfully retrofitted using countercultural and indigenous motifs and recycled materials. However, Hogan recognized that despite such trappings, there was no longer an effective alternative discourse at play in the lectures, workshops, exhibitions, lifestyle demonstrations, and other "happenings."

The marginal elements were indeed contained, managed, and policed at Jericho Beach, and their encounters with governments were carefully regulated. The UN even provided a central NGO space called "The Lobby" and staffed by the Friends of the Earth. Moreover, just as Maurice Strong commissioned *Only One Earth* and was behind the Distinguished Lecture Series at Stockholm, for Habitat, he commissioned Barbara Ward to write its sequel, *The Home of Man*, and helped put together another group of "world citizens"—the Vancouver Symposium—likewise to script discourses on human settlements for delegates, NGOs, media, and the public. "The whole damn Forum was rigged, pre-empted and upstaged," Hogan declared, "by the redoubtable Lady Jackson, alias Barbara Ward."[3] Closely aligned with the UN agenda, the "unanimous statement by these luminaries," he scoffed of the Vancouver Symposium's supposedly alternative declaration, also trumped other activities at the forum.

"There's no fringe fringe, as it were," Hogan lamented. "No, No! Vancouver City Fathers... would have called the whole thing off if they had been able to, what with Arab gunmen *and* hippies coming into town."[4] Although offensive in his casting of the Palestine Liberation Organization (PLO) delegates as "Arab gunmen," Hogan's cynical quip regarding the anxiety provoked by these two "unsettled" populations was not entirely unwarranted, nor was his characterization unique. In an equally insulting manner, Habitat Forum's daily newspaper *Jericho* blithely reported: "There was trouble with the PLO and with people wanting to camp near Habitat Forum. The idea of an invasion of nomadic Arabian campers settling their camels and goats on the West Coast (in a zoned residential area) proved just too much."[5] Strange as it might seem, the pending arrival of the PLO in official capacity as a UN observer group and the possible onrush of countercultural types thus were connected in the public imagination, seen as security risks in the months leading up to Habitat, and under the rubric of security, the city went as far as to institute a ban on tents, a point to which we will return.

Beyond recognizing that Habitat Forum retained little evident tension as a venue for NGOs and other alternative voices to address the UN conference—being both highly regulated and physically remote—Hogan identified another divide or point of slippage with profound ramifications. He noted that the "*technical* fixes" on display were distinctly out of sync with the "*societal* fixes" sought by Third World delegations, then increasingly powerful at UN conferences, not least on account of the rise of the Group of 77 (G77), a heterogeneous alliance of member states from the developing world. Hogan attributed the "technical fixation" of Habitat Forum to Canada's southern neighbor: the "blithering slide-show[s] of shingle domes... bush-bearded messiah's home-made answer[s]" and "endless little stalls with cranky messages," he concluded of the US countercultural presence, had little traction with the "social" concerns dominating the UN conference.[6] NGOs were in principle supposed to speak to such concerns.

The idea for a conference focused on housing and human settlements had emerged during the final days of the Stockholm conference, and Canada had offered to host the event. However, Habitat was not simply a "left-over tail-end," even if many critics invoked such a narrative. As Hogan and others recognized, the institutional structure, discursive frameworks, media tactics, and security apparatus put to work in Vancouver, as well as the mobilization of alternative architectures, remained indebted to that earlier event, and the political struggle between First and Third World groups was closely related, as well. Yet during that four-year interval the battleground had shifted, strategies had evolved. What Hogan called a "Third World show"[7] might be more accurately described, with reference to R. Buckminster Fuller's contemporaneous marketing of the World Game, as a Third World game. In the wake of the OPEC oil embargo and the Vietnam War, and with ongoing tensions in the Middle East and the rise of the G77, strategies related to and contesting the West's ambitions to global governance had ramped up since Stockholm.[8]

Habitat continued Stockholm's dual conference model—with intergovernmental discussions directed toward gaining consensus votes for prescripted documents (a declaration of principles, proposals for national action, and recommendations for international cooperation)[9] supplemented by a colorful forum intended to mobilize media and political will. The conference attracted 131 official delegations, 160 NGOs, 6 national liberation movements, and a vast international media (sixteen hundred journalists registered).[10] Habitat also sought to garner support, particularly among industrialized countries, for new policies and forms of governance by mobilizing fear of population growth in the Third World and with it the specters of scarcity, insecurity, and war.[11] Channeling this instrumental neo-Malthusian undertone, architect and urban planner Humphrey Carver summed up the sense of urgency regarding the developing world: "Beyond the magnitude of the human disaster, there is an apprehension that in these places of physical distress and intellectual degradation there would be a build-up of explosive forces, racial and class quarrels that might trigger the use of nuclear weapons. That might be the end of human life on earth. That's what the alarm is all about."[12] Yet what took place in Vancouver did not exactly follow the organizers' game plan, much to their dismay.

With reference to the primary concerns of the conference—population and urban growth, rural-to-urban migration, and the need for "shelter"—the Vancouver Action Plan cast the strategic challenge as how to build "another world on top of this one."[13] What that new world should look like and how it would be financed, managed, and governed, however, were not so easily agreed upon, given the heterogeneous interests and political conflicts among states, and Habitat was the first of the UN's world conferences to fail to come to a consensus. To many, this outcome marked the end of the initiative begun in Stockholm, a foreclosure blamed on the shifting geopolitical balance.[14] At Habitat, the Western media spoke of "truculent" Third World "mobs" threatening humanitarian agendas and unnecessarily politicizing discussions. Former Canadian prime minister John Diefenbaker saw the advent of Third World participation in the UN as nothing less than a form of emasculation: "What is happening is that as these small nations—gentlemen, they are ganging up together into blocs and cabals. They have emasculated the United Nations to such an extent that it no longer can carry out the principles of the charter. I'm not saying the United Nations has not done much for peace—it has. But that was before the multiplication of membership."[15] Causing panic in elderly establishment figures and among previously powerful blocs within the UN, Third World interventions once again took the form of creative and strategic resistance to extant hierarchies of power in a manner that warrants attention.[16]

The Playing Field

The G77 was formed in 1964 from nonaligned countries hoping to defend their interests in an institutional landscape driven by Cold War divides. By 1976, it had grown to 113 countries and represented a powerful voting bloc in the UN, much to the distress of the United States and other Western countries. In 1974, the G77 pushed through a vote to suspend South Africa from the General Assembly on account of apartheid, proposing similar action against Israel on account of the unjust and violent treatment of Palestinians. That same year, with support from the G77, UN General Assembly Resolution 3237 granted the PLO observer status, rendering them a nonvoting member. In response, the US secretary of state, Henry Kissinger, warned the new majority that US support for the UN was eroding on account of their actions as a bloc and that hence the very survival of the UN system was at stake. The future of the UN was "clouded," he posited, unless cooperation ensued. "The most solid bloc in the world today," he remarked, "is paradoxically the alignment of the nonaligned. This divides the world into categories of North and South, developing and developed, imperial and colonial, at the very moment in history when such categories have become irrelevant and misleading."[17] Acknowledging that US economic aid was driven not only by generosity, but because "our self-interest is bound up with the fate of all mankind," Kissinger stressed that within this condition of global interdependence, "our first responsibility abroad is to the great industrial democracies with whom we share our history, our prosperity, and our political ideals."[18]

Categories such as North and South, developing and developed, were indeed potentially misleading, given the complex topology of an emergent world order as it developed within and across states, but they were far from irrelevant in the globalizing context of the 1970s. This was painfully evident to the less developed South, particularly to countries struggling against colonial rule or its ongoing legacy. As Mwalimu Julius K. Nyerere, first president of Tanzania, put it, "Each of our economies has developed as a by-product and a subsidiary of development in the industrialized North.... We are not the prime movers of our destiny...economically we are dependencies—semi-colonies at best—not sovereign states."[19]

Michel Foucault offers some clues for understanding how the "ensemble of relations" at Habitat so quickly shifted.[20] He reminds us that societies would not exist without power relations and that within those relations, "there is necessarily the possibility of resistance because if there were no possibility of resistance (of violent resistance, flight, deception, strategies capable of reversing the situation), there would be no power relations at all."[21] Mediating between "strategic games between liberties" and "states of domination that people ordinarily call 'power,'" he posited, "you have technologies of government.... The analysis of these techniques is necessary because it is very often through such techniques that states of domination are established and maintained."[22] At stake was distinguishing the mutability of strategic positions from states of domination wherein "power relations are fixed in such a way that they are perpetually asymmetrical."[23] In principle, liberal forms of governance help to minimize the latter by opening fixed hierarchies up to creative struggle, facilitating a degree of freedom for ethical decisions, rendering power relations reversible. Foucault's point was to establish an ethos that "will allow us to play these games of power with as little domination as possible."[24]

At Habitat, the stakes were thus high not only for architects, in the conventional sense of the term, who hoped to help build that new world on top of the old one, but for competing factions who stood to profit or lose from how it was to be organized and regulated under the joint rubrics of humanitarian aid, scarcity, and security. Hailed as the most comprehensive of the UN's world's conferences—with the repeated claim that nothing less than life itself was at stake—Habitat offers a forceful reminder of the complex web of forces and governing techniques within which something as apparently harmless as a dwelling is embedded. In this volatile historical context, we can begin to read three key elements I have mentioned—the return appearance of British economist and celebrity spokesperson for Habitat, Barbara Ward; the countercultural trappings of Habitat Forum; and what Hogan characterized as the dissociation of social fixes desired by Third World delegates from technical ones promoted by figures such as Fuller, an attempted supplanting of politics by technology long championed by Fuller as a "revolution by design." All appear as strategic components of the UN's development apparatus as it sought to integrate Third World populations into the global economy. There was a reason, to cite *Washington Post* critic Wolf von Eckardt of the NGO forum, that "this time the folks out in the cold and drafty airplane hangars . . . had their issues, banners and sails all raised for them when they arrived."[25] Vancouver architect Donald Gutstein objected to the "greater penetration by the federal government of the NGO conference at Jericho, both in the physical preparations for the site and the programming content," as did local journalist Allen Garr, who saw the forum as "effectively subverted so that now it is little more than a front for government money and policy."[26]

In addition to these three trajectories, I want to trace the impact of the PLO's presence at Habitat: beyond facilitating the unlikely proximity of a national liberation organization and hippies, the entry of the Palestinian question onto this stage implicitly and explicitly disrupted the dominant development narrative, technocratic agenda, and rhetoric of human settlement at Habitat,[27] for the plight of Palestinians was anomalous to the ambition of integrating uprooted populations into the development apparatus in the service of global capitalism. Moreover, the policies driving their rural-to-urban migration—forceful eviction, colonial occupation, land seizure, and the attempted erasure of forms of life through the destruction of houses, villages, and farms—were more evidently violent and unjust and more evidently in violation of human rights than slower forms of dispossession at work in globalization. Although the Palestinian question was not officially on Habitat's agenda, it became a flash point in the larger North–South conflict playing out as countries in the developing world increasingly questioned the UN's domination by industrialized states and its repeated failure to act more forcefully on behalf of Palestinians. As the head of the PLO delegation to Habitat and a founding member of the PLO, Shafiq Al-Hout remarked of this new internationalism, "Palestinians have become a symbol for all oppressed masses in the Arab world, Latin America and the Far East."[28]

Inverting the presupposition that Jericho Beach would be the venue introducing radical voices and new questions into intergovernmental debates on human settlements, the interventions by and on behalf of the Palestinians' struggles brought political questions to the fore, interrupting the carefully scripted narratives of humanitarianism and goodwill. Mobilizing rights claims and institutional mechanisms such as resolutions and amendments, pro-Palestinian activism challenged the UN's claim that housing was a technical matter, for they sought actively to reverse injustices and extant hierarchies of power. Far from dreaming of a revolution by design, this nation in exile, as announced at Habitat, had "embarked on 'a revolution until victory' to create an independent secular state of Palestine."[29] We thus find a fascinating chiasmatic logic at work: while alternative and experimental strategies staged at Habitat Forum increasingly came to operate as technocratic agents in the service of the UN's development apparatus and hence in the service of US-driven global capital, UN debates regarding human settlements—wherein, as one critic anticipated, "diplomats will sit down with their multilingual earphones and argue over commas and tinker with the numbered paragraphs of the Documents"[30]—became increasingly radicalized and overtly politicized, despite efforts to the contrary.

Unsettlement

Anxieties about the PLO arriving in Vancouver, including claims that the city risked becoming an "armed camp," played out in the run-up to the conference. Angry pro-Zionist groups asserted pressure on various fronts. Threats ranged from disrupting the conference via anti-PLO rallies, marches, "teach-ins," and the staging of a "counter convention" and even an exhibition, to attempts to prohibit PLO presence as illegal.[31] The Canada-Israel Committee, for instance, planned "special exhibits designed to contrast the history of the PLO with Israeli achievements in the field of human settlements," as though the conflict was a competition to demonstrate higher levels of development. "The intention will be to place the history of what [our] people have done with basically a desert region compared to what their neighbors have done or have not done with theirs," a spokesperson explained.[32] The ensuing exhibition, *Israel: The Timeless Settlement*, was staged opposite the Queen Elizabeth Theater, the venue for UN plenary sessions. Its titular claim to situating Israel (a country then not thirty years old) outside of history forcefully reminds us that human settlements are not merely technical matters, but political ones, a point nowhere better demonstrated than in the centrality of territory, populations, and settlements to the Israel–Palestine conflict.[33] On June 2, after viewing *Israel: The Timeless Settlement*, Josef Burg, head of Israel's delegation to Habitat and its minister of the interior, described the PLO to reporters as "terrorists who kill people without discrimination,"[34] although the organization had avoided and condemned terror since the early 1970s. Under the inflammatory title "Habitat Will Let Murderers In," the *Vancouver Sun* reported that pro-Israel groups claimed that "under existing Canadian law the PLO is an outlawed organization and as such its members are inadmissible into Canada."[35] In late November 1975, the city council's Habitat Committee voted nine to one to petition the federal government to cancel the conference, arguing that it threatened to turn Vancouver into a "police state."[36] According to Gutstein, the plot to cancel the event was engineered by Mayor Phillips, whose development plans were stymied when a demonstration program was dropped from the Habitat agenda. Playing up "fears that Habitat could spark outbreaks of violence," he not only fooled the Habitat Committee into believing that a crisis was in the making, but successfully gained national press and extra police funding.[37]

Beyond attempts to position the PLO as outlaws or otherwise undermine their legitimacy, further arguments insisted that the Palestinians' plight was outside the framework of the conference, the *Chicago Tribune* reporting that "Israel and the US have asserted that the Palestinian question is a political matter and as such extraneous to the subject of human settlements."[38] UN Secretary-General Kurt Waldheim, the *Province* recounted, "issued a pointed reminder: 'The Palestinian question ... is not on the agenda of this conference.'"[39] In "Habitat's Palestinian Gambit," the reporter emoted, "the humane objectives of the Habitat conference could be subverted by those determined to use it as a forum for settling political scores,"[40] adding "all the best efforts of the sincere delegates to reach some common talking ground on the other great issues will have become shrouded in the Palestinian cloud."[41] As with the prohibition on questions of ecocide, colonialism, and neocolonialism in Stockholm, human settlement problems, it was repeatedly claimed, were technical, not political in nature, and the conference was an occasion for the exchange of information.

Figure 5.2 Demonstration against PLO presence at Habitat: The United Nations Conference on Human Settlements, Vancouver, June 9, 1976.

"What are we doing here at the UN Habitat conference?" Al-Hout queried rhetorically in response to ongoing accusations. "We, the Palestinians, are the last people to whom this question should be asked. We who represent those who have been inhumanly unsettled and uprooted from their country. We are here to contribute for a human settlement."[42] After all, as he put it, delegates were discussing "settlement," and there were around a million Palestinians "chased out from their own homeland, out of their own houses, from their own farms and it is because of that they have problems that are classified under the Habitat topics."[43] The *Toronto Star* added another potential relevance, noting widespread fear that "the human settlement theme of the conference provides Arab countries with a heaven-sent opportunity to bring up the topic of the Palestinian refugee camps."[44] Camps indeed marked the limits of "human settlement."

And apart from rhetorical attempts to stigmatize the PLO as outlaws and to marginalize their presence at the conference, there were many ways in which the PLO indeed could be said to exist outside the law, including the statelessness of many of its members (whether residing in camps or not) and their profound lack of effective recourse to legal protection, both civil and international. They lived in an ongoing state of emergency. As Edward Said noted of a prevalent perception in the West: "to be a Palestinian is in political terms to be an outlaw of sorts."[45] While what Said called "a vicious semiotic warfare conducted against the PLO as representative of the Palestinians" continued at Habitat, other frames of reference started to emerge, and cracks in Israel's near monopoly on Western perception and media rhetoric pertaining to the conflict surfaced.[46] The *Toronto Globe and Mail* reported, for instance: "There is anger when a frustrated Palestinian commits an act of terrorism, but nothing is said in Canada when Israeli Phantoms and Skyhawks attack Palestinian refugee camps."[47] Al-Hout underscored this asymmetry and the slippage between insurrection and acts of citizenship in "PLO Pledges Habitat Visit" by asking "whether Canadians would be called terrorists if they fought people who occupied their land."[48] *Jericho* even cited some numbers, noting: "The PLO representative claimed that in the last 28 years, 385 Palestinian villages have been destroyed and, in the last nine years alone, 18,000 homes."[49]

Soon after the city's Habitat Committee petitioned to cancel the conference, members went into overdrive regarding the supposed

Figure 5.3 Deserted Palestinian village in the Negev being patrolled by an Israeli Palmah unit, January 1, 1948 (UN Photo/LM).

Figure 5.4 United Nations Relief for Palestine Refugees, Khan Yunus Camp, south of Gaza, December 1, 1948 (UN Photo/R).

Figure 5.5 Prefabricated huts for Palestinian refugees, East Jordan, c.1972 (UN Photo/DB).

threat of a "tent city" at Jericho Beach, the second of the "two most hilarious acts in the city's farce," in Gutstein's estimation, and the source of the aforementioned connection made between the PLO and hippies. (Nowhere was it mentioned that the Palestinian city of Jericho—said to be the oldest urban settlement in the world—had been under Israeli occupation since 1967.) On January 9, a chief constable from the Vancouver Police Department's Bureau of Field Operations sent a letter to the City's Social Planning Department that was leaked to the *Vancouver Sun*.

> It must be firm in everyone's mind that the Vancouver police force is opposed to any form of "tent city" or "shanty town."... The problem in the past with this sort of living arrangement is quite clear. The habitation of Jericho in the past was a sordid site that invited almost every kind of vice and militant dissident. This led to a major confrontation with the Canadian Army, the R.C.M. [Royal Canadian Mounted] Police and the Vancouver police when transients who desired to remain as permanent residents, at the expense of the taxpayer, had to be evicted from the premises.[50]

Hugh Keenleyside, then associate commissioner-general of the Canadian Habitat Secretariat, estimated that Habitat Forum numbers would reach three times that of Stockholm, while "Ald.[erman] Mike Harcourt said he had heard that a San Francisco radio station has been unofficially promoting the conference for the last two months. 'We could end up with a Woodstock-flavored gathering,' he said."[51] Here we find ourselves back at the nexus of tent cities, hippies, and security threats launched by Stewart Brand in Stockholm. The Association in Canada Serving Organizations for Human Settlements (ACSOH), which was responsible for preparing and managing the site, responded to the "controversy swirling around allegations of possible violence, tent cities and 15,000 transients turning Jericho upside down," explaining that far from "vice and militant dissidents," those signed up to date were largely North American and European professionals and concerned citizens, including neighborhood associations, businessmen, academics, and the Women's World Conference.[52]

However, the rumors succeeded in extracting funding for security and in justifying tightened control over Habitat Forum events and displays. Ensuring that its agendas aligned closely with the UN mandate, Habitat Forum content was managed by the UN-appointed NGO Committee for Habitat under J. G. van Putten, the organizers working to ensure the message remained largely on script.[53] The organizers favored business, professional, and well-known humanitarian and environmental groups over citizen user groups or those with activist or political tendencies; issues considered political, rather than technical, were repeatedly excluded or, when they did appear, mobilized for good press. Among the NGOs admitted were the Union Internationale des Architects (UIA), the World Society of Ekistics, the Friends of the Earth, Greenpeace, the International Council of Societies of Industrial Design, the International Organization for Standardization, and the International Savings Banks Institute, along with the National Indian Brotherhood, Fourth World, the Ecology Action Institute, Chile Solidarity, Arcosanti, and the L-5 Society, a group dedicated to founding space colonies with which Brand was affiliated at that moment.[54] (Proposals by the Ant Farm collective, Martin Pawley, an International Women's Pavilion, and many others were rejected.)

Planetary Housekeeping

We will return to Habitat Forum and to the Israel/Palestine conflict as it played out at Habitat. But first I want to return to Barbara Ward's activities as they pertain to establishing the narrative for human settlements issues and to Fuller's contributions that effectively desublimated the underlying motivation of those issues.

In "'Lady Habitat' and the Unsettling Opposition," von Eckardt pointed with praise to Ward's position as a strategic fulcrum between the official UN conference and Habitat Forum. "She appears in both productions and also writes most of the script," he noted, identifying Maurice Strong, at this time chairman of the board of Petro-Canada, as her "fiendishly clever" "producer."[55] "Strong's plot calls for taking excessively rebellious winds out of the sails hoisted at Jericho while blowing fresh ideas into the hot-air proceedings downtown," he continued. Ward's "role as 'Lady Habitat,' a sequel to her role as 'Lady Spaceship Earth' at Stockholm," thus gave her "a worldwide audience" for "consciousness raising."[56] Like Hogan, von Eckardt identified both *The Home of Man* and the Vancouver Symposium as strategic elements in this plot, both repeat performances by "the Strong-Ward group." The book was dedicated to Constantin Doxiadis, founder of Ekistics, the science of human settlements, after which the conference was named. Among the symposium's "world citizens" were once again alumni of his famed cruises through the Aegean, notably Fuller and Margaret Mead.[57]

The Home of Man in part succeeded in establishing the ideological agenda for Habitat; Ward's formulations of a rising crisis and impending violence in the Third World surfaced over and over in discussions and press, as did her teleological narrative of rural-to-urban migration, substandard housing, sickness, disparity of wealth, food scarcity, child labor, and environmental degradation having shifted from Europe to the newly industrializing Global South. "Two-thirds of the world, in the slum-ridden cities of the developing countries," the *Guardian* reported, "is experiencing the crisis of early nineteenth-century industrialism and late twentieth-century high technology simultaneously. Which is why, at the Habitat conference, the rich and the poor, the developed, and the less developed, will find themselves sharing the same history."[58] Rich and poor nations were already often historically interconnected on account of colonial rule, but their relation to forces of industrialization was markedly distinct. The first-in-Europe-then-elsewhere evolutionary narrative implied that poor nations might catch up if they bought into the system. But catching up was not exactly the agenda.

Ward's involvement in Habitat dated at least to May 1973 when Strong (then at the United Nations Environmental Programme) appointed her to lead a seminar of experts to set the agenda. This included architects and planners—Kenzo Tange, Peter Oberlander, Michel Colot, Ernest Weissmann, and Adolf Ciborewski, the latter a representative of the UN's Center for Housing, Building and Planning—along with representatives of UN regional economic commissions and UNEP itself. Ward published her "personal account" of these discussions as *Human Settlements: Crisis and Opportunity*.[59] Its message: disaster was imminent amid the rapidly expanding urban populations in the Global South unless systems were put in place for "migrants to improve their own homes." Ward repeatedly connected the biopolitical function of a house to questions of security: after insisting that the house is "the starting point of all life in human settlements, in short, of human life itself," she declared: "Violence, apathy, aimless destruction, a busy police force and overcrowded penal institutions are all costs which need not be paid if citizens and their families feel, in the profoundest sense, that they are 'at home.'"[60] But, she argued, marking a departure from modern architectural ideals, the "uncritical cult of high technology and modernity" had to be rejected as out of place in such desperate contexts. That aspect of the narrative could not be afforded.[61]

Ekistics published an excerpt from *Human Settlements* in October 1974 that ambiguously pointed to issues of dispossession. "The very word 'settlement' is in some measure a contradiction," Ward wrote. "In many ways, modern man is dealing with continuous 'unsettlement.'"[62]

> Once the migrant arrives, any easy hope of betterment is brutally dispelled—by the absence of steady employment, the lack of shelter, the generally unsanitary nature of the squatter settlements.... The physical misery of these *favelas* or *calampas* or *bustees* or *bidonvilles* are a spreading blight on every continent. Yet it is false to see them only as disaster areas. There is enough experience now of the energy and the capacity of the squatters or, as some would call them, "urban pioneers" to suggest that the improvement and integration of squatter communities is possible even with virtually nothing more than the efforts of the people themselves.[63]

Tapping into the energy of the unsettled urban poor to provide their own housing, she concluded, was simply "a question, in fact, of treating citizens as assets." Dismissing previous attempts to deal with squatters, she added: "Bulldozing out the shacks does not send the squatters away. It simply destroys their faith in self-help."[64] What she called, with typical hubris, "the lemming-like surges of peasant to city which threatens to overwhelm even the bravest urban plans" thus had to be captured and regulated, fed into the system of global capital.[65] The house was to be quite literally a tool for what Foucault called the "calculated management of life," the place wherein domestic economics and political governance converge, the most intimate site for control over families, and hence, in Ward's analysis, over life itself.[66]

As will be discussed in the next chapter, which focuses on architects' involvement with this phenomenon, within the period's developmentalist matrix, self-help was not just about constructing a low-cost house; rather, it validated a precarious form of life and located those unsettled citizens and displaced persons, as well as their abodes, within a governing apparatus that could put them to work for profit. Whether talking of *favelas* in Brazil, *bustees* in India, shantytowns in the Philippines, *barriadas* in Peru, *calampas* or *colonias proletarias* in Mexico, or *bidonvilles* in Morocco, informal urbanisms came to stand as precedents for a bootstrapping solution that could be formalized in development paradigms such as "sites and services," aided self-help, and "core" housing projects.[67] Although self-help strategies had originated under slightly different circumstances decades earlier with the groundbreaking work of British architect John F. C. Turner, by the mid-1970s, they were firmly associated with institutions such as the World Bank, the Ford Foundation, USAID, the IMF, and so on, institutions long known to operate at the behest of multinational corporations under the rubric of "world peace." Not only did people "helping themselves" confirm that there was a huge pool of labor resources waiting to be tapped by global capital, it indicated that responsibility for housing and other services could shift from capitalist to worker. Standards could be lowered, profitability increased. This was the new world order against which calls for a new international economic order were then being voiced by many within nonaligned countries.

As in Stockholm, Ward was invited to address Habitat's plenary session, again the only private citizen to do so, and the Vancouver Symposium held a press conference at the UN media center, the only NGO afforded such a privilege. Ward used the occasion of her speech to reiterate that the horrors of Victorian England, familiar from Charles Dickens's novels, were now found in the slums of the Global South and to insist that the solution lay in replacing political approaches with the World Bank's sites and services and self-help housing strategies.[68] Europe, she conceded of this necessity, enjoyed "an element of chance and luck in history"; its "transition to the industrial economy" was "cushioned" by colonial exploitation of lands and peoples, a historical priority that, she stressed, reiterating her argument from Stockholm, could not be repeated in the South.[69] For Ward, it was all too easy to recognize Dickensian London in *favelas* or shantytowns. And she was largely correct that in the developing world, the shift from agricultural to urban economies would not be "cushioned" by the conquest and settlement of lands and peoples elsewhere. The opposite was typically true: almost invariably, poor countries were struggling with the persistent legacies of imperial expansion and colonial occupation and/or the realities of a neocolonial counterpart. Hence, in what was cast as "the most militant speech calling for a new economic order," the Cuban delegation to Habitat declared that "decorous living conditions in countries which at present are under-developed cannot be established, since these countries have been exploited and their national resources have for centuries been 'sacked by imperialistic consumer societies in the face of impoverished nations.' It was not easy to speak 'the language of international cooperation with those whose only law was exploiting in the interests of transnational companies.'"[70]

Beyond Europe's good fortune, Ward insisted, its historically assured dominance stemmed from "acts of policy," including sanitation and housing for the poor—from the recognition, even by conservative thinkers, that an element of reform and justice was necessary to maintain the social stability that succeeded in pacifying Europe and that these policy implementations could be replayed to avoid revolutionary struggles elsewhere. "Where these have been lacking," she threatened, "there has been social convulsion, violent revolution and an impetus to merciless worldwide war and conquest."[71] In an excerpt of *The Home of Man* published in the *Observer*, Ward underscored that at stake was not just peace, but, again, life itself, for, as she warned, "the bandits and terrorists and guerrillas of the next 'interregnum' might carry plutonium bombs."[72] Ward no doubt regarded her position as one of realpolitik: claiming urgency and commonsense solutions, she left little room for dialogue or alternative ideas. Her comments manifest not only elitism, but also, we might say, the shifting vicissitudes of power. Atomic weapons, Foucault argued of this topology, were the ultimate "counterpart of a power that exerts a positive influence on life, that endeavors to administer, optimize, and multiply it, subjecting it to precise controls and comprehensive regulations." Here was a form of power, or biopower, that came full circle from the sovereign right to take life to the power over life, the power over biological survival: "The atomic situation is now at the end point of this process: the power to expose a whole population to death is the underside of the power to guarantee an individual's continued existence."[73]

Key arguments from *Human Settlements* and *The Home of Man* appeared in the Declaration of the Vancouver Symposium, rendering the biopolitical agenda of Ward and her team explicit. With this document, the *Guardian* suggested, Ward "effectively opened" the

UN conference, handing a copy ceremoniously to the secretary-general of Habitat, Enrique Peñalosa, who spoke of the important role it would play.[74] "The Vancouver Conference is about the whole of life," the declaration began, noting its encompassing nature. Recalling the series of UN world conferences—on the environment in Stockholm, on population in Bucharest, on food in Rome, on the law of the sea in Caracas, and on women in Mexico City—it pronounced of what Didier Fassin and Mariella Pandolfi have called a "globalized biopolitics": "In the 1970s, the whole international community started to confront the realities of its planetary life."[75] With human settlements, it stated, "all other issues come together, to shape the daily life of the world's peoples."[76] What Ward called "planetary housekeeping" was indeed a sign of growing "togetherness"; it rendered visible the "close web of interdependence" necessary for globalized biopolitics, a web of relations that remained profoundly ambivalent.[77] Suspending that interdependence between the goals of world governance and the threats of insurrection, the declaration insisted that togetherness could lead to justice and happiness or to despair and "deepening conflict." Underscoring Ward's narrative of "a world of coming violence" emanating from the South, the declaration, too, made an analogy with European revolutions.

> There is no evidence in history that rich elites, entrenched in their wealth and unwilling to create the institutions and policies of wider sharing, will not be swept away by the growing revolt of the still oppressed. In Europe, at a comparable stage of technological development, the "Hungry Forties" led to the Year of Revolutions [1848]. Can we be sure that the "Hungry Eighties" will not confront the world with comparable disruption?[78]

The hope, of course, was ultimately that it would not, that the UN could help maintain the status quo in the name of peace. The ambition was not to ensure equity, but to institute a parallel modernity. This found a foothold in celebrating informality as a contemporary architectural vernacular: "The settlements built in this way do not conform to standards of 'excellence' borrowed from the norms of developed, industrialized societies," the declaration explained.

Hence, it was not surprising that, when the conference opened, we find the *New York Times* announcing of the new consensus, "Shantytowns of squatters, living on land that does not belong to them, are gaining a new respectability around the world." Given the extensiveness of shantytowns in the developing world and their ability to "exert formidable political and social pressures," the reporter continued, one of Habitat's "main aims is to crystallize new national policies regarding these 'unauthorized communities.'"[79] While many governments still responded by bulldozing, burning, and other violent techniques of forced displacement, others had moved toward strategies of participatory resettlement or improving services and accommodations. In a Habitat Forum panel, "Housing the Poor," *Jericho* reported, Vancouver Symposium member Otto Königsberger "had some advice for planners who want to resettle slum dwellers—don't do it... the answer was to upgrade slum settlements by providing water, electricity, and security of tenure.... Settlement not resettlement is the answer."[80] Writing for the *New Internationalist*, British journalist Jeremy Bugler announced with bemusement of this resemanticization, "Suddenly, it seems, the bulldozers have been called off from razing to the ground the shanty-towns around Third World cities. Huge monolithic government house programmes have been shredded or altered drastically. Instead, governments appear to have turned to involving the people themselves in the actual building of their houses and communities."[81] The Habitat conference served to shore up this narrative of assets, pioneers, and opportunities arising from such a deracinated condition and through it to help make the developing world safe for the penetration of US-style capitalism.

Like Hogan, others were less optimistic than Eckardt about Ward, Strong, and her new collaborators' ubiquitous role. Under the scathing title "Stockholm Spirit Withers at Forum," Patrick Nagle lamented that "another hatch of international groupies has been spawned," further "non-elected world changers" seeking to pressure politicians to adopt their position. The NGO forum, he posited of its counterrevolutionary character, had "become—in effect—a counter-counter conference," redirecting the focus from questions of inequity or injustice toward questions of clean water and a moratorium on nuclear power.[82] Hence, the much-hyped Water Day Walk spectacle, replete with Margaret Trudeau carrying empty buckets to demonstrate problems of the Third World and a march with a giant floppy H-bomb knitted from discarded videotape.

A little background to Strong's replacement is relevant here. In April 1974, Waldheim appointed Enrique Peñalosa as secretary-general of Habitat. Peñalosa trained as an economist in Bogota and worked briefly with Lauchlin Currie in the National Planning Department of Colombia. Following the 1953 military coup d'état, he spent 1954 in Washington, DC, in an economic development training course run by the World Bank, participating in missions to his native Colombia the following year. During the 1960s, he was in charge of the Colombian Institute for Agrarian Reform (INCORA) and served briefly as minister of agriculture before joining the Inter-American Development Bank (IDB) in 1970.[83] A member of World Bank's Permanent Advisory Panel on Agriculture and Rural Development, he takes us to the heart of the neoliberal ambitions of developmentalism. Both the INCORA and IDB jobs "were created as direct responses to the Cuban revolution of 1959," Gutstein reported. "Fearful that Castro-style revolution could spread to other Latin American countries," he recounted, "the Kennedy administration instituted the Alliance for Progress in 1961," which aimed "to promote a peaceful social and economic revolution in Latin America."[84] This pacification was to take place through and on account of projects stimulating foreign investment opportunities.

Under Peñalosa, what initially seemed to be a progressive land-reform scheme using supervised credit—wherein unused farmland was expropriated and distributed among the poor—almost exclusively benefited wealthier farmers, particularly those with good financial track records who were palatable to international financiers. As one report announced, noting that INCORA took over collective farms initiated by peasant invasions, "the overall passiveness of *parceleros*"—peasants given land—is "reinforced by the continued dependence on INCORA, which appears to become more pronounced over time."[85] Housing was not only a mechanism of social stability or counterinsurgency—people who owned their own home being less likely to revolt—but facilitated opportunities for foreign banks, multinational corporations, and industrialists. Peñalosa was the ideal man to follow Strong. Ready to play the game, he focused the conference agenda on technical and institutional terms through which to manage populations in the service of Western capital.

Architectures of Management

In addition to positioning self-help as an answer to threats arising from the developing world, the Declaration of the Vancouver

Symposium called for "new and appropriate methods of collecting and organizing data," including inventories on "types of land, natural eco-systems, mineral reserves, pressures and movements of population." While drawing from Stockholm's Earthwatch initiative, the reference was also to Fuller, a member of the symposium. "The answer need not be fear, anger and entrenched greed," it declared, "It can be a revolution not by violence but by design."[86] Citing World Bank calculations that if wealthy countries contributed toward necessary infrastructure—using "merely a tenth of what is spent each year on so-called defense and security"—weapons of destruction would be replaced by "the means of life," the declaration returns us to another Fullerism: not only would weaponry be converted to "livingry," as he would say, but technology would replace politics, as demonstrated in his World Game. At the Vancouver Symposium press conference, Fuller turned to his critique of the Club of Rome's *Limits to Growth* and of Jay Forrester's inadequate data pools, claiming that his public pronouncements of their inherent flaws after the Stockholm conference led to the group's reversal of Malthusian scarcity arguments. The World Game, Fuller's strategy game using a giant computerized electronic data-visualization map of global events, conditions, and resources, would by contrast render visible the inexhaustible wealth of Spaceship Earth's "four billion, billionaire heirs-apparent." In the World Game, the military application of a computerized, multiplayer logistical game—the War Game—was to be turned on its head: competing teams of players would "each develop their own theory of how to make the world work successfully for all of humanity," developing "grand world strategies" for the equitable distribution of resources to nomadic "citizens of the world."[87] Without nation-states vying for domination over world resources (since there was enough to go around), warfare and scarcity would simply become redundant. Indeed, to resort to war, in Fuller's words, to "use the war-waging equipment with which all national political systems maintain their sovereign power," was to lose the game, to be disqualified.[88] Fuller understood the strategic nature of what was at stake. As indicated by its military origin, the World Game was not an automatically evolving system, those "grand world strategies" not all alike.

Like Ward, Fuller circulated liberally between official governmental events and Habitat Forum and long had a foot in both camps.

As he recalled in "Accommodating Human Unsettlement," he traveled to Vancouver not only as a member of Ward's symposium, but as president of the World Society of Ekistics, as a guest of the City of Vancouver's Habitat Committee, and as the leader of the Now House Project on display at Habitat Forum. He also spoke in a forum panel, "Visions of the Future—Getting it Done," alongside Paolo Soleri of Arcosanti and Prabhat Poddar of Auroville. (Auroville was a "universal town" founded in India in 1968, built, like Arcosanti, using low-tech means and dedicated to "human unity.")[89] To Fuller, the "plurality of invitations" recognizing him "as the protagonist of a design science revolution by which to accommodate physically the now evident evolutionary insistence on world-around *unsettlement of humanity*" was in "marked contrast" to Habitat's "technological focus almost exclusively upon nationalistically emphasized, local, immobile, and 'one-off' tailoring of *human settlements*."[90] Despite this archaism, Fuller felt that the UN conference was "an historical watershed," demonstrating that after fifty years, "general evolutionary events" had come into alignment with his anticipatory designs for lightweight mobile housing. Habitat, as he put it, "marked the end of human settlement."[91]

For Fuller, the answer to sheltering unsettled populations did not lie in national governments or intergovernmental institutions adopting policies and technologies to provide fixed housing—he regarded laws, regulatory structures, and land ownership as anachronistic—but rather in developing housing appropriate for the mobility demanded by free-market capitalism. With a dream of freedom founded on overcoming troublesome legal codes and regulations (while he personally benefited from patent laws), Fuller's libertarianism appealed to both political conservatives and the counterculture alike. His initial solution—the universally applicable, mobile, and mass-produced Dymaxion Dwelling Machines—was updated for Habitat in the Now House, culminating his fifty-year campaign for an "air-deliverable, only-rentable, world-around dwelling machine." Sited amid other alternative energy and dwelling technologies in Habitat Forum's Appropriate Technology Village, the Now House was an outdoor exhibit produced in association with Earth Metabolic Design and destined for the International World Game Workshop, a US bicentennial celebration at the University of Pennsylvania called Design Revolution '76. The "now" in the title

Figure 5.6 R. Buckminster Fuller in front of Dymaxion Map at World Game headquarters, February 3, 1971 (AP Photo/Jim Palmer).

Figure 5.7 Now House Exhibit service dome in background during television interview of R. Buckminster Fuller In Vancouver by Los Angeles affiliate of NBC (courtesy of Department of Special Collections and University Archives, Stanford University Libraries; courtesy of the Estate of R. Buckminster Fuller).

referred to the fact that all components were already commercially available, the total cost running to $20,000, a significant amount in 1976. (It was conceived with what Brand called the "Fullerian wealth sanction," and they assumed that everyone would soon be able to afford such technology.)[92] Now Houses were to be high-tech and profitable. Stressing their integration into wider systems, Fuller argued that his dwellings demonstrated that performance criteria had ceased to be visible: one could now do so much more with so much less that "form is no longer following function. Functions have become formless."[93]

To demonstrate the mobility of Now Houses, ten World Gamers from the University of Pennsylvania and Yale University drove four fourteen-foot, five-eighths-sphere polyester fiberglass geodesic domes across the United States and into Canada in "one camper truck pulling one trailer" and lived in the installation for the duration of Habitat. In addition to the domes, which were sheathed in translucent or opaque fiberglass panels and could be rotated to capture or avoid heat gain from the sun, the exhibit included a "toilet which converted human waste into high-grade fertilizer," a solar panel water-heating device, a mobile greenhouse to grow food, and a windmill that converted power from DC to AC and could hook up to the grid to transmit unused power back to the system.[94] Also on site were two smaller geodesic North Face dome tents fabricated from aircraft aluminum and nylon: these could be disassembled and rolled into a two-foot-by-eight-inch pack weighing only eight pounds. Contemporary backpackers, Fuller posited, provided the model of world-around-dwellers overcoming sovereign borders and circulating freely by carrying their environmental control technologies on their person. Not only were World Game domes light, easily deployable, energy efficient, and able to be substituted one for the other (hence overcoming the need for individual ownership), but as "self-teaching devices," they harbored a disciplinary and normative function for training mobile world citizens to participate in this new global reality. Of central importance was that their use was no longer confined to military applications and other states of emergency, but would become normalized according to management criteria: weaponry would become livingry for an abstract humanity.

"Accommodating Human Unsettlement" situated the Now House within a narrative of transformations in capitalism to which it hoped to contribute. "Big money," as Fuller put it, "has left all the sovereignly locked-in, local-property-game-players 'holding the unmovable bags' of 'real estate,'" and in its place, "'know-how' has become the 'apple' of transnational capitalism's eye."[95] Dating the shift from "the monopolistic control of America's prime industrial establishment" to the rise of a knowledge economy and new management logic during the 1929 economic crisis, he went on: "All the great American corporations of yesterday have now moved out of America and their prime operations have become transnational and conglomerate and are essentially concerned with the game of selling their corporation's very complete, technical, managerial and vast credit handling and money making know-how."[96]

By 1952, Fuller argued, "Lawyer Desocialized and Strategied Supranational Managerial Capitalism" had largely "conquered" "governmental power," with corporate media holdings keeping governments distracted by creating "a smoke screen diverting attention from what they were doing."[97] Since power had shifted, "transnational conglomerate capitalism" had paid no heed to Habitat's obsolescent paradigm of shelter.

We can certainly question Fuller's faith in the end of real estate investment, let alone his celebration of neoliberal principles. Yet his reading of capitalist strategy during a moment when corporations were turning to the developing world manifest a Fulleresque insight. "While world news was spot-lighted on the Korean and Vietnam wars, the great USA corporations and banks were conglomerating and moving out of America into a world theater of operations. In 25 successive annual appropriations of Foreign Aid, totaling 100 billion dollars, 'riders' required that where a USA corporation was present in the country being aided, the aid funds had to be spent through those USA corporations."[98] US foreign aid, as noted earlier, was not driven by humanitarian goals or even by peace as a value, but indeed served such economic and political interests.

In "Accommodating Human Unsettlement," Fuller also joined Ward and others in celebrating squatter settlements, noting their inhabitants' ingenuity and ability to "improvise something to sleep under that sheds off the rain, whether it's three ply, corrugated paperboard or rusty corrugated iron." "In traveling around the world and visiting such squatter settlements," he wrote with unchecked romanticism, "I have observed their beautiful community life.

Figure 5.8 Now House Exhibit at Habitat Forum, Vancouver, June 1976. Showing media / dormitory dome and service dome in background, solar water heater in middle, and solar still in foreground (courtesy of Department of Special Collections and University Archives, Stanford University Libraries; © Estate of R. Buckminster Fuller).

Figures 5.9 & 5.10 Now House Exhibit at Habitat Forum, Vancouver, June 1976. Interior of media/dormitory dome with video equipment; packed up and being transported on Jeep (Tony Gwilliam).

People in trouble co-operate in a thoughtful and loving way. Their way of life is so beautiful that I have always said that if I ever have to retire, it will be into one of those squatter settlements."[99] Fuller did not question the global economic and political systems giving rise to such displacement, but only the racketeering that ensued from squatters' precarious condition, since they were "on land that by law 'belongs' to somebody else."[100] As a potential remedy, he singled out the Vancouver Symposium recommendation to cede land occupied by squatter settlements back to the public domain. Resonating with the dreams of Open Land communes and Earth People's Parks, this did not, however, simply entail free land once a squatter settlement had been incorporated within the development apparatus, but, as Peñalosa understood, different forms of regulation, keeping the inhabitants precariously on the edge of the system.

A year before Habitat, Fuller was invited by Senator Charles Percy (Republican, Illinois) to address the US Senate's Committee on Foreign Relations hearings on relations between the United States and the United Nations. "Nature is trying to integrate all humanity," Fuller posited, suggesting that the UN worked against such evolutionary trends by attending to the interests of sovereign nations and leaving people "locked into 150 national pens."[101] "All the world's great corporations have found sovereign nations' geographical confinement to be absolutely untenable wherefore they have all become supranational operations," he continued, noting, "Humans are experiencing exactly the opposite of political freedom."[102] Fuller called instead for "universal desovereignization," repeating his musings on the automatically evolving eradication of sovereign political boundaries that dated back to the late 1920s. National boundaries would simply wither away to engender a world without conflict, a world without politics. Senator Dick Clark (Democrat, Iowa) raised questions related to apartheid in South Africa and unjust trade regulations instituted by the United States, to which Fuller retorted that "my whole way of thinking is apolitical," that he wasn't interested in laws.[103] Asked by Senator Percy if he felt that "any form of world government is now in order or that we are moving toward it," Fuller responded by arguing that elections could regain "one-to-one correspondence" characteristic of older times through "electromagnetic communication." With the aid of satellite-mounted sensing devices and the capacity to tune in to humans' recently discovered electromagnetic broadcasts, "we may soon have the capability to directly sense how each and every human feels about each and every common human problem of the moment." Regarding data as transparent and centralized processing and programming protocols as without bias, Fuller quite literally argued that communications technology and management techniques could replace political discourse.[104] Assuming that other political actors would not step in to fill the vacuum of power left by the nation-state, Fuller stated of his "satellite harvested electromagnetic field sensing of how world democracy feels about any proposed solution of any given problem": "An incorruptible, true direct planetary democracy with all of humanity franchised and always voting may well render all humanity sustainable, successful. So those are my thoughts, sir."[105]

Fuller's "democracy" presciently outlined the emerging contours of a computer-interfaced surveillance apparatus and with it a global marketplace, mirroring the deterritorializing and reterritorializing forces of neoliberal capitalism.[106] There was little or no scope in this picture for democratic political or juridical processes or even for civil disobedience and rights struggles, but only their abandonment into the hands of corporations and computerized systems extracting and processing data, which, like his design-science revolution, was considered politically neutral or "incorruptible."

Beyond Fuller's outright rejection of politics as the cause of war was a more subtle elision operating in his notion of universal humanity. Promising a world without conflict, this notion is perhaps less efficacious as a tool in the service of peace and justice than it is as a rhetorical tool to overcome potential disagreement among nations and to institute a system foreclosing the ability of its citizens to question the technology underpinning it. Void of contestation, Fuller's scenario effectively ceded power to dominant economic and political forces driving the development apparatus as they sought to control world resources. That is to say: far from promoting a more just redirection of resources, such naturalization of technology as an evolutionary force implicitly supported and continues to support the logic driving the expanding military-industrial complex and its capacity to produce ever more extensively networked forms of global power.

While Fuller recognized the passage toward a postnational condition driven, in part, by US-led multinational corporations, hoping to synchronize his housing with this "desovereignization," what he didn't acknowledge was the rise of another form of sovereignty, what Michael Hardt and Antonio Negri theorized as "Empire," a super-sovereignty mediated through global networks of control, to which Fuller's dreams unwittingly ceded humanity's fate.[107] Far from realizing peace in the conventional sense, this paradigm is premised on a perpetual state of war, although no longer conventional or interstate war. As Hardt and Negri explain, "To the extent that the sovereign authority of nation-states, even the most dominant nation-states, is declining and there is instead emerging a new supranational form of sovereignty, a global Empire, the conditions and nature of war and political violence are necessarily changing. War is becoming a general phenomenon, global and interminable."[108]Moreover, although Fuller recognized the alignment of aid and development strategies with corporate profit, he did not critique a situation in which the UN and the World Bank, with celebrity support from Ward and others, served the *dispositif* of power it entailed. Far from 150 nation states separated into distinct pens, key players from powerful industrial states sought to exercise a hold over scripting policies at Habitat. Here, once again, is an image of Foucault's reversal of Clausewitz's famous notion, his suggestion that policy or politics is the extension of warfare by other means.[109]

Visions of the Future

When Fuller spoke at Habitat Forum, reiterating his technocratic and teleological narrative, he drew thousands of fans, evidence, as one reporter noted, of a Bucky cult.[110] He reiterated his ambition to "prove we have enough and make politics obsolete and war obsolete."[111] In contrast to his guaranteed celebrity during the previous decade, Fuller's talk did not make front-page news, even in *Jericho*, where he was relegated to a small column on the last page titled "Keeping the Sunny Side Up." Indeed, Fuller was both in and out of sync with Habitat Forum, his Now House installation marking a high-tech departure not only from Arcosanti and Auroville, but also from the do-it-yourself and funky aesthetic of the Jericho site.

When Habitat Forum opened on May 27, a few days in advance of the UN conference, visitors were presented with a widely celebrated, cost-effective transformation of a decrepit air force base once used to stage mock troop landings into a countercultural fantasy. The *Province* reported that it was "mindblowing" and "freaky."[112] Using driftwood and discarded timber from local logging operations, all salvaged from the beach and milled on-site, along with other recycled or donated materials, the five hangars were transformed into a large auditorium, several smaller theaters, conference and media rooms, exhibit halls, and a social center that housed ethnic food stands and a 242-foot-long yellow cedar bar. The spaces were furnished with rough-hewn stages, tiered seating and bleachers, and other furniture fashioned from recycled wood, their surfaces ornamented with colorful banners, flags, sculptures, and murals featuring Haida paintings characteristic of local indigenous people, for whom the site earlier had served as a potlatch meeting ground.[113] *Ekistics* referred to the setting as having a "frontier-like style": while tactlesssly alluding to British Columbia's settler period, the renovation followed a by then familiar countercultural or do-it-yourself aesthetic born of alternative lifestyle movements, like that Brand deployed in Stockholm. Habitat Forum even modeled its publications after the alternative press from that event, *Jericho* taking its cues from *Forum: Environment Is Politics* and *Forum: Your Guide to the People's Conference on Human Settlements* from Life Forum's *Open Options*. The ACSOH team on site at Jericho Beach produced *Habitat Forum Bulletin*, its executives, *Habitat Forum News*. All adopted the graphic language of the alternative press.

As with Life Forum activities in Stockholm, Habitat Forum read as a strange holdover or archaism from the optimism and cultural practices of the previous decade. Frederick Gutheim saw "a kind of environmental Woodstock,"[114] others a "great clapped-out audio-visual sit-down talk-in freak show."[115] Noting that the scene "could have been an anti-Vietnam war teach-in in the 1960s," *New York Times* architecture critic Paul Goldberger reiterated the cliché of the forum's radicalism, reporting that it "has taken on much of the air of a countercultural festival, while the official sessions are attended by gray-suited diplomats who spend most of their time arguing about the wording of resolutions."[116] *Ekistics* listed a heterogeneous, if familiar cast of characters:

> A group of indigenous American Indians publicized their grievances about land rights with drumming, chanting and dancing. A vociferous group of "Ban the Bomb" enthusiasts campaigned against the further use of nuclear energy. People in the Greenpeace movement were

> preparing for the annual launching of their expedition against whalers. "Brother Blue"... spoke, sang, chanted, mimed and danced his stories of love and joy before the Habitat crowds and his crew of cameramen. Others protested abortion or called for wider women's rights or proclaimed various new religions that would bring peace on earth.[117]

Finally, *Toronto Globe and Mail* reporter Malcolm Gray turned to a local hotbed of hippie culture: "The illusion is, once through the gates, that everyone inside has been frozen in time on a Kitsilano commune circa 1968. This could be the last refuge of the counter-culture, everyone who decided there was a better way in the 1960s than the nine-to-five routine gathered here to show they could do more than roll perfectly-tailored joints."[118] While harboring "'the last gasp of Vancouver's counter-culture'... seemingly everyone who dropped out during the 1960s," Habitat Forum was paradoxically not "the product of a commune work force," Gray clarified. Far from seeking participation, it was a "setting built by a workforce rigidly controlled from the top."[119]

Habitat Forum was not only populated by countercultural types, but as noted above, included the Vancouver Symposium, an array of NGOs, scholars, scientists, designers, and other prominent experts, such as Turner and the Self-Help and Low Cost Housing Symposium. Yet it was carefully styled to take on an alternative appearance. If, as von Eckardt recognized, "background music was provided by local Indians beating their drums for their cause and assorted barefoot fiddlers and rock combos, complete with their dazed young women and an occasional whiff of pot," these "counter trappings" were "superficial and the memories of anti-Vietnam teach-ins... deceptive. There was lots of hair and there were lots of blue jeans and protests. But there was also a great deal more." Beneath the trappings of dissent and alterity, he suggested, was technical know-how. "If the official delegates downtown, with their army-chauffeured cars, had their briefcases full of documents prepared by their foreign ministries, the citizen's representatives in blue jeans had the expertise."[120] In Stockholm, the agendas of Environment Forum, People's Forum, and Life Forum intersected in convoluted ways and were repeatedly collapsed in the media, public, and political imagination. Habitat Forum quite literally merged their functions, locations, and facilities, overcoming distinctions between official, radical, and countercultural groups.[121]

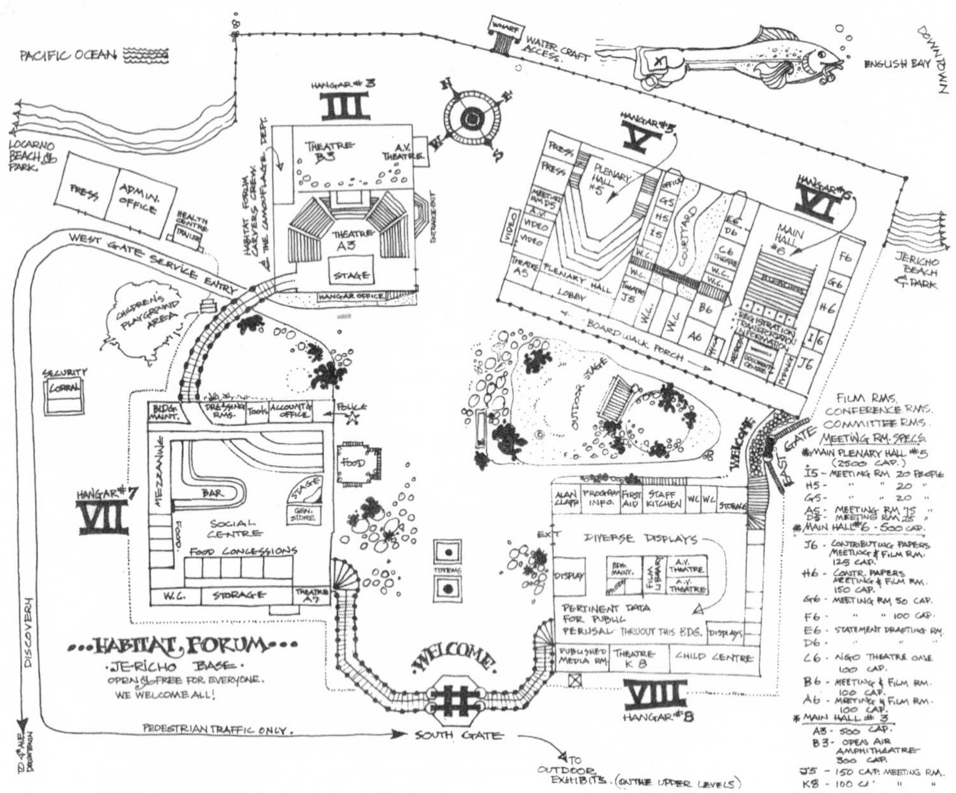

Figure 5.11 Habitat Forum map, 1976. From Conference of Non-governmental Organizations in Consultative Status with the UN Economic and Social Council Records 1948–1985 (Rare Book & Manuscript Library, Columbia University in the City of New York).

Figure 5.12 Entry gate to Habitat Forum, Vancouver, June 1976. From *Architectural Design*, October 1976.

No longer would the mixing of experts, minority groups, activists, and hippies occur by chance at the railway station or during major rallies or events. It was now to take place by design at Jericho Beach, visually marked as unofficial. While the mixing was productive for some, the trappings instituted other divides. "For the official delegates," a New York architect told Goldberger, "going to the forum was like slumming." The location, moreover, ensured that NGOs were "torn between getting their message to the media and lobbying the Habitat delegates."[122] Even if they chose the latter, there were few opportunities to cross paths.[123] As reported in *Ekistics*, "Contact between the caravanserai at the Forum and the 'official conference' in downtown Vancouver was almost completely nonexistent. Very few of the official delegates had the time or inclination to visit the Forum site. Many of those who did were somewhat shocked and disturbed by the 'riff-raff' they met there."[124]

In Gutstein's assessment, "site producer" Al Clapp, a media-savvy former BCTV news producer, had created "an elaborate stage set."[125] Representing the UIA on ACSOH's board, architect Jean-Louis Lalonde earlier had expressed concern that Clapp was "mainly concerned with the stage setting." He protested that as designed by a TV producer, "the enterprise at the moment is a 'happening' and can only prepare facilities for another happening."[126] Clapp was unapologetic. Familiar with media strategy not only from his time in television, but also, among other things, from producing the launch of Greenpeace's legendary antiwhaling action from the Jericho site the previous April, he explained to the *Vancouver Sun*, "'I built the thing like a film set—the whole idea was to make a film.'"[127] An ambiguous character, Clapp was known to be politically adept at mobilizing people, including precarious and unpaid labor. As Allen Garr explained, "Clapp had developed a reputation for being able to tap counter-culture energy. Freaks and government might not relish talking to each other, but sometimes they had mutual needs. When they did, Clapp was willing to play the role of interpreter."[128]

Well versed in the value of controversy, Clapp ensured that Habitat Forum received media attention.[129] Although an employee of ACSOH, he pursued his own agenda, including acting as gatekeeper and refusing access to approved exhibitors and even barring ACSOH's site-exhibit co-coordinator.[130] As one critic noted, "Mr. Clapp has worked himself into a position where he has absolute control over the site and no one can get on the base without his approval."[131] *Jericho* reported, for instance, that he decided to move the Muslim League exhibition that van Putten initally sited opposite *Aspects of Israel* to another site within the indoor display areas dedicated to alternative technology. "I'm embarrassed by it,' Clapp told *Jericho*. 'To put Moslems and Israelis next to each other is incredible. And where is Auroville supposed to go?"[132] *Jericho*'s Gremlin columnist retorted: "anyone a little closer to the Middle East might observe that things like this do happen. And what better place is there to encourage Muslims and Jews to rub shoulders rather than shake fists than in an ex-military hangar now converted to peace."[133]

Entering the Appropriate Technology Village, one found, alongside Fuller's Now House, a motley assortment of domes, teepees, tents, log huts, a plastic igloo, and houses made of sulfur blocks, polyurethane foam, mud, shipping containers, or cardboard, among other materials, cast, as the program announced, apparently without irony, as "low-cost shelter techniques—particularly those appropriate to the needs and resources of developing countries."[134] The *New York Times* reported on the "novel shelters on display" under the title "Dream Houses Become a Reality at UN Conference," seeing them as "illustrations of ways in which hundreds of millions of inadequately housed people around the world... could improve their lot."[135] While the exhibits' authors often stressed their utility as disaster and/or refugee housing, their relevance to developing countries remained unclear. (There were unrealized proposals for a sun-dried mud-brick vault and vernacular dome by the Iranian Development Workshop, among whose members was Taghi Farvar, and even for importing a team of Swazilanders to construct a circular house from rammed earth.) Few demonstrated evident connections to the needs, resources, or forms of life of developing countries, manifesting instead structures of identification "down" familiar from hippie culture. Although tent cities were banned by the local government, the outdoor exhibits in many regards replicated, stood in for, and regularized the alternative lifestyle demonstrations that Brand had staged at Stockholm, like them resonating ambiguously with itinerancy and less privileged forms of life.

In "The View from Jericho," Alfred Heller (an insightful reader of Brand's antics in 1972) noted that the forum's "parade ground" performed a somewhat allegorical function. He noted that Habitat

Figure 5.13 Al Clapp presenting Habitat Forum to Premier Bill Bennett, May 1976 (Ralph Bower / *Vancouver Sun*).

Forum was "inhabited by good-doers, mostly middle-class Canadians and Americans. These people don't have to stay there at night, and the water is pure, but they speak for those who live in slum cities; and somehow Jericho works as a symbol, a surrogate for the poor and the disposed. It is a daytime global village."[136] That is, the alternative forms of life on display at Habitat Forum stood in for and often spoke on behalf of Third World citizens, the poor, and others unable to attend (although some experts from developing countries were recruited by governments and paid for by Habitat Forum organizers.)[137] Turning to why governments might fund such a venture, Heller, too, pointed to security: "Why? It is a safety valve. Miles from the official center of action, people with no official conference status but who want to join the discussion can make the most outrageous, revolutionary statements, shout their heads off, even start a riot (they don't), and they can be controlled, isolated from the honorable delegates."[138] Despite such a controlled insertion of civil disobedience and dissent into the UN apparatus, Heller remained optimistic. "Jericho is more than a security man's dream," he concluded. "It takes on a life of its own. People from many villages meet there and discover they share interests that seem urgent, but that are ignored or swept aside by governments. They gain strength by coming together. Their idealism may spread, sooner or later, to governing councils."[139]

Involuntary Migration

While Heller rightfully observed that mechanisms of control could not entirely silence alternative and nongovernmental voices, implying that potential remained for the eruption of other types of claims into the public sphere, idealism was not necessarily the forum's most desirable contribution. Aligned with the dominant apparatus of power, Ward and Fuller's troping on "unsettlement" and their repeated insistence that technical and managerial strategies could replace politics as the domain of action exhibited plenty of idealism. In celebrating the prospect of a revolution by design, as I have tried to show, these "world citizens" each attempted to articulate strategies for a Third World game. Ward mobilized human unsettlement as marking both a crisis *and* an opportunity—as implying threats of insurrection *and* occasions for implementing policies to ensure global security in the wake of European and American colonialism.

Fuller celebrated dispossession as overcoming obsolete forms of sovereignty and as bringing dwellings into alignment with the deterritorializing forces of capitalism. Their strategies, however, were thrown into sharp relief by a group whose concerns were situated otherwise at the nexus of unsettlement, sovereignty, citizenship, land ownership, and colonial occupation: Palestinians.

Although idealism thus remained a motivating force for pursuing socioeconomic and political transformations, a better question perhaps lay in whether or not forms of creative resistance could effect reversals of power within the hierarchical apparatus that Ward and Fuller celebrated, reversals achieved not only through technical matters, but also through politics and in the name of rights and seeking justice. As noted above, catalyzed by the Israel/Palestine conflict, it was precisely this sort of claim that gained traction less within the NGO forum than within intergovernmental debates, prompting the *Chicago Tribune* to lament, "The good ship Habitat, a global attempt at improving mankind's living conditions, has run aground on the jagged reef of Arab-Israeli relations."[140] "What had seemed to be just a boring meeting of an editorial committee," Humphrey Carver reported of the breakdown in the anticipated consensus, "was transformed into a fragile and highly sensitive confrontation. Some observers have thought that the UN cannot survive if its conferences, like *Habitat*, are hijacked in the ideological war."[141]

Habitat, to be clear, was always and already a platform for an ideological war: the eruption of the Palestinian question simply rendered that explicit, the support from the G77 shifting the balance of voting power toward the nonaligned bloc. Much lamented by Western media, Habitat had been transformed into what one review called a "political battleground,"[142] another theater of "political warfare."[143] We might recast what took place not as the *introduction* of political warfare per se, but as the addition of another set of strategies within what had been launched as a Third World game. Moreover, the timing was crucial. Pointing to a controversial initiative sponsored by the G77 in defiance of US threats, Resolution 3379, the *Vancouver Sun* reported, "The first UN resolution equating Zionism with racism was last year's political bombshell. Now Habitat has provided the stage for yet another explosion."[144] Such rhetoric, as with much cited above, aimed to affiliate the PLO with violence, but the picture was much more complicated, and I want to outline

Israel's and Palestine's claims at Habitat before turning to a set of amendments that, operating at the center of the UN's procedural apparatus, targeted the structural asymmetry at work in the UN as it affected Palestinians. As the PLO's *National Report of Palestine* wryly explained of the UN's role in the founding of Israel as a Zionist state that from the outset discriminated against the majority of the indigenous population on the basis of religion and its subsequent ineffectiveness at protecting their human rights, the UN and the Palestinian question were "uniquely associated with each other."

In addition to initiating agencies and programs related to the conflict, the UN had issued multiple statements and resolutions in favor of the rights of Palestinians. For example, in 1974, UNESCO condemned Israel's "persistence in altering the historical features of the city of Jerusalem," arguing that it was "undertaking excavations which constitute a danger to its monuments, subsequent to the illegal occupation of the city."[145] Jerusalem, too, had become outlaw territory.

Israel's resultant expulsion from UNESCO's European regional group prompted the United States to terminate its financial contributions to the agency. Only a few months before Habitat, an increasingly isolated United States successfully vetoed resolutions in the Security Council condemning Israel's transformation of Jerusalem and its settlements in the Occupied Territories. But building upon earlier condemnations of Israel's alliance with apartheid South Africa and the colonial regime in Portugal, the November 1975 determination "that Zionism is a form of racism and racial discrimination" sparked expanded media attention to the underlying forces driving this long-standing conflict.[146] Many rejected the tactic of censuring Israel in this extreme manner, whether seeing it as inaccurate or as an undiplomatic attack on an allied country or questioning it as too inflammatory and likely to invoke a backlash.[147] Yet one outcome was that ensuing debates introduced historical facts and alternative perspectives, increasing the visibility of the Palestinians' plight, otherwise largely suppressed by Western media or presented solely in terms of terrorism and refugees. The public was reminded of Theodor Herzl's racist attitudes and of the privilege afforded to European settlers in the 1917 Balfour Declaration; critiques of Zionism were firmly distinguished from critiques of Judaism, refuting accusations of automatic anti-Semitism that long served to shut dialogue down.[148] "It is a moral myopia to try to solve Auschwitz by Deir Yassin (the 1948 massacre of 254 unarmed Arab villagers by Irgun and Stern Gang terrorists)," A. M. El-Messiri wrote in the *New York Times*, "and, in answer to Occidental concentration camps, propose the dispersion of the Palestinians." "One can even startle the American reader," he quipped, "by pointing out that there are non-Zionist and even anti-Zionist groups and public figures inside Israel itself."[149] At Habitat, the irreconcilability of narratives offered by Israel and Palestine, both known figures of victimhood, came to the fore. To introduce key points in these UN debates, at the risk of rehearsing two well-known stories that have been the subject of much important literature, I want briefly to outline each as told at Habitat.

Israel's national report, *Settlement in Israel*, rehearsed the narrative of revitalizing a neglected and underpopulated land—a land without a people for a people without land—and of making deserts bloom. It told the story of how "a sparsely-settled, under-developed country supporting a population of under half a million" developed into "one of the most highly urbanized and densely settled countries of the world, with a population of over 3 million.... Israel's experience in rural settlement," it suggested rather candidly, "shows ways of increasing the area suitable for settlement and of increasing the intensity of settlement" through policies geared toward increasing the absorptive capacity of the territory.[150] Most privately owned land, particularly agricultural land, the report acknowledged, remained in the hands of Arab and Druze populations. In addition to citing a "deep-rooted anti-city ideology" among many Israelis and outlining distinctions between plans for cities such as Tel Aviv and Jerusalem, new towns such as Kiryat-Gat, and rural settlements including kibbutzim and moshavim, *Settlement in Israel* detailed population dispersal strategies. These strategies, it indicated, sought to address concerns over regional imbalances of development and to open outlying settlements as "resource frontiers"; they also formed part of a national security strategy. Without apology, the report spoke of "occupying frontier regions for purposes of defense as well as to establish national presence and sovereignty over these areas."[151] Finally, and in defiance of UN resolutions, *Settlement in Israel* devoted significant attention to the redevelopment of Jerusalem "since reunification in 1967," stressing preservation efforts then underway in the Jewish quarter of the Old City and the role of heritage in strengthening "cultural links between the past and the present."[152]

When Josef Burg took the podium to deliver his statement to the plenary session on June 3, scores of delegates from the Middle East, Latin America, Asia, and Eastern Europe streamed out in protest of Israel's violation of human rights and destruction of Palestinian habitats.[153] Burg alluded to the "extraneous political disputes" that troubled UNESCO meetings in Europe, then presented Israel's national settlement policy as a strategy to absorb "large numbers of immigrants and refugees." As he explained, absorption took place through communal kibbutzim and cooperative moshavim that facilitated the "creation of new life styles," not mentioning lifestyles that were simultaneously destroyed in the project of building a Jewish state upon the negation of Palestine. Pointing to an alignment with Habitat, he explained, "The linchpin in Israel's settlement and development policies has been, and is, public control of land. 91 percent of all land is publically controlled." Israel's primary motivation, he claimed, was "the prevention of land speculation."[154] Prompted by the walkouts, he departed from his script to argue that the Syrian invasion of Lebanon earlier that year, aimed at limiting the power of Palestinian guerillas, gave rise to a "process not far from genocide"; Arabs fighting each other, he proposed, created "more victims than all wars since the proclamation of the State of Israel."[155] Reiterated by Burg and other Israeli delegates, such claims aimed to stress internal divides and violence and hence the inability of the PLO to govern.[156]

Al-Hout responded in his June 4 plenary address: to long and loud applause, "he condemned the PLO's 'Zionist American-armed adversary' and pledged support for a Trudeau-styled world of love."[157] The unexpected reference was to Canadian Prime Minister Pierre Trudeau's opening remarks at Habitat, wherein he called for a "'conspiracy' of love." (After celebrating the pioneering spirit of Canada's white settlers, Trudeau concluded by arguing that in the face of rapid population growth, "the only type of love which would be effective in the tightly-packed world we already live in would be a passionate love.")[158] Widely acknowledged as a clever tactic, Al-Hout's identification with Trudeau's remarks shifted the conversation from violence and religion to ethics and justice: it rendered love political.

> We share his belief. Ever since we initiated our struggle to restore our political, natural and legitimate rights in Palestine we offered

Figure 5.14 Gush Emunim settlers in front of tents erected in an attempt to establish the Elon Moreh settlement at Sebastia, December 8, 1975 (Moshe Milner/Government Press Office, State of Israel).

Figure 5.15 Members of a Nahal group in front of their prefabricated houses and bomb shelter entrance at Moshav Hamra in Eastern Samaria, October 5, 1972 (Moshe Milner/Government Press Office, State of Israel).

> as the objective of our struggles, love and coexistence on the basis of complete equality and justice. What more can the Palestinian, exiled from his homeland or oppressed within it, offer to his oppressor and expeller?... If this is not the love that Mr. Trudeau proposed, what is love?[159]

Al-Hout spoke the next day at an event to celebrate Palestine Day and Palestinian struggles for a democratic secular state, an event that was accompanied by an exhibit of photographs and films on the living conditions of Palestinians. It was also accompanied by "at least four plain clothes members of the R[oyal] C[anadian] M[ounted] P[olice]." He responded to Burg again, reading the invasion of Lebanon as a conspiracy provoked by the rise of Palestinian freedom fighters.[160] Reporting on the event, journalist Mordecai Briemberg invoked "the terror of Zionism" and indicated that many Jews, such as himself, supported the Palestinian cause.[161]

As an invited national liberation organization, the PLO was eligible to submit a national report, which the UN failed to distribute to the official conference, citing economic constraints.[162] Critiquing the UN for its role in the partition of Palestine and the founding of Israel as a nonsecular state, the *National Report of Palestine* outlined the shift from a "pluralist, multi-racial" society to a discriminatory social structure premised on the ideological principle of "Zionist exclusiveness" and the assumption of supremacy. Israel's colonial attitude, the report explained, was distinctly out of sync with the period's widespread rejection of colonialism and dismantling of colonial empires. Having pointed to the illegality of Israel's founding—in the refusal of the UN proposal and the assassination of UN mediator Folke Bernadotte by radical Zionist groups during the partition process—the PLO recalled that in 1948, "an organized and premeditated Zionist military and terrorist campaign seized four fifths of Palestine, emptied that area of 85–90 percent of its indigenous Arab population and turned almost a million people into refugees. Zionist exclusiveness, the fundamental Zionist credo that the integration of Jews with the rest of humanity is not possible, required an empty land."[163]

Land-grabbing strategies began well before the partition. "Already by the mid-1930s thousands of landless and jobless peasants were crowded in shacks on the edge of cities like Haifa," the PLO explained of ensuing shantytowns, reminding us that the massive tent cities of early refugee camps were not the only form of shelter arising from this process of dispossession.[164] The Jewish National Fund (JNF) purchased land decades earlier to facilitate settlements discriminating against the non-Jewish population, who could not buy, rent, or work on that land. This process was exacerbated after the founding of Israel by the adoption of laws intended to legitimate seizure of Palestinian-owned property or to create such deprivation that they were effectively compelled to leave. "Among the most important and cruel," the *National Report of Palestine* explained, was the Absentee Property Law, "which opened the way to the seizure of hundreds of thousands of dunums of land[165] and other properties (homes, shops, etc.) from Arabs considered to be Israeli citizens but held to be 'absentees,'" even if they left only temporarily to take refuge from the turmoil of the partition.[166] Under this law, *waqf* property—land considered under Islamic law to be implicitly owned by God—was confiscated, even though "God was not formally declared an absentee."[167] (Here we are reminded of the idealism of Open Land communes as they sought to cede land to God and hence to the commons under the rubric of *waqf*.)

Turning to the nexus of territory and security, the *National Report of Palestine* detailed the effects of Israel's use of defense laws instituted during the British mandate era for states of emergency. These empowered the government to appropriate property and control the movement, congregation, and even place of residence of Arab populations. "Expulsions can be done en masse without specifying people by name," it noted.

> In such circumstances [Palestinian] land soon became uncultivated and so under the Emergency Articles for Exploitation of Uncultivated Land, enacted in 1948, it was turned over to Jewish colonies "to ensure its cultivation." The 1949 Emergency Regulation (Security Zones) allowed similar measures to be applied to any area declared by the Minister of Defense to be a Security Zone. Such was the "legal" basis for many forcible expulsions and land seizures. After the 1967 war the Defense Laws were put in force in the West Bank and Gaza where they are applied even more ruthlessly than in the Arab areas of Israel itself.[168]

Such appropriation facilitated the establishment of dozens of illegal settlements in the Occupied Territories after the Six-Day War.

The report detailed how, employing the rhetoric of security, Israel implemented multiple forms of cultural and political repression of the indigenous population, producing an asymmetrical situation "maintained by the financial, military and political help granted it by a concert of Western powers, the U.S. in the lead."[169] But these techniques of power did not entirely succeed in crystallizing Israel's desired forms of sovereignty. Far from simply destroying Palestinian forms of life, Israel's strategies fomented a national consciousness and new, dispersed forms of community.[170]

> Camp inhabitants, still firmly attached to their villages in Palestine, divide the camps into sections, each section bearing the name of the Palestinian village from which they originated. Village ties draw others from the outside to join friends and relatives within the camps.
>
> Many villages that the Israelis razed to the ground in Palestine, in this way, still live as coherent social units in the refugee camps. Family, village and regional ties have not weakened. Social consciousness is perhaps greater. The camps in fact developed not in accordance with some UN plan but as spontaneous social formations in which the sense of being Palestinian burns as fiercely as ever. The sense of solidarity, a shared tradition, a common destiny—return to the home-land—has permitted the dispossessed to stand up to the long years of hardship and humiliation and to forge the bonds of a tightly knit and highly conscious community. To this extraordinarily tenacious social factor the arrival of the armed fedayeen added a growing national consciousness: for the first time the people in the camps accepted as their leaders persons not from their own villages or regions.
>
> Under the leadership of the Palestinian resistance movement the once frustrated and powerless refugees are becoming the masters of their own fate.[171]

Zionist strategies and the antagonisms they elicited, that is, produced new environmental and social formations and new political subjectivities, giving rise to creative forms of struggle and to modes of counterconduct.

Finally, the *National Report of Palestine* turned to Israel's refusal to honor UN resolutions, acts that, like the litany of violence outlined above, remain all too familiar today.[172] Pointing, among other instances, to attempts to shift the demographic balance and cultural identity of Jerusalem in Israel's favor, they noted that the Israeli Army continued to bomb the city following the withdrawal of Jordanian forces in 1967. Like the construction of settlements in the Occupied Territories, such illegal actions established facts on the ground, in this case, as the report detailed, razing the Maghrabi and Sa'diyah Quarters to make way for a parking lot in front of the Wailing Wall.[173]

Disagreement

The Palestinians' struggles received widespread support at Habitat, the conflict with Israel dominating international media reports and turning UN plenary sessions and committee meetings into a battlefield, as documented in the UN's official report and yearbook.[174] That Habitat would become a battlefield, exhibiting something like Foucault's "warlike clash between forces," was not unexpected.[175] Nor was it surprising that North American and Western European countries and their allies would rally around Israel as a country with a shared history and demographics and as a strategic foothold in the oil rich Middle East. Nevertheless, Palestinian struggles, aligned with the struggles of the G77, had become emblematic of and helped to reveal broader asymmetries and mechanisms of control between the wealthier industrialized and the developing states. The rhetoric of Spaceship Earth and planetary togetherness ceased to have traction. The aim of the United States and its allies, however, was not to produce overt or traditional states of domination—as the PLO noted, the colonial paradigm was out of favor—but to institute a governing apparatus and a set of rules or procedures through which to facilitate a neocolonial paradigm: in other words, to return to my title once more, a Third World game.[176] As we saw in the case of the Stockholm conference, it was through consensus decision making that powerful states pressured dissenting countries to compromise, compelling them to act against their own interests under the rubric of the good of humanity, a strategy effectively silencing or marginalizing alternative voices. Moreover, repeated claims that political issues were extraneous and the prescripting of debate by Strong, Ward, and others also served as attempts to structure the discourse and hence the platform of global governance and with it possible actions by its various players—to define the rules of the game. This is where the G77 came in, introducing amendments and resolutions to open up this framework to discussion and to redefine those rules from within.

To outline these initiatives briefly: Committee I debated the addition of a preamble to the Declaration of Principles recognizing the problem of "involuntary migration, politically, racially, and economically motivated relocation and expulsion of people from their national homeland." Moreover, alluding to UN Resolution 3379, Iraq sponsored an amendment indicating that it was "the duty of all governments to join the struggle against any form of colonialism, foreign aggression and occupation, domination, apartheid, and all forms of racism and racial discrimination referred to in the resolutions as adopted by the General Assembly of the United Nations." Another amendment referred to decades of ineffective resolutions, stating, "The establishment of settlements in territories occupied by force is illegal. It is condemned by the international community. However, action still remains to be taken against the establishment of such settlements."[177] Mysteriously, the Iraq amendment, which the United States and other Western countries protested, was eliminated from a draft forwarded to the plenary. The G77 responded by issuing a correction and a press release refuting claims that it was withdrawn. "One theory being voiced at Habitat," the *Vancouver Sun* reported, "is that the dropping of the amendment was merely a printer's error."[178] The declaration was adopted by the plenary with eighty-nine votes to fifteen, with ten abstentions. Those voting against it were Western European, North American, and British Commonwealth countries.

In Committee II, Cuba introduced an amendment on settlement planning that divided UN member states along similar lines. Stressing "respect for indigenous, cultural and social needs," it underscored the connection of settlement planning to human rights violations: "Settlement planning and implementation for the purpose of prolonging and consolidating occupation and subjugation in territories and lands acquired through coercion and intimidation must not be undertaken and must be condemned as a violation of United Nations principles and the Universal Declaration of Human Rights."[179]

With the committee unable to come to a consensus, the Canadian delegation brokered a compromise solution—sending the amendment to the plenary to avoid a split vote within the committee.[180] The amendment was approved seventy-seven to eight, with twenty abstentions. Media headlines read: "Israel Condemned: Vote Splits Habitat."[181]

In Committee III, Syria, on behalf of the Arab states and Uganda, proposed the following addition: "In all occupied territories, changes in the demographic composition or the transfer or uprooting of the native population, and the destruction of existing human settlements in these lands and/or the establishment of new settlements for intruders, is inadmissible. The heritage and national identity must be protected."[182]

Eliciting headlines such as "Dispute Erupts Again" and "Political Infighting Stalls Session,"[183] this amendment also was subjected to procedural irregularities, being shuffled from the committee to the plenary then bracketed from the first round to achieve a consensus vote on other paragraphs.[184] It was later adopted by sixty-nine votes to eight, with twenty-six abstentions, and as with the other decisions, it invoked angry reactions from Western countries and Israel.

Finally, Algeria and Egypt sponsored a resolution entitled "Living Conditions of the Palestinians in Occupied Territories." Expressing concern that Palestinians were "forced to abandon their indigenous homeland" and recognizing the "threat to international peace and security that will result from the willful destruction of their cultural habitat," it called upon a higher body, the General Assembly, to request that the secretary general prepare and submit a report.[185] Provoking anger from US delegates, who insisted that it was "not a matter either relevant or germane to the deliberations of this conference,"[186] and threats of noncompliance from Israel, it was forwarded to the plenary and adopted with seventy-three in favor and three against (Israel, Paraguay, and the United States), with forty-two abstentions, and was ratified in the following months.

Writing for *Audubon*, Philip Quigg recounted the drama with which concluding votes unfolded. "For two weeks the Palestine issue hung over the conference like smog," he lamented, "demanding an inordinate amount of delegates' time and energy. Until the end, it was hoped that the Muslim states (with Cuba riding shotgun) would rein in short of the brink, but they did not."[187] "In the final dramatic days and nights," he continued, referring to Urban Affairs Minister Barney Danson who presided over plenary sessions, and revealing further strategies to block the voting process,

> the Arabs and their allies completely outmaneuvered the officers of the conference and brought the plenary to the verge of chaos. Getting no

> help whatsoever from the secretariat's legal and parliamentary experts, the president of the conference, Canada's Barnett Danson, who is Jewish, finally made an arbitrary ruling for which he offered a highly emotional defense. Unable to make his ruling stick, he called a recess from which he did not return. When Father George K. Muhoho of Kenya, chairman of one of the committees, recalled the plenary to order, the simultaneous translation went amuck, a fire broke out in the ceiling, the lights went out, and the session was hastily adjourned.[188]

The plot was unsuccessful. Third World countries enjoyed a late night "sweeping victory," as one review put it, in "their bitter propaganda struggles against the developed world."[189]

Anxieties in the Western press were increasingly palpable. "A mob of Arab, African, Asian and Latin American countries and their bedfellows," the *Province* bemoaned with escalating rhetoric, "had their own agenda.... Their actions this week did create the grave danger that further alienation of the U.S. and other Western nations would make it that much harder for the West to co-operate in the desired solutions to human settlement problems."[190] The United States responded to being outmaneuvered by reiterating its displeasure and insisting on the extraneous nature of political discussions. "We came here for a serious purpose related to human settlements," US delegate Stanley Schiff declared, "We do not feel it would be appropriate for this conference to be addressing a political problem."[191] US delegates underscored earlier threats by Kissinger and others to undermine the UN. (It was implicit that US withdrawal would lead to that by other industrial countries.) The continuation of such tactics, Christian Herter threatened of the series inaugurated in Stockholm, "does not bode well for my country's support and participation in future U.N. conferences concerned with substantive global problems demanding international attention."[192] The departure from consensus was not in itself problematic. As Jon Tinker pointed out, "Most democratic institutions include majority voting among their procedures, so such a novelty can hardly be said to have sabotaged Habitat."[193] However, as evidence of disagreement, divided votes were both newsworthy and rendered evident the necessarily political nature of conference concerns. Human settlements, the amendments made clear, were not only the domain of ECOSOC or even UNEP.

Despite remaining a "nation-in-exile," at Habitat, Palestinians found an effective arena in which to state their claims, to render their struggles visible, and to articulate them with other political struggles and discourses. With intimate knowledge of the UN and its institutional apparatus—its procedures and communication formats, its language of resolutions and declarations, its relation to human rights and independence struggles, its hierarchies, its dependence on international media—the PLO identified a space within which to operate with a degree of liberty not afforded them in Israel or the Occupied Territories, even if they were aware of the unlikeliness of those discourses bridging back to facts on the ground in Palestine. Hence Al-Hout's haunting remark: "We Palestinians know that right which is not supported by freedom fighter guns will never be implemented."[194] But we should not underestimate the importance of interrupting dominant narratives, of opening up technocratic discourses to political questions, of the capacity of conflict and disagreements to displace or shift the conceptual terrain.

Living

In *The Question of Palestine*, Edward Said related the resilience of Palestinian identity not only to the "traumatic national encounter with Zionism," but to the common experience of "dispossession, exile and the absence of any territorial homeland."[195] He dated a Palestinian "national resurgence"—what he called "national reconstitution without a territory"—to the mid-1970s, noting the importance of the PLO as a representative body to this transformation. "The irony," he posited, "is that, as an expression of national self-determination, Palestinian activity was largely extra-territorial (without territorial sovereignty), and therefore always lived a sort of substitute life somewhere *other than* in Palestine."[196] Repeatedly condemning terrorist acts and the turn to violence, he expressed a wish "that there had been a less strident tone to Palestinian rhetoric about 'armed struggle,'" identifying it as symptomatic of the shift, also during the 1970s, from a liberation struggle to a national independence movement.[197] Critiquing airplane hijackings, assassinations, and other Palestinian "misadventures," he recalled: "that they occurred at all is not surprising; they are written, so to speak, into the scripts of every national movement (especially the Zionist one) trying to galvanize its people, attract attention, and impress itself on an inured world consciousness."[198] What remained unjust, he insisted, was the "invidious association" between acts of political terror and the entire Palestinian national movement.[199] On account of such misadventures, support for the Palestinian cause shifted dramatically soon after Habitat, with the June 27 hijacking of an Air France plane by the Popular Front for the Liberation of Palestine and the German urban guerilla group Revolutionäre Zellen (Revolutionary Cells) and the ensuing IDF raid of the Entebbe International Airport in Uganda where it landed, events to which we will return in the final chapter.

The first version of the UN General Assembly report *Living Conditions of the Palestinians in Occupied Territories* did not appear until October 1981, with earlier drafts repeatedly deemed not sufficiently analytical or not complete.[200] Confirming the *Palestine National Report* and drawing upon an extensive bibliography, including Said's *The Question of Palestine*, the report outlined the damaging effects of Israel's planning strategies: insecurity of land ownership due to appropriation and the ongoing destruction of houses and farms; the growing number of Jewish settlements and the diversion of resources such as water to serve them; infrastructure developed solely in the interest of Israel's military and security purposes; military governance by occupying forces and interference with local elections; forced economic and trade interdependence rendering Palestine subservient to Israel; and the deleterious effect of health and education policies. This litany of injustice also remains contemporary. Subsequent resolutions denounced Israel's lack of cooperation with the UN's designated group of experts (refusing access to East Jerusalem and the Occupied Territories), the ongoing expansion of settlements, and creation of conditions leading to further displacement and forced exodus of Palestinians.[201] In 1985, a new version appeared. Showing a heightened sense of insecurity and speaking of a second Palestinian exodus, it detailed the effects of "de-Palestinianization policies," the relocation of refugee camps, and the increasing violence of vigilante armed settlers and the "Terror against Terror" group's "aim of harassing, intimidating and terrorizing Palestinians and subsequently forcing them to abandon their domiciles."[202]

Architectures

Itself the scene of a complex, multiplayer logistical game, as I have tried to trace, Habitat situates us at the nexus of housing, life, alternative technologies, participatory planning, survival, and security, a biopolitical nexus already firmly entrenched in the narrative of Ward's *Human Settlements* and *The Home of Man* and in her claim, cited earlier, that the house forms "the starting point of all life in human settlements, in short, of human life itself." When Ward declared that "violence, apathy, aimless destruction, a busy police force and overcrowded penal institutions are all costs which need not be paid if citizens and their families feel, in the profoundest sense, that they are 'at home,'" she was not alluding to the Palestinian question, which remained bracketed as too political.[203] Instead, like the conference itself, she sought to bolster a development paradigm for managing rural-to-urban migration in the interests of global capital. In so doing, however, she made clear that the house was not seen as an isolated technology for shelter or defense against the environment. With the house and its integration into human settlements positioned as a central vehicle for development, Habitat (more than other UN world conferences) harbored the potential to render architects' expertise relevant, the house entering as the self-evident fulcrum for the discipline's contribution to urgent environmental and geopolitical questions.

As Hogan's reading of Habitat suggests, architects were not blind to the forces at work on this battleground. The editors of *Architectural Design* 's special post-Habitat issue also announced, "By all accounts, it was the official delegates from the Third World who called the tune at the UN Habitat Conference." Yet it was also evident that a structural reversal of power was unlikely. After suggesting that "the notion that the proceeds of all-out capitalist growth will 'trickle down' to the poorest sections of society has been discredited," the editors pointed to a call to order: "in a time of global economic recession, the haves—led by the multi-national corporations—are tightening their grip on the world resources they control."[204]

With multinational corporations and wealthier countries having long benefitted from structural inequities and access to resources, it is not difficult to fathom why they would work hard behind the scenes to maintain their strategic advantage, inventing new narratives of insecurity and techniques through which to govern. Architects' expertise—including once-utopian dreams of flexibility, open-endedness, recycling, and environmental care—became firmly inscribed within the protocols of these Third World games.

Consequently, we turn now to examine an exhibition and competition for self-help housing schemes launched for Habitat with the ambition to inscribe architecture firmly within and contribute to this development apparatus and its governing mandates. We find architects seeking out roles as designers alongside economists, planners, engineers, statisticians, politicians, and other technocrats hoping to harness the "ingenuity" of squatters and manage the precarious lives of the urban poor in what Turner called "uncontrolled urban settlements," not just in the name of helping people, but in the name of profit and security.[205] As we will see, management of the built environment and of the populations housed therein had not entirely escaped the domain of the architect.

CHAPTER SIX

"Cruel Habitats"

> One thing, it's true, hasn't changed—capitalism still keeps three quarters of humanity in extreme poverty, too poor to have debts and too numerous to be confined: control will have to deal not only with vanishing frontiers, but with mushrooming shantytowns and ghettos.
> —Gilles Deleuze, "Postscript on Control Societies," 1990

"Visitors to *Habitat: Toward Shelter* will see an important event in world architecture," proclaimed Frederick Gutheim of an exhibition at the Vancouver Art Gallery about self-help strategies in squatter settlements.[1] The principal attractions of the show were prize-winning and other notable entries from the International Design Competition for the Urban Environment of Developing Countries Focused on Manila. The competition was sponsored by the recently formed International Architectural Foundation of New York (IAF) on the occasion of Habitat: The United Nations Conference on Human Settlements. The exhibition's motto read: "Help Make a World Where Hope Makes Sense." Paraphrasing the widely cited UN statistic that squatter settlements "now comprise nearly half of the population of Third World Cities" and channeling the fear of growing insecurity born of demographic shifts as the rural poor migrated to urban slums, Gutheim proudly announced, "Here was a problem to which design could contribute solutions and that would give a new meaning to architecture."[2]

Demonstrating the role that architecture and design played or might play in the complex set of urban and territorial questions informing Habitat was the avowed motivation for the competition and its reformatting as an exhibition. Put forward as professional contributions to the UN conference and as expressions of support for its aims while knowingly benefitting from the expansive worldwide publicity and crowds who would come to Vancouver, both goals were also symptomatic of the degree to which architecture was largely a marginal concern for the UN. What, after all, could architecture do in the face of a humanitarian emergency born of millions of destitute persons "swarming" into cities in the Global South and bringing with them few resources? How could the discipline help to manage or contain such a destabilizing force? If, Gutheim speculated, the IAF could succeed in helping to shift the valence of architecture's contribution to housing and cities in developing countries, if it could demonstrate what "world architecture" might look like or what architecture could "mean" at a "world conference," perhaps the profession could find new relevance, even new work, within the rapidly globalizing world of the 1970s.

It was not that Western architects had previously failed to pay attention to the problem of "shelter" and informal settlements in the developing world or to the rapid urbanization of the rural poor and the environmental problems that ensued. Indeed, one only had to look at major European and North American magazines such as *Architectural Design*, *Casabella*, *L'Architecture d'Aujourd'hui*, and *Progressive Architecture* to see that research into squatter settlements, alternative and appropriate technologies, do-it-yourself and participatory strategies, environmental management, and recycling had proliferated over a number of years and in some cases decades. Yet if one could point to the catalytic effect upon architectural discourse of the work of CIAM-Alger in Algeria and of John F. C. Turner in Peru as far back as the 1950s or to the work of Martin Pawley in Chile, Yona Friedman in Africa and the Middle East, the Projecto Experimental de Vivienda (PREVI) competition in Peru, and "progressive" magazines such as *Architectural Design* or *The Whole Earth Catalog* in the 1960s and early 1970s, among many other examples, such practices remained peripheral, or at least alternative, within the profession as such.[3] But in the context of Habitat, those discourses and strategies joined technocratic counterparts (such as Otto Königsberger's work in India/Pakistan and the Philippines or Constantin Doxiadis's Ekistics) to become the highly visible talk of policy makers, developmentalist economists, and leaders of international institutions seeking new tools of global governance. As *New York Times* critic Paul Goldberger reported under the title "Radical

Planners Now Mainstream," at Habitat, such ideas "for the first time were given official government sanction on an international basis."[4]

The question of shelter, that is, appeared at the center of international political debate, or at least it was the UN's hope that it might. At stake for architects, then, was how to articulate the discipline's expertise and techniques with those political and regulatory apparatuses geared toward managing to productive ends Third World populations and the environments in which they lived. That is, how and to what ends could architecture interface with relevant institutional mandates, legal protocols, economic and technical paradigms, forms of data collection and analysis, territorial and geopolitical strategies, and discursive or media practices at work within this biopolitical apparatus?

Habitat: Toward Shelter and the self-help competition it displayed sought to answer such questions in a strategic manner for the profession, and in retrospect, they stand as telling attempts by the discipline's mainstream to claim a space for itself within the institutional structure of the UN in the 1970s and with it an expanding global client base of Third World governments. While the Union Internationale des Architects (UIA) proposed an updated "Charter of Habitat," defensively calling for an increased role for the aesthetic dimension of architecture, the IAF asked how, in response to emergency housing conditions, architecture could tend *toward* shelter, as the title of the exhibition suggested.[5] Moreover, the competition, exhibition, and accompanying publication, a special issue of *Architectural Record*, served a particular role at Habitat, one that NGOs were increasingly coming to play: that of broadcasting the emergency at hand, quite literally helping to "mobilize shame" and pressure governments to act, albeit with a functional twist.[6] As a medium slightly more legible or visibly compelling than endless statistical tables and data and seemingly more action oriented than photojournalism, architectural designs served as vehicles to capture and mobilize the public imagination. They projected not questions, but "solutions" to a humanitarian crisis that seemed poised to threaten world stability, solutions that avowedly would not be able to solve the problem, but rather would lend physical support to the approach being advanced by the UN's Second Development Decade.[7] Even as a media strategy, architecture offered a more material image of change. It was in this mediatic reflection and refraction of growing evidence of environmental injustice that Gutheim and his colleagues recognized an opportunity for architecture.

However, as Gutheim and his associates soon discovered, giving new meaning to architecture by staging an encounter with Third World cities for a UN conference was not quite as easy as promoting technical and semantic or even economic solutions to sheltering the urban poor. And as we will see, it is with the eruption once again of a political space within an ostensibly neutral technical or professional one that this story begins to get interesting. No one, not even Manila's poorest citizens, even those deprived of almost all rights and then living under martial law, likes to be evicted from their shelter under the promise of hope (to recall the exhibition's motto), no matter how precarious a life their current environment might seem to sustain. In what follows, I want to outline briefly the institutional situation and trace the ensuing resistance, and with it the emerging voices and claims, as architects attempted to offer their expertise, designing "solutions" to the humanitarian crisis that was the subject of Habitat. My point is not that architecture in its many facets—aesthetic, programmatic, discursive, institutional, or even technological—was irrelevant to the concerns of the conference and vice versa. Rather, the cynical relation of the exhibition to the political machinations informing the UN's promotion of development policies—those being advanced by the World Bank and its major shareholder, the United States—helps to render visible the contours of emerging techniques of power at play.

Experts

In May 1973, to recall, the executive director of the United Nations Environment Programme (UNEP), Maurice Strong, convened a seminar of experts chaired by Barbara Ward. It included Senator Helena Benitez of the Philippines, who had played an important role in initiating the Habitat conference four years earlier in Stockholm.[8] Benitez was appointed president of the Preparatory Planning Group in September, and it was in this context that the idea for the competition and for the founding of the IAF jointly emerged. Blake Hughes, owner of *Architectural Record*, regarded as problematic the lack of opportunities for architects at the UN and founded the IAF as a not-for-profit corporation to fill the perceived gap in architectural agencies associated with the institution. (If architects played a major role in resettling war-torn Europe after World War II, surely, it was hoped, they could play a larger role in the UN's development initiatives in the Third World.) The IAF received support from *Architectural Record* and its European partner in this venture, *L'Architecture d'Aujourd'hui*, as well as from American corporate architecture firms (The Architects Collaborative, Skidmore Owings and Merrill, and Harrison and Abramovitz), architectural foundations such the Graham Foundation, industrial and corporate giants, including Owens-Corning Fiberglass and Hyatt International Corporations, and the Rockefeller and Ford Foundations.[9] Benitez worked to ensure the choice of Manila as the competition site and to secure the support of her government, including a USD $100,000 commitment.[10]

Hughes commissioned Gutheim's recently formed consulting firm—Gutheim/Seelig/Erickson—to research and write the competition brief, administer judging, and organize the exhibition. Gutheim was a Washington, DC-based consultant and architecture critic. (In 1972, he contributed *A World of Cities* to Strong's Stockholm Conference series, Man's Home, small booklets funded by the Standard Oil Company of New Jersey with the hilarious caveat: "It is, of course, understood that the funding provided should not be interpreted as an endorsement of the views presented.")[11] Having trained at the Brookings Institute, Gutheim served as a UN housing and planning consultant and also listed as clients the Executive Office of the President of the United States and the Ford Foundation.[12] In 1971, he joined with Israeli architect and planner Michael Y. Seelig—who acted as project director for the competition—and prominent Vancouver architect Arthur Erickson.[13] Erickson was responsible for another manifestly architectural contribution to Habitat: a spectacular media and information center pavilion. Controversial on account of its cost, the pavilion was composed of hyperbolic paraboloid modules fabricated from cardboard tubes, to which thousands of school children applied papier-mâché from recycled newspapers and painted scenes. Finally, as required by professional bodies, the competition was administered through the UIA, a UN-accredited NGO, establishing guidelines and protocols that ensured that architects' labor would not be exploited.[14]

The competition and *Habitat: Toward Shelter* have left few traces in subsequent architectural debates beyond publications by the organizers. Competition results were presented in *Architectural Record* in May 1976, and Seelig published a book-length account as *The Architecture of Self-Help Communities*. Yet Gutheim was not mistaken in imagining the initiative to mark "an important event in world architecture." "The constant stream of information about the conference in newspapers around the world," Seelig recalled, "helped engender the general public's interest in the subject of urbanization and sustained the interest of the architects and planners who were actively responding to the competition program."[15] Architects in fact responded in unprecedented numbers—2,531 registrations from sixty-eight countries, with 476 final submissions from forty-six countries—which to the organizers ensured its "world character."[16] "While such problems exist in Latin America, Africa and the Near East," Gutheim proclaimed, justifying the site, "it is Asia which presents the most appalling spectacle of on-rushing urbanization and human misery in the homeless millions that surround almost every large city."[17] Furthermore, it was "the willingness of the government of the Philippines to support the competition, to identify a specific site, and to guarantee to build the winning design that caused the selection of the competition site at Dagat-Dagatan."[18] Competitors were asked to offer solutions for resettling residents from the Tondo Foreshore in Manila to an area a few miles north, known as Dagat-Dagatan, on land being reclaimed from fish ponds that the government claimed were little used. The Tondo Foreshore was home to approximately one hundred and seventy thousand people living on 184 hectares that the Marcos government wanted to develop through foreign investment as industrial fisheries and a shipping port.

Crisis and Opportunity

Although the fact was nowhere mentioned in the competition brief or exhibition material, the Philippines had been under martial law since September 1972, when President Ferdinand Marcos, facing the end of his second and final term as president, signed Proclamation 1081, suspending civil and political rights and placing the country under military rule in the name of national security and protecting democracy, with the avowed agenda of stimulating national economic development through foreign investment. Having effectively abolished habeas corpus the previous year, Philippine citizens, after decades of democracy, were denied rights afforded in their constitution, such as freedom of the press, free elections, freedom of speech, the ability to strike, the right to leave and return to the country, and more, with any sign of dissidence violently crushed as a threat to the state.[19] Having locked up his political opponents (including members of the press), and having taken ownership of the media, Marcos, as Bernard Wideman recalled, "told a nationwide radio and TV audience that the state was 'endangered by violent overthrow.' The imminent dangers which he cited were the communist insurgency in the north, and the Muslim insurgency in the south."[20] The US-trained Philippine military soon turned to the mass detention of rural insurgents and "launched campaigns in several provinces against the rebels—including the use of Vietnam style 'relocation' of villages—claiming considerable success."[21] By the mid-1970s, in the wake of the US-led war in Vietnam, the government's security concerns had shifted from suppressing armed rebellion by rural peasants fighting for economic justice, including minority groups and the Maoist New People's Army, to threats of urban instability. It was on the basis of counterinsurgency needs that Marcos argued successfully for an enormous increase in US military aid, multiplying troops and equipment. As many recognized, his brutal counterinsurgency strategies operated in the interest of making the country safe for foreign investment and hence in the national interest of the United States. Quelling insurgencies was good for business. Far from questioning evidence of massive human rights violations, under the dual guise of humanitarian aid and security, both the United States and the World Bank significantly increased aid after the 1972 declaration.[22]

As reported in *Architectural Record*, the Tondo Foreshore was reclaimed in the early 1940s, but delays in construction led to its takeover by squatters. "Through strong community organization, the Tondo squatters have developed a degree of political power, and have been difficult to dislodge," the *Record* explained. "To help solve this problem, the adjacent... Dagat-Dagatan site is being planned to rehouse them."[23] With no guarantee of secure land tenure for displaced residents or of adequate financial support for housing, architects were quite literally being asked to serve as a tool of globalization: under the rubric of humanitarian aid and security, they were to assist in the government's forced dispossession and displacement of the urban poor. And they were to do so in order to assist investment opportunities for multinational corporations and local

elites. This was not a unique story: the violent process of rendering not only the Philippines, but many developing countries safe for the expansion of "free market" capitalism was the "world" condition put into effect by the UN and its affiliated institutions such as the World Bank, itself the largest sponsor of the Dagat-Dagatan project, and an institution to which we will return.

The Philippine government's development plans involved moving a little more than half the current residents to the 430-hectare (1062-acre) relocation site. Within this, a 5-hectare portion was designated as the competition site. (Other areas were designated for World Bank "sites and services" initiatives and a government demonstration project.)[24] Designers were invited to offer a prototypical solution for a "new community" of 3,500 people, corresponding to the social and political unit called a *barangay*; they were given specifications to provide drawings ranging from the scale of the overall development area to individual dwellings and rooms. The brief repeatedly stressed the extremely low income levels of the community, the low-tech nature of an appropriate low-rise development, the lack of government resources anticipated for the project, and the need for innovative, affordable, and ecologically sound environmental systems, including waste disposal and energy production. "The housing units proposed in this competition," stated the brief, mirroring World Bank development policy, "must be applicable to a self-help program, one in which the entire community can be organized to help families build their own homes and the needed supporting services."[25] Responsibility, that is, had to be displaced from governments to squatters. As Gutheim put it, noting the centrality of unpaid labor: "Countries of the developing world may be poor in many respects but they are rich in manpower. To translate this resource into improved housing through self-help is the challenge the competition provided."[26]

Low-cost, industrially produced mass housing remained a much-celebrated figure of high modernism's *promesse du bonheur*, of architecture's utopian vocation within modernity. But Habitat was focused on a different population and, we might say, on a transformed modernity, raising paradoxes for such a narrative. The question here was not ensuring the happiness of slum dwellers—that was considered beyond the economic means of governments—but simply

Figures 6.1 & 6.2 Shanties in Tondo, Manila, c. 1976 (courtesy Vancouver Art Gallery Archives).

providing conditions for their basic subsistence. Foucault characterized the paradigm of liberal governance as ensuring not only that citizens would not die in great numbers, but that they would go from living to more than just living. Although this paradigm continued to inform the lives of many in both the industrial and developing world, with housing for the very poorest, we find ourselves faced with a more troubling situation. This reduced level of felicity was still to be, in Foucault's words, "constituted into state utility."[27] However, the goal was not to produce a growing middle class, or even a working class as such, but to manage a sector of the population who would remain "just living" on the brink of disaster. It was a carefully calibrated equation: offering just enough aid to pacify and allow squatters to function as productive bodies in the development process while maintaining their insecurity and hence their availability as extremely low-cost labor to attract foreign investment. In line with Ward and the World Bank, Gutheim posited: "Instead of deploring the squattaments, governments increasingly see them as an opportunity for social progress and urban development."[28]

For architects to perform this maneuver of care and its suspension, new concepts and expertise were needed: Architects had to retool, be reeducated. Here is where the competition came in. As Seelig explained, architectural competitions are "a traditional and accepted medium for educating architects and often for reorienting their professional practices."[29] In addition to providing architects a means of contributing to and bringing attention to Habitat through the project in Manila, the competition hoped to transform architects' terms of reference, advancing low-tech, minimum-cost regulatory strategies for self-help housing in the developing world. These, in turn, helped to legitimize squatter settlements, referred to by Gutheim as "once the 'untouchables' of the housing world."[30] Finally, according to Hughes, providing the financial incentives of prize money ($35,000 for the winning entry) and even the opportunity to build, the competition would "take this problem out of the realm of talk and into accomplishment."[31]

The organizers engaged social-science consultants to provide details concerning traditional rural nipa palm huts, thatched with the fonds of *Nypa fruticans*, with *silongs* (downstairs spaces), *silids* (dressing or private rooms) and *sala* (living rooms) furnished with *papag* (bamboo beds) and *dulang* (low wooden dining tables), the use of scavenged materials for squatter housing (flattened-out oil drums, rusty galvanized iron sheets, tin billboards from election campaigns), the condition of intense urban poverty, the stench of toilets in the shantytown and its lack of infrastructure (ten families sharing one tap, schools on three shifts with forty students per class), informal economies, forms of sociability, and political organizations in squatter communities. The brief also included a new vocabulary of urban terms and equipment: *barangay*, *purok* (ward), *sari-sari* (sundry or corner) store, *tulungan* (assistance or support) center, *talipapa* (local market), *suki* (regular customer), Jeepney, as well as a heroic story of day-to-day survival against all odds written by social scientist Aprodicio Laquian, "A Typical Day in the Life of the Cruz Family." "Community members are usually highly organized," competition registrants were warned, indicating possibility for resistance. "In Tondo, one may even say they are 'over-organized'—a study in 1968 identified no less than 29 organizations and associations in a community of 2,000 people."[32]

Armed with such information and a new vocabulary, teams of architects, most having never set foot in Manila, designed strategies for displacing the Tondo residents. A little social science and a few words in Tagalog were understood to go a long way as a script in the hands of an architect. It was not mentioned, for instance, that the precolonial term *barangay*, which once referred to a village or town, was only recently appropriated by the Marcos administration to replace the Spanish term *barrio* as a designation for a manageable scale of urban political organization. That the country was then under martial law, to reiterate, did not concern the IAF. After all, it was the suspension of democratic rights in the name of suppressing insurgencies and encouraging foreign investment that made it possible, safe, and even profitable for "world" architects to operate in the Philippines.

In early February 1976, the jury—Balkrishna Doshi, Eric Lyons, Moshe Safdie (a Vancouver Symposium member), Mildred Schmertz, William Whitfield, Takamasa Yosizaka, and Philippine General Gaudencio Tobias—convened in Vancouver. Tobias was the representative of the Philippine government's executive agency, the Tondo Foreshore Redevelopment Authority, who engineered preclusion of Tondo residents from participation in discussions with the World Bank.[33] Advisers included Blake, Gutheim, Seelig, and

Erikson, along with Laquian and Teresita Vicera, presented as a resident of Tondo.

With Laquian, then associate director of the International Development Research Center (IDRC) in Ottawa, we find ourselves again at the heart of developmentalist ideology. According to his personal narrative, his family escaped the violence of a Communist insurgency (the Huk Rebellion) in a small village to become squatters in Manila. After receiving a degree in public administration from the University of the Philippines, he received grants from the Asia, Rockefeller, and Ford Foundations to undertake urban studies at MIT, graduating with a PhD in political science supervised by Lucian W. Pye and dedicated to the role of urbanization in national development.[34]

The jury awarded first prize to New Zealand architect Ian Athfield.[35] Athfield's project was considered notable for two reasons: first, he proposed that the limited public funding be dedicated not to housing as such, but to providing each *barangay* with the means to construct a "working periphery," a continuous, linear, perimeter-wall-like structure to house nonpolluting light industry, workshops, small stores, a building cooperative, and community energy centers dedicated to alternative energy technologies and recycling, on top of which would be community gardens for growing vegetables. A gesture toward autonomy, this structure was intended both to enhance employment opportunities in the neighborhood and to give identity to individual communities. In the Philippines, Athfield explained, walls had served both as strong defining elements and as security mechanisms since Spanish colonial times.[36] Few commentators noted the wall's potential security functions from the perspective of the state, but we could imagine Tobias being pleased: there is nothing like walling in rowdy protestors to contain insurrectionary threats or regulate movement. Ian Hogan celebrated Athfield's project in *Architectural Design*, dismissing such concerns. "The idea of inclosing groups of potentially militant residents behind walls—given the political repression in the Philippines—created endless paranoia among critics of the scheme at Habitat," he recalled.[37] The proposal

Figures 6.3 & 6.4 Ian Athfield in front of his model at the exhibition *Habitat: Toward Shelter*, Vancouver Art Gallery, June 1976 (Ross Kenward / *The Province*); Ian Athfield, model in *Habitat: Toward Shelter*, exhibition at the Vancouver Art Gallery, May 31–July 4, 1976 (courtesy Vancouver Art Gallery Archives).

nevertheless resonates in an ambiguous zone between housing and prison camps, the specter of which haunted the project.

Second, desublimating the modern vernacular hybrid aesthetic implied by the brief, Athfield proposed that houses adopt the logic of rural nipa huts, but employ new techniques of fabrication, in this case, using coconut palm as a material, not the nipa palm, and not as thatching, but as logs or as by-products in the form of prefabricated panels, insulating board, plaster, and chip-based concrete blocks. These materials would be prepared in the working perimeter.[38] "The most interesting solution to the problem of 'squatter settlements' so far proposed to Habitat," professed architectural critic Wolf von Eckardt for the *Washington Post*, "are do-it-yourself houses made of coconut palms."[39] The architect's role in this self-help scheme would be reduced to controlling the distribution of materials, beginning with giving the squatters four poles and a choice of roof. Athfield prepared whimsical drawings suggesting a certain picturesque variety that might ensue from the squatters completing their houses within this basic module. Regulated uniformity of materials was important to him as a means of ensuring a coherent aesthetic, but there were aspects over which he hoped to cede responsibility. Sporting a long beard and late-hippie look, Athfield, we learn, "wants to leave the politics of the scheme to a Philippine architect—whether the squatters will own their houses through contributed labor, rent equity or some degree of subsidy. What this young blue-jeaned man wants to do is live on the site and work alongside the squatters with a saw and hammer."[40]

Athfield, like most competitors, had never been to Manila; indeed, he had never left New Zealand until traveling to Vancouver for Habitat. As reported by Mary Mountier, he "discovered exactly where the Philippines lay in relation to the rest of the Pacific" only after the results were announced. Yet his expertise regarding squatters' ways of life was widely celebrated. As Schmertz summed up in *Ekistics*, "Athfield's scheme won the competition because, of all the submissions, his exhibited the greatest respect and understanding of the culture, tradition, humanity and needs of the Philippine urban migrant. The most significant achievements of the IAF competition," she added, indicating a skewed priority, "were creating an opportunity for the hitherto unknown Athfield and awarding him first prize."[41] Athfield himself believed that the jury mistook him for a Philippine architect.[42] When Goldberger asked how he had "come to understand the needs of the Philippines so well," he responded by suggesting that he sought out what was "meaningful," offering "physical things to symbolize" what was familiar to them.[43] Recognizing connections to the rising postmodern paradigm, Goldberger likened Athfield's aesthetic to the populist work of Charles Moore, Hardy Holzman Pfeiffer Associates, and Venturi and Rauch. Here was an aesthetic that moved away from the abstraction of modernism and even the late modern corporate aesthetic of the competition's architectural sponsors toward the embrace of populist semantic tropes assumed to provide "meaning."

Athfield enjoyed enormous press coverage and was considered by the IAF to be a media asset; he was widely reported to be likeable, affable, and shy; his alternative dressing style and refusal of corporate ambitions were frequently commented upon, the fact that he just completed a building for the New Zealand Army less so. Goldberger described him as "obviously uncomfortable in the three-piece suit he had just put on to meet Imelda Marcos."[44] William Marlin likened him to Clym Yeobright from Thomas Hardy's *The Return of the Native* and in turn to "an inhabitant of Samuel Butler's fictional agrarian community Erewhon," suggesting that it was "almost as if he had taken his stylistic tenets from Hardy or Butler rather than from the 'masters' of modern architecture."[45] "One suspects," he concluded—ambiguously, given its dystopian undercurrent—"that Erewhon has finally found an architectural interpretation, and that it wasn't "nowhere' spelled sort of backward, after all." Marlin also told the story of Athfield being refused entry to New York's Yale Club on account of his "wide-brimmed leather hat, open shirt, and love beads." Why he sought entry to the Yale Club was not raised.

For Athfield, the Tondo slums provided a utopian condition for architectural work: as Mountier recalled, "One of the joys of the competition for Athfield was the complete absence of official codes and zoning: no fire, earthquake, roading or building regulations, which are the bane of his life in New Zealand."[46] Although, under martial law, the entire country had been declared under a state of emergency, the arbitrariness of the suspension of law and the protection it might afford citizens was felt particularly brutally in such shantytowns. Unlike the outlaw territory dreamed of by the Open Landers, where regulations were refused as harboring biopolitical mechanisms of control, in Dagat-Dagatan, no such agency or self-determination was afforded the resident; architects could operate at once beyond the law and in a register servicing global biopolitical regulation.

Hearts and Minds

Once the competition results were in, Gutheim/Seelig/Erickson and the curators at the Vancouver Art Gallery set about preparing the exhibition. As late as February 1976, there was still no consensus on a title. The working title, *The Right to Build*, invoked the language of rights, subtly transforming Article 25 (1) of the United Nations Universal Declaration of Human Rights from a right to the provision of housing, as provided by a government to its citizens, to that of building, an act to do oneself.[47] In a country where rights had been suspended by decree, the irony could not have been more pointed. Hughes indicated the IAF's displeasure, noting that the title "has implications that are inappropriate to what we are trying to do." He suggested instead *Building a Better World*, behind which architects could more easily rally for resettlement.[48] This would also be less likely to cause alarm among governments, particularly the government of the Philippines, which were not interested in expanding the rights of the urban poor. Far from seeking to empower squatters, especially already politicized ones, the underlying goal was development. While the rhetoric had to attend to improving the life of the poor—no doubt the sentiment under which many architects signed up for the competition—the message to governments was that support was available to provide minimal shelter to the low-cost labor pools needed for industrial development. Architecture offered the smiling face of this paradigm.

An interim report detailed a call to shift attention from political considerations to aesthetic ones. "Although the title, 'The Right to Build,' has a socio-political ring," it read, "the Vancouver Art Gallery exhibition would attempt to demonstrate that, given opportunity, encouragement and assistance, the poor and humble of the world are capable of expressing the fulfillment of the intrinsic need for shelter as a vigorous art form."[49] Beyond an ideology of innate creativity, such stress on aesthetics speaks to the uncomfortable fit of architecture in an art institution, also registering an anxiety that the aesthetic dimension of architects' work might fall victim to technocratic initiatives, a concern of the UIA and also expressed in an Iranian contribution to the Vancouver Habitat conference, *The Habitat Bill of Rights*. Another suggested title, *There Is a Solution*, was rejected by Seelig, who "justifiably objected to the word 'solution' because of its close association with Nazism."[50]

Alvin Balkind, chief curator at the gallery, explained that the question they now faced was "to edit, make decisions, and take responsibility for translating the competition project into a visual form." Hughes added of their media strategy that the task was "similar to producing the magazine; material has to be transformed into another medium."[51] Moreover, the plan was to supplement documents from the competition to dramatic effect, hoping "to sell information to the people" so that the show might "trigger [a] 'response mechanism'—'you can do it yourself.'" With unapologetic paternalism, Gutheim introduced the need to "present indigenous methods of building by primitive peoples; for instance present a Tondo community (Manila) to show how a community provides all its own necessary services."[52] This abdication of government responsibility was the key message he hoped to get across. That his strategic agenda extended beyond the plight of Tondo to align with US foreign policy quickly became manifest. As noted in the minutes, he "made an impassioned plea for [the] exhibit to change hearts and minds of architects, and, in turn, change the public attitude toward architecture."[53]

The rhetoric of hearts and minds had a long and at times troubled affiliation with counterinsurgency or counterrevolutionary campaigns, including struggles against colonial rule and neocolonial incursions. Although originating earlier, its contemporary usage is commonly dated to British counterinsurgency strategy during the Malayan Emergency in 1952. Conceived as well-intentioned means of avoiding extended warfare and hence bloodshed by winning hearts and minds through humanitarian aid or hope, this rhetoric was often tragically and violently contradicted by military action on the ground. Its well-known use by figures from John F. Kennedy regarding Latin America to Lyndon Johnson regarding Vietnam would not have been lost on Gutheim, especially in the wake of Peter Davis's searing 1974 documentary film on US involvement in Vietnam, *Hearts and Minds*.[54] Among the most devastating scenes in the film was General Westmoreland's claim that Asians place little value on human life. With the Philippine government then a testing ground for implementing urban counterinsurgency strategies, aided by the United States, Gutheim's mobilization of this rhetoric (seemingly without irony) to institute developmentalist aid reminds us once again, all too vividly, of Foucault's famous inversion of Clausewitz: policy or politics is warfare by other means.[55]

Open For Business

Habitat: Toward Shelter opened to great fanfare on May 30, on the eve of the official UN conference. Two thousand people attended the gala event.[56] As Schmertz reported of its successful engagement with the wider conference, a "private opening and dinner honoring Athfield was held for the leading dignitaries at the Habitat Conference."[57] Sited immediately opposite Erickson's Media Information Center and close to the Queen Elizabeth Theater and other Habitat venues, the exhibition drew sixteen thousand visitors during the period of the conference.[58] Visitors to the show learned that while it was "not possible for governments to construct and finance the housing for the massive numbers of squatters," this was not the end of the story, for "hope exists when people are given the opportunity to help themselves."[59] That Athfield subscribed to this bootstrapping logic was recorded in the press. "This is a project to be achieved with a great sense of pride over a period of time," he told the *Vancouver Sun*. "If you're given everything at once, you don't respect what has happened."[60]

Entering *Habitat: Toward Shelter*, the visitor was directed through preliminary exhibits before arriving at competition entries, providing a crafted narrative to naturalize the self-help paradigm and with it, we might say, the structural underdevelopment and inequity inherent in globalization. Upon entering, they were told, "architects around the world respond to Tondo's willingness to help itself."[61] After background information, visitors were presented with twenty-six large-format color photographs of vernacular architecture shot by Arthur Erickson and described as "'architecture without architects'—indigenous housing in underdeveloped countries."[62] The reference, of course, was to Bernard Rudofsky's 1964 exhibition, *Architecture without Architects*, which helped popularize the topic.[63] As the exhibition brochure proclaimed, "throughout history human society around the world has exhibited the capacity of people to create their own forms of shelter, appropriate to the environment, beautiful and serviceable." There was nothing like highly photogenic and visually seductive architectural vernaculars uprooted from their historical context to get this cynical message across: poor people can help themselves, and it can be aesthetically appealing, too.

Even if Tondo residents chose to identify with aspects of their traditional rural cultures, such forms of life were no longer open to them. This was not lost on the organizers, who neatly folded forces of modernization into their narrative. What the brochure cast as an *innate* "capacity of people for self-help" was now enhanced through research, they argued, in the service of an equally picturesque architectural aesthetic during "the rush for modernization" in the Third World.

> Only over long spans of centuries have the great building traditions that created the stone *trulli* of Alberobello or the *yurts* of the Mongolian nomads been able to express the collective wisdom. Now research can accelerate this slow process of evolution, and adapt such building techniques to the more immediate situation of contemporary urban communities. In many places throughout the world, new materials and tools have proliferated, do-it-yourself movements have sprung up, and a highly sophisticated search for an alternative architecture is well advanced. Architects are learning from the Cone of Cappadocia, the cave-land of central Turkey, and the North American Hopi Indians—as well as from Las Vegas. The time has come to apply this understanding to cities of the developing world.[64]

That Western architects could "learn from" vernacular examples as a means of tempering the shock of modernization dated at least back to the nineteenth century.[65] But more proximate to our concerns and informing the rhetoric of tools, do-it-yourselfism and "alternative" architecture were the new bibles of alternative lifestyles, such as Stewart Brand's *Whole Earth Catalog* and its offshoots in Lloyd Kahn's *Domebook* and *Shelter*, along with *Architectural Design* and other such publications. Across these pages, as noted in previous chapters, we find yurts, trulli, and other indigenous dwellings seamlessly associated with R. Buckminster Fuller's geodesic domes, plastics, cybernetics, and computerization. Equally symptomatic here, in addition to *Architecture without Architects*, is the invocation of Robert Venturi, Denise Scott-Brown, and Steven Izenour's legendary 1972

Figure 6.5 Installation view of *Habitat: Toward Shelter,* exhibition at the Vancouver Art Gallery, May 31–July 4, 1976. Section showing photographs of vernacular architecture by Arthur Erickson (courtesy Vancouver Art Gallery Archives).

Figure 6.6 Installation view of *Habitat: Toward Shelter,* exhibition at the Vancouver Art Gallery, May 31–July 4, 1976. Model in foreground by second prize winners, Mikiro Takagi, Kunihiko Hayakawa, Keiichiro Takashasi (courtesy Vancouver Art Gallery Archives).

book, *Learning from Las Vegas*, a widely cited embrace of the vernacular, inviting architects to celebrate unselfconscious manifestations of American capitalism. Why, we might ask, had the time come "to apply this understanding to cities of the developing world"?

Following Erickson's photographs were two slide shows presenting the problem of squatter settlements—*Squatters: A World Wide Problem* and *A Poor Squatter Settlement Today, a Housing Community Built by and for Squatters Tomorrow.* The former offered a panorama of rapid urbanization across the developing world—their ubiquity implying that squatter settlements were immanent or natural to the culture of the urban poor—the latter focused on the Tondo Foreshore as a "prototypical" example. With a little help from architects, the framing suggested, squatter settlements, too, might take on aesthetic qualities to become a new form of self-organizing urbanism from below. How it might do so was answered in the following galleries displaying world architecture. Nowhere in this material was the plight of Tondo squatters contextualized with respect to the legacy of colonialism, warfare, martial law, or globalization. But these images of shantytowns provided something close to the lesson of Las Vegas's celebration of capitalism, now applied to the developing world.

The main north gallery depicted "hope for the future" as demonstrated through self-help proposals generated by the IAF competition. Visitors were presented with photographic blowups of drawings for the three prize-winning designs and the four honorable mentions, along with details from other selected entries. Three scale models were constructed for the show: two by Athfield and one by the second-prize winner, the Takagi Design Team from Tokyo.[66] Browsing the galleries, visitors saw variegated attempts to regulate and regularize the "spontaneous" aesthetic and organizational logic of shantytowns within a process-oriented, self-help approach. Architects recognized that their task was not just to reflect extant culture, but productively to shift it, even rescript it, in response to contemporary forces. From systems-based modules of prefabricated panels, kits of parts using precast frames, and arcades aiming to serve as legible spines onto which informal structures could attach, to Yona Friedman's more enigmatic proposal for a giant open "self-design" megastructure with an "umbrella" roof and "habitacles" demarcated by matting, architecture was very much on display. Many projects cited rural nipa huts or adopted other vernacular tropes, and experimental environmental technologies were pervasive. A few projects foregrounded circulation infrastructure, such as roads or canals, and formal scaling techniques were tested repeatedly, including giant courtyard-house typologies. Reflecting the impact of recent urban theory, such as the work of Kevin Lynch and György Kepes at MIT, most offered strategies to produce cluster arrangements or patterns that would bring legible order to the environment, with the potential for achieving diversity or variation within a repetitious or modular framework being a repeated concern.[67] Some simply replicated the planning of suburban America. Only one departed dramatically from conventional architectural techniques: Brazilian architect Mauricio Roberto submitted in comic-book format, declaring his departure from architectural norms in other domains, as well: "The proposed solution is essentially social, economic, urbanistic and universal," he announced. "The contribution of architecture although ingenious, is relatively small."[68]

What sort of picture of "world architecture," to return to Gutheim's claim, was on display at *Habitat: Toward Shelter*? The competition produced a remarkable panorama of architectural trajectories and conceits familiar from the mid-1970s, whether formal, technical, experimental, mediatic, process oriented, semantic, romantic, regionalist, pseudovernacular, or whatever, each of these inflected or sometimes redirected through an encounter with the competition brief and hence, by extension, with Tondo.

What most, but not all entries shared is circumscription within the problems set by the competition organizers and the institutional frameworks and economic systems in the interest of which they functioned. I mention this not to excuse designers from responsibility, but to point to the apparatus at work. In being recruited for this mission, architects and planners not only responded to the call to offer solutions to what were indeed urgent humanitarian problems, but submitted their expertise to justifying and giving form (or at least process) to a paradigm of developmentalism then appealing to self-help. Roberto's scheme was among the few that spoke back, implying that even the most open-ended, least master-planned "non-plans" played into this apparatus. Prominently on display was the too-easy translation of architectural strategies into the context of Tondo, with few attempts to question or interrupt this narrative.

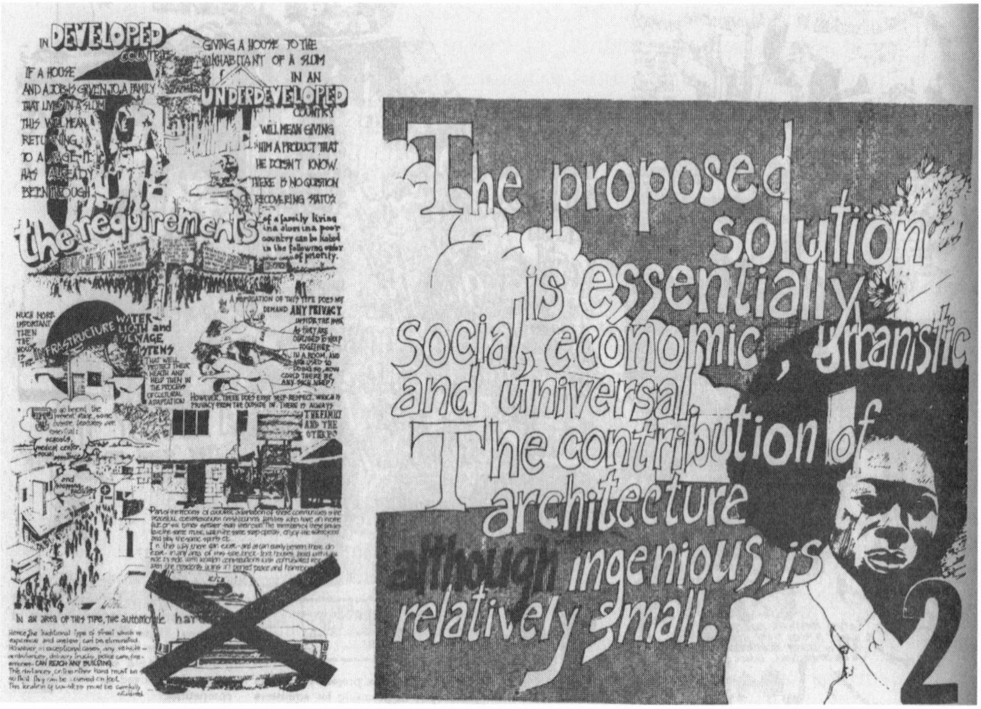

Figure 6.7 Mauricio Roberto, entry for the International Architectural Foundation's International Design Competition for the Urban Environment of Developing Countries Focused on Manila, 1976 (courtesy Marcio Roberto).

There was nothing more effective than the rhetoric of emergency, security, and a call to offer solutions and translate talk into buildings to incite architects to act without reflection.[69]

My point is not that, having participated in such a program, well-meaning architects should be dismissed as politically compromised (even if I do want to stress a pervasive naïveté), but to ask how, in retrospect, institutional structures seeking to mask political concerns as disciplinary, technical, or humanitarian could prevail to such an extent. Many entries did speak to social and political questions, such as the security of land tenure and economic injustice. The question is how that "reorientation" of architecture toward shelter, that carefully scripted reeducation of the profession through the competition, so effectively perpetuated a disconnection from questioning the underlying political apparatus at play in favor of providing solutions that might help win hearts and minds. Why were so many willing to participate in imagining the terms and forms of this imminent dispossession under the rubric of nongovernmental aid?

Speaking of Others

Writing for the *Times of India*, architect Charles Correa (another Vancouver Symposium member) singled out an aerial photograph of Tondo as emblematic of the importance of the upcoming Habitat conference.

> This photograph, without doubt, is going to be one of the monumental images of the last quarter of the century. As final, as simple, as devastating an icon as the great mushroom cloud that dominated the consciousness of man in the immediate post-war years. A great sea of squatters, stretching to the horizon. No open spaces. No schools. No trees. No roads. Down the center, an ironic stream of water reflecting the great open sky.[70]

The photograph, Correa suggested, intended not only to provoke action—like the threat of atomic warfare—but to speak on behalf of those not given a voice. It was shot by Patrick Crooke, a colleague of Turner's at London's Architectural Association who was also involved with self-help projects in Peru; it appeared both as a floor-to-ceiling installation in *Habitat: Toward Shelter* and as the cover of *Architectural Record*'s special issue on human settlements. In both

AN ISSUE ON ONE OF THE MOST
URGENT PROBLEMS OF OUR TIME
HUMAN SETTLEMENTS
WITH THE WINNING DESIGNS IN
THE INTERNATIONAL DESIGN COMPETITION
FOR THE URBAN ENVIRONMENT OF
DEVELOPING COUNTRIES—FOCUSED ON MANILA
ARCHITECTURAL RECORD
MAY 1976 5 A McGRAW-HILL PUBLICATION FIVE DOLLARS PER COPY

Figure 6.8 *Architectural Record*, May 1976, cover with aerial photograph of Tondo Foreshore (courtesy *Architectural Record*).

contexts, we need to ask how such an image spoke on behalf of those not given a voice and what it was being deployed to say about them.

Architectural Record cast their special issue as expert knowledge presented "to architects, planners, international aid and lending agencies, and government officials around the world—on behalf of the more than a billion people who live in urban slums."[71] Schmertz provided a telling overview. Picking up on Ward's alarmist rhetoric, she announced that "masses of humanity" were now "swarm[ing] into Seoul, Bombay, Mexico City and São Paolo," going on to list other cities suffering from an "incessant flow" of "unwanted migrants."[72] Quoting Laquian, she asserted that such people, visibly in poverty, "mock the aspirations of all those who yearn to make their cities sophisticated and modern."[73] "These human beings are unwelcome," Schmertz stated of their illegal acts, "because they build shacks on urban land to which they have no legal right." Although willing to concede why squatters might choose "urban squalor over rural misery" and why they maintained hope, her dominant concern was not the lack of infrastructure for their ventures, but their relation to crime and violence in the "host city," a term resonating ambiguously between hospitality and parasitism. Noting that not all squatters were optimistic or independent, she warned: "Criminals, fugitives, mental deficients, alcoholics, drug addicts, pimps, prostitutes, social outcasts and the indolent are found in every slum." "Slums have the potential," she added in escalating rhetoric, "for mob violence, crime, political revolution and other forms of social disruption."[74]

With squatter settlements thus situated on the brink of emergency, where the role of the police might imminently be replaced by the military, architects were called upon not just to alleviate problems of "flimsy construction" and poor sanitation, but "the danger to the human species posed by the spreading malignancy of squatter settlements." Schmertz's response resonated between panic prompted by an encounter with the Global South and a cynical mobilization of fear that might assure a role for architects. Her proposed solution, however, was clear: "The most promising alternative to government-built low-cost housing is the 'sites and services' approach combined with 'self-help.'" People were to be "counted as a resource."[75] Even in slums, where to her mind people were "apathetic, hostile and suspicious," ways and means could be found to motivate them toward self-help solutions advanced by the World Bank and promoted by the IAF.

Among the "world leaders" that the *Record* featured in the issue were Ward, Enrique Peñalosa, J. G. Van Putten, Benitez, and head of the World Bank, Robert S. McNamara. McNamara's text was excerpted from a speech to the World Bank's board of governors in which he stressed the bank's program of financing sites and services in place of providing finished housing. "The deprivation suffered by the poor is nowhere more visible than in the matter of housing," he announced.

> Even the most hardened and unsentimental observer from the developed world is shocked by the squalid slums and ramshackle shantytowns that ring the periphery of every major city in the developing countries of the world.
>
> But there is one thing worse than living in a slum or squatter settlement—and that is having one's slum or settlement bulldozed away by a government which has no shelter of any sort whatever to offer in its place. When that happens—and it happens often—there remains only the pavement itself, or some rocky hillside or parched plain, where the poor can once again begin to build out of packing crates and signboards and scraps of sheet-metal and cardboard a tiny hovel in which to house their families.[76]

Pointing to illegality while acknowledging the role of unjust economic circumstances, McNamara's answer to the problem of urban poverty was, of course, development, this time in the form of "policies and actions that will assist the poor to increase their productivity." He overtly called to integrate the poor more effectively within the extant socioeconomic matrix in order to boost national economies. Cities, he proposed, encouraging USAID and other agencies to do the same, should be "thought of as absorptive mechanisms for promoting productive employment."[77]

Like other development programs that the World Bank sponsored, such opportunities were not intended simply to aid the poor, and indeed rarely helped squatters, yet squatters were integral to the expansion of global capitalism. As Cheryl Payer explained in 1982, the bank was conceived "as a 'safe bridge' across which private investment could move again into distant and politically volatile territories," whether to gain access to resources and cheap labor pools or to provide often irrelevant industrial equipment, finance loans, and so on. Hence, she posited, it was no accident that so many of the countries receiving extensive aid from the World Bank during the 1970s were inegalitarian and "notorious for extremely inequitable income distribution and/or violations of human rights." This was "a natural consequence of the Bank's preference for lending to governments that offer favorable conditions for foreign investment, and of its unwillingness to jeopardize the power of such governments by exerting pressure on behalf of the underprivileged it champions in its rhetoric."[78] Developing the Tondo Foreshore for industrial fishing and export was a seminal case of World Bank ambitions to aid multinational corporations in accessing "underdeveloped" countries and to encourage production for export that benefitted corporations controlling international trade.

Demonstrations

On June 7, headlines for the *Guardian* read, "Filipino Protest Rocks Habitat." "The Tondo issue has come to Vancouver with a vengeance," reported Clyde Sanger, "because a main feature of Habitat has been an architectural contest to design homes for at least 500 squatter families in a Tondo resettlement area."[79] The protests were an unexpected turn of events for the IAF, which sought a different type of publicity for "world architecture"; it was a departure from the script. Given the importance attributed to citizen participation in the UN's goals, the lack of adequate consultation with Tondo residents targeted for resettling emerged as a contentious issue at Habitat Forum the previous week, but gained little press attention. With the impending arrival of Imelda Marcos for a presentation to the UN conference's plenary session and with her visit coming immediately in the wake of a mass arrest of protesters demonstrating against the Tondo Foreshore development in Manila, the plight of these people was suddenly news. As reported in a United Press International wire service, "Police arrested 2,000 slum dwellers and religious leaders who held a demonstration today timed to coincide with the United Nations conference on human settlements."[80] *Habitat Forum News* broadcast the UPI wire under the title "Tondo Squatters Answer Back," reporting: "A police official said 14 buses with a capacity of from 100 to 150 persons carried the arrested demonstrators to a suburban military camp."[81]

Answering back was not so easy to do in the Philippines, where by martial law decree, protests and squatting were criminal offenses, and publishing of antigovernment literature was banned, rendering any struggle for rights precarious, at best. This was not the first time Tondo squatters were arrested over the Dagat-Dagatan projects. In January 1976, squatter communities sought an audience with Imelda Marcos—recently appointed as governor of Metropolitan Manila—to discuss evictions and other grievances prompted by her beautification drive to restore Manila to its former state of (colonial) glory in order to attract tourism and investment. Mrs. Marcos met with community leaders, agreeing to halt demolition temporarily and to meet again four days later. However, as reported in *Southeast Asian Affairs*, "soon after this meeting was agreed to, the squatter leaders and organizers of the planned rally were arrested by the police." According to Marcos, the slums caused flooding; "obstructed the development of projects such as the Tondo Foreshoreland Development Plan, the Dagat-Dagatan Reclamation Project and the Marcos Highway; and the shantytowns were 'eyesores.'"[82] Organized resistance to their removal was met with mass arrests; some protestors were driven underground, while others joined the swelling ranks of political prisoners detained without due process. The Marcos regime insisted that protestors were being detained not because of their political views, but "because their activities are extralegal."

In solidarity with the Manila squatters, two protests were held in Vancouver. The first took place outside the Queen Elizabeth Theatre—official venue of Habitat plenary sessions—timed for Marcos's arrival and speech. With chants of "Down with the Marcos dictatorship" and "Squatting is not a crime,"[83] the rally was jointly sponsored by the Filipino coalition against martial law in Vancouver, the World Council of Churches, and the Self-Help and Low Cost Housing Symposium at Habitat Forum.[84] Noting the intense levels of security, newspaper reports indicated that forty or more protestors (some counted seventy) were met by an equivalent number of police, both uniformed and undercover, including Royal Canadian Mounted Police with walkie-talkies. "Police video tape cameras constantly panned the crowd as officers on nearby rooftops scanned office buildings with high-power binoculars," the *Province* reported.[85] The city council's unwarranted fear that the PLO's presence would

Figure 6.9 Demonstrations in support of Tondo squatters' rights during United Nations Conference on Human Settlements, Vancouver, June 1976 (Peter Hulbert/ *The Province*).

render Vancouver a police state was realized instead during Mrs. Marcos's visit, but her right to appear was never questioned. At Habitat Forum, twenty members of the Committee for Filipino-Canadian Understanding gathered for a quieter rally, protesting the forced-relocation scheme and the lack of consultation with residents, as well as the Philippine government's blocking of five Tondo community leaders from appearing at Habitat Forum as delegates under the auspices of the World Council of Churches.[86]

Governor Marcos insisted that reports of her husband detaining two thousand demonstrators were false, laughing at the idea that they had so many prisons available. Dismissing the Vancouver protests, she scoffed: "I did not see many Filipinos there, I think the rest were professional demonstrators."[87] She failed to mention that those who opposed martial law were considered "security risks" and refused clearance to leave the country.[88] Marcos's plenary session address attempted to shift the terms of the debate: she "blamed Manila's slums on the Second World War. She said much of Manila was leveled in fighting between U.S. and Japanese forces. 'The degree of devastation was equal only to Warsaw. . . . It's a city recent [sic] from the ruins and ashes of war, rebuilt with meager resources.'"[89] However, while she read the city's plight in terms of wartime breaches of sovereignty by dueling colonial powers, she cast its future as distinctly, if ambiguously, postsovereign, shifting from the rhetoric of Saint Augustine to 1960s ideology: "Our dream is to create in Manila a city of man. Our dream for man is to create cities for humanity. Our hope is that our earth will become a city of humanity," she began, then, turning to celebrate a world without borders, she added, "There is a growing realization that our spaceship earth is an inter-dependent life support system."[90] The allusion was to the ecological and environmental concerns of the late 1960s, when the rhetoric first took off as a potent image of vulnerability and global ecological interdependence. However, such tropes had taken on new valence by the mid-1970s. Following the 1973 OPEC oil crisis and the decision of the United States to abandon the convertibility of the dollar to gold, which terminated the Bretton Woods system of managing exchange rates by tying currency to gold, such language spoke to the economic fate of developing countries, particularly those that did not export oil, and to incursions on their sovereignty, as Geoff Payne noted in *Architectural Design*.[91] The

Philippine economy suffered significantly under the inflated price of oil, and the country was then battling export quotas for and commodity prices of sugar.[92]

Statements

As Governor Marcos was aware, her predicament in Vancouver was also tied to interdependency born of global media networks, such as those mobilized by the squatters and NGOs in the service of human rights claims. Tondo dwellers could be managed within the Philippines—their bodies detained, their critical voices contained, their texts banned—but under the intense media scrutiny of the conference, their plight began to circulate in the international press, operating beyond the domain of her control. In the context of Habitat, Tondo residents themselves answered back through print to acts of dispossession, silencing, and violence, issuing *Philippine Squatters and Martial Law Remedies* as an effective piece of counterpropaganda directed to the UN delegates and the press. Published by the Coordinating Council of People's Organizations of Tondo Foreshore, Navotas, Malabon (Ugnayan Tondo), and circumventing the ban on independent publications and debate, the pamphlet outlined the effects of government policies and actions bent on demolition and incarceration. Widely cited and helping to give traction to their concerns, it shifted the debate from terms scripted by the IAF in order to facilitate the voices and visibility of Tondo residents themselves, a media tactic exploding other facts and arguments into the public realm. (It entirely eclipsed the government's brochure on Imelda Marcos's "socio-civic endeavors," *Symbol of the Compassionate Society*, which celebrated her program to beautify Manila, as well as her support for the Green Revolution, Population and Environment Centers, funds for natural disasters, and a "resettlement program for Manila's slum-dwellers."[93] In a closed media environment, all could be pitched as humanitarian concerns.) What *Philippine Squatters and Martial Law Remedies* managed to do so effectively was to establish a platform upon which to articulate a distinct kind of political discourse about Tondo, a discourse in which the residents' plight was not simply a problem to be solved by innovative or low-cost design.[94] Moreover, the residents did not appear simply as abstractions of a universal humanity and a humanitarian crisis that could be substituted for similar phenomena in other parts of Asia, Latin America, or Africa.

However, Ugnayan Tondo did affiliate their plight with squatter settlements elsewhere, launching a different narrative of the interconnected global condition. While the IAF's insistence on the worldwide relevance of the architectural "solutions" on display reminds us that they embraced what Didier Fassin and Mariella Pandolfi have recently defined as a "globalized biopolitics," those who resisted it also recognized the network of forces at play.[95] Squatting, the council explained,

> is the natural outcome of the basic economic development schemes followed by many Third World countries, including the Philippines. In general, this basic policy is one of keeping farm income and urban wages low so as to both attract foreign capital investment and to produce foodstuffs within the budgets of the underpaid urban labor force. This results, in general, in rural peasants migrating to urban centers in search of the jobs provided by foreign investment.[96]

Given the structurally low wages concomitant with development policy enforced by martial law, they argued, poverty, urban migration, and slums composed of squatter shacks were the inevitable (if not exactly natural) outcome, one that would not be solved by lower-cost housing, but only by "a complete revision of developmental policies." At present, profit from industry benefitted only foreign investors and the conspicuous consumption of the Philippine elite.

Although Tondo residents were fighting for a right to housing, it was not a right to build that they were seeking, to return to the ill-conceived working title for the exhibition, let alone the right to build shelters themselves, again and again. They were fighting government plans to demolish their houses without or before providing even minimal shelter and their repeated displacement to unviable sites on the outskirts of the city. "Insecurity of domicile is a constant anxiety for the squatter," the pamphlet explained, "especially since the declaration of martial law in September 1972," after which "the government ordered stepped-up demolition of squatter shanties." In 1975, President Marcos repealed a 1965 congressional bill allowing squatters to purchase their land for a nominal fee, a bill that although ineffective, gave the expectation of security of tenure.

Self-help, Tondo residents understood, should not be confused with self-determination or political expression. Both were considered security risks by the Marcos administration, as *Philippine*

Squatters and Martial Law Remedies suggested, connecting government suppression directly to our story:

> [W]hen the World Bank, which is the projected source of funds for the Tondo Foreshore Development scheme, sent a mission to Manila to discuss the plan with government and community leaders in 1975, one of those leaders, Mrs. Trinidad Herrera, was arrested temporarily and locked in a military stockade until after the World Bank group had left. Mrs. Herrera was also scheduled to attend the UN Human Settlements design competition held in Vancouver last February, since the design was meant for housing in Tondo. But again, an order went out for her arrest, and she went into hiding, thus negating the possibility of attending the Vancouver meeting.[97]

Herrera was president of the Zone One Tondo Organization (ZOTO), a coalition of smaller organizations. In her absence, the 1975 World Bank mission declared, "General Tobias and his team are the best representatives in expressing the Tondo Foreshore peoples' needs and aspirations."[98] Herrera, like the other activists in Tondo, had a different idea of how to ease the problem. She might have questioned on whose behalf the IAF spoke, or might have rendered visible the structural violence inflicted on the squatters, or even might have raised rights claims in the context of martial law; that is, she might have shifted the terms of the arguments made during the judging. But precisely because the Philippines was chosen as the site for a Habitat demonstration project on account of the country's interest in "resettlement," it was constitutively not a place to demonstrate citizen participation in the expression of "people's needs and aspirations."

Philippine Squatters made one further media intervention that I want to outline before returning to the exhibition. It included Bernard Wideman's "Squatters: An Unsettling Problem," initially published in a Hong Kong weekly magazine. Wideman told the story of Anna and her friends. Squatting in the midst of tourists, businessmen, and diplomats, Anna was "44 years old, but looks 54, a testimony to her daily battle for existence," he began, reminding the reader that squatters' very bodies were at risk. Unlike Laquian's story of the Cruz family, who heroically scraped out a daily ritual in Tondo, Anna's family was forcibly resettled in Sapang Palay, on the outskirts of Manila, soon after the declaration of martial law.

Without food or hope of employment, they, like most of those relocated, returned to the city, recognizing life to be better in Manila "on the edge of the law and on the brink of disaster."[99] Referring to Marcos's beautification plan, Wideman positioned the government as "caught between trying to help the country's poor like Anna and wanting to turn Manila into an attractive metropolis." While Anna and her friends "pose[d] no real problem" to the state, squatters in Tondo, he conceded, had "become not only eyesores but also breeding grounds for political dissent." Tondo, he remarked, "represents a political powder keg. It is the only slum area with strong community organizations capable of galvanizing the people into action." Although Wideman set out an ambivalent picture—casting squatters as harmless victims of urban poverty and of a humanitarian crisis, on the one hand, and as potential threats to the state, on the other—his position was distinct from Schmertz's. Wideman, to be clear, was an avowed critic of martial law, and he underscored that squatter's concerns were not confined to forced relocation, but extended to the suspension of civil liberties and citizens rights under martial law. His point was not to cast squatters as potential terrorists, but to show them as actors with political representation whose insurrectionary acts took the form of demands for a space of political negotiation, such as might be provided through an NGO or the UN.

Unlike Tondo residents, Anna and her friends did not have access to political representation by community groups, and foreign media attention tragically prompted the government to respond with a counterattack. The week after Wideman's article appeared, they were "chased from their shanties by police and four of them were arrested and are currently on trial in Manila for disregarding a martial law decree which makes squatting a criminal offense." The first trial of its type, *Philippine Squatters* explained, it was watched with great interest for signs that the government planned to solve the problem of squatting simply by mass incarceration. The government's appropriation of Wideman's "Squatters: An Unsettling Problem" thus called attention to the structural ambivalence of media coverage subverting censorship in the Philippines and by implication the squatters' own use of print in an international forum such as Habitat. It also made evident that the squatters' battle for shelter and hence their bodies and lives were intimately connected to mass-media tactics: the media were not external to their plight or a disconnected representation of humanitarian agendas, but had real effects, if not always those anticipated. Having led to a public trial and hence to legal arguments on the question of squatting, this event constituted a moment when squatters paradoxically gained certain rights—as prisoners charged with a crime.[100]

In this media environment, *Habitat: Toward Shelter* soon assumed a new meaning. Although none of the IAF organizers found their livelihood or life at stake, they discovered the risks of media visibility. In response to the protests, Michael Seelig called a press conference at the gallery: "We feel this project is making a terribly important contribution to solving the problems of the poor around the world and we feel it's very unfortunate that it has been dragged into the political situation of the Philippines," he stated.[101] Pushed by journalists about the fate of Herrera, Seelig "confirmed that one of two Manila community leaders who had been invited to Vancouver in February to advise the panel of judges, went into hiding just before she was due to leave the Philippines," but denied her arrest. The government, he stressed, instead, "was very generous to offer us a site where they guaranteed they would construct the project. We wanted this to be a real competition, not just ideas." Politics and even human rights violations waned in relevance when building was involved.

Athfield proved an important media asset here, too. As reported in the *Guardian*, he seemed "bemused by all the dust being stirred up."[102] At the press conference, he clarified that he didn't want to force his ideas on the local populace: "If I am not accepted I will go home," he announced. "Filipinos have been 'in the minority' in the Vancouver demonstrations," he argued, reiterating Imelda Marcos's conspiracy claim. He insisted that "his project only provides squatters with 'four poles and a roof' and the rest is planned by the people themselves. 'I don't think that's imposing very much on people,' he said."[103] (If we recognize its similarity to Abbé Marc-Antoine Laugier's eighteenth-century figure of the primitive hut as an urform of architecture derived from nature, it becomes clear that quite a lot was being imposed.) Athfield, it appears, had not paid much attention to protestors' claims. For to reiterate, lack of consultation was only one aspect of the larger apparatus of oppression they struggled against. He did not seem to consider what drove a situation in which some Tondo inhabitants would be chosen to get four poles and a

Figure 6.10 Ian Athfield and Imelda Marcos at *Habitat: Toward Shelter,* exhibition at the Vancouver Art Gallery, May 31–July 4, 1976 (courtesy Vancouver Art Gallery Archives).

roof. Despite the belief, widespread among architects, that a degree of formal or organizational choice afforded to residents in completing their dwellings constituted agency, self-help, and political self-determination are not, to stress again, identical.

This persistent refusal or inability to situate the work within a larger context was not limited to Athfield. Mountier dismissed the protests as fomented by internal bickering among jealous architects, arguing that they were led "by a group of young American and British architects" who "attempted to force Ian Athfield . . . into endorsing their political demands." Refusing to be "bullied," she reported, he retreated to the Appropriate Technology Village at Habitat Forum: "Athfield quietly went about his business of putting together an on-the-spot illustration of his minimal Tondo house, made from old plywood, logs and disused timber and covered with plastered mesh."[104] Architecture, he believed, should and could stay outside the messy political fray.[105]

John F. C. Turner, a prominent spokesperson for the Self-Help and Low Cost Housing Symposium, recognized that more was at stake and spoke out, going to lengths to ensure that the competition not be confused with his ambitions for self-help and garnering media attention for himself in the process. Turner, the *Province* reported, "said economists, planners and architects unwittingly contribute to the situation in Tondo, where the people have no participation in decisions affecting their living conditions. 'The question is, who decides what for whom? Who is competent, who is able to decide for people, how and where they should live?'"[106] Raising the question of responsibility to "the people who will use their work," Turner pointed out to professionals, "theirs is not simply a technical job."[107] On June 8, the symposium issued a damning statement, drawing attention to the "wider implications" of the competition and its rejection by the Tondo community, structurally excluded from participation. "In displaying the results of the International Architectural Competition for Manila in a prominent downtown gallery, the UN Habitat Conference gives tacit approval to a project that was set up in violation of the goals expressed in the conference's declaration of principles."[108] Even if architects and planners were "well-intentioned," idealism was not an adequate substitute for taking responsibility. "Technological neutrality," he insisted, "is a myth."[109]

The Self-Help and Low Cost Housing Symposium enjoyed vast interest and support at Habitat Forum.[110] "On the morning of June 1, 500 people fill the amphitheater of Hangar 3, in biting cold, to hear John F. C. Turner on the subject 'Self-Help and Low-Cost Housing,'" Alfred Heller reported, noting that it was "the first of literally dozens of meetings on this single topic scheduled for Jericho."[111] Turner, as noted above, had worked in self-help housing and the informal sector for decades, establishing a model based on securing land tenure, offering technical assistance, financing, and facilitating minimal building codes. It was only more recently that the World Bank, the US Agency for International Development, and the Inter-American Development Bank adjusted their policies to conform to his model. As the *AIA Journal* reported,

> Turner's ideas have been a major influence on the turnaround to upgrading squatter settlements and sites and services projects in Asia, Africa and Latin America, and on the World Bank's financial support. It is essentially the success of these projects, documented in official films as well as in case study presentations in the symposium, which underlies the absence of controversy over this approach and to [sic] the clarity of language in the main conference's recommendation on construction by the "informal sector"—people building at small scale.[112]

In its statement, the symposium attempted to distance its paradigm from the World Bank, insisting that self-help be "understood as self-government or self-determination rather than the narrow sense of do-it-yourself home building." The issue, they stressed, "*is control*. User control demands a redistribution of power."[113]

On June 7, Turner arrived late to a Habitat Forum panel, "Housing the Poor," having been held up at a press conference on the Tondo protests. He walked in while Shafiq Al-Hout, head of the PLO delegation, answered a question about how to achieve a democratic secular state in Palestine. After expressing relief that he did not have to speak on the issues that Al-Hout raised, Turner told the audience that protestors in Manila were imprisoned in a "concentration camp." "We cannot ignore this sort of issue," he stressed, "because the principles on which the conference is based are at stake here."[114] (Likewise for Palestine, we might add.) However, Turner did not question the fundamental premise of self-help strategies, for which he would in turn be taken to task. Rod Burgess noted a few years later that "to those in the Third World ... rarely far from starvation, such appeals to be more self-reliant must seem a rather curious form of radicalism."[115]

Squatter settlements such as Tondo Foreshore did not emerge by direct force, but nevertheless were distillations of a forceful process of dispossession from rural lands by industrial development and of migrants' structural disenfranchisement from the mainstream economy of cities. The people of Tondo were not forced to live in these precarious legal zones, but arrived fleeing far worse conditions. Without legal recourse to dispute the ongoing process of displacement and with distinctions between police and military actions increasingly eroded, forced resettlement sites had become camps' haunting twins.[116] Expatriate Filipino journalist Ruben Cusipag noted this connection to camps. (Cusipag had been detained upon the declaration of martial law and then fled to Canada.) Tondo squatters, he argued, were caught between two forms of detention that were closely intertwined: on the one hand, the Marcos / World Bank / IAF scheme for incorporating them into the development process, and on the other, prison.[117] Under military rule, he stated at the Vancouver rally, "Tondo residents have only two choices: a 'forced' habitat—the new development—or prison camps. 'Mrs. Marcos will be building prison camps for them, not low-income housing,' he said. 'And unless she withdraws her iron fist, she will be developing not low income residents but a new breed of penitentiary tenants in slum prisons and new ghettos.'"[118]

Architectures of Security

Shortly after the Habitat conference, William Marlin, associate editor at *Architectural Record*, published "Helping to House Manila's Urban Poor," hoping to redeem the IAF project. "Trudging through the ramshackle squalor of Manila's Tondo Foreshore," he mused of its imminent disappearance, "it is hard to imagine that, in a few years, a minor revolution will probably have occurred here." Repeatedly condemning the adverse effect of political activists on government plans, he proclaimed in a distinctly Fulleresque tone that it was "going to be a revolution by design—design of sites, structures, and services—as some 140,000 people are relocated to the bleak flats and land-filled ponds of Dagat-Dagatan ... so that the Tondo can be transformed into an industrial-residential complex." In dreaming of a new gleaming city rising from the slums, Marlin was not, to be clear, lamenting displacement of the squatters. Rather, he was reveling in the capacity of architects to alleviate a potentially insurrectionary situation that would hold back development. According to him, *Architectural Record* established the IAF in order to calm a situation in which "the clash between the urban 'haves' and the 'have-nots' is reaching a crescendo, already creating upheavals or seismic social and political force."[119]

Architects are of course supposed to imagine and contribute to a better and more secure world; the discipline's dominant narratives are of social and material progress in line with Western Enlightenment thinking. Yet this was far from Marlin's concern. The competition did not ask architects to design housing or to address inequity between the haves and the have-nots, but to produce scenarios for minimal shelter that normalized such conditions, effectively scripting the troubling underside of that "industrial-residential complex." Whether knowingly or not, Marlin recognized the suspension of established standards to be connected to the same *dispositif* of power driving the rise of gleaming corporate towers. Here, the two sides of "world architecture" came together.

No longer would Western-trained architects and planners march back to their developing countries, Marlin speculated, "ready to conquer poverty with concoctions of metal, concrete, and brass," offering what he called "care packages" of modern architecture. Rather, what was appropriate for squatters in his estimation was a degree of architectural *modesty* that would serve as "a compliment to their potential as human beings." The IAF competition demonstrated that this could take the form of "a workable framework in which [squatters] can make the most of themselves through the exercise of innate energies." There would be no more grand hygienic housing estates, schools, or factories to discipline modern citizens, but an apparatus to put to work and manage those deemed of modest worth. To him, the competition demonstrated updated architectural metrics: "subjective preferences as to matters of form and shape seem to have been set aside, with priority given to more objective conditions of culture, climate, ecology, and the prevalent public opinion [that is, self-help] beyond the inflammatory tactics of certain political activists." Overlooking the persistence of aesthetic conceits, he laid stress on the sites-and-services paradigm, the need to remove squatters from prime development land, and enforcing technical solutions derived from an expanded field of scientific knowledge.[120]

What Marlin insightfully recognized and what he hoped to exploit was the unholy alliance between the informality of self-help architecture (or "workable frameworks") and strategies at work within neocolonial apparatuses of environmental governance. Both shared the ability to adapt to facts on the ground and to operate at once laterally and top-down. Informality was not simply a manifestation of the benevolent withdrawal of regulations such as architectural or planning codes in the face of extreme difficulties or a way of ceding agency to the user, as had been dreamed of by experimental architects such as Yona Friedman and other proponents of indeterminate structures. If fixed forms would give way to flexible frameworks, as Marlin recognized, a new type of top-down strategy emerged, one that was less evident and more dispersed. Inverting grassroots logics, he ambiguously announced that the self-help development marked "a new kind of revolution.... One in which people at the top are attempting to pull people at the bottom, not the other way around." Discerning the economic and political logics at work, he continued, "Though political obstacles and community contentiousness persist, swirling around the future of Dagat-Dagatan, the chances are good that at least 500 families are going to find a stake in something like that kind of freedom.... Four poles and a roof can create a revolution." Here, too, Marlin proves insightful, for the project indeed expressed the free-market paradigm driving neoliberal economic revolutions expanding into the Global South.

Other architectural critics responded very differently to this paradoxical or cynical schema, in which supposedly humanitarian interventions did little for the poor or even unwittingly participated in a process of dispossession. Docomomo founder Hubert-Jan Henket questioned architects' romantic attitude toward "the fantastic achievements of migrant minorities in their struggle against those in power." As he argued in "Cruel Habitats," "We often forget that our support for the self-help approach actually stimulates the policies which make these settlements necessary."[121] He clarified that squatters do not arrive in such places by choice.

> Many politicians in the third world will be well pleased to see the moral support colleagues are receiving for their actions from intellectuals

> of the industrialized world. If they follow the UN-sponsored Manila competition example, what they have to do is provide minimal infrastructures on the wastelands of their city peripheries and they can legitimately forget about the real issue at stake, which is that the poor shouldn't have to migrate to the cities in the first place.[122]

Questioning the statistically driven, bureaucratically implemented political process at work in Vancouver and the idealistic rhetoric at play, Henket referred to Habitat as a "mammoth council of war." Whether self-help solutions were motivated by economic gain or humanitarian factors, he argued, "ironically the ultimate victims will be precisely those who are now so loudly praised for their efforts: the urban poor."[123] Even Correa recognized that something was wrong with this picture. "Self-helpers depress me," he said to a taken-aback reporter from *Jericho*. "By this he has in mind well meaning efforts at 'moving people out to self-help schemes on the edge of cities where they become a ghetto of cheap labour.'"[124]

Evictions

Reporting on the self-help symposium for *Architectural Design*, Ian Hogan turned to Tondo, providing an account of the neighboring World Bank scheme to provide sites and services to about twenty thousand people on forty hectares of land, a density far lower than squatter settlements, with a correlative increase in cost. Each family would receive "a 12m x 4m plot with a 3m x 4m soil/cement floor and a 3m x 4m block wall, upon which are two cold taps, a sink and a W.C." Designed to ensure full cost recovery through leases, taxes, and so on, the so-called "project beneficiaries," Hogan posited, would be faced with a doubling of their housing costs, if not more. Hogan nevertheless found both the World Bank and Athfield's approaches "imaginative and commendable," but he, too, remained concerned that current residents might continue to raise controversy. "The people of Tondo themselves are vigorously represented and misrepresented by numerous clandestine activist groups, marxists and religious leaders," he scoffed. Adding, "there are numerous emigrant factions, left and right, propagandizing in the USA and Canada, putting out suspiciously elegant literature."[125] Squatters and their representatives, it seemed, were not supposed to inform development discourse.

While *Architectural Design*'s special issue, "Habitat Reconsidered," was on the newsstands, Tondo again made headlines. "Slum Evictions in Manila Embarrass the World Bank," the *New York Times* announced on October 7. In September, more than four hundred families were forcibly evicted from Tondo, their houses demolished as part of Governor Marcos's plan to beautify Manila in time for the arrival of thousands of foreigners for a meeting of the World Bank and International Monetary Fund. Some of these properties had legal titles—the squatters were legal property owners—a fact simply ignored, rendering the hope placed in land tenure effectively mute.[126] "Most of those displaced were carted, many in garbage trucks and with armed police at hand, to remote sites as far as 20 miles outside the city where they put up shanties no better than what they had left," the *Times* reported.[127] Five days before the IMF / World Bank meeting, Wideman reported in the *Washington Post* under the title "World Bank Embroiled in Manila Slum," "Manila officials demolished 50 shanties in Tondo to widen a road for the conference delegates' tour of the city. High wooden fences were erected around all of the shanty areas visible from the road."[128] The wall was not exactly the perimeter imagined by Athfield. But like these violent actions, the eruption of the wall resonates poignantly with the governor's aims of visual beautification and the disappearance of bodies. Like the shantytown itself, walls appear, we might say, following Wendy Brown, as a manifestation of a post-Westphalian world, a symptom of the waning of sovereignty.[129] The goal was not to keep foreign nationals, the stateless, or even squatters from entering the city. As with walls separating the United States from Mexico or Israel from occupied Palestinian territory (of which Brown writes) the logic was to regulate people's movement and keep the poor and their shanties out of sight. In this case, they had to be hidden from foreign bankers, diplomats, and journalists so as not to contradict the Philippine government's claims for the benefits of martial law: as President Marcos observed, "social injustice [was] incompatible with the goals of the New Society."[130] The *Washington Post* reported that he was "not at all embarrassed by the existence of martial law," which, he claimed, "not only makes the streets safe for citizens but the country safe for foreign investment."[131] Those streets, however, remained profoundly unsafe for vocal squatters.

McNamara cosigned an agreement for a $32 million loan for the development of Tondo Foreshore with Imelda Marcos in

Washington, DC, two days after her appearance at Habitat. At the time, World Bank policy explicitly refused loans to governments practicing slum clearance, prompting critics to applaud the bank for "for opposing a particularly inhumane practice of bulldozing slums out of existence."[132] Following this contractual breach, Tondo activists attempted to march to the IMF / World Bank conference and to arrange a meeting with McNamara or a bank representative in an unsuccessful attempt to request that the loan be withdrawn. At the time the largest financial contributor to the Philippines, the World Bank "thought it was politically inappropriate" to meet on account of "anti-martial law overtones."[133] The Marcoses' attempt at beautification also failed: the *Washington Post* reported that the "painfully apparent" suspension of democratic principles under martial law and the dramatic contrasts between the two hundred and sixty million dollars spent on new hotels owned by Marcos family members, as well as "an opulent convention center for the conference" and the nearby slums "almost sickened" many of the nearly four thousand delegates attending. Although some considered these fiscal priorities "obscene," others, such as "businessmen and bankers," were impressed: "Instead of visiting slums, they could attend performances of the Bolshoi and Australian ballets" under the patronage of Governor Marcos.[134]

Pushed by the press, a heavily guarded McNamara clarified that he did not question the lavish expenditure on facilities; "he defends it as a source of national pride, much like the Indian decision to build a nuclear bomb that the economy couldn't really afford."[135] Faced with the question of whether the bank should be "supporting a dictator and his martial law regime," McNamara held "the position that almost all developing countries, in one way or another, can be classed as authoritarian" and that to support the poor, such repressive governments had to be financed. What embarrassed the World Bank was that "Marcos had rigged the economic system in ways completely contrary to the free market philosophy espoused by the U.S. and other democracies."[136]

By 1976, McNamara and the World Bank had a track record of pushing industrial growth over equity or redistribution, pursuing projects working against the interests of the poorest of the poor, precisely those he identified as most in need. Self-help housing was no exception. In her chapter entitled "Urban 'Shelter' Projects,"

Payer turned to the Tondo Foreshore as exemplary of the World Bank's strategy of encouraging real estate speculation and the ability of investors to recuperate profit and develop a free-market system at the expense of the poor. Having determined (statistically) that even the "lowest standard of formal housing and services in the worst locations" would remain too expensive for such a sector in the developing world, the bank turned from housing to sites-and-services projects and squatter upgrading, understanding that any "betterment" improved land values and hence taxes. "It appears," Payer lamented, "that while the poor will not be bulldozed off the land they are occupying, they may well find that land 'improved' under their feet to the point where those who cannot afford to put it to 'productive' use... are evicted quietly by legal process."[137] With the majority of Tondo households relying on irregular sources of income and with eviction required by the bank after three months of defaulting, "those who cannot afford the betterment of Tondo will be forced to move elsewhere, according to the Bank's plan."[138] "Elsewhere" typically meant more precarious sites with riskier consequences. This quieter process of displacement was not an anomaly within World Bank strategy, but appeared in policy documents, with the Tondo project "justified in cost-benefit terms through the anticipated appreciation of property values."[139] The rhetoric of caring for the poor by providing "shelter," Payer concluded, masked the real priority of keeping "the territories of its borrowing countries open to capitalist penetration and their policies attractive to multinational corporations, or to aid the designs of an important member government."[140]

Camps

In another tragic twist to this story, World Bank and US support for the Philippine government was finally reconsidered, albeit only temporarily, in 1977, when human rights activists successfully mobilized a case of abuse as evidence of a wider, systematic use of political detention without filing charges and the routine practice of torture. The case was that of Mrs. Trinidad Herrera. On May 11, Wideman reported, "The best-known leader of Manila's 1 million slum dwellers has been under military detention for the past two weeks and her lawyer claims that she 'has been the victim of physical torture, specifically electric shock.'"[141] Herrera was arrested without notifying her lawyer or family on April 25, a few weeks prior to ZOTO's annual meeting. When her lawyer finally located her in Camp Crame, a military detention center, she could hardly recognize or speak to him. Inmates, Wideman wrote, "have smuggled out unconfirmed reports that Mrs. Herrera was given electrical shocks on very sensitive areas of the body, and that she could not feed or bathe herself for days after the torture. The reports said she would merely sit and stare blankly with tears rolling from her eyes."[142] Just as the Tondo project was paradigmatic of World Bank tactics for Payer, Herrera's torture became a paradigmatic case of Marcos regime violence and of potentials of human rights activism.

Marcos ordered Herrera's release two days after the story of her arrest and torture appeared in the US press, a story that prompted the US State Department to express "deep concern to the Philippines government." The World Bank postponed (but did not cancel) a $15 million resettlement loan, citing concerns about the connection of the arrest to Herrera's comments on the Tondo project.[143] The case continued to prove catalytic. On October 18, 1977, Representative Yvonne Burke (Democrat, California), read a powerful statement citing the case and questioning the escalation of US foreign aid to the Philippine military. Given the lack of delineation between military and police and with extensive evidence of torture, she argued, this aid was in violation of the prohibition on providing assistance to foreign police forces and prisons. Training Philippine military and military intelligence units at the US Military Police School and the Johns Hopkins School for Strategic Studies had to be questioned. "Even the Pentagon admits that the Philippines is not subject to any viable threat," she stated. "It seems that the defense envisioned is, rather, defense of the Marcos regime."[144]

Wideman detailed US congressional response along with Marcos's "all-out blitz to improve his regime's image before the Senate would uphold the House's action on his aid reduction."[145] The International Commission of Jurists also reported on Herrera's abuse in *The Decline of Democracy in the Philippines*.[146] Drawing on these documents, along with those of Amnesty International and other NGOs, Richard Claude, political scientist and founding editor of *Human Rights Quarterly*, picked up the case as exemplary of the political use of statistics in human rights activism and offered a gruesome account of Herrera's interpellation into Marcos's brutal military-police apparatus. "As Mrs. Herrera was walking down Chico Street, Quezon City, in late April 1977," he recounted, "she noticed some men in a car following her. One of them called out her name. When she turned to acknowledge him, she was hustled in the car and arrested."[147] After noting that Herrera accompanied Pope Paul VI on a 1970 visit to Tondo, he continued,

> On the day of her arrest Herrera was taken to Camp Crame for interrogation. There she denied membership in the Communist Party; acknowledged knowing two priests about whom she was interrogated; gave her correct address; and explained the relationships among several groups within ZOTO. Nevertheless, one of the interrogators suddenly shouted, "You are not cooperating!" Thereupon all but two interrogators quietly left the room. The remaining interrogators uncovered a box containing an army crank telephone. Trinidad Herrera was stripped of all her clothing. Wires were attached to her thumb and nipple. She was asked certain questions. Each time the interrogators did not like the answer, and even when they seemed to believe the response, they turned the crank on the field telephone. She could not help urinating from the intense pain. When they threatened to attach an electrode to her vagina, she agreed to sign any confession put before her.[148]

In another version, he added that during US congressional discussions, it was revealed that the hand-crank telephones were part of US aid to the dictatorship.[149]

I introduce these horrific details, which take us to the most intimate parts of Herrera's body, with hesitation. However, it was partially on account of the story's dramatic character, its coupling of bodies, urban environments, international media, the military, the police, detention centers, and international law and politics that it was able to "mobilize shame"—that rights denied Herrera under martial law could be claimed in an international arena. The case was not the first documented evidence refuting Marcos's 1975 declaration that "no one, but no one, has been tortured."[150] Rather, it was the confluence of details communicated to journalists that corroborated patterns of violation in numerous less documented cases and the connection to religious and human rights groups that rendered it catalytic.[151] When US embassy staff visited Herrera at the Bicutan rehabilitation center, Claude noted, they "said that if Herrera's interrogators had been aware of her contacts abroad in church

Figure 6.11 Pope Paul VI visiting Tondo, Manila, November 29, 1970 (© Bettman/CORBIS).

and human rights circles, they would have been more careful not to generate adverse public opinion."[152] The visibility provoked Marcos to order the court martial of military personnel accused of torturing her. They were acquitted on the basis that her documented injuries might have been self-inflicted, following the reputed practice of the Communist Party, the "leftist underground," and "subversive organizations."[153] However, Marcos had learned a lesson from media reportage: Noam Chomsky and Edward Herman made this point in *The Washington Connection and Third World Fascism* in 1979, also citing Herrera's case in their alarmist account of "repacification" and "constructive terror." Marcos now simply eliminated the evidence, turning to "unexplained 'disappearances'" of dissidents as common in other parts of what they characterized as the US neocolonial empire of brutal client states.[154]

Like You Give a Damn

The World Bank did not cancel its loan or the wider redevelopment project, which it pursued vigorously and profitably in close association with the Marcos regime and private developers during the coming years. Despite evidence of the lack of affordability, the bank celebrated the project, publishing an account of its success and that of projects like it in 1979 under the title "Revolutionary Ideas of 1972 Becoming Today's Convention."[155] The product of a slowly orchestrated global emergency, squatter settlements were now being rendered permanent by World Bank's embrace of informality as a revolutionary solution, one that Habitat and the UN sought to institutionalize as national policy and as international agreements and that the IAF hoped to codify as "world architecture." The visibility afforded by the exhibition did not ensure that Athfield's scheme was built, despite assurances by the Philippine government to the IAF and UIA. Reasons alluded to its lack of economic feasibility by World Bank standards, landfill and land-use issues in Dagat-Dagatan, and "socio-political conflicts in the squatter communities," along with the fact that it was not to the Marcoses' taste.[156] (The IAF dissolved in 1978.) We might imagine that Athfield's solution, like other IAF competition entries, contained too much architecture, too many amenities—that it manifested the discipline's inability to accede entirely to the regulatory domain or to reduce squatters' environments and with it their bodies to what Giorgio Agamben termed "bare life."[157] Perhaps architects were unable to abandon entirely modernism's utopian promise as articulated at the intersection of technology, aesthetics, and politics when faced with the often brutal conditions of Third World urbanism.

I am alluding here to the narrative of Kate Stohr's "100 Years of Humanitarian Design," in Architecture for Humanity's *Design Like You Give a Damn: Architectural Responses to Humanitarian Crises.*

> For decades architects have been called upon to provide solutions to the world's shelter crises. However, as designers embraced the idealism of the machine age, the increasingly technology-driven, often utopian ideas they proposed would carry little resonance for aid workers and others wrestling with the day-to-day realities of providing a roof, clean water, and sanitation to families in need. Over time, the worlds of relief and development became divorced from the worlds of architecture and design.[158]

Architecture's failure to bridge this gap is an ambivalent outcome, at best, but the causes need not be reduced to techno-utopianism, disciplinary autonomy, or even architecture's failure to be reduced to care for the body, although all remain relevant. For Stohr, this "disconnect" raised a set of questions: "What role should design play in providing basic shelter? How could architects best address the needs of the displaced and disenfranchised? And, at the heart of these questions: Should design be considered a luxury or a necessity?"[159] These are all good questions and in many regards are those that participants in the IAF competition attempted to answer.

But if we are to take the story I have been tracing as a case in point, a far more complicated and far more ambivalent, contradictory, and disjunctive picture of architecture's role in this humanitarian complex and its relation to the displaced and disenfranchised begins to emerge. Even the rather innocuous architectural exhibition that served as my starting point can be read as situated within a complex matrix of institutional, mediatic, economic, political, and geopolitical forces. At stake is not simply a choice between idealism and utopianism, on the one hand, and realpolitik solutions to facts on the ground, on the other. The exhibition and the competition were embedded in and contributed to a global apparatus of UN conferences, nongovernmental organizations, financial and military institutions, neoimperial development strategies, discourses and technologies of security, and media networks. Put forward as offering practical solutions to a perceived emergency while acknowledging that it posed problems that architecture could not solve, the IAF competition, *Habitat: Toward Shelter*, and *Architectural Record* attempted to harness emergent techniques of power by implementing and deploying dominant relationships of force, to paraphrase Foucault.[160] In responding to the competition brief, architects predominantly chose to operate within a global economic and geopolitical battlefield by offering solutions to problems scripted by the World Bank and the IAF, and even experimental work came to serve the interests of global capitalism. It was this alignment, I have been trying to argue, that constituted the "world architecture" on display at the Vancouver Art Gallery, with its attempted foreclosure of political dialogue in favor of technical demonstrations and images that might help win hearts and minds.

It was on the basis of an urgent humanitarian crisis—people were, and are, suffering—and of architecture's exclusion from it that architects were called upon by the IAF to engage with this biopolitical apparatus. For the IAF, architecture took on a mediatic function within it, assuming a role that NGOs came to play at this time: that of pressuring governments to act by mobilizing popular opinion. Given the cynical conjunction of architecture, territorial insecurity, and neoimperial economic strategies at play, it is an apparatus that would be impossible to negotiate "cleanly" or without taking risks. To reiterate, there are no easy "solutions" to the "problem of squatter settlements," forced resettlements, and other forms of dispossession arising in the context of globalization. The question here is which risks you choose to take and in which direction they tend.

We might still question whether architecture remains doomed simply to reflect such dominant apparatuses and techniques of power. In this case, the question is not whether architecture concerned with squatter settlements could or should escape this cynical and often opaque apparatus, but whether it operates within it to perpetuate the dominant sociopolitical order or, as I would hope, to speak back to, critique, or otherwise struggle against it. Faced with architecture's imbrication within such a *dispositif*, a better formulation might be to ask what else architects might have brought to the table, how else they might have operated within this battlefield, what other tactics remain open to them. For the ambivalence of this system suggests that architecture might also have a role to play in rendering visible and even recasting it, interrupting and redirecting forces at play. Utopian? Maybe.[161]

It is not incidental to my story that an expanded frame of reference recovers voices that recognized and resisted this conjunction of security claims and development while mobilizing the same apparatus—its institutions, key players, the use of media to effect political will—in attempting to effect a reversal in relations of power. The story of Tondo residents' struggles reminds us that despite the suspension of their rights under martial law and their reduction to humanitarian statistics to be housed on the order of "just living," they were not reduced to bare life, but emerged into visibility as political subjects who could interrupt dominant narratives. To cite Etienne Balibar, they "ceased to simply play the victims in order to become the actors of democratic politics." Balibar is speaking of a distinct struggle, that of the *sans-papier* in France during the 1990s, but his argument seems apt: "We owe them for having forced the barriers of communication, for having made themselves seen and heard for what they are: not specters of delinquency and invasion, but workers, families both from here and elsewhere, with their particularities and the universality of their condition as modern proletarians." Because of them, he posits, "we understand better what democracy is: an institution of collective debate, the conditions of which are never handed down from above."[162]

Herrera's case and the repeated dismissal of protests by the architectural fraternity remind us, however, of the violent and persistent resistance to such responses and of the relentless anxiety regarding insurgencies in a paradigm of security. But architects, too, left traces of dissent—Roberto's political cartoons, Henket's critique of the counterproductive effects of self-help on the poor, and Turner's insistence on self-determination, to name a few. The importance of their proliferation should not be underestimated.

Architecture, as I have been trying to demonstrate, has many tools—aesthetic, organizational, spatial, mediatic, discursive, documentary, institutional, technical, even temporal. And, at least in principle, it can mobilize them to different and tactical ends—it can turn to other registers of questioning and self-reflexivity: in addition to operating through design, it can reject the talk about rejecting talk in favor of urgent action or solutions and launch alternative theoretical concepts and research strategies into this domain. There is no question that people should be housed, that attempts should be made to alleviate suffering and support rights struggles. Nor is there any question that architects form part of this picture of an emergent and globalized biopolitics. The question is how architects might participate without rendering cynicism structural or ever more powerful, how they might interrupt this conjunction of emergency conditions, humanitarian aid, and militarism. Finally, to return to another repeated trope, the semantic instabilities and radical ambivalences that I have been stressing point not only to cynicism, but also to the potentials of harboring or broadcasting other "new meanings" for architecture. These, too, will be multiple. The ethical question remains: to what and whom might such meanings speak, who might speak them, and to what ends?

CHAPTER SEVEN

DISCOURSE, SEEK, INTERACT

Reporting to MIT President Howard W. Johnson on the state of the School of Architecture and Planning (SA+P) for the year 1968, Dean Lawrence B. Anderson noted the impact of the moment's turbulence as it was then being felt in the school. The profound "dislocations and adjustments" of society at large, he noted, had affected the ability of both architecture and planning to accumulate accurate knowledge of social needs or to predict future programs, troubling by extension the disciplines' assurance about their professional roles, which he described as "giving order to environmental and social change."[1] While, as he remarked, "traditional values in the environmental professions are fading rapidly," the counterpart of this waning was that "interaction with other professions intensifies." For Anderson, the rapid obsolescence of conventional expertise and established modes of practice were not cause for lament. Rather, such transformations provided the occasion for a strategic rethinking of the school's role within the institutional milieu of MIT as the institute strove to recalibrate its scientific and technical research in response to the so-called "urban crises" of the 1960s.[2] Acknowledging potential benefits, Anderson noted, "The continued awakening of the Institute as a whole toward urban problems is a spur to both departments." The school's encounter with that "awakening" left a profound mark on sectors of its architectural research and pedagogical initiatives in the years immediately following Anderson's report.

While interdisciplinary architectural and urban research had of course taken place during the previous decades at MIT, as elsewhere, we can recognize at this moment a significant shift in the very conception of architecture.[3] No longer were architects simply drawing upon multiple fields of expertise in order to facilitate their design work and scholarship. Rather, architecture would soon come to be regarded (and even to model itself) as one more parameter in a general systems paradigm geared toward environmental management and control, a paradigm that, like its forebears in the large-scale technoscientific research characteristic of MIT laboratories following World War II, was inextricably coupled with heavily funded research into the applications of computers and scientific knowledge. That is, architecture became inscribed within the domain of Big Science.[4] This did not, of course, affect the school in its entirety, and many other stories could be told about it during this period. However, the school's increased intimacy with the social sciences and computerization and its scripted interpolation within what Senator J. William Fulbright termed the "military-industrial-academic complex" at this moment, emerge as important symptoms of a larger historical transformation.[5]

To understand why the school was temporarily embraced as central to MIT's response to the period's social turbulence and related geopolitical insecurities, I want to trace some of the activities and the legacy of MIT's Urban Systems Laboratory (USL). As one official report retrospectively acknowledged, "M.I.T. responded to the urban crises of the 1960s by forming the Urban Systems Laboratory."[6] The USL was founded in 1968 following the recommendations of the Ad Hoc Faculty Committee on Urban Affairs convened by Johnson in late 1966. It was described as "a new interdepartmental and multidisciplinary activity to mobilize Institute-wide resources in the area of urban systems."[7] In February 1967, MIT submitted a 100-page proposal for a program in urban affairs to the Ford Foundation. The proposal included requests for funding "Development of Laboratories for Urban Problems." Cities, it argued "have become the focus for the most acute diseases of our society—poverty, racial discrimination, crime, social disintegration and the degeneration of public education"—problems that, it was believed, reiterating a common trope, "resemble those encountered in the traditional societies of less developed countries."[8] The institute was awarded a $3 million grant as part of the foundation's new program, "University Urban Studies," which replaced its urban extension program,[9] with $800,000 of the grant dedicated to founding the USL.

The initial aim of the USL was to develop an institutional framework and techniques of interdisciplinary coordination and to build up large urban data banks that together would facilitate collaboration and establish a framework for large-scale "mission-oriented" and "action-oriented" projects. Moreover, as the Ford Foundation proposal stressed, the lab would serve to educate "a generation of urban technologists who will have a language in common with those whose primary concerns are the political, social and economic aspects."[10] Before turning to the history and vicissitudes of the USL and to some of the architectural and urban research that took place under its sponsorship, I want to return to Anderson's 1968 report to President Johnson, which offers further clues regarding the historical contours of this encounter and the "urban technologists" it would produce.

Participation

Charting the school's move away from "old-style professionalism" toward the "catharsis" of "direct interaction with people in their environment," Anderson identified a series of "field activities in environmental development" concerned with the "dynamics of squatter settlement in cities in the have-not countries" that were, he suggested, related to work on race and poverty in the United States and particularly inner-city Boston.[11] In the Department of Architecture alone, as reported by its chair, Donlyn Lyndon, these field activities ranged from Robert Goodman's studio addressing the Lower Roxbury Community Corporation and Chester Sprague's ongoing work with Blackfeet Indians to Horacio Caminos's Ford Foundation–sponsored Program in Urban Settlement Design and recently appointed faculty member John C. Turner's work on squatter settlements in South America, as well as comparative studies of South American communities with "selected communities in Boston."[12] One might certainly question the too-easy or pseudomorphic conflation of development issues impacting the Global South and the socioeconomic inequities and environmental injustices characteristic of American inner cities following a period of rapid urbanization and "white flight." But the urban insecurities that emerged in both domains were connected in the minds—and hence in the development theories—of the State Department, the Department of Defense, and policy makers, as well as institutions such as the Ford Foundation, as they turned their attention to "urban affairs." Both domains were affected by the expanding reach and transforming

character of policies informing a largely US-driven capitalist globalization, and the nexus of policy, social scientific knowledge, managerial strategies, and technologies born of Cold War military research would come to be recognized as having strategic lessons not only for warfare and developmental aid, but also for domestic security applications in the form of technologies of environmental control.

After identifying the SA+P's attention to questions of urban instability, Anderson remarked, "Even more interesting (and disturbing to some) is M.I.T.'s own internal environmental ferment," manifest in widespread rejection of delegating decisions to experts and in people's growing desire, instead, to "participate." "It is important to recognize and to provide creative outlet for this wish," he proposed, ominously adding with reference to the protest movement: "Administrators who insist that things must continue as they always have lay their institutions open to destructive action, as has occurred in New York and Paris."[13] Although MIT had emerged relatively unscathed from the events of 1968, such attempts to offer palliative measures to the period's growing civil unrest through forms of participation would not succeed for long. The following year, political activism increasingly focused on the institute's role in the development of weaponry and military strategy for the war in Southeast Asia, and it would in turn become the target of such "destructive action," to which I will return.

Anderson identified some of these "creative outlets" that "manifest this new spirit in our School," noting that these "otherwise unrelated events" shared the capacity to "short-circuit conventional modes of representing action and go directly to the production of environmental change or artifact":

> First is the action on the part of an extraordinarily mature and demanding group of students to force the reformation of the curricular requirements for the [masters of city planning] degree. Second are the celebrated architectural "mezzanines," which, while trouble-making, are remarkable examples of a kind of mass will to create an environment.[14] Most public in character is the third example, the inspired commemoration of Martin Luther King, in which the design students chose to express their ideas by means of images arranged in space. Finally, I would mention the increasingly successful efforts of Professor Wayne

Figure 7.1 "The Mezzanines," fifth-year architecture students' studio space, MIT, 1968 (courtesy MIT Museum).

> V. Anderson, Professor Gyorgy Kepes, and the Fellows of the Center for Advanced Visual Studies to intensify the experience of the visual arts by involving the viewer in direct participation, as in the events designed by Hans Haacke and Otto Piene.[15]

Although each mode of "participation" exemplified for Anderson new, process-based relations between a subject and their environment, and although they seemed particularly relevant to rapid social change, he qualified his enthusiasm by noting a limitation within the institutional context. "Unless supported by disinterested monitoring and evaluation," he added, "they may be too visceral in character to meet the university's standards of objectivity."[16]

Such standards of "disinterested monitoring and evaluation", Anderson went on, could be found in a "complementary" side of the school's activities, which "spring[s] from the promise of new methodologies for problem solving, especially those supported by memory and retrieval systems and manipulative possibilities of the computer."[17] With the computer came the potential to eclipse architecture's subjective and aesthetic parameters—even to overcome the stasis and "overcodification" of "symbolic operations" burdening traditional conceptions—by adopting a feedback-based paradigm that, the dean proposed, "assures continued relevance" in a rapidly changing world. The computer provided tools for organizing complex data, allowing architects to "generate a richer choice of solutions." Architecture, that is, could move away from the intuitive toward the quantitative and hence toward what Anderson cast as a "rationalization" of "thinking patterns." If, as he recounted, architecture and planning were "slower than other professions in adopting the powerful tools of computation," that trend was "now in full swing." These methods were "now beginning to revolutionize environmental design," with developments in computer applications sponsored "through participation in the newly organized Urban Systems Laboratory."[18]

Urban Affairs

In October 1968, MIT's newsletter *Tech Talk* cast the recent founding of the Urban Systems Laboratory as a direct response to the period's domestic insecurity: "Civil unrest! Crisis in the cities! Scream the headlines almost daily." Identified as the "Institute's newest enterprise," the USL, they continued, "sprang into being last winter as an effort to initiate a systems approach—so effective in the space program—in alleviating some of the difficulties involved."[19] The USL brought to bear on the domestic front expertise developed in the institute's engineering and social-science labs—not only for the country's space program, but also for its military and intelligence agencies. And the character of this work would be marked by that legacy. "Much of the initial conceptual thinking about U.S.L.," its director, Charles L. Miller, reported to President Johnson at the end of the lab's first year, "was influenced by our experience with defense and space problem solving."[20] This transfer of skills, Miller explained, was not unique to a university setting. "Many technology-oriented companies are in the process of doing precisely what the Institute is doing: creating a mechanism whereby those skills and assets acquired working on the problems of defense and space can be transferred to the problems of cities," he remarked.[21]

In September 1969, *Progressive Architecture* published a profile on the USL entitled "In Search of Urban Expertise." "Can the university perform for the cities the same kind of research and development functions that it has so successfully performed for NASA and the Department of Defense? Can it work productively with city governments and industry to solve the difficult problems of the country's 'unmanageable' metropolitan centers?" Alis D. Runge asked rhetorically, adding that MIT "is setting out to prove that it can."[22] With the establishment of the USL, Runge went on, what constituted "urban expertise" in the university had fundamentally changed. The intimate triangulation of the military, industrial, and academic sectors was to her precisely what qualified MIT to operate at the forefront of defense against the "urban crisis": "The faculty is liberally salted with men whose careers straddle the academic-industrial consulting line, and includes a number of returnees from Washington's advisory elite who still contribute more than their share to the support of the Boston–Washington air routes."[23]

Runge stressed repeatedly that the USL's ambition was to institute "urban action" via the practical application of scientific knowledge and technology. "Designating the new urban unit as a 'laboratory' rather than a 'center' was not a random choice," she explained, since the terminology "reflects the action-oriented thinking that is everywhere affecting the form of American institutions. 'We are not to be simply another center studying the city, but a group of people that are trying to do something about the problems,'" she quoted Miller as asserting.[24] Miller characterized this application of academic research as making "technology work in the city," citing their goal of closing "an enormous gap between research—the university kind of research in particular—and the city."[25] According to Runge, somewhat inaccurately, this "shift in emphasis from study to action" distinguished the USL from the Joint Center for Urban Studies, which was also sponsored by the Ford Foundation and which had been founded in response to the destabilizing effects of rapid urbanization in both the United States and the developing world. The answer to why the Ford Foundation would fund, as Runge put it, "another urban unit in Cambridge," lay in the instrumental nature of USL research as it attempted to bridge the (controversial) gap between basic and applied research.[26] Miller stressed this action-oriented quality when interviewed in April 1968 by MIT's student newspaper, *The Tech*. As Jay Kunin reported in "Urban Lab to Aid America's Cities": "MIT's activities in urban research are somewhat unique, according to Miller. 'The style of the Institute is different,' from that of other universities. It is interested in being more than a 'city scholar,' and is actually closer to being action-oriented than other schools.'" Miller suggested that with the USL, "The main focal point of MIT's contribution to the nation is changing to solving the problems of cities," alluding to the conversion of military research to the domestic realm.[27]

To understand the Ford Foundation's funding, we need to ask just what types of technology and scientific research were to be put to work in the city, and of course for whom and to what ends. "Urban Lab to Aid America's Cities" appeared, symptomatically, adjacent to the issue's cover story, "Columbia Seized by Students." In his 1968 report, Miller indicated that the lab provided an outlet for such concerns: "Students turning to U.S.L. are particularly anxious to relate their academic study programs to real problems and issues, and they look to U.S.L. for a coupling with action in the cities."[28] The following year, he underscored the palliative nature of students' involvement: "In some ways, urban unrest and student unrest are connected. At least many students now view urban-oriented involvement as relevant and socially desirable, and their involvement in U.S.L. projects has always been high among our priorities."[29] With concern growing over the institute's contribution to the nation's burgeoning war machine, MIT now attempted to deploy "urban action" as a conciliatory mechanism—just as the arts and humanities previously were mobilized in response to rising fears of unchecked technocracy. It is important to recall that as noted in Chapter 1, the Ford Foundation had long been acknowledged as a CIA front for funding research, particularly in the applied social sciences; as Jennifer Light has argued, its efforts fed a national security strategy as it shifted its focus toward social engineering on the civilian front, both domestically and internationally.[30] Consequently, we find the USL situated precisely at a junction of urbanism, social engineering, development, communication, and citizen participation cast as mechanisms to ensure the goal of political stability or, in cybernetic terms, political "homeostasis."[31]

Although MIT had a long history of interdisciplinary collaboration in engineering and applied science, the USL was the first endeavor to script such an active interaction between architecture, planning, management, the social sciences, and engineering "on a major scale."[32] The problems of "the city and urban living," Miller suggested of this imperative, were the "broadest and most complex systems problems ever faced by the Institute," adding that "the commitment of the Institute is a long-term one, and work of U.S.L. will go on for several decades or more."[33] (It would actually close in 1974, as US involvement in Vietnam and hence military funding subsided.) As evident in the lab's name and as exemplified in projects it sponsored, such as Jay W. Forrester's Urban Dynamics, the conception of "urban" had undergone a significant transformation; the object of research no longer was the city, its history, or its inhabitants in the traditional sense, but rather multiple "urban systems" pursued through analysis and modeling or simulation. Following earlier definitions, the lab's annual report for 1968 attempted to clarify just what was meant in this regard: "The scope of urban systems is defined initially as the advancement and utilization of the methods of systems analysis, systems engineering, information systems, and related advanced capabilities and technologies applied to the planning, design, construction and management of the facilities and services required for urban living; including transportation, education, communications, environmental control, housing, health and others."[34] As the Ad Hoc Faculty Committee on Urban

Affairs concluded the previous year, it was in operations research, information science, and computerization that MIT could have its largest impact.[35]

This paradigm of science and technology being put to work in the service of environmental control and population management (through the domains of health, housing, circulation, education, productivity for capitalist ends, and more), situates us, again, in the realm of what Michel Foucault theorized in the 1970s as biopolitical regulation. With the USL, we find members of the academy, including architects, working to develop tools for advancing a form of governmental rationality and its micropolitical techniques of power that sought to govern the bodies and the psyches of contemporary subjects and populations in their everyday environments. And it is not incidental in this regard that Bedford-Stuyvesant in Brooklyn, New York, and Roxbury in Boston, both largely economically underprivileged African-American communities, became objects of USL analysis, strategic sites for such "urban systems" research, and potentially targets of its managerial tools.[36] As the USL report for 1969–1970 explained, Professor Frank Jones, associate director of the USL, ran the Technology, Race, and Poverty project, which worked with community organizers in Boston's South End and with the Metropolitan Applied Research Center, Inc. (MARC) in New York to "assist in a study of two urban ghettos as 'systems.'"[37]

Concluding her account of the USL in *Progressive Architecture*, Runge noted somewhat unexpectedly that "design excellence" and "the importance of aesthetics" were "duly recognized in USL studies, proposals, and reports"; however, she clarified that "finite, individual concerns are not the province of those whose task it is to devise universal patterns of order for complex social, physical, and economic systems. Still," she posited in closing, indicating a certain hesitation or unease, "one hopes that, somewhere along the way to the execution of large-scale dreams, there will be someone who will plug in the right architect at the right place."[38]

At stake here, in many regards, is precisely the question of what that "right architect" might look like at a moment characterized not only by increasing territorial insecurity, but, and not unrelatedly, by the expanding reach of information technology and the emergence of new, mediated forms of social and territorial organization, coupled with new techniques of management. In its contribution to the Ford Foundation proposal, the Department of Architecture suggested that under the impact of contemporary pressures, the designer no longer retained control over his product. "The elements that invite his manipulation are more extensive, no longer limited to the building as object," they explained, adding that "individual buildings become part of a continuum held together by structures at a macroscale, whose complexities must become part of the designer's vision."[39] How, then, we might ask, could any such architect or their vision "plug in" to such an expanded and increasingly less material apparatus of micropolitical control, a "continuum held together by structures at a macroscale"? How could they do so from a disciplinary perspective that we would still recognize as architecture? What role, that is, did (and might) architecture play once interpolated within a systems paradigm bent on the instrumentalization of disciplinary knowledge in the service of security?

Computer-Aided Design

Miller indicated that the "common denominator" of the USL's diverse activities was the computer, or "computer-based urban systems research."[40] "Access to an experimentally oriented computer," he explained, was "essential to new research in urban information systems, urban simulation, and urban design as planned by many groups associated with U.S.L."[41] In 1968, those computer resources took the form of an IBM System/360 Model 67 time-sharing computer, a mainframe to which the various USL groups had access via remote consoles. As announced in a press release, it was "operated under CP/67 and the Cambridge Monitor System, jointly developed by the M.I.T. Lincoln Laboratory and the IBM Cambridge Scientific Center."[42] At the time a highly advanced multiuser computer with the notable capacity to simulate multiple virtual machines, the S/360–67 was configured with the then-impressive statistics of "512 K bytes of core storage, high speed drum, and 2314 disk storage."[43]

As reported by the two associate directors affiliated with the school, Aaron Fleisher and Donlyn Lyndon, the School of Architecture and Planning hosted a number of USL-sponsored research projects in the lab's first year.[44] Fleischer recounted that SA+P supported four major projects in the Department of City and Regional Planning: William Porter's computer program DISCOURSE; Fleisher and his urban data laboratory's "urban data system" CHOICE; studies in the psychology of perception under Professors Stephen M. Carr, Mary C. Potter, and Kevin Lynch; and work on the Boston Model Cities Program in collaboration with the Department of Political Science.[45] In a December 1967 letter to Miller, political science professor Ithiel de Sola Pool identified the Boston Model Cities Program as a candidate for "one of the first investments of our Urban Systems Laboratories funds" on account of the potential value of the affiliated data bank and "situation room" to the experimental activities of the lab.[46] With the city and its population understood as components of information or cybernetic systems, computerized data banks were crucial resources, and citizen participation was the most effective means of feedback-based stabilization.[47] Pool was formerly affiliated with Stanford's Hoover Institution (where he acted as assistant director of the Program in Revolution and the Development of International Relations) and was the founding chair of MIT's Political Science Department; his research and the projects, centers, and the laboratories in which he participated exemplified the Stanford think tank and research center's focus on military and intelligence techniques and international development policy, as well as its transference of them to the domestic front in the wake of civil rights struggles. He was a key player in the 1969 establishment of Project Cambridge in the Center for International Studies (CIS), a DARPA-funded initiative to develop computer-based applications in the behavioral and social sciences.[48] Along with the USL, Project Cambridge cosponsored DISCOURSE, Porter's system of data storage and retrieval of urban information in the service of environmental design.[49]

Lyndon listed three primary areas of USL-sponsored research in architecture: "Communication in Urban Problem Solving, Computer-Aided Urban Design, and Environmental Planning for V/STOL (Vertical Short Takeoff and Landing) air transportation."[50] (V/STOL, also known as VSTOL and VTOL, was an Instrumentation Laboratory project that proved controversial for its counterinsurgency applications.)[51] Of these three research areas, Miller repeatedly singled out developments in the area of computer-aided urban design, announcing the following year that "work on the development of an architecture machine, a special-purpose satellite device with local memory and local processing ability, capable of interacting with the Institute's large IBM machine, the 360/67,

Figure 7.2 The Architecture Machine laboratory, Department of Architecture, Massachusetts Institute of Technology, 1973 (courtesy MIT Museum).

is being developed by Professors Nicholas P. Negroponte and Leon B. Groisser with U.S.L. support."[52] Although I will return, briefly, to other USL-sponsored projects, I want to focus on computer-aided urban design, for at stake is not simply the development of a computer-based graphic interface for design—something like the replication of a design process from sketching to working drawings (where it began)—but a much more thoroughgoing paradigm of data collection and management for the sake of environmental simulation in a virtual realm.

Negroponte and Groisser's research began in 1966 with URBAN2, developed in collaboration with the IBM Scientific Center in Cambridge, where Negroponte worked following his graduation that year from MIT's Master of Architecture program. (Negroponte's master's thesis, "The Computer Simulation of Perception during Motion in the Urban Environment," was presented as "an attempt at architectural research," and following his earlier interest in the question of population growth in the developing world, it forecast that a "new profession will evolve that must take the responsibility of handling the urbanization of millions and millions.")[53] URBAN2 provided the platform for Negroponte and Groisser's inaugural MIT course in fall 1967, "Special Problems in Computer Aided Urban Design." They explained that students would "work towards establishing a coordinated system that aids the direct design process we usually associate with yellow tracing paper." URBAN2 was to be a "conversational computer system" in which the computer was conceived as "a partner in this procedure *by providing a design service that monitors the process rather than optimizes or analyzes inputs*."[54] Students were given a prescripted graphical language using a ten-foot-cube building-block system operating within a three-dimensional orthogonal grid. "The manipulation of cubes provides a way of simulating the urban design process," the professors explained, adding that it "furnishes a 'frictionless-vacuum' environment in which to work."[55]

Sponsored by the USL and by then called URBAN5, the application made quite an impact at the first Design Methods Group conference in the spring of 1968. In his review, "Glass Box and Black Box," Jonathan Barnett declared it "the most spectacular example of blackboxmanship" at the conference, referring to the manner in which the application retained a conventional approach to design, simply augmenting it through new tools. ("Glass box" approaches, by contrast, were design-methods-oriented and sought transparency through a rationalization of analytical techniques.) Barnett pointed, in particular, to the device's inherent drive toward a conciliatory process, noting that it "provides a sophisticated and flexible format which actually adjusts to the idiosyncrasies of an individual designer." As he recounted, "Films, shown with three projectors, documented a novice's first encounter with URBAN5, which is programmed to make kindly comments like: 'I'm afraid you have a conflict here, Ted,' (the user types in his name when he sits down at the console) or 'Ted, how long are you going to postpone resolving this conflict?'"[56] Here indeed, as Lyndon suggested of the project's ambition, was "a new order of designer-machine interaction."[57]

URBAN5 was designed to be a monitoring device or "eavesdropping mechanism" that tried to eradicate conflicts by steering the architect toward a set of predetermined normative parameters while learning from interaction with the human user.[58] A few years later, Negroponte recalled that he initially understood the computer's role as "checking for violations in constraints and criteria" predetermined by the architect.[59] This modality of conversing with the computer might give us pause, because it seems not unrelated to the architects' desire to furnish a "'frictionless-vacuum' environment in which to work." For while they saw themselves as simply setting up a "launching vehicle" or "research toy" with which to test rather banal architectural parameters (number of bedrooms, structural feasibility, and so on), this experimental mode of simulating environments without the "friction" of the real world (which they likened to laboratory experiments in Newtonian mechanics) would inform the abstraction that came to characterize their environments.[60] In other words, the underlying technical logic of such systems translated all too easily into a paradigm in which historical and political valences were simply swept aside in favor of a smoothly functioning apparatus—whether architectural, administrative, political, or whatever. To eliminate conflict or "friction" is to close down spaces of contestatory negotiation.

Artificial Intelligence

Lawrence Anderson noted in his report as dean that "the Architecture Machine is a phantom in the minds of Professors Leon B.

Figure 7.3 The Architecture Machine, laboratory with SEEK in foreground, Department of Architecture, MIT, 1973 (courtesy MIT Museum).

Groisser and Nicholas P. Negroponte that is becoming concrete with disconcerting haste."[61] By 1969, as reported in *Progressive Architecture*, work on URBAN5 had been declared complete, and a "second generation of studies" was underway. As Runge explained: "One of the more interesting—though least practical—group of projects, under the leadership of Architecture Professor Nicholas Negroponte, is searching for nothing less than artificial design intelligence. The 'architecture machine,' as it is called, is to be a 'moral' animal and a design partner to the architect, capable of carrying on a man-machine dialogue in the manner of an associate having 'the potential for self-improvement.'"[62]

Now formalized as the Architecture Machine Group (ArcMac) and with research sponsored by the Ford Foundation and Interdata via the USL (sponsorship later supplemented by the Advanced Research Projects Agency of the Department of Defense [ARPA], the US Air Force, the Office of Naval Research, and others), Negroponte, Groisser, and their students, in association with Marvin Minsky, Oliver Selfridge, and Seymour Papert, had turned to questions of artificial intelligence that might be pertinent to design. The group's focus, Miller reported, was now on "the problem of interfacing, both between computer and man, and computer and real world."[63] Artificial intelligence, or what Negroponte referred to as "ultra-intelligence in computers,"[64] was approached by breaking down the design problem—understood as a process of monitoring and representing the environment—into systematic components: machine vision, sketch recognition, interfaces with nonprofessionals, computer graphics, tactile sensors and effectors, low-resolution interfacing, and three-dimensional input-output. While the ambition was to create "more flexible and more responsive" computer programs, what emerged was a mode of interface that required the extensive acquisition and processing of ever more detailed information of both "man" and his "real world." Even after collecting environmental data through those sensors in the "real world," the frictionless vacuum does not seem to have been replaced by sociohistorical material, but by other applications.

Under the subhead "Computers in Search of Identity," Runge offered a succinct description of research then underway as part of this shift towards artificial intelligence. "A computerized robot, GROPE," Runge begins,

> is a toy tank with photoelectric eyes that are being trained to search out "interesting" places (points of greatest diversity) on urban maps, and may someday lead to a mechanical design partner that can seek out information about the real world without human supervision; SEE is a computerized television camera that studies various groupings of 2" x 2" blocks (representing urban-scale modules), and then devises its own configurations. A program is being developed for a computer that can interview people about their urban environment, the ultimate goal being to hook it into the public phone system. Negroponte sees this as an important step towards universal advocacy: "The design of the city can start to reflect every single inhabitant—his needs and desires. This may seem completely ludicrous, but I don't think it is."[65]

Negroponte's step toward universal advocacy was illustrated by an image of an African-American man at a typewriterlike device. The caption reads: "Ghetto resident talks to computer about slum environment via typewriter computer terminal: Another of Architecture Professor Nicholas Negroponte's artificial intelligence projects."[66] As revealed in the September 1969 issue of *Architectural Design* dedicated to the discipline's interface with cybernetics and operations research, this project was titled INTERACT.

Edited by Royston Landau, the special issue of *Architectural Design* featured "Experiments in Computer Aided Design: Report from the Department of Architecture." Along with a report entitled "Space Arrangement," on research led by Tim Johnson, it covered USL-sponsored research, including Porter's DISCOURSE and John Boorn's CHOICE, as well as ArcMac's GROPE, SEE (soon to be called, more ominously, SEEK), and INTERACT. The introduction proposed that machines "and automation in general" might provide some of the "omitted and difficult-to-acquire information" needed for good design, information that was previously provided by human architects. But it stressed that information might still be missing. "Consequently, the Architecture Machine Group at MIT, are embarking on the construction of a machine that can work with missing information," a machine that could understand human metaphors, "solicit information on its own," "talk to a wide variety of people," acquire experience, and be intelligent.[67] The prospectus was followed by a reprint of Negroponte's "Toward a Humanism through Machines" of 1969, in which he described the desired process of mutual evolutionary exchange as an "acquaintanceship of two intelligent systems, the architect and the Architecture Machine," a relationship that would not take the form of master/slave, but rather that "of two associates which each have the potential for self-improvement." Computer-aided design, he stressed, distinguishing his group's work from simple processes of computerization, would not leave either party untouched, since, as he put it, it "concerns an ecology of mutual design complementation, augmentation, and substitution."[68]

Negroponte returned to questions of "responsiveness" and "participation" in "Concerning Responsive Architecture," his concluding remarks for "The Shirt-Sleeve Session in Responsive Housebuilding Technologies," a conference held at MIT in May 1972 and published as *The Responsive House*. He began by noting that there were many forms of responsiveness under discussion: there was "a responsive *design* technology that people are talking about—participation, advocacy planning"; responsive building technology; and, finally, what he was dreaming of, "responsive architecture itself." The latter, he clarified, entailed "the removal of all middlemen," including architects. To explain what he meant, he recalled having recently attended a conference on "design participation" in which he witnessed two primary orientations—the design methodologists and the "'Advocacy Planner' types."[69] The former sought information from the social sciences: "We want the psychologists, sociologists, and anthropologists to tell us more about what people want. We want people to fill out more questionnaires. We want to know *more*, so we can design better buildings," Negroponte ventriloquized. The latter took on an activist role, which he characterized as saying: "We're going to get people *heard*. We're going to help them to affect the design of their environments." Both, Negroponte assessed, were paternalistic, a category in which he now included URBAN5. His new solution: "a physical environment which has knowledge about *you*."[70] This idea was being provisionally tested on the lab's door with GREET, a device designed to recognize people through what cybernetician Gordon Pask called a "you-sensor." But as with URBAN5, GREET was only the first step: Negroponte was seeking an environment with the same predictive ability—with respect to his needs and desires—as his wife. It was not surprising, he speculated, that people remained suspicious, given the paucity of extant examples: "Unfortunately, examples such as floors that can tell how many people are walking on them, and doors that can recognize people, usually end up driving second-rate light shows, or doing very banal things in directing the physical environment." The one "genuine architectural response" he could point to was Sean Wellesley-Miller's "sculpture exhibit which counts the number of people that go into it and come out of it, and inflates or deflates additional sections of the building, depending on how many people are in the exhibit." (Wellesley-Miller was part of the Eventstructure Research Group, cofounded with Jeffrey Shaw and Theo Botschuijver.) Preempting contemporary personal-data-tracking applications, Negroponte concluded by pointing to operational responses that were more convincing, even if not yet realized—what he called "lots of little applications of a surrogate 'me.'" "I hate reading newspapers and looking at news on the television," he explained, "but I would love to have some sort of device which knew me well enough to synopsize the news each night, and tells me if there happens to be something interesting on television today or tomorrow, without having to read TV Guide."[71]

INTERACT

With ArcMac's INTERACT and the group's work on interfacing with nonprofessionals, we find ourselves at the crux of research into the urban crisis, computers, and social sciences fostered by the USL. INTERACT, as reported in *Architectural Design*, "faces the problem of soliciting information about the environment, about needs and desires, from the inhabitants themselves."[72] The little-documented project's primary researcher was Richard Hessdorfer, a recent graduate from MIT's architecture program who was "developing a 'consumer' item that could initiate a dialogue with inhabitants, build a model of [their] needs and desires (particular to the speaker) and report back to Architecture Machines." As the account in *Architectural Design* recalled, the experiment involved taking a "teletype writing device" into the South End, described as "Boston's ghetto area."

> Three inhabitants of the neighborhood were asked to converse with this machine about their local environment. Though the conversation was hampered by the necessity to type English sentences, the chat was smooth enough to reveal two important results. First, the three

> user-inhabitants said things to this machine they would probably not have said to a human, particularly a white planner or politician: to them the machine was not black, was not white, and surely had no prejudices. Second, the three residents had no qualms or suspicions about talking with a machine (in English about personal desires); they did not type uncalled for remarks, instead they immediately entered a discourse about slum landlords, highways, schools and the like.[73]

Although not revealed initially, the "user-inhabitants" were Maurice Jones, Barry Adams, and Robert Quarles, the latter wearing a "tenant power" badge.[74]

In July 1969, Negroponte included a further description in the inaugural issue of the school's new publication, *Research*. INTERACT, he explained,

> is a project that explores natural language communication between actual users (users-to-be) of a physical environment and machine "advocacy planners." The romantic notion of people designing their own houses, their own cities, their own physical environments (all within rapid change and growth) is the underlying goal.... At present the system exhibits a very false intelligence and is primarily a wordy conversationalist. However, the goal is to build a model of the speaker's needs and desires and to provide a mirror of his requirements and aspirations (and to get to know him).[75]

Negroponte's suggestion that the data-extraction system still exhibited a "false intelligence," that it remained a "wordy conversationalist," was perhaps a reference to a conceit at the heart of this project. As revealed parenthetically in *Architectural Design*: "The reader should know, as the three users did not, that this experiment was conducted over telephone lines with teletypes, with a human at the other end, not a machine. The same experiment will be rerun shortly—this time with a machine at the other end of the telephone line."[76] When in 1973 he mentioned the project in his contribution to "La Ville Totale," which appeared alongside projects by architects Kenzo Tange, R. Buckminster Fuller, and Yona Friedman in *2000: Revue de l'amanégement du territoire*, Negroponte revealed that the humans on the other end of the telephone line were architects.[77]

Negroponte's remarks on user participation and advocacy planning remind us that ArcMac's ambitions remained indebted to experimental architects whose work sought to be flexible and adaptable to users such as the Japanese Metabolists of the early 1960s and the Groupe d'Étude d'Architecture Mobile, a European collective founded in 1958 by Hungarian-born, Paris-based architect Yona Friedman. Following their initial meeting in 1964—when Negroponte, who could speak French, was sent to the airport to pick up the visiting lecturer—Friedman's "Une cité spatiale" became a key reference in Negroponte's undergraduate thesis of 1966, "Systems of Urban Growth," and Friedman became a long-standing collaborator with ArcMac.[78] The three-dimensional matrix structuring Friedman's spatial city was reiterated initially as a mechanical framework in Negroponte's three-dimensional "Mova-grid," adapted from the Metabolists. The larger "Mega-grid," in turn, "merely defines points in space that in turn describe potential volumes," within which components were jacked into place.[79] That matrix returned in the cubes of URBAN5 and other systems-based environments Negroponte built in that seemingly frictionless vacuum of the virtual realm, marking the degree to which the research uncannily harbored memory of the period's experimental practice while taking it in a very different direction.

Referring to Moshe Safdie's housing megastructure for Expo 67 in Montreal, Negroponte later acknowledged that URBAN5 had "mimicked the additive genre of composition, popular in school at the time and epitomized in Habitat. It did this comprehensively, smoothly, and expensively."[80] Moreover, he acknowledged that this desired shift to an advocacy model of user participation via the automation of artificial intelligence, and with it the eradication of the architect from the equation, "has received the serious attention only of Yona Friedman, in Paris, France."[81] But Negroponte's ambitions were distinctly out of sync with the utopian ideals of a liberatory environment motivating much experimental practice of this period. Introducing the English translation of Friedman's *Toward a Scientific Architecture* (1975), Negroponte alluded to the "paradoxical intersection of two academic streams—participatory design and scientific methods—too frequently held apart by the circumstances of our training," underscoring that his position was somewhat closer to the "scientific" side of this conflict. As he put it, "Yona Friedman has used a mathematical scaffolding to support philosophical positions in a manner which affords the reader the

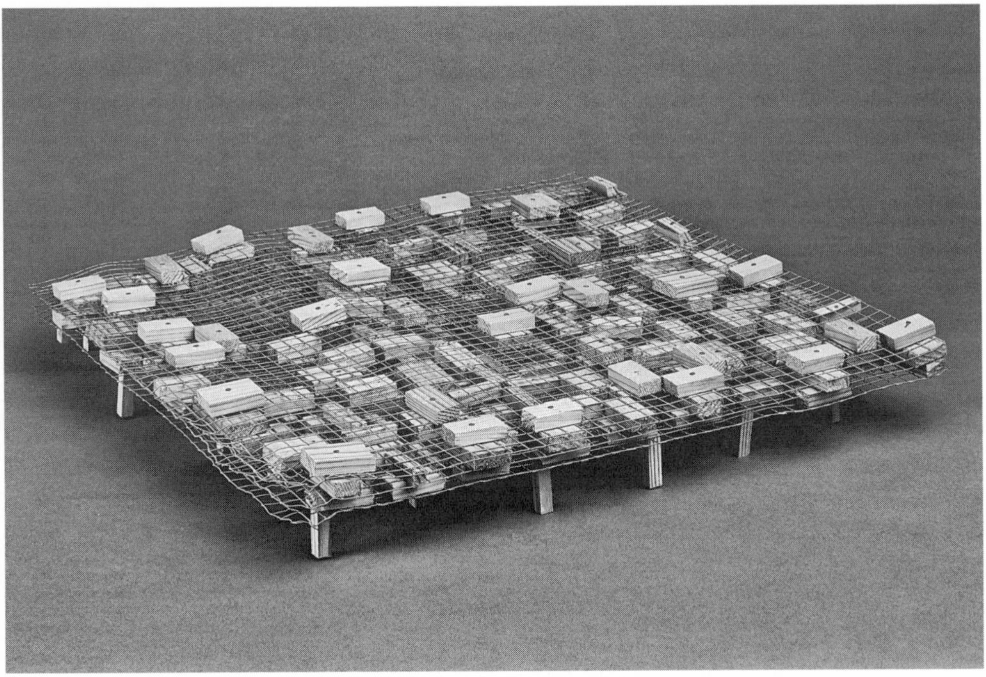

Figure 7.4 Yona Friedman, Untitled (Paris Spatial), 1960; wood, iron (Georges Meguerditchian, Musee National d'Art Moderne © 2015 Artists Rights Society [ARS], New York/ADAGP, Paris. © CNAC/MNAM/Dist. RMN-Grand Palais/Art Resource, NY).

opportunity to disagree with his utopian posture, but still benefit from his techniques."[82] That year, Friedman acted as a consultant to ArcMac on the Architecture-by-Yourself project. Related to Friedman's unrealized Flatwriter project, a keyboard-interfaced machine that would enable people to design their own homes within a giant megastructural framework, the application even adopted his name, YONA.[83]

By 1975, however, as Negroponte was likely aware, the trope of participation and the logic informing the feedback-based process of scientific methods were hardly so opposed. Any avowedly idealistic goal of user-controlled systems of organization was easily transposed into a form of participation in which an ever more precise constellation of data or information about human subjects—their needs and desires—could be extracted and fed back into a machine. Indeed, this was the most evident lesson of ArcMac's contribution to *Software: Information Technology, Its New Meaning for Art*, an exhibition of conceptual art held at the Jewish Museum in New York in 1970. *Software*, as curator Jack Burnham explained, responded to "life in a computerized environment," aiming to demonstrate "the effects of contemporary control and communication techniques in the hands of artists."[84] Research in Negroponte's experimental laboratory had little in common with the critical, artistic, and institutional questions driving conceptual art practices at the time. Nevertheless, it shared the exhibition's focus on systems-based and process-based work engaging communication technology and cybernetics through which individuals might interact with one another and with their environment.

Other contributors included Center for Advanced Visual Studies alumnus Hans Haacke, Sonia Sheridan, Vito Acconci, Les Levine, Allan Kaprow, Lawrence Weiner, and others. Haacke, for instance, presented *Visitors' Profile* and *News*, the former collecting, tabulating, and outputting data on visitors who interacted with the installation, the latter an active teletype printout of national and foreign news

Figure 7.5 Architecture Machine, *Seek*, 1969–70 in the Jewish Museum installation *Software—Information Technology: Its New Meaning for Art* (September 16–November 8, 1970) (Shunk-Kender © J. Paul Getty Trust. The Getty Research Institute, Los Angeles. [2014.R.20] Gift of the Roy Lichtenstein Foundation in memory of Harry Shunk and Janos Kender).

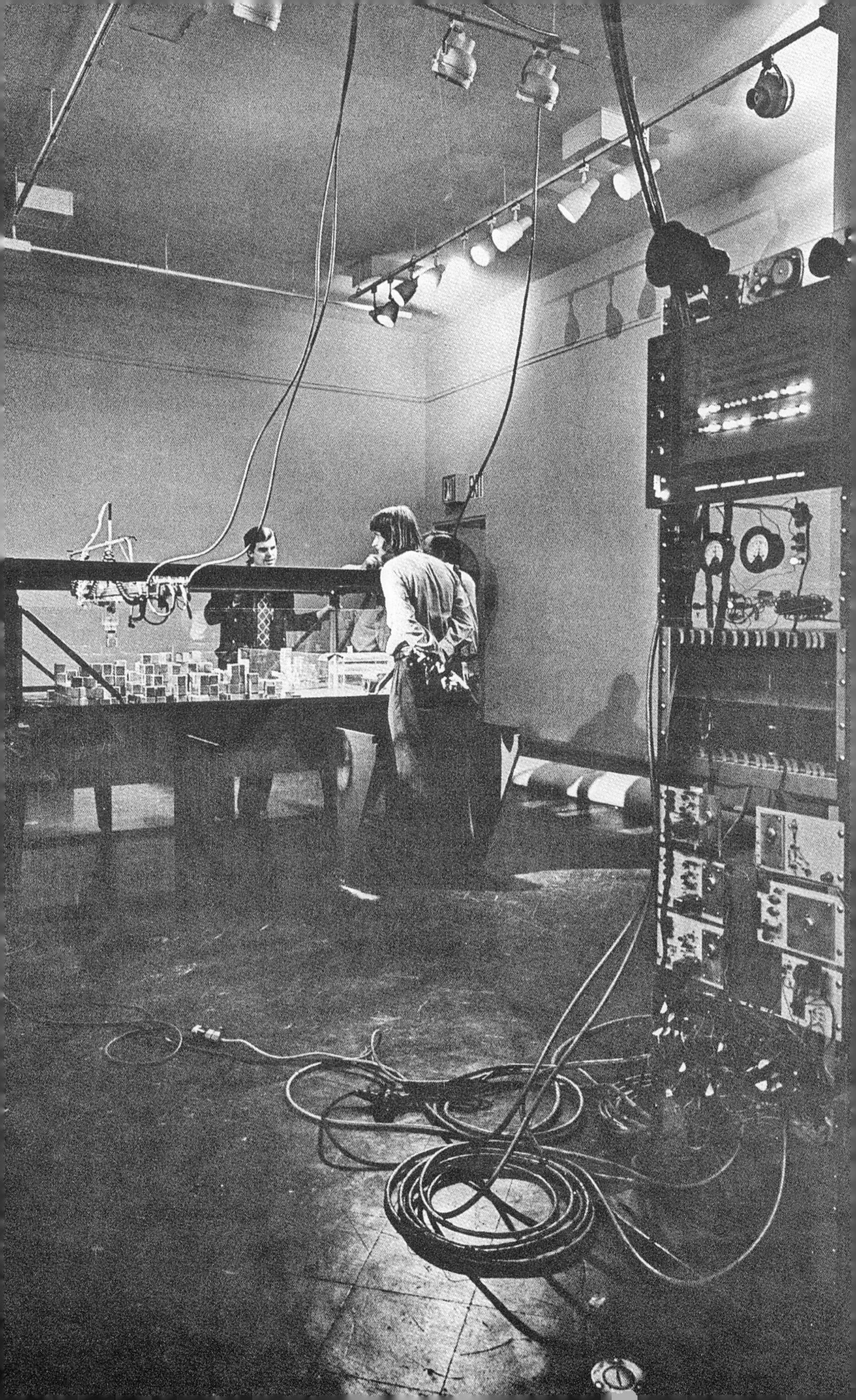

Figure 7.6 The Architecture Machine, *Seek*, 1969–70 in the Jewish Museum installation *Software—Information Technology: Its New Meaning for Art* (September 16–November 8, 1970) (Shunk-Kender © J. Paul Getty Trust. The Getty Research Institute, Los Angeles. [2014.R.20] Gift of the Roy Lichtenstein Foundation in memory of Harry Shunk and Janos Kender. The Jewish Museum, New York/Art Resource).

services. Levine installed *Systems Burn-off x Residual Software*, a work composed of photographs from the equally famous *Earth Works* exhibition the year before in Ithaca and speaking to the informatic residuals transmitted through media, along with *A.I.R.*—video feed from the artist's studio—and *Wire Tap*, speakers broadcasting his telephone conversations. In this context Negroponte presented SEEK, configured as a servomechanism connected to the Architecture Machine and designed to "handle local unexpected events" occurring within an environment composed of two-inch cubes that served as the habitat for a colony of gerbils. As he explained, SEEK "metaphorically goes beyond the real-world situation, where machines cannot respond to the unpredictable nature of people (gerbils). Today machines are poor at handling sudden changes in context in environment. This lack of adaptability is the problem *Seek* confronts in diminutive."[85]

Offered as an exercise in the benefits of artificial intelligence in which the computer architect had replaced the human architect, who was no longer able to deal with the complexity of the environment, SEEK hoped to demonstrate, in miniature, optimized relations between humans, their actions, and their computerized or virtual milieu. URBAN5's ten-foot blocks returned as 500 two-inch cubes to be tested in a five-by-seven-foot "real world" situation that was perhaps best understood as a simulation of environmental control. Negroponte's intelligent machine read the "desires" of the animals as registered by their random displacement of blocks, and then the computer-controlled prosthetic device straightened the blocks in the new locations. The outcome, he wrote, was "a constantly changing architecture that reflected the way the little animals used the place."[86] That is, the computer was supposed to learn to read indeterminate actions and the fluidity of the environment as possessing underlying meanings and then recalibrate the organization of blocks according to this newly detected set of parameters. In this pernicious circuit, it was precisely via interaction with the environment that the gerbil facilitated the computer's learning process and hence ceded his or her control over the transformation of the environment to the Architecture Machine. Negroponte later conceded that at the time of the show, the technology was not yet sophisticated enough for the Architecture Machine actually to learn in an "evolutionary sense"; it merely evaluated probabilities.[87] However, his attempts to produce such an environmental mechanism produced a perfect allegory of the potential evacuation of agency and of space for political negotiation at the hands of cybernetic machines as initially modeled by INTERACT.

When Negroponte described INTERACT in his book on early ArcMac research, *The Architecture Machine* (1970), he added the somewhat troubling suggestion that "with these domestic (domesticated) machines, the design task becomes one of blending the preferences of the individual with those of the group. Machines would monitor the propensity for change of the body politic. Large central processors, parent machines of some sort, could interpolate and extrapolate the local commonalities by overviewing a large population of 'consumer machines.'"[88]

The formulation of such a surveillance device, connected, as the group imagined, through the telephone system and avowedly dedicated to a normative ideal—"blending the preferences of the individual with those of the group"—is enough to make one nervous. Negroponte attempted to defer such a reaction by pointing to the machine's capacity to make ever more fine-grained distinctions among subjects, but in so doing, he may have instead revealed the project's disturbing proximity to domestic security applications. "What will remove these machines from a 'Brave New World,'" he remarked, "is that they will be able to (and must) search for the exception (in desire or need), the one in a million. In other words, when the generalization matches the local desire, our omnipresent machines will not be excited. It is when the particular varies from the group preferences that our machine will react, not to thwart it but to service it."[89] How, exactly, might the Architecture Machine's knowledge of your deviance or exception service your desires? What sort of decisions would such a computer, even if programmed to be an "ethical robot," really help you to make?

ArcMac returned to the question of interfacing with nonprofessionals, "the problem of interfacing . . . between computer and man," in "Computer Aids to Participatory Architecture," a 1971 proposal submitted to the National Science Foundation (NSF) for USL-affiliated research. The document concluded with SEEK, including the page from *Software* and details on six operations through which the software controlled the hardware—Generate, Degenerate, Fix it, Straighten, Find, Error Detect. The project abstract, published in the 1971 *USL Directory of Urban and Urban Related Research Projects at*

MIT, pointed to the task of data extraction, noting that "the outcome of a scenario with the system would be not so much an 'instant' house plan as it would be a model of the user, i.e., his needs and desires."[90] In the NSF proposal, the group went so far as to clarify that technology would replace politics: "*we are not proposing to do computer-aided advocacy planning*. We propose to take a step towards allowing the urban dweller to participate in the design of his own environment by multiplying the availability of design services rather than by mobilizing political power."[91] Again the group used photographs of INTERACT (though not naming the project in the proposal) to demonstrate their means of "eliciting information." "Since the basic premise of this proposal is that our users cannot express all their needs and desires explicitly, the machine must determine most of them implicitly."[92] Those needs and desires constituted precisely the data needed by the system to ensure (political) homeostasis. If, to stress the point, this inscription of the user within an ever more extensive data-driven feedback device was initially cast as a computer-mediated form of advocacy planning, such remarks, along with the trajectory of funding for such research, indicate that we might rightfully question a certain knowingness regarding its military potentials.[93] Years later, Negroponte suggested that he had become all too aware of such resonances, noting that "the idea is to encourage the most advanced media research, without the 'Dr. Jekyll and Mr. Hyde' tone implicit in arts and humanities research done conjointly with military and industrial sponsorships."[94]

This dream of a computer-controlled environment, replete with integrated sensor and surveillance technologies, computer-assisted data processing and evaluation, and automated prosthetic devices resonated with General Westmoreland's ambition of achieving a soldierless "battlefield of the future" in Vietnam, that superefficient, computerized, and totalizing "electronic battlefield" designed to respond to the asymmetrical tactics of guerilla warfare. As noted in Chapter 4, soldiers and military strategy were replaced by machines, reducing US military casualties and soothing certain aspects of antiwar protests; data were collected remotely and in increasingly microscopic detail; communication was instantaneous: it would be, as Paul Edwards writes, "knowledge without confrontation, power without friction."[95] Just as computers would run the wars of the future, so, it seems, would they manage future environments:

architects could now in effect man those guard towers, performing their environmental control while maintaining the appearance of having withdrawn from the operation. And all of this could be tested in the realm of simulation or modeling, in which, to cite Edwards again, "systems analysis linked choices about strategy directly to choices about technology," thus informing policy decisions and "inherently promot[ing] technological change."[96]

Arsenals of Democracy

To try to understand what was at stake in this Dr. Jekyll and Mr. Hyde dualism, this antinomy of good and evil inherent in certain trajectories of technological development, and why Negroponte recognized ArcMac to be haunted by such a morality tale, I want to come back to the USL, the Cambridge Project, and the politics of Big Science as MIT steered (or claimed to steer) research activity and resources away from war-related projects and toward the civilian domain. As the federal government became increasingly concerned with controlling or managing the urban crisis—including not only the physical basis of cities, but the social unrest rising in the face of social and environmental injustices, the Cold War arms race, and the ongoing war in Southeast Asia—things "urban" would for a short moment join military defense and space exploration as the new frontier of federal funding. MIT tried to situate itself at the forefront of this initiative, casting the USL's contribution as collecting data and developing programs, technologies, and ever more detailed forms of simulation. But funding proved not so easy to obtain, and as noted earlier, the program was dropped by 1974. That year *The Tech* published "Urban Systems Lab: Social Work since '68." "According to Miller," the retrospective note explained, "when the Urban Systems Lab was founded in 1968, 'there was the anticipation that urban problems would be approached on the basis of large scale, mission-oriented projects, as in the space program. These large scale projects never came about because of funding limitations. HUD never became the research equivalent of the Defense Department.'"[97] In the meantime, however, the DoD, like the Ford Foundation, emerged as a not-insignificant funding resource for certain types of urban studies, raising questions regarding both the character of the research pursued under such grants and its potential applications.

MIT's significant contributions to scientific and technological developments during World War II were typically greeted enthusiastically for their role in ensuring US and, hence, Allied supremacy against Axis forces. Norbert Wiener and others, however, famously raised the issue of science's social responsibility in the aftermath of the atomic bombing of Hiroshima and Nagasaki and refused military funding for subsequent research.[98] The Vietnam War was a different scenario. The institute emerged from the turbulent months of 1968 largely without incident. Yet beginning with a research stoppage on March 4, 1969, MIT was a target for and site of antiwar protests on account of the military-sponsored, often classified war-related research undertaken in its laboratories, in particular the off-campus "Special Laboratories"—the Lincoln and Instrumentation Laboratories.[99] (The former, to recall, operated the IBM System/360 mainframe computer, the latter cofunded VSTOL.) Not everyone was enamored of the institute's liberal "salting" with "men whose careers straddle the academic-industrial consulting line" or "returnees from Washington's advisory elite."[100] I want to turn now to two interrelated aspects of this story: first, the renaming, proposed conversion, and decision to divest the Instrumentation Laboratory (I-Lab), and second, protests over MIT's Center for International Studies(CIS) and with it Project Cambridge and Ithiel de Sola Pool. If these might read initially as detours or departures from the history of the SA+P, the first, as we will see, speaks to ongoing interactions between USL activities and war-related research, the second to the proximity of such research to the school.

In April 1969, following the March protests, President Johnson convened a review panel on the Special Laboratories; known as the Pounds Panel, it was charged with examining the role of military-funded and war-related research at MIT. The panel recommended continuing some defense-related research, but shifting the focus of work in the special labs "in the direction of domestic and social problems." The MIT Corporation, the university's governing body, accepted the recommendations and released a statement asserting that it "would be inappropriate for the Institute to incur new obligations in the design and development of systems that are intended for operational deployment as military weapons."[101] Distinguishing between basic and applied research, it clarified that this decision did not "mean that with its unique qualities the Institute should not continue to be involved in advancing the state of technology in areas which have defense applications."[102] In October, the faculty voted overwhelmingly in favor of Johnson's proposal to test the feasibility of the recommendations, and Johnson set up a standing committee, known as the Sheehan Committee, to establish whether funding would be available for such a shift in priorities.

Shortly afterward, Johnson appointed Charles L. Miller to succeed Charles S. Draper as the director of the I-Lab, now renamed the Charles Stark Draper Laboratory. As announced in *The Tech*, "According to a reliable source, Prof. Miller expects a major part of the Urban Systems Lab, which he also heads, to be absorbed into the new Draper Labs." "Transfer of on-going projects," the student reporter noted, "would pacify those who want the I-Labs to begin working on socially necessary projects now—even if those projects were a small part of the I-Lab total budget—and thus take away some support from the SACC [Science Action Coordinating Committee] drive to end war-related research at the labs."[103] But, he concluded, the "reorganization [gave] only the illusion of change."

> [T]his reporter was present when Prof. J. C. R. Licklider told Provost Jerome Wiesner in a phone conversation that appointing Miller to head the Draper Labs was "a stroke of genius." The whole thing is so pragmatic that Richard Nixon might have engineered it. I-Labs, with $50 million a year in volume, can swallow Urban Systems' $5 million whole—it will allow them, in fact, to keep people employed who might have had to leave now that the Apollo work is almost finished. But those projects can be used as a showcase effort. "See," MIT can say to us all, "the I-Labs are being converted to peaceful uses."[104]

The reporter was not the only one convinced that MIT's "plans to convert its laboratories from war-related research" were "nothing but a fraud" or that such claims to conversion were meant to counter criticism of Pentagon-related research.[105] These suspicions were fueled by the "liberation" of a memo from Miller to Johnson into the hands of the November Action Coalition (NAC), a coalition of about thirty activist groups from the Boston area that were planning militant action against the I-Lab. Miller wrote to Johnson with concerns about ongoing USL funding, concluding: "While wise use of Ford funds can help ease some of these, I feel it would be a mistake to ignore the critical needs of USL while giving a misleading illusion of 'converting' the I-lab."[106] The group took this statement as proof of disingenuousness.

As reported in the *New York Times*, on November 4, approximately one thousand NAC members "mounted the steps of the student center with Vietcong flags and a loudspeaker to begin their 'anti-imperialistic actions' against the Institute," later chanting "Ho, Ho, Ho Chi Minh, N.L.F. is going to win." In anticipation of the action, MIT administrators obtained a court order banning violence and disruption on campus; it was "believed to be the first taken by a college in advance of disorders."[107] The largely nonviolent protests continued for three days and were directed not only at the I-Lab, but at the CIS and its Cambridge Project. Protesters "also charged that two social science projects at the Center for International Studies and the so-called Cambridge Project are designed to counter revolutionary movements."[108]

In May 1969, the SACC launched a demonstration against the Cambridge Project, brainchild not only of Pool, but also of Licklider, a professor of electrical engineering and former director of the primary institutional support for artificial-intelligence research, the Information Processing Techniques Office (IPTO) of ARPA.[109] The *New York Times* reported that the SACC "asserted that the computer would be useful to the Pentagon for amassing data to be employed in suppressing popular movements." While the administration denied the assertion, insisting that the Cambridge Project was simply an unclassified project to develop computer analysis and modeling of research in the behavioral sciences, the project, the article revealed, "applied to the Behavioral Sciences Division of [ARPA], an arm of the Department of Defense."[110] Pool had a history of research on counterinsurgency and psychological-warfare techniques, some developed for Vietnam, and he believed in the value of the social sciences as a tool of government and national security, especially as a way of securing intelligence for US interests abroad.[111] "I can think of no greater contribution a social scientist could make to the intelligence of the US government," Pool argued in 1967, invoking Vietnamese villages, Dominican students, and Soviet writers, "than to help improve this effort at knowledge of the outside world."[112] In October 1969, the CIS was the target of a peaceful demonstration and "test occupation" promoted by the Rosa Luxemberg Students for a Democratic Society (RL-SDS), which interrupted work for about three hours.[113] Carrying the flags of the Vietnamese National Liberation Front, the students chanted, "We won't die for Pool and Pye," linking Pool with Lucien Pye, an MIT political scientist who worked on Southeast Asia, again claiming "the two were engaged in research on counter-revolutionary techniques and were funded by the Defense Department."[114] Pool's COMCOM program, which developed computer simulations of international communication patterns,[115] and the Cambridge Project were both condemned as part of an apparatus of "psychological warfare." A few weeks later, Dorothy Nelkin recounts in *The University and Military Research: Moral Politics at MIT*, Pool and three colleagues "were tried by a mock revolutionary tribunal and found guilty of 'crimes against humanity.'"[116]

Arguing that the I-Lab could not operate under the new constraints, Johnson announced his decision on May 20, 1970: "a divestment that protects this national asset, its personnel, and the Institute," for the country, he suggested, "looks to it as a shield." This separation allowed the lab to operate independently "and without the terms of the Corporation Executive Committee's directive."[117] As the reinstated Draper recounted in the lab's annual report, this "involved creating Charles Stark Draper Laboratory Division of M.I.T. with its own Board of Directors."[118] Miller joined the board and, quickly redeployed, returned to his duties as director of the USL.[119] An editorial in *The Tech* applauded the president's decision on account of the "current lack of funds for socially oriented research and the inability and unwillingness of the Draper Laboratory to change." "With the divestment of the Draper Lab and the gradual 'conversion' of the Lincoln Lab away from classified DOD research," they argued, "MIT will find itself out of the weapons systems development game."[120] It was evident to others that this divestment was again covering up for business as usual. Bruce Schwartz offered a dissenting voice in "D-Labs Inc.: Divestment as Cop-Out," which appeared on the same page of *The Tech* as the editorial, positing that MIT had simply washed its hands of the issue, hoping "to get war research protest as well as war research off campus" while the arms race continued with less oversight.

In 1972, as part of a reinvigorated campaign, the Committee on War-Related Research issued a statement. "War research has a long history at MIT," it began.

> America's interrelating complex of basic research, defense contracts, and weapons systems (with the corresponding profits), known as the military-industrial-university complex, has always held MIT close to its heart. The Institute's leadership role has always been recognized,

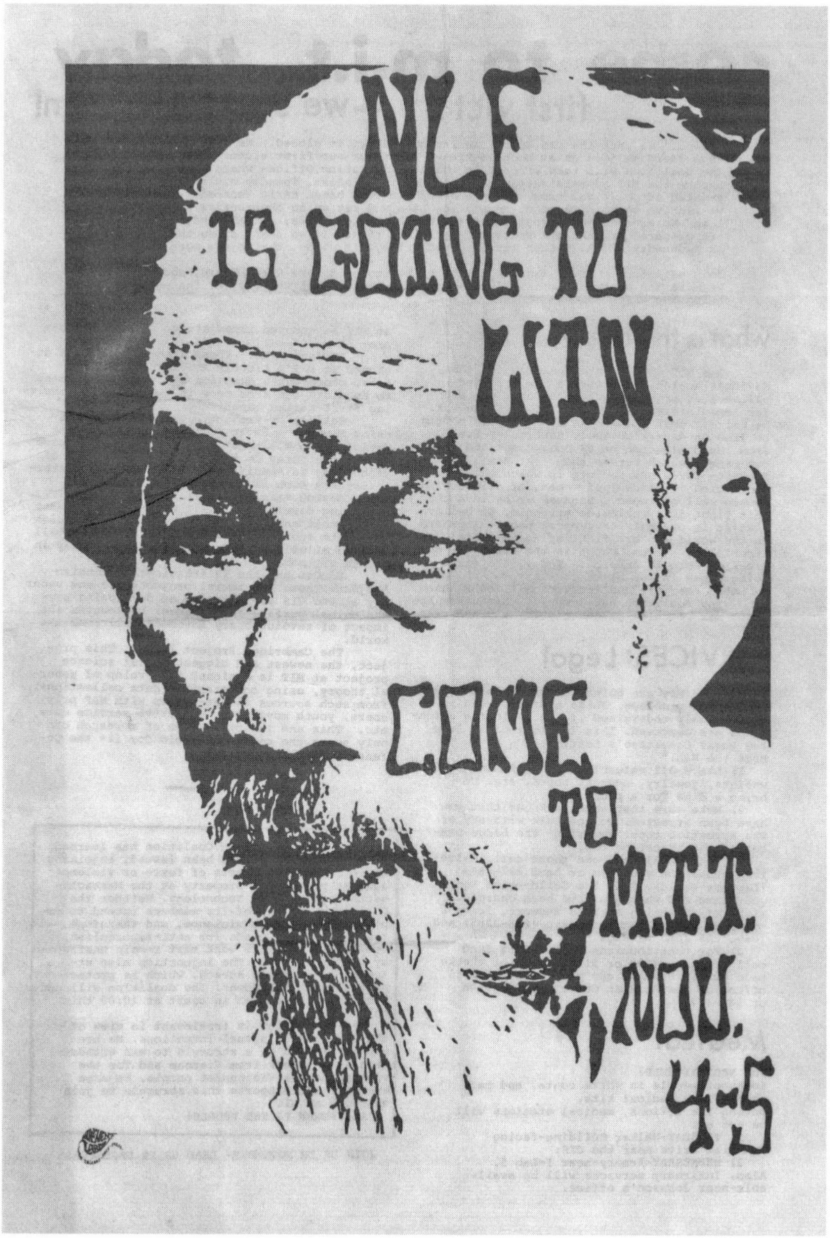

Figure 7.7 NLF is Going to Win, 1969; flyer (courtesy of MIT Libraries, Institute Archives and Special Collections, Cambridge, Massachusetts, Records of Vice President Constantine B. Simonides, 1960–1994).

Figure 7.8 Demonstrators march under a Viet Cong flag at MIT, November 6, 1969 (AP Photo).

> especially in war-time, and boasted of publicly. In 1966, J. B. Hanify, in a famous statement, defended MIT and its expansion in Cambridge by stating that it was an "arsenal of democracy." But times have changed, and the war in Indochina has increased the public's—particularly the student movement's—political awareness, to the point that now MIT has learned to hide behind the double-talk of innumerable committees, review panels, and false divestments.[121]

They continued: "*war research continues at MIT.* A little digging brings out a coherent picture that is not very different from what prompted Senator Fulbright to refer to MIT as 'the sixth wall of the Pentagon.'" When on May 8, 1972, President Nixon announced his decision to mine the harbors of North Vietnam, massive protests broke out against the escalation of the war; at MIT, riot police using clubs, dogs, and tear gas swept demonstrators from the campus.[122] The Draper Lab became independent the following year.

"The Little Pentagon"

In 1972, MIT-SDS launched a renewed battle against war-related research at the CIS. Pointing to its role in the suppression of popular movements struggling against US imperialism, they again targeted social-science research directed toward gathering intelligence, developing counterinsurgency techniques, and influencing government policy.[123] Moreover, demonstrators stressed the intimate coupling of social-science research with developments in engineering and computerization. As a pamphlet titled "Why CIS?" posited: "Many of the weapons systems developed by engineers at MIT's laboratories are deployed and used under the direction of MIT's social scientists."[124] Under the subtitle "The 'Little Pentagon,'" another pamphlet, "End MIT's War Complicity," argued: "The CIS provides analysis and strategy used in maintaining US economic domination and sympathetic governments all over the world. The US war machine is dependent on both the hardware and software developed at MIT." As detailed in "CIS Is CIA," the CIS was "founded in 1951, with CIA funding, under the directorship of the infamous W. W. Rostow... well-known as a key formulator of [President Lyndon B.] Johnson's policy in Vietnam" and a former major in the Office of Strategic Services, the forerunner of the CIA. The CIS was funded directly by the CIA until 1966, when, following protests, funding

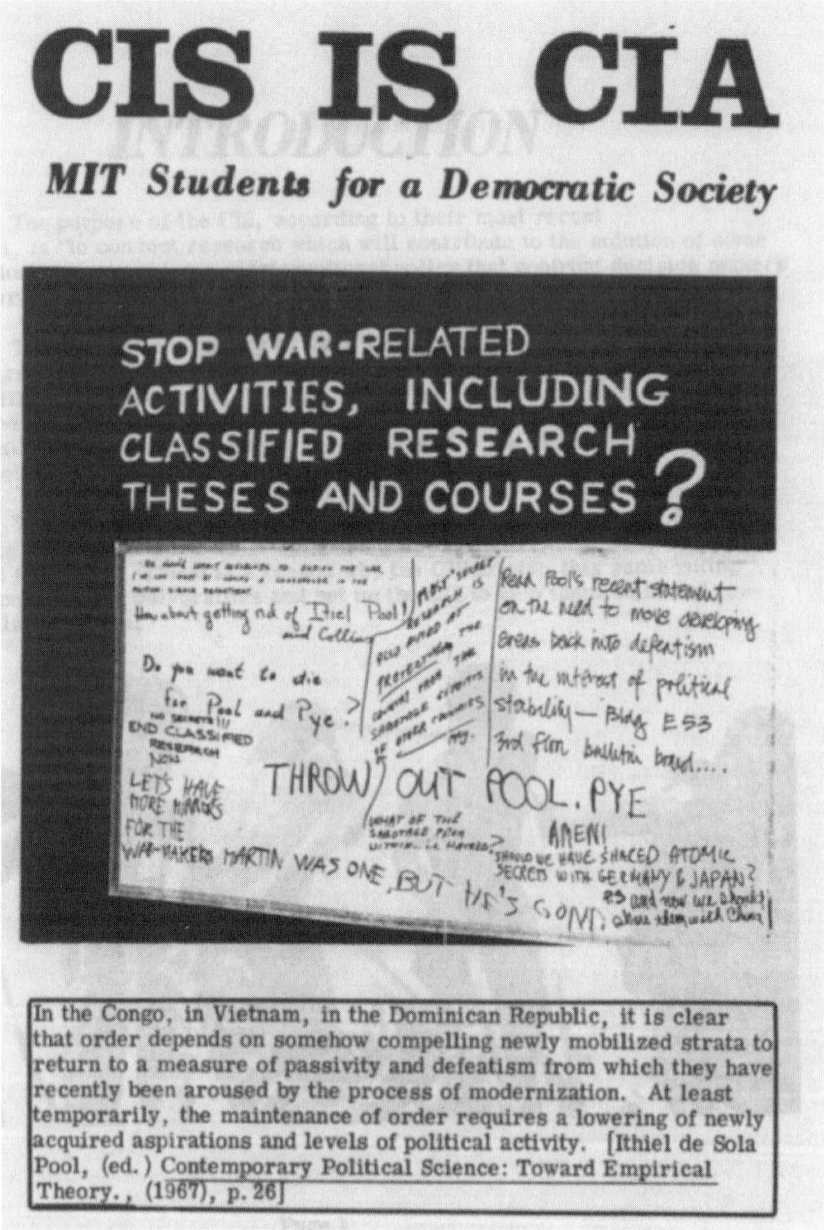

Figure 7.9 MIT Students for a Democratic Society, CIS IS CIA.

was taken over by the Ford Foundation and the Department of Defense. Little else had changed, they recognized. "The CIS," they concluded, "is, to this day, a CIA front."[125]

During the strikes of 1972, MIT-SDS declared de Sola Pool to be "People's Enemy No. 1." Pool and others at the CIS, they argued, "should be fired because they are essentially CIA agents in professors' clothing."[126] Pool had been a consultant at the RAND Corporation since 1951 and in 1959 founded Simulmatics, "a corporation to sell the software he developed to the government." Among Simulmatics's major contracts was the Strategic Hamlet program in Vietnam (in which, as we saw in Chapter 4, rural peasants were forcibly relocated into villages with secure perimeters to insulate them from contact with the Communist guerrilla insurgency) and "DoD's Project Agile/COIN (Counter-insurgency)."[127] Project Agile included "Research on Urban Insurgency," in part authored by Pool, and the "POLITICA-A Manual Countersubversion and Counterconspiracy Game," again coauthored by Pool and described as "a gaming project designed to investigate how the army could effectively deal with the guerilla movement in Vietnam." In addition, Project Agile entailed research on insurgency and counterinsurgency tactics in Guatemala, Peru, Ecuador, and Bolivia. From Project Agile, MIT-SDS suggested, Project Phoenix had emerged, an operation in which "teams of counter-insurgents went to villages in South Vietnam, and tortured or killed village chiefs who sympathized with the NLF (about 20,000 such village chiefs were murdered)."[128] Pool and his graduate students, moreover, were involved in preparatory field research, undertaking interviews with villagers to establish systems of political power and searching for "alternative organizations to the Viet Cong that would cooperate more readily with U.S. aims in Vietnam."[129]

According to Joseph Hanlon in the *New Scientist*, the DoD-funded Cambridge Project (operated under the CIS) was the key player in developing computer technologies for data collection and military-oriented and policy-oriented behavioral-science modeling for deployment in Southeast Asia. Hanlon cited a series of proposed areas of research and data sets from the original application to the DoD, a list that brings us back to the nexus of development and security: "Problems of the underdeveloped countries and on the conditions of stability"; "'A study of peasant attitudes' including: 'Under what conditions do peasants' protests become violent?"; "Studies on 'stability and disorder' in several countries"; "Analysis of several thousand interviews with Vietcong conducted by the Rand corporation"; along with "Public opinion polls from all countries"; "Cultural patterns on all tribes and peoples of the world"; "Data on youth movements"; "Mass unrest and political movements"; "Peasant attitudes and behavior"; and "Characteristics of Latin American countries." What Project Cambridge offered, Hanlon explained alluding to Jay Forrester's work, was the possibility of using data on villages to build a model of whether or not a village might be friendly to US interests or to predict what type of intervention might help gain its allegiance. Computers, he noted, "are already selecting bombing targets in Vietnam, so it is not inconceivable that the model would be used to select the most unfriendly villages for bombing." The tools developed by Project Cambridge aimed to facilitate more complex war-gaming models while simultaneously cutting simulation time down from months to a few hours, hence aiding decisions such as "whether or not to intervene in a foreign revolution or election."[130] As part of a USL "Summer Study" program, Pool worked simultaneously on developing computerized "Urban Information Systems" as "exercises in applied social science," this time dedicated to urban issues confronting the United States—"racial conflict, poverty, widespread physical decay, lack of low-cost housing, environmental pollution, and congested and wasteful transportation."[131]

Overlap

In 1974, the Cambridge Project was discontinued, or more properly, it was absorbed into the Overlap Project in the SA+P's newly founded Laboratory of Architecture and Planning (LAP). Funded by ARPA, the Overlap Project, as Porter, then dean of the school, explained without apology, was "an outgrowth of the Cambridge Project," and it was concerned with "devising ways of making inferences from textual and numerical data bases and automatically restructuring the data on the basis of these inferences (and vice versa)."[132] Given the long-standing relationship of Porter's USL-funded "urban data management language," DISCOURSE, to the Cambridge Project, Negroponte's presence on its board of directors since 1971,[133] and the interdisciplinary environmental research going on in the school, this transfer of the Cambridge Project to the architecture school seems hardly surprising. But it brings us back to the research's political coordinates. With Porter as primary director, the Overlap Project continued DISCOURSE, along with other data-management research.[134]

Porter established the LAP in July 1973 with the aim of promoting a "distinctive style of research and practice." In addition to stressing field-based research into physical and social environments, or "how people interact with each other and with these environments," research included "use of representations, or modeling," and "involvement in purposeful intervention," including role-playing and gaming exercises. "As more is known about society and the processes of social and environmental change," Porter explained, it became evident that "the environmental professional" was no longer adequately served by physical models and drawings of their buildings and needed to adopt the abstract modeling or simulation of the scientist, such as those inaugurated by Forrester. By "purposeful intervention," Porter hoped to express that what distinguished architects and planners from professionals in other fields "who try to understand existing social systems" was their roles as "agents of change." Architects and planners, he proposed, should concern themselves with "sensing opportunities, points of leverage, and mechanisms for change, and with ways of monitoring change."[135] In remarks at a March 1974 open house, Porter recalled that the idea for the LAP dated to an ill-fated 1971 proposal to the NSF to fund a "Center for the Human Environment," its name and timing seemingly pointed to the upcoming Stockholm conference. He stressed the similarity of the intended research to laboratory methods in the physical sciences, in which scientists construct representations of the real world "in order to permit experimentation where they cannot physically get at what they wish to investigate." In the LAP, he posited, faculty and students would make "interventions into carefully constructed representations of reality," using computer-based modeling to facilitate the simulation of complex urban and social environments through the incorporation of data.[136] Moreover, he stressed, being visually oriented, the school could bring additional visual skills to bear on quantitative data such as what fed Forrester's models: there was "considerable promise to some early efforts to combine the computer with other media for representing and manipulating environmental information."[137] Again MIT, Negroponte, and ArcMac were at the forefront of this development.

Like the Cambridge Project, the Urban Systems Lab ceased operations in 1974, when military spending was cut back due to the reduction of US involvement in Vietnam. But by then, as reflected in the LAP, as well as in the Interdisciplinary Environmental Design program founded in 1973 (absorbing the Urban Design program of 1966), and in the ongoing work of ArcMac, the school had so fully interpolated into its midst other aspects of scientific and technological research, as well as a systems-based paradigm of management, as to make such an interdisciplinary apparatus unnecessary.

What, then, might we learn from this story? I have been attempting to trace a series of interconnections—at the level of collaborations, of funding, of scientific methodology and technologies—that together suggest something more than simple homologies between research undertaken in the social sciences, management, and computer applications at MIT and that undertaken in architecture and urbanism. This, of course, is hardly strange, given the shared institutional milieu and its governing mandates, which structured the possibility for such heavily funded interdisciplinary research. (Other key players in the history of computers, such as Stanford University and Cal Tech, had no professional architectural programs.) To reiterate, I am not trying to suggest that we read all work undertaken at the School of Architecture as directed, wittingly or unwittingly, toward military ends or that the school necessarily or self-consciously operated in the service of national security and the broader geopolitical aims of the United States. But I do think we might ask whether, in some cases, architects, too, had become "defense intellectuals"—whether in the course of adopting modes of funding and alliances proper to Big Science and of collaborating with centers and laboratories at the forefront of counterinsurgency and other military operations in Southeast Asia and Latin America, these coordinates and skills had become so internalized or naturalized within the practice of the USL's "urban technologists" as to be pursued without questioning. The issue, once again, is not whether architects should engage with advanced forms of scientific knowledge and computer technology; such engagement has often characterized the discipline's vanguard, occasionally even its more radical avant-garde (although we are not concerned with avant-gardes here), and of course, tactical forms of practice continued to negotiate this territory with criticality and to politically progressive ends.[138] Rather, the question remains: How or to what ends might architects have engaged scientific and technological developments to progressive ends in a situation in which architectural and urban research in the university had become a targeted area of funding by the military and intelligence establishment and its allies such as the Ford Foundation?

Paul Edwards's argument that we should not dismiss the implied or actual military potentials of such research as simply "grantsmanship"—the "deliberate tailoring of grant proposals to the aims of funding agencies"—seems relevant here.[139] For even if such grantsmanship was initially intended as a convenient way to obtain necessary funding, its logic could shift to become what he calls "mutual orientation." In this scenario, just as the researchers start to imagine and even project the work's technical capacities into the military register to appeal for funding, the military agency comes to recognize new possibilities in the research, hence reorienting both sides of the equation. In 1967, Senator Fulbright cast this slightly differently in "The War and Its Effects: The Military-Industrial-Academic Complex." Referring to "an arrangement of convenience, providing the Government with politically usable knowledge and the universities with badly needed funds," he proposed that "a university which has become accustomed to the inflow of government contract funds is likely to emphasize activities which will attract those funds."[140]

This story reminds us, additionally, that the history of computers in architecture, or computer-aided design, is not merely a history of graphic interfaces and drawing or rendering techniques or of the experimental forms later facilitated by advances in software and hardware. To this we need to add the story of a paradigm shift put into effect during the discipline's inscription within new modalities of environmental management and control, the story of the role that architecture played (or was understood to play) within emergent paradigms of governmentality haunted by the Cold War and the rise of the Third World and refracted domestically with the threat of civil unrest. In the case of computer-aided design, Robin Evans's demonstration of how drawing techniques are not only descriptive tools, but formative mechanisms within the practice of architecture might thus be extended to suggest that what is at stake here is to understand and to intervene critically and politically in the ever-increasing structural alignment of the field and its tools with such mechanisms of control.[141] As the conception of architecture and the city came to be replaced by notions of environmental systems, we find that data on social organization and its physical matrix came to be understood simply as computational parameters with quantitative, rather than historical or political values. To invoke Forrester's work at the USL, insurrection was to be regarded as a momentary political instability before "urban dynamics" might be put to work to achieve a feedback-based stabilization that effectively quelled dissent.

I want to come back, then, to Dean Anderson's remark with which we began—his suggestion that the role of architecture and planning was that of "giving order to environmental and social change." The nature of that order had been radically altered. Architecture has long played a role in giving material form to the normative social mandates and welfare functions of the state as it both manages and cares for its citizens. And it has long operated semantically and even organizationally to achieve political ends. In the story we have been following, however, architecture was understood to function no longer simply (or not only) in the traditional sense of giving form and organization, or even aesthetic expression, to social needs or cultural identities, or even to enhance the quality of life. Architecture now offered tools with which to accumulate and deploy knowledge of the population who interacted with it and even a tactical arena in which to put those tools to work. Architectural research now operated in the service of advancing modes of global governmentality and hence micropolitical techniques of power; it became one agent among many in an expanded biopolitical regime and its security apparatus. The architect, and its updated version, the computer-architect, was imagined to be a protagonist in research feeding the proliferation of such political technologies, hence offering us a platform to identify the fine line distinguishing the discipline's progressive forms of experimentation—long a role played by schools of architecture—from its instrumental and normative function. Although architecture in some sense always treads this difficult line, we find here a shift to an operational paradigm in which decision making had ceded responsibilities to technologies of control and management which draw the user-participant ever more intricately into its machinations and that cynically mobilize the rhetoric of choice, participation, interaction, and even discourse, all now computer applications geared toward eradicating conflict.

CHAPTER EIGHT

Dataland (and Its Ghosts)

> And to think that some have heard of the "information superhighway" without sensing the total police surveillance to come.
> —Tiqqun, *This Is Not a Program*, 2011

"Research at the Architecture Machine Group continues to grow," N. John Habraken announced in his 1979 report as chairman of MIT's Department of Architecture. "The laboratory supports three major programs: Spatial Data Management, Mapping by Yourself, and Personalized Movies," he continued, noting "a major shift toward film and video, working intimately with the Film Section on a 'Movie Map.'"[1] Having spent many years developing tools (both hardware and software) to facilitate human-machine communication in the domain of architecture and urban design—including applications with computer-aided-design (CAD) such as YONA for Architecture-by-Yourself—ArcMac's research agenda turned to focus more extensively on regulating perception and amplifying interactivity with data. Referring to Nicholas Negroponte's Arts and Media Technology initiative, an intermediary between ArcMac, founded in the late 1960s, and the Media Lab launched out of it in the early 1980s,[2] Habraken posited that this transformation was "in part the beginning of a new Media Technology Program, embracing the larger interests of Film/Video and the Visible Language Workshop in particular."[3] By 1979, what might conventionally have been considered "architecture" or even "design" was no longer a motivating force for ArcMac, and even the "arts" in "arts and media technology" would be subsumed into "media" by the early 1980s. Indeed, as we will see, a lot was at stake in this shift.

Information Space

Clues to this shift toward mediated perception and human-machine interaction can be found in a November 1979 *New Scientist* article. Under the title "Alice in Dataland," it reported: "The potential scope for applying computers to military training and surveillance activities has been dramatically increased by experiments funded by the US Department of Defense which aim to improve the interaction between people and computers. The experiments are being conducted at [MIT by ArcMac,] which was originally established to study the use of computers in architecture."[4] The article focused on the Movie Map and Dataland. With the Movie Map, it explained, "not only does the computer enable the stranger to explore different routes along roads but it also permits interrogation of information files relating to particular buildings or areas," such as an "internal map of the building." Strangers could wander about and access intelligence. In Dataland, part of Spatial Data Management research, information was distributed into "data spaces... just as Disneyland is separated into discrete areas, each devoted to a particular theme." Its "obvious military potential" was exemplified for *New Scientist* in the presentation of LANDSAT images and "pictures of individuals." One could "focus on particular photos and... ask questions about that person, with answers coming from computerized data associated with that photo."[5] As revealed by ArcMac researcher Richard Bolt, this area was known as the "rogues' gallery," its demonstration model depicting ArcMac personnel.[6] Just in case the reader lost sight of Dataland's military relevance, Bolt's example of accessing territorial data used a map of Southeast Asia, zooming in on the intersection of China, Laos, and Vietnam.[7] "Alice in Dataland" stressed that both applications "depart radically from existing computer systems in avoiding the keyboard as the main method of communication between a person and a computer and in their mix of a variety of media, such as film, photographs and even sounds." Harnessing time-based multimedia components and audiovisual interfaces, ArcMac now operated at the forefront of military experiments with computer-driven tools for environmental control.

This new line of research led ArcMac to revamp its laboratory. As Habraken reported, the "renovation has been a specific attempt to match the physical environment to the research goals, making

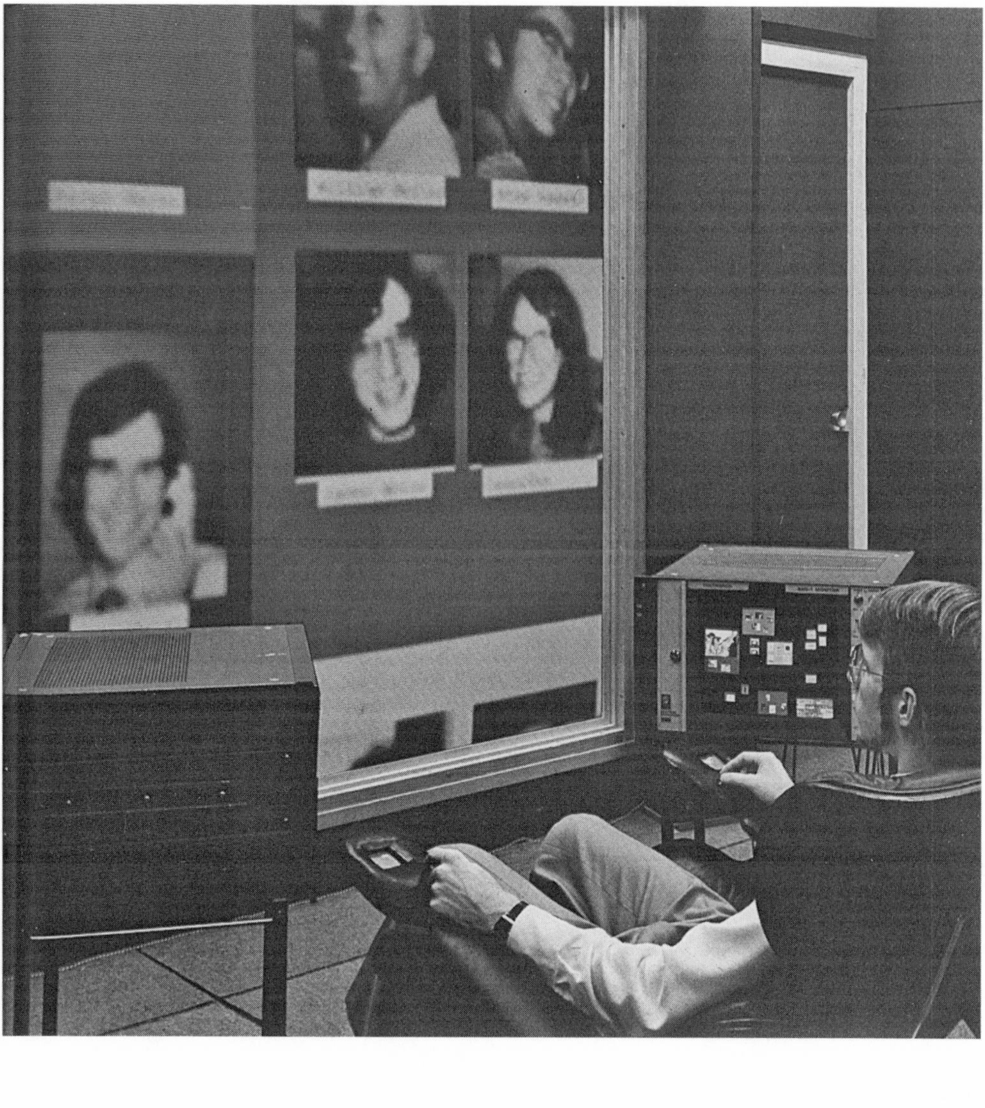

Figure 8.1 The Architecture Machine, demo of *Spatial Data Management System* with Bill Donelson in Media Room, MIT, c. 1979 (Hans-Christian Lischewski).

Figure 8.2 The Architecture Machine, demo of *The Interactive Movie Map: A Surrogate Travel System* in the Media Room, MIT, n.d. (Bob Mohl).

both a pleasant place and an electronic 'wired' milieu."[8] Called the "Media Room," the project was jointly funded by the Office of Naval Research (ONR) and the Cybernetics Technology Office at the Defense Advanced Research Projects Agency (DARPA); both sectors recognized potential in the shift from accessing data by name to traveling to it in (virtual) space. Alluding to the room's *unheimlich* character, Negroponte noted that it produced a "total immersion of cognitive and sensory apparatuses into an information space, convincingly real or uncannily imaginary." "Great concern," he specified of its departure from conventional planes of representation, "has been devoted to removing the sense of picture frame and to make the screen into a 'virtual wall.'"[9] This took the form of a floor-to-ceiling back-lit projection wall—served by a color-TV light-valve projection system located in an adjacent room. The Media Room was also furnished with a customized Eames chair and two touch-screen color video terminals. Sound came from an octaphonic sound system, with a speaker mounted at each corner of the large screen and four speakers situated behind the control chair. Furthermore, as Bolt noted, "automatic speech recognition and synthesized speech output facilities were present, enabling user and system to talk, each to the other."[10] Keyboards were polemically absent.

To Bolt, a trained psychologist, the atmosphere of the Media Room as a "multiple media information place" was not incidental to its function. "The relaxed ambiance conveyed by the presence of a chair of the Eames genre in lieu of something more utilitarian," he noted, "is intentional."

> It reflects convictions and positions about the nature and tone of human-computer interaction that we have attempted to actualize in the media room setting. Just as the hands-on immediacy of touch-sensitive pads suggests a literal impatience with intangibles about data, so the decor as epitomized in the selection of the style of chair rebuts the premise that system users must live in severe, ascetic settings.
>
> We have attempted to create an interface which is not a tiny, narrow-band "port-hole" into an information bank.... Rather, we have attempted radically to recast the setting as an "informational surround" wherein the user is directly engaged with data bodied forth in vision, sound, and touch, data inhabiting a spatially definite "virtual" world that can be interactively explored and navigated.[11]

The Media Room, Bolt explained to DARPA, "can be construed as an image of an office of the future," an office extending the transparency of the Ford Foundation Headquarters—with capacity to look both inward and outward and produce a secure, hermetic community—into another domain.[12]

From the Media Room's control seat, one could, for instance, zoom into satellite images embedded in Mapping by Yourself, revealing landscapes in increasing detail like *Powers of Ten*, the 1968 film by Charles and Ray Eames, to which ArcMac acknowledged their indebtedness. Yet unlike the film, *you* were in charge of zooming, instilling a sense of command. Reporting to DARPA on Mapping by Yourself, ArcMac posited that the Media Room facilitated "a media intensive surround which places the user *within* the information itself."[13] To this end, it operated at the nexus of bodily immersion and what they termed the "entrainment of attention." Their stated ambition in this context was to produce a computer-controlled information environment so detailed and "accurate" that "it would be indistinguishable from the 'real thing.'"[14] In a perverse instrumentalization of Walter Benjamin's reading of "tactile appropriation," ArcMac even sought to produce "*push-back* maps, namely those which physically impart forces to make the user respond; large scale *touch-sensitive* displays, those which engage full body movement with wall size displays; and *force feedback* about terrain, texture, climate and other variables." As they put it, "This proposal is about being there."[15]

The Spatial Data Management System (SDMS) put the Media Room to work slightly differently, "exploit[ing] the user's sense of spatiality for purposes of organizing and retrieving data."[16] As student-researcher William Donelson explained, the joystick-driven system allowed "the user to drive through the data base much as a pilot flies an airplane."[17] Recognizing how an individual organized information within his or her material world—distributing things spatially in piles and retrieving them through location, association, and a form of bodily or "motor" memory (what they called "haptic space")—it transposed that logic to a computer so that a user could "'zoom' around the information spaces of the data base."[18] "Automation," Donelson explained of the recalibration at work, "has transformed this natural spatial allocation system into a syntactically accessed compendium of data."[19] Bodies encountered a new set of rules—a new syntax—in this "electronic 'wired' milieu."

Bolt, principle research scientist for the SDMS, preferred the metaphor of "a helicopter-like flight," noting that in addition to using the joystick, users could "teleport" by touching an icon on the "world view" screen.[20] A worldview or *Weltanschauung* for a new world order was precisely what the SDMS aimed to create. While the apparatus gave the illusion of control over a vast arena, the technology was in fact geared to personalization. In *Computerworld*, Bolt explained that the Media Room "was about the size of a personal office" and that DARPA was interested in the system's "nonalphanumeric way of handling information" because it could be used by nonspecialists, citing "occasional users of terminals, like military officers." Dataland, Bolt stressed, was "a personal world of data belonging to this user. Your Dataland would look different from mine or everyone else's, reflecting our personal caches of data and individual interests." "Dataland is not a map of the data. It *is* the data," he insisted.[21] To Bolt, the SDMS had wide-ranging potential as a management tool, especially since "the modern manager cannot escape the fact that computers and computer based media are fast becoming the primary means of dealing with information and with people."[22] (Even libraries and books, he prophesized, would be browsed this way in the future. Real libraries and real books "otherwise [seem] doomed in the new electronic age.")[23] The intimate knowledge of users stored in the SDMS was indeed useful to managers, as is all too familiar today. Bolt also noted a military application: a "field version" was built for DARPA by the Computer Corporation of America and was "now operating aboard the U.S.'s newest nuclear carrier, the USS Carl Vinson."[24] (This supercarrier was deployed in Operation Desert Strike, Operation Iraqi Freedom, and Operation Enduring Freedom, and from its deck in 2011, the body of Osama bin Laden was disposed of into the sea.)

The Movie Map, which is the focus of this chapter, also deployed the Media Room to simulate movement and "place," but in this case, it simulated movement in urban space, coupled with maps and "data space." Commonly known as the Aspen Movie Map after the Colorado town serving as its test case, it brings us simultaneously closer to something we might recognize as architecture and further away. Student-researcher Robert Mohl underscored its use in unknown (read "foreign") territories, noting that users (implicitly, soldiers) "are able to learn about an unfamiliar urban space by 'traveling' around at will through sequences of photographic footage and 'helicoptering' above dynamic aerial photos and reference maps."[25] With regard to the anticipatory spatial knowledge that the interface was able to convey, he asserted, "movie map training leads to superior way-finding competence in the real setting."[26] Following Disneyland nomenclature, Mohl called its two primary modes of interface "travel land" and "map land," emphasizing the ease of switching between the two simulated environments, much as one might do at a theme park. It was even possible to switch between fall and winter via a "season knob," causing leaves to disappear and snow appear, and vice versa.[27] (Here, too, we find an uncanny updating of the experience of the Ford Foundation Headquarters opening onto two environments and two seasons, simultaneously.) Indeed, the Movie Map system aimed to refunction spatiotemporal distinctions such as here and there, near and far, now and then, real and virtual, all of which now seemed to belong to a preelectronic topology.

Aspects of the Movie Map's conception can be dated to Negroponte's 1966 master's thesis, "The Computer Simulation of Perception during Motion in the Urban Environment,"[28] which included experiments with film. Yet ArcMac's experiment in "surrogate travel" and the "demo" it produced are widely recalled as marking a pivotal moment not only in the group's research, but in the wider history of virtual and interactive digital environments. The project remains a landmark in the story of so-called "virtual space," a precursor to contemporary paradigms of spatially managed data and interactivity via computer interfaces. Stewart Brand, in his 1987 history of MIT's Media Lab, celebrated it as "a feat of virtuosity," noting that its implications for what computers might do "shook people," as did the sense of "how *un-authored* a creative work could become."[29] As Brand put it all too bluntly, "power was shifting from the material world to the immaterial world."[30] It was in this context that Brand returned to his 1971 formulation of an outlaw area in the *Whole Earth Catalog*. "Technology moves faster than laws. All new technologies are outlaw areas. All new communications technologies are political dynamite."[31] Technology could take the lead in lawlessness, too.

Scan. Freeze Frame

Not all commentators were quite so joyous in their reception of the Movie Map. Paul Virilio recognized in the shift from face-to-face communication to electronic human/machine interfaces a breakdown of "the very opposition 'intramural'/'extramural'" of cities effected by media technologies, a breakdown affiliated with new, militarized conceptions of the city and operative notions of "place."[32] "The way one gains access to the city," he argued in "The Overexposed City," indicating the waning of urban architecture's material role, "is no longer through a gate, an arch of triumph, but rather through an electronic audiencing system whose users are not so much inhabitants or privileged residents as they are interlocutors in permanent transit."[33] "The access protocol of telematics replaces that of the doorway," he proposed; the "threads" of the "technical culture" therein inaugurated were "no longer woven into the space of a constructed fabric, but into the sequences of an imperceptible planning of time in which the interface man/machine replaces the façades of buildings and the surfaces of ground on which they stand."[34] This urban condition was heralded for Virilio in the "derealization" of Disneyland, but informed a wider shift of attention from physical form to cinematic images. What he called the "'spectral' character of the city and its inhabitants" was most manifest *not* in "Venturi's Las Vegas," he concluded, citing a landmark in recent architectural research, but in Francis Ford Coppola's *One From the Heart*, wherein actors were inlaid "by an electronic process, in the filmic framework of a life-sized Las Vegas reconstructed in Zoetrope Company Studios."[35]

Haunting Virilio's reading of these spatiotemporal and perceptual logics, as well as these immaterial data banks, was the Aspen Movie Map.

> If aviation, which began the same year as cinematography, instigated a revision of point of view, a radical change in the perception of the world, infographic techniques will instigate, in their turn, a revision of reality and its representations. This process can also be seen in the "Tactical Mapping System," a videodisc created by the United States Defense Agency for Advanced Research Projects. [sic] This system provides a viewing of Aspen in continuity by accelerating or slowing down the procession pace of 54,000 images, changing direction or season as one changes television channels, transforming the little city into a sort of ballistic tunnel in which the function of eyesight and the function of weapons merge.[36]

Virilio returned to this "revision of reality" in concluding *War and Cinema: The Logistics of Perception*. Although again not citing its connection to architecture and noting only an applied version of the "basic" research undertaken by ArcMac, the Movie Map appears as a potent weapon in the American "perceptual arsenal," a new episode in the "fatal interdependence" of war and cinema.[37] "The small Colorado town of Aspen," he concluded, became a "ballistic tunnel for tank pilots, who use this method to train in street combat."[38] The Movie Map thus again situates us within a constellation of forces affecting architecture and the urban environment. The discipline contributed expertise to the configuration of these forces, a development that I want to trace further.

Insecurity

Research for the Movie Map was sponsored by DARPA's Cybernetics Technology Division.[39] "DARPA realized the need," principal investigator Andy Lippman recalled, "after Israeli soldiers practiced for the recovery of an airplane hijacked to Entebbe by using an abandoned airfield made up to look similar."[40] The reference was to Operation Thunderbolt, carried out by the Israel Defense Force (IDF), a much-celebrated nighttime raid to rescue not an airplane (as Lippman implied), but hostages held at the Entebbe airport, near Kampala in Uganda. The raid took place on July 3–4, 1976, coinciding with US bicentennial festivities. On Sunday, June 27, Air France Flight 139, originating in Tel Aviv and en route to Paris, was hijacked after a stop in Athens and diverted via Benghazi, Libya (where it refueled and released a pregnant passenger), to Entebbe. The hijackers included two members of the Popular Front for the Liberation of Palestine, Fayez Abdul-Rahim Jaber and Jayel Naji al-Arjam, and two members of the Revolutionäre Zellen, a West German urban guerrilla group, Brigitte Kuhlmann and Wilfried Böse, the latter an associate of Carlos the Jackal. Joined by others in Entebbe and calling for the release of Palestinian and pro-Palestinian prisoners in exchange for the hostages, the militant organizations sought through their violent methods to gain publicity for the Palestinian cause and to facilitate the end of Israel's occupation of Palestine.[41] This terrorist act was rightfully condemned by the international community and by the PLO. As mentioned by Lippman, in preparing for the raid, the IDF constructed a partial replica or material simulation

Figure 8.3 Model of Entebbe airport control tower and terminal building on display at parachutists' house in Ramat Gan, September 1, 1976 (Government Press Office, State of Israel).

Figure 8.4 Lieutenant General Mota Gur and Defense Minister Shimon Peres at Press Conference on Operation Thunderbolt, following rescue of hostages held at the Entebbe Airport, July 1976 (Israel Sun, Ltd.).

of the airport terminal where hostages were held in order for special-operations-unit soldiers from Sayeret Matkal (the top-secret General Staff Reconnaissance Unit) to practice their operation and familiarize themselves with the place. It was built from photographs and other intelligence gained from the airline industry and from blueprints provided by Solel Boneh, the Israeli company involved in modernizing the airport in the late 1960s, at which point the two countries enjoyed better relations.[42] "Made up of wooden posts and hessian screens to replicate the building layout," one account explained, "it was erected at the Sayeret Matkal base where rehearsals could take place."[43]

The raid, which succeeded in rescuing almost all of the hostages and in killing the terrorists, along with many Ugandan soldiers, was widely celebrated in the media: *Time* declared it "one of the most daring, spectacular rescues of modern times."[44] It would soon prove grist for Hollywood cinema, with *Victory at Entebbe* starring Burt Lancaster as Shimon Peres, Anthony Hopkins as Prime Minister Yitzhak Rabin, and Kirk Douglas and Elizabeth Taylor as Hershel and Edra Vilnofsky, appearing a few months later, and the TV movie *Raid on Entebbe* with Peter Finch as Rabin and Charles Bronson as Brigadier General Dan Shomron appearing the next year.[45] However, the raid would have a more complicated reception at the UN, to which I will return.[46]

According to many accounts, ArcMac's Movie Map project appealed to the DoD on the assumption that computers could achieve an environmental simulation much faster than such physical mock-ups and at much lower cost, allowing the military more effective advanced knowledge of hostile territories and allowing soldiers to familiarize themselves with a place before encountering it in person.[47] With the Movie Map, that is, the IDF's legendary physical mock-up of the airline terminal was to be replaced by a simulated foreign territory produced in electronic media. In Lippman's words, the goal of this hypercinematic technology "was to create so immersive and realistic a 'first visit' that newcomers would literally feel at home, or that they had been there before."[48]

Aspen Proving Grounds

To explain how the system worked: the Aspen Movie Map was a computer-controlled optical (analog) videodisc-based system that simulated movement by retrieving information from a multimedia, multichannel database. As Lippman explained in "Movie-Maps: An Application of the Optical Videodisc to Computer Graphics," the driver or "map reader" was presented either with sequential photographic images of Aspen or, by switching to another channel, with a digital animation produced by "computer synthesized replicas of those images." By controlling the speed, route, turning, viewpoint, and type of information accessed, the driver could undertake a simulated drive—what ArcMac termed "surrogate" or "vicarious" travel. Switching to an aerial-view routine, or map land, as noted earlier, he or she could also hover over the terrain and zoom in or out on maps stored in the database.

The user's movement was controlled initially via a customized joystick, but in subsequent iterations by a touch-sensitive screen developed by the firm Elographics. A precursor to a now common technology, the touch screen operated through a transparent plastic overlay that recorded the *x-y* position of the finger's touch, allowing the user to interface with computer-generated pictograms that indicated various actions, overlaid onto the videodisc image. Command icons included a central stop button; blue/green bars for the direction and speed of forward or reverse movement; arrows at the edges depicting turn options, which turned green to register acknowledgment of a command; and two "eyeballs" that allowed the user to switch viewpoints—from straight ahead, to the left, and to the right. When an option was not allowed, such as going forward at a T intersection, the pictogram was replaced by a symbol indicating that one could not proceed. In a later version, a navigation map appeared overlaid on the top portion of the screen. This traced the user's "real-time" trajectory and allowed the user to specify future directions through an "autopilot mode."[49] It was also an active portal through which to access map land.

To produce photographic images for surrogate travel, the ArcMac team went to Aspen and filmed every street using 16-millimeter Bolex El stop-frame cameras equipped with wide-angle lenses and set at 90-degree intervals—facing directly forward, to the right, to the left—mounted on a rig on the roof of an automobile. The cameras were triggered by a fifth wheel trailing behind to shoot one frame every ten feet, the trigger operating through an encoder that generated shutter-actuation pulses. Triggering the camera by

Figure 8.5 The Architecture Machine, *The Interactive Movie Map: A Surrogate Travel System*, January 1981. Screen shot showing Andrew Lipmann, Principal Investigator, interacting with screen.

Figures 8.6 & 8.7 The Architecture Machine, *The Interactive Movie Map: A Surrogate Travel System*, January 1981. Screen shot of Travel Land in film mode; screen shot of Travel Land in Quick and Dirty Animation System mode.

distance (not time, as would be conventional in a film) allowed for further manipulation over apparent speed by users of the Movie Map system. Travel velocity was thus independent of the rate of filming, being determined by the presentation rates of individual video frames, which came in multiples of thirty-three milliseconds (the normal rate for video). The ten-foot calibration of intervals, Mohl noted, was "an arbitrarily determined distance which would allow all the footage to fit within the 50,000 frames of one side of a single video disc."[50] Each round of shooting produced 15,000 frames for straight-ahead sequences and a further 12,000 documenting turns. While capable of allowing travel of, say, 200 miles per hour, the system was set to allow a maximum speed of 68.[51] What was important here, however, as we will see, was not just that the system could simulate space, but that users could experience the control of time.

The first round of filming took place in fall 1978, the results leading to a series of adjustments before returning to Aspen during the winter of 1978–79 and fall 1979. For instance, the team initially used four cameras until it was realized that this produced redundancy.[52] The team also learned that in order to minimize light and shadow distinctions upon turning, shooting had to be undertaken at a similar time each day, which was restricted to the interval between 10:00 a.m. and 2:00 p.m. They also added a gyroscopic stabilizer to minimize other visual discontinuities. These were particularly complicated during the filming of turns, which proved the most technically challenging to film. The team experimented with many variations, including: the "pivot turn," whereby the camera was rotated 360 degrees while fixed at the center of the intersection; the aerial pivot turn, using a cherry picker to obtain a more comprehensive perspective; the "truck turn," in which "the camera was fixed on axis with the direction of the filming vehicle as it executed a conventional turn"; "leading turns," integrating pivot and truck turns by "pivoting the camera in the direction of the anticipated turn in advance of the intersection"; the "tracking pivot turn," a variation on the previous turn; and "synthesized turns," which involved subsequent computer processing of the film footage.[53]

A master's student, Walter Bender, developed the animation component of the Movie Map system, the Quick and Dirty Animation System (QADAS), another "travel land" tool accessed by switching channels on the season knob. While most of the town appeared in the animation as a simple color-shaded, polygonal wire-frame CAD model, the facades of landmark buildings were superimposed or "billboarded" onto relevant surfaces via texture mapping. Deploying the same interactive navigation tools and spatiotemporal logic as its film-based component and with stills captured from the CAD database designed to match the film footage exactly through careful registration of frames, QADAS was developed, as Bender put it, specifically "as a supplement to the Movie Map." Unlike its filmic counterpart, however, QADAS could "fill in where practicality or reality leave off."[54] For instance, Lippman noted, it provided "the ability to drive in places where it is not possible to film" and allowed the subject to take a drive that was "more like a helicopter tour."[55]

Important here, too, was that unlike contemporary "real-time" flight simulators—notably the Novoview of computer graphics pioneers David Evans and Ivan Sutherland—storage of precomputed frames on the videodisc allowed ArcMac to process the images with a much higher visual density, then access them at rapid speed.[56] Moreover, the system permitted a level of editing or "systematic selection" not easily achieved in film, a capacity that could emphasize or deemphasize certain information and hence "direct attention." As Bender put it, "By resorting to digital or analog image processing techniques or manual intervention, it is possible to eliminate any aspect of an image which is misleading, redundant, distracting, irrelevant, or counter to whatever the system is attempting to elucidate."[57] For instance, the fact that the mountains around Aspen appeared smaller in the film because of the wide-angle lens was easily corrected, since "distances and scales are arbitrary." "With a quick manipulation of the database, the mountains are suddenly larger than life.... They 'feel' like the looming mountains of Aspen."[58] Mohl referred to this "billboarding" of the mountains as producing "monster facades standing far in the distance."[59] Here, indeed, was a new environmental syntax.

Map land not only provided a "You are here" function and a schematic map while in travel land, but also, as an independent channel, presented aerial photographs, maps, and so-called "landmark maps," each of which had been photographed in minute detail and at various distances using a laser guide for precise registration. These frames could then be recalled in particular sequences according to viewpoints distributed within two lattice-matrix systems in order

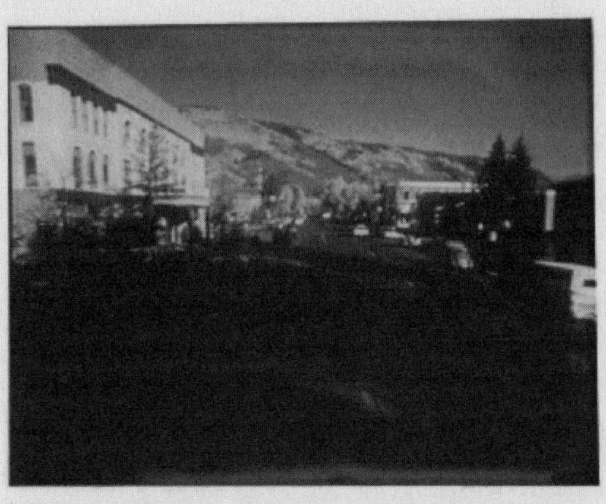

Figure 3: Main Street, Aspen Colorado.

Figure 4: Animated Main Street. [Note lack of traffic!]

23

Figure 8.8 Walter Bender, the Quick and Dirty Animation System, 1980 (courtesy Walter Bender).

to simulate the effect of helicoptering over an area, moving laterally or diagonally, or zooming in.[60] Since movement along the *z* axis, Mohl explained, did not produce perspective change, but only scale changes, it was in effect operating in two-and-a-half dimensions; the images were without parallax, and each vertical path had to be aligned with a particular crossing or node within the matrix. With their geometries and measurements taken from aerial photographs, the map frames superimposed exactly upon their photographic counterparts; hence, one could switch channels from one format to the other without discontinuity in registration, much as one can now do in Google Maps.

Through the Electronic Looking Glass

In addition to employing the two modes of surrogate travel and being able to helicopter above the aerial photographs and maps, Movie Map users could access ancillary data. Utilizing ArcMac's SDMS, the Movie Map thus also demonstrated potentials for storing, accessing, and managing data in a virtual three-dimensional space in which "the particular organization corresponds to the physical layout of real space." "In fact," Lippman explained of this experimental spatial filing system, now, of course, a ubiquitous computer interface experience, "this data is stored 'behind' the facades of buildings, or in locales, and is retrieved by 'driving' to it."[61] One could thus gain access to information not easily available to the naked eye of a visitor to Aspen; with adequate reconnaissance, that is, the system's data content was potentially higher than that of unaided vision or even of a local inhabitant. To retrieve data in travel land, the driver would touch a particular façade or live site, causing the driving sequence to stop, a close-up photograph of the building to appear as a transition to other data sources (or in the QADAS animation, the billboarded photograph to appear alone), a Votrax phonemic (voice) synthesizer to announce the building's name, and a new set of touch-sensitive pictograms to appear that listed available data. From map land, one could select such sites when maximally zoomed in, also causing the façade to appear, and so on.

Lippman referred to these façades, which were photographed to minimize registration shifts, hence producing apparently seamless transitions, as providing "a natural interface between driving and using the system as a means for accessing spatially stored data."[62]

Mohl simply noted that "façades served as the gateway transition between travel land or map land and cultural access."[63] Here, all too literally, and seemingly without irony, a building's façade was deployed in the new type of human/machine interface of which Virilio wrote, a transformation that, in retrospect, stands as a potent allegory of the loss of face-to-face interaction in the electronic milieu. "Constructed space," he posited, "now occurs within an electronic topology."[64]

The ancillary information accessible through facades in the Movie Map System included short films replete with analog sound—what ArcMac called "cinema verité" or "micro-documentaries"—typically in 16-millimeter format, but also 35-millimeter and 2-inch quad videotape; slide shows of historical photographs and interior shots; printed matter such as brochures and newspaper clippings; other sound recordings; synthesized speech (primarily to identify street and building names); and text-based "data data" on statistics such as "cases of beer consumed per week and number of beds."[65] Mohl called this material "cultural access routines."[66] The goal, indeed, was to provide access to cultural intelligence, not in the artistic sense, but rather knowledge derived from surveillance, statistics, and behavioral science. By way of example, Lippman pointed to the fact that "the telephone directory may be contained in the telephone exchange; the town's vital statistics are stored, naturally enough, at town hall."[67] The 1981 demo, *The Interactive Movie Map: A Surrogate Travel System*, spoke even more symptomatically of the system's inherent character. The only site visited in any detail was City Hall and its police facilities. After entering the façade, the viewer is shown, successively: a security guard, a T-shirt labeled "crime crusher," a "Suspect Description" form, the Aspen Police's *Crime Crusher's Text Book*, a police officer's belt buckle featuring a relief in the shape of a leaf from the area's famous Aspen tree, a man wielding a rifle, and a short interview. "I think we're treating police duties first as a human being, and then as professional police officers," he tells us. We then cut to a poster of the 1973 crime film *Serpico*, featuring Al Pacino as a good New York City cop who has gone undercover to weed out rogue elements in the force, then back out to the street. This was the example of ancillary data pointed to by Negroponte in his 1995 book *Being Digital*. "In 1978 the Aspen Project was magic. You could look out your side window, stop in

Figure 8.9 The Architecture Machine, *The Interactive Movie Map: A Surrogate Travel System*, January 1981. Screen shot inside Aspen City Hall.

front of a building (like the police station), go inside, have a conversation with the police chief, dial in different seasons... get guided tours, helicopter over maps, turn the city into animation."[68] If, as Negroponte argued, Sutherland's Sketchpad was "the big bang of computer graphics," the Aspen Movie Map marked the point where "*Multimedia* was born."[69]

Multimedia

Crucial to the Movie Map's multimedia capacities was the newly available videodisc, which allowed ArcMac to merge technologies from three industries key to the emerging field of "media technology": film and broadcasting, print and publishing, and computers.[70] A low-cost storage device, the optical videodisc was developed for stemming piracy in the home movie market.[71] Negroponte regarded the technology to be "potentially as important as the invention of the Gutenberg press," arguing that videodiscs "should be seen as 'books without pages,' and not just a delivery system to recycle old movies."[72] The Movie Map used videodiscs manufactured by DiscoVision Associates, a joint venture between Sony (TV), IBM (computers), and MCA (records); the then-standard capacity of 54,000 frames translated into half an hour of continuous video. Bender referred to videodiscs as a "video analog to a phonograph record," Lippman as a "record that stores television."[73] Although the videodisc had qualities not unlike a vinyl record, being composed of analog impressions in a reflective plastic substrate, its operation was different. As reported in "Videodisc: Ultimate Weapon of Video Revolution?" it was not an LP with pictures, but "a giant repository of information, a computer data bank filled with images"—"a new medium as different from videotape as movies were from radio."[74] With the Movie Map, we find videodiscs serving not as a weapon in a video revolution, but as arms for US counterinsurgency strategy.

It was not just the vast amounts of data stored that made videodiscs different. First, unlike an LP or videotape, information was not stored in a continuous groove or magnetic tape that required sequential retrieval, but as Bender noted, as "54,000 concentric tracks, each containing data for one video frame."[75] The discrete addresses of each track allowed random access to the data, with access rates of up to 30 million bits per second. Hence, videodiscs had capacities such as frame freezing without loss of image resolution, searching with accurate and quick access to individual frames by number (allowing for loops, nonsequential playback, and more), frame skipping, and easy reverse play. Once coupled with a computer, the videodisc allowed individual tracks or frames to be sequenced or edited together easily by the user. Using a match-cutting technique between straight-ahead sequences and turn sequences and retrieving the tracks at various rates, or even repeating them over and over, the Movie Map could generate the appearance of choosing one's route and speed while driving through the town. This capacity for nonlinear sequencing and real-time editing was key to the "personalization" sought by ArcMac. Although limited by data on the videodisc and the video-frame format itself, the system sought to give the impression that choice, even "freedom" of access to information, was facilitated through interactivity. In Negroponte's terms, "the user—the reader—can become an active agent, implicitly or explicitly calling forth personalized editions of information."[76]

Second, videodiscs were not medium specific: source material could bring together what Bender termed "previously immiscible media" in an "interactive manner." He listed these as "typography, raster-scan computer graphics, vector graphics, drawing, film, video and still photography."[77] "Vis-à-vis the arts," Negroponte announced enthusiastically of this capacity to modulate across formats, "one sees unique opportunity to experiment with a declassification of types, removing the vestigial boundaries between performance and image making, between artist and audience."[78] In a 1976 proposal to the National Science Foundation to fund the Graphical Conversation Theory project, ArcMac referred to the audiovisual aspects of multimedia systems as enhancing the computer's "liberality," claiming that the "computer is the most liberal of all available media." Unlike "a Turing representable machine," which was "restricted to the one-dimensional nature of the typewriter terminal" and thus limited people's notions of the computer, the group claimed, graphical interaction allowed people to "affect [sic] and be affected by machine operations" within a larger system and hence to more effectively "simulate 'worlds.'"[79] Negroponte insisted repeatedly that the use of graphical interfaces, rather than specialized languages, was key to simplifying the use of computers and hence to expanding their reach, noting the ability to "bring computers directly to generals, presidents of companies, and six-year-old children."[80]

Brand, too, was enthusiastic about this dissolution of boundaries and the convergence of modes (and subjectivities) in the multimedia work of the Media Lab. Echoing figures of neoliberalism, he wrote:

> With digitalization all of the media become translatable into each other—computer bits migrate merrily—and they escape from their traditional means of transmission. A movie, phone call, letter, or magazine article may be sent digitally via phone line, coaxial cable, fiberoptic cable, microwave, satellite, the broadcast air, or a physical storage medium such as tape or disk. If that's not revolution enough, with digitalization the content becomes totally plastic—any message, sound, or image may be edited from anything into anything else.[81]

"Only live face-to-face conversation," Brand concluded of its archaic character, would remain analog. Brand's primary referent here was *Technologies of Freedom* of 1983, written by Ithiel de Sola Pool, founder of MIT's Political Science Department. Like money in free-market capitalism, bits were free to travel anywhere.

Friedrich Kittler offered another reading of this multimedia "revolution," recognizing in the digital translation of "formerly distinct data flows" into "a standardized series of digitized numbers" the "farsighted planning" of electronic warfare.[82] Introducing *Gramophone, Film, Typewriter*, he speculated: "People will be hooked to an information channel that can be used for any medium—for the first time in history, or for its end.... The general digitization of channels and information erases the differences among individual media. Sound and image, voice and text are reduced to surface effects, known to consumers as interface."[83] Refuting end-of-history ideologies (and the overcoming of Turing machines), Kittler reminds us that older media technologies did not leave each apparatus unmarked: "The historical synchronicity of cinema, phonography, and typewriting separated optical, acoustic, and written data flows, thereby rendering them autonomous. That electric or electronic media can recombine them does not change the fact of their differentiation."[84] With the movie map, we are faced with a larger field than the technologies Kittler invoked in reading how "media determine our situation," yet all potentially fed into and haunted the system's new, heterotopic syntax and subjective effects.

Gap to Reality

Graphical interfaces have made interacting with a computer appear seamless, even easy—children can do it. For ArcMac, it was imperative that interaction appeared routine or ordinary, that the mechanism be obscured, or at least its operations naturalized. In the case of the Movie Map, they aimed to eliminate doubts or semantic uncertainties regarding the "reality" one encountered in the system. When one "chose" a target or even simply a direction in which to drive a tank, it should not be ambiguous or open to multiple interpretations, but read instead as a fact, regardless of how spectral it might be. The project sought, quite literally, to reverse long-standing avant-garde attempts to reveal the apparatus and in so doing speak to material conditions, social relations, and institutionalized structures of power. But the "electronic 'wired' milieu" of the Media Room and the spatiotemporal experience forged by the Movie Map were not ordinary places, and, as Kittler suggests, their multimedia character entailed a certain subjective and perceptual splitting that had to be accounted for. The new environmental syntax of the Movie Map and the distinct representational modes encountered as one switched between travel land and map land however, were not regarded by ArcMac researchers as detracting from the effectiveness of the system. If somewhat paradoxical at first, they were thought to help a user reconcile multiple forms of spatial knowledge in a more "synergistic" manner than unmediated vision allowed.

"No one is fooled into thinking the video display is a window onto a live reality," Mohl conceded, but to his mind, that "gap to reality" was not necessarily a limitation.[85] "Duality of representation," he reported, "allowed the integration of different understandings of the same thing (one of the conceptual threads of the movie map)."[86] "The dual representation," he reiterated, "seems to promote a synergistic cognitive mechanism."[87] Virtual space within the Movie Map, that is, was not understood to be identical to or merely a poor copy of real space, even if its two primary channels—travel land and map land—were believed to have affinities with the means by which subjects gained information about the environment. Mohl even argued that it could not "be taken for granted that the real environment is the best medium for conveying the most important information."[88] Here, indeed, was a new ordering of things.

For Lippman, employing the rhetoric of verisimilitude common to many accounts of the Movie Map, the integration of multiple data sources meant that the project might "provide a more responsive, visually complete representation of an environment."[89] He referred to the project's capacity to "explore the interface between real images and computer graphics," revealing through scientific research which aspects proved jarring to the user and which were simply overlooked. To this end, technical research was dedicated to establishing appropriate "ranges of realism" so this interchange could occur "with minimal real distortion and, ideally, no conceptual distortion."[90] Achieving this simultaneous splitting and realism/immersion proved challenging, and significant attention was dedicated to producing as smooth and information-rich an image as possible, particularly an image that could operate in "real time," or at least in the seemingly continuous flow of time familiar from the cinema. For instance, to overcome one limitation of the videodisc player, an MCA DiscoVision Model PR-7820 with a "seek time" of up to five seconds, the Movie Map system used two videodisc peripherals; while one retrieved the frames being displayed onscreen, the other, "invisible" unit was on standby, seeking ahead to anticipate possible turns that might need to be retrieved. Should a turn be requested, the system would switch to the other disc. Moreover, while the host machine used for data access and program execution—a 32-bit Perkin-Elmer minicomputer—far exceeded the necessary computational capacity for the system, there remained a certain "computational drag."[91]

ArcMac's attempts to achieve the appearance of a fully "dynamic" system within the Movie Map—the sense that one could drive anywhere in the town, determining speed, route, and view—remained haunted by a series of other limitations they sought to overcome. Limitations were apparent, for instance, with the initial use of a joystick as an input device, which implied more degrees of freedom than the system allowed.[92] In virtual Aspen, one had to drive down the center of a street at a position elevated approximately eleven feet (higher than a passenger in a car or even a van, but closer to a tank driver), move in discrete, ten-foot intervals, and look either directly in front or to either side. Moreover, as Bender indicated when noting the benefits of QADAS, uncanny visual anomalies and events emerged in virtual time as a result of the fact that Aspen could not be filmed in its entirety at a single moment. "Cars and pedestrians are constantly popping in and out of frames," he revealed. "Turning a corner, one can come face to face with a truck, materialized from the nothingness. The same pedestrians can be seen repeatedly throughout town. While travelling in reverse, cars and people move backwards also. All of this commotion is quite a distraction."[93] He referred to this phantomlike appearance of objects in the virtual world as a "now-you-see-it-now-you-don't" phenomenon.

On account of the discreteness of movement and filming time, Mohl noted, there was a "disconcerting separation of temporal and spatial linearity," later adding, "space and time do not obey the familiar rules... the environment is unevolving and scenes are repeated. It is interactive but not live."[94] That is, among other effects, certain "events" and scenes endlessly recurred without changing, even if the sequence of their appearance altered: the same dog appeared at the same corner, the same person entered the same building, the same car crossed the same street, and so on, mattering little whether the object was animal or machine. Here was a form of repetition without distinction, a form of iteration without drift or *différance*. Attempts to rid the system of those peculiar remainders of the material world captured while shooting film, of people and things that appeared to many as uncanny, Roadrunner-like ghosts, proved impossible, and they returned over and over, except in the more abstract, animated supplement QADAS, where one could selectively eliminate "any aspect of an image which is misleading, redundant, distracting, irrelevant or counter."

In virtual Aspen, there was also no imminent danger: "The user never has to worry about traffic and accidents, and driving down the middle of the street with seemingly reckless disregard for the pixilated crossing traffic may be exciting."[95] "Generally, when first-time users sit down to the movie map system," Mohl explained,

> the first thing they are struck by is the pixilated traffic. Cars zoom by in reckless burst [sic] of acceleration and deceleration. Typically users will make some comment indicating amusement at being in such a cartoon-like world (Roadrunner, etc.) where vehicles weave in and out at exaggerated speeds with absolute impunity. In this way users are immediately alerted to the fact that here is no ordinary flow of real time; and they are apparently able to accept this unusual convention of temporal flow quite readily.[96]

It was, as Mohl put it, a "unique model of reality," one in which events could not, strictly speaking, take place, but only return over and over.[97] As with the ghostly apparitions of the dead familiar from early accounts of technological reproduction, the Movie Map "always already provide[d] the appearance of specters."[98]

ArcMac's desire to achieve verisimilitude and continuity were driven by an underlying goal: symptomatic of the motivation to eliminate uncertainties, the ambition, Lippman wrote, "is to make a system so immersive, so visually clear and simple, that the map will substitute for the first visit. A user will be able to form such a complete model of the town that he will arrive a native. This will be accomplished through enhanced responsiveness and compelling visuals that allow no doubts and misinterpretations."[99] The substitution of one reality for another, that is, helped a stranger to feel like a "native."

Cognitive Space

In 1981, Mohl, a doctoral student in education and media technology at MIT, submitted his dissertation, "Cognitive Space in the Interactive Movie Map: An Investigation of Spatial Learning in Virtual Environments," from which I have been quoting. Supervised by Negroponte, it positioned the Movie Map not only as a device to facilitate surrogate travel, as we have been following, but also as a "research instrument" to investigate spatial cognition. Its "technical advantage" over other forms of simulating spatial experience, such as Donald Appleyard's Berkeley Simulator, he posited, "is the facility it provides for controlling precisely what a subject sees and repeating or varying those images."[100] Mohl's hypothesis was that by providing "a mechanism for pre-experiencing an unfamiliar locale" and by attempting to "convey the dynamic, interactive, and pictorial nature of everyday experience in moving through real spaces" (as distinct from "abstract representations" in the "hard copy medium of cartography"), interaction with the Movie Map could demonstrate "the processes by which the acqusition [sic] of spatial knowledge leads to the development of cognitive maps."[101] In this "novel form of spatial representation" that "substitutes for the actual experience," we find the "revision of reality" Virilio identified.[102]

As evident in the reference to "cognitive maps," Mohl's framework was indebted to MIT urban planning professor Kevin Lynch.[103]

After collaborating with György Kepes from 1954 to 1959 on a research project entitled "The Perceptual Form of the City," Lynch published *The Image of the City* in 1960—for Mohl, "perhaps the seminal work in modern cognitive mapping."[104] Mohl adopted Lynch's interviewing techniques—asking subjects to draw maps from memory—and set out to demonstrate Lynch's thesis that "internal models of the environment were constructed from five elements: landmarks, nodes, paths, edges, and districts."[105] To this theory of the acquisition of spatial knowledge he added a developmental component, drawing upon the work of Benjamin Kuipers, a student of artificial-intelligence pioneer Marvin Minsky. Following Piagetian stages of development, Kuipers argued that cognitive maps evolve from topological (known paths or routes) to projective (local orientation) to Euclidian (global or absolute orientation) modes.[106] He also drew upon the work of Lynch-inspired environmental psychologists Alexander Siegel and Sheldon White, who proposed a developmental hierarchy of way-finding techniques—from landmarks to routes to configurations, a sequence not unlike Foucault's reading of the shift in the organization of space from localization to extension to emplacement.[107] For Mohl, the seemingly persistent duality of small-scale spaces "encountered sequentially" versus large-scale spaces "apprehended simultaneously" seemed to fit nicely with the Movie Map's capacity to shift from travel land to map land. Yet his experimental trials yielded results casting doubt on the model's relevance. Subjective development in the Movie Map did not proceed in a linear manner from landmarks and routes in travel land to configurations in map land, but "each could mediate the others." Mohl concluded that "integration of multiple representations of space" was advantageous and even appeared to have affinities with a subject's learning process.[108] It was as though the brain worked through maps and movies: processes of translation could be eliminated, new worldviews produced.

Ben, Sally, Henry, and Kathy

Mohl's interest was not in cognitive maps per se, but in what he called "cognitive space," defined as "an internalized model, representation, or strategy which is useful in accounting for spatial relationships."[109] This transposition from maps to space entailed, first, a shift in focus from a fixed object to questions of process. Second, it facilitated expansion from a single to a multichannel or intermedia format. To test his hypotheses, Mohl designed cognitive experiments to evaluate if the Movie Map could help a subject "acquire accurate spatial knowledge that will help him find his way around a real place."[110] Seeking distinctions between local and global levels of "spatial learning"—pathfinding versus mapping—his method compared cognitive maps between those who learned about Aspen through the Movie Map and those who had "spatial knowledge of the real environment acquired first-hand." The experiment included eight test subjects, with five subsequently traveling to Aspen (and only four reporting back).[111] The Roadrunner pixilation of bodies and vehicles proved bemusing, and surrogate travelers were able to ignore the repetition of particular events as irrelevant to their task. However, a few glitches emerged. Turns proved disorienting, despite the extended attention dedicated to this part of the apparatus: many users lost their bearings and were unable to distinguish a 90-degree from a 180-degree turn. Many were also unable to determine how far they had traveled. More curiously, the most common strategy when initiating exploration of the system was entirely unanticipated. First-time users kept "striking out in an arbitrary direction and continuing more or less in that direction until it dead-ended at a movie map boundary at the edge of town." They did not seem to be "assimilating global spatial relations," he lamented. Rather, they sought "to sample the contents and find the edges. They wanted to find out how big the 'fish tank' was and what sort of things it was stocked with."[112] These tactics sought an exit or a weakness in the system to exploit.

For Mohl, the Movie Map's effectiveness was best demonstrated by four users who then went to Aspen for the first time—Ben, Sally, Henry, and Kathy. Each was assigned a destination previewed in the virtual system. After being picked up at the airport, they were instructed to direct the driver to that destination once inside the town limits. Three out of four, he reported, "gave virtually flawless directions.... They did not get lost once." Although occasionally uncertain during the approach, upon crossing into the town, they were confident that "they knew exactly where they were," he continued, and they made comments such as "'It almost felt like coming home; I had a strong sense of déjà-vu' to 'I feel like Robin Williams on Mork from Ork,'" or that it was "home ground."[113] Although Ben,

Sally, and Henry enjoyed success in way-finding and landmark identification following Movie Map training, the fourth subject, Kathy, did not, repeatedly getting lost and becoming increasingly frustrated and distressed.

As Mohl recounted, Kathy "recognized landmarks here and there that she has seen before but she couldn't place them in the context of any familiar points." Indeed, she seemed to see only the system's constructed nature: "As she colorfully put it, 'It was like a jigsaw puzzle thrown into the air.'"[114] The Movie Map system, as we have seen, was composed of abstract, dismembered components, and it was this discontinuous or discrete construction that Mary desublimated in her inability or refusal to participate in its syntax. In contrast to Lynch and Kepes's attempts to render coherent a cityscape shattered by forces of modernity, a disorienting environment that they sought to control through legible patterns or mental images that might alleviate the experience of chaos, Kathy, we might say, experienced a shattering of the imaginary born of this isolation of signifiers. I am thinking, here, of Fredric Jameson's 1984 reading of postmodern space, "The Cultural Logic of Late Capitalism," which created a wide audience for Lynch's analysis in its celebration of cognitive mapping as a panacea for disorientation.[115] Despite its indebtedness to Lynch, the Movie Map provided no secure "image of the city" for subjects like Kathy. To quote Mark Wigley, the ArcMac researchers failed in their role as "guardians of psychological security." They failed to domesticate this new kind of space by providing models or media through which the subject might reorient his or herself in an insecure territory.[116] What sort of knowledge, then, was being conveyed?

Event World

While Roadrunner-like specters—whether cars, people, or dogs—were easily overlooked by Movie Map users, they served as a subliminal reminder of the peculiar world the subject was encountering in this perceptual apparatus. Mohl revealed what might be at stake when he distinguished four "incarnations" of space in the system: real, virtual, playback, and cognitive. Unlike real space—the three-dimensional Euclidian world that is "continuous and uniform"—virtual spaces such as the Movie Map were seen as modular and discrete, built as a network of paths that appear volumetric through suspension within a three-dimensional lattice of points. Movement is linear within this matrix, and changes in direction risk producing discontinuities by jumps in registration.[117] Playback space was defined as the physical environment in which the virtual space is experienced, initially a single video monitor, but ultimately the immersive space of the Media Room. Finally, cognitive space, for Mohl, referred to how these all congeal into subjective knowledge. Each space also had a corresponding notion of time: real, virtual, playback, and cognitive. While "real time" felt continuous, or so Mohl believed, "virtual time" was discontinuous, nonlinear, and could also be reversible, as experienced in playback time: events took place "at a pace which users can never become a part of."[118] As he explained, "As users drive down the street real time may be 11:00 a.m. Monday. Turnin [sic] right, the real time may switch to 2:00 p.m. Tuesday," and so on.[119] Mohl dismissed the "cognitive consequences of such an idiosyncratic system of time" as minor, since from a perceptual perspective, time is experienced as a secondary dimension; the Movie Map user "perceives himself to be traveling in space, not in time."[120] History thus is replaced by geography. Users, Mohl noted, did not actually think they were traveling in a car and were "immediately alerted to the fact that here is no ordinary flow of real time."[121] While this might be obvious—the Movie Map driver was not in a car driving through Aspen, subject to normative space-time relations or endangered by the disjunctive qualities of bodies in the virtual environment—the implications of these spatiotemporal convolutions became troubling when understood in the realm of events.

The fact that triggering events was no longer a function of time, but of space, of emplacement within the system, gave rise to "the most significant cognitive implications" of the Movie Map. Although the filmed event retained a trace of the "real" time and space in which it occurred, when "pre-experienced" during surrogate travel, these two dimensions were decoupled. To explain the distinction, Mohl noted, "Events are fixed in this world [in time] almost as firmly as buildings are fixed in space."[122] Mohl's concern was that Movie Map readers might use the repetition of events—which were invariable—as orientation cues, just as one might use a building, hence becoming disoriented when in the physical site, or they might find that "a transitory cue they had relied upon would 'insert' itself into the real experience"; memory might play tricks.[123] He mused over the manner in which events—his example was a softball game in the park, but we can extrapolate to a terrorist popping up—could become in effect "dynamic landmarks," suggesting that landmarks were not only spatial, but temporal; hence, an "event world" had to be considered.[124]

The Movie Map's event world returns us to the "convincingly real or uncannily imaginary" quality of "information space" to which Negroponte alluded, a paradoxical coupling of which the researchers seemed partly aware. The spectral nature of events in this new electronic topology had implications for both the humans and environments that were the ultimate targets of such research in its military applications. In attempting to rid the system of those uncanny, Roadrunner-like ghosts that returned over and over, remaining marked by history, ArcMac produced an even more extreme form of abstraction through CAD animation, reducing places to the points, lines, and planes of a computer-simulated village. To invoke Thomas Keenan's analysis of the spectral logic of the commodity in Marx, we find ghostly residues emerging again during this process of abstraction. In Marx's case, Keenan argues, with the abstraction of use value and productive labor in the material world to exchange value, what we find is the abstraction of human difference underlying the notion "humanity." "This is the definition of humanity," Keenan writes, "abstract, similar, spectral."[125] In the Movie Map, too, ArcMac sought to vanquish the need to differentiate; QADAS implied those abstract, similar, spectral subjects—subjects without history or specificity. The problem is not that in a literal fashion the virtual world was mistaken for the real, but that as a training environment, the two became coupled in a manner that troubles such distinctions, just as it did with modes of "event." The inherent specificity of a subject or the singularity of an event in historical time and space—and hence the promise of opening onto new, unknown potentialities—was substituted for the promise of a computerized, interactive "freedom," as in the "personalized" choices one made while negotiating the system as it learned from you. It is an event world harboring a new type of ambivalence—not prompting ethical decisions, but rather training surrogate travelers to believe that people and environments do not warrant exercising one's responsibility. Here was a condition of absolute lawlessness, the simulation of an outlaw territory in which not only specificity or singularities, but even care and rights, could be suspended. We can only imagine what the "philosopher of the event" Gilles Deleuze might have thought of such a perversion.[126]

Being There

In 1998, Michael Naimark presented "Place Runs Deep: Virtuality, Place and Indigenousness" at the Virtual Museums Symposium. As a student at the Center for Advanced Visual Studies in the late 1970s, Naimark contributed to Movie Map cinematography. In the late 1990s, the media artist worked for the Interval Research Corporation in Silicon Valley. "Place Runs Deep" described a series of Movie Map projects, beginning with Aspen, then one for Karlsruhe (home of ZKM | Zentrum für Kunst und Medientechnologie), Banff (home of another media center), and related panorama projects such as *Be Now Here* (1977–1996) for UNESCO World Heritage Sites, including Jerusalem, Dubrovnik, Timbuktu, and Angkor. All attempted to simulate *place* and create modes of "telepresence," demonstrating "how new media can represent sense of place and its inhabitants." To situate his projects, Naimark traced a history of a global imaginary or "dream."

> From where I saw things, in the 1940s it was Gyorgy Kepes, MIT's first artist, and his vision of "The New Landscape." In the 1950s it was Arthur C. Clark and the concept of satellites, and Margaret Mead and Gregory Bateson applying cybernetic theory to global society. In the 1960s it was Buckminster Fuller and his idea of "Spaceship Earth" and Marshall McLuhan and the "Global Village." In the 1970s Stewart Brand and the "Whole Earth" movement and Gene Youngblood and the "Information Utility." We are not there yet, but it appears unstoppable.[127]

As Naimark's litany of characters reminds us, this is not just a story of technological advancement, but of the inscription of multiple arts, sciences, and communication technologies within a global imaginary with expansionist ideological agendas. Acknowledging, moreover, that computer simulations could not represent everything, that experience within them would "never be the same as 'being there,'" Naimark came to the conclusion that place, or its simulation, was not ultimately the point in attempts to represent a

Figure 8.10 The Architecture Machine, *Put That There*, c. 1981. From Richard A. Bolt, "Human Interfaces for Managers," *Computerworld*, July 16, 1984 (Barry Arons).

place and its indigenous inhabitants. As he put it, in terms that might give us pause: "Whoever controls representation, controls all."[128]

ArcMac's Put That There project further complicates what "being there" via computer interfaces could mean. Representing strategies of control over territory and resources, a 1981 demo video of this DARPA-funded project ran two scenarios. In the first, the user, after asking the system to "pay attention," requests a map of the Caribbean, going on to ask the computer to create, in turn, a red oil tanker, a blue cruise ship, a yellow sailboat, and a green freighter at locations of his choice before requesting that they are moved, copied, and so on, either by pointing to the screen using a watchband gesture-recognition device or by requesting specific locations by voice. "Copy the cruise ship south of Havana," he asks at one point, demonstrating the command of place, and implicitly of populations, available from the instrumented Eames chair. In the second scenario, he requests a map of Massachusetts Bay. "As you wish, I'm loading your picture now," the computer responds in a distinctly electronic drone, adding "Welcome to Boston" once it appears. Invoking narratives of European colonization, he asks the system to create, in sequence, a red Indian village, a blue garrison, a magenta church, and a yellow farmhouse, then requests it to "copy the farmhouse," demonstrating the spread of nonnative inhabitants. "The Media Room setting," Bolt explained in his report on the project, "in addition to its power to generate a convincing impression of interacting with an implicit 'virtual' world of data behind the frame of the physical interface, implies yet another realm or order of space rife with possibilities for interaction."[129] Here one gained a sense of omniscience over people, artifacts, and territory—colonial or neocolonial, take your choice.[130]

Simulating acts of choice and agency, the Movie Map, as Lippman explained to Stewart Brand, was the project from which ArcMac derived its definition of interactivity.[131] While deploying the rhetoric of choice and freedom, this interactivity involved suspending subjects within a control mechanism geared toward perceptual training and data extraction: it was a closed world masquerading as an open one and effectively eliminated indeterminacy at a higher level. And this was not the only collapse of oppositions. Negroponte himself connected the Movie Map not only to the police, as cited earlier, but, seemingly without irony, to the precedent of Hollywood cinema, noting that "whatever system was developed would need the full photorealism of a Hollywood stage set to convey a real sense of place."[132] Given their role in creating effects of cinematic derealization, Hollywood stage sets might not typically come to mind as environments that "convey a real sense of place." But at stake was overcoming or at least rearticulating binaries such as reality and representation, material and virtual, presence and "telepresence," native and stranger. Moreover, it was not just Hollywood illusions at work in the Movie Map, but a technique of switching back and forth between photographic or filmic representation, computer animations, and maps or satellite images, a switching that helped train users to think differently about such distinctions and in which animated-world doubles seemed, at least initially, to facilitate the disappearance of certain bodies.

Learning from Entebbe

Negroponte's account of the Aspen Movie Map in *Being Digital* appeared under the subtitle "Birth of Multimedia." "Late at night on July 3, 1976, the Israelis launched an extraordinarily successful strike on the Entebbe, Uganda, airport," his account of that birth began, going on to recall that the US military was so impressed that they sought "electronic ways in which American commandos could get the kind of training the Israelis had" with the IDF's full-scale physical model.[133] Having "practiced landings and takeoffs, as well as simulated assaults on this accurate mock-up," he noted, "by the time they arrived in Uganda for the 'real thing,' they had an extraordinarily keen spatial and experiential sense of the place, allowing them to perform like natives." The IDF special forces did not, of course, perform like native Ugandans in Entebbe, but like an invading army. But the reference reminds us of a central paradox of counterinsurgency struggles: "natives," while often weak in matériel, enjoy the advantages of home ground, something the IDF knew well from its suppression of certain indigenous populations of Palestine. "The idea as a physical embodiment was not extensible," Negroponte continued of the lesson of Entebbe, "in that we just could not build replicas of every potential hostage situation or terrorist targets like airports and embassies. We needed to do this with computers."[134] After outlining the basic elements of the Movie Map, he positioned the demo's relevance to contemporary security concerns by citing

Figure 8.11 Lockheed C-130 "Hercules" on film set for Menahem Golan's *Operation Thunderbolt*, December 21, 1976 (Sa'ar Ya'acov/Government Press Office, State of Israel).

a landmark failure in US strategy that erupted in November 1979: the Iran hostage crisis, known in Persian as the "conquest of the American spy den." In Negroponte's words, "military contractors were hired to build working prototypes for the field, with the idea of protecting airports and embassies against terrorists. Ironically, one of the first sites to be commissioned was Tehran. Alas, it was not done soon enough."[135]

Celebrating the IDF intervention in Uganda, Negroponte quoted uneven casualties as a sign of its success: "By the time the one-hour operation ended, twenty to forty Ugandan troops were killed and all seven hijackers were dead. Only one Israeli soldier and three hostages also lost their lives."[136] (That soldier was Yehonatan [Yoni] Netanyahu, brother of Israel's future prime minister, MIT Sloan School of Management–trained Benjamin Netanyahu). Not mentioned was the IDF's unprecedented breach of international laws protecting a country's territorial integrity and sovereignty, for which the raid is also often recalled; it was a signature instance of Israel's contempt for the UN Charter. Indeed, Entebbe demonstrated the value not only of an environmental simulation, but of lawlessness and selective disregard for sovereignty and human life.

The prime minister of Mauritius, Sir Harold Walter, recognized a dangerous precedent in Israel's doctrine of "limited sovereignty" by which Israel justified this violation of sovereignty in the name of fighting international terrorism. Then chairman of the Organization of African Unity, Walter noted that such a doctrine was likely to affect only Third World countries and petitioned to convene a session of the UN Security Council to condemn the "unprecedented aggression against Uganda by Israel."[137] Beyond calling for condemnation of Israel's breach of the UN Charter and the death and destruction it caused, he proposed a resolution involving reparations. Although it was evident from the start that the United States would veto the initiative, the proposal was put to lengthy debate in the UN Security Council on July 9, 1976. Attempting to shift the focus away from questions of international law, the United States, Great Britain, and Israel quickly drafted a counterresolution condemning terrorism and hijacking. Although the Western media remained overwhelmingly laudatory of the heroic and seemingly made-for-movies raid on Entebbe, subsequent debates at the UN complicated this picture.[138]

The Security Council debate was remarkable political theater; it demonstrated sharp divides and savvy tactics on this diplomatic battlefield and gave rise to fantastically irreconcilable accounts of the IDF raid, its justification, and its ramifications. While all parties condemned acts of terror as a means of addressing political grievances, perspectives diverged on whether the government of Uganda, and President Idi Amin, in particular, were aiding and abetting the terrorists, as claimed by the Israeli ambassador to the UN, Chaim Herzog, or working for their release, protecting them, and ensuring access to humanitarian aid, as claimed by Uganda's minister of foreign affairs, Lieutenant-Colonel Juma Oris Abdalla and supported by other accounts, including to some extent that of the French ambassador.[139] In the latter camp, Moulaye El Hassen, the Mauritanian ambassador to the UN, speaking on behalf of the Group of African States, pointedly situated his remarks on sovereignty in relation to contemporary celebrations. "The date of 4 July 1976 is of course an important date in the history of the United States," he pointed out. "It was quite rightly a joyous occasion for the great American people." But, he continued, noting the violation of law, the deception of public opinion, and the "death and destruction" wrought by the IDF, "for the people and Government of Uganda, and indeed for Africa as a whole, 4 July 1976 was a date of mourning and alarm." Disregarding the UN and the international community, Israel, as he put it, "preferred to take the law into its own hands."[140]

If the Air France airbus had been diverted not to Uganda, but to the United States, France, Belgium, or the United Kingdom, El Hassen queried rhetorically of the uneven status of sovereignty, "would those countries have simply folded their arms when confronted not only by the violation of their sovereignty but also by the death of the their fellow citizens, civilian and military?" He did not think so. Nor would Israel have been likely to invade. "But since we are dealing here with a third-world country," he noted, "an African country, there is a rush to claim victory, to lavish praise and even extend congratulations, flying in the face of logic and common sense. It seems, indeed, that there is applause for the introduction of the law of the jungle into international relations."[141]

Despite the evident limitations of his speculations, the IDF raid was, indeed, an example of "might makes right" ideology, an instance of frontier justice flying in the face of international law.

El Hassen underscored that he did not condone terror. "Even if in certain cases," he explained, pointing to Palestinian struggles, acts of hijacking and violence "reflect the despair of those who have been driven from their homes, of those who have had their dignity trodden down, and those who have been deprived of the most elementary human rights, no one can possibly approve the form, much less the consequences, of such violence." At stake, he concluded, especially for weaker states—those more reliant upon the UN and the notion of rights to protect them, those without equal access to arms—was the "outrage" when such unfortunate violence is not undertaken by uncontrollable persons, but instead "it is built into a system by a Government which not only publically assumes responsibility for it but even bases national pride on it. The act committed by the Tel Aviv authorities against the Republic of Uganda is a new form of violence infinitely more dangerous because it is the work of an organized authority which, moreover, is a Member of this Organization."[142]

Herzog told a very different story. Attempting to shift the conversation from the breach of sovereignty to terrorism, he proclaimed, "I am in no way sitting in the dock as the accused party. On the contrary. I stand here as an accuser on behalf of the free and decent people in this world." Suggesting that the room was full of terrorists and terrorist sympathizers, he offered a litany of targets:

> I stand here as an accuser of all those evil forces which in their inherent cowardice and abject craven attitude see blameless wayfarers and innocent women and children—yes, even babes in arms—as a legitimate target for their evil intentions.... I stand here as an accuser of this world Organization, the United Nations, which has been unable, because of the machinations of the Arab representatives and their supporters, to co-ordinate effective measures in order to combat the evil of world terrorism.[143]

With escalated, paranoid, and at times almost hysterical rhetoric, he attempted to undermine the reputations of the governments of Arab and African countries, recalling also Amin's notorious history of violence and anti-Semitism, before situating Israel's raid as a legitimate act of self-defense for which they were rightfully proud. In seeking the moral high ground, he even likened the raid to struggles against piracy, the slave trade, and Nazi Germany. Disingenuously stating that the plane was "hijacked by a group of PLO terrorists," he stated that Israel's actions in Entebbe "has given rise to a world-wide wave of support and approval.... The ordinary man and woman in the street have risen behind us and proclaimed 'enough' to this spectre of terror."[144]

Having presented Israel's actions as a beacon of hope in the fight against terror, Herzog ambiguously appealed to humanity, calling upon "nations of the world...to unite against this common enemy which recognizes no authority, knows no borders, respects no sovereignty, ignores all basic human decencies, and places no limits on human bestiality."[145] His comments serve as a tragically ironic critique of the Israeli government: refusing to recognize the authority of the UN and the moral norms of the international community, maintaining ambiguous territorial borders for Israel while forcibly bounding Palestinians, and claiming Israel's sovereignty over the territory while refusing to respect that of Palestine were and remain central strategies of Israel's occupation, as it continues to play out in Gaza, East Jerusalem, and the West Bank to this day.[146] Prefiguring the US government's response to the 9/11 hijackings twenty-five years later, Herzog called upon the Security Council "to declare war on international terror, to outlaw it and eradicate it wherever it may be."[147] International terrorism was of course already prohibited by law: it was unnecessary to outlaw it. In condoning a form of vigilante justice, however, and in arguing for Israel's right to operate outside the law, to take the law into its own hands in foreign territories, Herzog, as El Hassen implied, was calling for the institution of outlaw territories.

Walter reminded Herzog that sovereignty, not terrorism was under discussion, let alone the brutality of the Amin dictatorship, a charge with which most representatives agreed. Refuting Israel's claims, other ambassadors mobilized Herzog's framework to underscore symmetries between insurgencies and counterinsurgencies. Qatar's ambassador, then chairman of the Group of Arab States, pointed to the ramification of condoning Israel's acts of state terrorism, acts without a declaration of war: "We can no longer pretend to discuss world order and justice when the most flagrant acts of aggression are sanctioned by prominent Members of the United Nations and protected by the veto power of one of the permanent members of the Council, which is ignoring the racist Zionist danger confronting the developing nations and endangering world peace and security."[148] Ambassador Kikhia from the Libyan Arab Republic, his country called by Herzog the "paymaster of international terror movements," turned the tables again. Noting that Israel was angry at Uganda for revealing its collaboration with racist regimes in South Africa and Rhodesia, he reminded the council, "The history of the establishment of the Zionist State is a history of terrorism.... Who killed in cold blood the United Nations mediator, Count Bernadotte? Who assassinated Lord Moyne? Who made the killers of Count Bernadotte public heroes sitting in the Israeli Cabinet?... Who shot down a Libyan civilian aircraft, killing scores of people, including women and children?"[149]

Despite powerful allies, Israel thus had a shaky foundation upon which to base claims to fight terror, to protect innocent civilians, to defy the UN. Questioning Herzog's attempts to cast doubt on the PLO, Kikhia recalled that the organization was "recognized by the United Nations and by the majority of the world community as the legitimate representative of the Palestinian people" and had denounced the hijacking. "We are not paymasters to anybody," he concluded of the right to struggle against oppression: "We are trying to do our best to help our brothers, to help liberation movements. We help them, we train people who are fighting against colonialism, against imperialism, against racism, against *apartheid*, and we shall continue to do that."[150] Such struggles were often the only means for weaker parties to fight oppression and transform the status quo, as the United States had done two centuries earlier in gaining liberation from Britain; moreover, as noted in the debate, all liberation movements are described as terrorists by their oppressors. The semantic ambiguity was structural. What a mess.

Architecture, Technology, Bodies

Questions regarding how to manage complex environments and urban populations had been on Negroponte's mind at least since his 1965 thesis, "Systems of Urban Growth," research premised on the notion that "a new profession will evolve that must take the responsibility of handling the urbanization of millions and millions."[151] At that moment, Negroponte proposed to ameliorate the potential chaos or insecurity arising from such human unsettlement and the processes of urbanization associated with it by providing an open-ended lattice structure that facilitated growth while allowing for degrees of "freedom" within it. In setting out a systems-based solution avowedly indebted to Yona Friedman, whose own work drew upon Third World contexts, and in taking that paradigm into the digital domain, he came to conceive of architecture as a regulatory apparatus that, as we have seen, appeared to facilitate a level of choice and agency while simultaneously modeling dispersed systems of control.[152] By the late 1970s, Negroponte's research was no longer directed toward providing housing, or even physical systems of urban organization subject to feedback or "participation," no matter how complex. But his research remained dedicated to applied urban research, or what the Urban Systems Lab had celebrated as making technology work in the city. We can trace an arc from his early dreams of developing architectural tools with which to manage the urban impact of population growth in developing countries to late-1970s strategies of data visualization, bodily immersion, and the "entrainment of attention" via ArcMac's heavily funded technologies and programs for computerized monitoring, data collection, and regulation of environments. Although, with ongoing insurgencies and terrorist threats, ArcMac sought to develop computer simulations for training soldiers and other military personnel to intervene in "increasingly complex battlefields," the research was also understood to provide technologies for management that would soon infiltrate everyday life. In a 1976 reflection, "Return of the Sunday Painter, or the Computer in the Visual Arts," Negroponte forecast: "the major impact of computers in the visual arts will be on our daily lives, not necessarily on high and fine art. The observers will be participants. Processes will be products."[153]

At stake for Negroponte in bringing together architecture, art, science, and technology was not simply providing access to expanded domains of knowledge for those in the arts.[154] ArcMac's unsuccessful 1976 NSF application for Graphical Conversation Theory—to which was appended "Return of the Sunday Painter"—spoke of "professionalizing" the arts at MIT, practices "previously limited," as they put it, "to cultural, humanitarian, and introspective goals."[155] With the rejection of this grant, aesthetic concerns—even if only cultural, humanitarian, or introspective—waned even further as Negroponte turned his attention to the Arts and Media Technology venture, which soon dropped the term "art" and in turn even "technology" to become the Media Lab. With this transition came the dissolution of ArcMac into its research components and the withdrawal of the last traces in its name of its disciplinary origin in architecture.[156]

Situating the new Media Lab at the intersection of "information technologies and the human sciences," Negroponte indicated that "graduates will be required to pursue studies in epistemology, experimental psychology, filmmaking, holography, and signal processing, as well as in computer science."[157] Here, perhaps, was the new profession of which Negroponte dreamed in 1965, one able to "take the responsibility of handling the urbanization of millions and millions." This professionalizing, to reiterate, entailed a technoscientific paradigm born of interdisciplinary wartime research; like other heavily funded labs, by providing *relevant* expertise, these initiatives could draw enormous sponsorship from government bodies and institutions such as the Department of Defense and the Ford Foundation in the service of the military-industrial complex.

Fortunately, technologies now as ubiquitous as spatial data interfaces, data banks, and environmental simulations have in turn had other lives; some have even elicited counterconducts or opened onto new political spaces, more democratic alternatives, or even new claims to justice, as demonstrated by critical attempts, including by architects, to deploy such media otherwise, to redirect them to progressive ends, whether in the form of gaming strategies, data-visualization projects, alternative mapping and archive initiatives, or even in the "liberation" of data sets.[158]

ArcMac projects were not only architectural prosthetics, but also post-utopian spatiotemporal devices geared toward managing at once the milieu, the body, and cognition. Predominantly directed toward insecure territories and unsettled populations, all, we might say, were architectural technologies implicitly or explicitly generated by and often serving the interests of the violence and inequity at work in contemporary geopolitical transformations. This was rendered explicit when Negroponte situated the Movie Map simultaneously as the birth of multimedia and a legacy of the Entebbe raid. Coupling representation, technology, territory, and counterinsurgency, he reminds us, too, that such environmental simulations remain haunted by disappearing and reappearing bodies and by insecurities that dominant powers sought to control. During this period, that is, Third World populations repeatedly emerged as vectors, and as specters, of such geopolitical instability to be countered by counterinsurgency technologies; their voices and bodies were felt as a threatening presence by superpowers attempting to maintain control of the environment and its resources. "Create a magenta church... create a red tanker...." But voices and bodies did, of course, return, not only in the Movie Map's peculiar event world, but also in the material spaces those technologies sought to control. And they also returned elsewhere, such as at the UN and eventually in online platforms, wherein they sought to institute different discourses and to mobilize media, including multimedia, to other ends. Like bits, they too could travel. A specter, Derrida reminds us, "is always a *revenant*. One cannot control its comings and goings because it *begins by coming back*."[159]

Figure 9.1 View of Earth from the Moon, taken in 1966 by Lunar Orbiter 1 and restored from magnetic files in 2008 (NASA).

CONCLUSION

Passages and Passengers

> Hi-Seas has already conducted two four-month missions, and next year, six more people will reside for one year inside the dome.... It sits in an abandoned quarry at an altitude of 8,000 feet on Mauna Loa [Hawaii]. Like real astronauts, the Hi-Seas crew will be busy performing various scientific work, including excursions outside the dome in spacesuits.
> —Kenneth Chang, "In a Dome in Hawaii, a Mission to Mars," *New York Times*, October 21, 2014

During the 1960s and 1970s, a period (among others) experiencing widespread geopolitical insecurity and human unsettlement, questions of territory took on an enhanced valence.[1] In his seminal 1973 book, *The Significance of Territory*, Jean Gottmann posited that "the important aspect of territory as the unit in the political organization of space" is that it involves the "relationships between the community and its habitat on the one hand, and between the community and its neighbors on the other."[2] He situated traditional functions of territory at the chiasma of a "shelter for security" and a "springboard for opportunity," the former achieved through partitioning and the establishment of borders, the latter through forms of political organization and the regulation of access by outsiders in the interest of pursuing "the good life" of the people within. To him, traditional concepts of territory thus harbor a structural contradiction: while security seeks "relative isolation," opportunity thrives on a "degree of interdependence with the outside," giving rise to a persistent and irreconcilable duality that troubles governing institutions in a sovereign state.[3] In addition to being tied, quite literally, to the land or earth—as conveyed in the Latin root, *terra*—territorial sovereignty, he reasoned, "is not separable from a definite human will and purpose."[4] Hence the importance placed on human presence and settlement as factors linking sovereignty with territory. Striving beyond what Aristotle called "the bare needs of life," he explained of the expansionist impulse concomitant to the "good life," entails improving "resources and living conditions of the place" one called "home."[5]

Gottmann's reflections were prompted by the impact of forces further complicating this picture—automation; space travel; nuclear and long-range weapons; satellite, communication, and surveillance technologies; and the liberalization of international trade, migration, and travel. Territory remains central to a nation-state's ability to exercise sovereignty and to govern, he insisted, and it remains the cornerstone of international law at a moment when "practically all of the land area of the planet has been surveyed and apportioned to some national or international authority to administer."[6] Yet these technologies and the increasing fluidity of bodies and goods unsettle links between humans, sovereignty, and territory.[7] Automation, for instance, renders human presence redundant, since "all activities could be carried on by robots under remote control"; the planting of national emblems and flags on the moon raises the specter of conquest or colonization beyond Earth; airborne weapons and satellites circumnavigating the globe raise the issue of the vertical extension of sovereignty and undermined the relevance of borders to security strategies, and the list goes on. To the notion of airspace—an area remaining "under the sovereignty of the subjacent territory"—international law had recently added outer space, which, he wrote of a further uncoupling, now "became a sort of 'high seas' free for all."[8]

The New High Seas

Somewhat unexpectedly, Gottmann ended his list of challenges to territorial sovereignty by focusing on rural-to-urban migration, refracting concerns from the global or even extraterrestrial scope to the "massing of population in the cities." Urbanization and mobility, he argued, mark a "new order in the organization of the use of space as habitat," while the concomitant notion of territory has continued to shift back and forth between relations with outsiders and those internal to a border.[9] As *Outlaw Territories* has tried to demonstrate, relations between these various scales—as with those within and beyond borders—were difficult to untangle: insecurity seemed to arise simultaneously from within and without. Turning to urbanization, Gottmann's primary reference was the United States, then experiencing, as he put it, a "mechanized, automated age, in which information and knowledge were the main sources of prosperity," along with an increasing cosmopolitanism and "extraterritorial" urban behavior.[10] Such pressures, as we have seen, were increasingly felt not only in the United States, but throughout the world during this period of heightened globalization, a situation prompting symptomatic and distinctly neocolonial searches for a new "high seas."

A case in point: in 1977, after almost a decade proselytizing for mechanisms of population control to stem environmental catastrophe on Spaceship Earth, Stewart Brand published an anthology on his current fascination: *Space Colonies*. Many of the texts had appeared in *Co-Evolution Quarterly*, an offshoot of the *Whole Earth Catalog* that took its title from Paul Ehrlich's coevolution thesis (the coadaption of living organisms with each other). *Space Colonies* revolved around Princeton University physics professor Gerard O'Neill's proposals to colonize or settle the "high frontier," proposals presented, replete with elaborate architectural renderings and an enormous model, to the US House of Representatives Committee on Science and Technology in July 1975.[11] The book included a familiar cast of characters—Ken Kesey, R. Buckminster Fuller, Ehrlich, E. F. Schumacher, Stephanie Mills, Gary Snyder, Dennis Meadows, Garrett Hardin, and a host of alternative architects or alternative-technology figures—Paolo Soleri, Steve Durkee, Steve Baer, and John Todd. There was even an ironic contribution from the Ant Farm collective. To Paul and Anne Ehrlich, the initiative opened nothing less than a "new horizon for humanity"; in offering the prospect for reducing population density on Earth, they posited, "it might even make war obsolete."[12]

Seeking to escape a troubled Earth and territorial sovereignty entirely, space colonies promised liberation from extant environmental threats—such as population growth in the Third World—and political constraints, resonating ambiguously between utopian and dystopian agendas. Brand noted as much when recalling a semantic roadblock.

> [T]he use of the term "Space Colony" has been expressly forbidden by the U.S. State Department because of anti-colonial feelings around the world. So NASA has shrugged and adopted "Space Settlements"—

> unpoetic terminology since the last thing you do in Space is settle. We're sticking to "Space Colonies." It's more accurate. This time there's a difference in that no space natives are being colonized. And the term reminds us of things that went badly and went well in previous colonizations.[13]

The term "settlement" was indeed far from an enlightened substitute for "colony." As evident at Habitat: the United Nations Conference on Human Settlements of 1976, unsettlement remained the issue. What Brand recognized in space colonies was another potential "outlaw area" in which to "try stuff"—presumably what "went well in previous colonizations."[14] Recalling remarks by "a Navy man" he heard the previous night in California Governor Jerry Brown's office, he intimated that airplanes were less relevant to "the navigation, construction, command regimes, and life-onboard of space*ships*" than naval experience, pointing in turn to the precedent of "outlaw areas" such as the high seas of an earlier colonial era. Celebrating the capacity to function outside the law and beyond the reach of a political community, he wrote, for those "who believe with Buckminster Fuller that a culture's creativity requires an Outlaw Area, Free Space becomes what the oceans have ceased to be—Outlaw Area too big and dilute for national control."[15]

Brand might have been correct that "natives" would not directly suffer the effects of space colonization, while architects, engineers, and scientists developed new techniques of environmental control for those seeking to escape the chaos of Earth. Space colonies, he suggested, would provide the architecture of "*separate* whole systems."[16] With the departure of those privileged enough to enjoy such a passage to outer space, however, the threat of a certain withdrawal of care for Earth loomed, the impact of which would likely touch down unevenly on the planet. As with other examples traced in *Outlaw Territories*, the exceptional spaces that Brand celebrated were not only outlaw areas: bringing together humans, communities, and habitats or settlements, they were better understood as outlaw *territories*, spaces entailing governing bodies to regulate both internal and external relations.

Figures 9.2 & 9.3 Interior view of Bernal Space Colony for population of 10,000; interior view of agricultural module (multiple toroids) (NASA Ames Research Center; artwork by Rick Guidice).

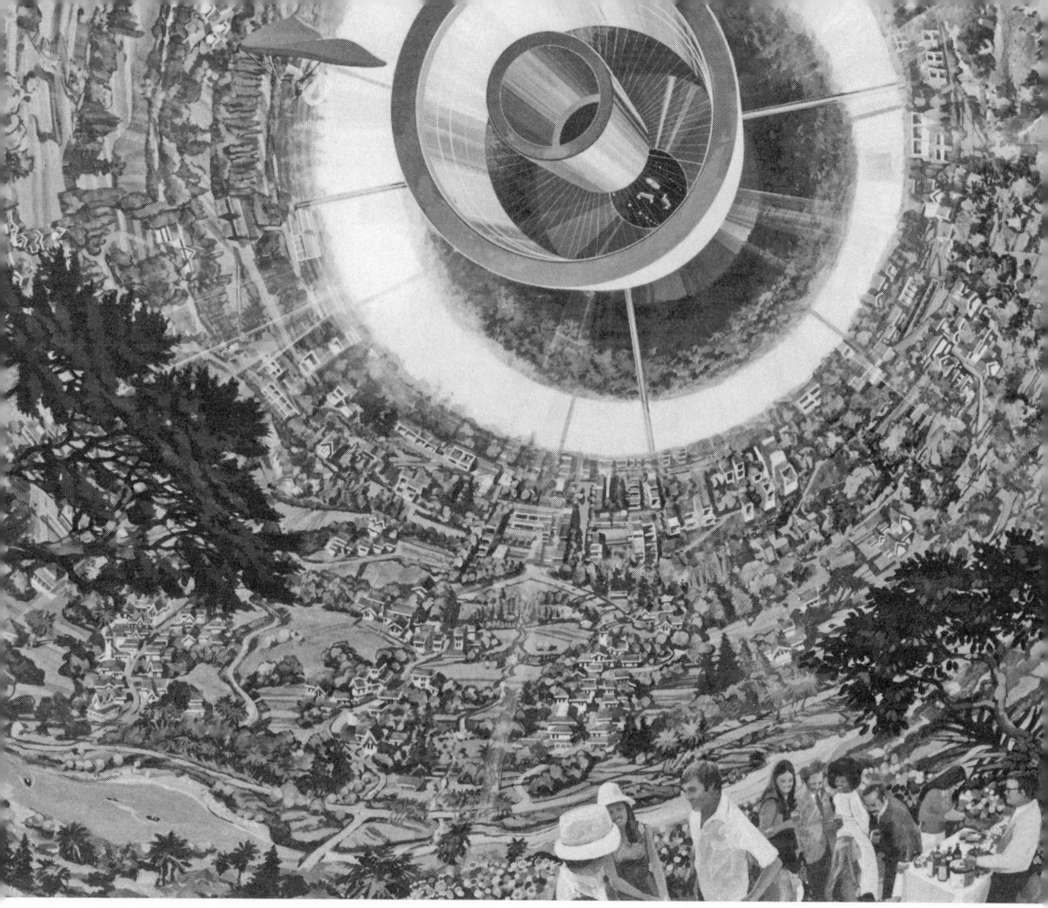

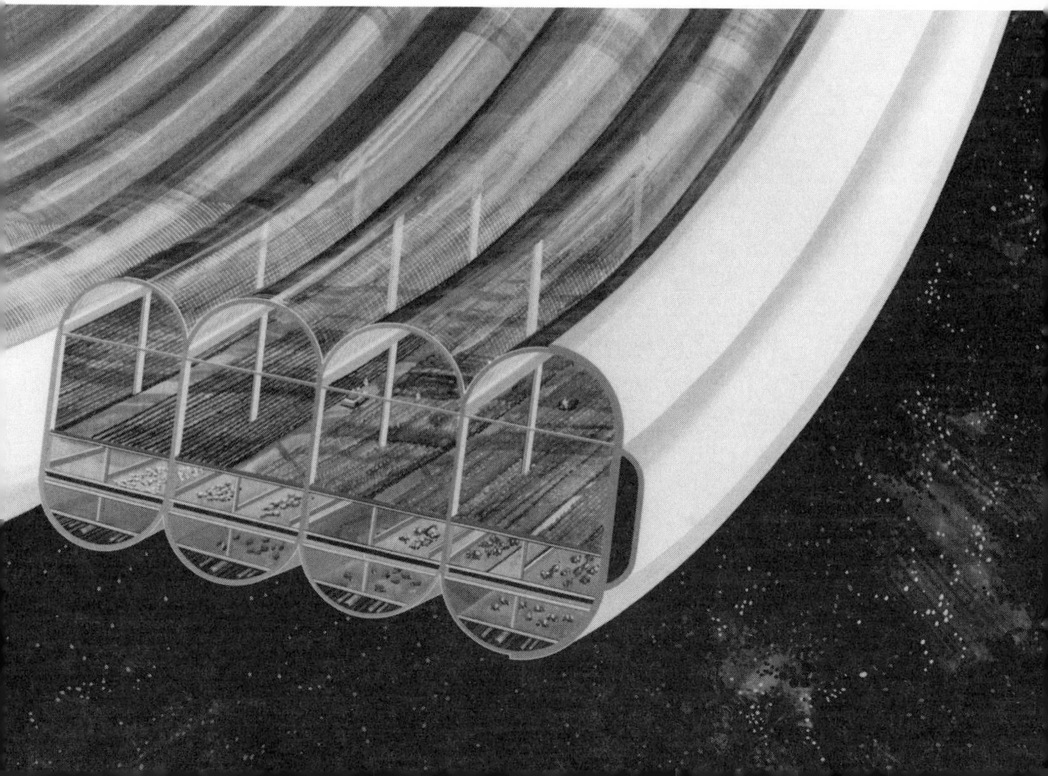

I invoke *Space Colonies* in concluding not only for the connection to Brand, where we began. Additionally, in resonating ambiguously between utopian and dystopian positions, the subject returns us to a conceptual stake derived from an earlier period of Michel Foucault's work that I want to unpack very briefly and at the risk of passing through well-known territory. In "Different Spaces," a lecture presented to the Architectural Studies Circle in Paris in March 1967, Foucault offered a theory of "emplacement" as an "ensemble of relations" that have superseded localization and extension as spatial paradigms.[17] When identifying spaces that were not simply utopian, but rather that served to unsettle distinctions or even to disrupt conventional ordering systems, he cited two forces: first, "contemporary engineering" as manifest in the storage of information, machine calculation, and discrete and coded elements associated with computerization, and, second, the demography at work in "human emplacement," a reference at once to ethnic or racial distribution and to the statistical analysis of human populations in terms of births, deaths, income, disease, and so on. As Foucault explained, invoking the period's widespread paranoia about population growth, it was "not just the question of knowing if there will be enough space for man in the world—a problem that is very important after all—but also the problem of knowing what relations of proximity, what type of storage, of circulation, of identification, of classification of human elements are to be preferentially retained."[18] This nexus of computers and information management, on the one hand, and populations and bodily circulation, on the other, has surfaced repeatedly in the stories related here.

What avowedly interested Foucault were not only ensembles of relations likely to be "preferentially retained" on account of their function in dominant systems, but also *different* emplacements, and he spoke of spaces that "suspend, neutralize, or reverse the set of relations that are designated, reflected or represented [*réflechis*]" in conventional modes of organization. "These different spaces, these other places," he noted, are connected to, but nevertheless outside normal spaces—they often mirror while disturbing their inherent divisions, hence also contesting extant structures of power.[19] Foucault had alluded to this dynamic the previous year in *Les mots et les choses*, translated as *The Order of Things*. Utopias, he posited, "have no real locality," but "there is nevertheless a fantastic, untroubled region in which they are able to unfold; they open up cities with vast avenues, superbly planted gardens, countries where life is easy, even though the road to them is chimerical."[20] It would be hard to find a better description of space colony designs in their reflection of privileged enclaves. Different spaces—heterotopias—by contrast, entail "tangled paths, strange places, secret passages, and unexpected communications."[21]

Foucault's preface famously opened with his encounter with Borges's Chinese encyclopedia, the radically unfamiliar contiguities and ordering of which—animals were divided into categories such as "frenzied," "embalmed," "drawn with a very fine camelhair brush," and so on—provoked a troubling laughter. When Foucault asked rhetorically, "Where else could they be juxtaposed except in the non-place of language?" he was not suggesting that language *only* was subject to disturbing propinquities and heterogeneities. The *tabula* informing systems of order, he posited, connects language to spaces, noting additionally that "our age-old distinction between the Same and the Other"—precisely the distinction threatened with collapse—bear the "stamp of our age and our geography."[22] That is, Foucault spoke to juxtapositions occurring with the mixing of bodies and with demographic shifts then transgressing traditional spatial and geographical divides. These divides—often marked racially, economically, and by sexuality or gender—organized not only conventional human emplacements, but structures of power: their disruption caused anxieties for those in power, hence proliferating attempts to control such transformations, attempts which, Foucault understood, were no laughing matter. If *different spaces* disturb such systems of order, if they "destroy 'syntax' in advance," they harbor the potential of opening up more heterogeneous places, spaces that do not serve to close down difference, but to foster radical forms of juxtaposition. It was this sort of threat that some of my protagonists—Brand, Maurice Strong, Kevin Roche, Sonoma County, Barbara Ward, the IAF, and Nicholas Negroponte—sought to quell, whether by instituting a new world order or by developing architectural paradigms to regulate such complexities.

Architecture

When in 1969 Kevin Roche proposed a bulletproof-glass bridge to span from the United Nations Headquarters to the United Nations

Figure 9.4 KRJDA, UN Center, New York, 1969; rendering (courtesy of KRJDA).

Plaza that he was designing across First Avenue, he imagined it might secure UN diplomats and visiting dignitaries as they crossed between these two extraterritorial spaces embedded in the city of New York. At once a gesture of connection and disconnection, of location and dislocation with respect to the city, the bridge responded to and harbored anxieties spanning (in a different sense) from the potential of urban insurrection in American cities to geopolitical tensions and insecurities at the international or even global scale—insecurities the UN sought to manage. Although both sides of Roche's bridge touched down in spaces that were exceptional, controlled, contained, and ostensibly secure, traversing between them required a passage through an outside, proximity to which entailed a certain risk. The bridge was dropped from the final scheme, and we might speculate that in addition to possible economic constraints or violations of city planning codes, this architectural element spoke too overtly to insecurity, the glowing, transparent, high-tech passage rendering it at once spectacular and cynical. The bridge's brief appearance in this story reminds us that even the enclosed environment that Roche designed for the UN required openings and control points to function within larger configurations.

The threats that such mechanisms for circulation sought to regulate have not been eliminated in the intervening decades, whether through architecture, technology, or political channels, but they have continued to generate new refuges and new outlets or passages in both the physical and virtual worlds. We might even say that Roche's transparent bridge finds uncanny counterparts, or inverse images, today in the proliferation of concrete tunnels constructed beneath Israel's "security" barrier around Gaza and in online digital portals and networks that breach other systems of order to claim a more differentiated global commons, portals interfaced graphically via computer terminals as once dreamed by the Architecture Machine Group.

Outlaw Territories has investigated the topologies of several exceptional sociospatial conditions from the 1960s and 1970s as they mirrored and departed from, while also informed or touched down in, the broader world. To do so, it has traced an arc from Roche's designs for two institutions of global governance—the Ford Foundation and the UN—to technoscientific research undertaken by architects at MIT and geared toward computerized control of both environments and populations. Between these end points, Open Land communes and UN "world conferences" dedicated to the "human environment" in Stockholm and to "human settlement" in Vancouver entered the picture as peculiar microcosms, spaces in which global geopolitical pressures and the technologies, laws, and systems of management proliferating to address them found expression in the form of testing grounds for implementing new modes of life, voluntary or otherwise. In each chapter, encounters with other populations and other spaces, whether born of identification with alterity, as with the Open Land communards, or in actual mixings of groups, as in the UN conferences (occasions for "world thinking" quite literally bringing voices from around the globe together), created unanticipated connections and points of conflict. These encounters either took place within or sponsored exceptional topologies as means of containing their effects—as in the enclosure of the Ford Foundation Headquarters or in the alliance of Brand's "environment yes, politics no" platform with the US delegation in Stockholm. Repeatedly, as multiple parties charted emplacements on complex, relational, fluid, and variegated battlefields, technologies, and discourses (including those derived from architecture, but increasingly those born of cybernetics and computerization) emerged as tools of biopolitical regulation and sites of political struggle, at times even providing platforms for the eruption of other voices and discourses and with them a new type of political space.

When faced with the very real, unsettling effects of technoscience or "tele-technology," Derrida argued in *Specters of Marx*, the point is not to call for return to a firm or somehow more true sense of place or territory, and with it the violence effected in the name of old frontiers "such as those of the blood, nationalism of native soil." Rather, he posits:

> It obliges us more than ever to think the virtualization of space and time, the possibility of virtual events whose movement and speed prohibit us more than ever... from opposing presence to its representation, "real time" to "deferred time," effectivity to its simulacrum, the living to the non-living, in short the living to the living-dead of ghosts. It obliges us to think, from there, another space for democracy. For democracy-to-come and thus for justice.[23]

Within the complex matrix of architecture, technology, territory, population, and science traced in *Outlaw Territories*, where such oppositions have frequently morphed into convoluted topologies that render conventional wisdom or disciplinary expertise helpless and hapless, such an obligation to think of another space and of other events has returned over and over. Undermining conventional oppositions, these topologies remind us that in demarcating subject matter deemed proper to the field, and in often seeking to uncouple (or to protect) architecture from the emergence of such a global biopolitical matrix, architectural history and criticism—sometimes knowingly, sometimes simply unwittingly—often serve as mechanisms of sanitization, even for the suppression of ghosts. Architecture, however, remains within the apparatus of globalization, as disheartening as that may be. The question these often messy stories pose, to reiterate, is not how architecture and its attendant discourses and practices might escape this violent apparatus, but how they might act within it without rendering cynicism structural or ever more powerful—how they might interrupt the conjunction of emergency, security, and militarism.

It is thus a wager of this study that within architecture, historical research remains subject to the sort of ethical obligation that Derrida identified. One can respond to contemporary pressures not by calls to order or attempts to retreat to familiar disciplinary formulations or narratives, with their attendant limits and own implicit violence, but by trying to articulate and render legible a more complex and variegated, if necessarily disjunctive picture of the network of forces at play. Investigating the deterritorializing forces of postindustrial technologies and neoliberal capitalism against the backdrop of architectural and urban discourses trying to *solve* the illegibility, disorganization, or "degradedness" of the American city (think György Kepes, Kevin Lynch, Jane Jacobs, Oscar Newman, Robert Venturi, and more), we have traced stories that both facilitate a reflection back upon the discipline of architecture *and* passages to its outside, mirroring Gottmann's chiasma with all its attendant contradictions and risks. Within this dynamic, specters from the Third World repeatedly return to visibility, reminding us that there remain many other stories to tell.

Like architecture itself, history can provide alternative maps, routes, conceptual tools, practices, technologies, and discourses;

it can identify inherent fluidities, ambiguities, and hence opportunities. At stake, then, is how to institute spaces of (or time for) reflection, witness, and analytical work, even new narratives and other histories that render visible and articulable the many forms of violence at play in order that they might be attended to differently. We might even argue that architecture is one of the most effective sites through which to enact political claims. It has a long history of interfacing with a broad matrix of players, discourses, and forces: financial, political, military, climatic, technical, artistic, scientific, environmental, geopolitical. The internal disjunctiveness or radical lack of autonomy in that history, as well as in architecture's present state and future prospects, can be put to productive ends for critical thinking and practice, employing the many media available to it, from buildings, drawings, exhibitions, magazines, books, photographs, to film, television, statistics, the Internet, and more. Such instabilities and ambivalences harbor the potential for being subject to a strategic reversal or power or tactically diverted to *other* ends.

Acknowledgments

This book has benefited greatly from the attention, ideas, support, and generosity of numerous individuals and institutions over a number of years, for which the gesture of acknowledgment never seems sufficient. At Zone Books, I want to sincerely thank Jonathan Crary, Michel Feher, Hal Foster, and Meighan Gale for both their confidence and their patience and Bud Bynack for his careful copyediting. I feel incredibly fortunate to have my work appear in a context that I have admired for so long. Thank you! At Columbia University I want to acknowledge Dean Mark Wigley, who fostered a remarkable culture of experiment and dialogue at the Graduate School of Architecture, Planning and Preservation, newly appointed Dean Amale Andraos for her ongoing support, and Senior Associate Dean David Hinkle for his assistance on so many fronts. The author also expresses appreciation to The Graham Foundation for Advanced Studies in the Fine Arts and the Schoff Fund at the University Seminars for their help in publication. Material in this work was presented to the University Seminar: Theory and History of Media. I also want to acknowledge the invaluable support of two fellowships, a Clark Fellowship at the Sterling and Francine Clark Art Institute in fall 2008 and the German Transatlantic Berlin Prize at the American Academic in Berlin in fall 2013. Not only did they enable precious time for writing; both also came with extraordinary colleagues (and wonderful meals), and I want to sincerely thank Michael Ann Holly, Mark Ledbury, and Gary Smith, as well as the staff and my fellow fellows from both contexts. As interlocutors, audiences, and friends, they have left important traces in the work. The many opportunities to present and discuss aspects of this research in public also proved critical during various stages of its development, and I want to sincerely thank everyone who invited me to speak or contributed to those discussions. I also want to acknowledge people involved with earlier publications related to this material. Sections of Chapter 3 appeared in *Sensible Politics: The Visual Culture of Nongovernmental Activism*, edited by Yates McKee and Meg McLagan (Zone Books, 2012); sections of Chapter 6 appeared in *Les Cahiers du Musée national d'art modern* 129 (Autumn 2014); sections of Chapter 8 appeared in *The Aspen Complex*, edited by Martin Beck (Sternberg Press, 2012); and an earlier version of Chapter 7 appeared in *A Second Modernism: Architecture and MIT in the PostWar*, edited by Arindam Dutta, Stephanie Tuerk, Michael Kubo, Jennifer Chuong, and Irena Chernyakova (MIT Press, 2013).

I feel especially indebted to Nora Akawi, Keller Easterling, Branden W. Joseph, Diana Martinez, and Marina Otero Verzier for reading parts of the manuscript as it neared completion and for their enthusiastic responses. To them I am enormously grateful. The development of this research and its intellectual coordinates over many years has also benefited from numerous other individuals and contexts, including participating in the University Seminar: Theory and History of Media run by Stefan Andriopoulos, Brian Larkin, and Noam Elcott; discussions with students in my seminars "Architecture, Human Rights, Spatial Politics" and "Histories and Modernities;" and especially from the long-standing collaboration with Branden W. Joseph and Reinhold Martin, as well as with Karen Beckman and Tom McDonough, on the journal *Grey Room*. Other key interlocutors, colleagues, students, and friends whom I want to warmly thank for their inspiration, dialogue, and support include Warwick Anderson, Thordis Arrhenius, Etienne Balibar, Daniel Barber, Martin Beck, Peter Brew, Beatriz Colomina, Tony Conrad, Arindum Dutta, Marco Fusinato, James Graham, Carol Greene, Sarah Herda, Sandi Hilal, Annabella Johnson, Thomas Keenan, Hollyamber Kennedy, Laura Kurgan, Adrian Lahoud, Alexandra Lawlor, Ayala Levin, Yates McKee, Detlef Mertins, Paul Minifie, Ulrike Müller, Ijlal Muzzafar, Ginger Nolan, Alessandro Petit, Anthony Vidler, Joseph Vogl, Mark Wasiuta, Eyal Weizman, Ines Weizman, Mark Wigley, and Mabel Wilson. Working through the material here in relation to each of these contexts and in dialogue with so many smart people has provided not only occasions for feedback and testing ideas, but discursive and critical footholds that helped clarify key stakes.

Thanks are also due to the many archivists, librarians, and their staffs who have facilitated my research: Yolande Korb at the American Academy in Berlin library; Chak Yung and other staff at the City of Vancouver Archives; Susan Roeper and Karen Bucky at the Clark Art Institute library; staff at the Rare Book and Manuscript Library as well as at Butler and Avery Libraries of Columbia University; Nicolette Lodico at the Ford Foundation Archives; staff at the Kungliga biblioteket in Stockholm; Nora Murphy and other staff at the Institute Archives and Special Collections at the MIT Libraries; Michelle Elligot and staff at the Museum of Modern Art Archives; Robert G. Trujillo, Tim Noakes, Mattie Taormina, and other staff at the Stanford University Libraries Special Collections; Katherine Kalsbeek, Kathryn Ferrante, and other staff at Rare Books and Special Collections as well as Erwin Wodarczak and Candice Bjur at the Archives of the University of British Columbia Library; Cheryl Siegel and Danielle Currie at the Vancouver Art Gallery; and Laura Tatum and other staff at the Yale University Library Manuscripts and Archives. My archival and image research has also benefited from individuals including Love Enqvist, Lars Gogman, Björn Gustafsson, Tony Gwilliam, Mary Jean Haley, Peter Harper, Henrik Henrikson, Ian Hogan, Per Janse, Jan Ökvist, Simon Scott, Ramon Sender, Pär Stolpe, Michael Leo Villardi, Anders Willgård, and Alexander Wood.

My family members have helped in many untold ways, and I want to sincerely thank my parents, Malcolm Scott and Ruth Scott, as well as my siblings, Fiona, Marcus, and Duncan, and their families for their support. Finally, endless gratitude is due to Branden W. Joseph for putting aspects of our lives on hold while I focused on such an enormous project.

This book is dedicated to my brother, Marcus Paul Elliston Scott (1964–2014), who in a heartbreaking moment in October, only weeks before he died, told me to "just hand it in; life is short." I did just that. You will always be in my heart.

Notes

INTRODUCTION

1. A cover note indicated that as part of its $1 series, the edition was technically a supplement, but due to post office regulations, it took the title *Whole Earth Catalog*.

2. Stewart Brand, "Apocalypse Juggernaut, Hello," *Whole Earth Catalog*, January 1970, p. 21.

3. R. Buckminster Fuller, quoted in *ibid*. See Calvin Tomkins, "In the Outlaw Area," *New Yorker*, January 8, 1966, pp. 35–97.

4. On this normalization of exception, see Giorgio Agamben, *State of Exception*, trans. Kevin Attell (Chicago: University of Chicago Press, 2005).

5. See Stewart Brand (ed.), *Space Colonies* (New York: Penguin, 1977). Many of the texts included had earlier appeared in *Co-Evolution Quarterly*, a Brand initiative following the *Whole Earth Catalog*.

6. Stewart Brand, "Loose Talk 1: The Outlaw Area," *Whole Earth Catalog*, January 1970, p. 21.

7. Stewart Brand, "Loose Talk 3: Mountain Fantasy," *Whole Earth Catalog*, January 1970, p. 22.

8. Walls, as Etienne Balibar reminds us, "are not passive structures" and are insufficient in themselves to halt movement across such divides. Rather, "They become a point, or a line of crystallization of permanent and additional violence, increasingly militarized, which also means that they tend to blur the distinction between normality and exception, or more precisely state of peace and state of war." Etienne Balibar, "Strangers as Enemies: Walls All Over the World, and How to Tear Them Down," *Mondi Migranti* (January 2012), pp. 9, 10.

9. *Ibid*., p. 12. Balibar is referring to the work of Sandro Mezzadra in this context.

10. On the notion and history of territory see Jean Gottmann, *The Significance of Territory* (Charlottesville: University of Virginia Press, 1973), and Stuart Elden, *The Birth of Territory* (Chicago: University of Chicago Press: Chicago, 2013).

11. Wendy Brown, *Walled States, Waning Sovereignty* (New York: Zone Books, 2010).

12. Walter Benjamin, "On the Concept of History," in *Walter Benjamin: Selected Writings, Volume 4: 1938–1940*, ed. Michael W. Jennings (Cambridge, MA: Harvard University Press, 2003), p. 392. On the Benjamin-Schmitt dialogue, see Hans Bredekamp, "From Walter Benjamin to Carl Schmitt, via Thomas Hobbes," trans. Melissa Thorson Hause and Jackson Bond, *Critical Inquiry* 25 (Winter 1999), pp. 247–66, and Agamben, *State of Exception.*

13. Hans Magnus Enzensberger, "A Critique of Political Ecology," *New Left Review* 84 (1974), p. 14.

14. See Michel Foucault, *The Birth of Biopolitics: Lectures at the Collège de France, 1978–1979*, trans. Graham Burchell (New York: Palgrave, 2008), and Timothy W. Luke, "Environmentality as Green Governmentality," in Eric Darier (ed.), *Discourses of the Environment* (Malden, MA: Blackwell, 1999), pp. 121–51. For a groundbreaking use of this notion in the context of northern India under British colonial rule, see Arun Agrawal, *Environmentality: Technologies of Government and the Making of Subjects* (Durham: Duke University Press, 2005).

15. For a different comparative approach, see James Ron, *Frontiers and Ghettos: State Violence in Serbia and Israel* (Berkeley: University of California Press, 2003). I thank Michel Feher for pointing me to this important study.

16. Among important landmarks in this regard, see Rafi Segal and Eyal Weizman (eds.), *A Civilian Occupation: The Politics of Israeli Architecture* (New York: Verso, 2003); Anselm Franke, Rafi Segal, and Eyal Weizman (eds.), *Territories, Islands, Camps and Other States of Utopia* (Cologne: Walter Koenig, 2003); Eduardo Cadava and Aaron Levy (eds.), *Cities without Citizens* (Philadelphia: Slought Books, 2004); Keller Easterling, *Enduring Innocence: Global Architecture and Its Political Masquerades* (Cambridge, MA: MIT Press, 2005); Ijlal M. Muzaffar, "The Periphery Within: Modern Architecture and the Making of the Third World," PhD diss., MIT, 2007; Eyal Weizman, *Hollow Land: Israel's Architecture of Occupation* (London: Verso, 2007); Paul Virilio and Raymond Depardon, *Native Land: Stop, Eject* (Paris: Fondation Cartier pour l'art contemporain and Thames and Hudson, 2008); and Laura Kurgan, *Close Up at a Distance: Mapping, Technology, and Politics* (New York: Zone Books, 2013). See also Reinhold Martin, *The Organizational Complex: Architecture, Media, and Corporate Space* (Cambridge, MA: MIT Press, 2003); and Aggregate Architectural History Collaborative, *Governing by Design: Architecture, Economy, and Politics in the Twentieth Century* (Pittsburgh: University of Pittsburgh Press, 2012).

17. See Le Corbusier, *The Radiant City: Elements of a Doctrine of Urbanism to Be Used as the Basis of Our Machine-Age Civilization* (1933; New York: Orion Press, 1967), p. 18. The mythology surrounding Le Corbusier's involvement with the

League of Nations competition was reiterated in his participation in the design of the United Nations Headquarters in New York almost two decades later.

18. On the complicated relation of CIAM, the UN, and the UIA, see Sarah Deyong, "Planetary Habitat: The Origins of a Phantom Movement," *Journal of Architecture* 6.2 (Summer 2001), pp. 113–28; and Muzaffar, "The Periphery Within."

19. Muzaffar, "The Periphery Within," p. 25.

20. Vladmir Bodiansky, "Notes on the Subject of a Habitat Charter," *Annals of Public and Cooperative Economics* 24.3 (October 1953), pp. 289–94. On CIAM's early attempts to embrace the language of "habitat" and the emergence of Team 10, see Max Risselada and Dirk van den Heuvel (eds.), *Team 10 1953–1981: In Search of a Utopia of the Present* (Rotterdam: nai010, 2005). On the occasion of the 1976 Habitat conference, the UIA also drafted a "Charter of Habitat." See Ken Jacobsen, "UIA Drafts a Charter on Human Settlements for Habitat '76," *Architectural Record* 159, March 1976, p. 37.

21. On the series of UN "world conferences" marking this trajectory, see Michael G. Schechter, *United Nations Global Conferences* (New York: Routledge, 2005). On the transformation of the UN during this period and its relation to developmentalism see Arturo Escobar, *Encountering Development: The Making and Unmaking of the Third World* (Princeton: Princeton University Press, 1995); Thomas G. Weiss, David P. Forsyth, and Roger A. Coate (eds.), *The United Nations and Changing World Politics* (Boulder: Westview Press, 1997); and Muzaffar, "The Periphery Within."

22. See, for instance, Le Corbusier, *Towards a New Architecture*, trans. Frederick Etchells (London: The Architectural Press, 1946), p. 269.

23. Gilles Deleuze, "What is a Dispositif?," in *Two Regimes of Madness: Texts and Interviews 1975–1995*, ed. David Lapoujade, trans. Ames Hodges and Mike Taormina (Los Angeles: Semiotext(e), 2006), p. 345. First published as Gilles Deleuze, "Qu'est-Ce Qu'un Dispositif?," in *Michel Foucault philosophe: Rencontre internationale Paris 9, 10, 11 Janvier 1988* (Paris: Seuil, 1988), pp. 185–95.

24. See Felicity D. Scott, *Architecture or Techno-Utopia: Politics after Modernism* (Cambridge, MA: MIT Press, 2007), and Reinhold Martin, *Utopia's Ghost: Architecture and Postmodernism, Again* (Minneapolis: University of Minnesota Press, 2010).

25. Barbara Ward, "The Home of Man: What Nations and the International Must Do," *Habitat: An International Journal* 1.2 (September 1976), p. 125.

26. Hence, earlier in 1976, during the Non-Aligned movement summit in Colombo, Sri Lanka, G77 members unsuccessfully proposed to establish alternatives to the World Bank and the IMF, both sources of profit to Western investors.

27. Stewart Brand, *The Media Lab: Inventing the Future at MIT* (New York: Penguin, 1988), p. 213.

28. Paul Virilio, "The Overexposed City," trans. Astrid Hustvedt, in *Zone 1/2: The Contemporary City* (New York: Zone Books, 1986), p. 25.

29. Paul Virilio, "The Suicidal State," trans. James Der Derian, Michael Degener, and Lauren Osepchuk, in James Der Derian (ed.), *The Virilio Reader* (Malden, MA: Blackwell, 1998), p. 30. Originally published in Paul Virilio, *L'insécurité du territoire* (1976; Paris: Galilée, 1993). See also Foucault, *The Birth of Biopolitics*.

30. Virilio, "The Suicidal State," p. 33.

31. *Ibid.*

32. *Ibid.*, p. 34.

33. *Ibid.*, p. 30.

34. *Ibid.*, p. 42.

35. See Jay W. Forrester, *World Dynamics* (Cambridge, MA: Wright-Allen Press, 1971), and Donella H. Meadows, et al., *The Limits to Growth: A Report for the Club of Rome's Project on the Predicament of Mankind* (New York: Universe Books, 1972).

36. Virilio, "The Suicidal State," pp. 42 and 43.

37. *Ibid.*, p. 44, n.9.

38. *Ibid.*, p. 41.

39. *Ibid.*, p. 32.

40. See Sandro Mezzadra and Brett Neilson (eds.), *Border as Method, or, the Multiplication of Labor* (Durham: Duke University Press, 2013).

41. Virilio, "The Suicidal State," p. 38.

42. See Daniel Defert, "Foucault, Space, and the Architects," in *Politics-Poetics: Documenta X—The Book* (Kassel: Cantz, 1997), pp. 274–83; Stuart Elden, "Strategy, Medicine and Habitat: Foucault in 1976," in Stuart Elden and Jeremy Crampton (eds.), *Space, Knowledge and Power: Foucault and Geography* (Burlington, VT: Ashgate, 2007), pp. 67–81; and Sven-Olov Wallenstein, "Foucault and the Genealogy of Modern Architecture," in Wallenstein, *Essays, Lectures* (Stockholm: Axl Books, 2007), 361–404.

43. Michel Foucault, "*Society Must Be Defended": Lectures at the Collège de France, 1975–76*, trans. David Macey (New York: Picador, 2003), pp. 244–45.

44. Michel Foucault, "The Right of Death and Power over Life," in *The History of Sexuality, Volume 1: An Introduction*, trans. Robert Hurley (New York: Random House, 1990), pp. 143–44.

45. *Ibid.*, p. 137.

46. Michel Foucault (ed.), *Politiques de l'habitat (1800–1850)* (Paris: Corda, 1977). See Elden, "Strategy, Medicine and Habitat," p. 72.

47. Michel Foucault, "Space, Knowledge and Power," in Sylvère Lotringer (ed.), *Foucault Live: Collected Interviews, 1961–1984* (New York: Semiotext(e), 1989), p. 335.

48. *Ibid.*, p. 336.

49. *Ibid.*, pp. 338 and 339.

50. *Ibid.*, p. 341.

51. Gilles Deleuze and Felix Guattari, *A Thousand Plateaus: Capitalism and Schizophrenia*, trans. Brian Massumi (Minneapolis: University of Minnesota Press, 1987).

52. Discourses, Foucault reminds us, function strategically within relations of power: the knowledge they harbor informs positions within strategic games and political struggles, it structures battlefields. "Discourse—the mere fact of speaking, of employing words, of using the words of others (even if it means returning them), words that the others understand and accept (and, possibly, return from their side)—this fact is in itself a force. Discourse is, with respect to the relation of forces, not merely a surface of inscription, but something that brings about effects." Michel Foucault, "Le discours ne doit pas être pris comme..." (1976), cited in Arnold I. Davidson, introduction to Foucault, *"Society Must Be Defended": Lectures at the Collège de France, 1975–76*, p. xx.

53. Maurizio Lazzarato, "From Biopower to Biopolitics," *Tailoring Biotechnologies* 2.2 (Summer–Fall 2006), p. 17.

54. The state of exception, as Balibar emphasizes, combines or collapses discourses and institutions of police with discourses of war, as exemplified in the "War on Terror," and blurs boundaries between criminal and enemy, legality and illegality, also destabilizing conventional notions of citizenship and territory. "This is already the case with illegal dimensions—often described as 'excesses'–of the use of police forces, which essentially derive from the fact that the legal rules police forces are supposed to observe even in the research and arrest of criminals (who must be *proved* to be criminals) are lifted when they are acting against enemies (who are supposed to be such *de facto*)." Balibar, "Strangers as Enemies," p. 16.

55. Michel Foucault, "Questions on Geography," in Colin Gordon (ed.), *Power/Knowledge: Selected Interviews and Other Writings, 1972–1977* (New York: Pantheon Books, 1980), p. 68.

CHAPTER ONE: INSTRUMENTS OF ENVIRONMENTAL CONTROL

1. Arthur Drexler, in conversation with Kevin Roche, untitled, undated transcript of interview, p. 1. Curatorial Exhibition Files, Exh. 940, *Work in Progress: Architecture by Philip Johnson, Kevin Roche, Paul Rudolph*, October 2, 1970–January 3, 1971, Museum of Modern Art Archives, New York.

2. On Roche's practice more generally, see Eeva-Liisa Pelkonen (ed.), *Kevin*

Roche: Architecture as Environment (New Haven: Yale University Press, 2011). For a more critical approach to Roche, see Reinhold Martin, *Utopia's Ghost: Architecture and Postmodernism, Again* (Minneapolis: University of Minnesota Press, 2010). Roche was born in 1922 in Dublin, Ireland, "during a civil war and at a time when my father was in jail serving a two-year sentence... for revolutionary activities," as he explained to Francesco Dal Co. He studied architecture while World War II raged in Europe and went on to work with Maxwell Fry and Jane Drew for a project in a British colony in Africa before heading to the United States, where he studied briefly with Ludwig Mies van der Rohe at the Illinois Institute of Technology before convincing the United Nations Headquarters Planning Office to hire him in 1949. It was through a UN connection that Eero Saarinen hired Roche in Spring of 1950, and through Saarinen, he came into contact with powerful figures in corporate America such as William S. Paley, chairman of the board of CBS, Frank Stanton, then president both of CBS and of the Rand Corporation, and Thomas J. Watson, president of IBM. See "Kevin Roche on Design and Building: Conversation with Francesco Dal Co," in Francesco Dal Co (ed.), *Kevin Roche* (New York: Rizzoli, 1985), p. 19.

3. Drexler, in conversation with Roche, p. 2.

4. *Ibid.*, pp. 4 and 5.

5. *Ibid.*, p. 6.

6. *Ibid.*, p. 8.

7. *Ibid.*, p. 20.

8. *Ibid.*, p. 22.

9. *Ibid.*, p. 24.

10. *Ibid.*, pp. 40 and 42–43.

11. On Mies's Seagram Building see Detlef Mertins, *Mies* (London: Phaidon, 2013); Phyllis Lambert, *Building Seagram* (New Haven: Yale University Press, 2013); Felicity D. Scott, "An Army of Soldiers or a Meadow: The Seagram Building and the 'Art of Modern Architecture,'" *Journal of the Society of Architectural Historians* 70.3 (September 2011), pp. 330–53.

12. Ada-Louise Huxtable, "Creations of 3 Top Architects Shown," *New York Times*, September 30, 1970, p. 38.

13. On the arson at Yale, see Tom McDonough, "The Surface as Stake: A Postscript to Timothy M. Rohan's 'Rendering the Surface'," *Grey Room* 5 (Fall 2001), pp. 102–11.

14. Drexler's wall text situated the exhibition as demonstrating "the idea that architecture, besides being technology, sociology and moral philosophy, must finally produce works of art if it is to be worth bothering about at all." Quoted in Huxtable, "Creations of 3 Top Architects Shown," p. 38.

15. Wolf von Eckardt, "Romantic Functionalism," *Washington Post*, October 17, 1970, pp. C1, and C5.

16. "Kevin Roche on Design and Building," p. 46. As Roche explained, "In any building, whether the client is the administration of the city or a private company or a wealthy individual, the client is always a source of power. That is what one has to work with. My objective is to use that power, which is always directed towards an immediate purpose originating from the client's needs, by solving his problem, but at the same time adding something more, and that more is frequently the provision of space for public use. So you knit the two things together," *ibid.*

17. Walter McQuade, "Structure and Design: The Ford Foundation's Mid-Manhattan Greenhouse," *Fortune*, October 1964, pp. 177–78.

18. McGeorge Bundy, quoted in Peter Bell, "The Ford Foundation as a Transnational Actor," in *Transnational Relations and World Politics* (Summer 1971), p. 476.

19. Henry Ford established the Ford Foundation in Detroit, Michigan, in 1936, concerned that inheritance tax laws would threaten his family's ownership of the Ford Motor Company. His son Edsel Ford, subsequent chairman of the Ford Motor Company, died prematurely in 1943, passing control to the founder's grandson, Henry Ford II, aka HF2. (Henry Ford, the founder, passed away in 1947.) It was under the younger Henry (with the help of Robert Strange McNamara, who joined the company in 1946 and instituted modern organization and management control systems, before departing in 1960 to become secretary of defense) that the Ford Motor Company began rapidly to expand after the war. On the history of the Ford Foundation and its relation to the Ford Motor Company, see Francis X. Sutton, "The Ford Foundation: The Early Years," *Daedalus* 116.1 (Winter 1987), pp. 41–91; Dwight McDonald, *The Ford Foundation: The Men and the Millions* (1955; New Brunswick: Transaction Publishers, 1989); Waldemar A. Nielsen, "Coming of Age in the Ford Foundation," in Nielsen, *The Big Foundation* (New York: Columbia University Press, 1972), pp. 79–98.

20. On Gaither, see McDonald, *The Ford Foundation*, pp. 8–13.

21. See Edward Berman, "Foundations and the Extension of American Hegemony," in Berman, *Ideology of Philanthropy: The Influence of the Carnegie, Ford and Rockefeller Foundations on American Foreign Policy* (Albany: State University of New York Press, 1983), pp. 11–40.

22. On the notion of "Total Peace," see Paul Virilio, "The Suicidal State," in James Der Derian (ed.), *The Virilio Reader* (Malden, MA: Blackwell, 1998), pp. 29–45.

23. Rowan Gaither et al., *Report of the Study for the Ford Foundation on Policy and Program* (Detroit: Ford Foundation, 1949), pp. 14–15.

24. See also Giuliana Gemelli (ed.), *The Ford Foundation and Europe*

(1950's–1970's): Cross-Fertilization of Learning in Social Science and Management, Memoirs of Europe (Brussels: European Interuniversity Press, 1998).

25. Michel Foucault, *"Society Must Be Defended": Lectures at the Collège de France, 1975–1976*, trans. David Macey (New York: Picador, 2003).

26. Antonio Negri, *Reflections on Empire*, trans. Ed Emery (Malden, MA: Polity, 2008), p. 65.

27. Gaither et al., *Report of the Study for the Ford Foundation*, p. 60.

28. Paul G. Hoffman, quoted in Kathleen D. McCarthy, "From Cold War to Cultural Development: The International Cultural Activities of the Ford Foundation, 1950–1980," *Daedalus* 116.1 (Winter 1987), p. 95. See also Hoffman, "The Peace We Fought for Is in Sight and We Can Win It," *Life*, July 18, 1955, pp. 94–107. On Hoffman, see Nielson, "Coming of Age in the Ford Foundation," p. 81, and McDonald, *The Ford Foundation*, p. 8.

29. Rowan Gaither, quoted in McCarthy, "From Cold War to Cultural Development," p. 94. She is quoting from Gaither et al., *Report of the Study for the Ford Foundation*.

30. Ford Foundation, *The Ford Foundation in the 1960s: Statement of the Board of Trustees on Policies, Programs, and Operations* (New York: Ford Foundation, 1962), p. 10.

31. Gaither et al., *Report of the Study for the Ford Foundation*, p. 93.

32. *Ibid.*, p. 96.

33. See the Introduction.

34. Gaither et al., *Report of the Study for the Ford Foundation*, p. 59.

35. See Joan Roelofs, *Foundations and Public Policy: The Mask of Pluralism* (Albany: State University of New York Press, 2003), and McCarthy, "From Cold War to Cultural Development," p. 98.

36. Bell, "The Ford Foundation as a Transnational Actor," p. 470.

37. Ford Foundation, *The Ford Foundation in the 1960s*, p. 3.

38. *Ibid.*, p. 11.

39. See Irving Louis Horowitz and Ruth Leonora Horowitz, "Tax-Exempt Foundations: Their Effects on National Policy," *Science* 168.3928 (April 10, 1970), pp. 220–28, and Gregory Raynor, "Engineering Social Reform: The Rise of the Ford Foundation and Cold War Liberalism, 1908–1959," Ph.D. diss., New York University, 2000.

40. Berman explains that many believed in "the need to create an international community of political elites, a 'world culture' in which modern (American) values became widely if not universally shared," noting that this viewpoint "was expressed by Harvard historian William Langer in a foundation-supported study issued in 1960. Langer had worked with the Office of Strategic Services during

World War II and for the CIA in the early 1950s. He also worked closely with Ford Foundation officials to help them define their overseas programs during this period." Berman, *Ideology of Philanthropy*, p. 113.

41. See McCarthy, "From Cold War to Cultural Development," pp. 105–107. See also Gemelli (ed.), *The Ford Foundation and Europe*, and Berman, *Ideology of Philanthropy*.

42. As Berman reminds us, "Foundation spokesmen have always stressed the altruistic nature of their institutions," and yet their "litany concerning the exclusively humanitarian nature of their work at home and abroad is simply not supported by internal foundation memoranda, letters, policy statements, and reminiscences left by their officers. These indicate unequivocally how foundation programs were designed to further foreign policy interests of the United States." Berman, *Ideology of Philanthropy*, pp. 2 and 3.

43. Details of the commissioning and design process come from documents in the Ford Foundation Archives. Belluschi advised against staging a competition and recommended five firms, which were contacted by Heald in May 1963: I. M. Pei and Associates, Skidmore Owings and Merrill, Harry Weese and Associates, Eero Saarinen and Associates, and Marcel Breuer and Associates. They interviewed three: SOM, Pei, and Roche of the Saarinen office. The Trustee's Building Committee for the project included J. Irwin Miller, head of the Cummins Engine Corporation and a renowned patron of modern architecture; Stephen Bechtel of the Bechtel Corporation, at the time, the world's largest engineering and construction firm, which held extensive Department of Defense contracts; Roy E. Larson, vice president of Time Inc.; Julius A. Stratton and Bethuel M. Webster, a lawyer and close advisor to Mayor John Lindsay. Miller suggested that Roche "might be expected to go a little deeper than most in searching out the actual needs of the client."

44. Kevin Roche, letter to R.H. McCarthy, director of buildings, planning, and construction, August 5, 1963, Ford Foundation records, Administration, Building Services, Ford Foundation Headquarters, New Building Planning and Construction Files, Series II, Design and Planning, 1951–1970, box 13, Rockefeller Archive Center. (Viewed in 2011 at the Ford Foundation Headquarters.)

45. "Five Attributes," anonymous four-page typescript. Ford Foundation records, Administration, Building Services, Ford Foundation Headquarters, New Building Planning and Construction Files, Series II, Design and Planning, 1951–1970, box 13, Rockefeller Archive Center. All citations are from this document.

46. See Ford Foundation, *The Ford Foundation Annual Report, October 1, 1966 to September 30, 1967* (New York: Ford Foundation, February 2, 1968), p. 35, and Horowitz and Horowitz, "Tax-Exempt Foundations." Grants were awarded to

Harvard, MIT, Columbia, and the University of Chicago. See also Richard Magat, "Urban Research and Training," in Magat, *The Ford Foundation at Work: Philanthropic Choices, Methods, and Styles* (New York: Plenum Press, 1979), pp. 99–101.

47. On this transition, see Nielsen, "Coming of Age in the Ford Foundation," p. 93. On the changes at Ford Foundation under Bundy, see "More Brainpower for Every Buck," *Business Week*, January 6, 1968, pp. 45–55.

48. Ford Foundation, *The Ford Foundation Annual Report, October 1, 1966 to September 30, 1967*, p. 2.

49. Nicholas von Hoffman, "Ford's Forest: Ever Green," *Washington Post*, July 23, 1969, p. B8. Nielson notes that soon afterward, Bundy attempted to diversify the makeup of the board. Nielson, "Coming of Age in the Ford Foundation," p. 95.

50. The figure of six million cubic feet comes from Kenneth Frampton, "A House of Ivy League Values," *Architectural Design*, July 1968, pp. 305–11.

51. See Jean-Louis Cohen, *Architecture in Uniform: Designing and Building for the Second World War* (New Haven and Montreal: Yale University Press and Canadian Center for Architecture, 2011), p. 386.

52. Steven V. Roberts, "Ford Fund's New Building Has Indoor Woods," *New York Times*, October 26, 1967, p. 49.

53. Joan Lee Faust, "The Outside-In Building," *New York Times*, March 17, 1968, p. D39.

54. Sara Davidson, "... Where You Go Inside to Get Outdoors," *Boston Globe*, February 10, 1968, p. 9. This was reiterated by a critic for *Baumeister*, who referred to a "permanent spring." "Fords feines Foyer: Ford Foundation Headquarters, Bürohaus in New York," *Baumeister* 65, May 1968, pp. 514–22.

55. Phil Roura, "June in January on East 43rd Street," *New York Daily News*, January 16, 1968, p. 14C. On the maintenance of the garden, see also Faust, "The Outside-In Building," and Rita Reif, "If You Lack a Green Thumb, Rent One," *New York Times*, April 5, 1972, p. 50. Details on the planting and maintenance system are derived from the Ford Foundation Archives.

56. Von Hoffman, "Ford's Forest: Ever Green," p. B1.

57. William Zinsser, "A Grant to Beauty," *Life*, March 29, 1968, p. 96.

58. Ed Wallace, "The Cleanest Air in Town ... and It's Polluted," *New York Sunday News*, February 15, 1970, pp. C24–25.

59. Wolf von Eckardt, "That's a Fine Thing Ford is Doing Up in Gotham," *Washington Post, Times Herald*, December 10, 1967, p. B3. On Roche's remarks about the building forging a sense of community, see also Davidson, "... Where You Go Inside to Get Outdoors."

60. Kevin Roche, quoted in Paul Heyer, *Architects on America: New Directions in Architecture* (New York: Walker and Company, 1966), p. 357.

61. Ada Louise Huxtable, "Bold Plan for Building Unveiled," *New York Times*, September 29, 1964, p. 45.

62. Joan Silver, "A Crystal Palace for Visible Man," *Village Voice*, January 25, 1968, p. 49.

63. Jim Burns and C. Ray Smith, "Charity Begins at Home," *Progressive Architecture*, February 1968, p. 102.

64. Kevin Roche, quoted in Zinsser, "A Grant to Beauty," p. 95.

65. Roche, in "Kevin Roche," in John W. Cook and Heinrich Klotz (eds.), *Conversations with Architects* (New York: Praeger, 1973), p. 70. On the Ford Foundation as a large house, see also Roche's comments in Alan Temko, "A Home to Work In," *New Yorker,* December 30, 1967, pp. 23–25. Here, indeed, was not simply a living room, but a figure of *Lebensraum* for US capitalism.

66. Alfred Friendly, quoted in Zinsser, "A Grant to Beauty," p. 96.

67. Zinsser, "A Grant to Beauty," p. 96.

68. Davidson, "Where You Go Inside to Get Outdoors," p. 9.

69. Roche, in *Conversations with Architects*, p. 67.

70. *Ibid.*, p. 70.

71. *Ibid.*, p. 71.

72. Klotz, in *Ibid.*

73. See, for instance, "View—A Garden Under Glass," *St. Louis Post-Dispatch*, February 25, 1968, pictures 1–5. Zinsser explained that although on the first day some employees closed their blinds in the face of such exposure, Bundy was entirely unconcerned at being seen and set the tone that they remained open. Some staff, he reckoned, "took it as a policy decision, or at least a strong hint, and now everybody has stuck with it—Bundy most of all. Today he is the Ford Foundation's most visible asset." Zinsser, "A Grant to Beauty," p. 96.

74. Silver, "A Crystal Palace for Visible Man," p. 11.

75. Manfredo Tafuri, *Architecture and Utopia: Design and Capitalist Development*, trans. Barbara Luigia La Penta (Cambridge, MA: MIT Press, 1976), p. 83.

76. See Félix Guattari, *Molecular Revolution: Psychiatry and Politics*, trans. Rosemary Sheed (1977; New York: Penguin Books, 1984), and Maurizio Lazzarato, *Signs and Machines: Capitalism and the Production of Subjectivity* (Los Angeles: Semiotext(e), 2014).

77. Ada Louise Huxtable, "Ford Flies High," *New York Times*, November 26, 1967, p. D25.

78. Lothar Buchar, quoted in Sigfried Giedion, *Space, Time, and Architecture: The Growth of a New Tradition*, 5th ed. (Cambridge, MA: Harvard University Press, 1967), p. 252.

79. Buchar, quoted in *ibid.*, p. 253.

80. *Ibid.*, p. 254.

81. Giedion, *Space, Time, and Architecture*, p. 254.

82. *Ibid.*, p. 245.

83. *Ibid.*, p. 246.

84. Giorgio Agamben, "Marx; or, The Universal Exposition," trans. Ronald L. Martinez, in Agamben, *Stanzas: Word and Phantasm in Western Culture* (Minneapolis: University of Minnesota Press, 1993), p. 39.

85. Paul Young, "Mission Impossible: Globalization and the Great Exhibition," in Jeffrey A. Auerbach and Peter H. Hoffenberg (eds.), *Britain, the Empire, and the World at the Great Exhibition of 1851* (Aldershot, UK: Ashgate, 2008), p. 5.

86. *Ibid.*, p. 20.

87. Timothy Luke writes, "In the ongoing struggle over economic competitiveness, environmental resistance can even be recast as a type of civil disobedience, which endangers national security, expresses unpatriotic sentiments, or embodies treasonous acts." Timothy W. Luke, "Environmentality as Green Governmentality," in Eric Darier (ed.), *Discourses of the Environment* (Malden, MA: Blackwell, 1999), pp. 124–25.

88. Frampton, "A House of Ivy League Values," p. 311.

89. See, for instance, Jonathan Barnett, "Innovation and Symbolism on 42nd Street," *Architectural Record*, February 1968, pp. 105–109.

90. Roche, in *Conversations with Architects*, p. 53.

91. Tafuri, *Architecture and Utopia*, p. 43.

92. On the design of the United Nations Headquarters, see Henry Stern Churchill, "United Nations Headquarters: A Description and Appraisal," *Architectural Record*, July 1952, pp. 105–121, and George Dudley, *A Workshop for Peace: Designing the United Nations Headquarters* (Cambridge, MA: MIT Press, 1994).

93. On account of the area's one-way streets and the site fronting onto busy Forty-Second Street, to approach the building's vehicular entrance on Forty-Third Street, as most of its visiting dignitaries would have done, one traversed along Forty-First Street, up a raised street within Tudor City—from where Ford is visible to the left, the UN Secretariat to the right—then turned left onto Forty-Third Street. With the addition of the UN Center, this connection was quite literally triangulated: Ford to the left, the UN to the right, and the new tower straight ahead.

94. Ralph G. Schwartz, Letter to Richard A. Bernstein, executive director of the City Planning Commission, May 13, 1966. Ford Foundation records, Administration, Building Services, Ford Foundation Headquarters, New Building Planning and Construction Files, series 2, Design and Planning, 1951–1970, box 13, Rockefeller Archive Center. See also, Norman J. Padelford, "United

Nations Headquarters: Alternatives for Expansion," *International Organization* 21.4 (Autumn 1967), pp. 768–85.

95. "U.N. Expansion Plan Protested Here," *New York Times*, December 20, 1969, p. 37.

96. That the Arab-Israeli War caused delays and concerns was noted by Padelford in "United Nations Headquarters."

97. United Nations Development Corporation, *The UN Center: A Development Program for UN Related Activities* (New York: United Nations Development Corporation, 1969), p. 3.

98. "A Crystal Palace for the UN," *Progressive Architecture*, January 1970, p. 24.

99. United Nations Development Corporation. "The UN Center," p. 17.

100. William Marlin, "A Friendly Neighborhood Skyscraper," *Architectural Record*, October 1976, p. 119.

101. Kathleen Teltsch, "Towers, Parks and Walkways are Included in Proposal for U.N. 'Campus,'" *New York Times*, April 21, 1968, p. 78.

102. Kathleen Teltsch, "New Building for U.N. Aims at Security Fears," *New York Times*, August 26, 1972, p. 27.

103. Roche, quoted in *ibid.*, p. 27.

104. Teltsch, "New Building for U.N.," p. 27.

105. Ada Louise Huxtable, "Proposed Monument Under Glass at the U.N.," *New York Times*, November 12, 1969, p. 37.

106. Diana Agrest, "Architecture of Mirror / Mirror of Architecture," *Oppositions*, no. 26 (Spring 1984), pp. 129 and 131. On mirror-glass buildings and their relation to flows of capital, see Reinhold Martin, "Materiality: Mirrors," in Martin, *Utopia's Ghost*, pp. 93–122.

107. Ada Louise Huxtable, "Sugar Coating a Bitter Pill," *New York Times*, February 15, 1970, p. 105.

108. *Ibid.*

109. Vincent Scully, "Thruway and Crystal Palace," *Architectural Forum* 140.2 (March 1974), p. 19.

110. *Ibid.*, pp. 20 and 24.

111. *Ibid.*, p. 24.

112. *Ibid.*

113. Paul Goldberger, "1 United Nations Plaza: A Serious Cause for Rejoicing," *New York Times*, June 8, 1976, p. 70.

114. Dal Co, *Kevin Roche*, p. 14.

115. William Marlin, "Giving a Boost to the 'Cliff Dwellers,'" *Washington Post*, April 3, 1977, p. 181. This article had previously appeared as a longer version in Marlin, "A Friendly Neighborhood Skyscraper."

116. Roche, in *Conversations with Architects*, p. 53.

117. Roche and Klotz, in *Conversations with Architects*, p. 83.

118. Henry-Russell Hitchcock, introduction to Yukio Futagawa (ed.), *Kevin Roche, John Dinkeloo and Associates 1962–1975* (Tokyo: ADA Edita, 1975 / trilingual edition, Fribourg: Office du Livre 1975), p. 17.

119. *Ibid.*

120. *Ibid.*, p. 19. Although Hitchcock alluded to social reform in his remarks, his dominant concern was not with Roche's departure from the leftist socioeconomic or political ideals of many modern architects, but rather what to him were ambiguous and often compromised aesthetics.

121. See Henry-Russell Hitchcock and Philip Johnson, *Modern Architecture—International Exhibition* (New York: Museum of Modern Art and W. W. Norton, 1932), and Henry Russell-Hitchcock and Philip Johnson, *The International Style: Architecture Since 1922* (New York: W. W. Norton, 1932).

122. Interview with Kevin Roche in *Office Age Special Edition 01: Kevin Roche / Seven Headquarters* (Tokyo: ITOKI, 1990), p. 11.

123. Manfredo Tafuri and Francesco Dal Co, *Modern Architecture*, ed. Pier Luigi Nervi, trans. Robert Erich Wolf (New York: Harry N. Abrams, 1979), p. 397.

124. Bundy, quoted in Bell, "The Ford Foundation as a Transnational Actor," p. 476.

CHAPTER TWO: CODE WARS

1. Earth People's Park literature, quoted in Sara Davidson, "Open Land: Getting Back to the Communal Garden," *Harper's*, June 1970, p. 102. Wheeler Ranch is sometimes called Wheeler Sheep Ridge Ranch, or simply Wheeler's.

2. This literature is extensive and includes Richard Fairfield, *Communes USA: A Personal Tour* (Baltimore: Penguin, 1972), a reprint and slight reworking of "Communes, USA," a special issue of *The Modern Utopian*, 5.2, and 5.3 (1971); Hugh Gardner, *The Children of Prosperity: Thirteen Modern American Communes* (New York: St. Martins Press, 1978); Dolores Hayden, "Edge City, Heart City, Drop City: Communal Building Today," in Hayden, *Seven American Utopias: The Architecture of Communitarian Socialism 1790–1975* (Cambridge, MA: MIT Press, 1976), pp. 320–47; William Hedgepeth and Dennis Stock, *The Alternative: Communal Life in New America* (New York: Collier Books, 1970); Robert Houriet, *Getting Back Together* (New York: Cowan, McCann and Geoghegan, 1971); Judson Jerome, *Families of Eden: Communes and the New Anarchism* (New York: Seabury Press, 1974); Rosabeth Moss Kanter, *Commitment and Community: Communes and Utopias in Sociological Perspective* (Cambridge, MA: Harvard University Press, 1972); Kanter, *Communes: Creating and Managing the Collective Life* (New York: Harper

and Row, 1973); Keith Melville, *Communes in the Counter-Culture: Origins, Theories, Styles of Life* (New York: Morrow, 1972); Ron E. Roberts, *The New Communes: Coming Together in America* (Englewood Cliffs: Prentice-Hall, 1971); Richard Todd, "'Walden Two': Three? Many More?," *New York Times Magazine*, March 15, 1970, pp. 24–25 and 114–26; "The Commune Comes to America," *Life*, July 18, 1969, pp. 16B–B23. See also John Curl (ed.), *History of Collectivity in the San Francisco Bay Area: From Indian Times to the Present* (Berkeley: Homeward Press, 1982), and Timothy Miller, *The 60s Communes: Hippies and Beyond* (Syracuse: Syracuse University Press, 1999).

3. Davidson, "Open Land," p. 92.

4. *Ibid.*, pp. 92 and 96.

5. *Ibid.*, p. 93.

6. Hedgepeth and Stock, *The Alternative*, p. 20.

7. See J.L. Austin, *How to Do Things with Words*, 2nd ed. (Cambridge, MA: Harvard University Press, 1975). See also Thomas Keenan, "Drift: Politics and the Simulation of Real Life," *Grey Room* 21 (Fall 2005), pp. 94–111.

8. Davidson, "Open Land," pp. 95 and 96.

9. As Davidson points out, Freedom Farm opened their land in 1963, but did not pose the same radical challenge to property rights.

10. Dick Torkelson, "Happiness People—II: Gratan Ranch Hippie Retreat," *Press Democrat* (1967), included in Unohoo, Coyote, Rick, and The Mighty Avengers (eds.), *The Morning Star Scrapbook: In the Pursuit of Happiness* (Occidental, CA: Friends of Morning Star, n.d. [c. 1973]), p. 26.

11. David W. Bernstein (ed.), *The San Francisco Tape Music Center: 1960s Counterculture and the Avant-garde* (Berkeley: University of California Press, 2008).

12. See Gardner, *Children of Prosperity*; Hedgepeth and Stock, *The Alternative*, p. 75; Felicity D. Scott, "Acid Visions," in Scott, *Architecture or Techno-Utopia: Politics After Modernism* (Cambridge, MA: MIT Press, 2007). See also Tuli Kupferberg, "The Hip and the Square: The Hippie Generation," in Jesse Kornbluth (ed.), *Notes from the New Underground* (New York: Viking, 1968), pp. 204–208, reprinted from *Berkeley Barb*, August 4, 1967.

13. Torkelson, "The Happiness People—II," p. 26.

14. On the notion of immaterial labor, see Maurizio Lazzarato, "Immaterial Labor," in Paolo Virno and Michael Hardt (eds.), *Radical Thought in Italy: A Potential Politics* (Minneapolis: University of Minnesota Press, 1996), pp. 133–47.

15. See Ramon Sender, "Morning Star Faith" in "Updated Directory of Communes," *The Modern Utopian* 4.3 and 4.4 (Summer–Fall 1970), p. 22.

16. See, for instance, Gardner, "The War of Sonoma County: Wheeler Ranch," in *Children of Prosperity*, pp. 134–49, and Ramon Sender Barayon, Gwen Leeds,

Near Morningstar, Bill Wheeler, et al., "Home Free Home: A History of Two Open-Door California Communes: Morning Star Ranch and Wheeler's (Ahimsa) Ranch," available online at http://www.diggers.org/home_free.htm. See also Ramon Sender's Web site, www.badabamama.com.

17. *Open Land: A Manifesto* (Bodega Bay, CA: Wheeler Ranch Defense Fund, c. 1969).

18. Gottlieb, quoted in Miller, *The 60s Communes*, p. 53.

19. Gottlieb, quoted in Ralph J. Gleason, "A Limeliter's New Thing," clipping reproduced in *The Morning Star Scrapbook*, p. 19.

20. Gottlieb, quoted in "Interview with Lou Gottlieb, Founder of Morning Star Ranch (February, 1971)," in "Communes, U.S.A.," p. 117.

21. Gottlieb, quoted in Davidson, "Open Land," p. 94. See also Miller, *The 60s Communes*, p. 53.

22. *The Morning Star Scrapbook*, p. 118.

23. Gottlieb, in "Interview with Lou Gottlieb," p. 117.

24. Gottlieb, quoted in Gleason, "A Limeliter's New Thing," p. 19.

25. See Boniface Saludes, "A 'Raid' by Officialdom," clipping in *The Morning Star Scrapbook*, p. 47. See also other clippings, pp. 42–46.

26. An important part of the story of rural communes during this period was the search for cheap land that remained less regulated by local and state authorities, whether on account of remoteness or lack of economic profitability for commercial land use. See Hugh Gardiner, "Love and Hate on Duncan's Mesa: Morning Star East and the Reality Construction Company," in *Children of Prosperity*, pp. 102–19.

27. Judge Kenneth Eymann, quoted in "Judge's Ruling: God Can't Own Morning Star," clipping reproduced in *The Morning Star Scrapbook*, p. 151. In the meantime, one woman had tried to sue God for damages after lightning hit her house; another man, claiming to be God, had attempted to obtain the title for himself.

28. See Bony Saludes, "Gottlieb Thunders against the Judge," clipping reproduced in *The Morning Star Scrapbook*, p. 149.

29. *Open Land: A Manifesto*, np.

30. See Stephen Graham, "Lessons in Urbicide," *New Left Review* 19 (January–February 2003), pp. 63–78 and its updated version as Stephen Graham, "Constructing Urbicide by Bulldozer in the Occupied Territories," in Graham (ed.), *Cities, War, and Terrorism: Towards an Urban Geopolitics* (Malden, MA: Blackwell, 2004), pp. 192–213; Eyal Weizman, *Hollow Land: Israel's Architecture of Occupation* (London: Verso, 2007); Andrew Herscher and András Riedlmayer, "The Destruction of Historic Architecture in Kosovo," *Grey Room* 1 (Fall 2000), pp. 108–22.

31. *Open Land: A Manifesto*, np.

32. "Gottlieb and County At It Again at Morning Star," April 25, 1971, clipping reproduced in *The Morning Star Scrapbook*, p. 161.

33. Bill Wheeler, "Wheeler Ranch," *Communitarian* 1 (March–April 1972), p. 53.

34. Gottlieb, quoted in Torkelson, "The Happiness People—II," p. 26.

35. On the Architectural Association's Department of Tropical Architecture and its later iterations, see Maxwell Fry and Jane Drew, *Tropical Architecture in the Humid Zone* (New York: Reinhold, 1956); Hannah Le Roux, "The Networks of Tropical Architecture," *Journal of Architecture* 8.3 (2003), pp. 337–54; Vandana Bawja, "A Pre-History of Green Architecture: Otto Koenigsberger and Tropical Architecture, from Princely Mysore to Post-Colonial London," Ph.D. diss., University of Michigan, 2008. On Doxiadis, see Ijlal M. Muzaffar, "The Periphery Within: Modern Architecture and the Making of the Third World," Ph.D. diss., MIT, 2007, and Jeannie Kim, "C. A. Doxiadis and the Ford Foundation," *Hunch* 13 (2010).

36. William Chaitkin, "The Alternatives," in Charles Jencks (ed.), *Architecture Today* (New York: Harry N. Abrams, 1982), p. 222.

37. See Gary Snyder, "Why Tribe," in *Earth House Hold* (New York: New Directions, 1969). pp. 113–16.

38. Chaitkin, "The Alternatives," p. 230.

39. See Charles W. Moore, "Plug It in Ramses, and See If It Lights Up, Because We Aren't Going to Keep It Unless It Works," *Perspecta* 11 (Fall 1967), pp. 32–43.

40. Bruce Hackett and Andrew Sun explained, "The function of these dwellings is to have some kind of meaning, not to necessarily be 'functional' in the conventional sense. The VW bus converted into a dwelling and the owner-built, hand-hewn tree-house utilizing only 'local' materials and only partially enclosed, both realize some or all of the appropriate values even if major conveniences are foregone. Consequently many of the structures lack the functionality of the normal house, but they have *meaning* directly related to the dweller because these structures are actually *extensions* of the self." Bruce Hackett and Andrew Sun, "Communal Architecture and Social Structure," paper presented at the Environmental Design Research Conference 3/AR8, 1972, p. 13-4-3.

41. On the tendency to stress adaptability, informality and flexibility, see *ibid.*

42. Richard Fairfield, "Morning Star," in "Communes, U.S.A.," p. 110. Fairfield's descriptions draw heavily on those of Davidson.

43. Davidson, "Open Land," p. 94. Brand blithely remarked to Davidson: "I admit we encourage starting from scratch. We don't say it will be easy, but education comes from making mistakes. Take delivering babies at home. That's hazardous! We carry books that tell how hazardous it is. People have lost babies that way,

but it won't hit the fan until we lose a few mothers. When it works, though, it's glorious." *Ibid.*, p. 96.

44. See, for instance, Michel Foucault, "*Society Must Be Defended*": *Lectures at the Collège de France, 1975–76*, trans. David Macey (New York: Picador, 2003).

45. Davidson, "Open Land," p. 94

46. Wheeler, quoted in *ibid.*

47. Davidson, "Open Land," p. 94.

48. Wheeler, quoted in *ibid.*

49. See "Communes, U.S.A," and James Reid, "Gottlieb Sentenced to Jail," clipping reproduced in *The Morning Star Scrapbook*, p. 124.

50. Gottlieb, quoted in Charles Phillips, "Visit to Morningstar: This Redwood Land Is Very Near to God," clipping reproduced in *The Morning Star Scrapbook*, p. 174.

51. *Open Land: A Manifesto*, n.p.

52. Gottlieb, quoted in Mitchell, *The 60s Communes*, p. 52.

53. *Ibid.*

54. Chuck Herrick, quoted in Fairfield, "Morning Star," p. 111.

55. Fairfield, "Morning Star," p. 112.

56. *Ibid.*

57. Gottlieb quoted in Saludes, "A 'Raid' by Officialdom," p. 47.

58. Gottlieb, in *The Morning Star Scrapbook*, p. 181

59. Chaitkin, "The Alternatives," pp. 226–27.

60. *Open Land: A Manifesto*, np. Questions of distributive justice were frequently acknowledged in the commune literature and typically questioned the inequity of America's use of world resources. See, for instance, "Communes, U.S.A.," pp. 173–77.

61. Davidson, "Open Land," p. 99.

62. Stewart Brand, quoted in *ibid.*

63. Gottlieb quoted in Gleason, "A Limelighter's New Thing," p. 19.

64. Gottlieb quoted in James E. Reid, "Lou Gottlieb Thunders as County again Plows Over 'God's Land,'" clipping reproduced in *The Morning Star Scrapbook*, p. 165. A *Los Angeles Times* article referred to one commune, with reference to overcrowding, overt poverty, and lack of food within makeshift communities in New Mexico, as a "ghetto in the wild." Charles T. Powers, "Communes: New Mexico's Stoned Society," *Los Angeles Times*, March 17, 1970, pp. 1, 3, 14.

65. Hedgepeth and Stock, *The Alternative*, caption, p. 5.

66. Karl Marx, *The Eighteenth Brumaire of Louis Bonaparte*, in Terrel Carver (ed.), *Marx: Later Political Writings* (Cambridge: Cambridge University Press, 1996), p. 32.

67. Walt Odets, foreword to *The Modern Utopian: Utopia U.S.A.* (San Francisco: The Alternatives Foundation, 1972), p. 3. It was not incidental that so many protagonists were white and typically middle class, their socioeconomic privilege and education facilitating their escape from the work ethic, normative lifestyles, and the culture of consumption.

68. Paul Lafargue, *The Right to Be Lazy* (Chicago: Charles Kerr and Co., Cooperative, 1883).

69. Paolo Virno, "Virtuosity and Revolution: The Political Theory of Exodus," in Paolo Virno and Michael Hardt (eds.), *Radical Thought in Italy: A Potential Politics* (Minneapolis: University of Minnesota Press, 1996), p. 199.

70. Virno was pointing to a paradox that, as early as 1848, confronted Karl Marx with respect to American capitalism. The "habit the immigrants assumed of abandoning the factory after a brief period, going West, penetrating the frontier," led to an impasse with respect to capitalist social relations. The "exasperated individualism of the frontiersman" and the expansionist impulse incited by the seemingly boundless territory led to a strange aberration, an "American enigma" manifest in the ongoing "cult of mobility." Here the experience of nature comes after that of the factory. Paolo Virno, "About Exodus," *Grey Room* 21 (2005), pp. 17 and 18.

71. Virno, "Virtuosity and Revolution," p. 199.

72. Albert O. Hirschman, *Exit, Voice, and Loyalty: Responses to Decline in Firms, Organizations, and States* (Cambridge, MA: Harvard University Press, 1970), p. 106. Hirschman's study primarily addressed economic processes, and he sought to produce a corrective model to a company's loss of revenue. Yet he came to understand these behaviors to have broader scope as a means of considering social and political issues in America.

73. Louis Hartz, quoted in *ibid.*, p. 107 n. 2.

74. Hirschman, *Exit, Voice, and Loyalty*, p. 107.

75. *Ibid.*

76. *Ibid.*, p. 108

77. Davidson, "Open Land," p. 94.

78. Hedgepeth and Stock, *The Alternative*, p. 184.

79. *Open Land: A Manifesto*, n.p.

80. Gottlieb, quoted in Davidson, "Open Land," p. 94.

81. Robert Ardrey, *The Territorial Imperative: A Personal Inquiry into the Animal Origins of Property and Nations* (New York: Atheneum, 1966). Ardrey believed that humans, just like other animals, have an instinctual drive to protect territory, a genetic predisposition to defend a space "as an exclusive preserve," and he argued that this survivalist instinct was not a product of culture, but of "our evolutionary past."

82. Davidson, "Open Land," p. 94.

83. Gottlieb, in "Interview with Lou Gottlieb," p. 116.

84. Gottlieb, quoted in "Lou Gottlieb Thunders," p. 165.

85. Gottlieb, quoted in Fairfield, "Morning Star," p. 113.

86. Wheeler, in "Interview with Bill Wheeler," p. 127.

87. Wheeler, in *ibid.*, p. 129

88. "A Fast Run-Through, Part Three," in *The Morning Star Scrapbook*, p. 40.

89. *Open Land: A Manifesto*, n.p.

90. Gottlieb, in "Interview with Lou Gottlieb," p. 115.

91. Giorgio Agamben, "What Is a Camp?," trans. Vincenzo Binetti and Cesare Casarino, in Agamben, *Means without End: Notes on Politics* (Minneapolis: University of Minnesota Press, 2000), pp. 37–45. Tied to the legacy of colonial wars and instituted during states of exception or martial law, camps were initially justified as quelling threats to the security of the state, but had become permanent spatial arrangements. See also Giorgio Agamben, *State of Exception*, trans. Kevin Attell (Chicago: University of Chicago Press, 2005).

92. See Hannah Arendt, "The Decline of the Nation State and the End of the Rights of Man," in Arendt, *The Origins of Totalitarianism* (San Diego: Harcourt Brace, 1966), pp. 267–302.

93. *The Morning Star Scrapbook*, p. 181.

94. "A Fast Run-Through, Part Three," in *The Morning Star Scrapbook*, p. 40.

95. Steve Durkee quoted in Hedgepeth and Stock, *The Alternative*, p. 164.

96. See, for instance, *This Is the Public Domain*, an art project by San Francisco–based artist Amy Balkin, www.thisisthepublicdomain.org; LAND, http://www.n55.dk/land.html; the project to renew People's Park, www.peoplespark.org; or organizations such as First Monday, www.firstmonday.org.

97. I am thinking, in particular, of a series of works undertaken between 2010 and 2013 and addressed to the American commune movement, including *Directions, Headlines, Painted Side Up, Irritating Behaviors, Turn Take Merge, Group, this time we'll keep it a secret, No Photographs: Visiting Hours Weekends Only 8AM to 8PM, rumors and murmurs, We Dismantle Abandoned Bridges. . .*, and *Incomplete Parts*—works realized as silkscreen prints, photographs, sculptures, wall installations, vitrines, texts, performances, and films.

98. Martin Beck, "Recent Exhibitions and Works," unpublished document. See also Michèle Thériault (ed.), *Martin Beck: The Particular Way in Which a Thing Exists* (Montreal: Galerie Leonard and Bina Ellen Art Gallery, Concordia University, 2013).

CHAPTER THREE: WOODSTOCKHOLM

1. Daniel Zwerdling, "Getting Back to Earth," *Washington Post and Times*

Herald, June 25, 1972, p. B3.

2. Barry Weisberg, "The Browning of Stockholm: America Takes Its Ecology Show Abroad," *Ramparts*, September 1972, p. 34.

3. Ross Gelbspan and David Gurin, "Woodstockholm '72: The Subject is Survival," *Village Voice*, May 11, 1972, pp. 29 and 34.

4. "The Big Cleanup: The Environmental Crisis '72," *Newsweek*, June 12, 1972, p. 38.

5. Friedel Ungeheuer, "Woodstockholm," *Time*, June 19, 1972, pp. 61–62.

6. Stewart Brand, quoted in Weisberg, "The Browning of Stockholm," p. 38.

7. Gelbspan and Gurin, "Woodstockholm '72," p. 34.

8. "Hog Farm," undated press release from the Life Forum, signed "Stewart Brand." Courtesy of Mary Jean Haley.

9. "The Big Cleanup," p. 36.

10. "The Big Cleanup," pp. 38 and 40. According to Barry Weisberg, "more attention was paid to events out at Skarpnick [sic], to the 'freak show,' than the political significance of what was happening at the Conference." He added, "The reporter from *Time* described the dynamic well: 'The editorial idea we had at the beginning was not to cover the Conference but to cover whatever groups like the Hog Farm, the Free Stage, other people produce as a way of dramatizing the issue. I'm really much more interested in this—I even have instructions from my senior editor.'" Weisberg, "The Browning of Stockholm," p. 39.

11. Frances Gendlin, "Voices from the Gallery," *Science and Public Affairs: Bulletin of the Atomic Scientists* 28.7 (September 1972), p. 26.

12. Mary Jean Haley, *Open Options: A Guide to Stockholm's Alternative Environmental Conferences* (Stockholm: Life Forum, 1972). In addition to detailed outlines of the alternative groups and information on living cheaply in Stockholm, *Open Options* provided a day-by-day calendar of events. Even the harshest critics of the Life Forum, such as Weisberg, acknowledged the value of this document, as would many in the mainstream press.

13. Michel Feher, "The Governed in Politics," in Michel Feher, with Gäelle Krikorian and Yates McKee (eds.), *Nongovernmental Politics* (New York: Zone Books, 2007), pp. 13–14.

14. The conference emblem took the form of a stylized human figure inscribed within a globe and surrounded by the UN wreath. See "U.N.'s '72 Motto: 'Only One Earth,'" *New York Times*, June 14, 1971, p. 7.

15. On the history of the conference see *Report of the United Nations Conference on the Human Environment, Stockholm, 5–16 June 1972* (New York: United Nations, 1973) / UN Document A/CONF.48/14/Rev.1; *Report on the United Nations Conference on the Human Environment* (Washington, DC: US Government Printing

Office, 1972); United Nations, "Questions Pertaining to the Environment," in *Yearbook of the United Nations 1972* (New York: Office of Public Information, United Nations, 1972), pp. 317–37; John McCormick, "The Stockholm Conference (1970–1972)," in McCormick, *Reclaiming Paradise: The Global Environmental Movement* (Bloomington: Indiana University Press, 1989), pp. 88–105; Lynton Keith Caldwell, "Evolution of an International Environment Movement: The Road to Stockholm," and "From Stockholm to Nairobi: The United Nations Environment Program, 1972–1982," in Caldwell, *International Environmental Policy: Emergence and Dimensions* (Durham: Duke University Press, 1984), pp. 19–48 and 49–81; Tony Brenton, "Stockholm Conference," in Brenton, *The Greening of Machiavelli: The Evolution of International Environmental Politics* (London: Earthscan and Royal Institute of International Affairs, 1994), pp. 35–50.

16. Strong's story of growing up in poverty and, by the age of thirty, running an oil company has been told a number of times, typically romanticizing his lack of education and his hardscrabble background as the source of empathy with developing nations. See, for instance, Wade Rowland, *The Plot to Save the World* (Toronto: Clarke, Irwin and Company, 1973), pp. 35–38.

17. See Gladwin Hill, "Sense of Accomplishment Buoys Delegates Leaving Ecology Talks," *New York Times*, June 18, 1972, p. 14.

18. Maurice Strong, quoted in Sally Jacobsen, "A Call to Environmental Order," *Science and Public Affairs: Bulletin of the Atomic Scientists* 28.7 (September 1972), pp. 21–22.

19. Hill, "Sense of Accomplishment Buoys Delegates."

20. Jacobsen, "A Call to Environmental Order," p. 22.

21. *Hearings Before the Committee on Foreign Relations, United States Senate, Ninety-Second Congress, Second Session on Preparations for and Prospects of the June 1972, U.N. Conference on the Human Environment (May 3, 4, and 5, 1972)* (Washington, DC: US Government Printing Office, 1972), p. 84. See also Richard N. Gardner, "The Hard Road to World Order," *Foreign Affairs* (April 1974), available at http://www.foreignaffairs.com/articles/24506/richard-n-gardner/the-hard-road-to-world-order.

22. Peter B. Stone, *Did We Save the Earth at Stockholm?: The People and Politics in the Conference on the Human Environment* (London: Earth Island, 1973), pp. 57 and 58. See also Robert J. Bazell, "Human Environment Conference: The Rush for Influence," *Science* 174, October 22, 1971, pp. 390–91.

23. Stone, *Did We Save the Earth at Stockholm?*, p. 63.

24. *Ibid.*, pp. 47–48.

25. Maurice Strong, "A Strong Reason for Hope," *Not Man Apart* 2.7, July 1972, p. 3.

26. Barbara Ward and Rene Dubos, *Only One Earth: The Care and Maintenance of a Small Planet* (New York: W. W. Norton, 1972). On the commissioning of *Only One Earth* as part of a larger publicity apparatus, see Stone, *Did We Save the Earth at Stockholm?*, pp. 45–46.

27. Ward and Dubos, *Only One Earth*, p. 44.

28. *Ibid.*, p. 11. According to David Satterthwaite, Strong's primary motivation in hiring Ward and Dubos to write the book was to head off the conflict between North and South. David Satterthwaite, *Barbara Ward and the Origins of Sustainable Development* (London: International Institute for Environment and Development [UK], 2006), p. 11.

29. See Sidney Hyman, *The Aspen Idea* (Norman: University of Oklahoma Press, 1975).

30. For instance, a 1971 workshop report, "The International Management of Environmental Problems," was adopted by the United States House of Representatives Committee on Foreign Affairs, its recommendations making their way into the UN conference's action plan documents and agenda items. Hyman, *The Aspen Idea*, pp. 288–90.

31. Ward and Dubos, *Only One Earth*, p. xviii.

32. See McCormick, *Reclaiming Paradise*, and Satterthwaite, *Barbara Ward*.

33. Adlai Stevenson, quoted in Albert Roland, Richard Wilson, and Michael Rahill (eds.), *Adlai Stevenson of the United Nations* (Manila: Free Nations Press, c. 1966), p. 224.

34. Barbara Ward, *Spaceship Earth* (New York: Columbia University Press, 1966), and R. Buckminster Fuller, *Operating Manual for Spaceship Earth* (Carbondale: Southern Illinois University Press, 1969).

35. In Stevenson's words, "We cannot maintain [Earth] half fortunate, half miserable, half confident, half despairing, half slave—to the ancient enemies of man—half free in the liberation of resources undreamed of until this day. No craft, no crew can travel safely with such vast contradictions." Stevenson, in Roland et al (eds.), *Adlai Stevenson of the United Nations*, p. 224.

36. Ward and Dubos, *Only One Earth*, p. 211.

37. Maurice Strong, preface to *Only One Earth*, p. viii.

38. Stone, *Did We Save the Earth at Stockholm?*, p. 45.

39. "Brief Summary of the General Debate," in *Report of the United Nations Conference on the Human Environment, Stockholm, 5–16 June 1972*, p. 45.

40. Maurice Strong (ed.), *Who Speaks for Earth?* (New York: W. W. Norton, 1973).

41. Sattherwaite, *Barbara Ward*, p.13. Strong's remarks appear on p. 16.

42. Published as "A Loved Yet Endangered Planet," *Science and Public Affairs:*

Bulletin of the Atomic Scientists 27.7 (September 1972), pp. 46–48.

43. President Richard Nixon, "Message on the Environment, February 8, 1972," in Department of State, *Safeguarding Our World Environment: The U.N. Conference on the Human Environment, Stockholm, June 1972* (Washington, DC: US Department of State, 1972), p. i.

44. On the release of NASA's images and their ramifications, see also Denis Cosgrove, "Contested Global Visions: *One-World, Whole-Earth*, and the Apollo Space Photographs," *Annals of the Association of American Geographers* 84.2 (June 1994), pp. 270–94; Paul Edwards, *A Vast Machine: Computer Models, Climate Data, and the Politics of Global Warming* (Cambridge, MA: MIT Press, 2010); Laura Kurgan, *Close Up at a Distance: Mapping, Technology and Politics* (New York: Zone Books, 2013).

45. Barry Commoner, "Motherhood in Stockholm," *Harper's*, June 1972, p. 54.

46. "A Special Report—What Happened at Stockholm," *Science and Public Affairs: Bulletin of the Atomic Scientists* 28.7 (September 1972), p. 16.

47. Gelbspan and Gurin, "Woodstockholm '72," p. 34.

48. See Fred Turner, *From Counterculture to Cyberculture: Stewart Brand, the Whole Earth Network, and the Rise of Digital Utopianism* (Chicago: University of Chicago Press, 2006), and Andrew G. Kirk, *Counterculture Green: The Whole Earth Catalog and American Environmentalism* (Lawrence: University Press of Kansas, 2007).

49. Stewart Brand, "Stockholm Preamble," *Clear Creek* 16, October 1972, p. 29.

50. Gelbspan and Gurin, "Woodstockholm '72," p. 34. See also Rowland, *The Plot to Save the World*, p. 123. Gun Zacharias reproduces sample pages of the *Whole Earth Catalog* that include information on drugs, carefully crossing out information for procurement. Gun Zacharias, *Skarpnäck, USA: En Bok om Droger och Politik* (Stockholm: Förbunder mot Droger, 1975).

51. See John Lambert, "Hog Farm Meets the Fanatics," *Forum: Environment Is Politics*, June 12, 1972, p. 6.

52. Weisberg, "The Browning of Stockholm," p. 38. Weisberg later added of this hubris that "the entire attitude of the American invasion of Stockholm was best summarized by Brand himself, who said 'Hi, we're here to help with all our juice, all our money and all our stuff, and we know what's happening and where do we plug in. And we'll take over here, and we'll run things there for you....'" Ibid., p. 39.

53. Correspondence with the author. See also Zacharias's account, "200.000:-bjudet!," in *Skarpnäck, USA*, p. 18.

54. See Foster Haley, "Kaplan Fund, Cited as C.I.A. 'Conduit,' Lists Unexplained $395,000 Grant," *New York Times*, September 3, 1964, p. 10; E.W.

Kenworthy, "Tax Case Held Up for C.I.A. Conduit: Inquiry into Kaplan Fund of New York Put Off 2 Years, but a Deal Is Denied," *New York Times*, March 5, 1967, pp. 1 and 38. Rowland, among others, notes funding from the Kaplan Foundation in *The Plot to Save the World*, p. 122.

55. On the Point Foundation, see Kirk, "On Point," in *Counterculture Green*, pp. 115–55. In addition to the Point Foundation, Brand channeled money from the Portola Institute, "organizational base for Stewart's WEC and Whole Earth Truck Store." "Life Forum," *Clear Creek* 16, October 1972, p. 32.

56. Brand, "Stockholm Preamble," p. 29.

57. Gelbspan and Gurin, "Woodstockholm '72," p. 34.

58. Russell Train, in *Hearings before the Committee on Foreign Relations, United States Senate, Ninety-Second Congress*, p. 18.

59. Weisberg recounts that Brand then approached the Environment Forum about the threat of "crowds of young people." Weisberg, "The Browning of Stockholm," p. 38.

60. John Lewallen, "Stockholm Revealed," *Clear Creek* 16, October 1972, p. 27.

61. The *New York Times* reported: "Despite some apprehension here over the influx of exotically dressed young people, the mood at Skarpnack has been good. An American traveling commune, Hog Farm, showed up, proclaimed its ability to organize campgrounds and counterculture groups, and has been cooperating with Swedish authorities to set up the tent city and make it a 'good ecological example.'" "Environment Conference Will Offer Some Sideshows," *New York Times*, June 5, 1972, p. 24. Stone, in *Did We Save the Earth at Stockholm?* noted of the Swedish authorities, "They had helped to bring Wavy Gravy and the Hog Farm (a 'family' about fifty strong) from the United States on the strength of a reputation of being able to keep order among youth," (p. 132). "The Hog Farm has offered its services to the local police to help keep order at Skarpnack and elsewhere." Alfred Heller, "A Visit to the Life Forum HQ," *San Francisco Chronicle*, June 9, 1972, p. 21.

62. Weisberg, "The Browning of Stockholm," p. 39.

63. When asked about a letter from a reader complaining "that in following Fuller's philosophy, the Catalog also held too closely to his withdrawn political views," Brand responded by noting that "he has puzzled in vain over a term, that could somehow combine the concepts of New Left and New Right to describe the catalog's political philosophy," adding "primarily, it is pragmatic and ecological." Thomas Albright, "The Environmentalists: The Whole Earth Catalog," *Rolling Stone*, December 13, 1969, p. 33.

64. Heller, "A Visit to the Life Forum HQ," p. 21.

65. Weisberg, "The Browning of Stockholm," p. 38. Weisberg described Brand as a "former merry prankster of Ken Kesey's salad days and now a millionaire

as a result of the Whole Earth Catalog." He noted that Life Forum's budget was $75,000, with funds coming from both Brand and the Kaplan Foundation.

66. *Ibid.*, p. 39.

67. *Ibid.*, p. 34.

68. Harold Gilliam, "Eco-Trips at Hog Farm," *San Francisco Chronicle*, June 14, 1972.

69. Brand, in "Hog Farm," undated press release from the Life Forum. Courtesy of Mary Jean Haley.

70. Gilliam, "Eco-Trips at Hog Farm."

71. Rowland, prologue to *The Plot to Save the World.*

72. Neal White and Peter Schjeldahl, "Living High on the Hog Farm," *Avant-Garde* 5, November 1968, pp. 45 and 46.

73. *Ibid.*, p. 51.

74. See Hugh Romney, "The Hog Farm," *The Realist* 86, November–December 1969, p. 18.

75. *Ibid.*, pp. 1–31. For an outline of Romney's relation to Kesey and the Pranksters, see Stephen Starger, "When Wavy Gravy Comes Home," *Hartford Courant*, May 10, 1970, p. 2M. See also William Hedgepeth and Dennis Stock, *The Alternative: Communal Life in New America* (New York: Collier Books, 1970), p. 78.

76. Brand, in "Hog Farm," undated press release from the Life Forum.

77. "Earth People's Park," *Whole Earth Catalog* supplement "The Outlaw Area," January 1970, p. 28. The account described participants as "people who had cooked at Woodstock, put up an overnight sound stage at Altamont, survived Liferaft Earth, doctored with the Hog Farm, built domes and tilled ground at innumerable communes, dodged tear gas canisters, smoked dope, been busted" (p. 28). See also Christopher McDermott, "Plans to Free a Piece of Mother Earth," *Los Angeles Free Press*, January 16, 1970, pp. 10 and 13.

78. "The Document," in *Whole Earth Catalog* supplement "The Outlaw Area," January 1970, p. 29.

79. Rodney Clarke, "Earth People's Park: 'Liberated' Land with a Mortgage," *Washington Post*, October 24, 1971, p. 178. A reporter for the *Hartford Courant* explained: "Romney's, and the Hog Farm's, mission now, he says, is to save the land and return it to the people. The communal group carries itself and its considerable equipment around the country in a caravan of multi-colored mural-painted buses, doing shows to raise money for the benefit of 'Earth People's Parks,' where people would be able to go and 'live the simple life.'" "Everything's Groovy Down on 'The Farm,'" *Hartford Courant*, March 13, 1970, p. 31E.

80. "Earth People's Park," *Whole Earth Catalog*, p. 28.

81. "Earth People's Park Abandons New Mexico," *Los Angeles Free Press*, March

6, 1970, p. 22.

82. Brand, in "Hog Farm," undated press release from the Life Forum.

83. "Liferaft Earth," *Whole Earth Catalog*, January 1970, pp. 23. On the inflatables related to this event, see Felicity D. Scott, *Living Archive 7: Ant Farm* (Barcelona: ACTAR Editorial, 2008).

84. *Whole Earth Catalog*, Fall 1969, p. 80.

85. Rick Field, commentary on Liferaft Earth, reprinted from *Berkeley Tribe*, October 17–23, 1969, in *Whole Earth Catalog* supplement "The Outlaw Area," January 1970, p. 24.

86. Turner, *From Counterculture to Cyberculture*, p. 43. See also Kirk, *Counterculture Green*.

87. Paul Ehrlich, *The Population Bomb* (New York: Ballantine, 1968), p. 1. See also Anne Chisholm, *Philosophers of the Earth: Conversations with Ecologists* (New York: E. P. Dutton, 1972).

88. Ehrlich, *The Population Bomb*, p. xii.

89. Wavy Gravy, *The Hog Farm and Friends, by Wavy Gravy as told to Hugh Romney and Vice Versa* (New York: Links, 1974), p. 132.

90. On mobilizing shame, see Thomas Keenan, "Mobilizing Shame," *South Atlantic Quarterly* 103.2–3 (Spring–Summer 2004), pp. 435–49.

91. Wavy Gravy, *The Hog Farm and Friends*, pp. 132 and 134.

92. Keenan, "Mobilizing Shame," p. 447.

93. Thomas Keenan, "Drift: Politics and the Simulation of Real Life," *Grey Room* 21 (Fall 2005), pp. 94–111.

94. "The Declaration of Cultural Evolution," *East Village Other*, May 31, 1968.

95. Sigmund Freud, *Civilization and Its Discontents*, ed. and trans. James Strachey (New York: W.W. Norton, 1961), p. 21.

96. I am thinking here of the thesis of Jacques Rancière, who argues, "The essence of politics resides in the modes of dissensual subjectification that reveal the difference of a society to itself. The essence of consensus is not peaceful discussion and reasonable agreement as opposed to conflict or violence. Its essence is the annulment of dissensus as the separation of the sensible from itself, the annulment of surplus subjects, the reduction of the people to the sum of the parts of the social body, and of the political community to the relationship of interests and aspirations of these different parts. Consensus is the reduction of politics to the police. In other words, it is the 'end of politics' and not the accomplishment of its ends but, simply, the return of the 'normal' state of things which is that of politics' non-existence." Jacques Rancière, "Ten Theses on Politics," *Theory and Event* 5.3 (2001), available at http://muse.jhu.edu/journals/theory_and_event/v005/5.3ranciere.html.

97. Carl Schmitt, *The Concept of the Political*, trans. George Schwab (Chicago: University of Chicago Press, 1996), p. 55.

98. *Ibid.*, p. 54.

99. Friedel Ungeheuer, "A Stockholm Notebook," *Time*, June 26, 1972.

100. Stone, *Did We Save the Earth at Stockholm?*, p. 127.

101. Paul Ehrlich, "A Crying Need for Quiet Conferences," *Bulletin of the Atomic Scientists* 28.7 (September 1972), p. 30.

102. Alissa J. Rubin, "As Iraq Takes Control, Puzzle over Prisoners," *New York Times*, Sunday October 25, 2008, pp. A1 and A8.

103. Heller, "A Visit to the Life Forum HQ," p. 21.

104. Romney, "The Hog Farm," p. 18.

105. Ian Hogan, quoted by Weisberg, "The Browning of Stockholm," p. 39.

106. See Hazel Whitman Hertzberg, "Indian Rights Movement, 1887–1973," in Wilcomb E. Washburn (ed.), *Handbook of North American Indians, Volume 4: History of Indian-White Relations* (Washington, DC: Smithsonian Institution Scholarly Press, 1988), p. 317.

107. See, for instance, Robert Venturi, Denise Scott Brown, and Steven Izenour, *Learning from Las Vegas* (Cambridge, MA: MIT Press, 1972).

108. Haley, *Open Options*, p. 20.

109. Caption in *Clear Creek* 16, October 1972, p. 31. Tom Scott reported, however, that Black Mesa events "held a great deal of interest for Europeans and Asians, who came in large numbers to watch films and slide shows and listen to Hopi and Navaho music." Tom Scott, "Other Groups; No Consensus," in *Not Man Apart* 2.7 (July 1972), p. 10.

110. On Stewart Brand and his interest in Native American culture, see Philip Deloria, "Counterculture Indians and the New Age," in Peter Braunstein and Michael William Doyle (eds.), *Imagine Nation: The American Counterculture of the 1960s and '70s* (New York: Routledge, 2001), pp. 159–88; Turner, *From Counterculture to Cyberculture*; and Kirk, *Counterculture Green*. See also Starger, "When Wavy Gravy Comes Home," p. 2. The following decade, Brand also told the story of the counterculture's "rediscovery of Indians," noting, "From a distance Indians looked perfect: ecologically aware, spiritual, tribal, anarchistic, drug-using, exotic, native, and wronged, the lone genuine holdouts against American conformity and success." Stewart Brand, "Indians and the Counterculture, 1960s–1970s," in *Handbook of North American Indians, Volume 4*, p. 570.

111. Ungeheuer "Woodstockholm."

112. Stone, *Did We Save the Earth at Stockholm?*, p. 133.

113. Michael McClure, "The Death of All Flesh: A Report on the U.N. Environmental Conference," *Rolling Stone*, August 3, 1972, pp. 18–19.

114. Stone, *Did We Save the Earth at Stockholm?*, p. 132. Walter Sullivan described the poem as partly being "ostensibly written by a whale, with prolonged moans and groans" in "Cry of the Vanishing Whale Heeded in Stockholm," *New York Times*, June 9, 1972, p. 3.

115. Sullivan, "Cry of the Vanishing Whale," p. 3.

116. "Hickel Order to Protect Whales Won't Be Suspended," *New York Times*, November 29, 1970, p. 40.

117. Gilliam, "Eco-Trips at Hog Farm."

118. *Ibid.*

119. Stone, *Did We Save the Earth at Stockholm?*, p. 133.

120. Sullivan, "Cry of the Vanishing Whale."

121. Zwerdling, "Getting Back to Earth," p. B3.

122. Gilliam, "Eco-Trips at Hog Farm."

123. "Whole Earth Conference," *Time*, May 22, 1972, available at http://www.time.com/time/magazine/article/0,9171,879105,00.html.

124. Despite UN support, the moratorium was vetoed by the IWC. See "Whaling Halt Urged in Stockholm," *New York Times*, June 10, 1972, p. 4. On the history of this initiative and of US support to ban commercial whaling, see Yasuhiro Sanada, "Turning the Tide: A Whaling Moratorium Proposal at the United Nations Conference on the Human Environment and the Bureaucratic Politics of Japan, the United States, and the United Kingdom," *International Studies Association 51st Annual Conference, Theory vs. Policy?: Connecting Scholars and Practitioners, February 17–20, 2010*, available at http://citation.allacademic.com//meta/p_mla_apa_research_citation/4/1/7/0/5/pages417050/p417050-1.php.

125. Founding vice president of the World Wildlife Fund (US) in the early 1960s, Train was appointed president of the Conservation Foundation in 1965 before being selected by president-elect Nixon in 1968 to lead his Task Force on Environment and in turn to be under secretary of the Department of the Interior.

126. Sullivan, "Cry of the Vanishing Whale," p. 3. On the side of the bus were the words "Maybe Dick." America, as thematized in *Moby-Dick*, was a major player in an unregulated global whaling enterprise. But after the mid-nineteenth century, petroleum products such as kerosene took over as a primary source of lighting fuel. The last American whaling vessel sailed in 1928, but by this time, the unchecked exploitation wrought by so-called Yankee whaling, long crucial to the American economy, had devastated the populations of many species, both in the Atlantic and in the Pacific.

127. Weisberg, "The Browning of Stockholm," p. 36.

128. *Ibid.*

129. Rowland, *The Plot to Save the World*, p. 124.

130. Ehrlich, "A Crying Need for Quiet Conferences," 32.

131. *Ibid.*

132. McClure, "The Death of All Flesh," p. 18.

133. Lewallen, "Stockholm Revealed," p. 28.

134. "Announcements: Hog Farm," *Forum* no. 8, June 13, 1972, p. 7.

135. "A Moratorium on Killing People," *Forum* no. 10, June 15, 1972, p. 2.

136. Rowland, *The Plot to Save the World*, pp. 122–23.

137. "Strong at Life Feast," *Forum* no. 10, June 15, 1972, p. 1.

138. *Ibid.*

139. "Doing Not Talking," *Forum* no. 2, June 6, 1972, pp. 4–5.

140. Mass media played a key role not only in spawning the Summer of Love in San Francisco in 1967, but also, according to many, in undermining the radical motivation of the movement. "Media created the Hippie with your hungry consent," the Diggers announced in their *Death of Hippie* march, a procession on October 7, 1967, to exorcise Haight-Ashbury from the Media Police. On the side of a coffin carried by masked performers were the words "Hippie—Son of Media."

141. R. Buckminster Fuller, "Proposal to the International Union of Architects," in Joachim Krausse and Claude Lichtenstein (eds.), *Your Private Sky: Discourse* (Baden, Switzerland: Lars Müller Publishers and Museum für Gestaltung, 2001), p. 248.

142. Gary Snyder, "Why Tribe," in Snyder, *Earth House Hold* (New York: New Directions, 1969), p. 113.

143. *Ibid.*

144. In *détournment*, "any elements, no matter where they are taken from, can serve in making new combinations." Thus, the elements of an existing system can be used against that system. See Guy-Ernest Debord, "Method of Détournement," available at http://library.nothingness.org/articles/SI/en/display/3; originally published in *Les livres nues* no. 8 (May 1956).

145. Sean Nazerali, "The Roma and Democracy: A Nation without a State," in Okwui Enwezor, et al. (eds.), *Democracy Unrealized: Documenta 11, Platform 1* (Ostfildern-Ruit: Hatje Cantz Publishers, 2002), p. 133.

146. Hannah Arendt, "The Decline of the Nation State and the End of the Rights of Man," in Arendt, *The Origins of Totalitarianism* (New York: Schocken, 2004), p. 358.

147. *Ibid.*, pp. 318, 383, 355, 361. Arendt's formulation would be famously pursued by Giorgio Agamben in his theorization of "bare" or "naked life," in which the camp is precisely the space that opens up when the nation-state is in crisis, when, in his words "the political system of the modern nation-state—founded on the functional nexus between a determinate localization (territory) and a

determinate order (the state), which was mediated by automatic regulations for the inscription of life (birth or nation)—enters a period of permanent crisis." Giorgio Agamben, "What is a Camp?," in *Means Without End: Notes on Politics* (Minneapolis: University of Minnesota Press, 2000), pp. 42–43.

148. *Ibid.*, p. 45.

149. Michel Foucault, "Confronting Governments: Human Rights," in *Essential Works of Foucault, 1954–1984*, vol. 3, *Power*, ed. James D Faubion (New York: New Press, 2000), pp. 475 and 476. See Thomas Keenan, *Fables of Responsibility: Aberrations and Predicaments in Ethics and Politics* (Stanford: Stanford University Press, 1997).

CHAPTER FOUR: BATTLE FOR THE EARTH

1. Barry Weisberg, "The Browning of Stockholm: America Takes Its Ecology Show Abroad," *Ramparts*, September 1972, p. 34.

2. *Ibid.*, pp. 37 and 34. See also Harold Gilliam, ""Eco-Trips at Hog Farm," *San Francisco Chronicle*, June 14, 1972.

3. Undated three-page press release entitled "Environment Forum," p. 1. Courtesy of Mary Jean Haley.

4. Hundreds of NGOs registered as participants, and with conference Secretary General Maurice Strong's support, some gained observer status at the UN conference. See Peter Willetts, "From Stockholm to Rio and Beyond: The Impact of the Environmental Movement on the United Nations Consultative Arrangements for NGOs," *Review of International Studies* 22.1 (January 1996), pp. 57–80; Terri Aaronson, "World Priorities," *Environment* 14.6 (July–August 1972), pp. 4–13; Frances Gendlin, in "Voices from the Gallery," *Science and Public Affairs: Bulletin of the Atomic Scientists* 28.7 (September 1972), pp. 26–29.

5. "Environment Forum," p. 2.

6. "A Funny Thing Happened to the Environment on its Way to the Forum," *Stockholm Conference Eco*, June 14, 1972, p. 59. See also Robert J. Bazell, "Human Environment Conference: The Rush for Influence," *Science*, October 22, 1971, pp. 390–91.

7. "Statement of Purpose of the OI Committee International," undated, four-page typescript manuscript, p. 2. Courtesy of Mary Jean Haley.

8. PowWow, *Newsletter*, February 1972, p. 14. See also Weisberg, "The Browning of Stockholm." On the founding of PowWow, see also Wade Rowland, *The Plot to Save the World* (Toronto: Clarke, Irwin and Company, 1973), p. 121.

9. Barry Commoner, "Motherhood in Stockholm," *Harper's*, June 1972, p. 54.

10. Barry Commoner, *The Closing Circle: Nature, Man, and Technology* (New York: Knopf, 1971). See also Michael Egan, *Barry Commoner and the Science of*

Survival: The Remaking of American Environmentalism (Cambridge, MA: MIT Press, 2007).

11. Friedel Ungeheuer, "Woodstockholm," *Time*, June 19, 1972, pp. 61–62. Commoner's words were also cited in "Man vs. Man Not Man vs. Nature: Commoner Tells Overflow Crowd," *Forum: Environment Is Politics*, June 6, 1972, p. 1.

12. Ian Hogan, quoted by Weisberg, in "The Browning of Stockholm," p. 39.

13. "Statement by Prime Minister Olof Palme in the Plenary Meeting, June 6, 1972," 12-page typescript, available at http://www.olofpalme.org/wp-content/dokument/720606a_fn_miljo.pdf. Quoted in Olof Palme, "The Outrage of Ecocide," *Science and Public Affairs: Bulletin of Atomic Scientists* 28.7 (September 1972), p. 44.

14. "Response of Russell E. Train, Chairman United States Delegation," *Science and Public Affairs: Bulletin of Atomic Scientists* 28.7 (September 1972), p. 45. See also Gladwin Hill, "U.S., at U.N. Parley on Environment, Rebukes Sweden for 'Politicizing' Talks," *New York Times*, June 8, 1972, p. 13, and "No Comment, It's Political," *Forum: Environment Is Politics*, June 6, 1972, p. 7.

15. See Fredrik Logevall, "The Swedish-American Conflict over Vietnam," *Diplomatic History* 17.3 (June–July 1993), pp. 421–45.

16. The International Commission of Enquiry into US Crimes in Indochina took place from June 2 to June 4, 1972. See David Zierler, "Going Global after Vietnam: The End of Agent Orange and the Rise of an International Environmental Regime," in Erika Marie Bsumek, David Kinkela, and Mark Atwood Lawrence (eds.), *Nation-States and the Global Environment: New Approaches to International Environmental History* (Oxford: Oxford University Press, 2013), p. 97.

17. See Richard A. Falk, "Environmental Warfare and Ecocide: Facts, Appraisal, and Proposals," *Bulletin of Peace Proposals* 4 (1973), pp. 80–96; and E. W. Kenworthy, "Some Delegates Critical of U.S. Approach to U.N. Conference on Ecology," *New York Times*, May 22, 1972, p. 23.

18. Gunnar Myrdal, preface to *The Effects of Modern Weapons on the Human Environment in Indochina* (Stockholm: International Commission of Enquiry into US Crimes in Indochina, 1972), p. ii.

19. See the documents collected in *ibid*. See also David Zierler, *The Invention of Ecocide: Agent Orange, Vietnam, and the Scientists Who Changed the Way We Think about the Environment* (Athens: University of Georgia Press, 2011).

20. See: E. W. Pfeiffer and Gordon H. Orians, "The Military Use of Herbicides in Vietnam," in J. B. Neilands (ed.), *Harvest of Death: Chemical Warfare in Vietnam and Cambodia* (New York: The Free Press, 1972); "Defoliation: Secret Army Study Urges Use in Future Wars," *Science and Government Reporter*, August 18, 1972, pp. 1–4; Jack Raymond, "Weed Killers Aid War on Viet Cong: They Are Used to

Destroy Reds' Shelter and Crops," *New York Times*, March 28, 1965, pp. 2 and 5. For an official account, see William A. Buckingham, *Operation Ranch Hand: The Air Force and Herbicides in Southeast Asia, 1961–1971* (Washington, DC: Office of Air Force History, 1982).

21. See Arthur Westing, "The Environmental Disruption of Indochina," and Westing, "Leveling the Jungle," in *The Effects of Modern Weapons on the Human Environment in Indochina*, pp. 1.1–1.11 and 6.1– 6.6.

22. See: Fred Branfman, "Air War: The Third Indochina War"; E. W. Pfeiffer, "Craterization and Impact on Land and Agriculture"; Arthur Westing, "The 7.5 Ton Bomb," all in *The Effects of Modern Weapons on the Human Environment in Indochina*, pp. 4.1–4.11, 5.1–5.8, 7.1–7.5.

23. See Noam Chomsky, "From After Pinkville," in Barry Weisberg (ed.), *Ecocide in Indochina: The Ecology of War* (San Francisco: Canfield Press, 1970), pp. 126–39.

24. See "... And a Plea to Ban Ecocide," editorial, *New York Times*, February 26, 1970, p. 38.

25. See, in particular, Hans Göran Franck, introduction to *The Effects of Modern Weapons on the Human Environment in Indochina*, pp. iii–vii, and John H. E. Fried, "War by Ecocide," in *ibid.*, pp. 2:1–2:26.

26. Weisberg, "The Browning of Stockholm," p. 36.

27. Barry Weisberg, introduction to *Ecocide in Indochina*, p. 4.

28. *Ibid.*, p. 6.

29. Barry Weisberg, preface to *Ecocide in Indochina*, p. vi.

30. Weisberg, introduction to *Ecocide in Indochina*, p. 12.

31. "What's on Today," *Forum: Environment Is Politics*, June 6, 1972.

32. "News in Brief," *Forum: Environment Is Politics*, June 12, 1972.

33. E-mail correspondence with John Lewallen, March 9, 2014, confirms that financing came from Brand and that he worked with Jen Brondum of Dai Dong.

34. John Lewallen, "Stockholm Revealed," *Clear Creek* 16, October 1972, p. 28.

35. Rowland, *The Plot to Save the World*, p. 131.

36. Lewallen, "Stockholm Revealed," p. 32.

37. Weisberg, "The Browning of Stockholm," p. 39.

38. Homer Page, "Ecocidal War: The Ideal Answer to Mass Destruction," *Not Man Apart*, 2.7, July 1972, p. 7.

39. Samuel P. Huntington, "The Bases of Accommodation," *Foreign Affairs* 46.4 (July 1, 1968), pp. 652–53, quoted in John Lewallen, "The Ecology of Devastation," manuscript for presentation at the Environment Forum, Stockholm, June 6, 1972, p. 3. Also quoted in John Lewallen, *Ecology of Devastation: Indochina* (Baltimore: Penguin Books, 1971), pp. 36–37.

40. Chomsky, "From After Pinkville," p. 128.

41. Falk, "Environmental Warfare and Ecocide," p. 20. Falk was author of *This Endangered Planet: Prospects and Proposals for Human Survival* (New York: Random House, 1971). His work at the time was focused on war crimes and the legality of the US war in Vietnam, along with security, disarmament, and emergent strategies and institutions of world order.

42. On the relationship between environmental knowledge and militarism, see Jacob Darwin Hamblin, *Arming Mother Nature: The Birth of Catastrophic Environmentalism* (Oxford: Oxford University Press, 2013). I thank Emily E. Scott for pointing out this reference.

43. Westing, "Leveling the Jungle," p. 6.2. Westing explained that the bulldozing operation was organized as five companies of three platoons each, each company operating thirty or more tractors and going under names such as Rome Runners, Land Barons, and Jungle Eaters. *Ibid.* Initiated in 1965, the bulldozing became organized by 1968 and escalated and came to replace the herbicidal assault after pressure from scientists reduced the chemical program.

44. Iver Peterson, "Giant U.S. 'Plows' Clear Scrub Along Foe's Route," *New York Times*, May 7, 1971, p. 5.

45. Falk, "Environmental Warfare and Ecocide," p. 15. See also Richard A. Falk, "United States Policy and the Vietnam War: A Second American Dilemma," *Stanford Journal of International Studies* 3 (1968), pp. 78–98.

46. As Lewallen summarized, "American military might was, and continues to be, deployed against the people of the countryside—indeed, against the countryside itself. Search-and-destroy operations cause the forced movement of people to urban centers. The establishment of so-called free-strike zones, which are designated areas where anything moving is fair game for passing troops and aircraft, drives villagers into population concentrations. The harassment-and-interdiction (H&I) artillery rounds, which thud quite randomly every night around the cities and towns of South Vietnam, encourage people to live inside the ring of fire. Then there are the nighttime 'squirrel hunts' and 'turkey shoots' by Huey choppers (helicopters) looking for human game in free-strike zones; the 'hosing' of targets by 'spooky birds', which are C-47 aircraft that can lay down 300 rounds per second from their .50 caliber Gatling guns; and the 'accidental' defoliation and deliberate chemical destruction of crops in remote areas. These and other tactics make much of rural South Vietnam hazardous to live in." Lewallen, *Ecology of Devastation*, pp. 33–34.

47. See John H. E. Fried, "War by Ecocide," in *The Effects of Modern Weapons on the Human Environment in Indochina*, pp. 2:1–2:26, and Don Luce, "Social Disruption," in *ibid.*, pp. 10:1–10:5.

48. Jean-Paul Sartre, "On Genocide," in *Ecocide in Indochina*, p. 40.

49. Lewallen, *Ecology of Devastation*, p. 36.

50. Lewallen, "The Ecology of Devastation," p. 2.

51. Jonathan Mirsky, "'Too Blind Stupid to See': The Tombs of Ben Suc," *Nation*, October 23, 1967, p. 398.

52. *Ibid.*, p. 399. He went on to note that the Americans in charge of the refugees "are fully dedicated to the welfare of the refugees." *Ibid.*

53. *Ibid.*, pp. 399–400.

54. Chomsky, "From After Pinkville," p. 136.

55. J. Robert Moskin, "Vietnam: Get Out Now," *Look*, November 18, 1969, pp. 73–88, quoted in Chomsky, "From After Pinkville," p. 136.

56. John Lewallen, "The Indochina War and Human Ecology," typescript of presentation at the Convention on Ecocidal War, June 13, 1972, p. 2. Courtesy of Mary Jean Haley.

57. *Ibid.*, p. 1.

58. *Ibid.*, p. 2.

59. *Ibid.*, p. 3.

60. William C. Westmoreland, "Address by General W. C. Westmoreland, Chief of Staff, United States Army, Annual Luncheon, Association of the United States Army, Sheraton Park Hotel, Washington, D.C. Tuesday, October 14, 1969," in Paul Dickson (ed.), *The Electronic Battlefield* (Bloomington: Indiana University Press, 1976), p. 223. For an insider's account of the development of this system, see Seymour J. Deitchman, "The 'Electronic Battlefield' in the Vietnam War," *Journal of Military History* 72.3 (July 2008), pp. 869–87. For an important historical account, see Paul N. Edwards, "From Operations Research to the Electronic Battlefield," in Edwards, *The Closed World: Computers and the Politics of Discourse in Cold War America* (Cambridge, MA: MIT Press, 1996), pp. 113–45.

61. Franck, introduction to *The Effects of Modern Weapons on the Human Environment in Indochina*, p. v.

62. See Branfman, "Air War: The Third Indochina War," pp. 4.9–4.10.

63. *Ibid.*, p. 4.10.

64. Lewallen, *Ecology of Devastation*, p. 147.

65. William Westmoreland, quoted in Lewallen, *Ecology of Devastation*, p. 147.

66. Leonard Sullivan, statement in the *Congressional Record* of August 11, 1969, quoted in Chomsky, "From After Pinkville," pp. 130–31.

67. Chomsky, "From After Pinkville," p. 131.

68. David Galula, *Pacification in Algeria, 1956–1958* (Santa Monica: RAND Corporation, 1963).

69. David Galula, *Counter-Insurgency Warfare: Theory and Practice* (New York: Frederick A. Praeger, 1964).

70. Another such doomsday report was *The Blueprint for Survival*, issued by the British magazine *The Ecologist* and likened by Peter Stone to Reformation era pamphleteering in *Did We Save the Earth at Stockholm?: The People and Politics in the Conference on the Human Environment* (London: Earth Island, 1973), pp. 8–9. On the "doomsday reports," see Norman J. Faramelli, "Toying with the Environment and the Poor: A Report on the Stockholm Environmental Conference," *Boston College Environmental Affairs Law Review* 2.3 (1972), pp. 469–86; Wilfred Beckerman, "The Myth of Environmental Catastrophe," *National Review*, November 24, 1972, pp. 1293–95; Robert Gillette, "The Limits to Growth: Hard Sell for a Computer View of Doomsday," *Science*, March 10, 1972, pp. 1088–92; Claire Sterling, "Club of Rome Tackles the Planet's 'Problematique,'" *Washington Post*, March 2, 1972, p. A18; Walter Sullivan, "Struggling against the Doomsday Timetable," *New York Times*, June 11, 1972, p. E7; Rowland, "Forecasts and Blueprints," in *The Plot to Save the World*; Robert Golub and Joe Townsend, "Malthus, Multinationals and the Club of Rome," *Social Studies of Science* 7.2 (May 1977), pp. 201–22; Francis Sandbach, "The Rise and Fall of the Limits of Growth Debate," *Social Studies of Science* 8.4 (November 1978), pp. 495–520; Paul Neurath, *From Malthus to the Club of Rome and Back: Problems of Limits to Growth, Population Control, and Migrations* (Armonk: M.E. Sharpe, 1994).

71. Faramelli, "Toying with the Environment and the Poor," p. 478. He is speaking of *The Limits to Growth* and *The Blueprint for Survival.*

72. See Stuart W. Leslie, *The Cold War and American Science: The Military-Industrial-Academic Complex at MIT and Stanford* (New York: Columbia University Press, 1993).

73. J.B. Neilands, "U.S. Policy Concerning CBW and Modern Methods of Warfare," submission to the International Commission of Enquiry into US Crimes in Indochina, June 1970.

74. The Club of Rome, "The Predicament of Mankind Proposal," June 1970. Jay Wright Forrester Papers, MC439, box 125. Massachusetts Institute of Technology, Institute Archives and Special Collections, Cambridge, MA. Henceforth "Forrester Papers." For an account of the Bern meeting, see Richard M. Koff, "An End to All This," *Playboy*, July 1971, pp. 112–14 and 206–208. On the Club of Rome, see also Samuel C. Florman, "Another Utopia Gone," *Harper's*, August 1976, pp. 29–36.

75. Press release no. 1, "What Is the Club of Rome," June 26, 1970, box 125, Forrester Papers.

76. "The Club of Rome Posture and Proposed Activity: Speech by Dr. A. Peccei at the Berne Conference of June 30, 1970," box 125, Forrester Papers.

77. The Club of Rome, "Statutes," June 16, 1970, p. 2, box 125, Forrester Papers.

78. The Club of Rome, "'Project 1970' as a first step in a coordinated effort to face the complex of global problems confronting mankind," November 6, 1969, pp. 2–3, box 125, Forrester Papers.

79. See Aurelio Peccei to Jay W. Forrester, March 17, 1970, and Forrester to Peccei, April 3, 1970, box 125, Forrester Papers.

80. Jay W. Forrester, *Urban Dynamics* (Cambridge, MA: MIT Press, 1969), p. 8.

81. *Ibid.*, p. 9.

82. *Ibid.*, p. 10.

83. Koff, "An End to All This," p. 114.

84. See, for instance, Charles Jencks, *The Language of Postmodern Architecture* (New York: Rizzoli, 1977). See also the remarkable reading of this phenomenon in Keller Easterling, *Subtraction* (Berlin: Sternberg, 2014).

85. See Rob Sauer, "World III: An Interview with Donella Meadows," *ZPG National Reporter* (October 1971), pp. 5–6, and; Jay W. Forrester interviewed by Jay McCulley, "Nous entrons dans une phase de transition entre la croissance exponentielle et l'équilibre," *Le Monde*, August 1, 1972, p. 11.

86. Jay W. Forrester, "DO," twelve-page handwritten document outlining concerns for seminar, undated, box 125, Forrester Papers.

87. Harvey Simmons, "Systems Dynamics and Technocracy," *Futures* 5.2 (April 1973), p. 219.

88. Jay W. Forrester, *World Dynamics* (Cambridge, MA.: Wright-Allen Press, 1971), p. ix.

89. *Ibid.*, p. 97.

90. On the humanitarian paradox, see David Rieff, *Slaughterhouse: Bosnia and the Failure of the West* (New York: Simon and Schuster, 1995); Adi Ophir, "The Sovereign, the Humanitarian, and the Terrorist," in Michel Feher, with Gäelle Krikorian and Yates McKee (eds.), *Nongovernmental Politics* (New York: Zone Books, 2007), pp. 161–81; Rony Brauman, "Learning from Dilemmas: Rony Brauman Interviewed by Michel Feher and Philippe Mangeot," in *Nongovernmental Politics*, pp. 131–47; Eyal Weizman, *Hollow Land: Israel's Architecture of Occupation* (London: Verso, 2007), p. 206; Mariella Pandolfi, "From Paradox to Paradigm: The Permanent State of Emergency in the Balkans," in Didier Fassin and Mariella Pandolfi (eds.), *Contemporary States of Emergency: The Politics of Military and Humanitarian Interventions* (New York: Zone Books, 2010), pp. 153–72.

91. Jay W. Forrester, "Urban Expert Says a City Can Exclude 'Immigrants,'" *Toronto Star*, January 16, 1973, p. 9.

92. *Ibid.* See also Walter Sullivan, "Probing Questions Too Tough for a Mere Brain," *New York Times*, December 6, 1970, p. 12. This pernicious reading was extended to food aid in Systems Dynamics Group researcher Dale Runge's paper

"The Potential Evil in Humanitarian Food-Relief Programs" of 1974. Runge's computer simulation demonstrated that from a "dynamic perspective," acts that might seem to have short-term benefits create "evil" side effects—in this case, increased population and increased dependency that put more people in potential jeopardy. "Over the long run," he argued, "the short-run goal of preventing starvation through food relief has produced greater suffering for a greater number of people. This effect is the potential 'evil' in humanitarian food relief" (pp. 8 and 13). The computer's answer: "only by lowering the birth rate can the humanitarian goal of providing a higher standard of living be reached," and only countries willing to do so should receive aid. Forrester Papers.

93. See Forrester, *World Dynamics*, pp. vii–x.

94. Caption to figure 26, "The World Model," in Donella H. Meadows, et al., *The Limits to Growth: A Report for the Club of Rome's Project on the Predicament of Mankind* (New York: Universe Books, 1972), p. 104.

95. Rowland, *The Plot to Save the World*, p. 9.

96. H. S. D. Cole et al. (eds.), *Models of Doom: A Critique of the Limits to Growth* (New York: Universe Books, 1973), p. 8.

97. "Blueprint Splits Forum," *Stockholm Conference Eco*, June 8, 1972, p. 22.

98. Robert McNamara quoted in John Lambert, "We Need a Bigger Earth," *Stockholm Conference Eco*, June 9, 1972, p. 2. For the full text of McNamara's speech, see Robert S. McNamara, "A Critical Truth," *Science and Public Affairs: Bulletin of the Atomic Scientists* 28.7 (September 1972), p. 40.

99. Lambert "We Need a Bigger Earth," p. 2.

100. McNamara, "A Critical Truth," p. 39.

101. *Ibid.*, pp. 42, 39, 40.

102. "Scenario for Year 2000," *Stockholm Conference Eco*, June 15, 1972, pp. 69–70, and "Yes, Dr Peccei, But...," *Forum: Environment Is Politics*, June 14, 1972, p. 3.

103. Aurelio Peccei, "Human Settlements," in Maurice Strong (ed.), *Who Speaks for Earth?* (New York: W. W. Norton, 1973), pp. 153–54.

104. *Ibid.*, p. 154.

105. *Ibid.*, pp. 157 and 159.

106. *Ibid.*, p. 160.

107. *Ibid.*

108. *Ibid.*, p. 162.

109. Garrett Hardin, "Lifeboat Ethics: The Case against Helping the Poor," *Psychology Today* 8, September 1974, pp. 38–43. See also Garrett Hardin, "Living on a Lifeboat," *Bioscience* 24, October 1, 1974, pp. 561–68.

110. Peccei, "Human Settlements," p. 165.

111. *Ibid.*, p. 165.

112. *Ibid.*, p. 167.

113. See Egan, *Barry Commoner*, chapter 4. On the Commoner-Ehrlich debate, see also Andrew Feenberg, "Environmentalism and the Politics of Technology," in Feenberg, *Questioning Technology* (New York: Routledge, 1999), pp. 45–70.

114. Commoner, "Motherhood in Stockholm," p. 49.

115. Garrett Hardin, "The Tragedy of the Commons," *Science*, December 13, 1968, pp. 1243–48.

116. Garret Hardin, quoted in Commoner, "Motherhood in Stockholm," p. 50, no original source noted.

117. Paul Ehrlich, *The Population Bomb* (New York: Ballantine, 1968), p. xii.

118. See Claire Sterling, "World Politics and Pollution Control: Rich and Poor Nations Collide," *Washington Post*, May 26, 1972, p. A24.

119. See Egan, *Barry Commoner*, pp. 122–23.

120. Oi Committee International, "An Independent and Critical Conference on Problems of the Human Environment and The Third World, June 4–22, 1972: A Description," n.d., p. 5.

121. See "Paying Oi's Way," *Village Voice*, May 11, 1972, p. 34.

122. Oi Committee, quoted in Gendlin, "Voices from the Gallery," p. 27.

123. "A Funny Thing Happened to the Environment on its Way to the Forum," p. 59. See also Rowland, *The Plot to Save the World*, p. 129.

124. A further panel with Ehrlich and seven other speakers was to follow that evening.

125. "Forum Comes to Life," *Forum: Environment Is Politics*, Saturday June 10, 1972, p. 2.

126. "A Funny Thing Happened to the Environment on its Way to the Forum," p. 59.

127. "Forum Comes to Life," p. 2. In Francis Gendlin's version, "When Ehrlich attempted to address a press conference and panel discussion, a group of Third Worlders seized the microphone and revised the panel, adding more Third World people and putting Dora Obi Chizea, a Nigerian medical student and Dai Dong member, in charge." Gendlin, "Voices from the Gallery," p. 28. The event is also mentioned by Lewallen as follows: "Taghi Farvar, Oi Committee leader and Commoner's student in St. Louis, rips a mike out of the hand of Paul Ehrlich—against whom Commoner has a long-term vendetta—Farvar claiming to represent the Third World thereby, though he's been in the States for some ten years." Lewallen, "Stockholm Revealed," p. 33.

128. Friedel Ungeheuer, "A Stockholm Notebook," *Time*, June 26, 1972. See also Faramelli, "Toying with the Environment and the Poor."

129. "A Funny Thing Happened to the Environment on its Way to the Forum," 59.

130. Gendlin, "Voices from the Gallery," p. 28.

131. Stone, *Did We Save the Earth at Stockholm?*, pp. 133 and 134.

132. David R. Brower, "Only Time Magazine Would Call It 'Woodstockholm,'" *Not Man Apart* 2.7, July 1972, p. 5.

133. Paul Ehrlich, "A Crying Need for Quiet Conferences: Personal Notes from Stockholm," *Science and Public Affairs: Bulletin of the Atomic Scientists* 27.7 (September 1972), p. 30.

134. Ehrlich, "A Crying Need for Quiet Conferences," p. 32.

135. See Farvar's editorial regarding *The Hamilton Documents: Proceeding of the International Youth Conference on the Human Environment*, Hamilton, Canada, August 20–30, 1971 (St. Louis: Oi Committee International, 1972) in Oi Committee International, and chairman M. Taghi Farvar (eds.), *International Development and the Human Environment: An Annotated Bibliography* (New York: Macmillan Information, 1974), np.

136. "Third World Ecology," in *Stockholm Conference Eco*, June 7, 1972, p. 13.

137. Herein lies the basis for critiques of the eighteenth-century French and American foundations of the notion of universal human rights that inform the UN's 1948 declaration. Although derived from Enlightenment philosophy, human rights claims and the institutions supporting them remain the most evident tools for pursuing international justice and have themselves become not simply models imposed from above, but vehicles of self-determination. See, for instance, Claude Lefort, "Human Rights and the Welfare State," in Lefort, *Democracy and Political Theory* (Minneapolis: University of Minnesota Press, 1988), pp. 21–44.

138. I am thinking here of Michael Hardt and Antonio Negri, *Empire* (Cambridge, MA: Harvard University Press, 2000).

139. Egan, *Barry Commoner and the Science of Survival*, p. 134.

140. Thomas Keenan, "Drift: Politics and the Simulation of Real Life," *Grey Room* 21 (Fall 2005), pp. 94–111.

141. *Ibid.*, p. 99

142. *Ibid.*, p. 102.

143. *Ibid.*, p. 99.

144. *Ibid.*, p. 106.

145. *United Nations Conference on the Human Environment: Report to the Senate by Senator Claiborne Pell and Senator Clifford Case, Members of the Delegation of the United States at the United Nations Conference on the Human Environment, Held in Stockholm, June 5–16, 1972* (Washington, DC: US Government Printing Office/Committee on Foreign Relations, July 1972), p. 4. See also Walter Sullivan,

"Earthwatch Voted to Check Habitability," *New York Times*, June 15, 1972, p. 12.

146. *Safeguarding our World Environment: The U.N. Conference on the Human Environment, Stockholm, June 1972* (Washington, DC: US Department of State, March 1972), p. 16.

147. Rowland, *The Plot to Save the World*, p. 3.

148. *United Nations Conference on the Human Environment*, p. 5.

149. Bengt Lundholm, "Remote Sensing and International Affairs," *Ambio* 1.5 (October 1972), p. 172.

150. As a contribution to the UN conference, Sven Bjork published a forty-page annotated version of Soleri's work, *Arcology: Alternative to Urban Disaster* (self-published, 1972), hoping to demonstrate the relevance of Soleri's ideas to the "environmental crisis" and to "advocate an alternative urban system."

151. "The ideal would be a string of towns separated by desert," Galula explained in *Pacification in Algeria*, p. 280.

152. Dana White, "Review: The Apocalyptic Vision of Paolo Soleri," *Technology and Culture* 12.1 (1971), p. 79. See also Donald Wall, *Paolo Soleri Documenta* (Washington, DC: Corcoran Gallery of Art, 1970).

153. White, "Review: The Apocalyptic Vision of Paolo Soleri," p. 77. He is citing Martin Meyerson's terms.

154. Reyner Banham, *Megastructure: Urban Futures of the Recent Past* (London: Thames and Hudson, 1976), p. 203.

155. See Paolo Soleri, *Arcology: The City in the Image of Man* (Cambridge, MA: MIT Press, 1969).

156. See William Irwin Thompson, "The Individual as Institution: The Example of Paolo Soleri," *Harper's*, September 1, 1972, pp. 48–62. Along with the Esalen Institute in California, and Auroville in India, Arcosanti served as a model for the establishment of Thompson's Lindisfarne Association in 1972.

157. See Weisberg, "The Browning of Stockholm," and Mary Jean Haley, *Open Options: A Guide to Stockholm's Alternative Environmental Conferences* (Stockholm: Life Forum, 1972).

158. A notable exception to this are the on-line accounts of Tord Björk. See Tord Björk, *Challenging Western Environmentalism at the United Nations Conference on Human Environment in Stockholm 1972*, available at http://aktivism.info/rapporter/ChallengingUN72.pdf.

159. This is recounted in "Environmental Parley Open Amid Hopes, Conflicting Proposals," *Wall Street Journal*, June 6, 1972, p. 8.

160. The exhibition ran from June 6 through August 28, 1972.

161. See "What Happened with the Art of the Strike?: An Art Project by Ingela Johansson," Tensta Konsthall, March 14 through May 26, 2013, program available

at http://www.tenstakonsthall.se/uploads/86-TK_%20I.Johansson%20EN.pdf.

162. PowWow, "Toward a People's Technology: An Exhibition," reproduced in Pär Stolpe, "Filialen Rapporten vid Moderna Museet I Stockholm 1.3 1971–1.7 1973," (1973), np.

163. "Alternative Technologies Exhibition: People's Forum—Alternative Technology Group, Details of Exhibition Projects," typescript, p. 6. Courtesy of Peter Harper.

164. Björn Eriksson and Peter Harper, "Alternative Technologies Project: Stockholm, Sweden, June 1972," two-page typescript. Courtesy of Peter Harper.

165. Peter Harper, "Alternative Technologies," *Forum: Environment Is Politics*, June 13, 1972, p. 6.

166. Eriksson and Harper, "Alternative Technologies Project," p. 2.

167. "Alternative Technologies Exhibition," p. 5.

168. See, for instance, Carroll Pursell, "The Rise and Fall of the Appropriate Technology Movement in the United States, 1965–1985," *Technology and Culture* 34.3 (July 1993), pp. 629–37.

169. "Global Viewpoint Needed for Cleaner Cities," *New York Times*, June 8, 1972, p. 6.

170."Alternative Technologies Exhibition," p. 1.

171. *Ibid.*

172. Harper, "Alternative Technologies."

173. Editorial note to Peter Harper's "Directory," in Godfrey Boyle and Peter Harper (eds.), *Radical Technology* (New York: Pantheon Books, 1976), p. 268.

174. Sandbach, "The Rise and Fall of the Limits of Growth Debate," p. 502.

175. See Pursell, "The Rise and Fall of the Appropriate Technology Movement."

176. PowWow, *Newsletter*, no. 1, February 1972, p. 15.

177. Stone, *Did We Save the Earth at Stockholm?*, pp. 129–30. See also Committee on Public Works, *Report on the United Nations Conference on the Human Environment* (Washington, DC: US Government Printing Office, 1972), pp. 6 and 13.

178. PowWow *Newsletter*, p. 10.

179. *Ibid.*, p. 12.

180. See Panayiota I. Pyla, "Planetary Home and Garden: Ekistics and Environmental-Developmental Politics," *Grey Room* 36 (Summer 2009), pp. 6–35.

181. See Mark Wigley, "Network Fever," *Grey Room* 4 (Summer 2001), pp. 82–122.

182. *Hearings Before the Committee on Foreign Relations, United States Senate, Ninety-Second Congress, Second Session on Preparations for and Prospects of the June 1972, U.N. Conference on the Human Environment (May 3, 4, and 5, 1972)* (Washington, DC: US Government Printing Office, 1972), pp. 19 and 130–31.

183. Barbara Ward and Rene Dubos, *Only One Earth: The Care and Maintenance of a Small Planet* (New York: W. W. Norton, 1972), p. 189.

184. *Ibid.*

185. See "Chapter X: Action on Reports of Committees and of the Working Group," in A/CONF.48/14/Rev.1, United Nations, "Report of the United Nations Conference on the Human Environment, Stockholm, 5–16 June 1972" (New York: United Nations, 1973), pp. 51 and 53–57.

186. Helena Z. Benitez, "Only One Earth: For Whom?," *Science and Public Affairs: Bulletin of the Atomic Scientists* 27.7 (September 1972), p. 56.

187. Maurice Strong, "One Year After Stockholm: An Ecological Approach to Management," *Foreign Affairs* 51 (July 1973), pp. 690–91.

188. *Ibid.*, p. 692.

189. *Ibid.*, p. 700.

190. *Ibid.*, p. 701.

191. *Ibid.*, p. 697.

192. *Ibid.*, p. 704.

193. *Ibid.*, p. 705.

194. *Ibid.*, p. 703.

195. Maurice Strong, quoted in Rowland, *The Plot to Save the World*, p. x.

196. See Timothy W. Luke, "Environmentality as Green Governmentality," in Eric Darier (ed.), *Discourses of the Environment* (Malden, MA: Blackwell, 1999), pp. 124 and 135.

197. Weisberg, "The Browning of Stockholm," p. 40.

198. World Commission on Environment and Development, *Our Common Future* (Oxford: Oxford University Press, 1987).

CHAPTER FIVE: THIRD WORLD GAME

1. Ian Hogan, "Ladies Bountiful, Tub-Thumpers and Ankle-Biters," *Architectural Design*, October 1976, p. 587.

2. *Ibid.*, p. 588.

3. *Ibid.* Hogan overlooked the degree to which relations between the official conference and other events were orchestrated by figures such as Strong and Stewart Brand in Stockholm.

4. *Ibid.*

5. Gremlin column, "On Hordes and Hosts . . . ," *Jericho: The Habitat Newspaper*, May 31, 1976, p. 8. The PLO was founded in 1964 to liberate Palestine from Zionism and fight for Palestinian self-determination and the right of return for the vast refugee and exile populations.

6. Hogan, "Ladies Bountiful," pp. 588 and 589.

7. *Ibid.*, pp. 586–89.

8. On the Group of 77, see Karl P. Sauvant, *The Group of 77: Evolution, Structure, Organization* (New York: Oceana Publications, 1981).

9. Official deliberations among delegates from participating nation states took place in grand venues, with plenary sessions held at Vancouver's Queen Elizabeth Theater and committee sessions in major downtown hotels. Coordinated by UN agencies including the United Nations Environment Programme (UNEP) and the Economic and Social Council's (ECOSOC) Center for Housing, Building and Planning (each struggling for leadership of the anticipated new program), as well as by the Canadian Host Secretariat, the agenda was established during numerous preparatory meetings and supplemented by a typical array of statistical documents, expert accounts, and national reports.

10. "Media Play Key Role in Impact of Conference," *Ottawa Bulletin*, no. 10 (August 1976), p. 20.

11. See, for instance, Karl Menck, "Habitat," *Intereconomics* 76 (September 1976), pp. 252–54.

12. Humphrey Carver, "Habitat 1976: The Home of Man. A Review Article," *Town Planning Review* 48.3 (July 1977), p. 283.

13. United Nations, "Vancouver Action Plan," Agenda Item 10 (a), 4, "Settlement Policies and Strategies," Report of Habitat: United Nations Conference on Human Settlements, Vancouver, Canada, May 31 to June 11, 1976.

14. Robert Allen, "The Last of the Megaconferences?," *Development Forum* 4 (July–August 1976), p. 3.

15. Alex Young, "Diefenbaker Sounds Alarm at Third World Gang-Up," *Province*, Saturday, June 12, 1976, p. 8.

16. Among the few exceptions to the alarmist responses was Jon Tinker, "Do Not Undervalue the Vision of Vancouver," *Jericho: The Habitat Newspaper* 11, June 1976, pp. 2–3.

17. Henry Kissinger, "The Global Challenge and International Cooperation [July 14, 1975]," *Department of State Bulletin* 73.1884 (August 4, 1975). p. 153. See also Kathleen Teltsch, "Kissinger Warns Majority in U.N. on U.S. Support," *New York Times*, July 15, 1975, p. 1.

18. Kissinger, "The Global Challenge and International Cooperation," p. 150. As reported in *Architectural Design*'s special issue on Habitat, recent General Agreement on Tariffs and Trade and United Nations Conference of Trade and Development meetings had made the West's intention to assume priority clear to nonaligned countries. Geoff Payne, "International Agencies and Third World Development," *Architectural Design*, October 1976, p. 602.

19. Mwalimu Julius K. Nyerere, Address to Fourth Ministerial Meeting of

the Group of 77, Arusha, February 1979, quoted in Sauvant, *The Group of 77*, p. 3.

20. Michel Foucault, "Different Spaces," trans. Robert Hurley, in James D. Faubion (ed.), *Michel Foucault: Aesthetics, Method, and Epistemology*, vol. 2 of *Essential Works of Foucault, 1954–1984* (New York: New Press, 1998), p. 178.

21. Michel Foucault, "The Ethics of the Concern for Self as a Practice of Freedom," in Paul Rabinow (ed.), *Ethics: Subjectivity and Truth*, vol. 1 of *Essential Works of Foucault, 1954–1984* (New York: New Press, 1997), p. 292.

22. *Ibid.*, pp. 292 and 299.

23. *Ibid.*, p. 292.

24. *Ibid.*, p. 298.

25. Wolf von Eckardt, "'Lady Habitat' and the Unsettling Opposition," *Washington Post*, June 9, 1976, p. A19.

26. Donald Gutstein, "Who's Who at Habitat," *City Magazine*, June 1976, p. 25, and Allen Garr, "The Irresistible Force of Habitat Forum," *Vancouver*, May 1976, p. 23.

27. The Israel/Palestine conflict and the centrality not only of political history, but of environmental and human settlement questions to it has been compellingly written about in great detail elsewhere. See, for instance, Edward Said, *The Question of Palestine* (London: Routledge and Paul, 1980); Rashid Khalidi, *Palestinian Identity: The Construction of Modern National Consciousness* (New York: Columbia University Press, 1997); Nadia Abu El-Haj, *Facts on the Ground: Archaeological Practice and Territorial Self-Fashioning in Israeli Society* (Chicago: University of Chicago Press, 2001); Rashid Khalidi, *The Iron Cage: The Story of the Palestinian Struggle for Statehood* (Boston: Beacon Press, 2006); Eyal Weizman, *Hollow Land: Israel's Architecture of Occupation* (London: Verso, 2007); and Adi Ophir, Michal Givoni, and Sari Hanafi (eds.), *The Power of Inclusive Exclusion: Anatomy of Israeli Rule in the Occupied Palestinian Territories* (New York: Zone Books, 2009).

28. "Palestinians Called Symbols for All Oppressed People," *Winnipeg Free Press*, June 7, 1976, p. 9.

29. *Ibid.*

30. Alfred Heller, "The View from Jericho," *Sierra Club Bulletin*, September 1976, pp. 11–13.

31. Paul Jackson, "Danson Critical of Jewish Stand on Habitat," *Province*, November 28, 1975, p. 15. See also Dorothea Katzenstein, "Vancouver Finds Hosting a UN Conference on Solving World's Woes Causes Many Woes," *Wall Street Journal*, March 18, 1976, p. 38.

32. Harvey Oberfeld, "Canadian Jews Drawing up Plans to Expose PLO," *Vancouver Sun*, February 6, 1976, p. 9.

33. See "Habitat Theater to Show Films of Israel Progress," *Vancouver Sun*, May

19, 1976, p. 53.

34. Moira Farrow, "Israel Lashes 'Smooth PLO Propaganda,'" *Vancouver Sun*, June 3, 1976, clipping in the City of Vancouver Archives, MSS.337, United Nations Conference on Human Settlements fonds, henceforth CVA.

35. "Habitat Will Let Murderers in, Jewish Leaders Claim," *Vancouver Sun*, December 4, 1975, p. 12.

36. Katzenstein, "Vancouver Finds Hosting... Causes Many Woes," p. 38.

37. Gutstein, "Who's Who at Habitat," pp. 26–27. See also Eileen Goodman, "Habitat: What the UN Conference Is All About," *Canadian Business*, March 1976, pp. 23–24.

38. Alan Merridew, "Conference Links Zionism, Racism," *Chicago Tribune*, June 12, 1976, p. 3.

39. "Habitat's Palestinian Gambit," *Province*, June 12, 1976, p. 1. On Waldheim's statement and position, see also "PLO Claim 'Not on Agenda,'" *Vancouver Sun*, June 1, 1976, clipping.

40. "Habitat's Palestinian Gambit," p. 1. See also Harvey Oberfeld, "Canadian Jews Drawing Up Plans to Expose PLO," *Vancouver Sun*, February 6, 1976, p. 9; and Moira Farrow, "Jews 'Support Habitat' Despite PLO Presence," *Vancouver Sun*, March 8, 1976, p. 3; Kay Alsop, "Habitat: A Way out of the Wilderness?," *Province*, April 8, 1976, p. 28; Tim Traynor, "Caution Won't Stop Arabs from Plugging Palestinian Cause," *Vancouver Sun*, June 4, 1976, p. 16; "The Lessons of Vancouver," *Washington Post*, June 19, 1976, p. A10.

41. "Habitat's Palestinian Gambit," p. 1. See also Wolf von Eckardt, "Habitat Approves Anti-Israel Stand," *Washington Post*, June 12, 1976, p. A15.

42. "Palestine Will Be a Key Habitat Issue," *Province*, May 31, 1976, clipping, CVA. See also Wolf von Eckardt, "U.N. Habitat Opens, Tackling 'Urgency' of Human Settlement," *Washington Post*, June 1, 1976, p. A12.

43. "Palestine Will Be a Key Habitat Issue."

44. Ross Howard and Frank Jones, "Political Storms Are Brewing Over UN Conference," *Toronto Star*, November 15, 1975, p. B4.

45. Said, *The Question of Palestine*, p. xliv.

46. *Ibid.*, p. xix. In Said's words, "Ever since its founding in 1948, Israel has enjoyed an astonishing dominance in matters of scholarship, political discourse, international presence, and valorization. Israel was taken to represent the best in Western and Biblical traditions... its miraculous transformation of an 'arid and empty land' gained universal admiration, and so on and on. In all this, Palestinians were either 'Arabs,' or anonymous creatures of the sort that could only disrupt and disfigure a wonderfully idyllic narrative." *Ibid.*, p. xiv.

47. "Canadian Arabs Will Pressure Business If PLO Barred, MacEachen Is

Warned," *Toronto Globe and Mail*, July 15, 1975, p. 9.

48. "PLO Pledges Habitat Visit," undated clipping, box 36, Association in Canada Serving Organizations for Human Settlements fonds, 1974–1976, Rare Books and Special Collections, University of British Columbia, henceforth UBC. See also "Not Group of Terrorists, PLO Representative Says," *Toronto Globe and Mail*, November 18, 1975, in which Al Hout stresses, "The PLO was responding to Zionist violence and Zionist attacks on Palestinian civilians. It steadfastly and courageously condemned kidnappings and aerial hijackings, concentrating its efforts against the state of Israel."

49. "PLO, Israel Talk in Peace," *Jericho: The Habitat Newspaper*, June 4, 1976, p. 2.

50. Letter from Deputy Chief Constable A. E. Oliver, Bureau of Field Operations, Vancouver Police Department, to Mr. M. Egan, Social Planning Department, City of Vancouver, January 9, 1976, published in "Police Warn Habitat Planners: No Tents," *Vancouver Sun*, January 24, 1976, p. 1.

51. Randy Glover, "Council in Quandary over Habitat Influx," *Vancouver Sun*, January 27, 1976, p. 1. See also Katzenstein, "Vancouver Finds Hosting... Causes Many Woes."

52. Moira Farrow, "Habitat Forum Running at Hectic Pace," *Vancouver Sun*, February 3, 1976, clipping, CVA.

53. The nine themes included the man-made and the natural environment, social justice and the question of differing values and cultures, sharing and managing the world's resources, national settlements policies, people's participation in planning and implementation, land use and ownership, community action for a better habitat, rural development, and appropriate technology.

54. On this connection see, for instance, Graham Chedd, "Space Colonies," *New Scientist*, June 10, 1976, pp. 598–99.

55. Von Eckardt, "'Lady Habitat' and the Unsettling Opposition," p. A19. Also published the next day as von Eckhardt, "Habitat a Show with a Superstar," *Vancouver Sun*, June 10, 1976.

56. Von Eckardt, "'Lady Habitat' and the Unsettling Opposition," p. A19.

57. The Vancouver symposium was sponsored by the Institute for Environment and Development (IIED), the Population Institute, and the Audubon Society. Its members included, in addition to Ward and Strong, anthropologist Margaret Mead, Catholic missionary Mother Teresa, and architect-planners R. Buckminster Fuller, Eduardo Terrazas, Jorge Hardoy, Juliusz Gorynski, Panayis Psomopoulos, Moshe Safdie, Charles Correa, and Otto Königsberger. Other members were geographers, development specialists, diplomats, NGO directors, and US real estate developer James Rouse. See also Leon Howell, "Habitat: An Elitist Approach to

Human Settlement Issues," *Christian Century*, August 4–11, 1976, pp. 677–79. On Doxiadis's cruises, see Mark Wigley, "Network Fever," *Grey Room* 4 (Summer 2001), pp. 82–122.

58. Thomas Harford, "Places for People: A Guardian Series for Habitat 1976," *Guardian*, March 1, 1976, p. 11.

59. Barbara Ward, *Human Settlements: Crisis and Opportunity* (Ottawa: Minister of State for Urban Affairs, 1974). Maurice Strong refers to it as a personal account in the preface, p. v.

60. Barbara Ward, in "Comments by World Leaders in the Struggle to Improve Conditions of Human Settlement around the World," *Architectural Record* 159, May 1976, p. 158.

61. As Ijlal Muzzafar has written of such ideologies, "We see in self-help projects the emerging contours of a new model of social intervention that professes, not the urgency of modernization, but the necessity of its delay to discover the optimum and sustainable 'pace' of historical change." Ijlal M. Muzaffar, "The Periphery Within: Modern Architecture and the Making of the Third World," PhD diss., MIT, 2007, p. 40.

62. Barbara Ward, "United Nations Conference–Exposition on Human Settlements," *Ekistics* 38.227 (October 1974), p. 237.

63. *Ibid.*

64. *Ibid.*, p. 238.

65. Barbara Ward, "The Home of Man: What Nations and the International Must Do," *Ekistics* 42.252 (November 1976), p. 277. Also published under the same title in *Habitat: An International Journal* 1.2 (September 1976), pp. 125–32.

66. Michel Foucault, "The Right of Death and Power over Life," in *The History of Sexuality, Volume I: An Introduction*, trans. Robert Hurley (New York: Random House, 1990), p. 141.

67. On this bootstrapping logic and on the self-help paradigm, see Muzaffar, "The Periphery Within," pp. 79–80. See also Helen Gyger, "The Informal as Project: Self-Help Housing in Peru, 1954–1986," PhD diss., Columbia University, 2012.

68. Ward, "The Home of Man," p. 277.

69. *Ibid.*, p. 275. See also Clyde Sanger, "Poorer Nations 'May Turn to Violence,'" *Guardian*, June 2, 1976, p. 3.

70. Margaret R. Biswas, "'Habitat' in Retrospective," *International Journal of Environmental Studies* 11.4 (1978), p. 271.

71. Ward, "The Home of Man," p. 276.

72. Barbara Ward, "The Road to Survival," *Observer*, May 30, 1976, p. 10.

73. Foucault, "The Right of Death and Power over Life," p. 137.

74. Clyde Sanger, "Habitat Receives Challenge to Act," *Guardian*, June 1, 1976, p. 2. The symposium also hosted lunchtime lectures and other events at Habitat Forum, all receiving significant media coverage.

75. Vancouver Symposium, "Declaration of the Vancouver Symposium," *Ekistics* 42.252 (November 1976), pp. 267–72. For a broad overview of these conferences, see *Habitat Guide* (Vancouver: Hometown Communications, 1976), pp. 5–6, and Michael G. Schechter, *United Nations Global Conferences* (New York: Routledge, 2005). On the notion of a globalized biopolitics, see Didier Fassin and Mariella Pandolfi (eds.), *Contemporary States of Emergency: The Politics of Military and Humanitarian Interventions* (New York: Zone Books, 2010).

76. Vancouver Symposium, "Declaration," p. 268.

77. See Ward, "The Home of Man."

78. Vancouver Symposium, "Declaration," p. 272.

79. Gladwin Hill, "View of World's Shantytowns Less Grim," *New York Times*, June 9, 1976, p. 4.

80. "Housing: It's Political," *Jericho: The Habitat Newspaper*, June 8, 1976, p. 3. See also Joseph Handwerger, "Meanwhile, the Nongovernmental Habitat Forum Emphasizes Self-Help and Smallness," *AIA Journal* (August 1976), pp. 42–44.

81. Jeremy Bugler, "Calling off the Bulldozers," *New Internationalist*, August 1, 1976, p. 14.

82. Patrick Nagle, "Stockholm Spirit Withers at Forum," *Vancouver Sun*, June 8, 1976, p. 20.

83. See: "Curriculum Vitae: Enrique Penalosa," CVA; biographical profile, "Enrique Penalosa," *Engineering Journal* 58 (July–August 1976), p. 64; "Enrique Penalosa of Colombia Appointed Secretary-General of Conference–Exposition on Human Settlements," United Nations Press Release SG/A/150, BIO/1091, HE/178, February 25, 1974. See also Roger James Sandilands, *The Life and Political Economy of Lauchlin Currie: New Dealer, Presidential Adviser, and Development Economist* (Durham: Duke University Press, 1990).

84. Gutstein, "Who's Who at Habitat," p. 20.

85. Rosemary E. Galli, "Columbia: Rural Development as Social and Economic Control," in Rosemary E. Galli (ed.), *Political Economy of Rural Development: Peasants, International Capital, and the State* (Albany: State University of New York Press, 1981), p. 59.

86. Vancouver Symposium, "Declaration," pp. 271 and 272.

87. R. Buckminster Fuller, "How It Came About (World Game)," in Joachim Krausse and Claude Lichtenstein (eds.), *Your Private Sky: R. Buckminster Fuller: The Art of Design Science* (Baden: Lars Müller, 2001), p. 473.

88. R. Buckminster Fuller, "The World Game: How to Make the World Work,"

in Fuller, *Utopia or Oblivion: The Prospects for Humanity* (New York: Bantam Books, 1969), p. 159.

89. "A.C. to V.P.—It's All Yours," *Jericho: The Habitat Newspaper*, June 1, 1976, p. 3.

90. R. Buckminster Fuller, "Accommodating Human Unsettlement," *Town Planning Review* 49.1 (January 1978), p. 52.

91. *Ibid.*

92. Thomas Albright, "The Environmentalists: The Whole Earth Catalog," *Rolling Stone*, December 13, 1969, pp. 30–33.

93. Fuller, "Accommodating Human Unsettlement," p. 56.

94. See Tim Traynor, "Windy-Day Gadget Pumps Power Back into Line," *Vancouver Sun*, May 4, 1976, p. 34. See also "The Now House—Introduction," ten-page typescript document, M1684, William Wolf collection of Buckminster Fuller papers pertaining to the World Game and Design Science Institute, Stanford University Department of Special Collections and University Archives.

95. Fuller, "Accommodating Human Unsettlement," p. 53.

96. *Ibid.*

97. *Ibid.*, p. 54.

98. *Ibid.*

99. *Ibid.*, pp. 54 and 55.

100. *Ibid.*, p. 54.

101. "Statement of Mr. R. Buckminster Fuller, Architect, Philadelphia, Pennsylvania," in *Hearings Before the Committee on Foreign Relations, United States Senate, Ninety-Fourth Congress, First Session on the United States and the United Nations and the Nomination of Daniel Patrick Moynihan to be U.S. Representative to the United Nations with the Rank of Ambassador* (Washington, DC: US Government Printing Office, 1975), pp. 194 and 195.

102. *Ibid.*, p. 195.

103. Fuller, in *Hearings Before the Committee on Foreign Relations*, p. 199.

104. Fuller speculated that feedback-based adjustments would have to be made on account of initial errors, just as with computer-controlled servomechanisms adjusting the steering mechanisms of airplanes or ships, or even spacecraft.

105. Fuller, in *Hearings Before the Committee on Foreign Relations*, p. 202.

106. For an opposite reading, see Alejandro Zaera-Polo, preface to Daniel Lopez-Perez (ed.), *R. Buckminster Fuller: World Man* (New York: Princeton Architectural Press, 2014), pp. 6–11.

107. See Michael Hardt and Antonio Negri, *Empire* (Cambridge, MA: Harvard University Press, 2000).

108. Michael Hardt and Antonio Negri, *Multitude: War and Democracy in the Age*

of Empire (New York: Penguin, 2004), p. 3.

109. Michel Foucault, *"Society Must Be Defended": Lectures at the Collège de France, 1975–76*, trans. David Macey (New York: Picador, 2003), p. 15.

110. Berton Woodward, "Plenty for All on Spaceship Earth, Says Fuller," *Province*, June 7, 1976, p. 25. On the Bucky cult, see Carver, "Habitat 1976," pp. 281–86.

111. "Keeping the Sunny Side Up," *Jericho: The Habitat Newspaper*, June 7, 1976, p. 8.

112. Nick Hills, "Great Expectations for the Forum," *Province*, May 27, 1976, p. 5.

113. On the transformation of the site, see Moira Farrow, "Habitat Showplace Grows at Jericho," *Vancouver Sun*, November 4, 1975, p. 68; Farrow, "Recycling Is a Way of Life at Jericho Habitat Site," *Vancouver Sun*, January 22, 1976, p. 39; Joan Haggerty, "Inside Habitat Forum," *Journal of Commerce*, May 31, 1976, p. 7; Harvey Southam, "Recycle City Is Magic in the Making," *Province*, March 1, 1976, clipping, CVA; John Braddock, "Habitat Forum Becomes Reality," *Province*, May 28, 1976, clipping, CVA; along with Gray, "Creation of Forum," Traynor, "Second Week," and Hills, "Great Expectations." On the history of the site, see also Rex Weyler, *Greenpeace: How a Group of Ecologists, Journalists, and Visionaries Changed the World* (Vancouver: Raincoast Books, 2004), and "The Story of Jericho" in Martha Miller (ed.), *Habitat Forum: Your Guide to the People's Conference on Human Settlements* (Vancouver: ACSOH, 1976), p. 3.

114. Frederick Gutheim, "Habitat: The United Nations Conference on Human Settlements. What Are the Results, Measured Against the Goals?" *Journal of Housing* 33 (August 1976), p. 374.

115. Eckardt, "Habitat: Where People Are the Answer," p. 4.

116. Paul Goldberger, "Informal Forum That Parallels the Habitat Conference Is a Youthful and Radically Different Affair," *New York Times*, June 9, 1976, p. 5.

117. "At the Forum," special issue, "Perspectives on Habitat," *Ekistics* 43.252 (November 1977), p. 283.

118. Gray, "Creation of Forum," clipping, CVA.

119. *Ibid.*

120. Von Eckardt, "Habitat: Where People Are the Answer," pp. B1 and B4.

121. That the organizers realized this departed from Stockholm was indicated in "Habitat Speeches: Short and Sweet—Hopefully," *Province*, April 10, 1976, clipping, CVA.

122. Gutheim, "Habitat," p. 374.

123. Van Putten hoped the relationship between the UN and NGOs would be symbiotic, noting that at Stockholm, the forum "was encouraged by the UN as

a method to obtain publicity and support for its activities. NGOs considered it a means by which they could express their points of view to the governments." J. G. Van Putten, "Report on the Habitat Forum, Vancouver 27 May–11 June, 1976," September 1976, p. 1. Columbia University Rare Books and Manuscript Library, Conference of Nongovernmental Organizations in Consultative Status with the UN Economic and Social Council Records 1948–1985, box 19.

124. "At the Forum," p. 284.

125. Gutstein, "Who's Who at Habitat," p. 18. See also *Habitat Forum Guide* (Vancouver: ACSOH, 1976).

126. Douglas Sagi, "Critic of Habitat Forum Progress Changes Views on Site Readiness," *Vancouver Sun*, February 12, 1976, p. 40.

127. Tim Traynor, "Second-Week Forum Crowds Expected," *Vancouver Sun*, May 8, 1976, p. 18.

128. Garr, "The Irresistible Force of Habitat Forum," p. 21.

129. See: Traynor, "Second-Week Forum Crowds Expected"; Garr, "The Irresistible Force of Habitat Forum"; Gutstein, "Who's Who at Habitat"; Moira Farrow, "Business, Unions 'Miserable, Petty' in Pondering Aid to Habitat Forum," *Vancouver Sun*, January 23, 1976, p. 2; Farrow, "Clapp Hits Park Board for Habitat Indifference," *Vancouver Sun*, January 30, 1976, p. 14; "Who's the Real Habitat Publicist," *Vancouver Sun*, May 12, 1976, clipping, CVA.

130. Garr, "The Irresistible Force of Habitat Forum," p. 19.

131. Malcolm Gray, "Creation of Forum Is Success Story of Habitat," *Toronto Globe and Mail*, May 26, 1976, clipping, CVA.

132. "A.C. to V.P.—It's All Yours," p. 3.

133. Gremlin column, "Busing: The Great Debate," *Jericho: The Habitat Newspaper*, June 2, 1976, p. 8.

134. Habitat Forum, "Program Outline," np, nd.

135. Gladwin Hill, "Dream Houses Become Reality at UN Conference," *New York Times*, June 6, 1976, p. 24. On the Appropriate Technology Village, see also Marcus Gee, "Dome Home Show," *Province*, May 27 1976, clipping, CVA, which describes it as "a community of pioneers in alternative housing and energy concepts."

136. Heller, "The View from Jericho," p. 12.

137. As Peggy Wireman notes, "At least at the Forum, the interactions with the Third World seemed to me to be almost too amicable. A Third World friend explained that most participants were at least indirectly financed by their governments or by other official institutions, and that they had been very carefully selected." Peggy Wireman, "Personal Reflections on the Forum," *HUD International* 40 (October 1976), p. 5.

138. Heller, "The View from Jericho," p. 12.

139. *Ibid.*

140. Alan Merridew, "UN's 'Habitat' Runs Afoul of Ill Will in Middle East," *Chicago Tribune*, June 13, 1976, p. 13.

141. Carver, "Habitat 1976," p. 285.

142. Howard and Jones, "Political Storms Are Brewing."

143. Tim Traynor, "Danson Slapped Down at Conference," *Vancouver Sun*, June 11, 1976, p. 1.

144. Moira Farrow, "Conference Leaves Bad Taste in U.S. Mouth," *Vancouver Sun*, June 12, 1976, p. 48. See also "The 77 Weigh In," *Jericho: The Habitat Newspaper*, June 7, 1976, p. 1. The previous year, Canada was put to shame over a similar panic launched in Toronto regarding the PLO's invitation to a UN conference on crime, as a result of which the conference was moved to Geneva and Arabic added to the official languages at Habitat at Canada's expense. See Charles Lynch, "Will History Blame Canada for UN Collapse?," *Province*, July 17, 1975, clipping, CVA; W. A. Wilson, "PLO Crunch Was Avoidable," *Vancouver Sun*, July 21, 1975, clipping, CVA; "Welcome, PLO Members—But Not Now," *Province*, July 26, 1975, p. 1; "PLO Intends to Send Observers to Habitat," *Vancouver Sun*, August 22, 1975, p. 2.

145. UNESCO Resolution 20C/7.6, November 20, 1974. Reiterating the degree to which Israel's colonial presence was out of sync with world trends, the report stated that the country "occupies Palestine only by 'right of military conquest.' This 'right' no longer exists. The consensus of the civilized community has established that military conquest is not a ground for acquisition of territory."

146. See, for instance, Howard and Jones, "Political Storms Are Brewing over UN Conference," and "UN Resolution on Zionism Angers Danson," *Toronto Star*, November 14, 1975, clipping. UBC.

147. See "The UN Resolution on Zionism," *Journal of Palestine Studies* 5.1–2 (Autumn–Winter 1975–76), pp. 252–54.

148. See, for instance, *Ibid.*, p. 253.

149. A. M. El-Messiri, quoted in "The UN Resolution on Zionism," p. 253.

150. Ministry of the Interior, *Settlement in Israel: Israel National Report to Habitat: United Nations Conference on Human Settlements* (Jerusalem: Environment Protection Service, 1976), p. 15.

151. *Ibid.*, p. 57.

152. *Ibid.*, p. 16. For an important critique from within architecture of these strategies, see Weizman, *Hollow Land*.

153. "Walkout Staged against Israel," *Vancouver Sun*, June 3, 1976, clipping, CVA; Ashley Ford, "Delegates Walk Out on Israel," *Province*, June 4, 1976,

clipping, CVA.

154. "Statement Delivered by Dr. Josef Burg, Minister of the Interior, Head of Delegation, on June 3, 1976." Mimeograph typescript, CVA. Quoted in Ford, "Delegates Walk Out on Israel." See also "PLO, Israel Talk in Peace," *Jericho: The Habitat Newspaper*, June 4, 1976, pp. 2 and 3.

155. Ford, "Delegates Walk Out on Israel." See also "Israel, PLO Trade Insults, Accusations at Conferences," *Vancouver Sun*, June 8, 1976, clipping, CVA, and Jim Joly, "PLO's Habitat Leader Raps 'Reactionary Arabs,'" *Vancouver Sun*, June 7, 1976, clipping, CVA.

156. See "Israel, PLO Trade Insults, Accusations at Conferences"; "Israel Wants No Confusion: Collusion Allusion Illusion," *Province*, June 8, 1976, p. 33 (Burg "defended the Jewish settlement of former Arab lands and said they were malaria-infested and unused by the Arabs as settlement sites"); "'Hatred' of PLO Counter-Attacked," *Vancouver Sun*, June 5, 1976, clipping, CVA. Mordecai Kidron argued that "the Palestinians had been instructed to leave [Israel] by Arab governments," who had then "left their brethren to rot and fester in camps." See also "Press Release: Delegation of Israel to Habitat, June 7th 1976," CVA.

157. Nick Hills, "Habitat War Dances May Feature Canadian Side-Step," *Province*, June 5, 1976, clipping, CVA.

158. "Notes for the Prime Minister's Speech at the Opening of Habitat: The United Nations Conference on Human Settlements in Vancouver, May 31, 1976," press release, Office of the Prime Minister (Canada), May 31, 1976, p. 10. See also "All You Need is Love," *Jericho: The Habitat Newspaper*, June 1, 1976, p. 1.

159. Hills, "Habitat War Dances May Feature Canadian Side-Step."

160. "Palestinians Called Symbols for All Oppressed People," p. 9.

161. Mordecai Briemberg, quoted in *ibid.*

162. "The PLO asked what had happened to the human settlements report on the Palestinians—which should have been presented to Habitat in accordance with Recommendation 3376 of the UN General Assembly. It could not be done, the PLO was told, because the secretariat and the economic Commission of Western Asia had decided there was no money to spare. This cavalier treatment did not satisfy the Palestinian representatives, but no national delegation protested." "This Week Could Heat Up," *Jericho: The Habitat Newspaper*, June 7, 1976, p. 2.

163. Palestine Liberation Organization, *National Report of Palestine*, 1976, p. 4.

164. *Ibid.*, p. 10.

165. A dunum is 1,000 square meters, or 10,764 square feet.

166. Palestine Liberation Organization, *National Report of Palestine*, p. 16.

167. *Ibid.*, p. 17.

168. *Ibid.*, p. 21.

169. *Ibid.*, p. 28.

170. Edward Said reflected on this phenomenon, for instance in *The Question of Palestine* and *After the Last Sky: Palestinian Lives* (New York: Columbia University Press, 1999).

171. *National Report of Palestine*, pp. 53–54.

172. On UN resolutions concerning Palestinians, see Regina Sharif, "The United Nations and Palestinian Rights, 1974–1979," *Journal of Palestine Studies* 9.1 (Autumn 1979), pp. 21–45.

173. On this transformation, see Abu El-Haj, *Facts on the Ground*, and Weizman, "Jerusalem: Petrifying the Holy City," in *Hollow Land*, pp. 25–52.

174. United Nations, *Report of Habitat: United Nations Conference on Human Settlements* (New York: United Nations, 1976), A/CONF.70/15, and "Questions Concerning Human Settlements," chapter 11 of *Yearbook of the United Nations 1978* (New York: United Nations Department of Public Information, 1981), p. 544.

175. See Foucault, *"Society Must Be Defended,"* p. 16.

176. Foucault, "The Ethics of the Concern for Self," p. 297. "The word 'game' can lead you astray: when I say 'game', I mean a set of rules by which truth is produced. It is not a game in the sense of amusement; it is a set of procedures that lead to a certain result, which, on the basis of its principles and rules of procedure, may be considered valid or invalid, winning or losing."

177. United Nations, *Report of Habitat*.

178. "Anti-Israel Resolution Back in Habitat List of Principles," *Vancouver Sun*, June 8, 1976, pp. 1 and 8. See also Nick Hills, "Canada Hopeful Habitat Will Shelve Zionist Issue," *Province*, June 7, 1976, clipping, CVA. See also Nick Hills, "Habitat's Success Still in Balance," *Province*, June 10, 1976, clipping, CVA; "Iraq Sets Stage for Debate on Delicate Israel Issue," *Province*, June 10, 1976, p. 49; Moira Farrow, "U.S. Objects to Racism in Resolutions," *Vancouver Sun*, June 11, 1976, p. 28.

179. United Nations, *Report of Habitat*, p. 164. See also A/CONF.70/L.3 *Report of the Second Committee*; and Clyde Sanger, "Israeli Target at Talks," *Guardian*, June 12, 1976, p. 3. Habitat Committee II was charged with three major subitems of "Recommendations for National Action"—settlement policies and strategies, settlement planning, and institutions and management.

180. Larry Still, "Canadian Compromise Overcomes Deadlock," *Vancouver Sun*, June 10, 1976, p. 80.

181. "Israel Condemned: Vote Splits Habitat," *Vancouver Sun*, June 11, 1976, p. 1.

182. United Nations, *Report of Habitat*, p. 171.

183. "Dispute Erupts Again," *Vancouver Sun*, June 8, 1976, p. 17, and Tim Traynor, "Political Infighting Stalls Session," *Vancouver Sun*, June 8, 1976, p. 16.

184. "Procedural Side-Step Helps Avert Flare-Up," *Vancouver Sun*, June 10,

1976, p. 80.

185. United Nations, *Report of Habitat*, p. 112.

186. US delegate Stanley Schiff, quoted in "Palestine Issue Erupts Again," *Vancouver Sun*, June 11, 1976, p. 28.

187. Philip Quigg, "Habitat: Important Gains Despite Political Chaos," *Audubon*, September 1976, p. 115.

188. Quigg, "Habitat: Important Gains," p. 115. See also von Eckardt, "Habitat Approves Anti-Israel Stand."

189. Farrow, "Conference Leaves Bad Taste," p. 48.

190. "Habitat's Palestinian Gambit," p. 1.

191. Stanley Schiff, quoted in "Palestine Issue Erupts Again," p. 28.

192. Merridew, "UN's 'Habitat' Runs Afoul," p. 13. See also Stanley Schiff, "U.N. Conference on Human Settlements," *Department of State Bulletin*, October 1976, p. 464; and Farrow, "Conference Leaves Bad Taste."

193. Tinker, "Do Not Undervalue the Vision of Vancouver," p. 2.

194. "Palestine Will Be a Key Habitat Issue."

195. Said, *The Question of Palestine*, pp. xxxv and 47. On Palestinian national identity, see also Khalidi, *Palestinian Identity.*

196. Said, *The Question of Palestine*, pp. xxxvi and xxviii.

197. *Ibid.*, p. xiii. "The actual significance of Palestinian armed struggle was complex, but on at least one level it also represented the end of liberation struggle and the beginning of a nationalist effort, in which arms (and armies) were used to protect a central national authority." *Ibid.*, p. 163.

198. *Ibid.*, pp. xx–xxi.

199. *Ibid.*, p. xxxvi.

200. United Nations General Assembly, *Living Conditions of the Palestinian People in the Occupied Arab Territories: Report of the Secretary General*, A/35/533, October 17, 1980. See Economic and Social Council resolution 2026 (LXI) of August 4, 1976 and 2100 (LXIII) of August 3, 1977; United Nations General Assembly, A/RES/31/110 of December 16, 1976; A/RES/32/171 of December 19, 1977; A/RES/33/110 of December 18, 1978; A/RES/34/113 of December 14, 1979; A/RES/35/75 of December 5, 1980. The secretary general prepared the report in collaboration with United Nations Relief and Works Agency for Palestine Refugees (UNRWA), the Economic Commission for Western Asia (ECWA), and the Special Committee to Investigate Israeli Practices Affecting the Human Rights of the Population of the Occupied Territories, among other agencies.

201. United Nations General Assembly, A/RES/36/73 of December 4, 1981; A/RES/37/222 of December 20, 1982; A/RES/ 38/166 of December 19, 1983.

202. United Nations General Assembly, *Living Conditions of the Palestinian*

People in the Occupied Territories, 1985, page 33. See also, as cited in the report, Janet L. Abu-Lughod, "The Demographic Consequences of the Occupation," in Naseer H. Aruri (ed.), *Occupation: Israel over Palestine* (Belmont, MA: AAUG, 1983), p. 255.

203. Ward, in "Comments by World Leaders," p. 158.

204. Editorial, "Habitat Redistributed," *Architectural Design*, October 1976, p. 580.

205. See John F. C. Turner, "Uncontrolled Urban Settlement: Problems and Policies," *International Social Development Review* 1 (1968), p. 119, and Turner, "A New Universe of Squatter-Builders," *UNESCO Courier*, June 1976, pp. 12–14.

CHAPTER SIX: "CRUEL HABITATS"

1. Frederick Gutheim, "Habitat: Toward Shelter," *Vanguard: The Vancouver Art Gallery* 5.5 (June–July 1976), p. 5.

2. *Ibid.*, p. 3. his language is repeated almost verbatim in Michael Seelig, *The Architecture of Self-Help Communities: The First International Competition for the Urban Environment of Developing Countries* (New York: Architectural Record Books, 1978).

3. See, for instance, "Signal Service," *Architectural Design*, October 1976, p. 580. On the work of John F. C. Turner in Peru, see Helen Gyger, "The Informal as Project: Self-Help Housing in Peru, 1954–1986," PhD diss., Columbia University, 2012. On architects' involvement with self-help and development, see Ijlal M. Muzaffar, "The Periphery Within: Modern Architecture and the Making of the Third World," PhD diss., MIT, 2007.

4. Paul Goldberger, "Radical Planners Now Mainstream," *New York Times*, June 13, 1976, p. 21.

5. See Ken Jacobsen, "UIA Defines Philosophy Behind Habitat 76," *Architectural Record*, November 1975, p. 38, and Jacobsen, "UIA Drafts a Charter on Human Settlements for Habitat '76,'" *Architectural Record*, March 1975, p. 37.

6. On the phenomenon of mobilizing shame in human rights activism, see Thomas Keenan, "Mobilizing Shame," *South Atlantic Quarterly* 103.2–3 (Spring–Summer 2004), pp. 435–49.

7. In announcing the competition, the editors of *Architectural Record* indicated that "we are not so naïve as to believe that architecture is the solution to all problems of the world; that good planning and design is a substitute for jobs that don't exist, or food that does not exist or is too dear. But housing and a sense of community are basic human needs—and that is the part of the problem that we know most about and can best do something about." Quoted in Walter F. Wagner, "Human Settlements," *Architectural Record*, May 1976, p. 95.

8. Benitez had earlier been a member of the governing council of ECOSOC's

Center for Housing, Building and Planning and went on to preside over UNEP's governing council.

9. Seelig, *The Architecture of Self-Help Communities*, p. 12.

10. See "The Winning Designs," *Architectural Record*, May 1976, p. 113. See also "Manila Became the Focus of the International Design Competition," *ibid.*, pp. 106–11.

11. Maurice Strong, quoted in Frederick Gutheim, *A World of Cities*, Man's Home no. 3 (New York: United Nations, 1972), frontispiece.

12. Office brochure sent to City Clerk's Office, City of Vancouver Archives, henceforth CVA, folder 548-A-2. Seelig noted that Gutheim came with "high level public service for the President and Congress of the United States." Seelig, *The Architecture of Self-Help Communities*, p. 12.

13. Seelig was born in Tel Aviv and received a diploma in architecture from Hammersmith University and a masters degree and PhD in community planning from the University of Pennsylvania. On his attitude toward the Israel/Palestine conflict, see Michael Seelig, "Palestine Revolution Article Questioned," *UBC Alumni Chronicle* 26.1 (Spring 1972), pp. 33–34.

14. Seelig, *The Architecture of Self-Help Communities*, pp. 10–14.

15. *Ibid.*, p. 5.

16. Wagner, "Human Settlements," p. 95.

17. Gutheim, "Habitat: Toward Shelter," p. 3.

18. *Ibid.*, p. 3.

19. Occupied by the United States during the Spanish-American War of 1898, the Philippines became a self-governing commonwealth in 1935, at which time a republican constitution went into effect. The Philippines officially gained independence from colonial tutelage on July 4, 1946. As in other former colonies, massive social inequity and ongoing economic ties born of colonialism persisted, largely to the benefit of multinational corporations and the local elite. Rich in natural resources, the Philippines exports sugar, timber, and coconut products, with the United States secured as a major market through colonial-era economic ties. Primary imports have included oil and machinery, driving the national debt and hence inflation.

20. Bernard Wideman, "The Philippines: Five Years of Martial Law," *AMPO: Japan Asia Quarterly Review* 9 (1977), p. 64.

21. David Wurfel, "Martial Law in the Philippines: The Methods of Regime Survival," *Pacific Affairs* 50.1 (Spring 1977), p. 6.

22. Cheryl Payer, *The World Bank: A Critical Analysis* (New York: Monthly Review Press, 1982), pp. 326–27.

23. "Manila Became the Focus of the International Design Competition,"

Architectural Record, May 1976, p. 107.

24. Imelda Marcos staged her own demonstration project in Dagat-Dagatan, launching government rental housing a few weeks before Habitat as a sign of her government's benevolence and "revolution against impoverishment." Priced at two to three times the squatters' current rate, it was less a solution than a media stunt, one requiring "soldiers of the Presidential Guard Battalion wearing combat fatigues and carrying M-16 rifles" and a government agent sweep of a neighboring slum, Barrio Boulevard, to mask the systematic dispossession taking place. See "Philippine Squatters and Martial Law Remedies," statement by Coordinating Council of People's Organizations of Tondo Foreshore, Navotas, Malabon, for the U.N. Human Settlements Conference, Vancouver, British Columbia, May–June 1976, np.

25. The competition guidelines are reprinted in Michael Seelig, "Tondo and the Competition Program," in *The Architecture of Self-Help Communities*, p. 30.

26. Gutheim, "Habitat: Toward Shelter," p. 3.

27. "This felicity, as the individual's better than just living," Foucault argued, "must in some way be drawn on and constituted into state utility: making men's happiness the state's utility, making men's happiness the very strength of the state." Michel Foucault, *Security, Territory, Population: Lectures at the Collège de France, 1977–1978,* trans. Graham Burchell (New York: Palgrave, 2007), p. 327.

28. Gutheim, "Habitat: Toward Shelter," p. 5.

29. Seelig, *The Architecture of Self-Help Communities*, p. 10.

30. Gutheim, "Habitat: Toward Shelter," p. 5.

31. Blake Hughes, quoted in "The Vancouver Art Gallery to Present Four-Part Program During Habitat," press release, April 2, 1976, p. 2, CVA.

32. "The International Design Competition for the Urban Environment of Developing Countries Focused on Manila," July 22, 1975, p. 8. Document sent to participants, Archives of the Vancouver Art Gallery, henceforth VAG. For an example of Tondo residents' engagement, see Zone One Tondo Organization, *People's Participation in Urban Development Planning* (Manila: Zone One Tondo Organization, 1975).

33. Payer, *The World Bank*, p. 328.

34. The Wilson Center, "Wilson Center Experts: Aprodicio Laquian," available at http://www.wilsoncenter.org/staff/aprodicio-laquian. See also biographical note in *Architectural Record*, May 1976, p. 101, and Aprodicio A. Laquian, "The City in Nation-Building: Politics in Metropolitan Manila," PhD diss., MIT, 1965.

35. Julia Gatley discusses Athfield in "Counterculture Themes in the Growth and Development of Athfield Architects," paper presented at the Society of Architectural Historians of Australia and New Zealand, Gold Coast, Queensland,

Australia, July 2–5, 2013, p. 30.

36. Athfield's design report explained, "A sense of place must be strongly defined . . . hence the use of a strong physical barrier around the Barangay . . . within which are housed the industrial and craft workshops. . . . This barrier would be a 'working periphery.'" Press release, p. 2.

37. Ian Hogan, "Self-Help / Tondo, Manila," *Architectural Design*, October 1976, p. 594.

38. For the most comprehensive accounts and images of Athfield's scheme, see Seelig, *The Architecture of Self-Help Communities*, pp. 37–47; *Architectural Record*, May 1976, pp. 114–23; Joan Lowndes, "New Zealander Exhibits Winning Settlement Design," *Vancouver Sun*, May 31, 1976, p. 35; Mildred Schmertz, "The 'Tondo' Competition: The International Architecture Foundation's Competition for Squatter Resettlement in Manila," *Ekistics* 43.252 (1975), pp. 292–95.

39. Wolf von Eckardt, "Squatters: A Palmy Solution," *Washington Post*, June 5, 1976, p. B1.

40. Lowndes, "New Zealander Exhibits Winning Settlement Design," p. 35.

41. Schmertz, "The 'Tondo' Competition," p. 295.

42. "'You know, before ripping open the sealed envelope to find out whom they had chosen, everyone on the jury was convinced that a Filipino was behind the design,' said Mr. Athfield recently, having never set foot outside New Zealand until his proposed community, or barangay, was a star exhibit at Habitat." William Marlin, "Ian Athfield—Architect Thinks of People First," *Christian Science Monitor*, August 13, 1976, p. 19.

43. Paul Goldberger, "New Zealand Architect Flouts Rules," *New York Times*, June 22, 1976, p. 30.

44. *Ibid.*

45. Marlin, "Ian Athfield—Architect Thinks of People First," p. 19.

46. Mary Mountier, "Self-Help Housing," *Designscape*, September 1976, pp. 29–30.

47. The Universal Declaration of Human Rights, Article 25 (1) reads: "Everyone has the right to a standard of living adequate for the health and well-being of himself and of his family, including food, clothing, housing and medical care and necessary social services."

48. Blake Hughes to Alvin Balkind, chief curator, Vancouver Art Gallery, September 24, 1975, VAG.

49. "The Right to Build," interim report, September 15, 1976, np, VAG.

50. "Habitat Meeting at the Vancouver Art Gallery, Feb. 18, 1976 at 10 a.m.," VAG.

51. Recounted in "Notes from Meeting held at Kovach's Office, Feb. 6, 1976

at 1:45 p.m. to discuss the Habitat exhibition to be displayed at the Vancouver Art Gallery, May 31–July 4, 1976," p. 4, VAG.

52. *Ibid.*, pp. 3 and 2.

53. *Ibid.*, p. 2.

54. *Hearts and Minds* received wide visibility at Cannes in 1974 before its release was delayed by a legal suit bought by interviewee Walt Rostow. On the film, see Peter Biskind, "Hearts and Minds," *Cineaste* 7.1 (1975), pp. 31–32, and Bernard Weiner, "Hearts and Minds," *Film Quarterly* 28.2 (Winter 1974–1975), pp. 60–63.

55. Michel Foucault, *"Society Must Be Defended": Lectures at the Collège de France, 1975–76*, trans. David Macey (New York: Picador, 2003), p. 15.

56. Seelig, *The Architecture of Self-Help Communities*, p. 18.

57. Mildred Schmertz, "Habitat: The U.N. Conference on Human Settlements in Vancouver Was Hampered by Political Posturing," *Architectural Record*, August 1976, p. 37.

58. Seelig points to this as a benefit in *The Architecture of Self-Help Communities*, p. 18.

59. *Habitat: Toward Shelter*, exhibition brochure, VAG.

60. Lowndes, "New Zealander Exhibits Winning Settlement Design," p. 35.

61. Video recording of John Turner, "Housing the Poor," lecture delivered at Habitat Forum, June 7, 1976, University of British Columbia Archives, Centre for Human Settlement fonds, videotape 517.

62. Gutheim, "Habitat: Toward Shelter," p. 5.

63. See Bernard Rudofsky, *Architecture without Architects* (New York: Museum of Modern Art, 1964).

64. *Habitat: Toward Shelter*, exhibition brochure.

65. See, for instance, Barry Bergdoll, foreword to Jean-François Lejeune and Michelangelo Sabatino (eds.), *Modern Architecture and the Mediterranean: Vernacular Dialogues and Contested Identities* (New York: Routledge, 2010), pp. xv–xix.

66. The third prize went to Sau Li Chan of Malaysia, with four further designs receiving honorable mentions: Holl, Tanner and Cropper of San Francisco; Robert F. Olwell and Jim Fong from San Francisco; Hector Giron de la Pena and his team from Mexico; and Akira Kuryu and his team from Japan.

67. See, for instance, György Kepes, *The New Landscape in Art and Science* (Chicago: Paul Theobold, 1956), and Kevin Lynch, *The Image of the City* (Cambridge, MA: MIT Press, 1960). See also Reinhold Martin, *The Organizational Complex: Architecture, Media, and Corporate Space* (Cambridge, MA: MIT Press, 2003).

68. Seelig, *The Architecture of Self-Help Communities*, p. 108.

69. Maybe some of the nearly two thousand registered competitors who failed

to submit did so as a form of refusal, although I have not yet found evidence to this effect.

70. Charles Correa, "Wall-to-Wall Squatters," *Times of India*, May 16, 1976, p. 10.

71. Wagner, "Human Settlements," p. 95.

72. Mildred Schmertz, "From Slum to Community, from Despair to Hope," *Architectural Record*, May 1976, p. 96.

73. Aprodicio Laquian, quoted in *ibid.*, p. 96.

74. Schmertz, "From Slum to Community," p. 97.

75. *Ibid.*, pp. 99 and 98.

76. Robert S. McNamara, in "Comments by World Leaders," *Architectural Record*, May 1976, p. 158.

77. *Ibid.*, and Robert S. McNamara, "The Significance of Habitat," *Finance and Development* 13.1, March 1, 1976, p. 5.

78. Payer, *The World Bank*, pp. 22 and 21.

79. Clyde Sanger, "Filipino Protest Rocks Habitat," *Guardian*, June 7, 1976, p. 4. See also "Imelda Marcos Dodges Demo to Speak of Manila Squatters," *Province*, June 8, 1976, clipping, CVA.

80. "2,000 Seized in Manila During Habitat Protest," *Vancouver Sun*, June 5, 1976, clipping, CVA. See also Sanger, "Filipino Protest Rocks Habitat," and "Marcos Opponents Schedule Demonstration," *Province*, June 7, 1976, p. 25.

81. "Tondo Squatters Answer Back," *Habitat Forum News*, June 11, 1976, p. 2.

82. R. Rajaretnam, "The Philippines: A Survey for 1976," *Southeast Asian Affairs* 4 (January 1977), p. 189.

83. "Mrs. Marcos Defends Gov't Slum Action," *Vancouver Sun*, June 7, 1976, p. 41.

84. "Imelda Marcos Dodges Demo."

85. *Ibid.*

86. "Filipino Raps Gov't: Plea for Place to Live," *Province*, June 10, 1976, clipping, CVA.

87. Anne Harvey, "Press Reports of 2,000 Jailed False, Mrs. Marcos Alleges," *Vancouver Sun*, June 8, 1976, p. 16.

88. Wideman, "The Philippines: Five Years of Martial Law," p. 66.

89. "Imelda Marcos Dodges Demo."

90. "Mrs. Marcos Defends Gov't Slum Action."

91. See Geoff Payne, "International Agencies and Third World Development," *Architectural Design*, October 1976, pp. 601–603.

92. See Wurfel, "Martial Law in the Philippines."

93. *Symbol of the Compassionate Society: Imelda Romualdez Marcos, First Lady of*

the Philippines, four-page brochure, np, nd.

94. I am thinking of the argument made by Thomas Keenan in "Drift: Politics and the Simulation of Real Life," *Grey Room* 21 (Fall 2005), pp. 94–111.

95. As they explain, "This state of exception is inscribed in a temporality of emergency, which may become perennial through successive plans and missions, confirming the impossibility of reestablishing normal order, and in a spatiality of exclusion manifested in relief corridors and protected enclaves within territories that are no longer subject to a state monopoly of legitimate violence." Didier Fassin and Mariella Pandolfi (eds.), *Contemporary States of Emergency: The Politics of Military and Humanitarian Interventions* (New York: Zone Books, 2010), p. 16.

96. "Philippine Squatters and Martial Law Remedies," np.

97. *Ibid.* See also Aprodicio Laquian, "Habitat: The End of the Beginning?" *IDRC Reports* 5.3 (1976), pp. 12–14, where he indicates that the IDRC sponsored the participation of Tondo residents in the judging without noting that Herrera had been blocked.

98. Payer, *The World Bank*, p. 328.

99. Bernard Wideman, "Squatters: An Unsettling Problem," *Far Eastern Economic Review*, March 5, 1976, reprinted in "Philippine Squatters and Martial Law Remedies." Wideman was also a correspondent for the *Washington Post*, and his reporting on the Philippines made him a target of attempted censorship.

100. I am thinking here of the argument made by Hannah Arendt in "The Decline of the Nation State and the End of the Rights of Man," in *The Origins of Totalitarianism* (San Diego: Harcourt Brace, 1966), pp. 267–302.

101. "Prize-Winning Architect Reacts to Slum Protest," *Vancouver Sun*, June 10, 1976, p. 81.

102. Sanger, "Filipino Protest Rocks Habitat," p. 4.

103. Ian Athfield, quoted in "Prize-Winning Architect Reacts to Slum Protest," p. 81.

104. Mary Mountier, editorial note accompanying "Self-Help Housing," p. 31.

105. Mildred Schmertz defended the Tondo competition in *Ekistics*. Although Dagat-Dagatan was to her largely "ideal" as a "prototypical site for an international design competition," she was forced to acknowledge that problems ensued. See Schmertz, "The 'Tondo' Competition," p. 292.

106. John F. C. Turner, quoted in "Marcos Opponents Schedule Demonstration," *The Province*, June 7, 1976, p. 25.

107. *Ibid.*

108. John F. C. Turner, "Local Participation Lacking in Tondo Competition," *Ekistics* 43.252 (November 1976), p. 296.

109. Turner, "Local Participation Lacking," p. 297.

110. Turner did not organize the Self-Help and Low Cost Housing Symposium. Through Monica Pidgeon at *Architectural Design*, in 1974, he proposed a related program to Habitat Forum under the rubric of the Architectural Association's Program on Alternatives in Housing, Local Building and Planning, but they were informed that foreign initiatives could not be funded by the Canadian government. The symposium was organized by two recent graduates from the University of British Columbia: Bruce Fairbairn (a planner) and Charles Haynes (an architect). As outlined in a brochure, their stated ambition was to take advantage of the vast numbers of people interested in self-help and low cost housing who would be attending the conference in order facilitate meeting, information exchange and the establishment of an ongoing network or international association. *Self Help & Low Cost Housing Symposium: Program Guide,* Association in Canada Serving Organizations for Human Settlements, Association in Canada Serving Organizations for Human Settlements fonds (aka Habitat Collection), University of British Columbia Library Rare Books and Special Collections, henceforth UBC.

111. Alfred Heller, "The View from Jericho," *Sierra Club Bulletin*, September 1976, p. 12.

112. Joseph Handwerger, "Meanwhile, the Nongovernmental Habitat Forum Emphasizes Self-Help and Smallness," *AIA Journal*, August 1976, p. 44.

113. "Habitat Forum Symposium on Self-Help and Low-Cost Housing," *Ekistics* 43.252 (November 1976), p. 296.

114. Video recording of Turner, "Housing the Poor."

115. Rod Burgess, "Petty-Commodity Housing or Dweller Control?: A Critique of John Turner's Views on Housing Policy," *World Development* 6. 9–6.10 (September–October 1978), p. 1130.

116. Giorgio Agamben, "What Is a Camp?," trans. Vincenzo Binetti and Cesare Casarino, in Agamben, *Means without End: Notes on Politics* (Minneapolis: University of Minnesota Press, 2000), pp. 37 and 39.

117. See, for instance, the obituary note on Cusipag by Ted Alcuitas, Balita, August 2, 2013, http://www.balita.ca/2013/08/ruben-cusipag-pumanaw.

118. "Local Filipino Group Protests Arrest of Squatters," *Vancouver Sun*, June 7, 1976, p. 41.

119. William Marlin, "Helping to House Manila's Urban Poor," *Christian Science Monitor*, August 6, 1976, p. 21.

120. Marlin even cast the IAF as "unusually attentive to the indigenous cultural character and deeply felt concerns of the people in defining the guidelines in consultation with the distinguished design and development firm of Gutheim/Seelig/Erickson." *Ibid.*, p. 21.

121. Hubert-Jan Henket, "Cruel Habitats," *Town and Country Planning* 44

(September 1976), pp. 390 and 391.

122. *Ibid.*, p. 392. Henket's more romantic solution was to encourage decentralization and to facilitate the preservation of traditional forms of life.

123. *Ibid.*, p. 390.

124. "Conference Profile," *Jericho: The Habitat Newspaper*, June 8, 1976, p. 3.

125. Hogan, "Self-Help / Tondo, Manila," p. 594.

126. Payer, *The World Bank*, p. 407 n. 26.

127. "Slum Evictions in Manila Embarrass the World Bank," *New York Times*, October 7, 1976, p. 69. "'What they said was that the First Lady said there are some tourists coming and we must have the place cleaned up,' he said," another squatter recounting that they were requested to paint their houses. "'The next morning,' he went on, 'the captain came down with some police and the civil engineers and they said our house was being demolished.'" They were then forced to live on the sidewalk for five days before being taken by dump trucks and garbage trucks to the outskirts of the city, three hours away from their work.

128. Bernard Wideman, "World Bank Embroiled in Manila Slum," *Washington Post*, October 6, 1976, p. A3.

129. See Wendy Brown, *Walled States, Waning Sovereignty* (New York: Zone Books, 2010).

130. "Philippine Squatters and Martial Law Remedies," np.

131. Hobart Rowen, "A Deep Divide in the Philippines," *Washington Post*, October 16, 1976, p. A15.

132. Payer, *The World Bank*, p. 319.

133. Wideman, "World Bank Embroiled in Manila Slum."

134. Rowen, "A Deep Divide in the Philippines."

135. *Ibid.*

136. *Ibid.*

137. Payer, *The World Bank*, p. 321 and 324.

138. *Ibid.*, p. 333

139. *Ibid.*, p. 338.

140. *Ibid.*, p. 345.

141. Bernard Wideman, "Manila Slum Leader Detained and Tortured, Lawyer Claims," *Washington Post*, May 11, 1977, p. A15.

142. *Ibid.*

143. "Philippines Slum Leader Freed after U.S. Protest," *Washington Post*, May 14, 1977, p. A4.

144. *US Congressional Record, House of Representatives*, H11211, daily edition October 18, 1977, p. 34113.

145. Wideman, "The Philippines: Five Years of Martial Law," p. 66.

146. William J. Butler, John P. Humphrey, and G.E. Bisson, *The Decline of Democracy in the Philippines* (Geneva: International Commission of Jurists, 1977).

147. Richard Pierre Claude, "The Decline of Human Rights in the Republic of the Philippines: A Case Study," *New York Law School Review* 24 (1978), p. 215.

148. *Ibid.*, pp. 215–16.

149. Richard Pierre Claude, "Information Technology and Statistics," chapter 6 in Claude, *Science in the Service of Human Rights* (Philadelphia: University of Pennsylvania Press, 2002), pp. 100–25.

150. Wideman, "The Philippines: Five Years of Martial Law," p. 66.

151. See Claude, "Information Technology and Statistics." As Claude explained, by 1976, the Task Force Detainees of the Philippines (TFDP), an NGO founded in 1974 by religious leaders, had six thousand dossiers detailing the systematic violation of human rights in the extensive network of political detention centers in the country.

152. Claude, "The Decline of Human Rights in the Philippines," p. 216.

153. *Ibid.*

154. Noam Chomsky and Edward S. Herman, *The Washington Connection and Third World Fascism* (Montreal: Black Rose Books, 1979), p. 237.

155. See Payer, *The World Bank*, pp. 333–39 on evidence documented by Dieter Obendorfer, and "Revolutionary Ideas of 1972 Becoming Today's Convention," *Report: News and Views from the World Bank*, September–October 1979, pp. 1, 3, 6.

156. See Seelig, *The Architecture of Self-Help Communities*, p. 183. In his August 4, 2009 obituary in *Architectural Record*, "Remembering Blake Hughes, A Noble Publisher," Martin Filler indicated that the project "was never implemented by the regime of Philippines president Ferdinand Marcos, who preferred to build more grandiose monuments to his rule," available at http://archrecord.construction.com/news/daily/archives/090804blake_hughes.asp(subscription required).

157. On bare life, see Giorgio Agamben, *Homo Sacer: Sovereign Power and Bare Life*, trans. Daniel Heller-Roazen (Stanford: Stanford University Press, 1998), and Agamben, *Means without End*. On subjects refusing to be reduced to bare life, see Judith Butler's remarks in Gayatri Chakravorty Spivak and Judith Butler, *Who Sings the Nation-State?: Language, Politics, Belonging* (London: Seagull Books, 2007).

158. Kate Stohr, "100 Years of Humanitarian Design," in Architecture for Humanity (eds.), *Design Like You Give a Damn: Architectural Responses to Humanitarian Crises* (New York: Metropolis Books, 2006), p. 34.

159. *Ibid.*

160. Power, as Foucault reminds us, is not a given, but the "implementation and deployment of a relationship of force." Foucault, *"Society Must Be Defended,"* p. 15.

161. For a compelling articulation of such dilemmas, see Alessandro Petti,

Sandi Hilal, and Eyal Weizman, *Architecture after Revolution* (Berlin: Sternberg Press, 2014).

162. Etienne Balibar, contribution to Emily Apter, Thomas Keenan, et al., "Humanism without Borders: A Dossier on the Human, Humanitarianism, and Human Rights," *Alphabet City: Social Insecurity* 7 (2000), pp. 43 and 42.

CHAPTER SEVEN: DISCOURSE, SEEK, INTERACT

1. Lawrence B. Anderson, "School of Architecture and Planning," in "Report of the President, 1968," *Massachusetts Institute of Technology Bulletin* 104.3 (December 1968), p. 29.

2. On the federal government's understanding of the "urban crises," see Senate Committee on Government Operations, United States Congress, Subcommittee on Executive Reorganization, *Federal Role in Urban Affairs, Hearings, Eighty-Ninth Congress, Second Session and Ninetieth Congress, First Session* (Washington, DC: US Government Printing Office, 1966–68).

3. To make this shift clear, we need only to mention the founding of the Center for Urban and Regional Studies in 1957 and, two years later and in collaboration with Harvard University, the establishment of the Joint Center for Urban Studies. Moreover, in October 1966, the Department of Architecture hosted a conference entitled "Inventing the Future Environment," which brought architects together with economists, political scientists, planners, philosophers, social psychologists, and "futurists." The proceedings were published as Stanford Anderson (ed.), *Planning for Diversity and Choice: Possible Futures and Their Relation to the Man-Controlled Environment* (Cambridge, MA: MIT Press, 1968).

4. See Stuart W. Leslie, *The Cold War and American Science: The Military-Industrial-Academic Complex at MIT and Stanford* (New York: Columbia University Press, 1993).

5. J. William Fulbright, "The War and Its Effects: The Military-Industrial-Academic Complex," in Herbert I. Schiller (ed.), *Super-State: Readings in the Military-Industrial Complex* (Urbana: University of Illinois Press, 1970), pp. 171–78. Reprinted from *Congressional Record*, 90th Congress, First Session, December 13, 1967, vol. 113, part 27, pp. 36181–84. Today, Fulbright explained, "Our country is becoming conditioned to permanent conflict. More and more our economy, our Government, and our universities are adapting themselves to the requirements of continuing war—total war, limited war, and cold war." *Ibid.*, pp. 173–74.

6. Charles L. Miller, "Urban System Laboratory," in "Report of the President and the Chancellor Issue, 1973–1974," *Massachusetts Institute of Technology Bulletin* 110.4 (November 1974), p. 122.

7. Charles L. Miller, "Urban Systems Laboratory," in "Report of the President,

1968," p. 489.

8. *A Proposal to the Ford Foundation for a Program in Urban Affairs at M.I.T.: Report of the Ad Hoc Faculty Committee on Urban Studies* (Cambridge, MA: MIT, 1967), p. I-1. The initial list of relevant resources began with the School of Architecture and Planning and ended with the Lincoln and Instrumentation Laboratories. "We can and do bring together the city planner, the engineer, the political scientist, the economist, the manager, the architect and artists whose combined perceptions are needed on urban problems," the report explained. *Ibid.*, p. I-3.

9. The urban extension program ran from 1959 to 1966. "University Urban Studies" was dedicated to establishing "long-term intellectual resources" and was avowedly a response to the "social ferment in the nation's cities." See Ford Foundation, "University Urban Studies," *Ford Foundation Annual Report 1967* (New York: Ford Foundation, 1967), p. 35. See also Ford Foundation, *Urban Extension: A Report on Experimental Programs Assisted by the Ford Foundation* (New York: Ford Foundation, 1966).

10. *A Proposal to the Ford Foundation*, p. I-2.

11. Anderson, "School of Architecture and Planning," in "Report of the President, 1968," pp. 30, 31, 30.

12. Donlyn Lyndon, "Department of Architecture," in "Report of the President, 1968," p. 36.

13. Anderson, "School of Architecture and Planning," in "Report of the President, 1968," p. 31.

14. In the spring of 1967, as reported by C. Ray Smith, MIT students had "overnight turned one of their design studios into an instant *barriada* by subdividing it with salvage timber and concrete blocks." Although supposedly outraging the administration, this act of taking charge was in fact quickly incorporated and neutralized. As Smith continued, "the following Fall, Donlyn Lyndon, newly appointed head of the department, gained the administration's agreement for first-, third-, and fourth-year students to involve themselves officially in subdividing, building, painting, and personalizing all their design studios as a 'Space/Use Workshop.'" C. Ray Smith, "The New Interiors: Fad or Fact?," *Progressive Architecture* (October 1968), p. 154. See also Lyndon, "Department of Architecture," p. 34. Hans Haacke's Hayden Gallery exhibition included early systems-based works, such as *Skyline*, *Wide White Flow*, *Weather Cube*, and others. See "Haacke Exhibit Features Systems of 'Grass,' 'Ice'," *The Tech*, October 20, 1967, pp. 1 and 3.

15. Anderson, "School of Architecture and Planning," in "Report of the President, 1968," p. 31.

16. *Ibid.* On the history of objectivity as the aspiration "to knowledge that bears no trace of the knower," see Lorraine Daston and Peter Galison, *Objectivity* (New

York: Zone Books, 2010), p. 17.

17. Anderson, "School of Architecture and Planning," in "Report of the President, 1968," pp. 31–32.

18. *Ibid.*, p. 32.

19. "MITUSL??," *Tech Talk*, October 30, 1968, p. 1.

20. Miller, "Urban Systems Laboratory," in "Report of the President, 1968," p. 499.

21. *Ibid.*, p. 492.

22. Alis D. Runge, "In Search of Urban Expertise," *Progressive Architecture*, September 1969, p. 125.

23. *Ibid.*

24. *Ibid.*

25. *Ibid.*

26. *Ibid.* The Joint Center for Urban Studies had initiated "action-oriented" research, as manifest perhaps most famously in the development project for Guyana, Venezuela, or its investment in urban renewal in US cities. Yet unlike the USL, from which the humanities were largely banished, historical scholarship continued to play a role in the center's research. See Eric Mumford, "From Master-Planning to Self-Build: The MIT-Harvard Joint Center for Urban Studies, 1959–1971," and Ijlal Muzaffar, "Fuzzy Images: The Problem of Third World Development and the New Ethics of Open-Ended Planning at the MIT-Harvard Joint Center for Urban Studies," both in Arindam Dutta et al. (eds.), *A Second Modernism: MIT, Architecture, and the 'Techno-Social' Moment* (Cambridge, MA: MIT Press, 2013), pp. 288–309 and 310–41, respectively.

27. Jay Kunin, "Urban Lab to Aid America's Cities," *The Tech*, April 30, 1968, pp. 2 and 1.

28. Miller, "Urban Systems Laboratory," in "Report of the President, 1968," p. 502.

29. Charles L. Miller, "Urban Systems Laboratory," in "Report of the President, 1969," *Massachusetts Institute of Technology Bulletin* 105.3 (December 1969), p. 481.

30. See Jennifer Light, *From Warfare to Welfare: Defense Intellectuals and Urban Problems in Cold War America* (Baltimore: Johns Hopkins University Press, 2003), p. 165.

31. *Ibid.*, p. 167.

32. Miller, "Urban Systems Laboratory," in "Report of the President, 1968," p. 490.

33. *Ibid.*

34. *Ibid.*, p. 491.

35. Ad Hoc Committee for Urban Affairs, quoted in *ibid.*, p. 490.

36. The archives of the USL include a memo dated March 25, 1969, regarding a trip to Bedford-Stuyvesant in Brooklyn as part of this research.

37. Charles L. Miller, "Urban Systems Laboratory," in "Report of the President for the Academic Year 1969–1970," *Massachusetts Institute of Technology Bulletin* 106.2 (September 1971), p. 99.

38. Runge, "In Search of Urban Expertise," p. 129.

39. *A Proposal to the Ford Foundation*, p. IV-A8.

40. Miller, "Urban Systems Laboratory," in "Report of the President, 1968," p. 500.

41. *Ibid.*, p. 501. In "Progress Report on the Role and Utilization of Grant Support from the IBM Corporation," in January 1971, Miller reiterated this, adding the remark that "the computer is the most important research tool of the Laboratory" (p. 4). Massachusetts Institute of Technology, Office of the Provost, records of Walter A. Rosenblith, AC7, box 2. MIT, Institute Archives and Special Collections, Cambridge, MA, hereafter AC7.

42. "Urban Systems Lab Installs New Computer," news release special to *The Tech*, September 23, 1968. Massachusetts Institute of Technology, Urban Systems Laboratory Records, 1968–1974, AC366, MIT Institute Archives and Special Collections, Cambridge, MA, hereafter AC366. On the history and importance of the IBM System/360, see Paul E. Ceruzzi, *A History of Modern Computing*, 2nd ed. (Cambridge, MA: MIT Press, 2003).

43. "Urban Systems Lab Installs New Computer."

44. In 1968, the USL had five associate directors. In addition to Fleisher and Lyndon, there were Richard L. de Neufville from the School of Engineering, Jerome Rothenberg (Economics), and Ithiel de Sola Pool (Political Science) from the School of Humanities and Social Science and Mason Haire from the Sloan School of Management.

45. Aaron Fleisher, quoted in Miller, "Urban System Laboratory," in "Report of the President, 1968," p. 493. Fleisher does not cite CHOICE by name, but it appears with this title in Urban Systems Laboratory, *Directory of Urban and Urban Related Research Projects at MIT* (Cambridge, MA: Urban Systems Laboratory, December 15, 1968), p. 20.

46. Letter from Ithiel de Sola Pool to Charles L. Miller, December 18, 1967, Massachusetts Institute of Technology, Office of the President, records of Vice President Constantine B. Simonides, AC276, box 29. MIT, Institute Archives and Special Collections, Cambridge, MA, hereafter AC276. See also memorandum from Leonard J. Fein to Ithiel Pool, "Proposal for MIT Relationship to the Boston Model Cities Program," December 14, 1967, AC276. On the Model Cities

Program, see Jennifer Light, "Taking Games Seriously," *Technology and Culture* 49.2 (April 2008), pp. 347–75.

47. See Light, *From Warfare to Welfare*, especially chapter 6, "Cable as a Cold War Technology."

48. This appears to be an outgrowth of research entitled ADMINS that Pool had previously undertaken in the USL. The 1968 *Directory of Urban and Urban Related Research Projects at MIT* lists ADMINS as an "experiment in computer methods for handling large data files in the social sciences" and notes that it was jointly funded by the National Science Foundation, the Department of Defense, the Advanced Research Projects Agency, and the Center for International Studies.

49. DISCOURSE was initiated with Porter's PhD thesis under Fleischer and Kevin Lynch. The project was under the general direction of Fleischer, with Katherine Lloyd and others working on the computer system design. See William Porter, Katherine Lloyd, and Aaron Fleisher, "DISCOURSE: A Language and System for Computer-Assisted City Design," in Gary T. Moore (ed.), *Emerging Methods in Environmental Design and Planning: Proceedings of The Design Methods Group First International Conference* (Cambridge, MA: MIT Press, 1968), pp. 92–104.

50. Donlyn Lyndon, quoted in Miller, "Urban Systems Laboratory," in "Report of the President, 1968," p. 497. The VSTOL research was under the supervision of Edward B. Allen; the Communication in Urban Problem Solving program was directed by Donlyn Lyndon and Marvin Manheim. The 1968 USL *Directory of Urban and Urban Related Research Projects at MIT* indicates that five additional projects were being conducted under the USL: Psychology of Place and Movement by John Myer; the establishment of a Group for Research in Environmental Design under William Porter and Robert J. Pelletier; Housing Issues in American Indian Communities by Chester Sprague, focusing on the Navajos; Building Design Issues Related to the Slope of the Ground by Waclaw Zalewski; and, the establishment of the Community Projects Laboratory by Myer and Porter, focused on low-income communities.

51. Dorothy Nelkin, *The University and Military Research: Moral Politics at M.I.T.* (Ithaca: Cornell University Press, 1972), p. 39. See also Committee on War-Related Research, "A Summary of War-Related Research at Draper Lab," AC276.

52. Miller, "Urban Systems Laboratory," in "Report of the President, 1969," pp. 480–81. On this time-sharing modality, see Nicholas Negroponte, "Toward a Humanism through Machines," *Architectural Design*, September 1969, p. 512.

53. Nicholas Negroponte, "The Computer Simulation of Perception during Motion in the Urban Environment," master's thesis, MIT, 1966, preface, np. Describing this new mode of research, he wrote: "There are no accompanying plans, sections, elevations, or models. The research has compelled me to become

more involved with the university and delve into other disciplines, some of them rarely associated with architecture." *Ibid.* On Negroponte's background in computing, see Negroponte (ed.), *Computer Aids to Design and Architecture* (New York: Mason and Lipscome, 1975), p. 8.

54. Nicholas Negroponte and Leon Groisser, *URBAN2* (Cambridge, MA: IBM Scientific Center, 1967), np. Emphasis in original.

55. *Ibid.*, np.

56. Jonathan Barnett, "Glass Box and Black Box," *Architectural Record*, July 1968, p. 127. See also: Nicholas Negroponte and L. B. Groisser, "URBAN5," *Ekistics* 24.142 (September 1967), pp. 289–91; Nicholas Negroponte and L. B. Groisser, "URBAN5: An On-line Urban Design Partner," in *IBM Report, 320–2012* (Cambridge, MA: IBM, 1967); Nicholas Negroponte, "URBAN5: An Experimental Urban Design Partner," in Murray Milne (ed.), *Computer Graphics in Architecture and Design* (New Haven: Yale School of Architecture, 1968).

57. Lyndon, "Department of Architecture," in "Report of the President, 1968," p. 497.

58. Nicholas Negroponte and Leon Groisser, "URBAN5: A Machine That Discusses Urban Design," in Gary T. Moore (ed.), *Emerging Methods in Environmental Design and Planning: Proceedings of The Design Methods Group First International Conference* (Cambridge, MA: MIT Press, 1970), p. 112.

59. Negroponte, in *Computer Aids to Design and Architecture*, p. 8.

60. Negroponte and Groisser, "URBAN5: A Machine That Discusses Urban Design," pp. 105–14.

61. Anderson, "School of Architecture and Planning," in "Report of the President, 1969," p. 34.

62. Runge, "In Search of Urban Expertise," p. 128. In a 1971 application to the National Science Foundation, the ArcMac group explained: "The academic year of 1968–1969 saw a dramatic transition of our basic attitude. Rather than cramming descriptions of the real world into the machine, we began to emphasize providing machines with interfaces to that world." They also note the importance of the founding of the USL and the Ford Foundation grant that was "able to sponsor a series of experiments in linguistics, self-organizing controllers, and machine vision." Nicholas Negroponte and Leon Groisser, *Computer Aids to Participatory Architecture* (Cambridge, MA: Massachusetts Institute of Technology, 1971), pp. 60–61, 60.

63. Charles Miller, "Urban System Laboratory," in "Report of the President for the Academic Year 1969–1970," *Massachusetts Institute of Technology Bulletin* 106.2 (September 1971), p. 100.

64. Negroponte, *Computer Aids to Design and Architecture*, p. 10.

65. Runge, "In Search of Urban Expertise," p. 129. As she presciently concluded of ArcMac: "if, as prognosticators of the future tell us, the day is coming when every man will have a computer terminal in his office and/or home, such efforts are building tools that may one day be accessible to all architects." Negroponte described these projects in Nicholas Negroponte, *The Architecture Machine: Toward a More Human Environment* (Cambridge, MA: MIT Press, 1970).

66. Runge, "In Search of Urban Expertise," p. 126.

67. Negroponte, "The Architecture Machine," *Architectural Design*, September 1969, p. 510.

68. Negroponte, "Toward a Humanism through Machines," pp. 511 and 512. This previously appeared in the April 1969 issue of *Technology Review*.

69. Nicholas Negroponte, "Concerning Responsive Architecture," in Edward Allen (ed.), *The Responsive House* (Cambridge, MA: MIT Press, 1974), pp. 302 and 303. See also Nicholas Negroponte, "Aspects of Living in an Architecture Machine," in Nigel Cross (ed.), *Design Participation* (London: Academy Editions, 1972), pp. 63–67. He later expanded on these ideas in Nicholas Negroponte, *Soft Architecture Machines* (Cambridge, MA: MIT Press, 1975).

70. Negroponte, "Concerning Responsive Architecture," pp. 303 and 304.

71. *Ibid.*, p. 305.

72. "Experiments in Computer Aided Design," p. 513.

73. *Ibid.*

74. Negroponte, *The Architecture Machine*, p. 56.

75. Nicholas Negroponte, "Five Experiments toward an Architecture Machine," *Research*, July 10, 1969, pp. 1–2.

76. "Experiments in Computer Aided Design," p. 513.

77. "La Ville Totale," *2000: Revue de l'aménagement du territoire* (1973), p. v.

78. Nicholas Negroponte, "Systems of Urban Growth," bachelor's thesis, MIT, 1965. A key "point of reference," as Negroponte explained, rehearsing the period's panic over population growth, was the question of populations, "generating a study of how populations live, what populations want, and primarily, how populations expand" (preface). The Architecture Machine Group drew upon Friedman's graph-theory design methods as set out in *Toward a Scientific Architecture* in developing the Architecture-by-Yourself project and the computer application for the self-design of habitations that they called YONA. See Guy Weinzapfel, "Report on Yona Friedman's Visit," *Architecture Machinations*, November 16, 1975, pp. 2–5; Guy Weinzapfel, "Architecture by Yourself," *Architecture Machinations*, May 23, 1976, pp. 5–9; and Yona Friedman, *Toward a Scientific Architecture* (Cambridge, MA: MIT Press, 1975), with introduction by Negroponte.

79. Negroponte, "Systems of Urban Growth," p. 76.

80. Negroponte, *Computer Aids to Design and Architecture*, p. 8.

81. *Ibid*, p. 10.

82. Nicholas Negroponte, forward to Friedman, *Toward a Scientific Architecture*, p. ix.

83. Yona Friedman, "The Flatwriter: Choice by Computer," *Progressive Architecture*, March 1971, pp. 98–101.

84. Jack Burnham, *Software—Information Technology: Its New Meaning for Art* (New York: Jewish Museum, 1970), p. 10.

85. Nicholas Negroponte, "The Architecture Machine Group, M.I.T.: Seek 1969–70," in *ibid.*, p. 23.

86. Negroponte, *Soft Architecture Machines*, p. 47. See also Nicholas Negroponte, "Semantics of Architecture Machines," *Architectural Forum*, October 1970, in which he notes, "Unknown to SEEK, the little animals are bumping into blocks, disrupting constructions, and toppling towers. The result is a substantial and continually changing mismatch between the three-dimensional reality and the computed remembrances residing in the core memory. SEEK's role is to deal with these inconsistencies" (p. 40).

87. Negroponte, "Aspects of Living in an Architecture Machine," p. 67.

88. Negroponte, *The Architecture Machine*, p. 57.

89. *Ibid.*

90. Nicholas Negroponte and Leon B. Groisser, "Computer Aids to Participatory Architecture," research project abstract, in Urban Systems Laboratory, *Directory of Urban and Urban Related Research Projects at M.I.T.*, 4th ed. (May 1, 1971), p. 49.

91. *Ibid.*, p. 13. Emphasis in the original.

92. *Ibid.*, p. 27.

93. See Paul Davidoff, "Democratic Planning," *Perspecta* 11 (1967), pp. 157–59.

94. Nicholas Negroponte, "Arts and Media Technology," *Plan* 11 (1980), p. 24.

95. Paul N. Edwards, *The Closed World: Computers and the Politics of Discourse in Cold War America* (Cambridge, MA: MIT Press, 1996), p. 144.

96. *Ibid.*, p. 120.

97. Greg Saltzman, "Urban Systems Lab: Social Work since '68," *The Tech*, May 17, 1974, pp. 2–3.

98. See "Universities: M.I.T. and the Pentagon," *Time*, November 7, 1969, pp. 52–53. See also Norbert Wiener, "A Scientist Rebels," *Atlantic Monthly*, January 1947, p. 46.

99. For a more detailed and general account of the protests at MIT, see Nelkin, *The University and Military Research*.

100. Runge, "In Search of Urban Expertise," p. 125. Nelkin indicated that MIT

faculty members had been administrators of Department of Defense research agencies, including ARPA, and that many, such as Pool, sat on advisory boards for the army, air force, and navy, as well as consulting for Pentagon and military contractors. A pamphlet from the antiwar faction—"Why CIS?"—cast this far less favorably, noting that "In addition to the official research projects, individual professors do a very substantial amount of consulting for the State Department, CIA, USIA, and other government agencies. There has been a long history of professors moving back and forth between the CIS and the government. Milliken, former director of the CIS, served as vice-director of the CIA. Griffith worked for Radio Free Europe, a CIA funded propaganda operation. Rostow, formerly of the CIS, served as national Security Advisor under Johnson and was responsible for many of the criminal policies pursued by the U.S. in Vietnam.... In addition the CIS has trained cycle after cycle of mandarins for the government. Military officers, State Dept. personnel and random other bureaucrats come to the CIS, study for a few years, learn new techniques of oppression, and return to their agencies with newly acquired skills." One-page typescript, no author noted. Appears to be from MIT—Students for a Democratic Society, c. 1972, AC276.

101. "Statement by President Howard W. Johnson on the Special Laboratories, October 22, 1969," MIT, *Institute Report* (October 24, 1969). Reprinted in Nelkin, *The University and Military Research*, p. 172.

102. *Ibid.*, p. 172.

103. Carson Agnew, "Notes on Conversion," *The Tech*, October 14, 1969, p. 4.

104. *Ibid.*, pp. 4 and 11.

105. Carol R. Sternhell, "M.I.T. Labs to Continue War Research, Says NAC," *Harvard Crimson*, October 29, 1969. See also Nelkin, *The University and Military Research*, p. 94.

106. Charles L. Miller, quoted in Sternhell, "M.I.T. Labs to Continue." Miller, Sternhell reports, was about to announce a $1 million Ford Foundation grant for converting the labs. She cites an NAC spokesman as saying: "This announcement of this grant for an illusory conversion is the apotheosis of M.I.T.'s attempts to head off our movement[.] Miller himself is down on the idea, both because he thinks it's a sop to radical students and because it is financially unfeasible."

107. Robert Reinhold, "1000 Stage a Peaceful Protest against War Research at M.I.T," *New York Times*, November 5, 1969, p. 18. On the November Action Coalition disruption, see also "Educator in a Dilemma: Howard Wesley Johnson," *New York Times*, November 4, 1969, p. 34; Robert Reinhold, "Police Disperse Demonstrators at M.I.T. Lab," *New York Times*, November 6, 1969, p. 26; Robert Reinhold, "150 Stage Sit-In as Protests against M.I.T. Research Continue," *New York Times*, November 7, 1969, p. 8; Fred M. Hechinger, "Colleges: Tension over

Issue of Defense Research," *New York Times*, November 9, 1969, p. E11. See also Robert Elkin, "Rally, Sit-In Protest War Research," *The Tech*, November 7, 1969, pp. 1 and 5, and numerous other articles in this issue of *The Tech*.

108. The Hermann Building, which housed the CIS, was preemptively closed and evacuated "because of the risk of violence." Reinhold, "1000 Stage a Peaceful Protest," p. 18. In 1971, the Hermann Building was actually the target of bombing, for which credit was taken by the Proud Eagle Tribe, "a revolutionary women's collective." The target had been William P. Bundy, a senior research associate at CIS and former advisor to President Lyndon B. Johnson, for his role in the escalation of the Vietnam War. See Bruce Schwartz, "Women's Collective Claims Role in Hermann Bombing," *The Tech*, October 19, 1971, pp. 1–2.

109. On Licklider, see Edwards, "Constructing Artificial Intelligence," chapter 8 in *The Closed World*, pp. 239–73.

110. John H. Fenton, "M.I.T. Group Assails Computer Plan," *New York Times*, May 7, 1969, p. 32.

111. Pool was part of an advisory committee of the National Research Council set up to encourage government programs in the behavioral sciences. In September 1968, the committee reported that "the behavioral sciences are an important source of information, analysis and explanation about group and individual behavior and are thus an increasingly relevant instrument of modern government," especially since, as the committee's chairman explained, "a very substantial portion of government policy decisions are directly concerned with the behavior of specific segments of the population." Harold M. Schmeck, "U.S. Urged to Rely on the Behavioral Sciences," *New York Times*, September 3, 1968, p. 16.

112. Ithiel de Sola Pool, "The Necessity for Social Scientists Doing Research for Governments," in Irving Louis Horowitz (ed.), *The Rise and Fall of Project Camelot: Studies in the Relationship between Social Science and Practical Politics* (Cambridge, MA: MIT Press, 1967), pp. 267–71. Quoted in MIT-Students for a Democratic Society, "CIS Is CIA," p. 11.

113. Greg Bernhardt, "150 Students Peacefully Disrupt CIS," *The Tech*, October 14, 1969, pp. 1 and 11.

114. "Demonstrators Protest MIT War Research," *New York Times*, October 11, 1969, p. 13.

115. COMCOM was developing "a model of the impact of foreign broadcasting on the Soviet Union, Communist China, and underdeveloped countries" and was used to "study the spread of news during the Cuban missile crisis." Joseph Hanlon, "The Implications of Project Cambridge," *New Scientist*, February 25, 1971, pp. 421–23, reprinted in MIT-Students for a Democratic Society, "CIS Is CIA," pp. 28–29.

116. Nelkin, *The University and Military Research*, pp. 110–11.

117. Howard W. Johnson, "Johnson Reports Draper Lab Divestment," *The Tech*, May 22, 1970, p. 5.

118. C. Stark Draper, "Charles Stark Draper Laboratory," in "Report of the President for the Academic Year 1969–1970," *Massachusetts Institute of Technology Bulletin* 106.2 (September 1971), p. 433.

119. "Johnson Reports Draper Lab Divestment," p. 5. The USL continued to play this PR role. See also Norman Sandler, "Lab Supports Efforts of Urban Researchers," *The Tech*, October 19, 1971, pp. 1 and 3.

120. "The Special Labs," *The Tech*, May 22, 1970, p. 4.

121. Committee on War-Related Research, "A Summary of War-Related Research at Draper Lab," four-page typescript, nd, AC276.

122. "Riot Police hit MIT Campus," *The Tech*, May 12, 1972, pp. 1 and 3.

123. The group outlined the charges as follows: "The purpose of the CIS, according to their most recent bulletin, is 'to conduct research which will contribute to the solution of some of the long-term problems of international policy that confront decision makers in government and private life'." They then continued, "The international policy of the US has long been to support fascist dictators (e.g. Spain, Greece, etc.); to suppress popular revolutions (e.g. the Philippines, Guatemala, Vietnam, and East Pakistan); and to engineer right-wing coups d'état (e.g. Cambodia, Argentina, and Indonesia, where 500,000 revolutionary peasants were massacred). We think that 'social science' research which aids this policy should be stopped. There is reason for this foreign policy: imperialism—the desire of a ruling class of bankers and businessmen in the US to extend their empire around the world. There is a reason why CIS exists: this same ruling class controls the universities and set up the CIS to help them build and preserve imperialism." MIT Students for a Democratic Society, "CIS Is CIA," p. 1.

124. MIT Students for a Democratic Society, "Why CIS?"

125. MIT Students for a Democratic Society, "End MIT's War Complicity," pamphlet, AC276.

126. MIT Students for a Democratic Society, "CIS Is CIA," p. 30.

127. The participation of Simulmatics in such research is confirmed in Philip Quarles van Ufford and Ananta Kumar Giri, *A Moral Critique of Development: In Search of Global Responsibilities* (London: Routledge, 2003). That Pool was unapologetic about this relation, as well as that between the CIS and the CIA, is evident in his rather alarming account, Pool, "The Necessity for Social Scientists Doing Research for Governments," pp. 267–80.

128. MIT Students for a Democratic Society, "CIS Is CIA," pp. 13 and 14.

129. MIT Students for a Democratic Society, "Why CIS?"

130. Hanlon, "The Implications of Project Cambridge," p. 422. "The project's leaders," Hanlon explained, "generally reflect the continuing military presence in the social sciences. The original proposal to DoD was written by Pool and MIT professor J. C. R. Licklider. Licklider was a staff member of the DoD Advanced Research Projects Agency (Arpa) and at MIT was connected with the Arpa funded Project Mac; Arpa is funding Project Cambridge. Pool has done counterinsurgency research for Arpa and he is a member of the MIT Center for International Studies, which was funded until 1966 by the Central Intelligence Agency. The present head of the project is Dr. Douwe Yntema, who was psychology group leader at the Air Force funded MIT Lincoln Laboratory." Hanlon, "The Implications of Project Cambridge," p. 422.

131. "Urban Information Systems: Report of M.I.T. Summer Study #2" (1968), AC7.

132. William L. Porter, "Laboratory of Architecture and Planning," in "Report of the President and the Chancellor Issue, 1974–1975," *Massachusetts Institute of Technology Bulletin* 111.4 (November 1975), pp. 162 and 163. In 1974–75, as Porter reported, the lab had a budget of "more than $480,000, mostly sponsored by the Department of Defense."

133. Nicholas Negroponte, résumé, in "Computer Aids to Participatory Architecture," p. 80.

134. See William L. Porter, "Laboratory of Architecture and Planning," in "Report of the President and the Chancellor Issue, 1975–1976," *Massachusetts Institute of Technology Bulletin* 112.4 (November 1976), p. 159.

135. William L. Porter, "Laboratory of Architecture and Planning," in "Report of the President and the Chancellor Issue, 1973–1974," *Massachusetts Institute of Technology Bulletin* 110.4 (November 1974), pp. 144 and 145.

136. "Welcoming Remarks made by Dean William Porter at the Open House of the Laboratory of Architecture and Planning, March 21, 1974," p. 2, Massachusetts Institute of Technology, School of Architecture and Planning, Office of the Dean, records, AC400, box 27. MIT, Institute Archives and Special Collections, Cambridge, MA, hereafter AC400.

137. Untitled five-page manuscript on letterhead from the Office of the Dean, p. 3, AC400, box 27.

138. See, for instance, Felicity D. Scott, *Living Archive 7: Ant Farm* (Barcelona: ACTAR Editorial, 2008).

139. Edwards, *The Closed World*, pp. 81–82.

140. Fulbright, "The War and Its Effects," pp. 175 and 176.

141. See Robin Evans, *The Projective Cast: Architecture and Its Three Geometries* (Cambridge: MIT Press, 1995).

CHAPTER EIGHT: DATALAND (AND ITS GHOSTS)

1. N. John Habraken, "Department of Architecture," in *Report of the President and the Chancellor, 1978–1979* (Cambridge, MA: MIT, 1979), p. 166. On these research programs, see, for instance, Richard A. Bolt, *Spatial Data-Management* (MIT, Architecture Machine Group, 1979); Architecture Machine Group, "Mapping by Yourself: A Multi-Media Paradigm for Computer-Based GeoGraphics" (Cambridge, MA: MIT Department of Architecture, Architecture Machine Group, 1977); John Carlos Correa, "A Personalized, Interactive Movie Manual," bachelor of science thesis, MIT, 1981.

2. See Nicholas Negroponte, "Arts and Media Technology," *Plan* 11 (1980), pp. 18–27.

3. Habraken, "Department of Architecture," p. 166.

4. "Alice in Dataland," *New Scientist*, November 15, 1979, p. 505. The title presumably refers to Ivan Sutherland's description of a computer monitor as "a window on Alice's Wonderland," as for instance in "Computer Displays," *Scientific American*, June 1970.

5. "Alice in Dataland," p. 506. For a related account of Dataland, see "Take a Lesson from a Machine," *Popular Science*, November 22, 1979, p. 610, where the term "data space" appears.

6. Bolt, *Spatial Data-Management*, p. 17. Bolt worked with The Cambridge Project and joined ArcMac in 1976 as a researcher for the Spatial Data Management System.

7. *Ibid.*, pp. 22–23.

8. Habraken, "Department of Architecture," p. 163.

9. Nicholas Negroponte, "Media Room," *Proceedings of the SID* 22.2 (1981), pp. 109 and 110 n. 3.

10. Richard A. Bolt, "Human Interfaces for Managers," *Computerworld*, July 16, 1984, p. ID6.

11. Bolt, *Spatial Data-Management*, p. 12.

12. *Ibid.*, p. 10.

13. Architecture Machine Group, "Mapping by Yourself," p. 39.

14. *Ibid.*, p. 7. The term "entrainment of attention" appears on p. 19.

15. *Ibid.*, pp. 5 and 8. Emphasis in the original. See Walter Benjamin, "The Work of Art in the Age of Its Technological Reproducibility (Second Version)," trans. Edmund Jephcott, in *Walter Benjamin: Selected Writings, Volume 3: 1935–1938*, ed. Michael W. Jennings (Cambridge, MA: Harvard University Press, 2002), pp. 101–33.

16. Bolt, *Spatial Data-Management*, p. 9.

17. William Campbell Donelson, "Spatial Management of Data," master of

science thesis, MIT, 1977, abstract.

18. *Ibid.*, p. 8.

19. *Ibid.*, p. 5.

20. Bolt, *Spatial Data-Management*, pp. 14 and 16.

21. Bolt, "Human Interfaces for Managers," p. ID6.

22. *Ibid.*, p. ID1.

23. *Ibid.*, p. ID8.

24. *Ibid.*, p. ID7.

25. Robert Mohl, "Cognitive Space in the Interactive Movie Map: An Investigation of Spatial Learning in Virtual Environments," PhD diss., MIT, 1981, p. i.

26. *Ibid.*

27. Andrew Lippman, "Movie-Maps: An Application of the Optical Videodisc to Computer Graphics," *ACM SIGGRAPH Computer Graphics* 14.3 (July 1980), p. 33. See also John Free, "Through the Electronic Looking Glass into Living Pictures: Videodiscs Are Combined with Computers for Create-it-Yourself TV," *Popular Science*, August 1981, pp. 68–70.

28. Nicholas Negroponte, "The Computer Simulation of Perception During Motion in the Urban Environment," master's thesis, MIT, 1966.

29. Stewart Brand, *The Media Lab: Inventing the Future at MIT* (New York: Penguin, 1988), p. 141. See also, for instance, Lev Manovich, *The Language of New Media* (Cambridge, MA: MIT Press, 2002), p. 259. As is often noted, the idea for the Movie Map began with Peter Clay, then an undergraduate, who "movemapped" the endless hallways of MIT in 1978.

30. Brand, *The Media Lab*, p. 42.

31. *Ibid.*, p. 213.

32. Paul Virilio, "The Overexposed City," trans. Astrid Hustvedt, in *Zone 1/2: The Contemporary City* (New York: Zone Books, 1986), p. 17.

33. *Ibid.*, p. 16.

34. *Ibid.*, p. 18.

35. *Ibid.*, p. 30.

36. *Ibid.*

37. Paul Virilio, *War and Cinema: The Logistics of Perception*, trans. Patrick Camiller (New York: Verso, 1989), p. 87. The term "perceptual arsenal" appears on p. 9.

38. *Ibid.*, p. 87.

39. Contract No. MDA-903-78-C-0039.

40. Andrew Lippman, quoted by Michael Naimark, "Aspen the Verb: Musings on Heritage and Virtuality," *Presence: Teleoperators and Virtual Environments* 15.3 (June 2006), p. 331.

41. See Alvin Shuster, "Israelis Say the Hijackers Included Key Guerrillas," *New York Times*, July 6, 1976, p. 3. The literature on the Entebbe raid is extensive and inconsistent and includes extensive press coverage during the event. See, for instance, Steven Carol, "The Entebbe Affair," in *From Jerusalem to the Lion of Judah and Beyond: Israel's Foreign Policy in East Africa* (Bloomington, IN: IUniverse, 2012), pp. 253–60, and Yesha'yahu Ben-Porat, Eitan Haber, and Zeev Schiff, *Entebbe Rescue*, trans. Louis Williams (New York: Delacorte Press, 1977).

42. On Solel Boneh's work in Africa, see Ayala Levin, "Exporting Zionism: Architectural Modernism in Israeli-African Technical Cooperation, 1958–1973," PhD diss., Columbia University, 2015.

43. This is noted in Simon Dunstan, *Israel's Lighting Strike: The Raid on Entebbe 1976* (Oxford: Osprey Publishing, 2009), p. 28.

44. "The Rescue: 'We Do the Impossible,'" *Time*, July 12, 1976. See also Kathleen Teltsch, "Rescue by Israel Acclaimed by U.S. at Debate in U.N.," *New York Times*, July 13, 1976, pp. 1 and 4. Teltsch quotes William W. Scranton, US chief delegate: "the Government of Israel invoked one of the most remarkable rescue missions in history, a combination of guts and brains that has seldom if ever been surpassed. It electrified millions everywhere, and I confess I was one of them."

45. On the race to make films on the subject, see Robert D. McFadden, "6 Film Studios Vie over Entebbe Raid," *New York Times*, July 26, 1976, p. 30.

46. See, for instance, Francis Anthony Boyle, "Part Two: International Law in Time of Crisis from the Entebbe Raid to the Hostages Convention," in Boyle, *World Politics and International Law* (Durham: Duke University Press, 1985), pp. 77–170.

47. ArcMac's Movie Map system was not the first use of computer-generated images to simulate movement. It was preceded by a system developed by Perceptronics, who produced a movie map "for the fictitious town of Dar-El-Mara." See Donald S. Ciccone, Betty Landee, and Gershon Weltman, *Use of Computer-Generated Movie Maps to Improve Tactical Map Performance* (Woodland Hills, CA: Perceptronics, 1978). According to Mohl, this was not interactive, like the Aspen Movie Map, and used primitive graphics, without the photographic input from a real site. See also Nicholas Negroponte, *Being Digital* (New York: Alfred A. Knopf, 1995), pp. 108–109.

48. Lippman, quoted cited in Naimark, "Aspen the Verb," p. 331.

49. See Mohl, "Cognitive Space in the Interactive Movie Map," p. 72.

50. *Ibid.*, p. 14. See also Lippman, "Movie-Maps."

51. Lippman, "Movie-Maps," p. 36. See also Michael Naimark, "A 3D Moviemap and a 3D Panorama," *SPIE Proceedings* 3012, "Stereoscopic Displays and Virtual Reality Systems IV" (May 15, 1997), p. 297.

52. Since travel was filmed in both directions, and since the vehicle traveled

down the center of the street, seeing "backward" could be achieved simply by running the film from the front camera in reverse.

53. Mohl, "Cognitive Space in the Interactive Movie Map," pp. 17–25, 43–48, 78–79.

54. Walter Bender, "Computer Animation via Optical Video Disc," master of science thesis, MIT, 1980, pp. 21 and 20.

55. Lippman, "Movie-Maps," pp. 37 and 39.

56. Bender, "Computer Animation via Optical Video Disc," p. 39. As he explained, "Each frame is generated on a Ramtek 9200 frame buffer, then recorded on 35mm film off a Matrix Color Graphics Camera. The film is subsequently transferred to optical video disc."

57. *Ibid.*, p. 22.

58. *Ibid.*, p. 30.

59. Mohl, "Cognitive Space in the Interactive Movie Map," p. 27.

60. *Ibid.*, pp. 82–83 and 91.

61. Lippman, "Movie-Maps," p. 33.

62. *Ibid.*, p. 37. On the process of photographing the facades, see Mohl, "Cognitive Space in the Interactive Movie Map," pp. 37–38.

63. Mohl, "Cognitive Space in the Interactive Movie Map," p. 84.

64. Virilio, "The Overexposed City," p. 18.

65. See Naimark, "Aspen the Verb," p. 331, and Mohl, "Cognitive Space in the Interactive Movie Map," p. 37.

66. Mohl, "Cognitive Space in the Interactive Movie Map," p. 58.

67. Lippman, "Movie-Maps," p. 33.

68. Negroponte, *Being Digital*, p. 67.

69. *Ibid.*, pp. 103 and 67.

70. Negroponte, "Arts and Media Technology," p. 20.

71. "Hollywood reruns," Bender explained, "are being transferred to disc, and sold at prices which undercut the costs of blackmarket and home-recorded video taped versions." Bender, "Computer Animation via Optical Video Disc," p. 6.

72. Negroponte, "Arts and Media Technology," p. 20.

73. Bender, "Computer Animation via Optical Video Disc," p. 6; Lippman, "Movie-Maps," p. 42.

74. Robert Abel, quoted in Bill Steigerwald, "Videodisc: Ultimate Weapon of Video Revolution?," *Los Angeles Times*, March 24, 1981, pp. H1 and H4. The article positioned their work as highly "futuristic," lamenting, however, that for the moment, "video revolutionaries must content themselves with discs of '1941' and Grateful Dead concerts." *Ibid.*, p. 4.

75. Bender, "Computer Animation via Optical Video Disc," pp. 7 and 8.

76. Negroponte, "Arts and Media Technology," p. 20.

77. Mohl, "Cognitive Space in the Interactive Movie Map," p. 7.

78. Negroponte, "Arts and Media Technology," p. 24.

79. R.A. Bolt, et al., *Computer Mediated Inter- and Intra-Personal Communication* (Cambridge, MA: MIT, Department of Architecture, Architecture Machine Group, 1976), p. 27.

80. Bolt, *Spatial Data-Management*, p. 5.

81. Brand, *The Media Lab*, p. 18. Brand championed Ronald Reagan for deregulating communications.

82. Friedrich A. Kittler, *Gramophone, Film, Typewriter*, trans. Geoffrey Winthrop-Young and Michael Wutz (Stanford: Stanford University Press, 1999), pp. 1 and 2.

83. *Ibid.*, p. 1.

84. *Ibid.*, p. 14.

85. Mohl, "Cognitive Space in the Interactive Movie Map," p. 196.

86. *Ibid.*, p. 83.

87. *Ibid.*, p. 196.

88. *Ibid.*, p. 92.

89. Lippman, "Movie-Maps," p. 32.

90. *Ibid.*, p. 33.

91. Mohl, "Cognitive Space in the Interactive Movie Map," p. 80.

92. *Ibid.* Mohl notes that they also tested the ROMPAMS body-tracking device and voice-input systems.

93. Bender, "Computer Animation via Optical Video Disc," p. 22.

94. Mohl, "Cognitive Space in the Interactive Movie Map," pp. 79 and 88. Quotes from p. 88 inverted.

95. *Ibid.*, p. 93.

96. *Ibid.*, p. 97.

97. *Ibid.*, p. 88.

98. Kittler, *Gramophone, Film, Typewriter*, p. 12.

99. Lippman, "Movie-Maps," p. 39. On the anamorphic system, see also Mohl, "Cognitive Space in the Interactive Movie Map," p. 189.

100. Mohl, "Cognitive Space in the Interactive Movie Map," p. 121.

101. *Ibid.*, pp. 2, 4, 5.

102. *Ibid.*, p. 2.

103. Mohl and his research associates adopted Lynch's interview technique, in which responses were written and tape-recorded and subjects were asked to draw maps from memory of the town and its main features and landmarks. Mohl acknowledged that theories of cognitive mapping were then very much in

fashion, and he traced the contours of a field divided "between those that model the experiential component of way-finding and those that address the function of navigational aides like maps," proposing that the Movie Map could offer a synthetic answer. *Ibid.*, p. 6.

104. *Ibid.*, p. 108. Kevin Lynch, *The Image of the City* (Cambridge, MA: MIT Press, 1960). Kepes went on to found the Center for Advanced Visual Studies, or CAVS, in 1967. Negroponte also situated his 1966 thesis experiments with altering perception through film in the lineage of Lynch and Kepes. Using a 16-millimeter camera, he tested varying shooting speed in order to speed up apparent playback velocity—a technique producing, as he put it a "slapstick" effect, heralding the later roadrunner effect of the movie map—and, for comparison, he used a still camera to attempt to simulate paradigms of human attentiveness to particular objects.

105. Mohl, "Cognitive Space in the Interactive Movie Map," p. 108.

106. *Ibid.*, p. 108. Drawing on Lynch's work, Kuipers's dissertation presented a computer model called TOUR, a device to investigate cognitive maps in humans. Discovering that his postdoctoral work on cognitive mapping at MIT, funded by DARPA, was of interest to military agencies on account of its potential contribution to war, Kuipers took a stand against military funding for computer science, refusing to accept it on pacifist grounds. See Benjamin Jack Kuipers, "Representing Knowledge of Large-Scale Space," PhD diss., MIT, 1977, published in 1977 as *Technical Report 418* of the MIT Artificial Intelligence Laboratory.

107. See Mohl, "Cognitive Space in the Interactive Movie Map," p. 109, and Alexander W. Siegel and Sheldon H. White, "The Development of Spatial Representations of Large-Scale Environments," *Advances in Child Development and Behavior* 10 (1975), pp. 9–55. See also Michel Foucault, "Different Spaces," trans. Robert Hurley, in *Michel Foucault: Aesthetics, Method, and Epistemology*, vol. 2 of *Essential Works of Foucault, 1954–1984*, ed. James D. Faubion (New York: New Press, 1998), pp. 175–85.

108. Mohl, "Cognitive Space in the Interactive Movie Map," p. 182.

109. *Ibid.*, p. 106.

110. *Ibid.*, p. 128.

111. To do this, he used four groups of test subjects—longtime residents of Aspen, first-time visitors to Aspen, Movie Map travelers with no experience of Aspen, and Movie Map travelers who subsequently visited Aspen for the first time. *Ibid.*, p. 129.

112. *Ibid.*, pp. 156 and 157.

113. *Ibid.*, p. 167. "One response was that by the second day or so, 'the reality of Aspen became a fact,' replacing the movie map version," even if "residual

recollections from the move [sic] map cropped up much later." *Ibid.*, p. 177.

114. *Ibid.*, p. 172.

115. Fredric Jameson, "The Cultural Logic of Late Capitalism," in Jameson, *Postmodernism, Or the Cultural Logic of Late Capitalism* (Durham: Duke University Press, 1991). The text was initially published in *New Left Review* in 1984.

116. Mark Wigley, "Lost in Space," in Michael Speaks (ed.), *The Critical Landscape* (Rotterdam: 010 Publishers, 1996), p. 35.

117. Mohl, "Cognitive Space in the Interactive Movie Map," pp. 89–90.

118. *Ibid.*, p. 98.

119. *Ibid.*, p. 96.

120. *Ibid.*

121. *Ibid.*, p. 97.

122. *Ibid.*, p. 99.

123. *Ibid.*, p. 101.

124. *Ibid.*, pp. 152 and 154.

125. Thomas Keenan, *Fables of Responsibility: Aberrations and Predicaments in Ethics and Politics* (Stanford: Stanford University Press, 1997), p. 121.

126. See Gilles Deleuze, "What Is an Event?," in Deleuze, *The Fold: Leibniz and the Baroque*, trans. Tom Conley (Minneapolis: University of Minnesota Press, 1992).

127. Michael Naimark, "Place Runs Deep: Virtuality, Place and Indigenousness," Virtual Museums Symposium, ARCH Foundation, Salzburg, Austria, 1998, available at http://www.naimark.net/writing/salzberg.html.

128. *Ibid.*

129. Richard A. Bolt, "'Put-That-There': Voice and Gesture at the Graphics Interface," *Computer Graphics* 4.3 (July 1980), p. 264.

130. The incipient militarism was rendered even more explicit in the "Graphical Input Techniques" research project of 1979. Undertaken for the U.S. Army's Research Institute for the Behavioral and Social Sciences, this "basic" research involved the design and testing of a graphics workstation that, with the aid of back projection, data tablets, and mirrors, allowed the user to "see through your hand." "Uses and benefits of the device," ArcMac explained, "are demonstrated by means of a set of games which simulate a situation where a user must interact with dynamically changing data and imagery." The first game, HIT, illustrated how the device might help identify targets for military situation analysis in a command-and-control station; the second, TRACK, was similarly conceived for moving targets; the third, DEFEND, was a combination of the former in which touching the first target caused others to move toward it. The foreword stressed the importance of "improving user-computer systems" due to the "increasingly complex battlefield," a task for

which interface technology, information management, and tactical data input and retrieval were regarded as critical aspects of improving "man-computer synergism." This was exactly the expertise ArcMac could provide, especially for battlefields and counterinsurgency operations where confrontations were not only between soldiers and insurgents, but between the city and its inhabitants, who had also literally become targets. See Nicholas Negroponte and Andrew Lippman, *Graphical Input Techniques* (Ft. Belvoir Defense Technical Information Center: MIT / US Army Research Institute for the Behavioral and Social Sciences, 1979), p. 6.

131. See Brand, *The Media Lab*, p. 49.

132. Negroponte, *Being Digital*, p. 66.

133. *Ibid.*, pp. 65–66.

134. *Ibid.*, p. 66.

135. *Ibid.*, p. 67.

136. *Ibid.*, p. 65.

137. Quoted in United Nations Security Council, *Official Records, Thirty-First Year, 1939th Meeting, July 20, 1976* (New York: United Nations, 1976), p. 1.

138. See Kathleen Teltsch, "U.S. Wants U.N. to Debate Hijacking as Well as Israeli Raid," *New York Times*, July 8, 1976, p. 4; Teltsch, "Uganda Bids U.N. Condemn Israel for Airport Raid," *New York Times*, July 10, 1976, pp. 1–2; "Hijacking in Reverse," *New York Times*, July 11, 1976, p. 123; and Teltsch, "Rescue by Israel Acclaimed by U.S. At Debate in U.N."; New Solidarity International Press Service, "The UN Security Council Debate on the Israeli Raid into Uganda," *Executive Intelligence Review*, July 20, 1976, pp. 24–26. For the reception of the Entebbe raid in the context of international law, see Boyle, "Part Two: International Law in Time of Crisis from the Entebbe Raid to the Hostages Convention"; and Tom Ruys, *'Armed Attack' and Article 51 of the UN Charter: Evolutions in Customary Law and Practice* (Cambridge: Cambridge University Press, 2010).

139. The French pilot of the hijacked plane also questioned Israel's story. See James F. Clarity, "Pilot Says Africans Didn't Stand In for Gunmen," *New York Times*, July 6, 1976, p. 4.

140. Moulaye El Hassen, representative of Mauritania, in United Nations Security Council, *Official Records, Thirty-First Year, 1939th Meeting, July 20, 1976* (New York: United Nations, 1976), pp. 6–7. In addition to killing soldiers and civilians and damaging Entebbe airport buildings, the IDF bombed landing strips and Ugandan aircraft, civilian and military.

141. *Ibid.*, p. 7.

142. *Ibid.*, p. 7.

143. Chaim Herzog, Israeli ambassador to the UN, in United Nations Security Council, *Official Records, Thirty-First Year, 1939th Meeting, July 20, 1976* (New York:

United Nations, 1976), pp. 7–8.

144. *Ibid.*, p. 8.

145. *Ibid.*, p. 16.

146. See Noam Chomsky, "Nightmare in Gaza," *Truthout*, published electronically August 3, 2014, at http://www.truth-out.org/opinion/item/25343-noam-chomsky-%7C-nightmare-in-gaza. See also Rashid Khalidi, "Collective Punishment in Gaza," *New Yorker* (2014), published electronically July 29, 2014, at http://www.newyorker.com/news/news-desk/collective-punishment-gaza.

147. Herzog in *Official Records*, p. 16.

148. "Statement by Mr. Jamal, representative of Qatar," in *Official Records*, p. 20.

149. Ambassador Kikhia, the Libyan Arab Republic, in *Official Records*, p. 25.

150. Kikhia, in *Official Records*, pp. 25 and 26.

151. Nicholas Negroponte, "Systems of Urban Growth," bachelor's thesis, MIT, 1965.

152. By the late 1970s, we might note, after experimenting with spatial-city paradigms in Europe and self-help housing in Africa, Friedman turned to developing manuals for self-help for UNESCO, including one that he prepared for the 1976 Habitat conference.

153. Nicholas Negroponte, "The Return of the Sunday Painter or the Computer in the Visual Arts," *Architecture Machinations*, May 2, 1976, p. 21.

154. There were many attempts to integrate art and technology during the 1960s, as is evident in the 1966 founding of Experiments in Art and Technology (EAT), Kepes's establishment of CAVS at MIT in 1967, and Maurice Tuchman's Art and Technology initiative at the Los Angeles County Museum of Art between 1967 and 1971, as well as other practices documented in Stewart Kranz's compendium, *Science and Technology in the Arts: A Tour through the Realm of Science + Art* (New York: Van Nostrand Reinhold, 1974).

155. Bolt, et al., *Computer Mediated Inter- and Intra-Personal Communication*," p. 252. Negroponte recalls his displeasure at the rejection of this proposal in "We Were Bricoleurs: Nicholas Negroponte in Interview with Molly Wright Steenson," in Arindam Dutta, et al. (eds), *A Second Modernism: MIT, Architecture, and the 'Techno-Social' Moment* (Cambridge, MA: MIT Press, 2013), pp. 794–809.

156. Negroponte, "Arts and Media Technology," p. 24.

157. Negroponte, quoted in Brand, *The Media Lab*, p. 11.

158. See, for instance, Alexander R. Galloway, *Protocol* (Cambridge, MA: MIT Press, 2004); Wendy Hui Kyong Chun and Thomas Keenan (eds.), *New Media, Old Media: A History and Theory Reader* (New York: Routledge, 2006); Thomas Y. Levin, Ursula Frohne, and Peter Weibel (eds.), *Ctrl [Space]: Rhetorics of Surveillance*

from Bentham to Big Brother (Karslruhe and Cambridge, MA: ZKM and MIT Press, 2002); Laura Kurgan, *Close Up at a Distance: Mapping, Technology and Politics* (New York: Zone Books, 2013); and Keller Easterling, *Subtraction* (Berlin: Sternberg, 2014).

159. Jacques Derrida, *Specters of Marx: The State of the Debt, the Work of Mourning, and the New International*, trans. Peggy Kamuf (New York: Routledge, 1994), p. 11.

CONCLUSION: PASSAGES AND PASSENGERS

1. See, for instance, Paul Virilio, *L'insécurité du territoire* (1976; Paris: Éditions Galilée, 1993), and Michel Foucault, *Security, Territory, Population: Lectures at the Collège de France, 1977–1978*, trans. Graham Burchell (New York: Palgrave, 2007).

2. Jean Gottmann, *The Significance of Territory* (Charlottesville: University of Virginia Press, 1973), p. ix. Gottmann outlines the multiple valences of the term territory: "To politicians, territory means the population and the resources therein, and sometimes also the point of honor of Irredentist claims. To the military, territory is topographic features conditioning tactical and strategic considerations as well as distance or space to be played with; occasionally it is also resources in terms of local supplies. To the jurist, territory is jurisdiction and delimitation; to the specialist in international law it is both an attribute and the spatial extent of sovereignty. To the geographer, it is the portion of space enclosed by boundary lines, the location and internal characteristics of which are to be described and explained. To the specialist interested in political geography, and I happen to be one, territory appears as a material, spatial notion establishing essential links between politics, people, and the natural setting. Under a purely analytical approach, the notion of territory would break up and dissolve into a multitude of different concepts such as location, natural resources, population density, settlement patterns, modes of life, and so forth." *Ibid.*

3. *Ibid.*, p. 14.

4. *Ibid.*, p. 5.

5. *Ibid.*, pp. 1–2.

6. *Ibid.*, p. 3.

7. Hence the proliferation of international institutions—the International Red Cross, the International Labor Organization, the United Nations, the International Court of Justice in the Hague, the International Monetary Fund, and so on.

8. Gottmann, *The Significance of Territory*, pp. 5, 131, 132.

9. *Ibid.*, p. 144.

10. *Ibid.*, pp. 144 and 154.

11. See Gerard O'Neill, "The High Frontier," in Stewart Brand (ed.), *Space*

Colonies (New York: Penguin Books, 1977), pp. 8–11. O'Neill's testimony to the US House of Representatives appears on pp. 12–21.

12. Paul and Anne Ehrlich, untitled comments in *Space Colonies*, p. 43.

13. Stewart Brand, "The Sky Starts at Your Feet," in *Space Colonies*.

14. See the Introduction.

15. Brand, "The Sky Starts at Your Feet," p. 6.

16. Stewart Brand, untitled comments in *Space Colonies*, p. 72.

17. Michel Foucault, "Different Spaces," trans. Robert Hurley, in *Michel Foucault: Aesthetics, Method, and Epistemology*, vol. 2 of *Essential Works of Foucault, 1954–1984*, ed. James D. Faubion (New York: New Press, 1998), p. 178.

18. *Ibid.*, pp. 176–77.

19. *Ibid.*, pp. 178 and 179.

20. Michel Foucault, *The Order of Things* (New York: Random House, 1970), p. xviii.

21. *Ibid.*, p. xix. For important readings of Foucault's 1967 talk and its relation to *The Order of Things*, see Daniel Defert, "Foucault, Space and the Architects," in Catherine David and Jean François Chevrier (eds.), *Politics-Poetics: Documenta X — The Book* (Kassel: Cantz, 1997), pp. 274–83, and Georges Teyssot, "Heterotopias and the History of Spaces," *A+U* 121, October 1980, pp. 79–106. Defert notes the relevance of Foucault's thinking to questions of colonialism and identity politics, a point I am trying to build upon with respect to the work's allusions to contemporary geopolitical concerns.

22. Foucault, *The Order of Things*, p. xv.

23. Jacques Derrida, *Specters of Marx: The State of the Debt, the Work of Mourning, and the New International*, trans. Peggy Kamuf (New York: Routledge, 1994). p. 169.

Index

ABDALLA, JUMA ORIS, 423.
Acconci, Vito, 362.
"Action Plan," for Stockholm conference, 122–23, 131.
Aesthetics, 93, 147, 324, 344; alternative, 112, 138, 207, 215, 258; of commune buildings, 74, 95; relative importance of, 37, 41, 147, 285–86, 334, 336, 348, 427; of Roche's designs, 64–66, 69; in self-built shelters, 296–298, 301, 304.
Agamben, Giorgio, 59, 164.
Agency, 31; self-built shelters and, 298, 321, 325; simulation of, 336, 419, 427.
Agrarian reform, 45, 246.
Agrest, Diana, 64.
Agriculture, 45, 175, 182, 246.
Aid: to developing countries, 26, 43; development, 23, 41, 44, 196, 222; economic, 229; foreign, 195, 252; humanitarian, 28, 146–47, 149–50, 199, 289; US to Philippines, 330–31; uses of, 23, 28, 70, 229.
Al-Arjam, Jayel Naji, 392.
Al-Hout, Shafiq, 231, 235, 268–71, 278, 322.
Algeria, 187.
Alternative conferences, to Stockholm conference, *see* Stockholm counterconferences.
"Alternative futures," Soleri on, 169.
Ami, Idi, 423–24.
Anderson, Lawrence B., 339–44, 353–54.
Ant Farm architectural collective, 143.
Antiwar protests: at MIT, 369–75, *373–74*; in Stockholm, *168*.
Antiwhaling activism, 121, 153–59.
Apparatus *(dispositif)*, 18, 30, 33, 69, 161, 341, 353; architecture's relation to, 18, 31, 67, 335–36; biopolitical, 112–13, 211; of ecological management, 158, 220–21; effort to escape grip of, 74–77; institutions of, 23, 231, 257, 264; tools of, 30, 110, 161; withdrawal from, 74–77, 111, 113, 164.
Appropriate Technology Village, Habitat Forum's, 248, 262.
Architects, 32, 286, 321, 349; attempts to address Third World problems, 284–85; *dispositif* of power and, 30–31, 38, 336; experimental, 360; in military-industrial-academic complex, 380–81; mission of, 324, 333–34, 339–40, 382; shelter competition and, 281, 288; at Stockholm conference, 205–209.
Architectural competitions, role of, 292.
Architectural Record: on shelter competition, 287–88; special issue on human settlements, 307–309.
Architecture, 70, 198, 340, 356; alternative, 300; ArcMac and Media Lab getting farther away from, 427–28; of communes, 93–95, 112; computers in, 23, 350-57, 358–59, 365–68, 380–81; computer-aided design in, 349–53, 355–57, 381, 383; contested image of, 20; corporate, 36, 70; as defense against environment, 18, 97; domestic, 29–30; high modernism in, 36; humanity becoming client of, 19–20; imbricated in *dispositif*, 11, 18, 30–31, 35–39, 335–36; influences on, 94–95; international style, 69; modern, 57; natural environment *vs.*, 26; pedagogy in, 35–36; politics and, 29, 321;

postmodernism in, 20, 95; power relations and, 20, 113; rejection of, 17–18, 91; research in, 350, 382; responsive, 357–58; roles of, 36–37, 67–68, 284, 382, 427; serving capitalist expansion, 70–71, 441–42; values of, 32, 37, 69; vernacular, 94–95, 206, 244, 300, *302*, 304–305.
Architecture-by-Yourself project, 362, 383.
Architecture Machine Group (ArcMac), at MIT, 23, 26, 350–55, *351*, *354*, *363–64*; concerns about, 366, 427; Media Room of, *386*, 387; projects of, 356, 383; Put That There project, *418*, 419; Spatial Data Management System of, 387–88. *See also* Movie Map.
Architecture without Architects (Rudofsky), 95, 206, 300.
Arcology, 205–209.
Arcosanti, 206–207.
Ardrey, Robert, 107.
Arendt, Hannah, 163–64.
Artificial intelligence, 355, 360.
Aspen Movie Map, *see* Movie Map.
Association in Canada Serving Organizations for Human Settlement (ACSOH), 238, 261.
Athfield, Ian, *320*; on Tondo protests, 319–21; winning self-help shelter competition, 294–97, *295*, 333.
Automation, 80, 206–207, 388.

BACK-TO-THE-LAND MOVEMENT, 9, 103, 117; values of, 74, 103–104. *See also* communes; Open Land movement; voluntary primitivism.
Balibar, Etienne, 15, 336.
Balkind, Alvin, 298–99.
Barnett, Jonathan, 352–53.
Bender, Walter, 399–400, *401*, 409.
Benitez, Helena Z., 218, 286.
Benjamin, Walter, 16, 56.
Bennett, Bill, *263*.
Bernadotte, Folke, 271, 426.
Bernal Space Colony, 435.
Big Data, 32.
Big Science, 23, 188, 340.
Biopolitics, 28–29, 161; apparatus of, 23, 25, 32, 70–71, 77, 112–13, 211, 285, 335; architecture in, 337, 382, 441; as control of people and environments, 28, 138, 165, 223, 240, 279–80; globalized, 244, 316, 441; regulation and, 43, 93, 111–12, 165, 298, 348, 440; withdrawal from apparatus of, 166, 211, 297–98.
Bodies, 95; relation to the land/environment, 97–98; in "wired" milieu, 388, 436.
Bolt, Richard, 384, 387–89.
Borders, 220, 432; envisioning lack of, 159, 251, 255, 314; life beyond, 12, 107.
Boyle, Godfrey, 209, 216.
Brand, Stewart, 13, 22, 27, 80, 101, 130, 145, 150, 159, 251, 407; accused of working with CIA, 177–78; Hog Farm and, 139–40; on Hog Farm's accomplishments, 140–43, 146, *160*, 161; on importance of "trying stuff," 9, 14; influence at Stockholm conference, 120, 132–34, *133*, 155–56; Life Forum at Stockholm conference and, 117–20, *119*, 131–32, 170; on outlaws and outlaw areas, 9–13, 23, 32–33, 390; promoting space colonies, 433–36; rejecting politics, 131, 137, 165, 178; use of media, 128, 138; values of, 12, 143, 177. *See also Whole Earth Catalog*.
Branfman, Fred, 175, 177.
British Empire, 59–60.
Building codes, 91, 248; lacking in Philippines, 297–98; used against communes, 77, 84–88, 87, 113.
Bundy, McGeorge, 41, 47–49, 70.
Burg, Josef, 233, 268.
Burgess, Rod, 322–23.
Business elites: influence on Stockholm conference, 125–27. *See also* corporations.

CAMBRIDGE PROJECT (MIT'S), 350, 369, 371, 375–78.
Camps: concentration camps, 181, 318, 323; connotations of shelters in, 149–50; internment, for displaced people, 164; as outlaw territories, 16; Palestinian refugee camps, 235, *236–37*, 273, 279; refugee camps, 16, 88, 150; resettlement camps, 16, 26, 182, *184*.
Capitalism, 23, 56; architecture and, 67, 95, 248; deterritorialization by, 256, 265; expansion of, 21, 70, 221–22, 291; Ford Foundation promoting, 42, 43, 70; global,

19, 280, 310–11, 329; ill-effects of, 59, 128, 178, 323; industrial, 59; influences on, 43, 84, 213; labor for, 28, 111, 310; neoliberal, 21; World Bank in expanding global, 310–11, 329.
Carver, Humphrey, 228, 265.
Center for Housing, Building and Planning, UN's, 240.
Center for International Studies (CIS, MIT's), 369, 371–72, 375–78, *376*.
Chaitkin, William, 93–94, 100.
Chemical agents, used in Vietnam War, 175, 180.
Chizea, Dora Obi, 200–202.
CHOICE program, 349, 356.
Chomsky, Noam, 180, 182, 187, 333.
CIA, 45, 347; Brand accused of working with, 132–34, 177–78; CIS's relation to, 375–77, *376*.
Citizens/the public, 225, 241; at Stockholm conference, 124, 127, 170.
Citizenship, Open Land movement and, 109–10.
City: changing model of, 30. *See also* urban areas.
Civil disobedience, *vs.* disregard of law, 110.
Civil rights, 25, 109.
Civil war areas, as outlaw territories, 16.
Civilians, in deterritorialized war, 175–76, 176–77.
Clapp, Al, 261–62, 263.
Claude, Richard, 330–32.
Client, architects', 41.
Closing Circle, The (Commoner), 171, 198.
Club of Rome, 125, 217; Forrester's World1 model for, 189, 192, 194; *The Limits to Growth* prepared for, 27, 188.
Cognitive space, 411–15.
Cold War, 13, 16, 42, 213.
Colonialism, 12, 275; economic, 42–43; effects of, 195, 199; legacy of, 218, 229, 242–43. *See also* decolonization struggles.
Colonies, as outlaw areas, 13.
Colonization, 152; Earth People's Park as, 142–43; of space, 432–34, *435*.
Commoner, Barry, 169; Ehrlich *vs.*, 167, 198–202; on environmental crisis as political issue, 170–71; at Environmental Forum, 199–200; on social justice clashing with ecology, 128–31.
Commons, efforts to maintain, 77, 83, 87, 113, 272, 439.
Communes, 9, 13, 79, 86; architecture of, 93–95; colonization of cheap land by, 102–103; criticisms of, 88, 207; hippies' fascination with kibbutzim in, 109; historical intentional communities and, 84; legacy of, 113; publications informing, 95–97; urban, 73. *See also* Open Land movement; specific communes.
Communication, 30, 95, 120, 132; in Ford Foundation's goals, 43; human-machine, 358–59, 366, 383–88, 387–88, 396, 402–405, 408; technological advances in, 204; technology advances in, 255–56, 362.
Community, Ford Foundation Headquarters as in-looking, 52, 54, 56.
Company headquarters, as outlaw territories, 16.
Computer-aided design, 349–53, 355–57, 381, 383.
Computers, 32, 436; environments controlled by, 367–68; Forrester's techniques on, 189, 192; in MIT's Urban Systems Lab, 344, 349–53; modeling by, 188, 427; Movie Map controlled by, 395–96; other uses, 378, 389, 406; people's interfaces with, 365–66, 408; in responsive design, 365–66; roles in architecture, 23, 355, 381 (*see also* computer-aided design); Systems Dynamics models by, 195, 198.
Conference on War and National Responsibility (1970), 176.
Congrès International d'Architecture Moderne (CIAM), 18–19, 93.
Consciousness, alternative, 80.
Convention on Ecocidal War, 170, 177, 182.
Corporations, 190; architecture for, 36, 70; development aid expanding, 196, 252; Green Revolution benefiting multinational, 45, 127; modernism as palatable to, 68–69; multinational, 60, 195, 252, 256–57, 280, 289–91, 311.
Correa, Charles, 307, 326.
Counterconducts, 21, 117.
Counterculture, American, 22, 73, 80, 110, 132; environmental consciousness of, 101,

128; ethics of personal responsibility in, 162–63; identification with Native Americans, 152–53, 162–63; influence at Habitat conference, 227, 258–59; "new tribalism" in, 94, 99, 101, 153; values of, 23, 74, 139. *See also* communes; hippies; lifestyles, alternative.
Counterdispositif, 138.
Counterinsurgency measures, 16, 47, 420; CIS and Cambridge Project in, 371–72, 375–78; ecocide as, 175–77; in Philippines, 289, 300; social-science research informing, 43, 377; US development and use of, 175, 178, 182–87; US strategy shifting to, 177; used in Third World, 187, 428–29.
Crimes against humanity, "ecocide" as, 175.
Crystal Palace, 56–59, *58*, 63–64, 66.
Cybernation, 95, 111.
Cybernetics, 190, 206–207, 356, 362.

DAGAT-DAGATAN PROJECT (MANILA), 291; Athfield's project not actually built in, 333; winning design of shelter competition to be built at, 288–89.
Dai Dong, 170, 177.
Dal Co, Francesco, 66, 70–71.
Data: gathering and generation of, 356, 358–59; gathering and generation of Movie Map's, 396–402, 409, 417; interactivity with, 383–87; tracking, 357–58.
Data management, 32, 247, 402; computers in, 23, 128, 204–205, 389; in DISCOURSE program, 349–50.
Dataland (MIT project), 384, 389.
Davidson, Sara, 97, 106; on Ford Foundation Headquarters, 50, 54; on Open Land movement, 73–74, 79, 107.
Declaration of the Vancouver Symposium, 243–44, 246–47.
Declaration on Human Rights, UN (1948), 122.
Declaration on the Human Environment, 122–23, 131.
Decolonization, 16–17, 27, 29, 44.
Defense, Department of (US), 368, 371–72, 377. *See also* military.
Deleuze, Gilles, 20, 31.
Democracy, 192, 256; US-led expansion of, 41, 42, 68.
Derrida, Jacques, 440–41.
Deterritorialization, 27, 60; by capitalism, 256, 265.
Developing countries, 17, 26, 126, 196, 245; calls for justice and self-determination in, 69, 125; effects of "Green Revolution" in, 45, 127; expansion of capitalism in, 23, 252, 291; fears about, 19, 44, 125; growing power of, 227–29; industrialization of, 240; legacy of colonialism in, 218, 229, 242–43; representatives at UN conferences, 218, 264; shelters in, 262; sovereignty of, 204, 314; West's desire for resources and labor from, 60, 83. *See also* Third World.
Development, 123; architecture's role in, 93–94, 305; effects of, 59–60, 316, 323; goals of, 246, 298, 310; narratives promoting, 23, 70, 246, 305; squatter settlements to be cleared for, 323–25.
Did We Save the Earth at Stockholm? (Stone), 123–24.
Dinkeloo, John, *see* Kevin Roche–John Dinkeloo and Associates.
Disaster relief encampments, 149–50.
DISCOURSE program, 349–50, 356, 378–79.
Dispositif, *see* apparatus (*dispositif*).
Dissent, effects on architecture, 35–36, 41.
Distributive justice, 22, 123, 138.
Do-it-youself, *see* self-help.
Domes: in Hog Farm's Tent City, 150; Now Houses', 251, *253–54*.
Donelson, Bill, *385*, 388.
Doxiadis, Constantin, 284; Ekistics project of, 93, 239–40; on human settlements, 126, 217–18.
Drexler, Arthur, 35–39.
"Dropping-out," 104–106.
Dubos, René, 124, 127, 153, 217–19. *See also* *Only One Earth: The Care and Maintenance of a Small Planet*.
Dymaxion Dwelling Machines, Fuller's, 248.

EARTH: AS CLOSED ECOLOGICAL SYSTEM, 128; photographs from space, 128, *129*, 219; view from the Moon, *430*.
Earth People's Park, 15, 143, 161, 164.

Earthwatch, 122, 128, 204–205.
East Pakistan (Bangladesh), 146.
Ecocide, 27, 172, 180; as counterinsurgency measures, 176–77; in Vietnam War, 22, 175, 180–81.
Ecological catastrophe, *see* environmental crisis.
Ecological interdependence, 125–28, 194, 219; spaceship earth as metaphor for, 126.
Ecology, 137; separating from political and economic roots, 157, 169; social justice clashing with, 128–31; systems-based, 100, 145, 158.
Ecology Action, 99–100.
Economic dependency, 229–30, 279.
Economic development, 196, 218. *See also* development.
Economic interdependence, 218.
Economic systems, 105, 157, 169.
Economy, 23, 59.
Edwards, Paul, 367–68, 381.
Ehrlich, Paul, 145, 194; Commoner *vs.*, 167, 198–202; at Environmental Forum, 149, 157–58, 200–202; on limited resources, 188, 200.
Ekistics project, of Doxiadis, 93, 217–18, 241.
El Hassen, Moulaye, 423–24.
Electronic battlefield, Westmoreland's vision of, 175, 185, 367.
Emergency, states of, 205, 235, 297; creation of outlaw territories in, 161; encampments associated with, 149–50; requiring drastic responses, 207, 307, *308*; as rule, not exception, 16.
Emplacements, 436–37, 440.
Encampments, *see* camps.
Enclosures: motives for, 38, 50; in Roche's designs, 38–39, 49–52.
Energy systems, 152, 222; alternative, 209; architecture and, 94, 251.
Entebbe International Airport (Uganda), 279; Israeli rescue of hostages at, 392–95, 420, *421*, 423–25, 428; model of, *393*, 395; UN discussing sanctions on Israel for rescue at, 422–26.
Environment: anxiety about, 19, 69, 77; architecture as defense against, 18, 97; built, 88, 93; in definition of outlaw territories, 16; electronic, 80; enclosures as conditioned, 38–39; humans' relationship with, 28–29, 83–84, 97, 379; influences on, 22, 178; insecurity of, 33, 74; politics *vs.*, 22, 171–72; responsibility for, 73, 115; simulations of, 352–53, 379; state of, 17, 122, 204; Vietnam's, 172–75, 182. *See also* Stockholm conference.
Environment Forum, at Stockholm conference, 177, 195; Americans and, 167, 171; Commoner-Ehrlich debate at, 198–202; purpose of, 124, 169–70; Soleri at, 206–209; Third World takeover of, 200–203.
Environmental control: computer-driven, 367–68, 384; enclosures and, 38–39, 50, 52; technology in, 343, 348.
Environmental crisis, 50, 69, 125, 171; causes of, 9, 117, 188, 198–202; impending, 121–22, 188; microcosms of, 100, 134; models of, 188, 194, 195; as political issue, 170–71; as security threat, 197–98.
Environmental damage, 99, 123; as cost of development, 23, 45, 196; as instrument of war, 175–76, 180, *183*, 187.
Environmental discourses, 21–22, 49, 123, 188.
Environmental management: apparatus of, 17, 158, 165, 340; Earthwatch gathering data for, 204; Hog Farm's, 118, 150, 161; Strong's vision of, 217, 220–21.
Environmental movement, 153, 178; shifting and tactical alliances of, 155–59, 170; Stockholm conference and, 124, 225–26.
Environmentalism, 32, 128, 223.
Environmentality, 17.
Erickson, Arthur, 287, 293–94, 298; photos of vernacular architecture, 300–301, *302*, 304.
Eriksson, Bjõrn, 209, 211, 215.
Ethics of care, 83, 98.
Europe, 26, 44; causes of dominance by, 242–43.
Exterritorial enclave, Open Land movement's attempts at, 109–10.

FAIRFIELD, RICHARD, 84, 97.
Falk, Richard A., 177, 180.
Famine, Liferaft Earth simulating, 143.
Farvar, Taghi, 200–202.
Faust, Joan Lee, 49–50.

Favelas, see squatter settlements.
First World, 16–17. *See also* West.
Fleischer, Aaron, 349–50.
Fõr en Teknik i Folkets Tjänst! (Toward a People's Technology), PowWow's exhibition of, 209–17, *212*, *214*.
Ford Foundation, 19, 45, 47, 60, 190, 213, 355; funding MIT's Urban Systems Lab, 341, 346; goals of, 41–47, 52–54, 70; Green Revolution and, 44–45, 127; influence of, 57, 60–61; as instrument of capitalist expansion, 60, 70; *Only One Earth* sponsored by, 124–25; UN and, 41, 61.
Ford Foundation Headquarters, 21, *39*, *53*, *55*; criticisms of design of, 60, 70; design of, 35, 38–39, 41, 45, 49, 60–61, 69; effects of working in, 52–56; garden of, 49–52, *51*; opening, 44; reviews of, 47–54, 65; Roche's goals for design of, 52–55, 69; UN Center's relation to, *62*, 63.
Foreign policy, US, 69.
Forrester, Jay W., 27, 186, 347; computer-based techniques of, 189–90, 192; models of, 192, *193*, 195; proposals of, 188, 190, 199.
Foucault, Michel, 17, 26, 42, 111–12, 165, 243, 292; on architecture, 30, 113; on emplacement, 436–37; on power, 28, 30–31, 113, 230.
Free trade, 59.
Freedom Farm, 73. *See also* Open Land movement.
Friedman, Yona, 284, 304, 360–62, *361*, 427.
Frontier mentality, in communal movement, 101–103.
Fuller, R. Buckminster, 38, 126, 247, *249*, *250*, 255; at Habitat conference, 247–56; influence of, 137, 147, 257; Now Houses of, 248–51; on outlaw areas, 11–12, 161; rejecting politics, 247, 255; on sovereignty as obsolete, 19, 265.
"Fullerian wealth sanction," 251.

Gaither Report, on Ford Foundation's goals, 42–44.
Galston, Arthur, 175–76.
Galula, David, 187.
Ganglands, as outlaw areas, 13.
Gelbspan, Ross, 117, 149.
"Getting Back to Earth" (Zwerdling), 115, 159.
Ghettos, urban, 16, 341, 348; INTERACT project and, 358–59. *See also* squatter settlements.
Giedion, Sigfried, 57–59, 64, 66.
Gilliam, Harold, 139, 155.
Global North/South, *see* North–South divide.
Globalization, 93, 108; architecture's role in, 441–42; neoliberalism and, 29, 36.
Goldberger, Paul, 66, 258, 284–85, 297.
Gottlieb, Lou, 80, 84, 106, 108; background of, 79–80; on benefits of Open Land movement, 91, 99, 101; charges against, 84–87; deeding land to God, 87–88, 100, 107, 111; expanding Open Land movement, 107–108; goals of, 79, 109; rejecting regulations, 98, 100.
Gottmann, Jean, 431–33.
Governance, tools of, 30.
Government, 36, 43, 77, 165, 252, 264; architecture as function of, 18, 29; art of, 29–30; exodus as response to, 104–105; Ford Foundation and, 44, 46; Morning Star Ranch *vs.*, 84–88, 101; outlaws and, 11; repression of Open Land movement, 107–108, 112–13; Stockholm conference and, 124, 170; urban crisis and, 328, 368; Wheeler Ranch commune *vs.*, 77–79; World Bank aid supporting, 311, 328.
Great Exhibition of the Works of Industry of All Nations, 57–59.
Green Revolution, 44–45, 95; criticism of, 126–27, 200.
GREET, 357–58.
Groisser, Leon B., 352, 353–55.
GROPE program, 355–56.
Group of 77 (G77, of developing countries), 23, 227, 229, 265; resolutions at Habitat conference, 274–77.
Growth, exponential, 27.
Guerilla insurgencies, 16–17.
Gur, Mota, *394*.
Gurin, David, 117, 149.
Gutheim, Frederick, 258, 283–84, 287, 293–94; *Habitat: Toward Shelter* exhibition and, 286, 298; on squatter settlements, 292, 299.
Gutstein, Donald, 231, 233, 238, 246.

HAACKE, HANS, 362–65.
Habitat, 19–20, 28, 87.
Habitat: The United Nations Conference on Human Settlements (1976), 21, 23, 121, 225, 230, 246, 264, 286; divisiveness over Israeli-Palestinian conflict at, 265, 274–77; efforts to cancel, 233; Fuller at, 247–56; G77 resolutions at, 274–77; goals of, 227–28, 240, 245; *Habitat: Toward Shelter* exhibition and, 283–84, 300; Israel's claims at, 266–67; lack of alternative voices at, 226–27, 231; lack of consensus at, 228, 265, 277; Palestinians' claims at, 278; PLO at, 231–33, *234*, 235; politicization of, 228, 231–33, 311; results of, 228, 277, 284–85; security at, 312–14; Third World participation in, 228, 280; trying to avoid politics, 274, 277; Ward's role at, 239–44. *See also* Habitat Forum.
Habitat: Toward Shelter exhibition, at Vancouver Art Gallery, 298–305, *302*, 304, 319; coinciding with Habitat conference, 283–84; lack of impact from, 287–88; layout of, 300–301; self-help competition generating exhibits for, 285–87; struggle over title for, 298–300.
Habitat du plus grand nombre project, of GAMMA, 19.
Habitat Forum, *224*, 227–28; alternative technology exhibit at, 216–17; Appropriate Technology Village and, 248, 262; focused on technical *vs.* societal fixes, 227, 245; Jericho Beach site for, 257–59, *260*, 261; lack of alternative discourse at, 226–27, 239; management of, 231, 238–39, 261–62, 264; merging roles of alternative conferences, 225, 259; participants at, 23, 225, 238, 239, 264; protests of Tondo resettlement plans and, 312–14; Self-Help and Low Cost Housing Symposium at, 321–22; self-help symposium at, 321–26.
Habraken, N. John, 383–87.
Haley, Mary Jean, 120–21, 134, 152.
Hanlon, Joseph, 377–78.
Hardin, Garret, 198–99
Harper, Peter, 209, 211, 215, 216.
Heald, Henry, 45–47.
Health/illness: diseases related to voluntary primitivism, 87, 98, 99; effects of contemporary society on, 98–99; effects of Green Revolution on, 45; state's role in ensuring, 79, 111.
Hedgepeth, William, 102, 106.
Heller, Alfred, 137, 262–64, 322.
Henket, Hubert-Jan, 325–26.
Herrera, Mrs. Trindad, 317, 319, 329–33.
Herrick, Chuck, 99–100.
Herzog, Chaim, 423–24.
Hickel, Walter, 153, 155, 157.
Hippies, 52, *92*, 109, 262; adopting trappings of pioneers, 101–103; colonization by, 102; as constituencies of outlaw areas, 12–13; "dropping-out" as option to dissatisfaction, 104–107; fear of invasion of UN conferences by, 134–37, 148–49, 238; identifying with Native Americans, 99, 100, 102–103; media coverage of, 84, 117; seen as threat, 104–106. *See also* communes; lifestyles.
Hirschman, Albert O., 105–106.
Hitchcock, Henry-Russell, 68–69.
Hog Farm, 73, 161; accomplishments of, 140–42, 146–47; Brand and, 139–42; development of, 138–40; free stage presentations at Skarpnäk, 153–59; goals at Skarpnäk, Sweden, 143, 165; "life shows" of, 159–61, *160*; Liferaft Earth of, 142–45; management by, 134, 161; politics and, 137–38, 140, 165; role of, 132; at Skarpnäk counterconference, 115–19, *116*, 134, *135*, 138–40, 149, *151*, 153; at Stockholm conference, 137, 159; values of, 138, 150, 159.
Hogan, Ian, 209, 326; on lack of alternative discourse at Habitat conference, 225–27; on Stockholm conference, 150, 171; on wall in Athfield's winning design, 294–96.
The Home of Man, commissioned before Habitat conference, 226, 239.
Housing, 190; affordable, 70; biopolitical function of, 232, 240–41, 246; demolition of Pruitt-Igoe project, 190, *191*; mobile, 248–51; to provide subsistence, not happiness, 291–92; as right, 298; as starting point of life, 280; traditional, in Philippines, 292–93. *See also* self-help; shelters.
Hughes, Blake, 286–87, 292, 298.
Human rights, 122, 146; denationalized people lacking, 163–64; housing as, 298;

violations of, 268, 275, 311, 329–33.
Human welfare, Ford Foundation on, 42, 45–46.
Humanitarian crises: encampments in actions by, 149–50; lack of housing as, 285–86
Humanitarianism: environmentalism and, 32; Forrester warning against, 190, 194. *See also* aid, humanitarian.
Humanity, 68, 148; becoming client of architecture, 19–20.
Hunger Show, *see* Liferaft Earth.
Huxtable, Ada-Louise, 35, 52, 56–57, 64–65.
Hygiene: in art of government, 29–30; lack of, 98–99.

IBM SCIENTIFIC CENTER, CAMBRIDGE, 349, 352.
Immigrants, Israel absorbing, 268.
Imperialism, 59–60, 148, 202.
India, 44, 145.
Indigenous people: appropriation of artifacts of, 152–53; opposition to Earth People's Park, 142.
Indochina, 29, 175–76; Ford Foundation sponsoring counterinsurgency measures in, 47. *See also* Vietnam War.
Industrialism, 83, 213; US profiting from expanding, 195–96.
Industrialization, 220; of developing countries, 195, 240; in imperialism, 59–60; problems caused by, 188, 195, 199, 242; Native Americans in Stockholm to publicize, 152; technology transfer in, 213.
Industry, 42, 190, 316; international exhibition of products of, 57–59.
Information: management, 436–37; revolution, 60; technologies, 95.
Information Age, intellectual property rights in, 113.
Infrastructure, 198, 279; squatter settlements and, 245, 293, 305.
Insecurity, 60, 128; of biopolitical apparatus, 112–13; causes of, 188, 283; responses to, 88, 221; of squatter settlements, 292, 316, 323, 329.
Instrumentation Laboratory (I-Lab, MIT's), 369; MIT divesting itself of, 372, 375; turning to nonmilitary research, 370–71.
Insurgencies, 16–17, 106, 187, 425; fear of, 33, 221, 336, 427; mechanisms to quell, 33, 289, 293. *See also* counterinsurgency measures.
INTERACT project, 356, 358, 366–67.
Interdependence, 14–15, 244, 315. *See also* ecological interdependence.
International Architectural Foundation of New York (IAF), 283–84, 298, 319, 324, 333; founding of, 286–87; promoting self-help solutions, 309–10, 315–16; self-help designs not challenging dominant narrative of, 334–35.
International Bank for Reconstruction and Development, *see* World Bank.
International Commission of Enquiry into US Crimes in Indochina, 172–76.
International Design Competition for the Urban Development of Developing Countries Focused on Manila, 283, 319; Athfield's winning design, 294–97, 295; *Habitat: Toward Shelter* exhibition of entries, 298–305; lack of impact of, 287–88, 334–35; specifications and background information for, 291–93, 324; vernacular architecture elements included in designs, 304–305.
International Institute for Environmental Affairs (IIEA), 125, 127. *See also* International Institute for Environment and Development (IIED).
International Monetary Fund (IMF), 327–28.
Internet, "ecological" systems on, 132.
Iraq War, 149–50.
Israel, 24, 266; acquisition of land by, 271–72; creation of, 271, 426; lack of cooperation with UN, 273–74, 279, 422; oppression of Palestinians by, 25, 268, 273; and Palestinian conflict at Habitat conference, 265, 266, 274–77; rescue of hostages at Entebbe, 392, 395, 420, *421*, 423–25; settlements of, *269–70*, 271–72; UN discussing sanctions for Entebbe rescue, 422–26. *See also* Occupied Territories, Palestinians'.
Izenour, Steven, 301–304.

JERICHO BEACH, AS HABITAT FORUM SITE, 226, 257–59, *260*, 261–62; tent cities banned at, 235–38, 262.

Jerusalem, 266–67, 273–74.
Johnson, Howard W., 339–40, 369–70.
Judicial system, *vs.* Open Land movement, 79, 84–87, 99.

KAPLAN FUND/FOUNDATION, 134, 178.
Keenan, Thomas, 147, 202–203, 416.
Kepes, Gyõrgy, 305, 412.
Kevin Roche–John Dinkeloo and Associates, 35, 68. *See also* Roche, Kevin.
Kibbutzim, 109.
Kiley, Dan, 49, *51*.
Klotz, Heinrich, 55–56.
Kõnigsberger, Otto, 245, 284.

LA CHARTE DE L'HABITAT, CIAM'S, 19.
Labor, 95; "dropping-out" of, 104; squatters,' 291; technology's effects on, 80, 111; voluntary primitivism increasing, 80, 97; West's desire for developing countries', 28, 60, 83, 181, 196.
Laboratory of Architecture and Planning (MIT), 378–79.
Lama commune, 113.
Land, 99, 268, 275; allowing flight as American alternative to revolution, 105; communards' search for cheap, 102–103; dispossession from, 323, 329; Gottlieb deeding to God, 100, 111; Israel's acquisition of, 271–72, 279; ownership of, 83–84, 266, 309; propertyless relation to, 110, 142; rural, 246, 323; use, 95.
Laquian, Aprodicio, 293–94, 309, 317.
Latin America, 29, 246; counterinsurgency measures in, 47, 187; Ford Foundation in, 44, 47.
LATWIDN principle, of Open Land movement, 83–84.
Law, Tom, 73, 142. *See also* Open Land movement.
Laws, as obstacle to "trying everything," 11.
Le Corbusier, 18–19, 68, 70.
Left, 106, 188.
Levine, Les, 362–65.
Lewallen, John, 178; on counterinsurgency measures, 182–85; on ecocide, 170, 177, 182, 186–87; on Stockholm conference, 137, 159.
Liberation movements, called terrorism, 426.
Life Forum, as alternative to Stockholm conference, 117–20, *119*, 137, 170, 258; accused of association with CIA, 177–78; goals for, 131–34; programs at, 120–21.
Liferaft Earth (Hunger Show), 142–45, *144*, 161.
Lifestyles: alternative, 91, 111, 300; counterculture's rejection of modern, 74, 164; demonstration of alternative, 118–20, 131–32, 138–40, 159, 262; "dropping-out" of normative, 104; meaning to communards, 88; of voluntary primitivism, 80–83, 97–98, 101.
The Limits to Growth: A Report for the Club of Rome's Project on the Predicament of Mankind, 27, 188, 194–96.
L'insécurité du territoire (Virilio), 26, 28, 31.
Lippman, Andy, 392; on Movie Map, 395–96, *397*, 402, 405, 409, 411, 419–20.
Lorien commune, *102*.
Love: Hog Farm promoting, 146–48, 159; Trudeau calling for, 268–71.
Luce, Don, 175, 177, 181.
Lynch, Kevin, 305, 350, 411–12, 414.
Lyndon, Donlyn, 349–50, 353.

MACHINES, 80, 97.
Management, 22, 190; global, 21, 171, 192, 257; systems for, 29, 192. *See also* data management; environmental management.
Manila, Philippines: beautification of, 314, 318, 327–28; as site for architects' competition, 286. *See also* Dagat-Dagatan project; Tondo Foreshore (squatter settlement).
Mapping by Yourself program, 388.
Marcos, Ferdinand, 328, 330; dissidents and, 330, 333; martial law under, 288–89, 327.
Marcos, Imelda, *320*; addressing Habitat conference, 311, 314–15; Tondo redevelopment and, 312, 327–28.
Marlin, William, 66, 297, 323–25.
Martial law: outlaw territories under, 16; in the Philippines, 293, 297–98, 318, 327; Philippines squelching protests under, 311–12, 315, 318, 322, 329–33.
Marx, Karl, 59, 103.
Massachusetts Institute of Technology (MIT), 188; antiwar protests at, 369–72,

373–74; backing off military research, 368, 369–72; demonstrations against CIS and Cambridge Project at, 375–78; "direct participation" models at, 343–44; ferment at, 339, 343; in forefront of military-industrial-academic complex, 188, 372–75; "The Mezzanines" of, *342*; military research at, 345, 372–75; research and development work at, 22, 192, 345; research on human-machine communication, 383–88; School of Architecture and Planning at, 339–40. *See also* Architecture Machine Group; Urban Systems Lab.
Materials: for Athfield's design for squatter settlements, 296; in commune architecture, 94, 95; innovative uses of, 61; salvaged, 95, 258, 293; for traditional housing in Philippines, 292–93.
McCloy, John J., 45–47, 61.
McClure, Michael, 121, 153–55, 157–58.
McNamara, Robert, 23, *174*, 195–96; at World Bank, 180, 196, 310, 327–28.
Mead, Margaret, 125, 127.
Meadows, Dennis, 192, 194.
Meadows, Donella, 194.
Media, 15, 97, 315, 417; on Habitat conference, 265, 274–76; Habitat Forum and, 258–59, 261–62; on Hog Farm's counterconducts, 117, 143, 159; on Hog Farm's "life shows," 140, 159–61; lack of attention by, 215; on Open Land movement, 79; on protests of Tondo resettlement, 315, 318–19, 327; on Stockholm conference, 124; on Stockholm's counterconferences, 117–18, 153, 169; on torture of Herrera, 330, 333; use of, 124, 138, 222, 228.
Media Lab (MIT's), 383, 389–90, 407.
Medicine, 97, 146.
Mies van der Rohe, Ludwig, 37, 45.
Migration: of African Americans to cities, 47; causes of rural to urban, 45, 316; effects of rural to urban, 125, 241, 283, 309; forced, 25–26; rural to urban, 219, 228, 231, 280, 326; US tactics in Vietnam forcing, 181–82; white flight, 47. *See also* unsettlement.
Milieu: destruction of Vietnam's, 181–82; industrial, 57; war of *vs.* war on, 27.
Militarization, of everyday milieu, 12.
Military, 149, 187; Architecture Machine research used by, 355, 384, 387–88, 427; Israeli, 392–95, 420, *421*, 423–25; MIT trying to steer research away from, 368, 369–72; MIT's research and development for, 343, 345, 347, 369, 372–75; Philippines, 330–31; police and, 25, 35; research at MIT for, 389–90, 392, 395; technology of, 12, 161, 175, 367.
Military-industrial-academic complex, 42, 70, 169; architects in, 380–81; MIT in forefront of, 188, 345, 372–75.
Miller, Charles L., 345–47, 349, 355, 370, 372.
Mills, Stephanie, 121, 143.
Minority populations, civil rights of, 25.
Minsky, Marvin, 355, 412.
Mirrored buildings, effects of, 64, 66.
Mirsky, Jonathan, 181–82.
Mobility, of shelters, 95, 100.
Mobilization of fear, 27–28, 188, 309.
Mobilization of shame, 146, 285, 331.
Modern Architecture: International Exhibition (MoMA), 68–69.
Modernism, 66; high, 291; industrial, 70; as palatable to corporations, 68–69.
Modernity, counterculture's rejection of, 74, 91–93.
Modernization, 70; in imperialism, 44, 59–60, 178.
Mohl, Robert, 389, 402–403; on cognitive space, 411–14; on four incarnations of space, 414–16; on Movie Map, 408, 410–11.
Moore, Charles, 94–95.
Morning Star Ranch, 79, 80, 84, 99, 100, 113; ethos of openness at, 83–84; members of, 84, *85*, 86; shelters at, 80, *90*, *96*; shelters bulldozed by county, 84, *89*; shelters' meaning to communards, 88, 91; signed over to God, *86*, 87; suppression of, 79, 84, 101; voluntary primitivism at, 80–83, 97.
Movie Map (MIT project), 23, 384, *386*, *397–98, 404*; capabilities and limitations of, 403–11; computer-controlled, 395–96; creation of, 420–21, 428; criticism of, 390–92; flow of time in, 410, 415; gathering data for, 396–402; goals for, 411, 420–21; human-machine communication

in, 396, 402–405, 408, 419; military uses of, 389–90, 395; use in acquiring spatial knowledge, 412–14.
Multimedia, 403–11, 428.
Mystic Arts commune, *82*.
Mysticism, 98.

NAIMARK, MICHAEL, 417–19.
Nation-states, 163, 221, 257.
National Report of Palestine, prepared for Habitat conference, 271–74.
Nationalism, 47, 163.
Native Americans: counterculture's identification with, 99, 100, 152–53, 162–63; hippies' relation to, 102–103; Tent City referencing, 150–53.
Natural resources, *see* resources.
Nature: mysticism surrounding, 98; systems-based ecology of, 100.
Negri, Antonio, 43, 257.
Negroponte, Nicholas P., 352, 405, 420, 426–28; Architecture Machine of, 353–56, 387; on computer-aided design, 356–57; Friedman's influence on, 360–62; INTERACT project of, 359–60, 366; SEEK in *Software* exhibition, 365.
Neo-Malthusians, 143, 146, 166, 167; on limits to growth, 22, 188; Peccei as, 197–98.
Neocolonialism, 25, 29, 187, 274.
Neoimperialism, US, 60, 69, 77.
Neoliberalism, 29, 36, 44, 143, 246, 325, 407.
Nepal, Hog Farm's trip to, 146–47.
New York City, as headquarters for United Nations, 63, 65.
Nixon, Richard, 128, 157, 375.
Nongovernmental organizations (NGOs), 21; alternative declaration at Stockholm conference, 127; Environment Forum as semiofficial conference for, 124, 169–70, 200; Habitat Forum for, 23, 225, 239, 261; Stockholm conference and, 124; "The Lobby" at Habitat conference for, 226.
North–South divide, 16, 41, 156, 229, 242; causes of, 125, 240, 244; Stockholm conference and, 122–23.
Now Houses, Fuller's, 248–51, *250*, *253–54*.
Nyerere, Mwalimu Julius K., 229–30.

OCCUPATION, 42–43, 73–74, 79.
Occupied territories: as outlaw territories, 16; settlements in, 275–76.
Occupied Territories, Palestinians', 266; living conditions of Palestinians in, 25, 279; settlements in, 272, 274, 279.
Odets, Walt, 103–104.
Oi Committee, at Environment Forum, 152, 169, 199, 203.
One United Nations Plaza, 21, *62*, 66.
Only One Earth: The Care and Maintenance of a Small Planet (Ward and Dubos), 124, 171, 188; on human settlements, 217–19; on managing conflict over wealth disparities, 126–27; select contributors to, 125–26.
Open Land: A Manifesto, 83, 88–91, 98–99.
Open Land movement, 21, 71; architecture of, 95, 112–13; attempt to create territory beyond statutes, 109–10, 113; expansionism of, 107–108; principles of, 73–74, 83–84; repression of, 107–108; voluntary primitivism in, 97–100; as withdrawal from system, 111, 113. *See also* Morning Star Ranch; Wheeler Ranch.
Open Options: A Guide to Stockholm's Alternative Environmental Conferences (Haley), 120–21, 152.
Operating Manual for Spaceship Earth (Fuller), 126, 161.
"Outlaw Area," in *Whole Earth Catalog*, 9, 161, 390.
Outlaw areas, 33, 390; Brand on, 9–12; constituencies of, 12–13; examples of, 13, 15–16; outlaw territories *vs.*, 434; R. Buckminster Fuller on, 11–12.
Outlaw territories, 161, 266; definition of, 16; Movie Maps as, 416–17; outlaw areas *vs.*, 434; space as, 434; Wheeler and Morning Star ranches as, 109, 113.
Outlaws, 103; Brand's call for better, 32–33; denationalized people as, 163–64; government and, 11, 109; PLO as, 233, 235, 278–79; squatters as, 309, 318–19.
Overpopulation, Ehrlich *vs.* Commoner on, 198–202.

PADWA, DAVID, 132–34.
Palestine Liberation Organization (PLO),

23, 229, 268, 392; at Habitat conference, 226–27, 231–33, *234*, 235, 312–14; as outlaws, 233, 235, 278–79; UN not circulating report by, 271.
Palestinians, 279; claims at Habitat conference, 266–67, 278; Israel's occupation of territory of, 25, 278; Israel's oppression of, 272–73; in refugee camps, *237*, 273; UN's failure to act on behalf of, 231, 279; unsettlement of, 231, 235, *236*. *See also* Occupied Territories, Palestinian's.
Palme, Olaf, 171–72.
Paul VI, Pope, *332*.
Paxton, Joseph, 56–57.
Payer, Cheryl, 310, 328–29.
Peace, 33; Ford Foundation promoting, 43–44.
Peace-keeping, Hog Farm's, 134, 137, 142.
Peccei, Aurelio, 188, 189; at Stockholm conference, 125, 127, 197–98.
Pell, Claiborne, 203–*204*, 218.
Peñalosa, Enrique, 244–46.
People's Forum, as Stockholm counterconference, 132, 137, 177–78; PowWow at, 209–17; seen as too extreme, 169–70, 217.
Perception, regulating/mediated, 383–84.
Peres, Shimo, *394*.
Perpetual peace, as control over resources, 171.
Pfeiffer, Egbert W., 172, 175, 177.
Philippine Squatters and Martial Law Remedies (Tondo residents), 315–18.
Philippines: architects' ignorance of, 293, 296; development in, 298, 316; economy of, 314–15, 328; under martial law, 288–89, 293, 297–98, 318, 327; protests squelched under martial law, 311–12, 315, 318, 322, 329–33; self-help design competition and, 319, 333; Tondo Foreshore Redevelopment Authority of, 293–94; torture of human rights activists in, 329–33; vernacular architecture of, 292–93, 300, *302*.
"Philosophy of architecture," of Open Land movement, 91–93, 111.
Pioneers, American, 101–103.
Place Company, 13–15, 17.
Plazas, *vs.* enclosures, 39, 50.
Police: military and, 25, 35, 330; Morning Star Ranch *vs.*, 84; race riots and, *48*; squelching Tondo protests, 311–14; at Stockholm conference, *136*, 137, 148; Vancouver, 238; Wheeler Ranch commune *vs.*, 77–79.
Politics, 194; architecture and, 29, 36, 321; Brand's rejection of, 131, 137, 165; in definition of outlaw territories, 16; ecology and, 137, 157, 169; environment *vs.*, 22; environmental, 120; at Habitat conference, 231–33; Habitat conference trying to avoid, 274, 277; Hog Farm and, 137–38, 140, 165; ignored in self-help shelter design competition, 292–93, 300, 305–307; obsolescence of, 190, 247, 256; in Open Land communities, 110; PowWow's agenda, 213–15; rejection of, 148, 165, 255; Stockholm conference trying to avoid, 120, 123, 217; technology and, 29, 205, 247; uninvited taking rightful place in, 202–203; as warfare by other means, 42, 257, 300.
Politics of alterity, 161.
Pollution, 50, 52, 125, 204.
Pool, Ithiel de Sola, 350, 371–72, 377, 407.
Popular Front for the Liberation of Palestine, 279, 392.
The Population Bomb (Ehrlich), 100, 143, 145; anxiety caused by, 188, 199.
Population control, 143–45, 192, 199, 219–20.
Population dispersal, in Israel, 266.
Population explosion: metaphors for, 197–98; at Morning Star Ranch, 84, 100. *See also* overpopulation, Ehrlich *vs.* Commoner on.
Population growth, 16, 202, 240; anxiety about, 44, 100, 166, 199, 228; architecture and, 36, 198; causes of, 199; effects of, 9, 125, 192, 197–98; exponential, 195, 197–98.
Populations: in definition of outlaw territories, 16; environment's effects on, 28–29; forced migrations of, 25–26; management of, 17, 93, 348, 436; Third World input on debates, 21–22.
Porter, William, 349–50, 378–79.
Postsovereign territory, 19.
Poverty, 171, 196, 309–10.
Power: access to, 35–36, 217; of American institutions and corporations, 67, 252;

architecture in matrix of, 35–39, 41, 113; asymmetry of, 128, 187; as disembodied, 65–66; hierarchies of, 161, 220–21, 229; Open Landers withdrawing from system of, 110–11, 113; relations of, 20, 29, 31, 33; resistance to, 31, 229; techniques of, 26–28, 30–31, 37, 71, 112; territory and, 30, 33. *See also* apparatus (*dispositif*).
PowWow, 171, 217, 222; People's Forum and, 169–70, 209–17.
Prisons, as outlaw areas, 13.
Privacy, lack of, 54–56.
Project Jonah (antiwhaling activism), 121, 153.
Property, communal, 74.
Property rights, 113; attempts to cede, 73, 77. *See also* land and Open Land Movement.
Protests, 45, 91, 126; effects of, 69, 106. *See also* Tondo Foreshore (squatter settlement, Manila); Vietnam War.
Pruitt-Igoe housing project, demolition of, 190, *191*.
Public domain, 77, 87. *See also* commons, efforts to maintain.
Put That There project, *418*, 419.
Pye, Lucien, 371–72.

RACE, 171, 348.
Race relations, 47–49.
Race riots, 47, *48*.
Racism, Zionism called, 266, 271–72.
RAND Corporation, 42, 178, 187.
Rationalization, building, 93.
Rauch, John K., 94–95.
Real estate speculation, 329.
Refugees: Israel and, 268, 271; in US war on Vietnam, 175, 181–82. *See also* camps.
Regulations, 98; biopolitical, 93, 111–12; efforts to escape, 74–77, 88, 103, 109–10, 113; of human habitations, 79, 93; lacking in Philippines, 297–98; rejection of, 100, 248. *See also* building codes; health codes.
Remote sensing, Earthwatch's, 128.
Research, 377; architectural, 382; on artificial intelligence, 355–56; on computers' interfaces with people, 366–67; social-science, 43; technoscientific, 42. *See also* Massachusetts Institute of Technology.
Resistance, 31–33.
Resources, 115; access to, 35–36, 60, 125, 222; anxiety about depletion of, 77, 167, 188; control over, 171, 222; data as, 204–205; depletion of, 37, 188, 200; exploitation of, 74, 77; management of, 120, 122, 127, 280; squatters as, 292, 309, 310; uneven distribution of, 220; war as waste of, 171–72.
Responsibility: counterculture ethic of personal, 115, 159, 162–63; for environment, 115, 221; government passing to squatters, 291, 299–300, 324; scientists', 169; shifting from capitalist to worker, 242.
Responsive design, 357–58, 365–66.
Revolution, 70; fear of impending, 197–98, 244; flight as American alternative to, 105; resistance to, 108–109, 371–72; squatter settlements breeding, 318, 324.
Revolutionäre Zellen (Revolutionary Cells), 279, 392.
Rights, 37; squatters', *313*, 317–19. *See also* civil rights; human rights.
Risk capital, Ford Foundation's, 46–47.
Roberto, Mauricio, 305, *306*.
Roche, Kevin, 21, 61; criticisms of, 41, 65–66; Ford Foundation Headquarters designed by, 45, 52, 61, 69; goals of, 54–55, 61, 69; on role of architecture, 35–39, 67–68, 70; UN Center designed by, 63–64, 69, 437–39. *See also* Kevin Roche–John Dinkeloo and Associates.
Rockefeller Foundation, sponsoring "Green Revolution," 44–45.
Romney, Hugh, *see* Wavy Gravy.
Rowland, Wade, 139, 157, 178, 195, 204.
Runge, Alis D., 345–46, 348, 355–56.

SAFDIE, MOSHE, 293, 360.
Said, Edward, 235, 278.
Savage, Melissa, 132, 137.
Savane, Landing, 195, 200.
Scale, inhuman, 65–66.
Scarcity, effects of, 172, 188, 247.
Schiff, Stanley, 277.
Schmertz, Mildred, 293, 296, 300, 309.
School of Architecture and Planning (MIT), 339–40, 349–50, 378.
Science/scientists, 348; influence on Stockholm conference, 123–26; responsibility of, 169, 369; Third World input, 152, 169.
Scientists' Institute for Public Information

(SIPI), 169, 178.
Scott, Peter, 153, 200–201.
Scott-Brown, Denise, 94–95, 301–304.
Scully, Vincent, 65–66.
Seagram Building, 39, 50.
Second Development Decade, UN's, 285.
Security, 16, 205, 222, 431; addressing threats to, 25, 149–50, 172, 420–21; Ford Foundation Headquarters providing, 49, 52–54, 60; at Habitat conference, 226–27; at Habitat Forum, 238–39; housing promoting, 240–41, 246; Israel seizing property for, 266, 272–73; militarization for, 12, 42; social sciences as tools in, 347, 371; sources of, 68, 171; at Stockholm conference, 134–37, *136*, 148–49; threats to, 69, 88, 175, 188, 197–98, 336; tools in, 172, 289, 347, 371; UN as instrument of, 19, 44; UN Center's need for, 63–64; urban, 23, 47.
SEE[K] program (MIT's), 356, *363–64*, 365.
Seelig, Michael Y., 287–88, 292–94, 319; *Habitat: Toward Shelter exhibition* and, 298–99.
Self-help, *see* International Design Competition for the Urban Development of Developing Countries Focused on Manila.
Self-Help and Low Cost Housing Symposium, 321–26.
Self-help paradigm, 241–42; encouraging causes of squatter settlements, 325–26; promotion as Third World solution, 246, 322–23; self-determination *vs.*, 316, 321–22.
Self-help shelters, 300, 322; Architecture-by-Yourself project, 362; *Habitat: Toward Shelter* exhibition of, 285, 300–301; for squatter settlements, 283, 296, 309–10, 321.
Sender, Ramon, 79–80, *81*, 83, 100, 107.
Settlement in Israel, report for Habitat conference, 266.
Settlements, 79; efforts to forbid destruction of, 275–76; Israel destroying Palestinian, 268, 273–74, 279; Israeli, *269–70*, 271–72, 274, 279; Peccei lecturing on, 197–98; as political as well as technical, 26, 231–33, 275; Stockholm conference and, 121, 126; US planned, 181; war targeting, 180. *See also* unsettlement. *See also* Habitat: The United Nations Conference on Human Settlements (1976).
Shantytowns, *see* squatter settlements.
Shelters, 95; in camps, 164, *237*; at Habitat Forum, 227, 262; Hog Farm's, 139–40; meaning to communards, 88, 91, 94–95, 100; at Morning Star Ranch, 80, 84, 87–88, *89–90*, *96*; need for, 228; self-built, 112–13, 298; in squatter settlements, 252–53, *290*, 296 (*see also* International Design Competition for the Urban Development of Developing Countries Focused on Manila); in Tent City at Skarpnäk, 115, *116*, *135*, 139, 149, *151*, 215; at Wheeler Ranch, 73–74, *75*, 77–79. *See also* housing; self-help shelters.
Silver, Joan, 52, 56.
Sites-and-services paradigm, 324–25.
Skarpnäk, Sweden, Stockholm counterconference at, 115–19, *116*, 134, *135*, 138–40, 139, 143, 149–53, *151*, 153, 164, 165; free stage presentations at, 153–59.
Snyder, Gary, 121, 162–63.
Social engineering, 43, 192, 347.
Social injustice, 69; identification with victims of, 83, 100–101, 103.
Social justice, 138, 190; clashing with ecology, 128–31; modernist aesthetics and, 68–69.
Social sciences, 43, 125, 350, 371; architecture and, 36, 347, 357; laboratories as outlaw territories, 16.
Socialism, 45.
Society: architecture as appendage of, 67; "dropping-out" as option to dissatisfaction with, 104–106; free rent in transformation of, 84, 99, 110; illness from contemporary, 98–99, 109.
Software: Information Technology, Its New Meaning for Art exhibition (Jewish Museum), 362–65, *363–64*.
Soleri, Paolo, 169, 205–209, 208.
Sonoma County, California: communes in, 79, 113; Morning Star Ranch *vs.*, 84, 87–88, 108–109; Wheeler Ranch commune *vs.*, *78*, 79.
Sovereignty, 21; Fuller criticizing, 255, 265; Israeli military violating Uganda's, 422–24; need to redefine, 127, 221;

postnational condition *vs.*, 256–57; territory and, 431–32; violations of Third World countries', 204, 314, 423.
Space, colonization of, 12, 432–34, *435*, 437.
Spaceship earth metaphor, 126, 128, 147, 161, 196, 219, 314.
Spatial Data Management System (SDMS), *385*, 388–89, 402.
Squatter settlements, 218–19, 304, 333, 341; Athfield's winning self-help design for, 294–96; bare subsistence in, 292, 293; to be cleared for development, 324–25; breeding discontent, 318, 324; causes of, 323, 325–26; destruction of, 310, 316, 327; forcible resettlement of, 317–19, 323; gaining respectability, 244–45, 252–53, 292; insecurity of, 316, 329; organizations and associations in, 293, 315, 317; as outlaw territories, 16; self-help in, 283, 287–88 (*see also* International Design Competition for the Urban Development of Developing Countries Focused on Manila). *See also* Tondo Foreshore.
Squatters: as outlaws, 318–19; as resource, 310.
Standards of living, 192, 195.
State, Department of (US), 128, 204.
Stockholm conference, UN (1972), 21, 26–27, 115, 120, 159, 209; anti-Americanism at, 171–72; architects at, 205–209; counterconferences and, 115–20, 124, 131–34, 152, 167, 169–70, 177, 259; Distinguished Lecture Series, 127; dominated by Western interests, 199–200; fear about counterculture invasion of, 134, 148–49; goals of, 122–23, 156; influences on, 125–26, 157–58, 188, 195; NGOs at, 127, 157–58; *Only One Earth* setting narrative for, 124; outcomes of, 131, 217, 219, 287; participants at, 117–18, 127, 157, 167, 218; police presence at, *136*; PowWow at, 209–17; prefabricated documents at, 122–24; shifting and tactical alliances at, 155–59, 170; Strong's goals for, 128, 171; Third World's counterdeclaration at, 199–200; trying to avoid politics, 180, 217; US blocking discussion of Vietnam War at, 172, 176; US delegation to, 128, 153, 157, 172, 203–204; US dominating, 167, 169, 171; Ward's role at, 124, 127, 239. *See also* Environment Forum; Life Forum; People's Forum.
Stone, Peter, 124, 127, 148–49, 153.
Stratton, Julius A., 45, 47.
Strong, Maurice, *160*, 223, 239; on global management, 123, 127, 171, 217; goals for Stockholm conference, 124, 128, 171; *Only One Earth* commissioned by, 125, 127; Peñalosa replacing as secretary general of Habitat conference, 245–46; preparing for Habitat conference, 226, 240, 286; publications based on Stockholm conference, 127, 219; as secretary general of Earth Summit, 223; as secretary general of Stockholm conference, 122–23, 159; Stockholm conference and, 124, 131; trying to create consensus, 131, 171; at Whale Night, *154*, 155–57.
Students, desire for action, 346–47.
Surveillance, 25, 204.
Survivalism, 101.
Sweden, 132, 177. *See also* Stockholm conference, UN (1972).
Systems approach, to urban crisis, 344–45.
Systems-based paradigms, 22–23, 221.
Systems Dynamics, 192, 198; Forrester's models from, 189–90, 194–95.
Systems theory, 182–87, 189.

TAFURI, MANFREDO, 56, 61, 70–71.
Takagi Design Team, *303*, 304.
Tange, Kenzo, 126, 240.
Technology, 45, 123, 343, 405–406; alternative, 209–17, 210; in communication, 255–56, 362; in dispersed global *dispositif* of power, 161–62; effects of, 80, 162, 198–202; military, 12, 161, 175, 185; MIT's, 345–46; new, as outlaw areas, 23, 390; politics and, 18, 205, 247; rejection of, 93, 97, 101.
Technology transfer, 213, 345.
Tent City, *see* Hog Farm, at Stockholm conference.
Territorial imperative, Open Land movement *vs.*, 107–108.
Territory, 30, 44, 104; importance of, 431; insecurity of, 26, 33, 164; lack of, 163–64, 278; power relations and, 20, 30, 33; sovereignty and, 431–32.

Terrorism: hijacking of plane to Entebbe as, 279, 420; liberation movements called, 426; sovereignty *vs.*, 422–25.
Third World, 195, 291; focus on modernization and development of, 70, 213, 222; influence of, 195, 280; politicizing Habitat conference, 228, 277; in population discussions, 21–22, 188, 199, 202; problems of, 17, 240, 283, 284; seen as threat by First World, 16, 44, 188; at Stockholm conference, 199–200, 200–202; treatment of, 70, 423, 428–29. *See also* developing countries.
Third World (Oi Committee) session of Alternative Conference, *see* Oi Committee, at Environment Forum.
Thompson, William Irwin, 207–209.
Todd, Lou, 139, 159.
Tomkins, Calvin, 11–12.
Tondo Foreshore (squatter settlement, Manila), *290*, 297, 300, *332*; to be cleared for development, 311, 323–24; evictions from, 327; organizations of, 293, 315, 317–18, 326; photos of, 304, 307, *308*; protests of resettlement plans, 311–21, 328–33, 336; residents not consulted on resettlement plans, 311, 317, 321; residents to be relocated to Dagat-Dagatan, 288–89.
Total peace, maintenance of security as, 26–27, 42.
"Total war," 26–27.
Train, Russell, 157, 172.
Tribalism: in counterculture, 94, 99, 101, 153; ethic of personal responsibility and, 162–63; from propertyless relation to land, 110.
Trips Festival, 80, *81*, 153.
Trudeau, Margaret, 245
Trudeau, Pierre, 268–71.
Turner, John F. C., 242, 284, 321–22.

UGANDA, SOVEREIGNTY OF, 422–24.
UN Center, *62*, 437–39, *438*; Ford Foundation and, 41, 63; reviews of, 64–65, 70; Roche's design for, 35, 38, 41, 63–64, 69.
UN Conference on Environment and Development (Earth Summit, 1992), 223.
UN conferences, 19, 244; power relations at, 227, 231, 274. *See also* Habitat: The United Nations Conference on Human Settlements; Stockholm conference (1972).
UN Relief for Palestine Refugees, *236*.
Underdevelopment, replacing conventional occupation, 42–43.
Union Internationale des Architectes (UIA), 18–19, 285.
United Nations (UN), 19, 27, 120, 121, 159, 176, 257; architecture and, 18–19, 284, 286; discussing sanctions on Israel for Entebbe rescue, 422–26; environmental activities of, 128, 223; expansion of, 16, 61; focus on development, 23, 41, 70, 218, 231, 285; Ford Foundation and, 44, 61; founded on national sovereignty, 21, 255; in Israel's creation, 266, 271, 426; Israel's lack of cooperation with, 273–74, 279, 422; NGOs' role in, 21, 155; Palestinians and, 231, 279; power relations within, 228–29, 231; resolution on whaling moratorium, 156–57; roles of, 44, 70; US relations with, 255, 277.
United Nations Conference on the Human Environment. *See* Stockholm conference (1972).
United Nations Development Corporation (UNDC), 35, 61, 63, 65.
United Nations Economic and Social Council (ECOSOC), 121–22.
United Nations Environment Program (UNEP), 128.
United Nations Environment Programme, 223.
United Nations Headquarters, 61, *62*, 63.
United States, 17, 25, 200, 274; counterinsurgency measures of, 178, 182–87; ecocide in Vietnam War, 172–76, *173*, 180; economic expansion of, 36, 42, 68, 195–96; leading antiwhaling movement, 157–58; motives for aid by, 229, 289; at Stockholm conference, 120, 167, 171, 176; UN and, 22–23, 61, 255, 277; use of exit option in response to dissatisfaction, 105, 107.
United States Agency for International Development (USAID), 44–45.
Universal advocacy, 356, 359–60, 367.
Unsettlement, 23, 164, 245, 426, 434; causes of, 181–82, 241; of Palestinians, 235–36,

279.
URBAN5, 349–53, 355, 357, 360, 365.
Urban areas, 74; efforts to improve, 47, 345; Forrester's models for, 190; migration flooding, 219, 240, 241, 309; in visions of exponential population growth, 197–98.
Urban crisis: efforts to control, 47, 340–41, 344–45, 368; unrest in, 17, 69, 99.
Urban Dynamics (Forrester), 190, 192.
Urban renewal, 88.
Urban studies, 47, 368.
Urban Systems Lab (USL, MIT's), 23, 340–41, 348, 370, 380; computer-aided design at, 349–53; founding of, 344–45; funding for, 47, 368; goals for, 345–47, 356.
Urbanism, in art of government, 19, 29–30.
Urbanization, 125, 288, 432–33; need to manage, 426, 428; as strategy against wars of national liberation, 178; US tactics in Vietnam forcing, 175–76, 181–82.
Urbicide, 88.
Utopias, 20, 140, 436–37; architecture's promise of, 280, 291, 333, 336, 360–62; arcology proposed as, 206–207; Open Land movement as experiment in, 79–80, 108–109, 114, 436–37; space colonies as, 433, 436.

VANCOUVER ACTION PLAN, 228.
Vancouver Art Gallery, *Habitat: Toward Shelter* exhibition at, 298–305.
Vancouver conference, *see* Habitat: The United Nations Conference on Human Settlements (1976).
Vancouver Symposium, alternative declaration by, 226, 243–44, 259.
Venturi, Robert, 94–95, 301–304.
"Vernacular nostalgia," commune architecture as, 94.
Vers une architecture (Le Corbusier), 68, 70.
Vietnam: environment before war, 182; environmental damage to, *179*, *183*; resettlement camps, *184*.
Vietnam War, 178; ecocide in, 22, 172–75, *173*, 180–81; environmental dimensions of, 172–75, 180; escalation of, 45, 47, 375; MIT research used in, 343, 375–77; opposition to, 177, 180, 186, 369; US focus on counterinsurgency, 88, 177.
Violence, 196; Open Land movement and, 74, 99, 108.
Virilio, Paul, 26–28, 390–92.
Virno, Paolo, 104–105.
Visibility, in Ford Foundation Headquarters, 54–56.
Voluntary primitivism, 21, 97–100, 101, 110; Hog Farm's, 138; at Morning Star Ranch, 80–83; PowWow's alternative technology *vs.*, 215. *See also* back-to-the-land movement.
Von Eckardt, Wolf, 41, 231, 239, 259.
Von Hoffman, Nicholas, 47–50.

WALDHEIM, KURT, 231, 245–46.
Walls: around shanty towns, 327; in Athfield's winning self-help shelter design, 294–96; proliferation of, 26.
Walter, Harold, 422, 425.
War, 43, 247; depersonalization of, 186–87; ecocide as, 176–77, 180, 187, 204; electronic battlefield in, 175, 185; nonmilitary domains of, 26, 42, 180; politics as warfare by other means, 108, 257, 300; relation to environmental crisis, 171, 198; unsettlement as weapon of, 181–82; as waste of resources, 171–72. *See also* Vietnam War.
War crimes, "ecocide" proposed as, 176.
War on Terror, 24–25.
Ward, Barbara, 23, 125–26, 280; on human settlements, 124, 217–19; role at Habitat conference, 226, 239–43, 286; at Stockholm conference, 127. *See also Only One Earth: The Care and Maintenance of a Small Planet.*
Wars of national liberation, 178, 187.
Water Day Walk, 245.
Wavy Gravy, as spokesperson for Hog Farm, 73, 140, 159; in Stockholm, 139, *141*, 155–56; on trip to East Pakistan, 146–47.
Wealth disparities, 126, 128, 196, 311, 324.
Weisberg, Barry, 117, 157, 222; on Hog Farm, 137–38; on Stockholm conference, 122, 167, 171, 176.
Welfare, 87–88, 111, 199.
West, 16, 44, 227; Stockholm conference dominated by, 199–200; supporting Israel, 273, 274; wanting continued access to resources, 60, 222.

Westing, Arthur H., 172, 175, 177, 181.
Westmoreland, William, 175, 185, 367.
Whale Night, hosted by life Forum, 153–59.
Wheeler, Bill and Gay, *76*, 79, 91; on relation to the land, 97–98; on Sonoma County's repression of Ranch, 108–109.
Wheeler Ranch: Davidson on, 73–74; government *vs.*, 77–79, *78*, 107; as outlaw area, 13; residents of, 86, *92*; shelters at, *10*, 73–74, *75*, 77–79, 91; values of, 77, 97. *See also* Open Land movement.
White, Dana, 206–207.
Whole Earth Catalog, *10*, 137; influence on counterculture, 95–97, 132; "Outlaw Area" in, 9, 161, 390; products in, 100–101, 145.
Wideman, Bernard, 289, 317–19, 327, 329–30
Woodstock, 134, 140.
Work in Progress: Philip Johnson, Kevin Roche, Paul Randolph exhibit, 35, 39–41, *40*.
World1, Forrester's, *193*.
World2, Forrester's, 192, *193*.
World3 (or the World Model), 194.
World Bank, 257, 326, 327–28; development apparatus of, 23, 310; forbidding loans to governments eradicating slums, 327–28; McNamara at, 180, 196; *Only One Earth* sponsored by, 124–25; power through aid, 28, 127; role in expanding global capitalism, 310–11, 329; self-help competition designs not challenging dominant narrative of, 334–35; squatter settlements and, 291, 293–94, 309–10, 328, 333.
World Dynamics (Forrester), 188, 192.
World Game, Fuller's, 186, 227, 247.
World1 model, Forrester's, 192.
World War II, 26, 42, 60, 164.
"World War IV" game, 14.

XEHAEDRON MODEL, Soleri's, *208*.

ZINSSER, WILLIAM, 50, 54.
Zone One Tondo Organization (ZOTO), 317.
Zoning, uses of, 38–39, 297.
Zwerdling, Daniel, 115, 159.

This project funded in part by a generous grant from
The Graham Foundation for Advanced Studies in the Fine Arts

Graham Foundation

Zone Books series design by Bruce Mau
Typesetting by Meighan Gale
Image placement and production by Julie Fry
Printed and bound by Maple Press

ZONE BOOKS
near futures
ONLINE

This online forum is dedicated to the analysis of the challenges borne out of national governments' and international institutions' responses to some critical events — the financial crisis of 2008, the "Arab Springs" of 2011 — as well as ongoing developments such as climate change and soaring inequalities. Organized around a specific question, each issue of NFO brings together scholars, journalists, political activists, and artists, and includes contributions belonging to different genres and using a variety of media — essays and reportages, interviews and dialogues, photo essays and videos.

SPRING 2016

Issue #1: Europe at a Crossroads

www.nearfuturesonline.org